The Western Heritage

The Western Heritage

Brief Edition

Donald Kagan
Yale University

Steven Ozment
Harvard University

Frank M. Turner
Yale University

with the assistance of
A. Daniel Frankforter
Pennsylvania State University, Behrend College

PRENTICE HALL, Upper Saddle River, New Jersey 07458

The Library of Congress has catalogued the full edition of this work as follows:

Library of Congress Cataloging-in-Publication Data

Kagan, Donald.
   The Western Heritage/Donald Kagan, Steven Ozment, Frank M.
Turner.—5th ed.
    p.   cm.
   "Combined volume."
   Includes bibliographical references and index.
   ISBN 0-02-363262-3
   1: Civilization, Western.   I. Ozment, Steven.   II. Turner, Frank
M. (Frank Miller).   III. Title.
   CB245.K28 1995
   909'.09812—dc20   94-20481
                                   CIP

Acquisitions Editor: *Sally Constable*
Editorial Director: *Charlyce Jones Owen*
Development Editor: *David Chodoff*
Production Editor: *Barbara Reilly*
Director of Marketing: *Lauren Ward*
Marketing Manager: *Alison Pendergast*
Copy Editor: *Eleanor Walter*
Editorial Assistant: *Tamara Mann*
Buyer: *Nick Sklitsis*
Design Director: *Anne Bonanno Nieglos*
Interior Design: *Lorraine Mullaney*
Cover Design: *Thomas Nery*
Cover Art: Giovanni Antonio Canaletto, *The Basin of Saint Marco with the Buccintoro* (Scala/Art Resource)
Photo Editor: *Melinda Reo*
Photo Research: *Joelle Burrows*

© 1996 by Prentice-Hall, Inc.
Simon & Schuster/A Viacom Company
Upper Saddle River, New Jersey 07458

Printed in the United States of America

10 9 8 7 6 5 4 3 2

ISBN 0-02-361872-8

Prentice-Hall International (UK) Limited, *London*
Prentice-Hall of Australia Pty. Limited, *Sydney*
Prentice-Hall Canada Inc., *Toronto*
Prentice-Hall Hispanoamericana, S.A., *Mexico*
Prentice-Hall of India Private Limited, *New Delhi*
Prentice-Hall of Japan, Inc., *Tokyo*
Simon & Schuster Asia Pte. Ltd., *Singapore*
Editora Prentice-Hall do Brasil, Ltda., *Rio de Janeiro*

Brief Contents

Contents

4 Rome: From Republic to Empire 78

The Middle Ages, 476–1300

5 The Roman Empire 106

The Middle Ages, 476–1300

Europe in Transition, 1300–1750

12   The Age of Religious Wars *282*

13   Paths to Constitutionalism and Absolutism: England and France in the Seventeenth Century *305*

14   New Directions in Thought and Culture in the Sixteenth and Seventeenth Centuries *329*

Enlightenment and Revolution

Toward the Modern World

23 The Age of Nation-States *536*

24 The Building of European Supremacy: Society and Politics to World War I *560*

28 Europe and the Great Depression of the 1930s *661*

Global Conflict, Cold War, and New Directions

29 World War II *679*

Index   I-1

Maps

Documents

Preface

The heritage of Western civilization has perhaps never been the focus of so much interest and controversy as it is today. Many commentators criticize it, many praise it, but for all it is a subject of intense discussion. *The Western Heritage* helps teachers introduce students to the subject of that discussion. It presents an overview of Western civilization, including its strengths, its weaknesses, and the controversies surrounding it.

On campus after campus, every aspect of Western civilization has become an object of scrutiny and debate. Many participants in this debate fail to recognize that such self-criticism is characteristic of Western civilization and an important part of its heritage. We welcome the debate and hope that this book can help raise its quality.

The collapse of communism has left the people of half of Europe struggling to reorganize their political institutions and their social and economic lives. The choices they are making and the future they are forging will reflect in large measure their understanding of their heritage. To follow and participate in that process we too need to understand that heritage.

This brief edition of *The Western Heritage* is designed to meet the needs of those who want a succinct overview of Western civilization for quarter and semester courses and those who plan to supplement their courses with extensive outside readings. Although this version of *The Western Heritage* is indeed shorter than the full version, it covers all the same topics with the same overall organization. Our colleague Dan Frankforter has skillfully reworked the entire text for brevity, ensuring that it retains a consistent voice and a coherent narrative.

∼ Goals of the Text

Since *The Western Heritage* first appeared, we have sought to provide our readers with a work that does justice to the richness and variety of Western civilization. Our primary goal has been to present a strong, clear, narrative account of the key developments in Western history. We have also chosen to call attention to certain critical themes:

 The development of political freedom, constitutional government, and concern for the rule of law and individual rights;

 The shifting relations among religion, society, and the state;

 The development of science and technology and their expanding impact on thought, social institutions, and everyday life;

 The major religious and intellectual currents that have shaped Western culture.

We believe that these themes have been fundamental in Western civilization, shaping the past and exerting a continuing influence on the present.

Balanced and Flexible Presentation. History has many facets, no one of which alone can account for its development. Any attempt to tell the story of the West from a single overarching perspective, no matter how timely, is bound to neglect or suppress some important part of that story. Our goal in this text has been to present Western civilization fairly, accurately, and in a way that does justice to its great variety. We have designed the text to accommodate many approaches to a course in Western civilization, allowing teachers to stress what is most important to them.

We do not believe that a history of the West should be limited to politics and international relations, but we share the conviction that political events have shaped the Western experience in fundamental and powerful ways. Recent events in central and eastern Europe and the former Soviet Union have strengthened that belief. We have also been told repeatedly by teachers that no matter what their own specialties, they believe that a political narrative best equips students to begin building an understanding of the past.

The Western Heritage, brief edition, also provides a rich account of the social history of the West, with strong coverage of family life, the roles of women, and the place of the family in relation to broader economic, political, and social developments. This coverage reflects the explosive growth in social historical research in the last quarter century.

Finally, no other brief survey text presents so full an account of the religious and intellectual development of the West. People may be political and social beings, but they are also reasoning and spiritual beings. What they think and believe are among the most important things we can know about them. Their ideas about God, society, law, gender, human nature, and the physical world have changed over the

centuries and continue to change. We cannot fully grasp our own approach to the world without understanding the intellectual currents of the past and their influence on our thoughts and conceptual categories.

Clarity and Accessibility. Good narrative history requires clear, vigorous prose. A survey text especially must engage students if it hopes to keep them reading. Throughout this brief edition of *The Western Heritage,* we have sought to make our presentation fully accessible to students without compromising on vocabulary or conceptual level.

Recent Scholarship. This edition of *The Western Heritage,* like all others, reflects our determination to incorporate the most recent developments in historical scholarship and the expanding concerns of professional historians.

⁓ Features of the Brief Edition

The Western Heritage, brief edition, has several distinctive features designed to make it accessible to students and reinforce key concepts. Each chapter includes:

● An opening *outline;*

● A *key topics* list that gives a succinct overview of the chapter;

● *Introductory* and *concluding sections;*

● One or more *timelines* that help students build a chronological framework;

● A *primary source document* that augments the narrative and helps acquaint students with the raw material of history;

● *Questions* accompanying the source document that direct students toward important, thought-provoking issues and help them relate the document to the material in the text. These questions can be used to stimulate class discussion or as topics for essays and study groups;

  Chapter review questions that help students review the material in the chapter and relate it to broader themes. These too can be used for class discussion and essay topics;

  A *suggested readings* list that directs students to more detailed sources on particular topics.

Maps and Illustrations. The abundant *maps* throughout the text are carefully cued to the narrative. *Photographs* and other illustrations enrich the text and help draw students in to it. *Color inserts* provide examples of fine art from the paleolithic age to the twentieth century.

⁓ Ancillary Instructional Materials

The Western Heritage, brief edition, comes with an extensive package of ancillary materials.

  An **Instructor's Manual** with Test Items prepared by Perry M. Rogers of Ohio State University. This includes chapter summaries, key points and vital concepts, identification questions, multiple-choice questions, essay questions, and suggested films.

  Map Transparencies in full color. These include all the maps in the brief edition as well many others.

  A **Study Guide** prepared by Anthony M. Brescia of Nassau Community College that includes commentary, identifications, map exercises, short-answer exercises, and essay questions.

  A **Computerized Study Guide** con-

sisting of 15 multiple-choice questions from each chapter with reinforcing feedback on correct answers and clarifying feedback on wrong answers. All answers are cross-referenced to the text.

  A **Computerized Test Bank** consisting of more than 1500 multiple-choice and essay questions from the Instructor's Manual for IBM compatible and Macintosh systems.

  The Hammond **Historical Atlas of the World,** available with the text at a special discounted price. Please contact your local Prentice Hall sales representative for details

⁓Acknowledgments

We are grateful to the scholars and teachers whose thoughtful and often detailed comments have helped shape *The Western Heritage.* We would also like to thank the many dedicated people at Prentice Hall who helped produce this edition. Our acquisitions editor, Sally Constable, and our development editor, David Chodoff, convinced us of the value of a brief edition and prodded us to see it through. Tamara Mann, editorial assistant, helped coordinate the many pieces of the project. Alison Pendergast, our marketing manager, provided valuable suggestions for the book's overall format. Lorraine Mullaney produced the book's handsome design and Joelle Burrows helped us with photo research. Finally, Barbara Reilly, our production supervisor, and Nick Sklitsis, our manufacturing buyer, oversaw the sometimes rocky transition from manuscript to bound book with unfailing professionalism and good humor.

  D.K.
  S.O.
  F.M.T.

About the Authors

Donald Kagan is Bass Professor of History and Classics and Western Civilization at Yale University, where he has taught since 1969. He received the A.B. degree in history from Brooklyn College, the M.A. in classics from Brown University, and the Ph.D. in history from Ohio State University. During 1958–1959 he studied at the American School of Classical Studies as a Fulbright Scholar. He has received three awards for undergraduate teaching at Cornell and Yale. He is the author of a history of Greek political thought, *The Great Dialogue* (1965); a four-volume history of the Peloponnesian war, *The Origins of the Peloponnesian War* (1969); *The Archidamian War* (1974); *The Peace of Nicias and the Sicilian Expedition* 1981; *The Fall of the Athenian Empire* (1987); and a biography of Pericles, *Pericles of Athens and the Birth of Democracy* (1991). With Brian Tierney and L. Pearce Williams, he is the editor of *Great Issues in Western Civilization*, a collection of readings.

Steven Ozment is McLean Professor of Ancient and Modern History at Harvard University. He has taught courses in Western civilization at Yale, Stanford, and Harvard. He is the author of eight books. *The Age of Reform, 1250–1550* (1980) won the Schaff Prize and was nominated for the 1981 American Book Award. *Magdalena and Balthasar: An Intimate Portrait of Life in Sixteenth Century Europe* (1986) and *Three Behaim Boys: Growing Up in Early Modern Germany* (1990) were selections of the History Book club, as is also his most recent book, *Protestants: The Birth of a Revolution*, an interpretation of the German Reformation.

Frank M. Turner is John Hay Whitney Professor of History at Yale University, where he served as University Provost from 1988 to 1992. He received his B.A. degree at the College of William and Mary and his Ph.D. from Yale. He has received the Yale College Award for Distinguished Undergraduate Teaching. He has directed a National Endowment for the Humanities Summer Institute. His scholarly research has received the support of fellowships from the National Endowment for the Humanities and the Guggenheim Foundation. He is the author of *Between Science and Religion: The Reaction to Scientific Naturalism in Late Victorian England* (1974), *The Greek Heritage in Victorian Britain* (1981), which received the British Council Prize of the Conference on British Studies and the Yale Press Governors Award, and *Contesting Cultural Authority: Essays in Victorian Intellectual Life* (1993). He has also contributed numerous articles to journals and has served on the editorial advisory boards of *The Journal of Modern History, Isis,* and *Victorian Studies.*

A. Daniel Frankforter is Professor of Medieval History at the Pennsylvania State University. He holds degrees from Franklin and Marshall College, Drew University, and the Pennsylvania State University, where he has taught since 1970. His books include *A History of the Christian Movement; Civilization and Survival; The Shakespeare Name Dictionary;* and a translation and edition of François Poullain de la Barre's *De l'Égalité des Deux Sexes.* He has received four awards for excellence in teaching and research from the Pennsylvania State University.

The
Western
Heritage

1

The Birth of Civilization

KEY TOPICS IN THIS CHAPTER

~ The earliest history of humanity, the origins of human culture in the Paleolithic Age, the shift from food gathering to food production, and the emergence of civilizations

~ The ancient civilizations of Mesopotamia and Egypt

~ The Assyrians and the first great Middle Eastern empires

~ The ancient Middle Eastern civilization compared with that of the ancient Greeks

---

For hundreds of thousands of years, people lived by hunting and gathering what nature provided. Only about 10,000 years ago did they learn to cultivate plants and domesticate animals. These discoveries transformed human beings from harvesters to producers and made settled life possible. About 5,000 years ago the Sumerians, who lived in the area that the Greeks named "Mesopotamia" ("between the rivers," the Tigris and Euphrates), and the Egyptians, who dwelt in the Nile Valley, pioneered Western civilization. By the fourteenth century B.C. powerful empires had begun to struggle for control of the Middle East. But of more lasting significance than any of them was the tiny nation of Israel, which began the evolution of the West's religions: Judaism, Christianity, and Islam.

～ Early Human Beings and Their Culture

Scientists estimate that the earth may be 6 billion years old and that creatures very much like humans may have appeared 3 to 5 million years ago, probably in Africa. Some 1 to 2 million years ago, erect, tool-using beings spread over much of Africa, Europe, and Asia. Our own species, *Homo sapiens,* probably emerged some 200,000 years ago, and the earliest remains of fully modern humans date to about 90,000 years ago.

Humans, unlike other animals, are cultural beings. *Culture* may be defined as a way of living developed by a group and passed on from one generation to another. It includes material things (tools, clothing, and shelter) as well as ideas, institutions, and beliefs. Because culture is learned and not inherited, it permits more rapid adaptation to changing conditions than biological evolution.

The Paleolithic Age

Anthropologists identify early human cultures by the styles of their stone tools—the major artifacts they have left us. The first period—the Paleolithic (from Greek, "old stone")—dates from the earliest use of stone tools some 1 million years ago to about 10,000 B.C. During this immensely long time, people were hunters, fishers, and gatherers, but not producers, of food.

These early humans, dependent on nature for food, vulnerable to wild beasts and natural disasters, may have developed responses to the world rooted in fear of the unknown—of the uncertainties of human life and the overpowering forces of nature. Religious and magical beliefs and practices may have emerged in an effort to propitiate or coerce the superhuman powers thought to animate or direct the natural world. Evidence of religious faith and practice, as well as magic, goes as far back as archaeology can take us. Fear or awe, exultation, gratitude, and empathy with the natural world must all have figured in the cave art and in the ritual practices, such as burial, that we find evidenced at Paleolithic sites around the globe. The sense that there is more to the world than meets the eye—the religious response to life—seems to be as old as humankind.

Human life in the Paleolithic Age was probably characterized by a division of labor by sex. Men ranged far afield on the hunt. Women, less mobile because of the burdens of childbearing and nursing, gathered edibles near a base camp. The technologies of the Paleolithic period could support only a small human population. People were subject to the same natural and ecological constraints that maintain balances between packs of wolves and the deer on which they prey.

The Neolithic Age

Some 10,000 years ago parts of what we now call the Middle (or Near) East began to shift from a hunter-gatherer culture to a settled agricultural one. Because the shift to agriculture coincided with advances in stone tool technology—

the development of precise carving and grinding—this period is called the Neolithic ("new stone") Age. Humans became dependent on domesticated plants and animals. Since crops required constant care from planting to harvest, farmers settled in villages. Settled life encouraged the invention of new materials, like pottery, and of building techniques.

The Neolithic revolution was a major step toward human control of nature, and it was a vital precondition for the emergence of civilization. The earliest Neolithic communities appeared in the Middle East about 8000 B.C., in India about 3600 B.C., and in China about 4000 B.C. The Neolithic economy of the Middle East and India was based on species of wheat—the wild forebears of which were native to the foothills of the mountains north and east of the Tigris and Euphrates river valleys.

The Bronze Age and the Birth of Civilization

Neolithic farmers and herders gradually replaced Paleolithic cultures over much of the world. Then, first in Mesopotamia along the Tigris and Euphrates rivers (in modern Iraq) and later in the valley of the Nile in Egypt, another major shift occurred. Urban life appeared—and with it techniques for writing and for smelting metals. These are characteristics of the advanced form of human culture called *civilization.*

∽ Early Civilizations to About 1000 B.C.

About 4000 B.C., large numbers of people began to migrate into the river-watered lowlands of Mesopotamia and Egypt. By 3000 B.C., when the invention of writing gave birth to history, centralized states had been established along the Tigris and Euphrates rivers and in the valley of the Nile (see Map 1-1).

Since cities are home to many people who do not grow their own food, urban life is possible only where farmers can produce a surplus beyond their own needs. The first cities sprang up on land whose fertility was renewed by annually flooding rivers, but in dry climates that required farmers to irrigate their fields. Some people believe that urban life, literacy, and the first centralized states were a response to a need for a strong authority capable of constructing irrigation and flood control systems and managing the distribution of water. But recent research suggests that this theory may be simplistic. Water management was probably the responsibility of local officials, not central governments. The earliest written records deal with land, not water, management; the care of animals; and trade.

The great temple complexes that were central to Mesopotamian cities produced many kinds of texts that reveal the complexity of urban society. Temples employed large staffs of people who had all kinds of duties. Commerce was important enough to support an urban merchant class. Since scripts were very complicated and took many years to learn, each city also had a small group of professional scribes. The collection into cities of people with

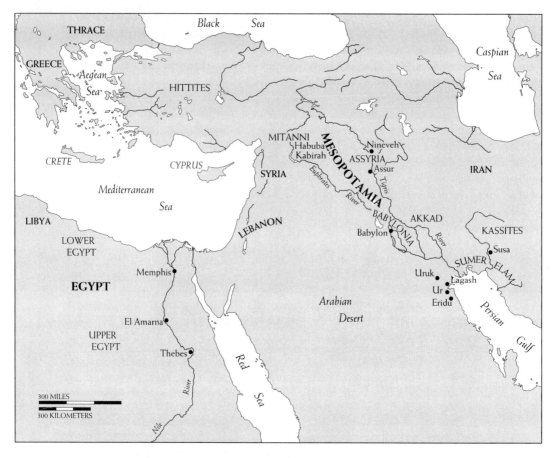

MAP 1-1 The Ancient Middle East *There were two ancient river valley civilizations. While Egypt early was united into a single state, Mesopotamia was long divided into a number of city-states.*

different interests and educations made life in cities much more complex and stimulating than life in farming villages.

Cities that drew water for the irrigation of their fields from the same river were forced into close association. The logic of nature promoted unification of a river's dependencies, for central control put the river's water to the most efficient use and prevented destructive competition. This process consolidated neighboring cities into a kingdom.

The typical king in a river-valley civilization, who was regarded either as a god or as the delegate of a god, occupied the pinnacle of a hierarchy composed of rigidly defined social classes: soldier-aristocrats, priests, merchants, professionals, free peasants, and slaves. Cities were centers of administrative, commercial, religious, and military activity. Most of a community's farmers lived in outlying villages. Much of the land they worked was owned

Significant Dates from Ancient Mesopotamian History

ca. 3500 B.C.	*Earliest Sumerian settlements*
ca. 2800–2370 B.C.	*Sumerian city-states, Early Dynastic Period*
ca. 2370 B.C.	*Sargon establishes Semitic dynasty at Akkad*
ca. 2125–2027 B.C.	*Third Dynasty of Ur*
ca. 1900 B.C.	*Old Babylonian Dynasty of the Amorites*
1792–1750 B.C.	*Reign of Hammurabi*
ca. 1600 B.C.	*Hittite and Kassite invasions of Babylon*

by the upper classes. These cultural patterns formed early, and since they were assumed to be part of the natural order, they changed only slowly and grudgingly.

Mesopotamian Civilization

Civilization seems to have appeared first in Mesopotamia. The region contains two ecological zones: the south (Sumer), where irrigation is vital, and the north (Assyria), where agriculture depends more on rainfall and wells. A people called the Sumerians founded the first Mesopotamian cities about 3000 B.C., close to the head of the Persian Gulf. For a long time Uruk, which lies in that region, was the earliest known Sumerian site. Recent discoveries in northern Syria, notably at Habuba Kabirah, have brought to light other settlements of the same period.

During the early dynastic period (2800 B.C. to 2370 B.C.) city-states such as Ur, Uruk, Lagash, and Eridu—each controlling about 100 square miles—dotted the landscape of southern Mesopotamia. Quarrels over water rights and frontiers led to incessant fighting among them, and in time the stronger towns consolidated the weaker ones into kingdoms.

The land upstream from the principal Sumerian city-states was settled by a people who probably came from North Syria. Although they absorbed Sumerian culture, unlike the Sumerians they spoke a Semitic language (that is, a language from the same family as Arabic and Hebrew). These people established a kingdom with a capital at Akkad, near the site of the later city of Babylon. About 2370 B.C. Sargon, the most famous Akkadian king, conquered the Sumerian cities and created an empire that may have extended to Lebanon and the coast of the Mediterranean Sea. His dynasty ruled Sumer and Akkad for two centuries.

About 2125 B.C. the Akkadian state collapsed, and the city of Ur restored Sumerian dominance. The kings of the Third Dynasty of Ur inaugurated a renaissance of Sumerian culture that lasted until an invasion ended their rule in 2000 B.C. The Sumerians never recovered from that defeat. Sumerian faded away as a living language, but survived as a scholar's tongue used by priests and scribes who cherished Sumer's cultural legacy.

After the fall of Ur, leadership passed to a people called the Amorites, who (ca. 1900 B.C.) founded the city of Babylon. The Amorite, or Old Babylonian, dynasty dominated Mesopotamia for about 300 years. Its high point was the reign of Hammurabi (ca. 1792–1750 B.C.), who is best known for a code of laws that bears his name. (Earlier collections of laws were made by the Sumerians, but Hammurabi's code is our most complete account of ancient Mesopotamian legal practice.)

The Babylonian kingdom declined about 1600 B.C. under the impact of invasions from the north and east by the Hittites and the Kassites. The Hittites plundered what they could and then withdrew to their home in Asia Minor. The Kassites occupied Babylon and ruled Mesopotamia for five centuries.

Government. Although some scholars have suggested that the Sumerian cities were first governed as "primitive democracies," the evidence for this thesis is poetry that is hard to interpret. The earliest historical records speak of kings whose power, even in early times, may have been little checked by their subjects. Kings led armies, administered economies, sat as judges, and served as intermediaries between their people and the gods. Kings were usually thought of as human representatives of the gods, but occasionally kings were worshiped as divine.

A union of church and state (to use modern terminology) in the person of a king reflected a centralization of power typical of Mesopotamian life. Royal governments carefully managed the state's economy. Each year the land was surveyed, fields were assigned to specific farmers, and the amount of seed to be used was designated. The government estimated the size of the crop and planned its distribution even before it was planted.

This process required a large, competent staff equipped with a system of writing and a good knowledge of mathematics. The Sumerians invented a script known as *cuneiform* (from Latin *cuneus*, "wedge," because a scribe's stylus made wedge-shaped impressions on the clay tablets used as writing material). Sumerians pioneered a sophisticated system of mathematics and computed a calendar that reconciled the lunar and solar years by adding extra months at regular intervals.

Religion. A typical Sumerian god was identified with a natural phenomenon, but conceived in human form. Gods were assumed to be frivolous, quarrelsome, selfish, and often childish creatures, who differed from humans only in their greater power and their immortality. The people of Mesopotamia expected little from a life after death. Their religion dealt with problems of this world, which they tried to solve using prayer, sacrifice, and magic. A large priesthood existed to provide expert advice on ways to influence the gods, and a high percentage of the cuneiform tablets that have come to light is devoted to religious texts (prayers, incantations, curses, and omens).

The Babylonians cultivated many methods of divination to discover the will of the gods. Their search for clues to divine action in the movements of the heavenly bodies gave birth to astrology. They also examined the entrails of sacrificial animals for significant abnormalities, and armies of scribes kept elaborate records of omens for interpretation by learned priests.

This Neo-Hittite relief carving dates to the ninth century B.C. It comes from the citadel at Binjirli in modern Turkey and shows two banqueters. [Erich Lessing/Art Resource, N.Y.]

The stories ancient peoples told about their gods became a mythology that had a lasting impact on Western literature and art. The Babylonians composed tales of the creation of the world, of a great flood that almost destroyed humanity, of an island paradise from which the god Enki was expelled for eating forbidden plants, and of a hero named Gilgamesh who performed great feats as he struggled to come to terms with his mortality.

Religion also inspired the greatest of Mesopotamia's architectural achievements, the ziggurat. The ziggurat was a stepped mound of mud-brick surmounted by a temple. The eroded remains of these monumental structures still dot the Iraqi landscape.

Society. Tens of thousands of cuneiform texts give us a detailed picture of the way people in ancient Mesopotamia conducted their lives. The evidence from the reign of Hammurabi is particularly good. It reveals a society legally divided into three classes: nobles, commoners, and slaves. The harshness of a punishment for a crime varied according to the class or classes to which the criminal and the victim belonged.

The laws recorded in Hammurabi's code reflect the priorities and concerns of his people. The third largest category of laws in the code deals with commerce. Regulations governing debts, rates of interest, security, default, and the quality of professional services (from contractors, surgeons, etc.) testify to the sophistication

The Babylonian Story of the Flood

This passage is part of the Babylonian Epic of Gilgamesh, *which may have been written before 2000 B.C. Its hero, Gilgamesh, becomes aware of his mortality when his friend and companion dies. Gilgamesh then seeks the secret of immortality from Utnapishtim. This man and his wife were the sole survivors of a great flood that destroyed the rest of humanity and the only two mortals known to have been granted eternal life. The tale is similar to, but diverges in significant ways from, the biblical story of Noah.*

~ How is this tale similar to the story of Noah in the Book of Genesis in the Hebrew Bible? How is it different? How does the presence of many divinities shape this story differently from the one in Genesis?

"For six days and (seven) nights the wind blew, and the flood and the storm swept the land. But the seventh day arriving did the rainstorm subside and the flood which had heaved like a woman in travail; there quieted the sea, and the storm-wind stood still, the flood stayed her flowing. I opened a vent and the fresh air moved over my cheek-bones. And I looked at the sea; there was silence, the tide-way lay flat as a roof-top—but the whole of mankind had returned unto clay. I bowed low: I sat and I wept: o'er my cheek-bones my tears kept on running.

"When I looked out again in the directions, across the expanse of the sea, mountain ranges had emerged in twelve places and on Mount Nisir the vessel had grounded. Mount Nisir held the vessel fast nor allowed any movement. For a first day and a second, fast Mount Nisir held the vessel nor allowed of any move-ment. For a third day and a fourth day, fast Mount Nisir held the vessel nor allowed of any movement. For a fifth day and a sixth day, held Mount Nisir fast the vessel nor allowed of any movement.

"On the seventh day's arriving, I freed a dove and did release him. Forth went the dove but came back to me: there was not yet a resting-place and he came returning. Then I set free a swallow and did release him. Forth went the swallow but came back to me: there was not yet a resting-place and he came returning. So I set free a raven and did release him. Forth went the raven—and he saw again the natural flowing of the waters, and he ate and he flew about and he croaked, and came not returning.

"So all set I free to the four winds of heaven, and I poured a libation, and scattered a food-offering, on the height of the mountain. Seven and seven did I lay the

of Babylonian commercial life. The second largest group of laws concerns land tenure, and the largest deals with the maintenance and protection of families.

Parents arranged marriages for their children. The groom made a bridal payment, and the father of the bride provided a dowry for his daughter. A marriage started out monogamous, but a husband whose wife was childless or ill for a long time could take a second wife. Extramarital relations for men with concubines, slaves, and prostitutes were common and accepted.

vessels, heaped into their incense-basins sweet-cane, cedarwood and myrtle. And the gods smelled the savour, the gods smelled the sweet savour, the gods gathered like flies about the priest of the offering.

"Then, as soon as the Mother-goddess arrived, she lifted up the great jewels which, (in childhood, her father) Anu had made as a plaything for her: 'O ye gods here present, as I still do not forget these lapis stones of my neck, so shall I remember these days—shall not forever forget them! If it please now the gods to come here to the offering, never shall Enlil come here to the offering, for without any discrimination he brought on the deluge, even (the whole of) my people consigned to destruction.'

"But as soon as Enlil arrived, he saw only the vessel—-and furious was Enlil, he was filled with anger against the (heaven-) gods, the Igigi: 'Has aught of living-kind escaped? Not a man should have survived the destruction!'

"Ninurta opened his mouth and spake unto warrior Enlil: 'Who except Ea could have designed such a craft? For Ea doth know every skill of invention.'

"Then Ea opened his mouth and spake unto warrior Enlil: 'O warrior, thou wisest among gods, how thus indiscriminately couldst thou bring about this deluge? (Had thou counselled): On the sinner lay his sin, on the transgressor lay his transgression: loosen (the rope) that his life be not cut off, yet pull tight (on the rope) that he do not [escape]: then instead of thy sending a Flood would that the lion had come and diminished mankind: instead of thy sending a Flood that the wolf had come and diminished mankind: instead of thy sending a Flood would that a famine had occurred and impoverished mankind: instead of thy sending a Flood would that a pestilence had come and smitten mankind. And I, since I could not oppose the decision of the great gods, did reveal unto the Exceeding-Wise a (magic) dream, and thus did he hear the gods' decision. Wherefore now take thee counsel concerning him.'

"Thereupon Enlil went up into the vessel: he took hold of my hand and made me go aboard, he bade my wife go aboard and made her kneel at my side. Standing between us, he touched our foreheads and did bless us, saying: 'Hitherto Utnapishtim has been but a man; but now Utnapishtim and his wife shall be as gods like ourselves. In the Far Distance, at the mouth of the Rivers, Utnapishtim shall dwell.'

"So they took me and did make me to dwell in the Far Distance, at the mouth of the Rivers. . . ."

Trans. by J. V. Kinnier Wilson in Documents from Old Testament Times, *D. Winton Thomas, ed. (London: Thomas Nelson and Sons, Ltd., 1958), lines 145–198, pp. 22–24.*

Women did not have similar sexual privileges, but a wife had rights protected by the law. Divorce was relatively easy and not entirely inequitable. Women divorced by their husbands without good cause received their dowries back. A woman initiating a divorce could also recover her dowry if her husband could not convict her of wrongdoing. A woman's primary duty, however, was to her home. The law stated that if a wife "has made up her mind to leave in order to engage in business, thus neglecting her house and humiliating her husband, he may divorce her without compensation."

Although true chattel slavery did not become common until late in Mesopotamian history (in the Neo-Babylonian period, 612–539 B.C.), the practice of enslaving foreigners captured in wars was ancient. Babylonians might also become slaves to other Babylonians. Parents could sell their children into slavery or pledge themselves and their families as surety for loans. And slavery was the punishment decreed for certain crimes—such as kicking one's mother or striking an elder brother. Laws against fugitive slaves or slaves who defied their masters were harsh, but in some respects, Mesopotamian slavery was more enlightened than other slave systems in history and offered slaves limited legal protection. Slaves could engage in business and, with certain restrictions, acquire property with which to buy their freedom. They could marry free men or women, and the children of these unions were considered free persons. Children of a slave by her master might also be allowed to share in his property after his death.

Egyptian Civilization

As Mesopotamian civilization evolved along the banks of the Tigris and Euphrates rivers, another great civilization emerged in Egypt. Its focus was the Nile. From its source in central Africa the Nile runs north some 4,000 miles to the Mediterranean. Ancient Egypt was shaped like a funnel with two distinct parts. A 150-mile-wide by 100-mile-deep triangular delta at the mouth of the Nile was home to Lower (downstream, northern) Egypt. Upper (upstream, southern) Egypt occupied a narrow valley stretching 650 miles from the delta to the First Cataract, a set of rapids that were a barrier to navigation.

The Nile alone made life possible in the almost rainless deserts of Egypt. Annually the river's floods covered the land and deposited fertile mud that enabled farmers to bring in two crops a year. Egypt's agricultural prosperity was unmatched in the ancient world.

Although Egypt was a long, narrow country, the Nile was a highway promoting its unification. The city-states of Mesopotamia competed among themselves for dominance, but Upper and Lower Egypt had become a single state as early as 3100 B.C., the start of Egypt's recorded history. The people on the open plains of the Tigris-Euphrates lived in constant fear of storm, flood, earthquake, and invasion, but nature protected the Egyptians. The Nile's unnavigable cataracts, the sea, and the desert made it difficult for foreigners to reach Egypt, and Egypt's climate was sunny and predictable. Consequently, Egypt was far more peaceful and secure than Mesopotamia, and Egyptian culture reflected an optimistic outlook that contrasted vividly with the pessimism expressed in Mesopotamian literature.

Events in the more than 3,000-year span of ancient Egyptian history are traditionally dated by reference to the reigns of thirty-one royal dynasties, which modern historians have clustered into eight periods (see chronology chart). The first dynasty was founded by Menes, the unifier of Upper and Lower Egypt, and the last, by a Greek conqueror, Alexander the Great (332 B.C.). For

Significant Dates from Ancient Egyptian History (Dynasties in Roman Numerals)

ca. 3100–2700 B.C.   *Early Dynastic Period (I–II)*
2700–2200 B.C.   *Old Kingdom (III–IV)*
2200–2052 B.C.   *I Intermediate Period (VII–X)*
2052–1786 B.C.   *Middle Kingdom (XI–XII)*
1786–1575 B.C.   *II Intermediate Period (XIII–XVII)*
ca. 1700 B.C.   *Hyksos invasion*
1575–1087 B.C.   *New Kingdom (Empire) (XVIII–XX)*
1087–30 B.C.   *Post-Empire (XXI–XXXI)*

most of its long history Egypt maintained its unity, for central management was vital to the success of its irrigation-based agriculture.

The Old Kingdom (2700–2200 B.C.). By the time of the Third Dynasty, Egypt's kings had achieved full supremacy. Ruling from their capital at Memphis, on the border between Upper and Lower Egypt, they had the resources of a huge, prosperous nation at their disposal. Royal power was absolute. The king or pharaoh (a title that evolved later from a term meaning "great house" or "palace") staffed his government with members of his family, appointing and removing them at his pleasure. Peasants were carefully regulated. Their movement was limited, and they were taxed heavily (perhaps as much as one-fifth of what they produced).

Egyptians believed their king to be a living god on whom their lives, safety, and prosperity depended. Since he was the direct source of law and justice, Egypt needed no law codes. Government was merely an aspect of the religion that dominated Egyptian life. The gods of Egypt took many forms: as animals, humans, and natural forces. In time, Re, the sun god, came to have the dominant place, but for centuries there was little order to the Egyptian pantheon.

Unlike the Mesopotamians, the Egyptians had a rather clear idea of an afterlife. They had elaborate conventions for the burial of their dead and supplied graves with all kinds of things they thought the departed would need for pleasant lives after death. At first, only kings were thought to achieve eternal life. Then nobles were included, and finally all Egyptians—if properly embalmed and buried with the requisite spells—laid claim to immortality. Bodies were preserved as mummies. Tombs were beautifully decorated, and offerings of food were made to the deceased on a regular basis. Some royal tombs were provided with full-sized ships for the voyage to heaven.

Egypt's land was the ruler's personal possession, and Egypt's people were his servants. The extent of royal power is demonstrated by the Old Kingdom's most famous monuments, the pyramids that were used as tombs for the kings of the Fourth Dynasty. Although many pyramids were built, the largest, that of

Khufu, has cast all others in its shade. It contained 2,300,000 blocks of stone averaging 2.5 tons each. It originally rose to a height of 481 feet from a base whose sides were 756 feet long. The Greek historian Herodotus claimed that it was constructed in a mere twenty years by a work force of 100,000 men. The pyramids are remarkable for the great technical skill they demonstrate, but even more so for the evidence they provide of the strength of Egypt's royal government.

The Egyptians developed a system of writing not much later than the Sumerians. Though the idea of writing may have come from Mesopotamia, Egyptian script developed independently. It began as picture writing and later combined pictographs with phonetic symbols. The result was a difficult and complicated script that the Greeks called *hieroglyph* ("sacred carvings"). Egyptian writing was designed to be done with pen and ink on a paper made from reeds (papyrus) that grew in the delta, not, like cuneiform, to be impressed with a stylus onto mud tablets.

Egyptian literature consisted of hymns, myths, magical formulas, tales of travel, and "wisdom literature" (bits of advice to help one succeed in the world). But Egyptian society, happier and simpler than that of Mesopotamia, produced nothing as serious and probing as Mesopotamia's epic of Gilgamesh.

The Middle Kingdom (2052–1786 B.C.). The power of the kings of the Old Kingdom waned as priests and nobles gained independence. The governors of *nomes*, Egypt's administrative districts, established hereditary rights to their offices that made it difficult for the central government to control them. About 2200 B.C. the Old Kingdom collapsed. After an era of confusion (the First Intermediate Period, ca. 2200–2052 B.C.) created by struggles among the nobles, the nomarchs (governors) of Thebes in Upper Egypt unified the country and established the Middle Kingdom (2052 B.C.).

The rulers of the Twelfth Dynasty restored Egypt's central government from their base at Thebes—though their power over the nobles who ruled the *nomes* remained limited. The kings of this period emphasized their role as dispensers of justice, and their statues often depicted them burdened with care for their people. Tales of the period stress the king's concern for justice and the welfare of ordinary folk. Order, peace, and prosperity characterized the Middle Kingdom. Trade expanded, and Egypt's influence extended north to Palestine and south to Ethiopia. The seat of government eventually shifted from Thebes back to the more defensible site at Memphis, but the patron god of Thebes, Amon, grew in importance. He was identified with Re, the sun god, and evolved into Amon-Re, Egypt's chief deity.

The New Kingdom (Empire) (1575–1087 B.C.) and After. The resurgent power of the nobility eroded the central authority of the Thirteenth Dynasty and inaugurated the II Intermediate Period (1786–1575 B.C.). About 1700 B.C., Egypt, already weakened, was invaded. A collection of Semitic peoples (probably from Palestine and Syria) whom the Egyptians called the Hyksos crossed the Sinai and occupied the delta. They dominated Egypt until 1575 B.C., when the no-

The Egyptians believed in the possibility of life after death through the god Osiris. The character of each person's life had to be tested by forty-two assessor-gods before the person could be presented to Osiris. In this scene from an illustration of the Book of the Dead, the deceased and his wife (on the left) watch the scales of justice weighing his heart (on the left side of the scales) against the feather of truth. The jackal-faced god Anubis also watches the scales, while the ibis-headed god Thoth keeps the records. [Courtesy of the Trustees of the British Museum]

marchs of Thebes rallied their countrymen to drive out the Hyksos and founded the New Kingdom or Empire Period.

Contact with the Hyksos brought the Egyptians new military techniques and weapons. The rulers of the New Kingdom built a powerful army to defend Egypt and pushed out Egypt's frontiers to the south and the east. The Eighteenth Dynasty, whose most prominent pharaoh was Thutmose III (r. 1490–1436 B.C.), extended Egypt's power across Palestine and Syria, to the upper Euphrates (see Map 1-2). Egypt's expansion was not checked until the pharaoh's armies made contact with the powerful Hittite empire of Asia Minor. The struggle that ensued weakened both nations, and as the New Kingdom declined, the glory of ancient Egypt faded. During the Post-Empire period (1087–30 B.C.) Egypt repeatedly suffered foreign invasion and foreign dominance.

Near the end of the Eighteenth Dynasty, when Egypt's empire was at its peak, an interesting struggle took place. The power of the priests of Amon had increased to the point where the pharaoh felt threatened. When young Amenhotep IV (r. 1367–1350 B.C.) came to the throne, he apparently decided to resist the priesthood of Amon. Supported by his family and advisers, he made a clean break with the worship of Amon-Re and devoted himself to the worship of the god Aton. He changed his name to Akhnaton ("it pleases Aton")

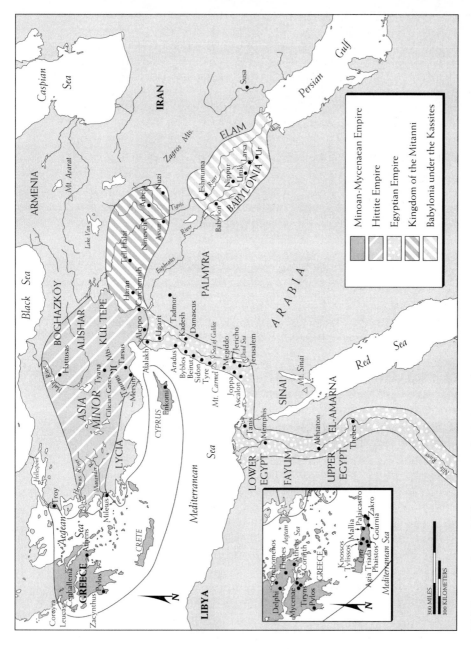

MAP 1-2 The Middle East and Greece About 1400 B.C. *About 1400 B.C. the Middle East was divided among four empires. Egypt went south to Nubia and north through Palestine and Phoenicia. Kassites ruled in Mesopotamia, Hittites in Asia Minor, and the Mitannians in Assyrian lands. In the Aegean the Mycenaean kingdoms were at their height.*

and moved his capital from Thebes, the center of Amon worship, to an entirely new city—Akhtaton—about 300 miles to the north at a place now called El Amarna.

The new god was different from any that had come before him, for he was believed to be universal, not merely Egyptian. But only the pharaoh and his family worshiped Aton directly. The people honored him through worship of the pharaoh. Unlike other gods, Aton had no cult statue but was represented in painting and relief sculpture as the disk of the sun. The universal claims made for Aton implied intolerance of the worship of other gods. Their temples were shut down, and the name of Amon-Re, Egypt's former high god, was chiseled from monuments. The priests of the old cults were deprived of their posts, and the pharaoh chose new people—even some foreigners—to serve him.

Akhnaton's preoccupation with religion apparently led him to make the disastrous mistake of ignoring foreign affairs. Egypt's Asian possessions fell away, and the economic consequences of the loss presumably increased hostility to the new religion. When the king died, a strong counterrevolution swept away his life's work.

His chosen successor was soon replaced by Tutankhamon (r. 1347–1339 B.C.), the young husband of a daughter of Akhnaton and his beautiful wife, Nefertiti. The new pharaoh restored the old religion and tried to wipe out the memory of the worship of Aton. He restored Amon to the center of the Egyptian pantheon, abandoned El Amarna, and returned the capital to Thebes. Although Tutankhamon died young and was a relatively minor pharaoh, he is very well known today. The magnificent treasures of his tomb remarkably survived undisturbed until their discovery in 1922.

The fall of Akhnaton restored power to the priests of Amon and to Egypt's military. A general named Horemhab became king (r. 1335–1308? B.C.) and recovered much of the lost empire. He branded his predecessor "the criminal of Akhtaton" and erased his name from the records. Akhnaton's city and memory disappeared for over 3,000 years, to be rediscovered only by chance about a century ago.

Although Egypt returned to its traditional gods and culture, its confidence was shaken. *The Book of the Dead*, a product of this late period, collected spells to help the dead reach the next world safely, avoiding destruction by a hideous monster. The text was a metaphor for the fate that threatened the nation—the approach of powerful, menacing enemies.

∾ Ancient Middle Eastern Empires

While the Eighteenth Dynasty ruled Egypt, new peoples who spoke Indo-European languages established themselves in the Middle East: the Kassites in Babylonia, the Hittites in Asia Minor, and the Mitannians in northern Mesopotamia. The Kassites and Mitannians were small warrior castes who ruled more civilized folk whose cultures they absorbed unchanged. The

Hittites established a kingdom of their own and built an empire that lasted 200 years.

The Hittites

The Hittites arrived in Asia Minor about 2000 B.C. By about 1500 B.C. they had established a strong, centralized government with a capital at Hattusas (near Ankara, the capital of modern Turkey). Between 1400 and 1200 B.C. they contested Egypt's control of Palestine and Syria. And by 1265 B.C. they were strong enough to merit a dynastic marriage with the daughter of the powerful Nineteenth Dynasty pharaoh, Ramses II. The Hittite kingdom was gone by 1200 B.C., swept away by new Indo-European migrations. But Neo-Hittite centers flourished in Asia Minor and Mesopotamia for a few centuries longer.

The Hittites adopted the Mesopotamian culture that dominated the east, but there were unique aspects to their society. Hittite kings did not claim to be divine or even to be the chosen representatives of the gods. In the early period a king's power was checked by a council of nobles, and the assembled army had to ratify his succession to the throne. The Hittites were also responsible for bringing a great technological advance to the east, the smelting of iron. Some of their importance in history derives from their role as transmitters of the cultures of Mesopotamia and Egypt to the Greeks, who lived on their frontiers.

The Assyrians

The Assyrians, who followed the Hittites, spoke a Semitic language and had ancient cultural roots in Mesopotamia. They established the first of several powerful empires that united the peoples of the Middle East and extended their ancient civilizations to new areas. The Assyrian homeland was the hill country of northern Mesopotamia and the area east of the Tigris River. Of the capitals of the Assyrian Empire, the best known was Nineveh (modern Iraq's Mosul).

Before its rise to empire Assyria had been ruled by Akkadians, Sumerians, Amorites, and Mitannians. A Hittite defeat of the Mitannians in the fourteenth century B.C. effectively liberated Assyria. About 1000 B.C. the Assyrians began a period of steady expansion, which by 665 B.C. brought them control of Mesopotamia, much of Asia Minor, Syria, Palestine, and Egypt. They succeeded thanks to a large, well-disciplined army and a society that promoted military virtues. Fierce and cruel, they boasted of their brutality—a strategy designed to terrorize real and potential enemies.

Unlike earlier empires, the Assyrian Empire systematically and profitably exploited the people it conquered. Some were forced simply to pay tribute. Others endured the stationing of garrisons on their territory. A few were broken up and driven from their homelands (a fate that befell the people of the kingdom of Israel). The administration of something as vast and diverse as the Assyrian Empire required great skill. But in addition to maintaining the empire, the Assyrians had to defend it against the barbarians on its frontiers. In the seventh century B.C. these tasks drained the overextended empire and made it vulnerable to internal rebellion. A new dynasty in Babylon threw off Assyrian rule, joined with the rising kingdom of Media to the east (in modern Iran), and defeated the Assyrians.

Nineveh was destroyed in 612 B.C., but the victorious Chaldean—or Neo-Babylonian—and Median kingdoms did not last long. By 539 B.C., they had been gathered into a new eastern empire, Persia.

～ Palestine

None of the empires of the ancient Middle East had as much influence on the future of Western civilization as the little nation of Israel that evolved in Palestine, a small stretch of land between Syria and Egypt. Its people produced the Hebrew Bible and set in motion events that created the modern West's religions: Judaism, Christianity, and Islam.

Canaanites and Phoenicians

Before the Israelites arrived in the land they believed their God had promised them, it was inhabited by people speaking a Semitic language, Canaanite. The Canaanites lived in walled cities and practiced a polytheistic religion. Their way of life followed the ordinary pattern of Mesopotamian cultures. When the Israelites appeared, the Canaanites were driven north to settle among similar people in the coastal district called Phoenicia.

The Phoenicians had played an important role in commerce from a very early time. Their writing system is among the earliest decipherable examples of a nearly alphabetic script, a simplified form of writing that relies on a small number of symbols to spell out the sounds of spoken language. They founded colonies along the African coast of the Mediterranean as far west as Spain. The most famous of these was Carthage, near modern Tunis in North Africa. The Phoenician cities dominated major trade routes and transmitted culture from east to west.

The Israelites

The history of the Israelites must be pieced together from various sources. Since they are rarely mentioned in the records of their neighbors, we must rely chiefly on the literature they have left us, the Bible. It is not a history in our sense, but a collection of historical narratives and bits of wisdom literature, poetry, law, and religious proclamation. Scholars once tended to dismiss it as a historical source, but the most recent trend is to take it seriously and use it with caution.

According to tradition, the patriarch Abraham came from Ur about 1900 B.C. and wandered west to tend his flocks in the land of the Canaanites. Some of his people settled there, and others drifted into Egypt, perhaps with

Significant Dates from the Early History of the Hebrew Nation

ca. 1000–961 B.C.	*Reign of King David*
ca. 961–922 B.C.	*Reign of King Solomon*
722 B.C.	*Assyrian conquest of Israel, the northern kingdom*
586 B.C.	*Chaldean conquest of Judah, the southern kingdom*
586–539 B.C.	*The Exile (the "Babylonian Captivity")*
539 B.C.	*Restoration of Jerusalem*

the Hyksos. By the thirteenth century B.C., led by Moses, they had left Egypt and wandered in the desert until they reached Canaan. They established a united kingdom that reached its peak under David and Solomon in the tenth century B.C. The sons of Solomon could not maintain the unity of the kingdom, and it split into two parts: Israel, the north, and Judah, the south, containing the old capital at Jerusalem (see Map 1-3). The northern kingdom fell to the Assyrians in 722 B.C., and its people—the "ten lost tribes"—were scattered and lost forever. Since the people of Judah alone survived, from this time forth it is appropriate to speak of the Israelites as Jews.

In 586 B.C. Judah was defeated by the Neo-Babylonian king Nebuchadnezzar II. He destroyed the great temple built by Solomon and carried thousands of hostages off to Babylon. When the Persians defeated Babylonia, they ended the period of the Exile or "Babylonian Captivity" of the Jews and allowed them to return to Jerusalem. But the land that had once belonged to the kingdom of the Jews remained under the dominance of other peoples for some 2,500 years until the establishment of the State of Israel in A.D. 1948.

The Jewish Religion

The fate of the tiny nation of Israel would be of little interest were it not for its unique religious achievement. The Jews' belief in one universal God—the all-powerful creator, the father of all people, and a just ruler demanding righteousness and obedience from humankind—became a central part of the Western heritage. The Jewish God is not a natural force, nor is He like human beings or any other creatures. He is so elevated that those who believe in Him may not picture Him in any form.

The Jewish faith established a unique link between ethics and religion. Jews believe that God made a covenant with Abraham that his progeny would be a chosen people who would be rewarded for following His revealed law. God is a severe but just judge. Ritual and sacrifice are not enough to win His approval. God binds Himself to act righteously, and His people, too, must be righteous. The Jewish prophets constantly criticized any falling away from the law and the path of justice. They blamed the misfortunes of their nation on a just God's necessary interventions in history to punish the sins of His people. The prophets also promised the Jews God's mercy when they repented.

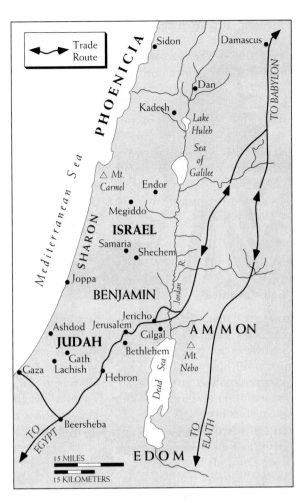

MAP 1-3 Ancient Palestine
The Hebrews established a unified kingdom in Palestine under kings David and Solomon in the tenth century B.C. After the death of Solomon, however, the kingdom was divided into two parts—Israel in the north and Judah, with its capital Jerusalem, in the south. North of Israel were the great commercial cities of Phoenicia.

The prophets expected the redemption of their people to be the work of a Messiah who would restore the house of David. Christianity, emerging from this tradition, holds that Jesus of Nazareth was that Messiah.

～ General Outlook of Middle Eastern Cultures

The various cultures of the Middle East differed in many ways. But they all taught points of view that were clearly distinct from those of the Greeks, the ancient people who had the greatest influence on the formation of the Western tradition. The contrasts between Greece and the Middle East appear when we compare what each culture thought about a human being's relationships to nature, to the gods, and to the human community.

Humans and Nature

The peoples of the Middle East were not aware of any gulf dividing humans from nature or animate creatures from inanimate objects. Since all things partook of life and spirit, the universe was the arena for a chaotic war of wills. Because the natural world appeared to have little order, the gods seemed capricious.

An Egyptian text defined human beings as "cattle of god," and the Babylonian story of creation said that humanity's function was to serve the gods. In a world ruled by powerful deities for their own benefit, human existence was precarious. Even disasters such as war, which we think of as human in origin, the Mesopotamians saw as the products of divine wills.

The helplessness of humankind in the face of irrational divine powers is the point of both the Egyptian and the Babylonian versions of the story of a great primeval flood that nearly extinguished the human race. In the Egyptian tale, Re, the god who created humans, decides for some unexplained reason to loose the vicious goddess Sekhmet on his hapless creatures. Re then changes his mind and pours 7,000 barrels of blood-colored beer in Sekhmet's path. Humanity is saved when the goddess becomes drunk. In the Babylonian story, the noise made by increasing hordes of human beings leads the gods to decree their destruction. The species is spared only because Enki, god of wisdom, decides to rescue the family of his friend Utnapishtim. In a world where such things were possible, humans could not hope to understand or control nature. At best, they might resort to magic to pit one mysterious force against another.

Humans and the Gods, Law, and Justice

Since the gods could destroy humankind—and might do so at any time for no good reason—people tried to win the gods over by offering prayer and sacrifice. But there was no guarantee of success, for gods were not bound by reason or conscience.

Human beings were different. In the earliest civilized societies human relations were guided by laws. The challenge for a lawgiver was to justify his authority: Why, apart from a lawgiver's power to coerce obedience, should anyone obey the law? The Egyptians simply asserted that the law came from the king, and since the king was a god, he could do as he wished. The Mesopotamians agreed. Their kings were representatives of gods who delegated them authority to command the people.

The Hebrews had a more subtle understanding of law. Their God was capable of destructive rages, but He was also open to rational discourse and subject to a moral law He imposed on Himself. In the biblical version of the flood story the Hebrew God is wrathful, but not arbitrary. He decides to destroy His creatures as just punishment for their sin. And when He repents and saves Noah, He does so because Noah is a good man. The Hebrews believed that God willed human beings to live in just relationships with each other and was Himself an advocate for justice.

⌁ Toward the Greeks and Western Thought

The Greeks devised original approaches to the perennial human problems addressed in ancient Middle Eastern literature, but it is important to recognize that most Greeks held many ideas in common with earlier peoples. The Greek gods had most of the characteristics of the Mesopotamian deities; magic and incantations played a part in the lives of most Greeks; and Greek law, like that of other states, often derived its authority from gods. Many, if not most, Greeks in the ancient world must have thought about life in the same way as their neighbors to the east. The surprising thing is that some Greeks were exceptions. They developed strikingly original ideas that set a part of humankind on an entirely new path.

As early as the sixth century B.C., Greek thinkers living along the coast of Asia Minor began an intellectual revolution. Thales, the first Greek philosopher, and his followers sought to explain natural events by referring them to each other, not to supernatural powers. Their search for a naturalistic explanation of cause and effect marked the start of Western science.

Rationalism transformed the way Greeks thought about everything. Xenophanes of Colophon, Thales' contemporary, pointed out that people had no real grounds for conceiving of the gods in human form. He argued that if oxen could paint, they would draw gods who looked like themselves. Ultimately such thoughts might lead to skepticism, but they could also produce valuable insights. In the fifth century B.C., Thucydides of Athens began to explain human history as a function of human nature and chance—never citing the gods as causes of events. He may have been influenced by Hippocrates of Cos, who founded a school of medicine that diagnosed and treated disease without any reference to the supernatural. The same absence of divine causality also characterized Greek views of law and justice.

Although the Greeks' sharp departure from the thinking of earlier peoples marked the beginning of the unusual experience that we call Western civilization, we should not forget that the Greeks built on a foundation of lore that people in the Middle East had accumulated over millennia. Phoenicia gave the Greeks a writing system, and from ancient Mesopotamia and Egypt the Greeks acquired vital technical information and models that stimulated the development of mathematics, astronomy, art, and literature. The discontinuities between the culture of the Greeks and those of their eastern neighbors are, however, more striking than the continuities.

A secular, reasoned quest for an understanding of the world that sought explanations for events in the natural order of things rather than in the supernatural acts of gods was not characteristic of pre-Greek cultures. Nor would it appear in similar societies at other times in other parts of the world. The new way of looking at things was uniquely the product of the Greeks. Was there something special in their experience that made them raise fundamental questions in an original way?

✑ Review Questions

1. How would you define *history*? What different academic disciplines do historians rely on for information? Why is the study of history important?

2. How was life during the Paleolithic Age different from that in the Neolithic Age? What advances in agriculture and human development had taken place by the end of the Neolithic era? Do they warrant referring to the period as the "Neolithic Revolution"?

3. What differences do you see in the political and intellectual outlooks of the Egyptian and Mesopotamian civilizations? How do their religious views compare? How did the geography of each region influence its religious outlook?

4. How did the monotheism of Akhnaton differ from that of the Hebrews? How did religious faith help bind the Hebrews together politically? Why did Middle Eastern civilizations regard the concept of monotheism as a radical idea?

5. Why were the Assyrians so successful in building an empire? How did their empire differ from that of the Hittites or Egyptians? How did their empire benefit the civilized Middle East? What caused its failure?

6. How did Greek thinkers depart from the assumptions that guided intellectuals schooled in the Middle Eastern civilizations?

✑ Suggested Readings

V. G. CHILDE, *What Happened in History* (1946). A pioneering study of human prehistory before the Greeks, from an anthropological point of view.

H. FRANKFORT et al., *Before Philosophy* (1949). A brilliant examination of the mind of the ancients, from the Stone Age to the Greeks.

A. GARDINER, *Egypt of the Pharaohs* (1961). A sound narrative history.

O. R. GURNEY, *The Hittites* (1954). A good general survey.

D. C. JOHNSON AND M. R. EDEY, *Lucy: The Beginnings of Mankind* (1981). A study of the first human creatures, based on remains found in Africa.

S. N. KRAMER, *The Sumerians: Their History, Culture and Character* (1963). A readable general account of Sumerian history.

J. OATES, *Babylon*, rev. ed. (1986). An introduction to the history and archaeology of Babylonia, revised to make use of newly discovered evidence.

H. M. ORLINSKY, *Ancient Israel* (1960). Chiefly a political survey.

J. N. POSTGATE, *Early Mesopotamia* (1992). An excellent study of Mesopotamian economy and society, from the earliest times to about 1500 B.C., helpfully illustrated with drawings, pictures, and translated documents.

J. B. PRITCHARD (ed.), *Ancient Near Eastern Texts Relating to the Old Testament* (1969). A good collection of documents in translation, with useful introductory material.

C. L. REDMAN, *The Rise of Civilization* (1978). An attempt to use the evidence provided by anthropology, archaeology, and the physical sciences to illuminate the development of early urban society.

W. F. SAGGS, *The Might That Was Assyria* (1984). A history of the northern Mesopotamian empire and a worthy companion to the author's account of the Babylonian empire in the south.

S. SANDMEL, *The Hebrew Scriptures* (1963). An examination of the Bible's value as history and literature.

B. G. TRIGGER et al., *Ancient Egypt: A Social History* (1982).

2

The Rise of Greek Civilization

The Bronze Age on Crete and on the Mainland to About 1150 B.C.
The Minoans
The Mycenaeans

The Greek "Middle Ages" to About 750 B.C.
Greek Migrations
The Age of Homer

The Polis
Development of the Polis
The Hoplite Phalanx

Expansion of the Greek World
The Greek Colony
The Tyrants (About 700–500 B.C.)

The Major States
Sparta
Athens

Life in Archaic Greece
Society
Religion
Poetry

The Persian Wars
The Persian Empire
The Ionian Rebellion
The War in Greece

KEY TOPICS IN THIS CHAPTER

- The Bronze Age civilizations that ruled the Aegean area before the development of Hellenic civilization
- The rise, development, and expansion of the *polis*, the characteristic political unit of Hellenic Greece
- The early history of Sparta and Athens
- The wars between the Greeks and the Persians

About 2000 B.C., Greek-speaking peoples settled the lands surrounding the Aegean Sea and established a culture that became one of the most powerful forces shaping the Western way of life. Their location at the eastern end of the Mediterranean put the Greeks in touch, early in their history, with Mesopotamia, Egypt, Asia Minor, and Syria-Palestine. The Greeks acknowledged their debt to their predecessors, but were well aware of the importance of their own contributions to civilization.

The Bronze Age on Crete and on the Mainland to About 1150 B.C.

During the Bronze Age, civilizations developed in three parts of the Aegean world: on the island of Crete, on the smaller islands of the Aegean Sea, and on the mainland of Greece.

The Minoans

Crete was a cultural bridge between the older civilizations of the east and the lands settled by the Greeks. The Minoan civilization of Crete (which modern historians have named for Minos, a legendary king of Crete) was the Aegean's earliest—flourishing during the third and second millennia B.C.

During the periods in history known as Middle and Late Minoan (2100–1150 B.C.), the cities of eastern and central Crete evolved a unique civilization. The palaces modern archaeologists have uncovered at Phaestus, Haghia Triada, and Cnossus were its most striking creations. Sections of the palace at Cnossus, the most important of the Minoan monuments, were four

(a)

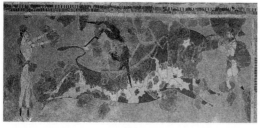

(b)

(a) The Minoan-period Palace at Cnossus on the island of Crete. (b) A fresco painting from the east wing of the palace. The fresco shows acrobats leaping over a charging bull. It is not known whether such acrobatic displays were only for entertainment or part of some religious ritual. [(a) D. A. Harissiadis, Athens; (b) Scala/Art Resource, N.Y.]

Significant Dates from the Era of the Rise of Greece

ca. 2900–1150 B.C.	*Minoan period*
ca. 1900 B.C.	*Migration of the Greeks to the mainland*
ca. 1600–1150 B.C.	*Mycenaean period*
ca. 1250 B.C.	*Sack of Troy (?)*
ca. 1200–750 B.C.	*Dark Ages*
ca. 725–700 B.C.	*Homer and Hesiod*
ca. 700–500 B.C.	*Major period of Greek tyranny*
ca. 650–625 B.C.	*Spartan constitution*
594 B.C.	*Solon's reforms at Athens*
546–527 B.C.	*Pisistratus' tyranny at Athens*
ca. 508–501 B.C.	*Clisthenes' democratic reforms at Athens*
490 B.C.	*Battle of Marathon*
480–479 B.C.	*Xerxes' invasion of Greece*
480 B.C.	*Battles of Thermopylae and Salamis*
479 B.C.	*Battles of Plataea and Mycale*

stories high. The building was a labyrinth of rooms organized around great courtyards. The main and upper floors contained living quarters as well as workshops for making pottery and jewelry. The cellars had elaborate storage facilities for oil and grain. There were sitting rooms and even bathrooms, to which water was piped. Ceilings were supported by columns of a unique design—tapering gracefully downward. Many walls carried murals showing landscapes, seascapes, festivals, and sports. Minoan art reflects eastern influences, but it has a style and quality all its own.

Since Minoan palaces and settlements were wealthy, they would have been attractive targets for raiders. But, surprisingly, the great Minoan structures lacked defensive walls. Some scholars, relying on theories about Minoan religion, have argued that the civilizations of Crete were strongly influenced by women and were, therefore, inherently pacific. Other experts have suggested that the protection provided by the sea made the fortification of buildings on Crete unnecessary.

The Minoans wrote on clay tablets like those found in Mesopotamia. Most of the extant specimens were preserved accidentally when they were baked by a great fire that destroyed the palace at Cnossus. The Cnossus tablets are inscribed with three distinct kinds of writing: hieroglyphic (picture writing) and two different linear scripts (A and B). At this point only Linear B has been deciphered. It records an early form of Greek.

The Linear B tablets are fairly pedestrian documents—inventories, the working papers of the kind of elaborate bureaucracy that was characteristic of an ancient eastern monarchy. The greatest mystery posed by the tablets is their language. Why should Minoans, who were not Greek, write in a language not their own? How was Crete related to the Bronze Age ("Helladic") cultures of the Greek mainland?

The Mycenaeans

During the Early Helladic Period (the third millennium B.C.) most of the Greek mainland was occupied by a people who knew how to use metal, who constructed impressive buildings, and who had trade contacts with Crete and the islands of the Aegean. Some of the names they gave to places have survived. The names prove that these people were not Greeks, for the names do not fit the pattern of the Indo-European languages to which Greek belongs.

Sometime after 2000 B.C., many of the Early Helladic sites were destroyed, abandoned, or occupied by a new people. These signs of invasion probably signal the arrival of the Greeks. The invaders won control of the entire mainland and, during the Late Helladic era (1580–1150 B.C.), developed a civilization that modern historians have named for Mycenae, one of its cities. The Linear B tablets found at Cnossus suggest that at the height of Mycenaean power (1400–1200 B.C.), Greeks conquered Crete and ruled it until the end of the Bronze Age.

Mycenaean Culture. The Mycenaean world contained a number of independent, powerful, and well-organized kingdoms. Excavations at Mycenaean sites suggest that the culture of the Mycenaeans was influenced by, but very different from, that of the Minoans. Unlike the Minoans, the Mycenaeans were preoccupied with war. The walls of their palaces were decorated with paintings depicting scenes of battle and hunting, and defensible sites were chosen for their cities. The need for defense probably promoted the development of strong, centralized monarchies.

By 1500 B.C. Mycenaean kings were constructing monumental tombs that testify to their wealth and to their power to command. The *tholos* tombs of the Mycenaeans were of a unique design—beehivelike chambers, built of enormous cut and fitted stones, buried beneath an artificial mound. The wealth that financed the construction of these monuments probably came from raids and trade. Mycenaean ships ventured west to Italy and Sicily, but most Greek commerce was with the islands of the Aegean, the coast of Asia Minor, and the cities of Syria, Egypt, and Crete.

The Rise and Fall of Mycenaean Power. At the height of their power (1400–1200 B.C.), the Mycenaeans enlarged their cities, expanded their trade, and established commercial colonies in the east. Mycenaeans are mentioned in the archives of the Hittite kings of Asia Minor and in Egyptian records— as marauders of the Nile Delta. About 1250 B.C., the Mycenaeans probably sacked a city called Troy on the coast of northwestern Asia Minor (see Map 2-1). This campaign gave rise to a most important body of literature (Homer's epics, the *Iliad* and the *Odyssey*). And it may have been the Mycenaeans' last great adventure. By 1200 B.C., their world was in trouble; by 1100 B.C., it was gone.

What happened? Recently, some scholars have suggested that a volcanic eruption on the Aegean island of Thera (modern Santorini) may have triggered the fall of Bronze Age civilization in the Aegean, but their argument is not

MAP 2-1 The Aegean Area in the Bronze Age *The Bronze Age in the Aegean area lasted from about 1900 to about 1100 B.C. Its culture on Crete is called Minoan and was at its height from about 1900 to about 1400 B.C. Bronze Age Helladic culture on the mainland flourished from about 1600 to about 1200 B.C.*

convincing. The Mycenaean towns were not destroyed at one time; many fell around 1200 B.C., but some flourished for another century, and some places, such as Athens, were never destroyed or abandoned. No natural disaster could account for this pattern.

The Dorian Invasion. The ancient Greeks preserved a legend that told of an attack on the Peloponnesus (the southern Greek peninsula) by Dorians, a rude people from the north whose Greek dialect was different from that of the Mycenaeans. Archaeology has not yet been able to confirm this story, and it is impossible to say with certainty what happened at the end of the Aegean Bronze Age.

Mycenaean civilization faded during the century between 1200 B.C. and 1100 B.C., and its end may have been the result of a combination of conflicts among the Mycenaean kings and pressure from outsiders—like the Dorians. The rigid, bureaucratic organization of the Mycenaean kingdoms may have limited their flexibility, sapped their vitality, and increased their vulnerability to invasion.

∽ The Greek "Middle Ages" to About 750 B.C.

The immediate effects of the Dorian invasion were disastrous for the inhabitants of the Mycenaean world. The palaces and the kings and bureaucrats who managed them were destroyed. The wealth and social order that made it possible for artists and merchants to thrive were swept away. Many villages were abandoned and never resettled. The chaos resulting from the collapse of the highly centralized palace governments produced severe depopulation and widespread poverty that lasted for a long time.

Greek Migrations

As a result of the invasion, Greek people migrated from the mainland to the Aegean islands and the coast of Asia Minor. The Dorians themselves, after occupying most of the Peloponnesus, swept across the Aegean to occupy the southern islands and neighboring parts of the Anatolian coast.

These migrations made the Aegean a Greek lake. But Greek trade, both internal and with the old civilizations of the Middle East, declined with the fall of the Minoan and Mycenaean civilizations. The Greeks turned inward, and each community was left largely to its own devices. At this time the Middle East was also in disarray, so no great power was poised to take advantage of the confusion in the Aegean. Consequently, the Greeks had time to recover and freedom to evolve a unique way of life. We, however, know little about this crucial era in their history. Since writing disappeared with the fall of Mycenae and was not reinvented until after 750 B.C., no contemporary authors shed light on this "dark age." And excavation reveals no architecture, sculpture, or painting until after 750 B.C.

The Age of Homer

Homer's epics, the *Iliad* and the *Odyssey,* are our best sources of information on the Greek dark ages. They are the end products of a tradition of oral poetry with roots in the Mycenaean era. For generations bards sang tales of the heroes who fought at Troy. Since singers used rhythmic formulas to aid the accurate memorization of their verses, some very old material was preserved until the poems attributed to Homer were finally written down in the eighth century B.C. Although the poems narrate the adventures of Mycenaean heroes, the society the verses describe is not purely Mycenaean. Homer's warriors are not buried in *tholos* tombs but are cremated; they worship gods in temples, whereas the Mycenaeans had no temples; they have chariots but do not know their proper use in warfare. Homer's epics combine information about the ancient Mycenaeans with material drawn from the very different worlds of their descendants of the tenth and ninth centuries B.C.

Government. The kings Homer describes had much less power than real Mycenaean monarchs. Homeric kings had to consult a council of nobles when making important decisions. Their nobles felt free to discuss matters in vigorous language and to oppose the king's wishes. In the *Iliad*, Achilles does not hesitate to accuse Agamemnon, the "most kingly" commander of the Trojan expedition, of having "a dog's face and a deer's heart." Such language may have been impolite, but it was not treasonous.

The right to speak in council was limited to noblemen, but the common people could not be ignored. If a king planned a war or a major change of policy during a campaign, he would not fail to call the common soldiers to an assembly. They could listen and express their feelings by acclamation, even though they could not take part in debate. The evidence from Homer shows that even in these early times the Greeks, unlike their predecessors and contemporaries, practiced limited forms of popular government.

Society. Homeric society was sharply divided into classes. We do not know the origin of the distinction between noble and commoner, but there is no doubt that the Greek world was dominated by a hereditary aristocracy. There were three groups of commoners: the *thetes,* the landless laborers, and the slaves. The *thetes* may have owned the land they worked outright, or they may have worked hereditary plots that belonged to their clans (and which they were not free to sell). The worst condition was that of the free, but landless, agricultural laborer. Attachment to a household guaranteed a slave protection and food. But free workers were desperately vulnerable, for they were loners in communities where membership in a settled group was the only source of security. Slaves were few in number and mostly women who served as maids and concubines. Some male slaves worked as shepherds, but agriculture depended on free labor throughout Greek history.

Homeric Values. The Homeric poems reflect an aristocratic code of values that powerfully influenced all later Greek thinkers. In classical times Homer was the schoolbook of the Greeks. They memorized his texts, cherished his values, and emulated the behavior he described: physical prowess; courage; fierce protection of one's family, friends, and property; and, above all, defense of one's honor. Speed of foot, strength of arm, and, most of all, excellence at fighting established a man's reputation. Honor was his supreme value. The *Iliad* is the story of a fight over honor. When Agamemnon, the king who presided over the Greek army besieging Troy, wounds the honor of his most important warrior, Achilles, Achilles refuses to fight and persuades the gods to heap defeat on the Greeks. When Achilles finally returns to the battlefield, he is not motivated by a sense of duty to his country, but by a personal obligation to avenge the death of a friend, Patroclus.

The highest virtue in Homeric society was *arete*—manliness, courage, the excellence proper to a hero. A man demonstrated this quality by engaging in a contest with a worthy opponent. Homeric battles are usually individual struggles between great champions, not group combats. Homeric festivals are often athletic competitions. The *Iliad* ends with the description of such an event, staged in honor of the burial of Achilles' friend, Patroclus.

Homer's central ethical idea is found in the advice Achilles' father gives him as he departs for Troy: "Always be the best and distinguished above others." The father of another Homeric hero adds a codicil to this prescription: "Do not bring shame on the family of your fathers." Here in a nutshell we have the chief values of the aristocrats of Homer's world: to vie for individual supremacy in *arete* and to defend and increase the honor of the family. These remained prominent aristocratic values long after Homeric society was only a memory.

～ The *Polis*

The characteristic Greek institution was the *polis* (plural, *poleis*). The common translation of that word as "city-state" is misleading, for it says too much and too little. Since all Greek *poleis* began as small agricultural villages or towns (and many stayed that way), the word "city" is inappropriate. All of them were states in the sense of being independent political units, but they were more than that. The *polis* was thought of as a community of relatives; all its citizens were theoretically descended from a common ancestor. Its families were organized into various hereditary subgroups—such as fighting brotherhoods *(phratries)*, clans, and tribes—defined by common religious ceremonies.

In the fourth century B.C., hundreds of years after the *polis* came into existence, the philosopher Aristotle described the assumptions that had guided its evolution from the beginning. He argued that the human being was by nature "an animal who lives in a *polis*," for the attributes that define humanity—the power of speech and the ability to distinguish good from bad and right from wrong—require us to live together. He said that "the sharing of these things is what makes a household and a *polis*," and people who are incapable of such sharing or who are so self-sufficient that they have no need of it are not truly human. They are either beasts or gods.

Development of the *Polis*

Originally the word *polis* referred only to a citadel, an elevated, defensible rock to which the farmers of an area could retreat in case of attack. (The Acropolis in Athens and the hill called Acrocorinth in Corinth are examples.) For some time such places and the adjacent farms comprised the *polis*. Towns grew gradually and without planning, and for centuries they had no walls. Unlike the city-states of the Middle East, they were not often situated, for the convenience of traders, on rivers and seacoasts. The availability of farmland and of a natural fortress determined their location, and, when possible, they were located well inland to avoid raids by pirates. Only later and gradually did an *agora*—a marketplace and civic center—appear within the *polis*. The *agora*, the spot where citizens most conveniently met for formal and informal discussions, became the center of Greek urban life.

Some *poleis* probably came into existence early in the eighth century B.C. They were widespread by the middle of that century, for all the colonies that the Greeks established in the years after 750 B.C. were *poleis*. With the appearance of the *polis*, monarchy disappeared. Vestigial kings survived in some places, but they were almost always ceremonial figures without power. The *polis* was usually a republic dominated by an aristocracy that monopolized government offices. But there were developments that encouraged wider participation in politics. About 750 B.C., coincident with the development of the *polis*, the Greeks borrowed a writing system from one of the Semitic scripts and added vowels to create the first true alphabet. Since this alphabet was easier to learn than any earlier script, it promoted much wider literacy. At the same time changes in military technology similarly empowered the common man and contributed to the development of the *polis*.

The Hoplite Phalanx

Earlier Greek warfare was conducted by small troops of cavalry and individual "champions" who first cast spears and then came to close quarters with swords. But at the end of the eighth century B.C., a kind of infantry developed. The hoplite was a heavily armed footsoldier who fought with a spear and large shield. A hoplite fought in a tightly ordered formation called a phalanx—usually a block of men at least eight ranks deep. The success of a phalanx depended on the discipline, strength, and courage of the individuals who composed it. A phalanx could withstand cavalry charges and defeat much larger companies of less disciplined men. Until the more flexible Roman legion appeared, the phalanx was the dominant military force in the eastern Mediterranean.

A phalanx was a communal project that relied not on the extraordinary actions of a few individuals but on the courage of a considerable portion of the citizens of a *polis*. These men committed themselves to brief, violent encounters with their enemies that were designed to resolve disputes quickly with minimal threat to houses, livestock, and the capital on which the citizens of a *polis* depended.

Although Homeric warfare had been an aristocratic prerogative, the new infantry units were not limited to noblemen. As the size of armies grew and farmers working relatively small holdings were recruited as hoplites, kings and aristocrats declined in importance. The rise of the hoplite phalanx created a bond between the aristocrats and the yeoman family farmers who fought at their side. And shared military responsibilities led inevitably to demands for shared political privileges.

∽ Expansion of the Greek World

About the middle of the eighth century B.C., the Greeks began to extend the territory they controlled, and their colonists spread *poleis* from Spain to the Black Sea. Syria and other eastern lands were too strong to penetrate, but Greeks moved into regions that were sparsely settled or whose natives were not well organized to resist: the southern coast of Macedonia, the Chalcidic peninsula, southern Italy, eastern Sicily, and the Mediterranean coasts of France and Spain. (There were so many Greek colonies in Italy and Sicily that the Romans called the whole region *Magna Graecia*, "Great Greece.") By the seventh century B.C., the Greeks had outposts scattered throughout the Mediterranean world.

The Greek Colony

The pressures of overpopulation probably explain why thousands of Greeks left the cities of their births to found new *poleis*. Emigration was difficult, but it could be very rewarding. Colonists copied the constitutions and the religious rites of their mother cities, and they traded with them. But a colony was established for the good of its residents, not the homeland.

By scattering the Greeks, colonization strengthened Greek civilization. By providing outlets for excess population, colonies helped Greeks live together in peace. And colonies heightened the Greeks' awareness of their culture by bringing them into contact with alien peoples. *Poleis* across the Mediterranean established games and festivals to celebrate their common Panhellenic ("all-Greek") heritage. (Those held at Olympia, Delphi, Corinth, and Nemea were particularly famous.)

Colonization encouraged economic activity that changed the lives not only of colonists but of the Greeks who remained in the homeland. An influx of wealth from abroad and an increased market for trade goods stimulated more intensive use of the land and development of crops for export (chiefly olives and wine grapes). The manufacture of pottery, tools, weapons, and fine artistic metalwork was also encouraged. These economic opportunities created a new class of independent commoners who resented the aristocrats' traditional monopoly of governmental authority. The result, in a small percentage of the more than 1,000 Greek *poleis*, was increasing political tension that sometimes resulted in the establishment of a tyranny.

The Tyrants (About 700–500 B.C.)

A tyrant was a monarch who had gained power unconstitutionally, but usually with widespread popular support. The founder of a tyranny was usually an aristocrat who broke with his class and seized control of a city with the help of those who were unhappy with aristocratic rule (the poor and the politically disenfranchised farmer-soldiers). He often expelled his aristocratic opponents, distributed their land among his backers, and devised policies to foster economic development benefiting the masses.

A tyrant's rule was secured by a personal bodyguard and by mercenary soldiers, but it was not necessarily oppressive. Since a policy of aggression against other states required the training of a citizen army that might turn on its leader, tyrants usually avoided war and concentrated on domestic development. They financed useful public works projects that provided employment for the poor, sponsored festivals that promoted civic pride, and generously supported the arts.

Despite the contributions some tyrants made to the development of some *poleis*, tyranny faded from the Greek world at the end of the sixth century B.C. There was something about tyranny that was inimical to the traditions on which *poleis* were founded. A *polis* was defended by all its citizens. They looked to it for justice, and the aristocratic values they inherited made tyranny seem alien and offensive. The rule of a tyrant, however beneficent, was unacceptable, for it was arbitrary and not answerable to the will of the citizens. But by breaking the grip of the aristocracy and putting the productive powers of the most talented citizens fully at the service of the *polis*, tyrants contributed to the development of popular government.

~ The Major States

It is impossible to describe all of the *poleis*. But two—Sparta and Athens— were of such historical importance that they require special attention.

The temple of Hera at Paestum in southern Italy (sixth century B.C.) is considered the finest surviving example of Doric architecture. [Hirmer Verlag, Munich]

Sparta

About 725 B.C., Sparta embarked on a path that made it the strongest state in the Peloponnesus and Greece's most respected military power. The need for space to accommodate a growing population led the Spartans to invade their western neighbor, Messenia. The conquest of Messenia and the enslavement of its people solved Sparta's economic problems, but created a dangerous political situation. The Spartans were outnumbered ten to one by their slaves (the Helots), and about 650 B.C. a slave revolt nearly destroyed Sparta. To maintain control of the situation the Spartans embarked on a program of total military mobilization.

Spartan Society. The new system was designed to subordinate natural feelings of devotion to family to the interests of the state. The state's concern was to turn all of its men into superb soldiers. Privacy, luxury, and comfort were sacrificed to the purpose of producing soldiers whose physical powers, training, and discipline made them the best in the world. Nothing that might turn the mind away from duty was permitted.

The *polis* controlled the life of each Spartan from birth. Only infants that officials of the state judged to be physically fit were raised. At the age of seven Spartan boys left their mothers and began their military training. They learned to fight, to endure privation, to bear physical pain, and to live off the land. At twenty they joined the army in the field and resided in barracks until the age of thirty. Marriages were permitted, but not home lives. Young Spartan husbands visited their wives only infrequently and by stealth. At thirty a man acquired full citizen rights. Though he lived at home, he took his meals at a public mess in the company of fifteen comrades. His food, a simple diet with little meat or wine, was provided by a grant from the state—a plot of land worked by Helots. At age sixty a Spartan could finally retire from active service.

Spartan females were also trained to serve the state. Female infants were examined for fitness in the same way as males. Girls were given athletic training, and since Spartan men were often absent from home and preoccupied with military affairs, Spartan women had greater freedom of movement and wider responsibilities than other Greek women.

Spartan Government. The Spartan constitution mixed elements of monarchy, oligarchy, and democracy. There were two kings whose functions were chiefly religious and military. A Spartan army rarely left home without one of its kings in command, but the kings did not govern Sparta. An oligarchic council, consisting of the kings and twenty-eight men over the age of sixty who were elected for life, devised policy and sat as a high court. All Spartan males over thirty could participate in the democratic assembly. Theoretically they were the final authority, but they could only consider proposals previously approved by the council. Since they voted by acclamation rather than ballot, their function was to ratify decisions already taken or to decide between positions favored by their leaders.

The administration of Sparta was facilitated by a board of ephors: five men elected annually by the assembly. They controlled foreign policy, oversaw the generalship of the kings, presided at the assembly, and policed the Helots.

The Peloponnesian League. Since suppression of the Helots required all the energy Sparta had, the Spartans chose not to expand. Instead of conquering and assimilating potentially troublesome neighbors, the Spartans forced them into an alliance that left them free internally but subservient to Sparta's foreign policy. The resulting Peloponnesian League eventually enrolled every Peloponnesian state but Argos and made Sparta the most powerful *polis* before the rise of Athens.

Athens

The environment of Athens caused it to evolve more slowly than Sparta. Athens had a large area (about 1,000 square miles) that absorbed population growth and retarded unification of villages as a single *polis* until the seventh century B.C. Economic development was hampered by the fact that it was not situated on the leading trade routes of the eighth and seventh centuries B.C.

Aristocratic Rule. The government of Athens in the seventh century B.C. was aristocratic. Aristocratic families held the most and best land and led the tribes, clans, and brotherhoods (phratries) that structured Athenian society. There was no written law. The state was governed by the Areopagus, a council of nobles that annually elected nine magistrates, called archons.

Pressure for Change. In the seventh century B.C. an agrarian crisis accelerated Athens' political evolution. Many Athenians obtained their livings from family farms planted in wheat, the staple crop. After years of consistent cultivation without rotating fields or sufficient fertilization, productivity declined. Shifting to more intensive agricultural techniques and to the planting of trees and vines required capital. To survive, some farmers had to borrow from wealthy neighbors by mortgaging future crops—and by pledging themselves as surety for new loans. Many defaulted and were enslaved. Some were even sold abroad. The disgruntled poor resented their loss of status and began to demand the abolition of debt and a redistribution of the land.

In 632 B.C., a nobleman named Cylon tried unsuccessfully to establish himself as tyrant. He was thwarted, but Athens' leaders saw the danger he represented and attempted a compromise to head off other revolutionaries. In 621 B.C., they gave a certain Draco special authority to codify and publish Athens' laws. Draco acquired a reputation for extreme harshness, but his laws were probably limited to cases concerning homicide. They were primarily intended to end blood feuds among clans, but they laid the foundation for a public law that established a common standard of justice for all Athenians.

Reforms of Solon. In the year 594 B.C., the Athenians elected Solon sole archon and gave him extraordinary powers to reform their institutions. He attacked the agrarian problem by canceling debts and forbidding loans secured by the person of the borrower. He freed those enslaved for debt in Athens and brought home many Athenians who had been sold abroad. He did not, however, alienate the rich and play to the poor by redistributing the land. Instead he tried to provide for the poor by expanding Athens' economy. He forbade the export of wheat, but not olive oil. This made wheat more available in Attica, the region around Athens, and encouraged the cultivation of cash crops. He facilitated trade by changing the Athenian standards of weights and measures to conform with those of Corinth and Euboea and the cities of the east. And he promoted industry by offering citizenship to foreign artisans who set up shop in Athens.

Solon also decreed major political reforms. He divided Athens' citizens

The Development of the Athenian *Polis*

When the Spartans invaded Attica at the beginning of the Peloponnesian War, the Athenians were forced to leave their homes in the country to seek safety behind the walls of Athens. While explaining this, the historian Thucydides takes the opportunity to describe the development of the Athenian polis *from a collection of separate towns into a single political unit. He wrote several centuries after the unification of Athens, and the details of the event are legendary, but the general outlines of what took place are credible.*

⮑ What kind of evidence does Thucydides give for his history of early Attica? Does it seem sufficient and reliable enough to provide an accurate account? How does he create a coherent and plausible explanation with so few facts? How does the picture given here of early kingship in Athens compare with kingship in the ancient Middle East, Mycenaean Greece, and Homeric Greece?

The Athenians . . . began to carry in their wives and children from the country, and all their household furniture, even to the woodwork of their houses which they took down. Their sheep and cattle they sent over to Euboea and the adjacent islands. But they found it hard to move, as most of them had been always used to live in the country.

From very early times this had been more the case with the Athenians than with others. Under Cecrops and the first kings, down to the reign of Theseus, Attica had always consisted of a number of independent townships, each with its own town hall and magistrates. Except in times of danger the king at Athens was not consulted; in ordinary seasons they

into four classes on the basis of wealth. Only members of the two richest classes could hold the archonship, the chief magistracy in Athens, and thus win membership on the Areopagus. Men of the third class could serve as hoplites and be elected to a council of 400 chosen by all the citizens (100 from each tribe). Solon intended this council to serve as a check on the Areopagus, for it oversaw all proposals that were put before the assembly of all adult male citizens. The poorest class, the *thetes*, voted in the assembly. They participated in the election of archons and sat on a new popular court of appeal.

Pisistratus the Tyrant. Solon's reforms failed to ease political tensions in Athens, and on several occasions fights among factions prevented the election of the archons. In 546 B.C. (following unsuccessful attempts at coups in 560 B.C. and 556 B.C.) Pisistratus, a nobleman, faction leader, and military hero, profited from the confusion. He entered Athens at the head of a mercenary army

carried on their government and settled their affairs without his interference; sometimes they even waged war against him, as in the case of the Eleusinians with Eumolpus against Erechtheus. In Theseus, however, they had a king of equal intelligence and power; and one of the chief features in his organization of the country was to abolish the council chambers and magistrates of the petty cities, and to merge them in the single council chamber and town hall of the present capital. Individuals might still enjoy their private property just as before, but they were henceforth compelled to have only one political centre, viz. Athens, which thus counted all the inhabitants of Attica among her citizens, so that when Theseus died he left a great state behind him. Indeed, from him dates the Synoecia, or Feast of Union, which is paid for by the state, and which the Athenians still keep in honour of the goddess. Before this city consisted of the present citadel and the district beneath it looking rather towards the south. This is shown by the fact that the temples of the other deities, besides that of Athene, are on the citadel; . . . Again, from their old residence in that quarter, the citadel is still known among Athenians as the *city*.

The Athenians thus long lived scattered over Attica in independent townships. Even after the centralization of Theseus, old habit still prevailed; and from the early times down to the present war most Athenians still lived in the country with their families and households, and were consequently not at all inclined to move now, especially as they had only just restored their establishments after the Median invasion. Deep was their trouble and discontent at abandoning their houses and the hereditary temples of the ancient constitution, and at having to change their habits of life and to bid farewell to what each regarded as his native city.

Thucydides, The Peloponnesian War, 2.14–16, trans. by *Richard Crawley, Vol. 1, ed. by F. R. B. Godolphin in* The Greek Historians *(New York: Random House, 1942).*

and established a tyranny. At his death in 527 B.C., his authority passed to his son Hippias, who led Athens until he was driven from the city by a competitor in 510 B.C.

Like the tyrants of other Greek cities, Pisistratus courted the people as a way of dominating them. He sponsored public works programs, urban development, and civic festivals. He employed poets and artists to add cultural luster to his court. Although he made no formal change in Solon's constitution, he devised ways to increase the power of the central government at the expense of the nobility. Assembly, councils, and courts met; magistrates and councils were elected. But Pisistratus saw to it that his supporters dominated these bodies. This blunted the sharp edge of tyranny with the appearance of constitutional government and won Pisistratus a reputation as a popular, gentle ruler. The strategy also gave the Athenians experience in the procedures of self-government and increased their taste for it.

Spartan Intervention. Hippias, Pisistratus' elder son, tried to follow his father's example. In 514 B.C., however, the murder of his brother, Hipparchus, in a private quarrel inflamed his suspicious nature. As his government became increasingly harsh, the Alcmaeonids, one of the noble clans that Hippias and Hipparchus had exiled, saw an opportunity. They persuaded the Spartans to march into Athenian territory in 510 B.C. and drive out Hippias.

In Athens the Spartans put in power a party led by a man named Isagoras. Isagoras hoped to make Athens more like Sparta by restoring a version of the pre-Solonian aristocratic state. As part of his plan, he purged the citizen lists, removing those who had been enfranchised by Solon or Pisistratus. When Clisthenes, the Alcmaeonid leader, opposed this motion by making a direct appeal to the people, Isagoras called in the Spartans again. The people refused to tolerate a second Spartan intervention in their affairs, rallied to Clisthenes, and drove out Isagoras.

Clisthenes, the Founder of Democracy. Clisthenes curtailed the activities of the regional political machines that were the bases for the power of the aristocratic factions. In 508 B.C., he divided Attica into *demes*—equivalents of small towns in the country or wards in the city. *Demes* were grouped together to form the tribal organizations that formed Athens' army and elected its government, and care was taken to make sure that each tribe was composed of *demes* representing a variety of regions. This prevented a tribe from identifying with a region and coming under the control of a local baron.

A council of 500 replaced Solon's council of 400. Its chief responsibility was preparation of legislation for discussion by the assembly, but it also received foreign emissaries and managed some fiscal affairs. Final authority in all things rested with the assembly composed of all adult male Athenian citizens. Debate in the assembly was free and open; any Athenian could submit legislation, offer amendments, or argue the merits of any question.

As a result of the work of Solon, Pisistratus, and Clisthenes, Athens entered the fifth century B.C. well on the way to prosperity and democracy. It was finally prepared to take its place as one of Greece's leading *poleis.*

⟅ Life in Archaic Greece

Society

The features that were to distinguish Greek society emerged at the end of the "dark ages." The great majority of people made their living from the land, but artisans and merchants increased in importance as contact with the non-Hellenic world improved.

Farmers. Ordinary country people rarely leave a record of their thoughts or activities. But the poet Hesiod (ca. 700 B.C.), who claimed in his *Works and Days* to be a small farmer, gives us some idea what their lives were like. Their common crops included barley, some wheat, grapes for wine, olives mainly for oil (used for cooking, lighting, and washing), green vegetables, beans, and fruit. Sheep and goats provided milk and cheese. Since land fertile enough to provide fodder for cattle was needed to grow grain, the only meat most people tasted was the flesh of the animals sacrificed to the gods at religious festivals.

Farmers worked hard. Hesiod had the help of oxen and mules and occasional hired laborers, but his life was one of continuous toil. The toughest season began with October's rains, the time for the first plowing. Plows were iron-tipped, but light and fragile. Even with the help of a team of oxen it was difficult to break the sod. During autumn and winter, wood was cut and repairs made to buildings and equipment. Vines needed attention in late winter. Grain was harvested in May. At the height of summer's heat there was time for a little rest. But in September grapes had to be harvested and pressed, and then the round of yearly tasks began again. Hesiod says nothing about pleasures or entertainments, but the existence of his poetry testifies to the presence in Greece of a rural population more dynamic and confident than we know of anywhere else in the ancient world.

Aristocrats. Wealthy aristocrats had hired laborers, sharecroppers, and slaves to work their extensive lands. They, therefore, had leisure for other activities. Aristocratic social life centered on the "symposium," a men's drinking party. It was not simply an opportunity for inebriation. Sessions began with prayers and libations to the gods. Usually there were games, such as dice or *kottabos*, in which wine was flicked from cups at various targets. Sometimes dancing girls or flute girls offered entertainment. Frequently the guests provided their own amusements with songs, poetry, or philosophical disputes. There was usually a prize for the winner, for aristocratic values emphasized competition and the need to excel, whatever the arena.

Athletic contests became widespread early in the sixth century. Games usually included running events, the long jump, the discus and javelin throws, boxing, wrestling, and the chariot race. Only the rich could afford to raise, train, and race horses, so the chariot race was the special preserve of the nobility. Wrestling was also favored by the upper classes, and the *palaestra* where they practiced became an important social center. There was a great contrast between the drab life of farmers and the cultivated existence of the leisured aristocracy.

Religion

The Greeks were polytheists whose religion permeated every aspect of their culture. Religion organized the civic life of the *polis* and shaped its art and literature.

Olympian Gods. Twelve deities formed the Greek pantheon, a divine family that lived on Mount Olympus. Zeus, the sky god, presided over a lively company composed of his siblings and offspring. He had three sisters: Hera, his wife; Hestia, goddess of the hearth; and Demeter, goddess of agriculture and marriage. Poseidon, his brother, was god of the seas and earthquakes. By various mates he had an assortment of children: Aphrodite, goddess of love and beauty; Apollo, god of the sun, music, poetry, and prophecy; Ares, god of war; Artemis, goddess of the moon and the hunt; Athena, goddess of wisdom and the arts; Hephaestus, god of fire and metallurgy; and Hermes, messenger of the gods, connected with commerce and cunning.

Gods were assumed, apart from their superhuman strength and immortality, to be much like mortals. Zeus was believed to be a defender of justice, but he and the other gods were not omnipotent. They were subject to the Fates, personifications of the inviolable order of the universe. Each *polis* honored one of the Olympians as its special guardian, but religion was Panhellenic. In the eighth and seventh centuries B.C. shrines sacred to all Greeks were established at Olympia (Zeus), Delphi (Apollo), Corinth (Poseidon), and Nemea (Zeus). Each sanctuary sponsored athletic contests in honor of its god, to which all Greeks were invited and for which a sacred truce was declared.

In the sixth century B.C., the shrine of Apollo at Delphi achieved great and lasting fame for its oracle, the most important of several that the Greeks consulted for guidance about their futures. Delphian Apollo endorsed the pursuit of self-knowledge and self-control *(sophrosynē)*. "Know thyself" and "Nothing in excess" were Apollo's mottos. Arrogance *(hubris)* brought on by excessive wealth or good fortune was the most dangerous of human failings, for it created moral blindness and called forth divine vengeance. This theme was explored again and again in Greek literature.

Immortality and Morality. In addition to the Olympians the Greeks worshiped countless lesser deities connected with local shrines. Some were human heroes, real and legendary, whose great deeds had won them divine status. But ordinary people had no expectation of immortality. For them, religion was a matter of prayers and gifts beseeching divine help for this life.

The moral order the gods enforced was simple. Virtue consisted of paying one's debts, doing good to one's friends, and opposing one's enemies. Civic responsibility required participation in the cult of the state deities, performing public service, and fighting to defend the state.

The Cult of Dionysus and the Orphic Cult. The cults of the Olympian gods were state religions not intended primarily to speak to the personal needs of individuals. For private devotions the Greeks turned to rites of a different kind. The most popular of these honored a fertility deity associated with the grape vine—Dionysus, god of drunkenness and sexual abandon. He was particularly popular with women. His female devotees (maenads) cavorted by night and were reputed, when possessed by the god, to tear to pieces and devour any creatures they encountered.

The Orphic cult, named for Orpheus, a mythical poet, offered the prospect of some form of life after death. Cult followers are thought to have refused to kill animals or eat their flesh and to have believed in the transmigration of souls.

Poetry

The great changes that were sweeping through the Greek world by the sixth century B.C. were reflected in poetry. The era favored lyric poetry that was meant to be sung. The songs of Sappho of Lesbos, Anacreon of Teos, and Simonides of Cos were intimately personal—often describing the pleasure and agony of love. Alcaeus of Mytilene, an aristocrat driven from his city by a tyrant, wrote bitter invectives. But from a political point of view the most interesting poet of the century was Theognis of Megara. Theognis was the spokesman for the aristocracy of birth that was losing ground in most *poleis.* He believed that only nobles could aspire to virtue, for only nobles possessed the crucial sense of honor. Such a quality could not be taught; it was innate and had to be protected against loss by eschewing marriage with base commoners. Although the political privileges of the old nobility were reduced in most Greek states, these antique ideas remained dear to aristocratic hearts and greatly influenced important thinkers like Plato.

∽ The Persian Wars

The Greeks' period of freedom from interference from the outside world came to an end in the middle of the sixth century B.C. The Greek colonies, which had flourished on the coast of Asia Minor since the eleventh century B.C., first came under the control of Croesus (ca. 560–546 B.C.), king of the Anatolian nation of Lydia. Then in 546 B.C. Lydia and its dependencies passed into the hands of the Persians.

The Persian Empire

The Persian Empire had been created in a single generation by Cyrus the Great, founder of the Achaemenid dynasty. In 559 B.C., he came to the throne of Persia, then a small kingdom well to the east of the lower Mesopotamian valley. In succeeding years he expanded his empire in all directions. He ultimately reached Asia Minor, defeated Croesus, and occupied Lydia. Most of the Greek cities of Asia Minor resisted the Persians, but by 540 B.C., they had all been subdued.

The Ionian Rebellion

The Greeks of Ionia (on the west coast of Asia Minor) had been moving toward democracy and were not pleased to find themselves subservient to Persia. But the Persians were clever empire builders. They appointed Greek "tyrants" to govern the Greek cities. And since these native leaders usually ruled benignly and Persian tribute was not excessive, the Greeks were soon reconciled to life in Persia's empire. Neither the death of Cyrus in 530 B.C., nor the suicide of his successor Cambyses, nor the civil war that followed it in 522–521 B.C. prompted the Greeks to revolt. When Darius emerged as Great King (as the Persian rulers styled themselves) in 521 B.C., Ionia was perfectly obedient.

The personal difficulties of Aristagoras, the ambitious tyrant of Miletus, ended this era of peace and cooperation. In 499 B.C., to avoid punishment by the Persians for his part in stirring up an attack on the island of Naxos, he organized a rebellion of Ionian cities. He won local backers by helping to overthrow tyrannies and proclaim democratic constitutions. Then he turned to the mainland states for help. The Spartans refused his appeal. They had no close ties with the Ionians, no national interest in the region, and no wish to send their army abroad and leave their homeland undefended against its Helots.

The Athenians, who were related to the Ionians, lent Aristagoras a more sympathetic ear. They had reasons of their own to fear the Persians. Hippias, the deposed tyrant of Athens, was an honored guest at Darius' court, and the Great King made it plain that he favored returning Athens to Hippias' control. The Persians also held both shores of the Hellespont, Athens' route to the grain fields beyond the Black Sea. Consequently, the Athenian assembly decided to risk sending a fleet of twenty ships to help the rebels.

In 498 B.C., the Athenians and their allies made a surprise attack on Sardis, the old capital of Lydia and the seat of the "satrap," the Persian governor. The sack of Sardis encouraged revolt to spread, but the Ionians did not follow up their victory. The Athenians withdrew, and gradually the Persians recovered the ground they had lost. In 495 B.C., they defeated the Ionian fleet at Lade, and a year later they wiped out Miletus.

The War in Greece

In 490 B.C., the Persians launched an expedition to punish Athens, to restore Hippias, and to gain control of the Aegean Sea (see Map 2-2). They landed their infantry and cavalry forces first at Naxos, destroying it for its successful resistance in 499 B.C. Then they deported the people of Eretria, who had followed Athens' lead in going to the aid of Miletus.

Despite the risk of suffering the same fate as the Eretrians, the Atheni-

MAP 2-2 The Persian Invasion of Greece *This map traces the route taken by the Persian king Xerxes in his invasion of Greece in 480 B.C. The light gray arrows show movements of his army, the darker arrows of his fleet.*

ans refused to submit to Persian demands. Miltiades, an Athenian who had fled from Persian service, was chosen to lead the city's army into battle with the Persians at Marathon. A Persian victory would have led eventually to the conquest of all the mainland Greeks and would have changed forever the nature of Greek civilization. But the Athenians confounded the odds and decisively defeated the Persians. Their success instilled them with a sense of confidence and pride in their *polis*, themselves, and their new democracy.

The Great Invasion. Internal troubles prevented the Persians from taking swift revenge for their loss at Marathon. Almost ten years elapsed before Darius' successor, Xerxes, in 481 B.C. assembled an army of at least 150,000 men and a navy of more than 600 ships for the conquest of Greece.

By then a significant development had occurred in Athens. Themistocles, the city's leading politician, had launched a program designed to make Athens into a naval power. During his archonship in 493 B.C., Athens had built a fortified port at Piraeus. A decade later the Athenians used the profit from a rich vein of silver discovered in the state mines to finance the construction of a new fleet. By 480 B.C., Athens had over 200 ships. These ships were to be the salvation of Greece.

Of the hundreds of Greek states, only thirty-one (led by Sparta, Athens, Corinth, and Aegina) were willing to fight when the Persian army gathered south of the Hellespont in the spring of 480 B.C. Xerxes' strategy was to march into Greece and overwhelm the Greek forces with superior numbers. But Themistocles believed that the huge Persian army had a vulnerable point. It needed to keep in touch with its fleet for supplies. If the Persian navy was defeated, the Persian army could not remain in Greece. Themistocles, therefore, hoped to win the war by means of a naval engagement.

The Greek League, founded specifically to resist the Persian invasion, met at Corinth as the Persians prepared to cross the Hellespont. It chose Sparta as its leader and decided first to confront the Persians at Thermopylae (the "hot gates") on land and off Artemisium at sea. The opening between the mountains and the sea at Thermopylae was so narrow that it could be held by a smaller army against a much larger one. The Spartan king, Leonidas, commanded an army of about 9,000 Greek allies—including 300 of his fellow citizens.

Storms wrecked a large number of Persian ships while the Greek fleet waited safely in a protected harbor. Then Xerxes attacked Thermopylae. For two days the Greeks butchered his best troops without serious loss to themselves. On the third day, however, a traitor showed the Persians a mountain trail that permitted them to come on the Greeks from behind. Many allies escaped, but Leonidas and his 300 Spartans chose to stand their ground and die fighting. Simultaneously the Greek and Persian fleets fought an indecisive battle at Artemisium.

The Persian army then moved into Attica and burned Athens. If an inscription discovered in 1959 is authentic, Themistocles had foreseen this possibility and begun the evacuation of Athens before the fleet sailed to Artemisium.

The fate of Greece was decided in a sea battle in the narrow waters to the east of the island of Salamis to which the Greek fleet withdrew after the battle of Artemisium. The Peloponnesians were reluctant to confront the Persian fleet at this spot, but Themistocles persuaded them to stay by threatening to remove all the Athenians from Greece and settle them anew in Italy. The Spartans knew that the Greeks could not hope to win without the aid of the Athenian navy. In the ensuing battle the Persians lost more than half their ships. Xerxes retreated to Asia with a good part of his army, but the danger was not over.

The Persian general Mardonius spent the winter in central Greece. In the summer of 479 B.C., the Spartan regent, Pausanias, assembled the largest army the Greeks had ever put into the field. It met Mardonius' forces at Plataea in Boeotia, and the Persians suffered a decisive defeat. Mardonius died in battle and his army dispersed.

Meanwhile the Ionian Greeks urged King Leotychidas, the Spartan commander of the Greek navy, to take the offensive against the Persian fleet. At Mycale, on the coast near Samos, Leotychidas routed the enemy, and the Persians fled the Aegean and Ionia. For the moment, the Persian threat retreated.

Hellenic civilization, which powerfully influenced the modern West, was shaped by inheritances from the Bronze Age cultures of Minoan Crete and Mycenae. These early Aegean states more closely resembled Egypt, Mesopotamia, and Palestine-Syria than the Hellenic communities that sprang from them. They had urban institutions, systems of writing, centralized monarchies, large administrative bureaucracies, hierarchical social systems, professional standing armies, and systems of taxation. They were similar to each other and changed little over time. Hellenic civilization was quite different.

The collapse of the Mycenaean world sent the Greeks into cultural decline. Cities were replaced by villages. Trade all but ended. Communication among the Greeks and between them and other peoples was curtailed. The art of writing was lost. And for the duration of their "dark age" the Greeks were ignored by their neighbors.

Between 1100 and 750 B.C. the Greeks laid the foundations for their great achievements. The new Greek way of life focused on the polis, the Hellenic city-state. There were hundreds of poleis, and most were fiercely independent. Rivalries among them led to a dynamic, often chaotic, competition for excellence. An agonal (competitive) quality has characterized Greek life throughout history. It has prompted strife and warfare, but it has also encouraged extraordinary achievements in literature and art.

Monarchy faded with the Mycenaean world, and the poleis evolved as republics. Since the Greeks were poor and differences in wealth among them were relatively small, class distinctions were less marked than in other societies. The development of infantry—the hoplite phalanx—had further leveling effects. Armies were made up of citizen-soldiers who were not paid, but whose services gave them the right to demand a role in the governments of the cities that depended on them for protection. Most states imposed no regular taxation. They had no bureaucracy to stifle individual initiatives. They had no castes of priests to enforce religious orthodoxy. These varied, dynamic, secular, and remarkably free communities created conditions favorable to the rise of speculative natural philosophy, the root of modern science.

Review Questions

1. What was the Minoan civilization of Crete like? How did Mycenaean differ from Minoan civilization?

2. From what ancient sources do we derive our knowledge of Minoan and Mycenaean history? What is Linear B? What problems are involved in using it to reconstruct Bronze Age history? How reliable are the Homeric epics as sources of early Greek history?

3. What was involved in the ancient Greek concept of a *polis*? What role did geography play in its development? Why did the Greeks consider it a unique and valuable institution?

4. How did the fundamental political, social, and economic institutions of Athens and Sparta compare about 500 B.C.? Why did Sparta develop a unique form of government?

5. Through what stages did Athens pass between 600 and 500 B.C. as it evolved from an aristocratic state into a democracy? What did Draco, Solon, Pisistratus, and Clisthenes each contribute to the process?

6. Why did the Greeks and Persians go to war in 490 and 480 B.C.? What benefit would the Persians have derived from conquering Greece? Why were the Greeks able to defeat the Persians? What effect did victory have on them?

Suggested Readings

A. ANDREWES, *The Greeks* (1967). A thoughtful general survey.

J. BOARDMAN, *The Greeks Overseas* (1964). A study of the relations between the Greeks and other peoples.

A. R. BURN, *The Lyric Age of Greece* (1960). A discussion of early Greece that uses the evidence of poetry and archaeology to fill out the sparse historical record.

A. R. BURN, *Persia and the Greeks,* 2nd ed. (1984). A thorough narrative and analysis of the conflict between the Persians and the Greeks down to 479 B.C.

J. CHADWICK, *The Mycenaean World* (1976). A readable account, by a man who helped decipher Mycenaean writing.

R. DREWS, *The Coming of the Greeks* (1988). A fine study of the arrival of the Greeks as part of the movement of Indo-European peoples.

V. EHRENBERG, *The Greek State* (1964). A good handbook of constitutional history.

M. I. FINLEY, *World of Odysseus,* rev. ed. (1965). A fascinating attempt to reconstruct Homeric society.

W. G. FORREST, *A History of Sparta, 950–192 B.C.* (1968). A brief but shrewd account.

V. D. HANSON, *The Western Way of War* (1989). A brilliant and lively discussion of the rise and character of the hoplite phalanx and its influence on Greek society.

J. M. HURWIT, *The Art and Culture of Early Greece* (1985). A fascinating study of the art of early Greece in its literary and cultural context.

D. KAGAN, *The Great Dialogue: A History of Greek Political Thought from Homer to Polybius* (1965). A discussion of the relationship between the Greek historical experience and political theory.

H. D. F. KITTO, *The Greeks* (1951). A personal and illuminating interpretation of Greek culture.

B. SNELL, *Discovery of the Mind* (1960). An important study of Greek intellectual development.

C. G. STARR, *The Economic and Social Growth of Early Greece, 800–500 B.C.* (1977).

E. VERMEULE, *Greece in the Bronze Age* (1972). A study of the Mycenaean period.

3

Classical and Hellenistic Greece

KEY TOPICS IN THIS CHAPTER

∼ The Peloponnesian War and the struggle between Athens and Sparta

∼ Democracy and empire in fifth-century-B.C. Athens

∼ Culture and society in Classical Greece

∼ The struggle for dominance in Greece after the Peloponnesian War

∼ The Hellenistic world

The Greeks' victory over the Persians in 480–479 B.C. marked the start of an era of great achievement. The Spartans refused to assume responsibilities that would take them away from their homeland, but the Athenians were eager to expand. They organized the Delian League, an alliance of Greeks who wanted to defend the Aegean against future Persian incursions, and used the league to build an Athenian empire. Although imperial abroad, at home Athens evolved a radically democratic form of government. States that feared the ambitions of the Athenians allied themselves with Sparta. Polarization of the Greek world was a prelude to a civil war that impoverished Greece and again made it vulnerable to conquest. In 338 B.C. Philip of Macedon imposed his rule on the Greek states and ended the age of the polis.

～ Aftermath of Victory

The Greeks had found it difficult to remain united even while struggling for their lives against the Persians. Within two years of Persia's retreat the Greeks had split into two camps, one led by Sparta and the other by Athens.

The Delian League

The Spartans had led the Greeks to victory against the Persian invaders, but they were not prepared to assume responsibility for defending the Greeks against the return of the Persians. Sparta could not afford to station troops far from home for long periods of time, and Sparta did not have the navy that was needed to guard the Aegean.

Athens was Greece's leading naval power. The Athenians were also related to the Ionians who lived in districts still threatened by Persia: the Hellespont and the islands and coasts of the Aegean. In the winter of 478–477 B.C. the Greeks who wanted to continue the war with Persia met on the sacred island of Delos and swore oaths of alliance (see Map 3-1). The aims of the Delian League were to free those Greeks who were under Persian rule, to defend against a Persian return, and to obtain compensation from the Persians by raiding their lands.

The league was remarkably successful. The Persians were steadily driven back, and the Aegean was cleared of pirates. In 467 B.C., the league won a great victory over the Persians at the Eurymedon River in Asia Minor. These successes prompted some cities to assume that the league had served its purpose, but the league refused to allow them to resign. What began as a voluntary association of free states ended as an empire dominated by Athens.

The Rise of Cimon

Following the Persian Wars, Themistocles was driven from power, and for two decades Athens was led by Cimon, son of Miltiades, the hero of Marathon. At home, Cimon defended a limited version of Clisthenes' democratic constitution. Abroad, he pursued a policy of aggressive attacks on Persia and friendly relations with Sparta.

MAP 3-1 Classical Greece *Greece in the Classical period (ca. 480–338 B.C.)
centered on the Aegean Sea. Although there were important Greek settlements
in Italy, Sicily, and all around the Black Sea, the area shown in this general
reference map embraced the vast majority of Greek states.*

～ The First Peloponnesian War: Athens Against Sparta

The Rise of Pericles

In 465 B.C. the island of Thasos rebelled against the Delian League. Cimon,
who ran the league in Athens' interests, was away from Athens for two years
commanding the siege that ended the revolt. When he returned, he was charged
with taking bribes. The trial—which acquitted him—was only an attempt by
his political opponents to reduce his influence. They accused him of being too
friendly to Sparta and to Athens' aristocratic factions. The radical democrats
who opposed Cimon were led by Ephialtes. But the man chosen to prosecute
him was Pericles, a member of a distinguished Athenian family, who was to
become Athens' most famous democratic leader.

Significant Dates from Greek History: The Persian Wars to Alexander

478–477 B.C.	*Delian League founded*
462 B.C.	*Pericles rises to leadership*
449 B.C.	*Peace with Persia*
435 B.C.	*Civil war on Corcyra*
432 B.C.	*Sparta declares war on Athens*
421 B.C.	*Peace of Nicias*
415–413 B.C.	*Athens invades Sicily*
404 B.C.	*Athens surrenders to Sparta*
404–403 B.C.	*Thirty Tyrants rule at Athens*
401 B.C.	*Expedition of Greek mercenaries to Persia*
382 B.C.	*Sparta seizes Thebes*
378 B.C.	*Second Athenian Confederation founded*
371 B.C.	*Thebans defeat Sparta at Leuctra*
362 B.C.	*Battle of Mantinea (end of Theban hegemony)*
359–336 B.C.	*Reign of Philip II of Macedon*
338 B.C.	*Battle of Chaeronea (Philip conquers Greece)*
338 B.C.	*Founding of League of Corinth*
336–323 B.C.	*Reign of Alexander III of Macedon, the Great*
334 B.C.	*Alexander invades Asia*
333 B.C.	*Battle of Issus*
331 B.C.	*Battle of Gaugamela*
327 B.C.	*Alexander reaches Indus Valley*
323 B.C.	*Death of Alexander*

At the start of their rebellion, the Thasians had asked Sparta to assist them by invading Athens. Sparta was willing, but an earthquake sparked a Helot revolt that kept the Spartan army tied up at home and persuaded the Spartans to call on Athens for help. Cimon persuaded the Athenians to go to Sparta's aid. This proved to be a fatal mistake. The Spartans reconsidered the wisdom of inviting an Athenian army into their land and ordered Cimon to go home. The angry Athenians promptly exiled Cimon (461 B.C.) and reversed his policies by allying themselves with Argos, Sparta's traditional enemy. Since Ephialtes had been assassinated in 462 B.C., Pericles probably engineered these developments.

The Division of Greece

Pericles was confident and ambitious. He persuaded Athens to support the city of Megara when it withdrew from the Peloponnesian League. Megara wanted to escape exploitation by its neighbor, Corinth. Athens saw a great strategic advantage in maintaining a presence in Megara. Megara straddled the route between the Peloponnesus and Athens. Sparta opposed these developments, and the result was the outbreak of the First Peloponnesian War, the beginning of what was to be a long and disastrous Greek civil war.

The Athenians were initially victorious—conquering Aegina and winning control of Boeotia. But about 455 B.C., an Athenian fleet that had gone to Egypt to stir up trouble for Persia was destroyed. This setback inspired subjects of Athens' empire to rebel, and the threat to the empire forced Athens to curtail other military engagements. Sparta agreed to a truce, and in 449 B.C. Athens ended hostilities against Persia.

In 446 B.C., the war on the Greek mainland broke out again. Pericles, the commander of the Athenian army, chose not to fight. In exchange for a treaty promising peace for thirty years, he abandoned Athens' possessions on the Greek mainland outside of Attica. In return, the Spartans formally recognized the Athenian Empire. This effectively divided Greece into two power blocs: Sparta leading its allies on the mainland and Athens ruling its empire in the Aegean.

⁓ Classical Greece

The Athenian Empire

After the Egyptian disaster the Athenians moved the Delian League's treasury to Athens and began to keep one-sixtieth of the annual revenues for themselves. By 445 B.C., when the Thirty Years' Peace gave formal recognition to an Athenian empire, only Chios, Lesbos, and Samos still provided their own ships for the league's navy. All the other states paid tribute. Athenian propaganda suggested that henceforth the allies would be treated as colonies and Athens as their mother city, the whole to be held together by good feeling and common religious observances. But although the empire had many friends among the lower classes and the democratic politicians in the subject cities, nothing could cloak the fact that Athens was the master and its allies mere subjects. Athenian prosperity and security had come to depend on the empire, and the Athenians were determined to defend it at any cost.

Athenian Democracy

As the Athenians tightened their hold on the subjects of their empire, they increased their own democratic freedoms.

Democratic Legislation. The hoplite class became eligible for the archonship, and, in practice, the property qualification for holding this office was suspended. Pericles sponsored a law providing pay for jury members. This made it possible for the poor to serve. Pericles revived the custom of sending circuit judges into the countryside to make justice available to the rural poor. He also persuaded the electorate to limit citizenship to those who had two citizen parents. Democracy made citizenship a valuable commodity, and it was in the self-interest of the electorate to increase the significance of each vote by limiting the number of voters. Participation in government in all the Greek states was denied to slaves, resident aliens, and women.

The Acropolis was both the religious and the civic center of Athens. In its final form it is the work of Pericles and his successors in the late fifth century B.C. This photograph shows the Parthenon and to its left the Erechtheum. [Meredith Pillon, Greek National Tourist Organization]

How Did the Democracy Work? Athenian democracy gave citizens extensive powers. Every decision of the state had to be approved by the popular assembly—by the voters themselves, not their representatives. Every judicial decision was subject to appeal to a popular court of not fewer than 51 and as many as 1,501 citizens representative of the Athenian population at large. Most officials were selected by lot without regard to class. Successful candidates for the chief offices—such as the generals (who had both political and military authority) and the imperial treasurers—were usually wealthy aristocrats, but the voters were free to elect anyone. All public officials were subject to scrutiny before taking office, could be called to account and removed from office during their tenure, and were subject to a strict accounting at the end of their term. Since there was no standing army and no police force (open or secret), there was no way to coerce voters.

Pericles was elected to the generalship fifteen years in a row and thirty times in all, not because he was a dictator but because he was a persuasive and respected leader. After the defeat of the Athenian fleet in the Egyptian campaign and the failure of Athens' continental campaigns, Pericles favored a conservative policy that aimed at retaining the empire in the Aegean and living at peace with the Spartans. In 443 B.C. he was at the height of his power as the guardian of Athens' imperial democracy.

The Women of Athens—Two Views

Greek society, like most all over the world throughout history, was dominated by men. But the actual position of women in democratic Athens has been the subject of much controversy.

Subjection. The bulk of the evidence suggests that women were excluded from most aspects of public life. They could not take any direct part in politics—that is, debate, vote, or hold office. In the private sphere they were always subject to the authority of male guardians: a father, a husband, or some other male relative. They married young, usually between the ages of twelve and eighteen. Since men often did not marry until they were in their thirties, husbands probably treated wives like dependent children. Marriages were arranged—often without consulting the bride. Women were assigned dowries, but they had no control over their property. Divorce was difficult for a woman to obtain, for she needed to find a male relative to assume responsibility for her after the dissolution of her marriage.

The chief responsibility of a respectable Athenian woman of a citizen family was to produce male heirs for her husband's household *(oikos)*. But if a woman's father died without leaving a male heir, she became an *epikleros*, the heiress to the family estate. Such a woman was required by law to terminate any previous marriage and to wed one of her father's relatives. A son born of this union re-established her father's *oikos*.

Because political privileges were passed down in citizen families, the legitimacy of children was important. Athenian males ranged free and openly consorted with prostitutes. But citizen women were confined to special quarters in their houses and were denied contact with any men but close relatives. Women spent their days raising children, cooking, weaving, and managing their households. Occasionally they had important roles to play in the state religion. But for the most part, Athenian women were expected to be invisible. In a frequently quoted speech, Pericles declared that "the greatest glory of women is to be least talked about by men, whether for good or bad."

Power. Evidence from mythology and especially from the tragedies and comedies of the great Athenian dramatists implies that the roles played by Athenian women may have been more complex than their legal status suggests. The central characters of plays are often women. Clytemnestra in Aeschylus's tragedy *Agamemnon*, for example, arranges the murder of her husband, the king, and establishes her lover (whom she dominates) as tyrant in his place. *Medea*, one of Euripides' tragedies, examines the contradictions in women's roles. Medea complains bitterly of the subjugation of women, but she is herself a powerful figure who manipulates kings. Medea is simultaneously pitiable, as a victim of injustice, and terrifying, in her pursuit of vengeance. She is anything but the creature "least talked about by men, whether for good or bad."

Slavery

The Greeks practiced various kinds of slavery from the earliest times. The most common forms of bondage were varieties of serfdom characteristic of backward areas such as Crete, Thessaly, and Sparta. When the Spartans conquered the natives of their region, they reduced them to the status of Helots—subjects who belonged to the Spartan state and worked the land for Spartan masters. Default on a debt could lead to temporary bondage *(hektemoroi)* or sale into true slavery outside one's homeland. About 600 B.C., Solon put an end to this practice in Athens.

Chattel slavery proper began to increase about 500 B.C. and remained important to Greek society thereafter. Most slaves were taken as prisoners of war or abducted by pirates and slave traders. The Greeks regarded foreigners as inferior. (They called foreigners "barbarians" because their speech sounded like unintelligible mumbling: "bar bar.") Most slaves working for the Greeks were foreigners. Greeks sometimes enslaved Greeks, but not to serve in their home territories.

Most Greek farmers worked small holdings too poor to support more than one slave. The upper class had more land, but it was usually let to free tenant farmers. If it was worked by slaves (under an overseer who was often himself a slave), their numbers were modest. Wealthy men owned farms scattered about the *polis*. They had no use for the hordes of slaves that appear where there are plantation systems.

Slaves were used in greater numbers in industry—especially mining. The largest slaveowner on record was Nicias, an Athenian of the fifth century B.C. who was prominent during the Great Peloponnesian War. He owned 1,000 slaves, whom he rented to a mining contractor. A family of resident aliens in Athens employed about 120 slaves in a shield factory, but most manufacturing was on a much smaller scale. Slaves worked as craftsmen in almost every trade, and, like agricultural slaves on small farms, they worked alongside their masters. Slaves were used as domestic servants. Many were shepherds. Publicly owned slaves served as policemen, prison attendants, clerks, and secretaries.

There are no reliable figures for the absolute number of slaves or their percentage of the free population for any city except Athens. Estimates of the slave population of Athens in the fifth and fourth centuries B.C. range from 20,000 to 100,000. If the accurate number is the mean between the extremes—60,000—and the city had about 40,000 households, there were fewer than two slaves per family. If some families owned many, there must have been quite a few who had none. By comparison, during the period before the American Civil War slaves made up less than one-third of the population of the south, and three-quarters of free southerners had no slaves. The proportion of slaves to free citizens in ancient Athens was similar.

Despite a numerical similarity, Athenian slavery did not resemble the American model. The Athenian economy was mixed. It did not depend on a single cash crop produced by exploiting slave labor. Greek slaves did not differ from their masters in skin color, and Athenian slaves walked the streets with such ease as to offend class-conscious Athenians (like Plato). The emancipation of slaves, which was rare in America, was common in Greece. On occasion the Athenians contemplated the liberation of all their slaves. In 406 B.C., when Athens faced defeat in the Peloponnesian War, all slaves of military age were freed and citizenship was granted to those who rowed the ships that won the battle of Arginusae. Similar proposals were made on two other occasions, although without success.

∼ The Great Peloponnesian War

The Thirty Years' Peace that Sparta and Athens agreed to in 445 B.C. ended prematurely. About 435 B.C., a dispute in a remote part of the Greek world began a war that shook the foundations of Greek civilization.

Causes

The spark that ignited the conflict was a civil war at Epidamnus that led to a quarrel between Corinth and Corcyra, an island at the entrance to the Adriatic Sea. The fight within the colony invited intervention by both states. Since the Corcyraean fleet was second in size only to that of Athens, the Athenians feared that its capture by Corinth would upset the balance of power and threaten Athenian interests. Athens decided, therefore, to support Corcyra against Corinth. A series of crises in the years 433--432 B.C. sent Corinth, a member of the Peloponnesian League, running to Sparta for help.

In the summer of 432 B.C., the Spartans hosted a conference to consider the grievances of their allies. Persuaded by the Corinthians that Athens was an insatiably aggressive power, the Peloponnesian League voted for war. In the spring of 431 B.C. its army marched into Attica.

Strategic Stalemate

The Spartan strategy was traditional: to invade the opponent's country, threaten his crops, and force him to defend them in a hoplite battle. Since the Spartans and their allies had the better army and outnumbered the Athenians by more than two to one, they were confident of victory.

Any ordinary *polis* would have yielded or been quickly defeated. Athens, however, had unique resources: the income from an empire, a vast reserve fund, and walls that created a fortified highway between the inland city and its port at Piraeus. So long as the Athenians had their enormous navy, they could supply themselves from the sea. And, secure behind their walls, they could demonstrate that the Spartans had no power to hurt them by refusing to accept Sparta's challenge to a fight. Meanwhile the Athenian fleet could raid the Peloponnesian coast to prove that Sparta could not protect its allies. Pericles expected that this strategy would force the Peloponnesians, within a year or two, to recognize the hopelessness of the situation and sue for peace.

The plan was intelligent, although success was far from certain. It required Athens' democratic assembly to exercise great self-control, and so long as Pericles provided inspired leadership, the city stayed the course. But in 429 B.C., in the wake of a devastating plague, Pericles died.

None of the politicians who followed him could hold the Athenians to a consistent course. Two factions appeared: one, led by Nicias, wanted to continue the defensive strategy; the other, led by Cleon, preferred to take the offensive. In 425 B.C., Athens captured 400 Spartans in a skirmish in the Peloponnese. Sparta offered peace to get them back. But Cleon's party persuaded the Athenians to continue the war. When assaults on Megara and Boeotia failed in 424 B.C., the Athenian electorate's confidence in the aggressive policy was shaken. Meanwhile, Sparta's ablest general, Brasidas, took a small army to Thrace and Macedonia and captured Amphipolis, the most important Athenian colony in the region. (Thucydides, the commander of the Athenian fleet in those waters, was discharged as punishment for the loss. His exile gave him the time to win lasting fame as the great historian of the war.) In 422 B.C., Cleon led an assault on Amphipolis, and both he and Brasidas died in battle. The deaths of the leaders of the aggressive factions in both cities paved the way, in the spring of 421 B.C., for the Peace of Nicias, a treaty named for its chief negotiator.

The Fall of Athens

The agreement between Athens and Sparta was supposed to guarantee peace for fifty years, but neither side carried out all its commitments. Despite the precariousness of the situation, in 415 B.C. an ambitious young Athenian politician named Alcibiades persuaded the Athenians to send an army to intervene in the complicated affairs of Sicily. In 413 B.C., the entire expedition was destroyed. Athens lost 200 ships and 4,500 men. Her allies lost almost ten times as many. Rebellions erupted in the Athenian empire, and Persia exploited Athens' difficulties by offering assistance to Sparta.

Remarkably, the Athenians found the strength to continue fighting. But their financial resources were no match for the aid their enemies received from Persia. In 405 B.C., Athens' fleet was caught napping at Aegospotami and was destroyed, and the city could not afford to replace it. Lysander, the Spartan general who had obtained Persia's support, cut off Athens' food supply, and starved the city into submission in 404 B.C. Athens was allowed to survive, but was stripped of its fleet and empire.

～ Competition for Leadership in the Fourth Century B.C.

Sparta was not able to take Athens' place as leader of the Aegean world. From 404 B.C. until 338 B.C., the Greeks fought among themselves, squandered their resources, and made themselves vulnerable to conquest.

The Hegemony of Sparta

Sparta's limited population, Helot problem, and traditional conservatism made it a less than ideal state to succeed Athens at the head of a maritime empire. Sparta first ceded the Greek cities of Asia Minor to Persia to pay the debt it had incurred for Persia's help in the war. Lysander then made a mockery of Sparta's promise to free the Greeks from Athenian dominance by attempting to build a Spartan empire. In the cities he "liberated," Lysander installed boards of local oligarchs who were loyal to him. He backed them up with Spartan garrisons and demanded tribute comparable to what Athens had collected. These policies alienated Thebes and Corinth, Sparta's most powerful allies, and worried conservative Spartans.

In 404 B.C., Lysander installed an oligarchic government in Athens. The behavior of its leaders earned them the title "Thirty Tyrants." Their democratic opponents took refuge in Thebes and Corinth and raised an army to retake the city. Sparta's cautious king, Pausanias, restored order by recalling Lysander and allowing Athens to revert to democracy. So long as Athenian foreign policy remained under Spartan control, Sparta was willing to allow Athens to have any government it wanted.

Persia's ability to continue to involve itself in Greek affairs was hampered by internal problems. In 405 B.C., Darius II of Persia died. Cyrus, a young prince, received Spartan help in recruiting a Greek mercenary army to contest the succession of his brother, Artaxerxes II. In 401 B.C., the Greeks defeated the Persians at Cunaxa in Mesopotamia, but Cyrus's death in battle doomed their cause. The Greeks succeeded in fighting their way back to the Black Sea and safety, but the cities of Asia Minor that had supported Cyrus now faced the threat of Artaxerxes' revenge. The Spartans raised an army to defend them, and in 396 B.C. they appointed their new king, Agesilaus, its commander.

The Persians countered Agesilaus's aggressive policies by offering aid to any Greek state willing to help them against Sparta. By 395 B.C., Thebes had organized an alliance that included Argos, Corinth, and a resurgent Athens. The Corinthian War (395–387 B.C.) that followed ended Sparta's Asian adventure; in 394 B.C., the Persian fleet destroyed Sparta's maritime empire. The Athenians seized the opportunity to rebuild their walls, enlarge their navy, and recover some of their foreign possessions.

The Persians, who believed that Athens was potentially a greater threat than Sparta, supported Sparta's ambitions on the mainland. Agesilaus broke up all alliances except Sparta's Peloponnesian League, and in 382 B.C. he seized Thebes in a surprise attack. In 379 B.C., shortly after the Thebans had reclaimed their independence, a Spartan army attempted unsuccessfully to occupy Athens.

In 371 B.C. the Thebans, led by their great general Epaminondas, defeated the Spartans at Leuctra. The Thebans freed the Helots, and helped them found a city of their own. By depriving Sparta of much of its farmland and of the people who worked it and by hemming Sparta in with hostile neighbors, Thebes ended Sparta's hope of ever again being a power of the first rank.

The Hegemony of Thebes: The Second Athenian Empire

Thebes' victories over Sparta opened the way for the city to become the dominant power in Greece, and Epaminondas proceeded to win control of all the Greek states north of Athens and those of the Corinthian Gulf. Theban expansion threatened many Greeks, and Athens was able to recruit help in opposing it. In 362 B.C., Epaminondas took a Boeotian army into the Peloponnesus to confront Athens' allies. His men routed them at the battle of Mantinea, but he was killed. Since no comparable leader rose to take his place, his death ended the era of Theban dominance.

Sixteen years earlier (in 378 B.C., shortly after Sparta's attack on Thebes and Athens), an alliance known as the Second Athenian Confederation had been organized to guard against Spartan aggression in the Aegean. Although its constitution was meant to prevent the abuses of power of which Athens had been guilty in the days of the Delian League, Athens soon alienated the confederates. When the collapse of Sparta and Thebes and the restraint of Persia removed motives for voluntary membership, Athens' allies revolted. By 355 B.C., Athens had again lost most of its empire. Two centuries of almost continuous warfare thus left the Greek world as chaotic and disorganized as it had been in the days before the founding of the Peloponnesian League.

✍ The Culture of Classical Greece

The repulse of the Persian invasion released a flood of creative activity in Greece that was rarely, if ever, matched anywhere at any time. It produced achievements of such quality as to justify the designation of the era as the "classical period." Ironically, the term *classical* often suggests calm and serenity, but the products of Greece's Classical Period reflect tension.

The Fifth Century B.C.

Two sources of tension shaped the work of Greek artists of the fifth century B.C. One originated in the conflict between the soaring hopes of individuals and the limit put on private ambition by the duties of citizenship in the *polis*. The other sprang from the conflict between the Greeks' pride in their accomplishments and their fear that excessive striving was punished by divine retribution. The Greeks' faith in themselves had been strengthened by victory over Persia, but at the same time the Greeks worried that the punishment that had humbled Xerxes' ambition awaited them if they overreached themselves. Attic tragedy, which emerged as a major literary form in the fifth century B.C., pondered this problem as Athens and Sparta marshalled the *poleis* into mutually hostile camps.

Attic Tragedy. Greek plays were written to be staged as part of public festivals honoring the god Dionysus. The festivals were contests among play-

Xenophon Recounts How Greece Brought Itself to Chaos

The confusion in Greece in the fourth century B.C. peaked with the inconclusive battle of Mantinea and the death of the Theban leader Epaminondas in 362. No one arose to take his place and to provide the leadership Greece needed. Xenophon, a contemporary, described the near chaos in Greek affairs—the condition that invited intervention by Philip of Macedon.

〜 What does this passage reveal about the nature of ancient Greek warfare and the customs surrounding it? How decisive were most battles in ancient Greece? Before the Macedonian conquest of Greece in 338 B.C., why was no state able to impose its rule over the others? Why did they succeed in doing so elsewhere?

The effective result of these achievements was the very opposite of that which the world at large anticipated. Here, where well-nigh the whole of Hellas was met together in one field, and the combatants stood rank against rank confronted, there was no one who doubted that, in the event of battle, the conquerors this day would rule; and that those who lost would be their subjects. But god so ordered it that both belligerents alike set up trophies as claiming victory, and neither interfered with the other in the act. Both parties alike gave back their enemy's dead under a truce, and in right of victory; both alike, in symbol of defeat, under a truce took back their dead. And though both claimed to have won the day, neither could show that he had thereby gained any accession of territory, or state, or empire, or was better situated than before the battle. Uncertainty and confusion, indeed, had gained ground, being tenfold greater throughout the length and breadth of Hellas after the battle than before.

Xenophon, Hellenica, trans. by H. G. Dakyns, in The Greek Historians, ed. by F. R. B. Godolphin (New York: Random House, 1942), p. 221.

wrights. Each poet who wished to compete submitted three tragedies (which might or might not have a common subject) and a concluding satyr play (a comic choral dialogue with Dionysus). An archon chose the three authors who were to compete and assigned each three actors and a chorus. The actors were paid by the state, and the chorus was sponsored by a donation from a wealthy citizen (the *choregos*). Most plays were performed in the temple of Dionysus, an amphitheater of 30,000 seats on the south side of the Acropolis. A jury of Athenians, chosen by lot, determined the best author, actor, and *choregos*.

Attic theater provided poets with a forum where they could challenge their fellow citizens to ponder vital issues of the day. On rare occasions the subject of a play might be a contemporary or historical event, but usually a playwright chose a tale from mythology that illuminated current affairs. The plays of Aeschylus and Sophocles, our earliest extant examples, deal with public issues of religion, politics, and ethics. The plays of Euripides, which were written a little later, show an emerging awareness of individual psychology.

Old Comedy. Comedies were added to the Dionysian festival early in the fifth century B.C. Cratinus, Eupolis, and Aristophanes (ca. 450–ca. 385 B.C.), the great master of Old Comedy and the author of the only surviving complete plays, wrote humorously about serious political issues. They used scathing invective and satire to lampoon contemporary figures—including Pericles, Cleon, Socrates, and Euripides.

Architecture and Sculpture. Like the plays Pericles witnessed, the buildings his city erected reveal the creative tension that existed in his generation between civic responsibility and the transcendent genius of individual artists. In 448 B.C., Pericles inaugurated a great building program on the Acropolis that was financed by income from the empire. The plan included new tem-

The three orders of Greek architecture, Doric, Ionic, and Corinthian, have had an enduring impact on Western architecture.

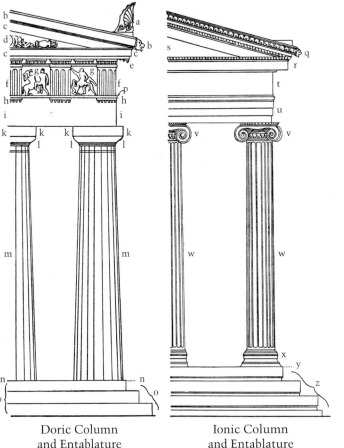

a Corner akroterion
b Sima with a lion's head as waterspout
c Geison (cornice)
d Tympanum
e Mutule with guttae(drops)
f Triglyphs
g Metopes
h Regulae with guttae
i Architrave or epistyle
k Albacus
l Echinus
m Shaft with 20 sharp-edged flutings
n Stylobate
o Krepts or krepidoma
p Taenia
q Sima
r Geison (cornice)
s Tympanum
t Frieze
u Architrave or epistyle
   (in three parts)
v Capital with volutes
w Shaft with 24 flutings
   separated by fillets
x Attic base with double
   torus and a trochilos
y Stylobate
z Krepis or krepidoma

Doric Column
and Entablature

Ionic Column
and Entablature

Corinthian Capital

ples to honor the city's gods and an imposing gateway for the sacred precinct. Pericles' intent was to represent visually the political power and intellectual greatness of Athens—to make Athens, in his words, "the school of Hellas."

Philosophy. The art of the fifth century B.C. attempted to define the human being and explore its relation to the natural world order. Curiosity about these questions also spawned the invention of philosophy. Philosophy began in the sixth century B.C. when a thinker named Thales proposed a theory to explain how a world composed of changing phenomena could function as a stable, coherent whole. He suggested that the changes we see are nothing but alterations in the state of a single underlying universal substance. But when no such substance could be proven to exist, later thinkers suggested that Thales had been naive in assuming that change and permanence could exist in the same world.

Heraclitus argued that permanence was an illusion produced by our perception of slow change. Parmenides of Elea and his pupil Zeno countered that since the concept of change implied that something arose from nothing, change was a logical absurdity. Empedocles of Acragas proposed a compromise by suggesting that there were unchanging elements (fire, water, earth, and air) whose combinations changed. Similarly, Leucippus of Miletus and Democritus of Abdera imagined the world to be composed of innumerable tiny, solid, indivisible particles (*atomos*, in Greek) that move about in a void. The size of the atoms and the shapes of the clumps they form account for the things our senses perceive.

The atomists regarded "soul" or mind as material and believed that purely physical laws explained everything. Anaxagoras of Clazomenae, their older contemporary, accepted the existence of tiny fundamental particles called "seeds," but claimed that these were controlled by a rational force, *nous* ("mind"). At issue here was the debate between materialism and idealism that still continues.

These speculations were too abstract to interest many people, but the Sophists, a group of professional teachers who emerged in the mid-fifth century B.C., attracted much attention. They were paid to develop and teach a practical skill, rhetoric. Arts of persuasion were much valued in democracies, where many issues were resolved through open debate.

Some Sophists claimed to teach wisdom and virtue. They refrained from speculations about the physical universe, but used reason to analyze human beliefs and institutions. In the process they identified a central problem of human social life: the conflict between nature and custom. The more traditional among them argued that laws were of divine origin and in accord with nature, but others argued that laws were merely conventions—arbitrary agreements among people. The most extreme Sophists argued that law was contrary to nature—a device to reverse the natural order and enable the weak to dominate the strong. Critias, an Athenian oligarch, went so far as to say that the gods themselves had been invented to deter people from doing what they wished. Such speculations undermined the concept of justice on which the *polis* was founded. The effort to refute them called forth the philosophical responses of Plato and Aristotle in the next century.

History. Herodotus—"the father of history," as he has been deservedly called—was born shortly before the outbreak of the Persian Wars. The description he wrote of those wars goes far beyond all earlier prose accounts, in chronicles, genealogies, and geographical studies, in attempting to explain human actions. Although his *History* was completed about 425 B.C. and shows a few traces of Sophist influence, its spirit is that of an earlier time. Herodotus accepted, although not uncritically, information taken from legends and oracles, and he often credited events to interventions by gods. But his work is typical of its time in celebrating the crucial role of human intelligence in determining the course of human events. Nor was Herodotus unaware of the importance of institutions. He credited Greece's victory over Persia to the love of liberty the *polis* instilled in its citizens.

Thucydides, the historian of the Peloponnesian War, was born about 460 B.C. and died a few years after the end of the war he spent his life studying. His thought was influenced by the secular, human-centered, skeptical rationalism of the Sophists of the late fifth century B.C. And he shared the scientific attitudes that characterized the work of contemporaries like Hippocrates of Cos. (The Hippocratic school of medicine advocated careful observation and rational inference as strategies for diagnosing and treating disease.) Thucydides took great pains to achieve factual accuracy, and he searched his evidence for significant patterns of human behavior. He hoped that these patterns would enable people to foresee events. Since human nature was, he believed, essentially unchanging, similar circumstances produced similar responses. But Thucydides admitted that even the wisest student of history could be mistaken, for an element of randomness—chance—affects all human affairs.

The Fourth Century B.C.

The Peloponnesian War marked the passing of the *polis* as an effective form of government. The Greeks of the fourth century B.C. may not fully have grasped this fact, but they did realize that their traditional way of life was threatened. Some tried to shore up the weakened structure of the *polis*; others looked for alternatives to the *polis*; and still others averted their gaze from the public arena altogether.

Drama. The poetry of the fourth century B.C. reveals the disillusionment some Greeks felt with the *polis*. The popular subjects are no longer drawn from politics and public life, but from the private concerns of ordinary people—things relating to the family and the interior life of the individual. Old Comedy, which focused on political issues and matters of public policy, yielded to Middle Comedy, a comic-realistic depiction of daily life, plots of intrigue, and mild satire of domestic situations. The role of the chorus, which in some way represented the *polis*, was very much diminished. New Comedy pushed farther in these directions. Menander (342–291 B.C.), its pioneer, wrote domestic tragi-comedy: gentle satires of the foibles of ordinary people and tales of temporarily thwarted lovers—subjects fit for modern situation comedies.

Tragedy, which had been inspired by the robust political life of the *polis*, declined during the fourth century. No plays from the period have survived. The theatrical producers of the period may have sensed decline, for they began to revive the plays of the previous century. Euripides' tragedies, which had rarely won top honors when first produced, became increasingly popular. More than the other great playwrights of his age, Euripides had been interested in the psychology and behavior of individual human beings. Some of his late plays look like forerunners of New Comedy: *Helena, Andromeda*, and *Iphigenia in Tauris* are more like fairy tales, fantasy adventures, or love stories than tragedies.

Sculpture. The same movement away from the grand, the ideal, and the general and toward the ordinary, the real, and the individual is apparent in the evolution of Greek sculpture. To see this, one has only to compare the work of Polycleitus (ca. 450–440 B.C.) with that of Praxiteles (ca. 340–330 B.C.) or Lysippus (ca. 330 B.C.).

Philosophy and the Crisis of the *Polis*

Socrates. The life and teachings of Socrates (469–399 B.C.) reflect an early awareness of the crises that were developing for the *polis*. Socrates recognized the difficulties and criticized the shortcomings of the *polis*, and he turned away from an active political life. But he did not abandon the idea of the *polis*. He fought as a soldier in its defense, obeyed its laws, and sought a sound rational foundation for its values.

Since Socrates wrote nothing, our knowledge of him depends on the reports of his disciples, Plato and Xenophon, and later commentators. As a young man, they say, he studied the theories about the physical world developed by the first philosophers, but his interests soon shifted to the interior world: the explication of the processes of human understanding and decision making. Unlike some Sophists, he believed in the existence of truth and the power of reason to search it out.

Socrates sought truth by cross-examining people who were reputed to know something—craftsmen, poets, and politicians. His conversations with them always ended the same way. He demonstrated that, apart from technical information and skills, they had little knowledge of the fundamental principles of human behavior. It is not surprising that Athenians, whose opinions were challenged by his rigorous logical critiques, concluded that he was undermining the beliefs and values of the *polis*. Socrates also did not conceal his contempt for democracy—a system of government that empowered amateurs to make important political decisions about issues of which they were ignorant.

In 399 B.C. Athens, its confidence shaken by the loss of the Peloponnesian

War, decided that it could no longer afford to be tolerant of Socrates. He was condemned to death on charges that implied that he was undercutting the traditions on which the survival of the *polis* depended. He was given a chance to escape, but Plato says that he refused because of his respect for the laws of the city. In taking this stand Socrates demonstrated that he was not a Sophist or an irresponsible skeptic. He had faith that the *polis* and its laws were more than arbitrary human conventions. Although he had not succeeded in grounding that faith in reason, he defended it in the most convincing fashion.

The Cynics. Socrates had advocated concern with personal morality and the state of one's soul, disdain of worldly pleasure and wealth, and withdrawal from political life. After his death these ideas were developed as a program for a group of extremist philosophers known as the Cynics. Antisthenes (ca. 455–ca. 360 B.C.), a follower of Socrates, was the first, but the most famous was Diogenes of Sinope (ca. 400–ca. 325 B.C.)—whom Plato characterized as Socrates gone mad.

Diogenes believed that happiness lay in satisfying natural needs in the simplest and most direct way. He dismissed all civilized constraints on the individual as nothing more than arbitrary social convention. Diogenes adopted a way of life to demonstrate his contempt for convention. He begged for his bread, wore rags, lived in a tub, openly performed intimate acts of personal hygiene, and ridiculed all religious observances.

Although the Cynics claimed to follow Socrates, they contradicted some of his beliefs. Socrates said that virtue was a matter of knowledge—that people do wrong only through ignorance of what is right. The Cynics, on the contrary, argued that wisdom and happiness derived from actions (a proper style of life), not from knowledge (philosophy). Where Socrates had criticized but ultimately defended the *polis*, the Cynics abandoned it. When Diogenes was asked about his citizenship, he answered that he was *kosmopolites*, a citizen of the world.

Plato. Plato (429–347 B.C.), the most important of Socrates' associates, is the perfect example of the pupil who becomes greater than his master. Plato was the first systematic philosopher—the first to lay out a consistent worldview that provided a context for all fundamental questions. He was also a brilliant writer. His twenty-six philosophical discussions—most cast in the form of dialogues—are artistic masterpieces that make the analysis of complicated philosophical ideas dramatic and entertaining.

Plato, like other members of his aristocratic Athenian family, planned a career in politics. But the excesses of the Thirty Tyrants and Socrates' execution discouraged him. He made two trips to Sicily, where he hoped that the tyrants of Syracuse (Dionysius I and II) would allow him to guide them in building a model state. When this project failed, he returned to Athens to found the Academy (386 B.C.), a center for research and a school for training statesmen and citizens. The Academy survived until a Christian government closed it in the sixth century A.D.

Like Socrates and unlike the radical Sophists, Plato believed in the *polis*. He thought that it was consistent with human nature and was an instrument for creating good people. But Socrates' insistence that virtue was a kind of knowledge led Plato to reject democracy as an ideal form of government for a *polis*. Justice, Plato said, consists in each man doing only that to which his nature is best suited. The true knowledge on which virtue is based is beyond most people. It is *episteme*—science, the unchanging wisdom achieved by a few highly trained and specially gifted individuals. Only these "philosopher kings" can be trusted with political power, for only they are capable of subordinating private interests to the good of the community. Only they can restore harmony to the *polis* by eliminating the causes of strife: private property, the family, and anything that distracts individuals from their public duties.

Concern for the redemption of the *polis* was central to Plato's philosophy. Since the survival of the *polis* depended on its ability to produce good citizens, Plato had to define goodness. Because Plato believed that goodness was a kind of knowledge, he had to develop a theory of knowledge. And this led him into the realm of metaphysics. Thus Plato's purely logical and metaphysical work springs from his interest in politics. His search for a satisfactory foundation for the beleaguered *polis* culminated in the birth of systematic philosophy.

Aristotle. Aristotle (384–322 B.C.) was born at Stagirus in the Chalcidice, the son of the physician to the court of Macedon. As a youth he went to Athens to study at the Academy and remained there until Plato's death. He then conducted research in marine biology at Assos and at Mytilene in Asia Minor. In 342 B.C., he accepted an appointment as tutor to Alexander, son of King Philip of Macedon. In 336 B.C., he returned to Athens and founded his own school, the Lyceum or the Peripatos—a reference to a covered walkway on its grounds. (In later years Aristotle's followers were called *Peripatetics*.) After Alexander's death in 323 B.C., the Athenians turned against the Macedonians, and Aristotle found it wise to leave. He died at Chalcis in Euboea a year later.

The program of the Lyceum was different from that of the Academy. Plato's students were preoccupied with mathematics; Aristotle was interested in gathering, ordering, and analyzing data relating to all fields of human knowledge. He and his students assembled collections of materials to support various scientific studies. The loose organization and style of much of Aristotle's prose suggests that we have his lecture notes, not his polished treatises. The range of subjects Aristotle taught is astonishing: logic, physics, astronomy, biology, ethics, rhetoric, literary criticism, and politics.

Aristotle began the study of every subject the same way. He gathered empirical evidence. Sometimes the evidence was physical; sometimes it was anecdotal—a garnering of common opinions. The evidence was then rationally analyzed to see if it could be consistently explained. Metaphysical principles ultimately emerged as Aristotle wrestled to resolve inconsistencies.

Like Plato, Aristotle viewed things teleologically; that is, he explained things in terms of their ultimate ends or purposes. Plato described these ends as universal ideas or forms—transcendent realities that shaped the world, but that were not part of human experience. Aristotle, however, inferred the purposes of most things from their behavior in the world. His most striking characteristic is his common sense. In his view, matter existed to achieve an end. It evolved until it articulated the form that was its end. Being was a constant process of development from matter to form, from potentiality to actuality.

This metaphysical model is at the heart of Aristotle's thinking about the *polis*. He rejected the Sophists' claim that social life was a convention that frustrated the true nature of individuals. He believed that the *polis* was natural because it was necessary for the realization of human potential. Human survival and happiness depended on group life: family, village, and *polis*. The primitive instincts of individuality were the human "matter" from which human social potentials emerged as people were formed by the experience of life in a *polis*. The purpose of the *polis* was, therefore, not economic or military. It was moral: it made possible the good life.

Aristotle was less interested in theorizing about the perfect state than in designing the best state practically possible. To determine what this was, he assembled a collection of 158 constitutions. (Only the *Constitution of the Athenians* has come down to us.) He concluded that a *politeia*, not the best constitution but the one best suited to most states, was characterized by moderation. It empowered neither the rich nor the poor, but the middle class. A large middle class was essential for political stability, for this class was not tempted to the arrogance of the rich nor infected by the malice that resentment of their circumstances created in the poor. Stable constitutions were also usually "mixed"—blending aspects of democracy and oligarchy.

All the political thinkers of the fourth century B.C. recognized that the *polis* was in danger, and all hoped to save it. All recognized the economic and social troubles that threatened it. But few made such realistic proposals for its reform as did Aristotle. It is ironic that the ablest defense of the *polis* came just before its demise.

ᔑ The Hellenistic World

The term *Hellenistic* was coined in the nineteenth century to describe the period in Greek history that began when a Macedonian dynasty conquered Greece and the Persian Empire. This brought elements of Greek and Middle Eastern culture together to create a new, more cosmopolitan civilization.

The Macedonian Conquest

The quarrels among the Greeks made them vulnerable to conquest by Macedon, the northernmost of the mainland Greek states. By Greek standards Macedon was a backward, semibarbaric land. It had no *poleis*, but was ruled by a king who, like Homer's Agamemnon, depended upon the cooperation of his nation's powerful aristocratic families. Hampered by constant wars with barbarian tribes on its northern frontier, internal strife, loose organization, and lack of money, Macedon played no great part in Greek affairs until the fourth century B.C.

Philip of Macedon. The Macedonian king who conquered Greece was Philip II (359–336 B.C.). As a youth, Philip had spent several years (367–364 B.C.) as a hostage in Thebes. There he learned much about Greek politics and warfare under the tutelage of Epaminondas, the general who defeated Sparta. Philip's talent and training made him the ablest king in Macedonian history. He solidified his hold on his throne, pacified the tribes on his frontiers, and challenged Athens' position in the northern Aegean. Conquest of Amphipolis gave him control of the gold and silver mines of Mount Pangaeus. With this wealth he elevated the level of culture in Macedon, founded new cities, won friends abroad, and turned his army into the world's finest fighting force.

The Macedonian Army. Philip's army was national, but more professional than the amateur armies of citizen-soldiers who fought for the individual *poleis.* Its infantry was recruited from Macedon's farming class and feisty hill people. Infantrymen were armed with thirteen-foot pikes instead of the hoplite's more common nine-foot weapon. This enabled them to spread out and form a more open, flexible phalanx than was customary. The Macedonian cavalry was recruited from the aristocracy. Its members, the "Companions," lived with the king and developed a special loyalty to him. Philip also employed mercenaries who knew the latest tactics and were familiar with the most sophisticated siege machinery. Altogether he could field an army of about 40,000 men.

The Invasion of Greece. The Greeks themselves gave Philip the excuse he needed to intervene in their affairs. The people of Thessaly invited Philip to lead them in a war they had been fighting with the Phocians since 355 B.C. Philip won the war, treacherously occupied Thessaly, and marched on Thrace to take control of the northern Aegean coast and the Hellespont.

These actions threatened the vital interests of Athens, but although Athens had a formidable fleet of 300 ships, it was not the Athens of 350 B.C. or the Athens of Pericles. Its population was smaller than in the fifth century, and it had no empire from which to draw funds to support a major war. As a result, the Athenians were uncertain how to respond to Philip.

Eubulus, a financial official and conservative political leader, favored a cautious policy of cooperation with Philip in the hope that his aims were limited and no real threat to Athens. The leading opponent to appeasement of Macedon was Demosthenes (384–322 B.C.), one of the greatest orators in Greek history. He was convinced that Philip was a threat to Greece, and he spent most of his career urging the Athenians to fight. Other Athenian leaders saw Philip as the savior of Greece. Isocrates (436–338 B.C.), the head of an important rhetorical and philosophical school in Athens, looked to Philip to provide the unity and leadership needed for a Panhellenic campaign against Persia. He and other orators believed that the conquest of Asia Minor would solve the economic, social, and political problems that had brought poverty and civil war to the Greek cities ever since the Peloponnesian War.

In 349 B.C., Philip attacked several cities in northern and central Greece and firmly planted Macedonian power in those regions. The years between 346 B.C. and 340 B.C. were spent in diplomatic maneuvering until, at last, Philip attacked Perinthus and Byzantium, the lifeline of Athenian commerce. When the Athenian fleet saved both, Philip marched into Greece. Demosthenes convinced Thebes to take Athens' side. But in 338 B.C., a cavalry charge led by Philip's eighteen-year-old son, Alexander, defeated the allied forces at Chaeronea in Boeotia.

The Macedonian Government of Greece. The Macedonian settlement of Greek affairs was not as harsh as many had feared. Athens was spared from attack on condition that it accept Macedonian leadership, and Macedonian garrisons were stationed around Greece to guard against rebellions. In 338 B.C., Philip called the Greek states to Corinth and announced the formation of a federation: the League of Corinth. The constitution of the league provided for autonomy, freedom from tribute and garrisons, and cooperation in suppressing piracy and civil war. This was a facade that enabled the Greeks to submit with dignity to Macedonian occupation. The defeat at Chaeronea had ended Greek freedom and the autonomy of the *polis*.

Philip choose Corinth as the seat of his new confederacy because it was at Corinth that the Greeks had gathered almost 150 years earlier to plan their strategy for the Persian Wars. And it was there, in 337 B.C., that Philip announced his intention to lead the Greeks in a new war with Persia. In the spring of 336 B.C., however, as Philip was about to launch this campaign, he was assassinated.

Alexander the Great

Philip's first son, Alexander III (356–323 B.C.), who was to be known as "the Great," succeeded his father at the age of twenty. The young king was committed to carrying out his father's plans for invading Persia.

The Conquest of the Persian Empire. Although the Persian Empire was vast and its resources enormous, its size and the diversity of its subjects made it hard to control. Persia's rulers faced constant troubles along far-flung frontiers and constant intrigues within the royal palace. At the time of Philip II's death in 336 B.C., Persia's new king, Darius III, was inexperienced. But with a navy that dominated the sea, a huge army, and vast wealth, Darius was a formidable opponent.

In 334 B.C., when Alexander crossed the Hellespont into Asia, he had no navy and little money (see Map 3-2). His army consisted of about 30,000 infantry and 5,000 cavalry. The Greeks could not risk heading inland from the coast until they had neutralized the Persian navy by taking all its ports, but

This sculpture of Alexander the Great, king of Macedon and conqueror of the Persian Empire, was made in the second century B.C. and found at the ancient city of Magnesia in Asia Minor. Alexander's conquests spread Greek culture far from its homeland, laying the foundation of the Hellenistic world. [Erich Lessing/Art Resource, N.Y.]

they needed some quick victories over the Persian army to win the booty required to finance the war. Memnon, the commander of the Persian navy, proposed an excellent strategy for defeating the Greeks: retreat, scorch the earth, avoid all but guerrilla engagements, and deprive the enemy of supplies. Pride, however, led the Persians to reject his advice.

The Persians gave Alexander the battle he needed at the Granicus River on the coast of Asia Minor. Alexander led a cavalry charge across the river into the teeth of the enemy. He nearly lost his life, but his courage inspired his soldiers, and their victory opened all of Asia Minor to conquest.

In 333 B.C., Alexander marched out of Asia Minor into Syria to meet the main Persian army under Darius. At Issus, Alexander led a cavalry charge that broke the Persian line. But instead of pursuing Darius as he retreated inland, Alexander continued south along the coast, assaulting Persia's naval bases. When he arrived in Egypt, he was greeted as liberator and proclaimed pharaoh. Like all of Egypt's divine kings, he was hailed as son of Re, the god who, as head of the Egyptian pantheon, was equated with Zeus.

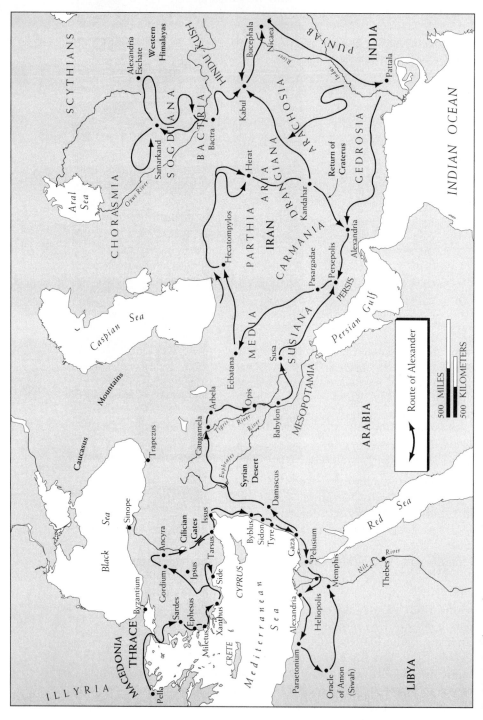

MAP 3-2 Alexander's Campaigns *The route taken by Alexander the Great in his conquest of the Persian Empire, 334–323 B.C. Starting from the Macedonian capital at Pella, he reached the Indus Valley before being turned back by his own restive troops. He died of fever in Mesopotamia.*

In the spring of 331 B.C., Alexander marched into Mesopotamia to meet an army Darius had assembled at Gaugamela (near the ancient Assyrian city of Nineveh). Once again the Persian line broke, and Darius was forced to flee. Alexander occupied Babylon, and in January of 330 B.C., he entered Persepolis, the Persian capital. Conquest of Persia's treasure cities ended Alexander's financial problems, and the gold he began to shower on his troops loosed vast sums of money to circulate—a development whose economic effects were felt for centuries.

Since the new regime could not be secure while Darius was at large, Alexander again set out to capture him. But the Persian nobles deprived the Greeks of that victory. Having lost faith in Darius, they killed him and recognized Bessus, one of his relatives, as his successor. Alexander pursued Bessus into the east. Although Bessus was caught, Alexander's longing to explore foreign lands caused him to press on to the frontiers of India.

Near Samarkand, in the land of the Scythians, he founded the city of Alexandria Eschate ("Farthest Alexandria"), one of many cities Alexander created as part of a plan to secure the future of the empire. Alexander hoped to hold the empire he was winning by scattering Greeks through it and amalgamating its diverse peoples. To set an example, he married a Bactrian princess, Roxane, and recruited 30,000 young Bactrians to be trained for service in his army.

In 327 B.C., the Greeks crossed the Khyber Pass and entered the territory of modern Pakistan. Although Porus, the native king, submitted, Alexander still was not content. He ordered the army east to find the river called Ocean that Greek geographers believed encircled the world. At this point his exhausted men mutinied and forced him to take them home for a rest. By the spring of 324 B.C., they were back at the Persian Gulf and celebrating, in true Macedonian style, with a drunken spree.

The Death of Alexander. Alexander, at age thirty-three, was filled with plans for the future, but in Babylon in June of 323 B.C., he succumbed to a fever and died. He quickly became the subject of myth, legend, romance, and controversy among historians. Some have seen him as a man of grand and noble vision who transcended the narrow limits of Greek and Macedonian ethnocentrism—seeking to create a great world state that would realize the brotherhood of humankind. Others have depicted him as a calculating despot, given to drunken brawls, brutality, and murder. The truth probably lies in between. No one disputes that Alexander was one of history's greatest generals and a man of rare organizational talent. Even he, however, would have had difficulty holding together the vast empire he had created.

The Successors

Nobody was prepared for Alexander's sudden death, and he left no obvious successor. His nearest adult male relative was a weak-minded half-brother, and although Roxane, his queen, bore him a son soon after his death, an infant heir to the throne could not rule. Alexander's Macedonian generals planned to hold the empire for his son by making themselves governors of its various provinces. But conflicting ambitions soon had them at each other's throats. In the ensuing battles all of the direct members of the Macedonian royal house were destroyed. The deaths of Roxane and her son in 310 B.C. removed the last restraints on the surviving governors, who in 306 B.C. and 305 B.C. proclaimed themselves independent kings.

Three Macedonian dynasties emerged as heirs to major portions of Alexander's empire. Ptolemy I (367?–283 B.C.) claimed Egypt and founded its thirty-first dynasty. (Cleopatra, who died in 30 B.C., was the last of the Ptolemies.) Seleucus I (358?–280 B.C.) created the Seleucid dynasty that ruled Mesopotamia. And Antigonus I (382–301 B.C.) established the Antigonid family that reigned over Asia Minor and Macedon.

For about seventy-five years after Alexander's death the world economy expanded. The money that Alexander had loosed to circulate increased the level of economic activity. The opening of vast new territories to Greek trade, the increased demand for Greek products, the enhanced availability of goods, and the enlightened economic policies of the Hellenistic kings helped the growth of commerce. Problems of overpopulation on the Greek mainland were solved by opportunities to emigrate to new cities in the east.

The new prosperity was not evenly distributed. Urban Greeks, Macedonians, and Hellenized natives—the upper and middle classes—lived comfortable, even luxurious, lives, while the standard of living for rural laborers declined. The independent men who owned and worked the small farms that formed the early *poleis* disappeared. Arable land was consolidated into large plantations, and farmers were reduced to the status of dependent peasants. During prosperous times their lot was bearable, but the costs of continuing wars, inflation, and a gradual lessening of the positive effects of the introduction of Persian wealth steadily eroded the economy. Kings bore down heavily on the middle class, which shifted the burden to the peasants and the city laborers. They responded by slowing their work and by striking. In Greece economic pressures brought clashes between rich and poor and demands for the abolition of debt and the redistribution of land. In places civil war erupted.

These internal problems—and the strain of endemic warfare—increased the vulnerability of the Hellenistic kingdoms to invasion. And by the middle of the second century B.C. they had all, except for Egypt, succumbed to an expanding Italian power, Rome. In the two centuries that separated Alexander and the Roman conquest, however, Greece and the east had grown together politically, economically, and culturally.

～ Hellenistic Culture

Alexander the Great's life marked a turning point in the history of Greek literature, philosophy, religion, and art. His empire and its successor kingdoms ended the role that the *polis* had played in shaping Greek culture. *Poleis* continued to exist throughout the Hellenistic period (and might have had successors in the Roman *municipia*), but these communities were mere shadows of the vital *poleis* of the Hellenic era. Hellenistic cities were not free, sovereign states, but municipal towns submerged within great military empires.

As the freedoms central to the life of the *polis* faded, Greeks lost interest in pursuing political solutions for their problems. They abandoned public affairs and resorted to religion, philosophy, and magic for help in dealing with their private hopes and fears. The confident humanism of the fifth century B.C. gave way to a kind of resignation to fate, a recognition of helplessness before forces too great for humans to manage.

Philosophy

Athens survived as the center of philosophical studies during the Hellenistic era. Plato's Academy and Aristotle's Lyceum continued in operation and were joined by schools that developed the most popular new philosophies of the era: Epicureanism and Stoicism.

The Lyceum abandoned the scientific interests of its founder and became a center for literary and historical studies. The Academy was even more radically transformed. It adopted the Skepticism taught by Pyrrho of Elis. Skeptics specialized in pointing out fallacies and weaknesses in all schools of philosophy and concluded that nothing could be known. They advised people, in lieu of a better option, to accept conventional morality and the world as it was. The Cynics drew a more radical conclusion from the inevitability of human ignorance. They denounced convention and advocated a life in accordance with nature's crude impulses.

None of these views appealed much to the middle-class city dwellers of the third century B.C. They were searching for the kind of dignity and meaning that the *polis* had provided for the lives of their ancestors.

The Epicureans. Like many thinkers of his day, Epicurus of Athens (342–271 B.C.) doubted that human beings could obtain knowledge. The atomists, Democritus and Leucippus, convinced him that the world was nothing more than a swirl of atoms continually falling through a void. Knowledge was, therefore, nothing more than the impressions atoms left on human sense organs. Since Epicurus believed that the atoms did not obey permanent laws of motion, but swerved in arbitrary, unpredictable ways, he concluded that their behavior could produce no certain knowledge in us.

Epicurus concluded from this that philosophers ought not to seek knowledge of the world, but insights that would ensure human happiness. For instance, Epicurus believed that philosophy could free people from the fear of death. When people understood that death was merely the dispersal of the atoms of body and soul, they realized that nothing of themselves survived to suffer pain or loss. The gods, too, were no threat. They were material beings who appeared to have no interest in human affairs.

The proper pursuit of humankind was pleasure in the sense of *ataraxia,* a state of being undisturbed, without trouble, pain, or responsibility. The happiest people were those who withdrew from the world, avoided business concerns, and stayed free of the duties of family and public life. Epicurus's ideal was the genteel, disciplined selfishness of intellectual men of means. It was a dream not calculated to be widely attractive.

The Stoics. Soon after Epicurus began teaching in Athens, Zeno of Citium (335–263 B.C.) established the Stoic school—named for the *Stoa Poikile,* the Painted Portico in the Athenian agora (marketplace) where Zeno met with his disciples. Zeno and his successors owed much, by way of the Cynics, to Socrates and to Eastern thinkers.

Like the Epicureans, the Stoics sought the happiness of the individual, but Stoic philosophy relied more on religious images. Stoics believed that human fulfillment lay in living in harmony with nature, and Stoics claimed that nature was a manifestation of divine *logos*—an eternal principle of reason that was the "fire" of life. Every human being had a spark of this divine fire, and at death it returned to its source in the eternal spirit. Like other living beings, the whole world, on occasion, died in a great conflagration and was born anew.

Human happiness was the product of a virtuous life—a life that was fulfilled because it was lived in accordance with natural law. To live such a life a person had to understand which things in life were good and evil and which were morally "indifferent." Things like prudence, justice, courage, and temperance were good. Things like folly, injustice, and cowardice were evil. Some things—like life, health, pleasure, beauty, strength, and wealth—were morally neutral, for by themselves they did not produce either happiness or misery. Misery was the result of passion, a disease of the soul that arose from attachment to wrong things. Happy people achieved *apatheia,* freedom from passion.

The Stoics saw the world as a single *polis* in which all people were equally children of god. Despite the fact that politics invited preoccupation with things that were morally indifferent, many Stoics led active public lives. Their aim was to live in accordance with the divine will. Thus they fatalistically accepted their places in life and sought to play out the roles in which they found themselves while cultivating a form of apathy. This fit well with the reality of post-Alexandrian life, where docile submission was more important than active participation.

Literature

Alexandria became the center of literary production in the third and second centuries B.C. Its intellectuals, unlike the creative thinkers who were citizens of a *polis,* were preoccupied with the past more than with current affairs over which they had little influence. The Ptolemies supported a "museum," a great research institute that collected Greek literature of every kind for scholars to

This is a Roman copy of one of the masterpieces of Hellenistic sculpture, the Lao- coön. *According to legend, Laocoön was a priest who warned the Trojans not to take the Greeks' wooden horse within their city. This sculpture depicts his punishment. Great serpents sent by the goddess Athena, who was on the side of the Greeks, devoured Laocoön and his sons before the horrified people of Troy. [Vatican Museum]*

edit and interpret. Some of their work was dry and petty, but without them much of what we have today would have been lost.

Architecture and Sculpture

Hellenistic kings could afford conspicuous displays of royal patronage to artists and architects as well as scholars. Many new cities were built or rebuilt—usually laid out on the grid plan introduced in the fifth century B.C. by Hippodamus of Miletus. Famous artists traveled the world, fulfilling commissions and creating a kind of uniform international style. It favored a sentimental, emotional realism rather than the idealism popular during the age of the *polis.*

Mathematics and Science

The most spectacular and remarkable intellectual achievements of the Hellenistic age were in mathematics and science. The scholars of Alexandria amassed the greater part of the scientific knowledge available to the Western world until the scientific revolution of the sixteenth and seventeenth centuries A.D.

Euclid's *Elements* (written early in the third century B.C.) remained the textbook of plane and solid geometry until recent times. Archimedes of Syracuse (ca. 287–212 B.C.) established the theory of the lever in mechanics and invented hydrostatics. Heraclides of Pontus (ca. 390–310 B.C.) advanced a heliocentric theory of the universe that was fully articulated by Aristarchus of Samos (ca. 310–230 B.C.). Since Hellenistic technology could not provide data to confirm this theory, it did not take hold. A geocentric model advanced by Hipparchus of Nicaea (born ca. 190 B.C.) and refined by Ptolemy of Alexandria (second century A.D.) acquired currency and remained dominant until the work of Copernicus in the sixteenth century A.D. The scholars of the age knew that the earth was round, and Eratosthenes of Cyrene (ca. 275–195 B.C.) calculated its circumference within about 200 miles. His maps were more accurate than those that were standard in the Middle Ages.

The achievements of Greece's Classical Age were unparalleled. To a great degree they sprang from the unique political experiences provided by the poleis, *the independent city-states. Democratic imperial Athens nurtured the greatest artists and intellectuals. The freedoms Athens gave its citizens (its native-born males) bred respect for the human individual and curiosity about human potential. Philosophy, science, drama, and history evolved to explore this potential, and a naturalistic style of art evolved to show human beings first as they ideally might look, and then as they really did look.*

The Classical Period came to an end with the Macedonian conquest. As the polis *faded and the Greeks established great national states or empires, the Hellenistic Age began. Greek culture spread over a wide area and evolved to adjust to a new cosmopolitan context. Syncretism of thought and belief made understanding and accord more likely among peoples who were very different and paved the way for the great Roman Empire.*

~ Review Questions

1. How was the Delian League transformed into an Athenian empire during the fifth century B.C.? Did Athens' empire offer any advantages to its subjects? Why was there such resistance to Athenian efforts to unify the Greek world in the fifth and fourth centuries B.C.?

2. Why did Athens and Sparta come to blows in the Great Peloponnesian War? What was each side's strategy for victory? Why did Sparta win the war?

3. In what ways were the tensions that characterized Greek life in the Classical Period reflected in its art, literature, and philosophy? How does Hellenistic art differ from that of the Classical Period?

4. Between 431 and 362 B.C., Athens, Sparta, and Thebes each tried to impose hegemony over the city-states of Greece, but none succeeded except for short periods of time. Why did each state fail? What does your analysis tell you about the components of successful rule?

5. How and why did Philip II conquer

Greece between 359 and 338 B.C.? How was he able to turn Macedon into a formidable military and political power? Why was Athens unable to defend itself against Macedon? Did Philip's success result from Macedon's strength or from the weakness of the Greek city-states?

6. What were the major consequences of Alexander's early death? What were Alexander's achievements? Was he a conscious promoter of Greek civilization or only an egomaniac devoted to conquest?

∼ Suggested Readings

J. BUCKLER, *The Theban Hegemony, 371–362 B.C.* (1980). A study of Thebes at the height of its power.

W. BURKERT, *Greek Religion* (1985). A fine general study.

P. CARTLEDGE, *Agesilaus and the Crisis of Sparta* (1987). More than a biography of the Spartan king, it is a thorough study of Spartan society.

W. R. CONNOR, *The New Politicians of Fifth-Century Athens* (1971). A study on changes in political style and their significance for Athenian society.

J. M. COOK, *The Persian Empire* (1983). A solid history that makes good use of archaeological evidence.

J. R. ELLIS, *Philip II and Macedonian Imperialism* (1976). A study of the career of the founder of Macedonian power.

J. FERGUSON, *The Heritage of Hellenism* (1973). A good survey.

P. GREEN, *From Alexander to Actium* (1990). A brilliant new synthesis of the Hellenistic period.

R. JUST, *Women in Athenian Law and Life* (1988). A good study of the place of women in Athenian life.

D. KAGAN, *The Fall of the Athenian Empire* (1987). The last period of the war.

D. KAGAN, *The Outbreak of the Peloponnesian War* (1969). A study of the period from the foundation of the Delian League to the coming of the Peloponnesian War that argues that war could have been avoided.

H. D. F. KITTO, *Greek Tragedy* (1966). A good introduction.

J. LEAR, *Aristotle: The Desire to Understand* (1988). A brilliant yet comprehensible introduction to the work of the philosopher.

A. A. LONG, *Hellenistic Philosophy: Stoics, Epicureans, Skeptics* (1974). A solid study.

R. MEIGGS, *The Athenian Empire* (1972). A fine study of the rise and fall of the empire, making excellent use of inscriptions.

M. I. ROSTOVTZEFF, *Social and Economic History of the Hellenistic World*, 3 vols. (1941). A masterpiece of synthesis by a great historian.

B. S. STRAUSS, *Athens After the Peloponnesian War* (1987). An excellent discussion of Athens' postwar recovery and of the nature of Athenian society and politics in the fourth century B.C.

W. W. TARN, *Alexander the Great*, 2 vols. (1948). The first volume is a narrative account; the second, a series of detailed studies.

G. VLASTOS, *The Philosophy of Socrates* (1971). A splendid collection of essays illuminating the problems presented by this remarkable man.

F. W. WALBANK, *The Hellenistic World* (1981). A solid history.

A. E. ZIMMERN, *The Greek Commonwealth* (1961). A study of political, social, and economic conditions in fifth-century Athens.

4

Rome: From Republic to Empire

KEY TOPICS IN THIS CHAPTER

~ The emergence of the Roman Republic

~ The development of the republican constitution

~ Roman expansion and imperialism

~ The character of Roman society in the republican era

~ The fall of the republic

The Romans, who started with nothing but a small village in central Italy, achieved remarkable things. They united the peoples of the Western world and maintained the longest period of peace in Western history. By adapting and spreading aspects of Greek culture through their empire, the Romans created a universal Graeco-Roman tradition that remains at the heart of western civilization to this day.

Significant Dates from Rome's Republican Era

509 B.C.	*Republic founded*
392 B.C.	*Fall of Veii; Etruscans defeated*
387 B.C.	*Gauls burn Rome*
338 B.C.	*Latin League defeated*
295 B.C.	*Samnites defeated*
287 B.C.	*Plebeian Assembly wins power to legislate*
275 B.C.	*Pyrrhus evacuates Italy*
264–241 B.C.	*First Punic War*
218–202 B.C.	*Second Punic War*
215–205 B.C.	*First Macedonian War*
200–197 B.C.	*Second Macedonian War*
189 B.C.	*Antiochus defeated; Asia Minor conquered*
172–168 B.C.	*Third Macedonian War*
149–146 B.C.	*Third Punic War*
133 B.C.	*Tribunate of Tiberius Gracchus*
123–122 B.C.	*Tribunates of Gaius Gracchus*
111–105 B.C.	*Jugurthine War and Marius*
90–88 B.C.	*War against the Italian allies*
88 B.C.	*Sulla's march on Rome*
60 B.C.	*Formation of First Triumvirate*
58–50 B.C.	*Caesar conquers Gaul*
49–48 B.C.	*Civil war between Caesar and Pompey*
46–44 B.C.	*Caesar's dictatorship*
43 B.C.	*Formation of Second Triumvirate*
31 B.C.	*Octavian's victory over Antony at Actium*

Prehistoric Italy

Italy's cultural evolution began slowly. The Paleolithic era lingered in Italy until 2500 B.C., and Italy did not feel the effects of the Bronze Age until 1500 B.C. About 1000 B.C., the Umbrians, Sabines, Samnites, and Latins—the peoples whose Italic languages gave the peninsula its name—began to immigrate from the east. The newcomers pioneered Italy's Iron Age. By 800 B.C., they had occupied the highland pastures of the Apennines, the mountain range that runs the length of Italy, and had begun to challenge earlier settlers for control of the western coastal plains (see Map 4-1).

The Etruscans

About 800 B.C., a mysterious people whose language was not Italic settled in Etruria (Tuscany) on a plain west of the Apennines between the Arno and Tiber rivers. Although the background of the Etruscan people is unknown, aspects of their civilization suggest an eastern origin. They had a powerful influence on the development of Rome.

MAP 4-1 Ancient Italy *This map of ancient Italy and its neighbors before the expansion of Rome shows major cities and towns as well as a number of geographical regions and the locations of some of the Italic and non-Italic peoples.*

Government

Etruscan communities were independent, self-governing city-states loosely linked in a religious confederation. Aristocratic landowners soon banished kings from most cities and set up governments run by councils and annually elected magistrates. The Etruscans were the militarized ruling class of their nation. They subjected the peoples they conquered in Italy and took to the sea as traders and pirates. They competed with the other maritime powers of the western Mediterranean, the Carthaginians of north Africa and Italy's Greek colonists.

Dominion

In the seventh and sixth centuries B.C., the Etruscans extended their power north to Italy's Po Valley and overseas to the islands of Corsica and Elba. They also moved south into Latium (a region that included the small town of Rome) and Campania (a plain that the Greeks of Naples had begun to colonize). These conquests were the work of independent Etruscan chieftains who rarely supported each other. As a result, they were short-lived.

Etruscan power peaked before 500 B.C. By 400 B.C., Celts from Gaul (modern France) had driven the Etruscans from the Po Valley, an area the Romans later called Cisalpine Gaul (Gaul on "this" side of the Alps). Gradually the cities of Etruria lost their independence, and their language ceased to be a living tongue. Their culture was not forgotten, however, and had a profound effect on Rome.

Roman religion shows the clearest evidence of Etruscan influence. The Etruscans believed that innumerable supernatural beings had the power to intervene in human affairs. Since Romans were convinced that human survival depended on understanding and placating these spirits (many of whom were evil), they preserved the Etruscan rites for divining the wills and interpreting the omens of the gods.

～ Royal Rome

The Latin peoples who settled Rome may have been attracted by its location. Rome was established fifteen miles from the sea at the point where the Tiber River emerges from the foothills of the Apennines. An island in the Tiber southwest of Rome's Capitoline Hill made the river fordable and made Rome the center for Italy's inland communication and trade.

Government

Rome's potential was not realized until the sixth century B.C., when Etruscan kings established themselves in Rome and conquered most of Latium. Although one family monopolized the royal office, kingship was technically elective. The Roman Senate, an aristocratic council, had to approve a candidate for the throne. And only the assembly of the Roman people could bestow on him his unique power—the *imperium*, the right to enforce commands by fines, arrests, and corporal or capital punishment. The king was Rome's chief priest, high judge, and supreme military commander.

According to legend, Rome's Senate originated when Romulus, Rome's founder, chose 100 of Rome's leading men to advise him. (The Senate of the Roman Republic had 300 members.) The early Senate had no formal executive or legislative authority. It met only when the king convened it to ask for advice. In practice, however, the Senate was very influential. Since it was composed of the most powerful men in the state, a king could not safely ignore its will.

The curiate assembly, an organization to which all citizens belonged, was the third organ of government. It met only when summoned by the king, who determined its agenda and decided who could address it. Its job was to listen and approve. Romans voted, not as individuals, but as members of groups. Citizens were registered in thirty groups. Each group had one vote. It was cast according to the will of its majority.

The Family

Family organizations were the basic units of Roman society. The head of a family was its "king," the holder of *imperium* over it. Like the king at the head of the state religion, the father supervised Rome's most important rites, the family's daily worship of its ancestors. Like the king, a father could sell even his adult children into slavery or order their execution. Since his wife was protected by the family of her birth, he had less authority over her. And she could not be divorced unless convicted of certain serious offenses by a court of her male blood relatives. A Roman wife had a respected position as the administrator of her husband's household.

Clientage

The power of a family organization was enhanced by the institution of clientage: an exchange of mutual obligations between a client and a patron that was sanctioned by custom and eventually codified in law. A patron provided a client with physical and legal protection and, if necessary, with economic assistance. A client might subsist on daily handouts, receive a grant of land, become a tenant farmer, or labor on his patron's estate. In return a client fought for his patron, voted as his patron ordered, and did any jobs that were requested of him. It was not uncommon for wealthy, ambitious members of the upper classes to become clients of great families that could bring them the support of powerful political machines.

Patricians and Plebeians

From the start, a distinction of birth divided Roman citizens into two classes. A "patrician" upper class monopolized power, for only its members could serve as priests, sit in the Senate, or hold office. The lower "plebeian" class may originally have consisted of small farmers, laborers, and artisans who were clients of the patricians. But wealth alone did not define the classes. From very early times there were rich plebeians, and incompetence and bad luck must have produced some poor patricians. The patricians, however, guarded their rights by forbidding marriages with plebeian families. Plebeians had to struggle for over two centuries to win political equality.

～ The Republic

According to Roman tradition, in 509 B.C. an atrocity committed by a member of the royal family sparked a revolt that drove the last Etruscan king from

Busts of a Roman couple from the period of the republic. Although some people have identified the individuals as Cato the Younger and his daughter Porcia, no solid evidence confirms this claim. [Scala/Art Resource, N. Y.]

the city. The patricians refused to appoint a successor to him and set up a republic to govern Rome.

Its Constitution

The Consuls. The Roman Republic evolved a very conservative, unwritten constitution with strong links to Rome's past. It assigned the duties and trappings of monarchy to republican magistrates.

Two patricians were annually elected consuls and vested with *imperium.* Like the former kings, they led the army, oversaw the state religion, and sat as judges. They even used the traditional symbols of royalty—purple robes, ivory chairs, and *lictors* (guards who accompanied them bearing the rods and axe that signified their power to discipline and execute). A consul was, however, not a king. He remained in office for only a year. He had an equal, a colleague who could prevent him from taking independent action. And his *imperium* was limited. Consuls could execute citizens who were serving with the army outside the city, but when at home citizens had the right to appeal all cases involving capital punishment to the popular assembly.

The checks on consular action prevented initiative, swift action, and change, and this was just what a conservative, aristocratic republic wanted. But since a divided command could create serious problems for an army in the field, the Romans usually sent only one consul at a time into battle—or assigned consuls sole command on alternate days. If this proved too unwieldy, the consuls could, with the advice of the Senate, step down and appoint a single dictator. His term of office was limited to six months, but his *imperium* was valid inside and outside the city and unlimited by any right of appeal.

These devices worked well enough for a small city whose wars were short skirmishes fought near home. But as Rome's wars grew longer and more difficult, adaptations had to be made. In 325 B.C., proconsulships were invented to extend the terms of consuls serving in the field. This maintained continuity of command during a long war, but it provided ambitious men with an opportunity to monopolize political power.

Consuls were assisted by financial officers called *quaestors* (originally two, but ultimately eight). A need for more military commanders led to the introduction of other aides, *praetors*. The praetor's primary function was judicial, but he could also be granted a general's *imperium* and have his term of service in the field extended beyond a year. In the second half of the fifth century B.C., the consuls' responsibility for enrolling and keeping track of citizens was delegated to new officials, two *censors*. Since they determined the status and, therefore, the tax liability of each citizen, they had to be men of unimpeachable reputation. They were usually senior senators who viewed the office as the pinnacle of their careers. By the fourth century B.C., censors had the right to strike from the rolls of the Senate members who were deemed a disgrace to that body.

The Senate and the Assembly. The Senate was the only deliberative body continuously in session in the Roman Republic. Senators were prominent patricians, often leaders of clans and patrons with many clients. Consequently, the Senate won control of the state's finances and of foreign policy, and its advice was not lightly ignored by magistrates or by popular assemblies.

The centuriate assembly—the Roman army when convened to deliberate rather than fight—was the early republic's most important popular assembly. It elected the consuls and several other magistrates, voted on bills the Senate put before it, made decisions of war and peace, and served as a court of appeal for citizens convicted of serious offenses. The centuriate assembly was named for the "centuries" in which its members voted. A century was, in theory, a unit of 100 soldiers who fought with the same kind of equipment. Because each man bought his own equipment, centuries grouped citizens into classes according to wealth. Each century cast a single vote, and votes were tallied beginning with the richest centuries, those of the cavalry.

The Struggle of the Orders. Patricians monopolized power in the early republic. Plebeians were barred from all political and religious offices. They could not serve as judges. They could not even know the law, for the law was an oral tradition maintained by patrician magistrates. When Rome acquired new land by conquest, patricians were in position to reward themselves most generously. They dominated the assemblies and the Senate. And they refused to sanction marriages outside their caste that would have permitted at least the most wealthy plebeian families to share their privileges.

The plebeians responded to the intransigence of the patricians by launching the "struggle of the orders," a fight for political, legal, and social equality that lasted for 200 years. Plebeians had weight in their negotiations with the patricians, for plebeians made up a large part of the republic's army. According to tradition, early in the republic's history the plebeians withdrew from the city and refused to fight until the patricians granted them a concession. The plebeians formed a political organization of their own, the plebeian tribal assembly, and elected "tribunes," officials with the power to protect plebeians from abuse by patrician magistrates. In effect, a tribune could veto any action of a magistrate or any bill in a Roman assembly or the Senate.

The protection of plebeian rights required that Rome's law be fixed and opened to public scrutiny. In 450 B.C., the Twelve Tables were published, the first attempt to codify Rome's harsh customs. In 445 B.C., plebeians won the right to marry patricians, but they were still barred from many public offices. It was not until 367 B.C. that one of the consuls was allowed to be of plebeian rank. Gradually other offices, even the dictatorship and the censorship, were opened to them, and in 300 B.C., they were admitted to the most important priesthoods. In 287 B.C., the plebeians completed their triumph by securing passage of a law that made decisions of the plebeian assembly binding on all Romans.

The plebeians' victory did not make Rome a democracy. It simply cleared the way for wealthy plebeian families to enter politics and share the privileges of the patrician aristocracy. The *nobiles*, a small group of rich and powerful families of both patrician and plebeian rank, monopolized the republic's highest offices. Since there was no secret ballot, the numerous clients of the wealthy *nobiles* could easily be intimidated into voting as their patrons ordered. This permitted the great families to build political machines and maintain their hold on offices. From 233 to 133 B.C., twenty-six families produced 80 percent of the consuls; ten of those families accounted for almost 50 percent of the successful candidates. Since the politically dominant families were all represented in the Senate, the Senate became the republic's chief deliberative body. The product of the struggle of the orders was, therefore, a republican constitution dominated by a senatorial aristocracy. Most Romans accepted it, for it led Rome well in the wars that won Rome an empire.

The Conquest of Italy

Not long after the birth of the republic in 509 B.C., a coalition of Romans, Latins, and Greeks defeated the Etruscans and drove them out of Latium. Rome's neighbor, the Etruscan city of Veii, continued to be a problem. But in 392 B.C., after a long siege, Rome destroyed Veii. The territory Rome annexed doubled its size.

Romans used both inducements and menaces when coming to terms with their foes. Friendly alliances with former enemies brought additional soldiers into Rome's army. If land belonging to a defeated people had to be annexed, the result was the same. Distribution of newly won land, to poor Romans as well as the rich, brought them the income they needed to equip themselves for military service. This helped give the Roman poor a stake in their government and reconciled them to the aristocratic regime. The long siege of Veii, which kept soldiers from working their farms, prompted the Romans to begin paying men for military service. This, too, was popular with the poor and improved the quality of the army.

Gallic Invasion of Italy and Roman Reaction. Early in the fourth century B.C., Rome suffered a dramatic setback. In 387 B.C., the Gauls marched south from the Po Valley, defeated the Roman army, and burned Rome. The Romans had to pay the Gauls to evacuate the city. Rome quickly recovered from this humiliation, but in 340 B.C., the city's Latin neighbors, the Latin League, tried to curtail its expansion. In 338 B.C., Rome defeated and dissolved the League. The terms by which this war ended set a precedent for Rome's future reorganization of Italy.

Roman Policy Toward the Conquered. The Romans did not destroy any of the Latin cities, nor did they treat them all alike. Some were given full Roman citizenship. Others were granted municipal privileges: internal self-government, the right to intermarry and trade with Romans—but not to take part in Roman politics unless they moved to Rome and applied for citizenship. The treaties by which other states became allies of Rome differed from city to city. Some were given the private rights of intermarriage and commerce with Romans; some were not. (Allied states were always forbidden to exercise these rights with one another.) Some states, but not all, were allowed local autonomy. Land was taken from some, but not from others. All the allies supplied troops to Rome's army under Roman officers, but they did not pay taxes to Rome.

The Romans planted colonies of veteran soldiers on some of the land they annexed. The colonists retained their Roman citizenship and served as a kind of permanent garrison to deter rebellion. A network of military roads was built to connect the colonies with Rome and guarantee that a Roman army could swiftly reinforce an embattled colony and put down an uprising.

The Roman settlement of Latium reveals the strategy that the Romans developed to extend their dominance. Rome used diplomacy and military actions to separate enemies. It cultivated a reputation for harsh, speedy punishment of rebels. But it was also generous to those who submitted. The status given a newly conquered city was not a permanent sentence. Loyal allies could improve their prospects—even achieve full Roman citizenship. This policy gave Rome's allies a stake in Rome's future and a sense of being colleagues rather than subjects. Consequently, most of Rome's allies remained loyal even when put to severe tests.

Defeat of the Samnites. After the struggle with the Latin League, Rome's next challenge was a series of wars with the tough mountain people of the southern Apennines, the Samnites. Some of Rome's allies joined the Samnites—as did various Etruscans and Gauls. But most of the allies remained loyal, and by 280 B.C., Rome's victories over these assorted opponents had won the city mastery of central Italy.

Rome's expanded territory was in direct contact with the Greek cities of southern Italy. Roman intervention in a quarrel between two of these cities led to a war with a Greek mercenary, Pyrrhus, king of Epirus and probably the best general of his day. The Greeks hired Pyrrhus to fight the Romans. He defeated them twice but suffered so many casualties that he decided that he could not afford to see the war through to its conclusion. Judging his "Pyrrhic" victory not worth the cost, he withdrew, and his Greek employers had to join the Roman confederation. By 265 B.C., Rome ruled all of Italy south of the Po River, an area of 47,200 square miles. And victory over Pyrrhus brought Rome international recognition as a power in the Hellenistic world.

Rome and Carthage

Late in the ninth century B.C., the Phoenician city of Tyre had planted a colony called Carthage ("New City") on the coast of northern Africa near modern Tunis (see Map 4-2). In the sixth century B.C., the conquest of Tyre by the Assyrians liberated the Carthaginians to develop the opportunities offered by

MAP 4-2 The Western Mediterranean Area During the Rise of Rome *This map covers the theater of conflict between the growing Roman dominions and those of Carthage in the third century B.C. The Carthaginian Empire stretched westward from the city (in modern Tunisia) along the North African coast and into southern Spain.*

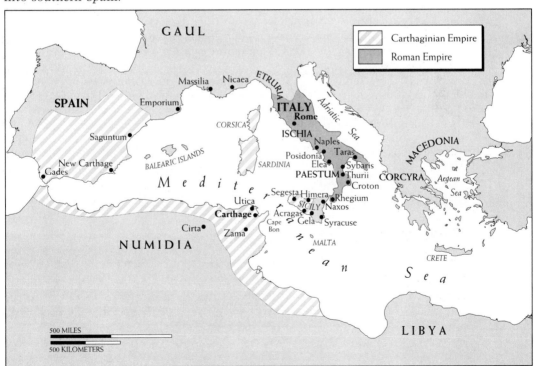

their strategic location. The city had an excellent harbor and commanded rich lands that it worked with slave labor.

In the sixth century B.C., Carthage's domain expanded westward along the coast of northern Africa beyond the Straits of Gibraltar and eastward into Libya. Parts of southern Spain, Sardinia, Corsica, Malta, the Balearic Islands, and western Sicily also came under the city's control. The natives of these lands became subjects of the Carthaginian Empire. They served in the Carthaginian army or navy and paid tribute. Carthage also claimed exclusive rights to trade in the western Mediterranean.

Rome and Carthage became entangled when Hiero, tyrant of Syracuse, attacked the Sicilian city of Messana. Messana, which commanded the straits between Italy and Sicily, had been seized by a group of Italian mercenaries who styled themselves Mamertines ("sons of Mars"). The Mamertines asked Carthage for help in fending off Hiero. Because of the importance of the straits, Carthage agreed. But the Mamertines then tried to check Carthage by also inviting the Romans to send them aid. Rome realized that if it did not intervene, it was ceding control of the straits and of Sicily to Carthage. Conse-

A Roman warship. Rome became a naval power late in its history, in the course of the First Punic War. Roman sailors initially lacked the skill and experience in sea warfare of their Cathaginian opponents, who could maneuver their oared ships to ram the enemy. To compensate for this disadvantage, the Romans sought to make a sea battle more like an encounter on land by devising ways to grapple enemy ships and board them with armed troops. In time, they also mastered the skillful use of the ram. This picture shows a Roman ship, propelled by oars, with both ram and soldiers, ready for either kind of fight. [Vatican Museum]

quently, in 264 B.C., the assembly voted to send an army to Messana. Since the Romans called the Carthaginians *Poeni* or *Puni* (Latin for "Phoenician"), the ensuing conflict came to be known as the Punic War.

The First Punic War (264–241 B.C.). The Romans made no progress against Carthage until they built a fleet to blockade the Carthaginian ports at the western end of Sicily. In 241 B.C., after a long war of attrition, Carthage capitulated. It surrendered Sicily and the islands between Italy and Sicily to Rome and agreed to pay a war indemnity. In 238 B.C., while Carthage struggled to put down a revolt led by her unpaid mercenary soldiers, Rome seized Sardinia and Corsica and demanded an additional indemnity. This was a provocative action on the part of Rome that was to cost Rome a second war with Carthage.

It is hard to understand why Rome sought more territory, for the administration of lands outside of Italy was difficult. Sicily, Sardinia, and Corsica were turned over to military governors as the first provinces of a Roman empire. Since Rome had no way of overseeing the behavior of magistrates outside the city, provincial governors had ample opportunity to abuse their offices. The traditional policy of extending citizenship—and with it, loyalty to Rome—was not applied beyond the borders of Italy. The residents of the provinces were neither Roman citizens nor allies; they were subjects who paid tribute in lieu of serving in the army. Rome collected this tribute by "farming" out the right to gather money in the provinces to the highest bidder. The provinces soon became a source of corruption that undermined the machinery of the Roman Republic.

While Rome struggled to adjust to its new situation, Hamilcar Barca, the Carthaginian governor of Spain (237–229 B.C.), put Carthage on the road to recovery. His plan was to build a Punic empire in Spain that would make up for the lands Carthage had lost to Rome. Hasdrubal, Hamilcar's son-in-law and successor, continued his policies with such success that he alarmed the Romans. They imposed a treaty in which he promised not to expand north of Spain's Ebro River. He doubtless assumed that if Carthage accepted the Ebro as its northern frontier, the Romans would grant Carthage a free hand in the south. He was wrong. Within a few years the Romans had violated, at least in spirit, the Ebro treaty by accepting an offer of an alliance from the people of Saguntum, a Spanish town 100 miles south of the Ebro.

The Second Punic War (218–202 B.C.). Hasdrubal was assassinated in 221 B.C., and the army chose Hannibal, the twenty-five-year-old son of Hamilcar Barca, to succeed him. Hannibal quickly consolidated and extended the Punic empire in Spain. At first, he avoided any action against Saguntum, but the Saguntines, confident of Rome's protection, began to stir up trouble for him. When Hannibal besieged and captured the town, the Romans sent an ultimatum to Carthage demanding Hannibal's surrender. Carthage refused, and Rome declared war (218 B.C.).

Rome had repeatedly provoked Carthage, but had taken no steps to prevent Carthage from rebuilding its empire—and made no plans to defend itself against a Punic attack. Hannibal exacted a high price for these blunders. In the fall of 218 B.C., he crossed the Alps into Italy with an army to which the Gauls were eager to contribute. Hannibal defeated the Romans at the Ticinus River and crushed the joint consular armies at the Trebia River. In 217 B.C., he outmaneuvered and trapped another army at Lake Trasimene. He could not take Rome, however, unless he could persuade its allies to defect. Despite his efforts to court them, most of the allies remained firm.

Sobered by their defeats, the Romans suspended consular government and chose a dictator: Quintus Fabius Maximus. Since time and supplies were on Rome's side, his strategy was to avoid pitched battles and wear Hannibal's army down by harassing its flanks. In 216 B.C. Hannibal attacked a grain depot at Cannae in Apulia to tempt the Romans into an open fight. They took the bait and suffered the worst defeat in their history. Hannibal obliterated the army of 80,000 men they sent against him.

Rome's prestige was shattered. Most of the allies in southern Italy—and the crucial port of Syracuse in Sicily—went over to Hannibal. For the next decade no Roman army dared confront Hannibal directly. But Hannibal had neither the numbers nor the supplies to blockade walled cities, nor did he have the equipment to take them by assault. If the Romans refused to fight him, there was little he could do to bring the war to an end.

The Romans devised a plan to defeat Hannibal outside of Italy. Publius Cornelius Scipio (237–183 B.C.), later called Africanus, set out to conquer Spain and prevent it from sending reinforcements to Hannibal. Scipio was not yet twenty-five, but he was a general almost as talented as Hannibal. Within a few years he had taken Spain and won the Senate's permission to open a front in Africa. In 204 B.C., Scipio landed in Africa, defeated the Carthaginians, and forced them to order Hannibal to withdraw from Italy. Hannibal had won every battle but lost the war. His fatal error was to underestimate the determination of Rome and the loyalty of its allies. When Hannibal returned to Carthage, hostilities flared up again. In 202 B.C., Scipio and Hannibal met at the battle of Zama. The day was decided for Rome by the generalship of Scipio and the desertion of Hannibal's mercenaries. Rome reduced Carthage to the status of a dependent ally and emerged as the undisputed ruler of the western Mediterranean.

The Republic's Conquest of the Hellenistic World

The East. By the middle of the third century B.C., the three great Hellenistic kingdoms that dominated the eastern Mediterranean had achieved equilibrium. The balance of power among them was threatened, however, by the attempts that Philip V of Macedon (221–179 B.C.) and Antiochus III, the Seleucid ruler (223–187 B.C.), made to expand their domains. Philip had allied himself with Carthage during the Second Punic War—provoking Rome to stir up a conflict in the Aegean called the First Macedonian War (215–205 B.C.). Once the Second Punic War was over, Rome determined to make sure that Macedon did not succeed Carthage as a threat to Italy. In 200 B.C., the Romans challenged Philip by ordering him to cease preying on the Greek cities. Two years later the Romans demanded that Philip withdraw from Greece entirely. Philip refused, and Rome declared the Second Macedonian War. In 197 B.C., Flamininus, a gifted young general, defeated Philip at Cynoscephalae in Thessaly, and the following year (196 B.C.) Flamininus surprised the Greeks by restoring the autonomy of the city-states and pulling Rome's troops out of Greece.

Philip's retreat offered Antiochus an opportunity to advance. On the pretext of freeing the Greeks from Roman domination, he invaded the Greek mainland. The Romans quickly drove him from Greece, and in 189 B.C., they crushed his army at Magnesia in Asia Minor. The peace of Apamia in the next year deprived Antiochus of his war-elephants and his navy and imposed a huge indemnity on him. Again, the Romans annexed no territory, but they treated Greece and Asia Minor as protectorates in whose affairs they could freely intervene. This benign policy was to change as the influence of Cato, a conservative and ruthlessly businesslike censor, increased in Rome.

In 179 B.C., Perseus succeeded Philip V as king of Macedon. His popularity with democratic, revolutionary elements in the Greek cities convinced the Romans that he was a threat to the stability of the Aegean. The result was the Third Macedonian War (172–168 B.C.) and a harsher Roman policy. Macedon was divided into four separate republics, whose citizens were forbidden to intermarry or do business with each other, and leaders of anti-Roman factions in the Greek cities were punished severely. Aemilius Paullus, the Roman general who defeated Perseus, brought so much booty home that Rome abolished some taxes on its citizens. Romans were discovering that foreign campaigns could be profitable for the state, its soldiers, and its generals.

The West. Rome's worst abuses of power were directed not against the Greeks, but against the people of the Iberian Peninsula, whom the Romans considered barbarians. In 154 B.C., the natives of Iberia launched a fierce guerrilla campaign against their oppressors. By the time Scipio Aemilianus took the city of Numantia and brought the war to a conclusion in 134 B.C., Rome was having difficulty finding soldiers willing to go to Spain.

Carthage fared much worse. Carthage scrupulously observed the terms of its treaty with Rome and posed no threat to Rome, but fear and hatred of Carthage were deeply ingrained in some Romans. Cato is said to have ended all his speeches in the Senate with the same sentence: "Besides, I think that Carthage must be destroyed." The Romans finally took advantage of a technical breach of the peace to declare war on Carthage, and in 146 B.C., Scipio Aemilianus destroyed the city. A province of Africa was then added to the five existing Roman provinces: Sicily, Sardinia-Corsica, Macedonia, Hither Spain, and Further Spain.

⁓ Civilization in the Early Roman Republic

The Roman attitude toward the Greeks ranged from admiration for their culture to contempt for their political squabbling and money grubbing. Conservatives like Cato spoke contemptuously of the Greeks, but, as Roman life was transformed by association with the Greeks, even he learned Greek. The education of the Roman upper classes became bilingual, and young Roman nobles studied Greek rhetoric, literature, and sometimes philosophy. Greek refined the Latin language, and Greek models—such as Livius Andronicus' third-century B.C. translation of the *Odyssey*—prompted the birth of Latin literature.

Religion

The Romans identified their ancestral gods with the Greek deities and worked Greek mythology into their own traditions. But Roman religious practice was little affected until new Eastern influences were felt in the third century B.C. In 205 B.C., the Senate approved the public worship of Cybele, the Great Mother goddess from Phrygia. But since Cybele's cult involved rites that shocked and outraged conservative Romans, the Senate soon reversed itself. For similar reasons, it banned the worship of Dionysus, or Bacchus, in 186 B.C. And in 139 B.C., the Senate drove from Rome Babylonian astrologers whom it believed to be unhealthy influences.

Education

In the early centuries of the Roman Republic, education was entirely the responsibility of the family—a father teaching his sons at home. (Daughters may or may not have been schooled in those days; they were later on.) The curriculum was designed to equip men with vocational skills, to elevate their moral standards, and to inspire them with respect for Roman tradition. Boys were taught to read, write, calculate, and farm. They memorized the laws of the Twelve Tables, practiced religious rites, learned the legends of early Roman history—particularly those involving their ancestors—and trained for military service.

Hellenized Education. Contact with the Greeks of southern Italy in the third century B.C. produced momentous changes in Roman education. Greek teachers introduced the Romans to the study of language, literature, and philosophy—and to what the Romans called *humanitas,* the broad training and critical habits of mind that are the characteristics of a liberal education.

Since Rome did not yet have a literature of its own, elementary education involved learning Greek as a preparation for the advanced study of rhetoric, the art of speaking and writing well. Philosophy was at the heart of Greek education, but the practical Romans preferred rhetoric. It was of great use in legal disputes and political life.

This carved relief from the second century A.D. *shows a schoolmaster and his pupils. The one at the right is arriving late. [Alinari/Art Resource, N.Y.]*

Some important Romans were powerful advocates of Greek literature and philosophy. Scipio Aemilianus, the man who destroyed Carthage, was the patron of Greek intellectuals like the historian Polybius and the philosopher Panaetius. Cato the Elder spoke for the conservative Romans who feared that Greek learning would weaken Roman moral fiber. On occasion the Senate was persuaded to drive philosophers and teachers of rhetoric out of Rome, but Rome could not return to its simple agrarian past. If Romans were to deal with the sophisticated world of the Hellenistic Greeks, which they had come to dominate, they needed the new education.

In the late republic, Roman education, though still entirely private, became more formal and organized. From the ages of seven to twelve, boys went to elementary school accompanied by a Greek slave called a *paedagogus* (whence our term "pedagogue") who looked after them and with whom they practiced conversing in Greek. Boys learned to read, to write—using a wax tablet and a stylus—and to do simple arithmetic with the aid of an abacus and pebbles (*calculi*). From twelve to sixteen, boys studied Greek and Latin literature with a *grammaticus*. He gave them a liberal education involving dialectic, arithmetic, geometry, astronomy, music, and some elements of rhetoric. Some boys went on to advanced study in rhetoric. A few, like the great orator Cicero, undertook what we might call postgraduate study by traveling abroad to work with the great teachers of the Greek world.

Education for Women. Though the evidence is limited, it is certain that girls of the upper classes received an education equivalent at least to the early stages of a boy's education. They were probably taught at home by tutors, not sent out to school as was increasingly common for their brothers in the late republic. Young women did not study with philosophers and rhetoricians, for they were usually married at the age at which men pursued higher education. Still, some women found ways to continue their studies. Some became prose writers or poets. By the first century A.D. there were women in aristocratic

A Women's Uprising in Republican Rome

In 195 B.C., Roman women made a rare group appearance on the stage of republican political life. They demanded the repeal of a law (passed two decades earlier during the Second Punic War) that they judged to limit their rights unfairly. Livy (59 B.C.–A.D. 17) describes the affair and the response of the traditionalist Marcus Portius Cato (234–149 B.C.).

~ Of what did the women complain? How did they try to achieve their goals? Which of Cato's objections to their behavior do you think were most important? Since women did not vote or sit in assemblies, how can the outcome of the affair be explained?

Amid the anxieties of great wars, either scarce finished or soon to come, an incident occurred, trivial to relate, but which, by reason of the passions it aroused, developed into a violent contention. Marcus Fundanius and Lucius Valerius, tribunes of the people, proposed to the assembly the abrogation of the Oppian law. The tribune Gaius Oppius had carried this law in the heat of the Punic War in the consulship of Quintus Fabius and Tiberius Sempronius, that no woman should possess more than half an ounce of gold or wear a parti-coloured garment or ride in a carriage in the City or in a town within a mile thereof, except on the occasion of a religious festival. The tribunes Marcus and Publius Iunius Brutus were supporting the Oppian law, and averred that they would not permit its repeal; many distinguished men came forward to speak for and against it; the Capitoline was filled with crowds of supporters and opponents of the bill. The matrons could not be kept at home by advice or modesty or their husbands' orders, but blocked all the streets and approaches to the Forum, begging the men as they came down to the Forum that, in the prosperous condition of the state, when the private fortunes of all men were daily increasing, they should allow the women too to have their former distinctions restored. The crowd of women grew larger day by day; for they were now coming in from the towns and rural districts. Soon they dared even to approach and appeal to the consuls, the praetors, and the other officials, but one consul, at least, they found adamant, Marcus Porcius Cato, who spoke thus in favour of the law whose repeal was being urged.

"If each of us, citizens, had determined to assert his rights and dignity as a husband with respect to his own spouse, we circles who were famous or—as conservative males saw it—infamous for their learning.

Slavery

The Romans, like most ancient peoples, had always had slaves. But the shepherds and family-farmers of early Rome owned few. Slavery became fundamental to the Roman way of life only during the second century B.C., in the wake of Rome's conquests. Between 264 B.C. and 133 B.C., the Romans en-

should have less trouble with the sex as a whole; as it is, our liberty, destroyed at home by female violence, even here in the Forum is crushed and trodden underfoot, and because we have not kept them individually under control, we dread them collectively. . . . But from no class is there not the greatest danger if you permit them meetings and gatherings and secret consultations. . . .

"I should have said, 'What sort of practice is this, of running out into the streets and blocking the roads and speaking to other women's husbands? Could you not have made the same requests, each of your own husband, at home? Or are you more attractive outside and to other women's husbands than to your own? And yet, not even at home, if modesty would keep matrons within the limits of their proper rights, did it become you to concern yourselves with the question of what laws should be adopted in this place or repealed.' Our ancestors permitted no woman to conduct even personal business without a guardian to intervene in her behalf; they wished them to be under the control of fathers, brothers, husbands; we (Heaven help us!) allow them now even to interfere in public affairs, yes, and to visit the Forum and our informal and formal sessions. What else are they doing now on the streets and at the corners except urging the bill of the tribunes and voting for the repeal of the law? Give loose rein to their uncontrollable nature and to this untamed creature and expect that they will themselves set bounds to their licence; unless you act, this is the least of the things enjoined upon women by custom or law and to which they submit with a feeling of injustice. It is complete liberty or, rather, if we wish to speak the truth, complete licence that they desire.

"If they win in this, what will they not attempt? Review all the laws with which your forefathers restrained their licence and made them subject to their husbands; even with all these bounds you can scarcely control them. What of this? If you suffer them to seize these bounds one by one and wrench themselves free and finally to be placed on a parity with their husbands, do you think that you will be able to endure them? The moment they begin to be your equals, they will be your superiors."

. . .The next day an even greater crowd of women appeared in public, and all of them in a body beset the doors of those tribunes, who were vetoing their colleagues' proposal, and they did not desist until the threat of veto was withdrawn by the tribunes. After that there was no question that all the tribes would vote to repeal the law. The law was repealed twenty years after it was passed.

From Livy, trans. by Evan T. Stage (Cambridge, Mass: Harvard University Press, 1935), XXXIV, i–iii; viii, pp. 413–419, 439.

slaved some 250,000 prisoners of war. Slaves could marry, and their children increased the slave population.

In Rome as in Greece, domestic slaves and those engaged in crafts and commerce were permitted to earn money with which to purchase their freedom. The freeing of slaves was very common among the Romans. After a time a considerable portion of the Roman population was made up of people who had been slaves or whose ancestors had been slaves. It was not uncommon to see a freedman son or grandson of a slave become wealthy and the slave himself or his son become a Roman citizen. By importing slaves from all over the

Mediterranean world and freeing them, the Romans transformed the ethnic composition of their population.

A unique contribution of the Romans to slavery was the invention of an agricultural system that depended on vast numbers of unfree workers. At the end of the republic there were 2 million to 3 million slaves in Italy, about 35 percent to 40 percent of the total population. Most belonged to great slave gangs working vast plantations (*latifundia*). These estates produced capital-intensive cash crops (wool, wine, olive oil, cattle) rather than the grain that small farmers raised. The lives of agricultural workers were harder than those of other kinds of slaves, for *latifundia* were designed to produce maximum profits. Slaves, who were simply a means to that end, were fed cheaply, treated like machines, and discarded when they were no longer useful.

Harsh treatment spawned slave rebellions of a kind unknown in other ancient societies. A rebellion in Sicily in 134 B.C. kept that island in turmoil for over two years. In 73 B.C., a gladiator named Spartacus raised an army of 70,000 fugitive slaves from the Italian countryside and repeatedly defeated the Roman legions. When the Romans finally defeated him, they crucified 6,000 of his men along the road from Capua to Rome.

∼ Roman Imperialism: The Late Republic

Rome followed no plan in building its empire. Territories were acquired as a result of wars that the Romans believed were either defensive or preventive. Roman foreign policy was designed to provide security for Rome on Rome's terms. Since these terms were often unacceptable to other nations, conflicts arose; intentional or not, the ensuing expansion brought Rome an empire (see Map 4-3).

The empire undercut the very republic it was built to protect. The constitution of the republic had been designed for a city-state. It was well adapted to the mastery of Italy, but not to the responsibilities entailed in governing an empire beyond the seas.

The Aftermath of Conquest

Before the Punic Wars most Italians owned their own farms and were largely self-sufficient. Some families had larger holdings than others, but they grew the same crops (grain) and used free laborers rather than slaves. The Punic Wars changed this. For fourteen years Hannibal marauded through Italy, doing terrible damage to its farmland. Many veterans returned from the wars to find that they did not have enough capital to get their devastated farms back into production. Some moved to Rome seeking work as day laborers. Most stayed in the country and became tenant farmers or hired hands. The land they abandoned was gathered into large parcels by the wealthy who had the capital to convert it to crops profitable on a world market (olives, grapes, and cattle). The upper classes had plenty of capital to invest, for the political of-

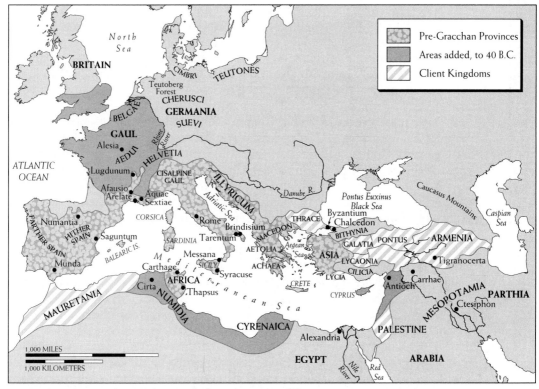

MAP 4-3 Roman Dominions of the Late Republic *The Roman Republic's conquest of Mediterranean lands—and beyond—until the death of Julius Caesar is shown here. Areas conquered before Tiberius Gracchus (ca. 133 B.C.) are distinguished from later ones and from client areas owing allegiance to Rome.*

fices they monopolized enabled them to exploit Rome's new provinces. The economy that evolved with the empire separated the people of Rome and Italy more sharply into rich and poor, landed and landless, privileged and deprived. The result was an increasingly tense situation that threatened the survival of the republic.

The Gracchi

By the middle of the second century B.C., perceptive Roman nobles were aware that institutions fundamental to the republic were collapsing. The decline of the peasant farmer was shrinking the class from which Rome drew its soldiers. And the patron-client organizations that had structured Roman society were weakening. Patrons found it hard to control clients once the latter were no longer tied to the land. The introduction of the secret ballot in the 130s B.C. further weakened the traditional ties of clientage.

Tiberius Gracchus. In 133 B.C. Tiberius Gracchus, a tribune, tried to solve these problems by proposing a program of land reform. He suggested reclaiming public land that was being held illegally. Current holders of this land were to be allowed to retain as many as 300 acres in clear title as private property, but the state would take the rest and redistribute it, at low rents and in small lots, to the poor. Those who received farms were not to be allowed to sell them.

Tiberius's proposal aroused great hostility. Many wealthy senators would be hurt by its passage. Others feared the precedent set by any interference with property rights. Still others feared the political gains that Tiberius would make if the beneficiaries of his legislation were properly grateful to its drafter.

When Tiberius put his land reform bill before the tribal assembly, one of his fellow tribunes, M. Octavius, vetoed it. This left Tiberius with the choice of dropping the matter or attempting a maneuver that would undercut the checks and balances of Rome's constitution. Tiberius decided to challenge the constitution. He cleared the way for discussion of his popular bill by persuading the assembly to remove Octavius from office. At this point many of Tiberius's powerful senatorial allies deserted him. If the assembly could pass laws opposed by the Senate and vetoed by a tribune, if they could remove magistrates, then Rome would no longer be an oligarchical republic, but a democracy like Athens.

Tiberius, giving up hope of conciliating the Senate, passed a second bill that was harsher than the first and more appealing to the people. It contained a scheme for funding a commission to carry out land redistribution. King Attalus of Pergamum had just died and left his kingdom to Rome. Tiberius's suggestion that this revenue be used to finance implementation of land reform was a second assault on the constitution: a challenge to the Senate's control of finances and foreign affairs.

Tiberius knew that he would be in great personal danger once he lost the protection the tribunal office gave him, so he announced his candidacy for a second successive term. This was another blow to tradition, and his opponents feared that he intended to hold office indefinitely, ruling Rome as a demagogic tyrant. At the elections a riot broke out, and a mob of senators and their clients killed Tiberius and some 300 of his followers. The Senate put down the threat to its rule, but at the price of the first internal bloodshed in Rome's political history.

The tribunate of Tiberius Gracchus permanently changed the thinking of Roman politicians. Heretofore Roman politics had been a struggle among great families for honor and reputation. Fundamental issues were rarely at stake. Tiberius's revolutionary proposals and the senatorial resort to bloodshed created a new situation. Tiberius, despite his failure, had shown how the tribunate could be used to challenge senatorial rule. He had demonstrated that a man could acquire power, not by courting the aristocracy, but by appealing directly to the people with a popular issue. Politicians who took this route came to be known as *populares*. Those who supported the traditional role of the Senate were the *optimates* ("the best men").

These groups were not political parties with formal programs and party discipline, but they were more than vehicles for the political ambitions of unorthodox office seekers. The Roman people needed to debate fundamental issues that had the potential to divide them. Some of their leaders were interested only in advancing their own careers. Some were sincere advocates of principled positions. Most, no doubt, were a mixture of the two.

Gaius Gracchus. In 123 B.C., ten years after the death of Tiberius, his brother Gaius Gracchus became a tribune. Gaius dominated Roman politics by proposing legislation that appealed to different groups. He revived efforts to redistribute public land; when supplies of land proved insufficient, he proposed new colonies; and he put through a law stabilizing the price of grain in Rome. Gaius also weakened the rich by setting the two wealthiest classes in the republic against each other. The Senate usually had the support of the equestrians—the rich men who could qualify for the Roman cavalry, the most expensive form of military service. Many equestrians were businessmen with interests in the provinces. In 129 B.C., when Pergamum became the province of Asia, Gaius gave the equestrian order the privilege of collecting its revenue. He also barred senators from serving on the courts that tried provincial governors. This prevented the senators from sitting in judgment on themselves, but it did not improve the administration of the provinces. No senator dared interfere with the equestrian tax collectors in his province lest he find himself dragged before their court.

In 122 B.C., Gaius celebrated his reelection to the tribunate—which was now legal—by proposing that Rome's Italian allies be given citizens' rights. The allies, who had not received a fair share of the profits from the empire they had helped Rome win, were becoming a threat to Italy's stability, but the ordinary Roman did not want to share his citizenship. The Senate used this to drive a wedge between Gaius and his supporters, and Gaius lost the election of 121 B.C. The Senate then trumped up a charge against him, killed him, and put to death without trial some 3,000 of his followers. Once again, the senatorial oligarchy triumphed over the *populares*, but the struggle was by no means over. Gaius's death simply taught the *populares* that they would have to oppose the Senate's violence with violence of their own. Marius, an officer who rose to prominence in the Jugurthine War, showed them the way.

Marius

In 111 B.C., a group of Italian businessmen who were working in Numidia, a client kingdom in Africa, were caught in the crossfire of a dispute over succession to the throne. The Roman electorate promptly declared war against Jugurtha, the perpetrator of this assault on their nation's honor. The war dragged on longer than expected, and rumors circulated that Rome's generals were being bought off.

In 107 B.C., the assembly elected C. Marius (157–86 B.C.) to a consulship and usurped the Senate's right to direct foreign policy by commissioning him to end the Jugurthine War. Marius was a *novus homo*, a "new man"—that is, the first of his family to hold a consulship. He was outside the closed circle of the old Roman aristocracy and something of a political maverick.

Marius quickly defeated Jugurtha, and the grateful Romans elected him to a second consulship to deal with another problem. In 105 B.C., two barbaric tribes, the Cimbri and the Teutones, had crushed a Roman army in the Rhone valley. The struggle to contain them kept Marius in office for five consecutive terms (until 100 B.C.).

Marius's success derived from changes he made in the army. He convinced the assembly to drop the property qualification for military service. This was a popular idea for it opened the way to a career for the impoverished citizens whose problems had not been solved by the Gracchi. Marius's reforms built a strong army, but they also altered the balance of power in Roman politics. Marius's soldiers were semiprofessional clients of their general. They were dependent on him for their pay and for the grants of land on which they would retire as veterans. They looked to him, not to the state, for their rewards. And he used them to frighten the Senate into giving him whatever he needed to keep them happy.

Sulla

Marius's example inspired imitation, and competitors soon appeared to challenge him. The most successful was L. Cornelius Sulla (138–78 B.C.), an impoverished aristocrat who had served under Marius in the Jugurthine War. Sulla made his mark in a campaign that Gaius Gracchus had tried to prevent: a struggle between Rome and its Italian allies. In 90 B.C., the allies gave up hope of receiving fair treatment from Rome and established a separate confederation with its own capital and its own coinage. Rome immediately offered citizenship to those cities that remained loyal and to the rebels who laid down their arms. Even then, hard fighting was needed to put down the uprising. By 88 B.C., the war was over, and all the Italians became Roman citizens.

Sulla's performance in the war brought him the consulship for 88 B.C. and command of a war against Mithridates, a native king who was leading an uprising in Asia. Marius, although he was seventy years old, suddenly emerged from obscurity to demand this assignment for himself. When the assembly acquiesced to Marius, Sulla marched his army against Rome. Marius had brought the army into Roman politics, and now for the first time a Roman general used military force against his fellow citizens. Sulla regained his command. But when he left for Asia, Marius and the consul Cinna occupied Rome with their armies. Marius died soon after his election to a seventh consulship in 86 B.C., and Cinna became the leader of Marius's party. In 83 B.C., Sulla, who had forced Mithridates to retreat and agree to a truce, returned to Rome. Sulla drove Marius's followers from Italy and assumed dictatorial powers.

His first step was to wipe out the opposition. He posted lists of names of men who were "proscribed" as enemies of the state. Proscribed men could be executed on sight, and those who killed them were rewarded by the state. Sulla confiscated their property and used it to reward his own men. As many as 100,000 Romans may have died in Sulla's purge.

Sulla could have made himself the permanent ruler of Rome, but he saw himself as the republic's savior, not its enemy. Once in power, he set about restructuring and restoring traditional senatorial government. The Senate's political privileges were reaffirmed, and the powers of the office of tribune, which the Gracchi had used to attack senatorial rule, were severely curtailed. In 79 B.C., Sulla declared his work complete and retired from public life. He could not, however, undo the effect of his own example, an example that brought on civil war and the end of the republic

∼ Fall of the Republic

Pompey, Crassus, Caesar, and Cicero

Within a year of Sulla's death (78 B.C.), the Senate found it necessary to ignore the very rules Sulla had designed to defend the Senate's dominance of the republic. To deal with emergencies the Senate created "special" commands that were free of the constitutional restrictions that bound the regularly elected magistrates. The most important of these went to a trusted young general, Pompey (106–48 B.C.), who at the age of twenty-eight had never been elected to any office.

Pompey spent several years subduing a Marian army that had occupied Spain. In 73 B.C., the Senate appointed him and Marcus Licinius Crassus, a wealthy senator, to put down the slave rebellion led by the gladiator Spartacus. Crassus and Pompey, though they were jealous of each other, joined forces in repealing most of Sulla's constitution. This opened the way for ambitious generals and demagogic tribunes to collaborate in attacks on the Senate.

In 67 B.C., a special law aimed at the suppression of piracy gave Pompey *imperium* for three years over the entire Mediterranean and its coast inland for fifty miles. In three months Pompey cleared the seas of pirates, but meanwhile a new war had broken out with Mithridates. In 66 B.C., the assembly granted Pompey even more authority to deal with that threat. Once again Pompey justified his appointment. He defeated Mithridates, drove him to suicide, and extended Rome's frontier to the Euphrates River.

When Pompey returned to Rome in 62 B.C., he had more power than any Roman in history. The Senate had reason to fear that he might emulate Sulla and establish his own rule. Crassus was foremost among those who feared Pompey. Although rich and influential, he did not have the kind of military support needed to rival Pompey. During the 60s B.C., therefore, he allied himself with various popular leaders.

The ablest of these men was Gaius Julius Caesar (100–44 B.C.), a descendant of an old but obscure patrician family. Despite his noble lineage, Caesar was connected to the popular party. His aunt was the wife of Marius, and he married Cornelia, the daughter of Cinna. Caesar's rhetorical skill made him a valuable ally for Crassus in winning the discontented of every class to the cause of the *populares*. Each man needed the help of the other to win the significant military assignments that would enable them to build armies to compete with Pompey's.

Cicero (106–43 B.C.), a "new man" from Marius's home town of Arpinum, marshalled the opposition to Crassus and Caesar. Although he was an outsider to the senatorial aristocracy, he was no *popularis*. He hoped to create a "harmony of the orders" between the Senate and the equestrians that would secure the power of the propertied classes. His plan did not appeal to the Senate, but the Senate backed him to block the rise of Catiline, an extremist linked with Crassus.

When Cicero defeated Catiline for the consulship in 63 B.C., Catiline hatched a plot to take over the state. News of it leaked to Cicero, who quickly suppressed the plot. Cicero's action inconvenienced Pompey.

Formation of the First Triumvirate

Toward the end of 62 B.C., Pompey landed at Brundisium. He had delayed his return, hoping to find Italy in such a state as to justify his keeping his army. But Cicero's quick suppression of Catiline deprived him of any pretext, and Pompey had to disband his army to avoid the appearance of treason.

Pompey had achieved amazing things for Rome and expected the Senate to show its gratitude by deferring to him. He wanted the Senate to approve the treaties he had negotiated in the east and to give him land for his veterans. If prudent, the Senate would have granted his reasonable requests. Instead it tried to sap his power by denying him what he wanted. This drove him into an alliance with his natural enemies, Crassus and Caesar. They joined him in an informal political arrangement, the First Triumvirate, that brought them control of the republic.

Julius Caesar and His Government of Rome

With the aid of his colleagues, Caesar was elected to the consulship for 59 B.C. and saw to it that each of the triumvirs got what he wanted. Pompey obtained land for his veterans and confirmation of his eastern treaties. Crassus won valuable tax concessions for the equestrians who were his chief supporters. Caesar got a special command that gave him a chance to rival Pompey. When Caesar's consulship ended, the triumvirs secured their gains by arranging for the election of friendly consuls and by forcing their enemies to leave Rome.

Caesar's special command gave him authority, for five years, over Cisalpine Gaul in the Po Valley and Narbonese Gaul on the other side of the Alps. From these provinces, Caesar set about conquering the rest of Gaul. In

56 B.C., he bought himself additional time, by persuading Crassus and Pompey to renew the triumvirate. By 50 B.C., Caesar had completed the conquest of Gaul and acquired the wealth, fame, and military power he needed to compete against Pompey.

By this time the Triumvirate had dissolved. Crassus had died (in 53 B.C.) while invading Parthia, the successor to the Persian Empire. And Pompey saw no reason to sit idly by while Caesar's star rose. In the late 50s B.C., the Senate appointed Pompey sole consul with authority to quell rioting among the city's political factions. The Senate had concluded that Pompey was less of a threat than Caesar and was eager to help Pompey bring Caesar down.

Caesar searched for some way to retain an office that would allow him to keep his army, but the Senate refused to compromise. In January of 49 B.C., it ordered him to lay down his command. For Caesar this meant exile or death. Preferring treason, he ordered his legions to cross the Rubicon River, the boundary of his province, and march on Rome. The result was a civil war that Caesar fought to a successful conclusion in 45 B.C.

Caesar made few changes in the government of Rome. In theory, the Senate continued to play its role. But Caesar increased its size and packed it with his supporters. His monopoly of military power made a sham of senatorial decrees. In 46 B.C., Caesar was appointed dictator for ten years and in the next year for life. His enemies concluded that he was aiming at monarchy, and they began to plot his destruction. Gaius Cassius Longinus and Marcus Junius Brutus recruited some sixty senators, and as the Senate was convening on March 15, 44 B.C., they mobbed and assassinated Caesar. The assassins simply expected that once Caesar was dead the republic would automatically flourish. Instead, their act precipitated thirteen more years of civil war that finally buried the republic.

The Second Triumvirate and the Emergence of Octavian

Caesar had named his eighteen-year-old grandnephew, Gaius Octavian (63 B.C.– A.D. 14), as his heir. At first, the Senate tried to use the sickly, inexperienced young man against Mark Antony, the second-in-command to whom Caesar's men had spontaneously turned for leadership. But Octavian broke with the Senate, marched on Rome, assumed the consulship for 43 B.C., and declared war on Caesar's assassins. Mark Antony and another of Caesar's officers, M. Aemilius Lepidus, joined him in the Second Triumvirate, a legally established shared dictatorship charged, ostensibly, with the restoration of the republic.

In 42 B.C., the triumviral army defeated Brutus and Cassius at Philippi in Macedonia. Each of the triumvirs then rewarded himself with a command. The weakest member, Lepidus, was given Africa. Octavian took the west— and the troubles that went with it: a war with one of Pompey's sons, the settlement of some 100,000 veterans, and the restoration of order in Italy. Antony received the most promising assignment: command of the east. This gave him a chance to invade Parthia and win an army with which to sweep aside his fellow triumvirs.

In 36 B.C., Antony attacked Parthia, with disastrous results. His soldiers' faith in him was further undercut when Octavian mounted a propaganda campaign to convince them that Antony had become the pawn of Egypt's queen, Cleopatra. By 32 B.C., all pretense of cooperation came to an end. Lepidus had been put aside some years earlier, and at Actium in western Greece in 31 B.C., Octavian defeated Antony.

The suicides of Antony and Cleopatra ended the civil war and left Octavian, at the age of thirty-two, absolute master of the Mediterranean world. His power was enormous, but so was the task that faced him. To restore peace, prosperity, and stability to Rome he needed to create a form of government that could handle the empire without violating the republican traditions to which the Romans were passionately attached.

The Roman Republic, at its start, resembled the poleis of the Greek dark ages. The Romans were influenced by more advanced neighbors, like the urbanized Etruscans, but long remained a nation of farmers and herdsmen to whom trade was relatively unimportant. As Rome organized itself for war, the traditional distinctions that divided Romans into patrician and plebeian castes became less important than distinctions based on wealth. The republic needed a strong army, for it was engaged in virtually continuous warfare in defense of its lands and allies.

The Romans were a very pragmatic, conservative people who placed great importance on the maintenance of traditional codes of conduct. Their laws derived from experience, common sense, and a commitment to equity. Law helped them create something unique: an empire ruled by a republic. Rome controlled an area as large as the great empires of the East, but it needed no king or bureaucracy. It acquired and managed its territory as a state guided by an aristocratic Senate and governed by magistrates elected annually by its citizens. It achieved *world dominion with an army composed of those citizens and their allies.*

The temptations and responsibilities of governing an empire eventually proved too much for the republican constitution. As trade increased, a class of merchants and financiers (the equestrians) grew strong enough to inject their commercial interests into Roman politics. Masses of slaves captured in war undermined the small farmers who had been the backbone of the Roman state and its army. Many of them moved to Rome, where they lived by selling their only asset: their vote. Conscripted armies of farmers serving relatively short terms gave way to volunteer armies of landless men who were professional soldiers. They expected to be rewarded for their services with gifts of land or money. These men gave their generals the power to ignore constitutional restraints. As their leaders jostled for advantage, Rome began a long civil war that ended in the destruction of the republic. Despite itself, Rome drifted toward the monarchical institutions that had characterized the ancient states of Egypt and Mesopotamia.

Review Questions

1. In what ways did the institutions of family and clientage and the establishment of patrician and plebeian classes contribute to the stability of the early Roman Republic? How important was education to the success of the republic? How essential was the institution of slavery?

2. What was "the struggle of the orders"? What methods did plebeians use to get what they wanted? How was Roman society different after the struggle ended?

3. Until 265 B.C., what were the motives for and the stages in the expansion of Roman territory? How was Rome able to conquer and to control Italy? How did Rome's desires for security, wealth, power, and fame shape its relations with Greece and Asia Minor in the second century B.C.?

4. Why did Romans and Carthaginians clash in the First and Second Punic wars? Could the wars have been avoided? How did Rome profit from its victory over Carthage? What problems did the victory create for Rome?

5. What social, economic, and political problems did Italy have in the second century B.C.? How did Tiberius and Gaius Gracchus propose to solve them? What questions about Roman society did the Gracchan reform program raise? Why did it fail?

6. What were the problems that plagued the Roman Republic in the last century B.C.? What caused these problems, and how did the Romans try to solve them? To what extent were ambitious, power-hungry generals responsible for the destruction of the republic?

Suggested Readings

F. E. ADCOCK, *The Roman Art of War Under the Republic* (1940).

E. BADIAN, *Roman Imperialism in the Late Republic*, 2nd ed. (1968).

A. H. BERNSTEIN, *Tiberius Sempronius Gracchus: Tradition and Apostasy* (1978). A new interpretation of Tiberius's place in Roman politics.

T. CORNELL and J. MATTHEWS, *Atlas of the Roman World* (1982). Much more than the title indicates, this book presents a comprehensive view of the Roman world in its physical and cultural setting.

M. GELZER, *Caesar: Politician and Statesman*, trans. by P. Needham (1968). The best biography of Caesar.

L. P. HOMO, *Primitive Italy and the Beginning of Roman Imperialism* (1967). A study of early Roman relations with the peoples of Italy.

J. F. LAZENBY, *Hannibal's War* (1978). An excellent military history of the Second Punic War.

F. B. MARSH, *A History of the Roman World from 146 to 30 B.C.*, 3rd ed., rev. by H. H.

Scullard (1963). An excellent narrative account.

M. PALLOTTINO, *The Etruscans*, 6th ed. (1974). Makes especially good use of archaeological evidence.

E. T. SALMON, *The Making of Roman Italy* (1980). The story of Roman expansion on the Italian peninsula.

H. H. SCULLARD, *A History of the Roman World 753–146 B.C.*, 4th ed. (1980). An unusually fine narrative history with useful critical notes.

H. H. SCULLARD, *From the Gracchi to Nero*, 5th ed. (1982). A work of the same character and quality.

L. R. TAYLOR, *Party Policies in the Age of Caesar* (1949). A fascinating analysis of Roman political practices.

B. H. WARMINGTON, *Carthage* (1960). A good survey.

G. WILLIAMS, *The Nature of Roman Poetry* (1970). An unusually graceful and perceptive literary study.

5

The Roman Empire

KEY TOPICS IN THIS CHAPTER

~ The Augustan constitution

~ The organization and government of the Roman Empire

~ Culture and civilization from the late republic through the imperial period

~ The early history of Christianity

~ The decline and fall of Rome

The victory of Octavian over Mark Antony at Actium ended a century of civil strife that had begun with the murder of Tiberius Gracchus. Octavian (subsequently known as Augustus) brought peace to Rome by establishing a monarchy hidden behind a republican facade. The unification of the Mediterranean world under one government facilitated economic expansion. The administration of the empire improved. The spread of Latin and Greek as the empire's official languages promoted growth of a common "classical" culture. This classical tradition had a great influence on the development of Christianity, which appeared in the first century A.D. as one of the empire's competing Eastern cults.

In the third century A.D. Rome's institutions began to fail. Some emperors resorted to drastic measures in an effort to restore order. The result was increasing centralization and militarization leading to authoritarian government. At last, a wave of barbarian attacks in the second half of the fifth century brought the Roman Empire, in the West, to an end.

~ The Augustan Principate

The memory of Julius Caesar's fate was fresh in Octavian's mind in 31 B.C. as he pondered what to do with the empire he had won. Octavian had united all of Rome's armies under his command. He had located loyal, capable assistants. He had amassed ample capital by confiscating Egypt's treasury. He believed that the people of Italy were prepared to accept a strong ruler who would end civil war and restore order. But he knew that it would be dangerous to disregard their republican traditions.

Slowly Octavian pieced together a new constitution that was both acceptable to the Romans and capable of running an empire. Despite republican trappings and an apparent sharing of authority with the Senate, it was a monarchy. All real power, both civil and military, lay with the ruler. Octavian disguised this fact by referring to himself simply as *princeps* ("first citizen") or

This statue of Emperor Augustus (r. 27 B.C.–A.D. 14), now in the Vatican, stood in the villa of Augustus's wife Livia. The figures on the elaborate breastplate are all of symbolic significance. At the top, for example, Dawn in her chariot brings in a new day under the protective mantle of the sky god; in the center, Tiberius, Augustus's future successor, accepts the return of captured Roman army standards from a barbarian prince; and at the bottom, Mother Earth offers a horn of plenty. [Charitable Foundation, Leonard von Matt]

Significant Dates from the Imperial Era

The Julio-Claudian Dynasty

27 B.C.–A.D. 14	*Augustus*
[ca. 4 B.C.–A.D. 30	*Jesus of Nazareth]*
A.D. 14–37	*Tiberius*
A.D. 37–41	*Gaius (Caligula)*
A.D. 41–54	*Claudius*
A.D. 54–68	*Nero*
A.D. 69	*Year of the Four Emperors*

The Flavian Dynasty

A.D. 69–79	*Vespasian*
[ca. A.D. 70–100	*Gospels written]*
A.D. 79–81	*Titus*
A.D. 81–96	*Domitian*

The "Good Emperors"

A.D. 96–98	*Nerva*
A.D. 98–117	*Trajan*
A.D. 117–138	*Hadrian*
A.D. 138–161	*Antoninus Pius*
A.D.161–180	*Marcus Aurelius*

Selected Late Emperors

A.D. 180–192	*Commodus*
A.D. 193–211	*Septimius Severus*
A.D. 222–235	*Alexander Severus*
A.D. 249–251	*Decius*
A.D. 253–260	*Valerian*
A.D. 253–268	*Gallienus*
A.D. 268–270	*Claudius II Gothicus*
A.D. 270–275	*Aurelian*
A.D. 284–305	*Diocletian*
A.D. 306–337	*Constantine*
[A.D. 311	*Edict of Toleration]*
A.D. 337–361	*Constantius II*
A.D. 361–363	*Julian the Apostate*
A.D. 364–375	*Valentinian*
A.D. 364–378	*Valens*
A.D. 379–395	*Theodosius*

imperator ("commander-in-chief"), but these titles soon acquired connotations of royalty that accurately reflected the power of his office.

During the civil war Octavian's legal authority derived from the triumvirate, a temporary dictatorship set up to restore the republic. After his victory in the civil war terminated the triumvirate, Octavian governed by holding consecutive consulships. This was, however, an unpopular violation of Roman tradition, and he sought an alternative to it. On January 13, 27 B.C., at a dramatic Senate meeting, Octavian resigned most of his offices—except for the governorships of Spain, Gaul, and Syria—and returned command of the other provinces to the Senate. This was less magnanimous than it seems, for Octavian's provinces were the border lands that contained twenty of Rome's twenty-six legions. The Senate, however, declared this to be the restoration of the republic and thanked Octavian by granting him a new title—"Augustus" ("revered"). (Historians have used this title to indicate Octavian's role as Rome's first emperor and the founder of its royal government, the "Principate.") In 23 B.C., Octavian Augustus made another republican gesture. He resigned the consulship. Henceforth his authority rested on two special powers: proconsular *imperium maius* (supreme military command) and the political privileges of an honorary tribune.

Administration

The Romans were willing to go along with Augustus, for his government brought them many benefits. He weeded out inefficient and corrupt administrators. He blocked ambitious politicians and generals who might otherwise have disturbed the peace. He eased tension among classes and between Romans and provincials. And he fostered rapid economic development.

The Senate took on most of the political functions of the assemblies, but it became a less parochial institution. Augustus manipulated elections to offices in the republic and saw to it that promising young men, whatever their origin, had opportunities to serve the state. Those who did well were rewarded with appointments to the Senate. This allowed equestrians and Italians who had no connection with the old Roman aristocracy to earn Senate membership, and it ensured that the Senate was composed of talented, experienced statesmen.

Augustus was careful to court the politically volatile residents of Rome. He founded the city's first public fire department and police force. He organized grain distribution for the poor and set up an office to oversee the municipal water supply. The empire's rapidly expanding economy also enabled him to fund a vast and popular program of public works.

The provinces, too, benefited from Augustus's union of political and military power. For the first time, Rome had a central government that was able to oversee the conduct of the men who administered its provinces. Good governors were appointed. Those who abused their power were disciplined, and the provincials themselves were granted a greater degree of political autonomy.

The Army and Defense

Augustus professionalized the military and reduced its numbers to about 300,000 men—a force barely adequate to hold the frontiers. The legions were recruited from Italians, but auxiliary companies admitted provincials. The term of enlistment was twenty years. Pay was good, with occasional bonuses and the promise of a pension on retirement. Armies were permanently based in the provinces where they were likely to be needed, and their presence helped introduce native peoples to Roman culture. Soldiers married local women and settled new towns. Eventually, provincials qualified for Roman citizenship and developed a commitment to the empire that strengthened its defenses.

Augustus's chief military problem was the defense of the empire's northern frontier. Very little Roman territory protected Italy from invasion by the barbarians who wandered about Germany. Augustus's plan was to push forward into central Europe to create a shorter and more defensible border for the empire. But in A.D. 9 a German tribal leader, Herrmann (or Arminius, in Latin), ambushed and destroyed three Roman legions, and the aged Augustus abandoned the campaign.

Religion and Morality

Augustus tried to repair the damage that a century of political strife had done to Rome's fundamental institutions. He devised a program to restore traditional values of family and religion. Laws curbed adultery and divorce and encouraged early marriage and large families. He set a personal example of austere behavior and banished Julia, his only child, when she persisted in immoral behavior.

Augustus restored the dignity of formal Roman religion, building many temples, reviving old cults, invigorating the priestly colleges, and banning the worship of some foreign gods. He did not accept divine honors during his lifetime, but, like his step-father, Julius Caesar, he was deified after his death and honored with a state cult.

∼ Civilization of the Ciceronian and Augustan Ages

Roman civilization reached its high point in the last century of the republic and during the principate of Augustus. Hellenistic Greek influences were strong, but the spirit and sometimes the form of Roman art and literature were unique.

The Late Republic

Cicero. Cicero (106–43 B.C.) was the most important literary figure of the late republic. He wrote treatises on rhetoric, ethics, and politics, and developed Latin as an instrument for philosophical disputation. But it is his orations, delivered in the law courts and in the Senate, and his private letters, which survive in large numbers, that are most important. They provide us with a better insight into his mind than we have into the mind of any other figure from antiquity.

Cicero's thinking was pragmatic and conservative. He believed that the world was governed by a divine natural law that human reason could comprehend and use to guide the development of civilized institutions. His respect for law, custom, and tradition as guarantors of stability and liberty led him to champion the Senate against *populares* leaders like Mark Antony.

When the Second Triumvirate seized power and began its purges, it marked Cicero for execution.

History. Much of the work of the historians who wrote during the last century of the republic has been lost. A few pamphlets on the Jugurthine War and the Catilinarian conspiracy of 63 B.C. are all that survive from the pen of the man reputed to be the greatest historian of his generation: Sallust (86–35 B.C.). Julius Caesar wrote treatises on the Gallic and civil wars. They are military narratives that Caesar developed for use as political propaganda. Since their direct, simple, and vigorous style still makes them persuasive reading, they must have been most effective with their intended audience.

Law. Before the generation of the Gracchi, Roman law evolved case by case from juridical decisions. However, contact with foreign peoples and the influence of Greek ideas forced a change. The edicts of praetors began to expand a Roman legal code and the decisions of the magistrates who dealt with foreigners developed the idea of the *jus gentium*—the law of all peoples, as opposed to the law that reflected only Roman experience. In the first century B.C., Greek thought promoted the concept of the *jus naturale,* a natural law that lay behind the customary laws of different nations. This law reflected the principles of divine reason that Cicero and the Stoics believed to be at work in the world.

Poetry. Lucretius (ca. 99–ca. 55 B.C.) and Catullus (ca. 84–ca. 54 B.C.)—two of Rome's greatest poets, each representing a different aspect of Rome's poetic tradition—were Cicero's contemporaries. The Hellenistic poets and literary theorists taught the Romans that poets ought to be both entertainers and educators. That was Lucretius's intent in his epic poem, *De Rerum Natura (On the Nature of Things).* Lucretius hoped to save his generation from fear and superstition by converting it to the materialistic philosophies of Epicurus and Democritus, who claimed that living things were nothing more than temporary agglomerations of lumps of matter.

Catullus's poems were personal, even autobiographical, descriptions of the joys and pains of love. He hurled invective at important contemporaries like Julius Caesar, and he amused himself in witty poetic exchanges. But he offered no moral lessons. His celebration of himself was an affirmation of the importance of the individual, one of the characteristics of the Hellenistic era.

The Age of Augustus

The age of Augustus was the Golden Age of Roman literature. The great poets of the era relied on the patronage of the *princeps,* and their dependence on him limited their freedom of expression. But although their work glorified him and served his political agenda, they were not mere propagandists. They were grateful for what he had done for Rome and sang his praises with sincerity.

Vergil. The first pieces by Vergil (70–19 B.C.), the most important of the Augustan poets, were somewhat artificial pastoral idylls (the *Eclogues* or *Bucolics*). Maecenas, Augustus's chief cultural adviser, seems to have suggested the subject for Vergil's *Georgics*, a reworking of Hesiod's *Works and Days*. Vergil transformed the early Greek poet's praise of simple labor into a hymn to heroic human effort—the struggle to wrest civilization from the brutal world of nature. The compliment Vergil intended to the cults, traditions, and greatness of Italy became the theme of his most important work, the *Aeneid*.

During the civil war, Augustus rallied the Romans to his side by persuading them that Mark Antony was succumbing to Eastern influences (namely, Cleopatra). Since Augustus represented himself as the guardian of Italy's culture, he had to defend Italy's special status in the empire. The *Aeneid* explained Rome's origin and greatness by grounding Roman history in the founding myth of Hellenic civilization, the *Iliad*'s account of the Trojan War. But Vergil's hero, the Trojan prince Aeneas, is not motivated by the lust for personal honor and excellence that Homer describes. He personifies Roman qualities: duty, responsibility, and patriotism—the civic virtues of men, like Augustus, who maintained the peace and prosperity of the empire.

Horace. Horace (65–8 B.C.), the son of a freed man, was a highly skillful lyric poet. His *Satires* are genial and humorous. His *Odes*, which ingeniously adapt Latin to the forms of Greek verse, glorify the new Augustan order.

Ovid. Ovid (43 B.C.–A.D. 18), who wrote light love elegies, was the only one of the great poets to run spectacularly afoul of Augustus's program. His celebration of the loose sexual mores of certain sophisticated Roman aristocrats was not consistent with the serious, family-centered life Augustus was advocating, and Ovid's poetic textbook on the art of seduction, *Ars Amatoria*, confirmed Augustus's decision to exile the poet in A.D. 8. Ovid tried, but failed, to recover favor by switching to less sensitive themes. His *Fasti* was a poetic essay on Roman religious festivals. His most popular work, the *Metamorphoses*, was a charming survey of Greek mythology.

History. Augustus's emphasis on tradition and his desire to increase Rome's reverence for its unique cultural traditions encouraged historical and antiquarian prose writers. The most important of them was Livy (59 B.C.–A.D. 17), an Italian from Padua. His *History of Rome*, a quarter of which survives, treated the period from the legendary origins of Rome until 9 B.C. Livy based his history on secondary accounts and did little original research, but he was a gifted narrator. His sketches of historical figures provide us with perennially popular models of good and bad behavior and compelling lessons in patriotism.

Architecture and Sculpture. Augustus embarked on a building program designed to make Rome worthy of its history. The Campus Martius and the Roman Forum were rebuilt. Augustus constructed a new forum of his own to

Ruins of the Roman Forum. From the earliest days of the city, the Forum was the center of Roman life. Augustus had it rebuilt, and it was frequently rebuilt and refurbished by his successors, so most of the surviving buildings date to the imperial period. [The Bettmann Archive]

celebrate his victory in the civil war. A splendid temple to his patron god, Apollo, rose on Rome's Palatine Hill. Most of the new building conformed to the Greek classical style, which aimed at serenity and the ideal type. The same attributes are visible in the best surviving portrait sculpture of Augustus and his family: the reliefs carved for the Altar of Peace, which Augustus dedicated in 9 B.C.

~ Imperial Rome A.D. 14–180

The Emperors

Because Augustus was ostensibly only the "first citizen" of a restored republic, he had no public office to which he could openly appoint an heir. Tiberius (r. A.D. 14–37), his step-son and immediate successor, tried at first to follow Augustus's example and cloak the monarchical nature of his government. But as the Romans became accustomed to the new order, there was less reason to conceal its true nature. The terms *imperator* and "Caesar" began to be used as titles for men whose connection with Julius Caesar's family brought them the military power to run the Roman world.

Tiberius was followed by his nephew, Gaius Caligula (r. A.D. 37–41). Caligula was succeeded by his uncle Claudius (r. A.D. 41–54), and Claudius left the throne to his step-son Nero (r. A.D. 54–68). Nero, who was not equal to the responsibility of his job, committed suicide when a rebellion in Gaul convinced him that he had lost control of the army. He was the last of the Julio-Claudians, the descendants of Augustus or his wife Livia.

The year 69 saw four different emperors assume power in quick succession as different Roman armies marched on Rome. The victor, Vespasian (r. A.D. 69–79), and his sons, Titus (r. A.D. 79–81) and Domitian (r. A.D. 81–96), compose the Flavian dynasty. Vespasian was the first emperor who had no connection with the old Roman nobility. He was a tough soldier from the Italian middle class. His sons inherited his excellent administrative talents, but Domitian may have succumbed to paranoia. His increasingly tyrannical behavior alarmed his intimates and led to his assassination.

Domitian had no close relative to succeed him, and his assassins were not foolish enough to try to turn the clock back to the days of the republic. They appealed to the Senate to avoid chaos by choosing a new emperor. The Senate elected one of its own, Nerva (r. A.D. 96–98). Nerva was the first of the "good emperors": Trajan (r. A.D. 98–117), Hadrian (r. A.D. 117–138), Antoninus Pius (r. A.D. 138–161), and Marcus Aurelius (r. A.D. 161–180). None of the first four men had a son to succeed him, so each followed the example set by Nerva—each adopted an heir. This system of succession was a fortunate historical accident, for it guaranteed that worthy men were promoted to power. It produced a century of peaceful, competent government that ended when Marcus Aurelius allowed his unworthy son, Commodus (r. A.D. 180–192), to follow him to the throne.

The Administration of the Empire

Although some of the emperors tried to enlist the cooperation of the senatorial class—as counselors, judges, and department heads—in running the empire, the imperial government was largely staffed by professionals. These career bureaucrats were, in many ways, an improvement over the amateurs who annually exchanged the offices of the republic.

The provinces (see Map 5-1), in particular, benefited from imperial government. Once exploitation by governors was curbed, the economic advantages of being part of a huge empire were felt. Rome's policy was to unify the empire and its various peoples while respecting local customs and differences. By A.D. 212, citizenship had been extended to almost every inhabitant of the empire. The spread of *Romanitas* ("Roman-ness") was more than nominal, for senators and even emperors began to be drawn from provincial families.

Local Municipalities. Administratively, the empire was structured as a federation of cities and towns. The typical city had about 20,000 inhabitants. Only three or four had a population of more than 75,000. Rome, however, certainly had more than 500,000 residents—perhaps more than a million. The central government dealt with city governments and had little contact with rural populations in the countryside. A typical municipal charter left much responsibility in the hands of local councils and magistrates. The holding of a magistracy, and later a seat on a municipal council, earned a man Roman citizenship. In this way the Romans enlisted the upper classes of the provinces in their own government, spread Roman law and culture, and won the loyalty of influential people.

Rome's policy of assimilation did not succeed everywhere. Jews, who on religious grounds refused to compromise with Rome, rebelled in A.D. 66–70,

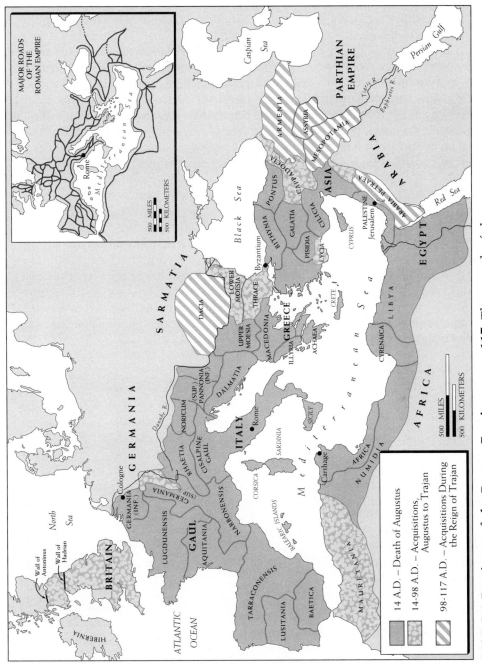

MAP 5-1 Provinces of the Roman Empire to A.D. 117 *The growth of the empire to its greatest extent is here shown in three stages—at the death of Augustus in A.D. 14, at the death of Nerva in A.D. 98, and at the death of Trajan in A.D. 117. The division into provinces is also indicated. The insert shows the main roads that tied the far-flung empire together.*

115–117, and 132–135. They were savagely suppressed. Egypt's peasants were exploited with exceptional ruthlessness and not offered the opportunity to integrate.

The emperors took a broad view of their responsibility for the welfare of their subjects. Nerva conceived and Trajan introduced the *alimenta,* a program of public assistance aiding the children of indigent parents. More and more the emperors intervened when municipalities got into difficulties—sending imperial troubleshooters to deal with problems that were usually financial. As a result, the autonomy of the municipalities declined, and the central administration took on more and more functions. This caused the provincial aristocracy to lose interest in public service and to regard it as a burden rather than an opportunity. The price paid for the increased efficiency offered by centralized control was a loss of vitality by the empire's local governments.

Foreign Policy. Augustus's successors, for the most part, accepted his conservative, defensive foreign policy. Trajan was the first to return to the offensive. He crossed the Danube and mounted a campaign (A.D. 101–106) that added a new province to the empire: Dacia. His intent was probably to defend the empire by driving wedges into the territory of threatening barbarians. The same reasoning justified an invasion of the Parthian Empire in the East (A.D. 113–117). Trajan initially succeeded in establishing three more eastern provinces: Armenia, Assyria, and Mesopotamia. But his lines were overextended, and successful rebellions forced him to retreat. He died on his way back to Rome.

This is a reconstruction of a typical Roman apartment house found at Ostia, Rome's port. The ground floor contained shops, and the stories above it held many apartments. [Scala/Art Resource, N.Y.]

Hadrian, Trajan's successor, developed a new policy for the defense of Rome's frontiers. Heretofore, the Romans had taken the initiative against the barbarians. Although they rarely sought new territory, they conducted frequent military maneuvers to chastise and pacify troublesome tribes. Hadrian hardened Rome's defenses, building a stone wall in the south of Scotland and a wooden one across the Rhine-Danube triangle. As Rome's defensive strategy grew rigid, initiative passed to the barbarians. Marcus Aurelius had to spend most of his reign fending off dangerous attacks in the East and on the Danube frontier.

***Agriculture: The Decline of Slave Labor and the Rise of* Coloni.** The defense of the empire's frontiers made enormous demands on its resources, but the effect was not immediately felt. Economic growth continued well into the reigns of the "good emperors." Internal peace and efficient administration benefited agriculture as well as trade and industry, for they made it easier to market farm products at a distance.

Small farms continued to exist, but more and more large estates, managed by absentee owners and growing cash crops, came to dominate agriculture. At first, these estates were worked by slaves, but in the first century A.D. this began to change. Economic pressures forced many members of the lower classes to become *coloni* (tenant farmers), and *coloni* steadily replaced slaves as the mainstay of agricultural labor. These sharecroppers paid rent in cash, in labor, or in kind. Eventually their movements were restricted, and they were tied to the land they worked. The economic importance of slavery declined in the second century as the *coloni* took over, but slavery survived and continued beyond the fall of Rome's empire.

The Culture of the Early Empire

Literature. The years between the death of Augustus and the time of Marcus Aurelius (A.D. 14–180) are known as the Silver Age of Latin literature. In contrast to the hopeful, optimistic outlook of the Augustan authors, the writers of the Silver Age were gloomy and pessimistic. Their works are freighted with complaints and satires that reveal their hostility to the growing power and personal excesses of the emperors.

The writers of the second century A.D. avoided commenting on contemporary affairs and events in recent history that might irritate imperial sensibilities. Historical writing about remote periods was safe. Scholarship was encouraged, but little poetry was produced. In the third century A.D., Greek romances became popular. They suggest that the readers of the age sought entertainment and escape from contemporary realities.

Architecture. Advances in engineering enabled Rome's architects to design new kinds of buildings—great public baths (like those of Diocletian and Caracalla), and huge free-standing amphitheaters (like the Flavian Colosseum). Romans continued the tradition of post-and-lintel construction pioneered by the Greeks, but supplemented it with the semicircular arch developed by the Etruscans. Romans were also the first to exploit fully a Hellenistic invention: concrete. The Pantheon, the only major Roman temple to survive intact, combines all these elements. They are also visible in multitudes of mundane but useful structures, like bridges and aqueducts.

Society. The Roman Empire was at its peak during the first two centuries A.D., but by the second century A.D. it was clear that difficult times lay ahead. The literature of the era expresses a desire to flee the present—to retreat from reality and the public realm to the remote past, to romance, and to private concerns.

The age's declining interest in public affairs correlates with a loss of vitality in the government of the empire's cities. In the first century A.D., members of the upper classes vied with one another for election to municipal office and for the honor of serving their communities. By the second century A.D., the emperors had to intervene to force unwilling citizens to accept public office. Reluctance to serve was understandable, for the central government had begun to hold local magistrates personally responsible for the revenues due from their towns. Men sometimes fled to avoid office and the risk of confiscation of their property.

The central government's extreme fiscal measures were a response to a declining economy. Rome's prosperity, created by the end of civil war and the influx of wealth looted from the East, diminished in the first half of the second century A.D. For reasons that are unknown, population also seems to have shrunk. Meanwhile, however, the cost of government kept rising. An ever-increasing need for money compelled the emperors to raise taxes and to bring on inflation by debasing the coinage. These policies precipitated crises that ultimately destroyed the empire.

The Rise of Christianity

Jesus of Nazareth

One of the most important developments of the imperial era was the rise of Christianity, the religion that came to dominate Western civilization. The new faith originated in Judaea, a remote province of the empire, in response to the life of an obscure Jew, Jesus of Nazareth. The Gospels tell us all we know about him. The earliest, by Mark, is dated about A.D. 70 (perhaps forty years after Jesus' death), and the latest, by John, about A.D. 100. The Gospels were never intended to be read as simple historical narratives of a man's life. They were designed to proclaim the faith that Jesus was the son of God who had come into the world to redeem humanity and to bring immortality to those who believed in him.

Jesus, who was born during Augustus's reign, was a most effective teacher in the tradition of the Hebrew prophets. Some of the prophets had spoken of

Juvenal on Life in Rome

The satirical poet Juvenal lived and worked in Rome in the late first and early second centuries A.D. His poems present a vivid picture of the material and cultural world of the Romans of his time. In the following passages, he tells of the discomforts and dangers of life in the city, both indoors and out.

∾ According to Juvenal, what dangers awaited pedestrians in the Rome of his day? Who had responsibility for the condition of Rome? If the situation was as bad as he says, why was nothing done about it? Why did people choose to live in Rome at all, and especially in the conditions he describes?

Who, in Praeneste's cool, or the wooded
    Volsinian uplands,
Who, on Tivoli's heights, or a small
    town like Gabii, say,
Fears the collapse of his house? But
    Rome is supported on pipestems,
Matchsticks; it's cheaper, so, for the
    landlord to shore up his ruins,
Patch up the old cracked walls, and
    notify all the tenants
They can sleep secure, though the
    beams are in ruins above them.
No, the place to live is out there, where
    no cry of *Fire!*
Sounds the alarm of the night, with a
    neighbor yelling for water,
Moving his chattels and goods, and the
    whole third story is smoking.
This you'll never know: for if the
    ground floor is scared first,
You are the last to burn, up there
    where the eaves of the attic
Keep off the rain, and the doves are
    brooding over their nest eggs.

Look at other things, the various dangers
    of nighttime.
How high it is to the cornice that breaks,
    and a chunk beats my brains out,
Or some slob heaves a jar, broken or
    cracked, from a window.
Bang! It comes down with a crash and
    proves its weight on the sidewalk.
You are a thoughtless fool, unmindful
    of sudden disaster,
If you don't make your will before you
    go out to have dinner.
There are as many deaths in the night
    as there are open windows
Where you pass by; if you're wise, you
    will pray, in your wretched devotions,
People may be content with no more
    than emptying slop jars.

Juvenal, The Satires of Juvenal, trans. by Rolfe Humphries (Bloomington: Indiana University Press, 1958), pp. 40, 43.

a Messiah, a redeemer who would bring Israel victory over its enemies and establish the kingdom of God on earth. Jesus modified this message—claiming that the Messiah would not establish an earthly kingdom but would bring an end to the world as human beings knew it at the Day of Judgment. On that day God would reward the righteous with immortality and happiness in heaven and condemn the wicked to eternal suffering in hell. While the faithful awaited the apocalyptic event, which they believed was imminent, Jesus

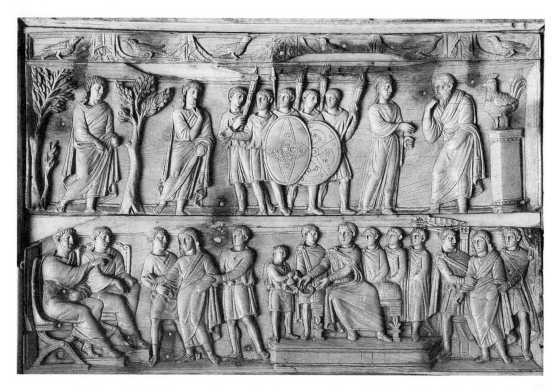

This early Christian art shows Christ arrested by soldiers on the night before his crucifixion. Note that Christ is portrayed clean-shaven and dressed in the toga of a Roman aristocrat. [Hirmer Verlag, Munich]

advised them to abandon sin and worldly concerns: to trust in him and practice love, charity, and humility.

Jesus won a considerable following, and his criticism of the cultic practices associated with the temple at Jerusalem provoked the hostility of the Jewish religious establishment. The Roman governor of Judaea concluded that Jesus and his followers were a threat to the peace and ordered his crucifixion (probably in A.D. 30). His followers believed that he was resurrected on the third day after his death and that the resurrection proved him to have been the Christ (*christos*, the Greek term for "Messiah").

Paul of Tarsus

The most important missionary at work in the generation that founded the Christian church was Paul (born Saul), a Roman citizen and native of the city of Tarsus in Asia Minor. Paul was at first a Pharisee, a member of a Jewish sect known for strict adherence to the Jewish law. And he was an ardent opponent of Christianity until his mysterious, precipitous conversion on the road to Damascus about A.D. 35.

To define themselves the early Christians had to define their relationship to Judaism. James, the brother of Jesus, led those who believed that the new faith was a version of Judaism and, therefore, that its members had to adhere to the Jewish law. The less conservative Hellenized Jews saw Christianity as a new universal religion. They believed that the imposition of the Jewish law—with its many technicalities, dietary prohibitions, and alarming practice of circumcision—would be a tremendous and unnecessary deterrent to conversion. Paul agreed with them and had great success making converts among the gentiles. The triumph of his point of view in the church greatly facilitated the work of its missionaries.

Paul began the development of Christian theology. He believed that the followers of Jesus had to spread the gospel, the "good news" of God's gift of the Messiah. But he warned that faith in Jesus as the Christ was a necessary but not sufficient agent of salvation. Salvation was a gift of God's grace that could not be earned by good deeds.

Organization

Christianity had a unique appeal that enabled it to spread throughout the Roman Empire and beyond its borders. Christ's declaration of the spiritual importance of love and charity focused the Christian community's attention on the needs of the weak, the sick, and the unprotected. Consequently, early churches were characterized by a warmth and a human appeal that stood in marked contrast to the coldness and impersonality of the pagan cults. The Christian promise of salvation, which confirmed the importance of each individual human soul to God, also implied the spiritual equality of all believers, no matter what their social class or gender.

At first, Christianity appealed most to the uneducated urban poor, and its early rites were simple ceremonies congruent with the poverty of its people. Baptism by water brought converts into the community by cleansing them of original sin (the state of alienation from God into which they had been born). The central ritual of the church was a common meal (the *agape* or "love feast") followed by a *eucharist* ("thanksgiving"), a celebration of the Lord's Supper in which bread and wine were blessed and consumed. Prayers, hymns, and readings from the Gospels were also part of worship.

The church owed its success in part to the unique organization it evolved. At first, Christian groups had little formal structure, and Christianity was in danger of dissolving into a gaggle of tiny sects. But the need to support missionary preachers and to administer charities prompted churches to elect officers: *presbyters* ("elders") and *deacons* ("those who serve"). By the second century A.D., when converts had increased to the point where a city was likely to have many churches, an "overseer" (*episkopos*, "bishop") was chosen to coordinate their activities. Bishops then extended their authority over the Christian communities in outlying towns and the countryside. Bishops acting together in councils could resolve disputes and preserve the unity of the church, and it was soon accepted that the powers that Jesus had given his original disciples were passed on in the church from one generation of bishops to another (the doctrine of Apostolic Succession). It is unlikely that Christianity could have survived the travails of its early years without the strong government provided by its bishops.

The Persecution of Christians

The Roman authorities could not at first distinguish Christians from Jews and, therefore, gave Christians the same protection under the law as Jews. It soon became clear, however, that Christians were different in potentially dangerous ways. Christians and Jews both incurred suspicion by their hostility to aspects of Roman tradition. (Both denied the existence of the pagan gods and refused to take part in the state cult of the emperor.) But while the Jews were not eager to spread their ancient faith, Christians were ardent missionaries, proclaiming an imminent end to the Roman world. They had a network of local associations spreading across the empire, and they were oddly secretive about the rituals they practiced.

Romans traditionally disliked secret organizations—particularly those of a religious nature. Claudius expelled Christians from the city of Rome, and Nero made them scapegoats for the great fire that struck the city in A.D. 64. But for the most part the Roman government did not take the initiative in attacking Christians in the first two centuries. Most of the persecutions in this period were the work of mobs, not governmental officials. Christians alarmed their pagan neighbors by ridiculing the ancient cults on which the state had always depended for its security. When misfortunes befell communities, therefore, Christians were blamed and sometimes attacked. Persecution was in some ways good for the church. It weeded out weaklings, united the faithful, and created the martyrs who became the heroes of Christian legend.

The Emergence of Catholicism

The survival of the church was threatened as much by internal disputes as by external persecution. The simple beliefs held by the great majority of Christians were open to a wide range of interpretations and left many questions unanswered. As a result, differences of opinion about the content of orthodox ("correct") faith developed. Minorities who disagreed with the Catholic ("universal") majority were branded heretics ("takers" of unique positions) and driven out of the church.

The need to combat heretics compelled the orthodox to formulate their own views more clearly. By the end of the second century A.D., the church had agreed upon the core of a canon (a "standard" set of holy books): the Old Testament, the Gospels, and the Epistles of Paul. (It took at least two more centuries before consensus was reached on the rest of the Scriptures.) The church also drew up creeds, brief statements of faith to which true Christians were expected to adhere, and empowered its bishops to enforce conformity of opinion within its ranks. Whatever the shortcomings of this development, it ensured the clarity of doctrine, unity of purpose, and discipline needed for survival.

Rome as a Center of the Early Church

During this period, when the church's administrative structures were evolving, the bishop of the city of Rome began to lay claim to "primacy" (highest rank among bishops). Rome was, after all, the capital of the empire, and it had the largest number of Christians of any city. Rome also claimed to be the place where Peter and Paul, the two most important missionaries of the early church, were martyred. Peter, who was said to have been the first bishop of Rome, was an especially important figure. The Gospel of Matthew (16:18) says that Peter was the first of the apostles to recognize Jesus as Messiah. Jesus acknowledged his faith by saying: "Thou art Peter [*Petros*, in Greek] and upon this rock [*petra*] I will build my church." Eventually the bishops of Rome would come to interpret this passage as granting Peter—and his episcopal successors in Rome—supremacy over the church.

∼ The Crisis of the Third Century

Barbarian Invasions

The pressure on Rome's frontiers, already serious in the time of Marcus Aurelius (d. A.D. 180), reached massive proportions in the third century. The eastern frontiers were threatened by a new power arising in the lands that had belonged to the Persians and their successors, the Parthians. In A.D. 224 a new Iranian dynasty, the Sassanians, seized control from the Parthians and began to make raids deep into Roman provinces. In A.D. 260, they captured and imprisoned a Roman emperor (Valerian).

On the western and northern frontiers the pressure came from an ever-increasing number of semi-nomadic German tribes. Though they had been in contact with the Romans since the second century B.C., they had not been much affected by civilization. German males were hunters, fighters, and carousers. The limited farming Germans engaged in was done by women and slaves. Tribes were led by chiefs, usually elected from the princes of a royal family by an assembly of fighting men. A chief headed a fraternity (*comitatus*, in Latin) of warriors pledged by oath to his personal service. Eager for plunder, these career raiders were attracted by the delights they knew to exist in the civilized lands across the Rhine and Danube rivers.

The most aggressive of the Germans were the Goths. By the third century A.D., they had wandered from the coast of the Baltic Sea, their original home, into southern Russia. From there they launched attacks on Rome's Danube frontier, and, about A.D. 250, they overran the Balkan provinces. To meet the threats posed by the Goths and the Persian Sassanids, the Romans transferred soldiers from their western to their eastern armies. This weakened the defenses of the west and made it easier for the Franks and the Alemanni to cross the Rhine frontier.

Rome's internal weakness invited an unprecedented number of simultaneous attacks. By the second century A.D., the Roman army was made up mostly of Romanized provincials. A manpower shortage, brought on by a plague, had forced Marcus Aurelius to resort to the conscription of slaves, gladiators, barbarians, and brigands. Consequently, the training, discipline, and professionalism of Rome's forces had begun to decline.

Septimius Severus, who followed Marcus Aurelius's son Commodus to the throne (r. A.D. 193–211), played a crucial role in the transformation of the character of the Roman army. Septimius was a military usurper who owed everything to the support of his soldiers, many of whom were peasants from the less civilized provinces. He was prepared to make Rome into an undisguised military monarchy.

Economic Difficulties

The financial crisis exacerbated by the barbarian attacks also forced changes in Rome's military. Inflation had forced Commodus to raise the soldiers' pay, and the Severan emperors had to double it to keep up with prices. This increased the imperial budget by as much as 25 percent. To raise money, emperors resorted to new taxes, debased the coinage, and even sold the palace furniture. To attract men into the army, Septimius relaxed its discipline and made military service the path to social advancement.

The same developments that caused problems for the army did damage to other parts of society. As emperors devoted their attention to the defense of the empire's frontiers, they were less able to preserve internal order. Piracy, brigandage, and the neglect of roads and harbors all hampered trade—as did the debasement of the coinage and inflation. Taxation confiscated property that was badly needed as capital for commercial enterprises, and a shortage of workers reduced agricultural production.

More and more the government had to compel people to provide the food, supplies, money, and labor needed to sustain the armies. As the state began to demand that urban magistrates meet deficits in tax revenue out of their own pockets, the upper classes fled the cities. And in the countryside, peasants abandoned farms that taxes rendered unproductive to work.

The Social Order

The new conditions led to changes in the social order. The senatorial and ruling classes were decimated by direct attacks from hostile emperors and by economic losses. Their ranks were filled by men coming up through the army. As a result, the state took on an increasingly military appearance. Classes had been distinguished by dress since the days of the republic, but in the third and fourth centuries A.D. the people's everyday clothing became a kind of uniform that precisely declared their status. Titles were assigned to ranks in society as to ranks in the army. Septimius Severus drew a sharp line between the *honestiores* (senators, equestrians, the municipal aristocracy, and the soldiers) and the lower classes, the *humiliores.* The *honestiores* enjoyed legal privileges: lighter punishments for crimes, immunity from torture, and a right of appeal to the emperor. As time passed, it became more difficult to move from the lower order to the higher. Peasants were tied to their lands, artisans to their crafts, soldiers to the army, and merchants and shipowners to the service of the state. Freedom and private initiative declined as the state expanded its control over its citizens.

Civil Disorder

In A.D. 235 the death of Alexander Severus, the last member of the dynasty founded by Septimius Severus, brought on a half-century of internal anarchy that invited foreign invasion. The empire teetered on the brink of collapse as conspirators overthrew and replaced emperors in rapid succession. A few able men appeared. Claudius II Gothicus (r. A.D. 268–270) and Aurelian (r. A.D. 270–275) drove back the barbarians and restored some discipline. But the soldiers who followed Aurelian on the throne developed strategies for defending the empire that acknowledged that it was losing ground. They built walls around Rome, Athens, and other cities and drew back their best troops from the frontiers. Their armies were mobile infantry and heavy cavalry that functioned as a kind of expanded imperial bodyguard. They recruited their soldiers from the least civilized provinces and even from the German tribes. Military service made these men the new aristocracy of the empire. They dominated its government and even ascended its throne. In effect, the Roman people succumbed to the control of an army of foreign mercenaries they hired to protect them.

~ The Late Empire

The Fourth Century and Imperial Reorganization

At the start of the fourth century an effort was made to save the empire by extensively reorganizing it (see Map 5-2). The Emperor Diocletian (r. A.D. 284–305), a native of the Balkan province of Illyria, was a man of undistinguished birth who rose through the ranks of the army. Recent history convinced him that the job of defending and governing the empire was too great for one man. Therefore, he set up a tetrarchy—a committee of four rulers, each of whom had responsibility for a different part of the empire. Diocletian administered the provinces of Thrace, Asia, and Egypt. He assigned Italy, Africa, and Spain to his friend, Maximian. Those two men were the senior members of the tetrarchy and shared the title "Augustus." Their two subordinates, the "Caesars," were Galerius, in charge of the Danube frontier and the Balkans, and Constantius, governor of Britain and Gaul.

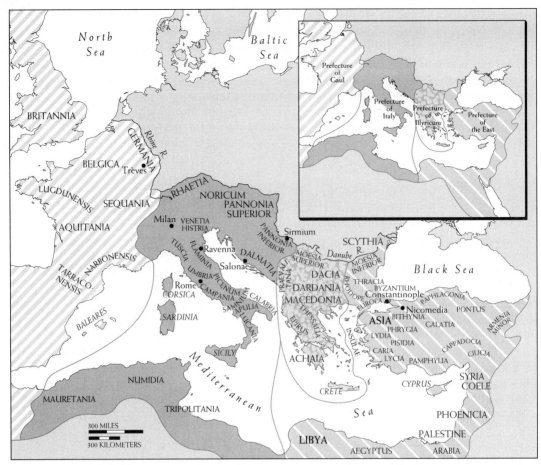

MAP 5-2 Divisions of the Roman Empire Under Diocletian *Diocletian divided the sprawling empire into four prefectures for more effective government and defense. The inset map shows their boundaries, and the larger map gives some details of regions and provinces. The major division between East and West was along the line running south between Pannonia and Moesia.*

The tetrarchy stabilized the empire by giving four powerful men a stake in the *status quo* and by providing for an orderly process of succession to the throne. The Caesars, who were appointed by the Augusti, were recognized as successors to the Augusti, and their loyalty was enhanced by dynastic marriages. The system was a return, in a way, to the precedent set by the "good emperors" of A.D. 96–180, who adopted their successors from the ranks of the ablest men.

Each tetrarch established a residence at a place convenient for frontier defense. No one chose Rome. Maximian's base at Milan, which commanded the Alpine passes, became the effective capital of Italy. Diocletian donated monumental baths to Rome, but he visited the city only once and resided at Nicomedia in Bithynia.

In A.D. 305, Diocletian retired and compelled Maximian to do the same, but the hope for a smooth succession faded when Constantius died and his son, Constantine, claimed his father's throne. Other pretenders followed his example, and by A.D. 310 there were five Augusti and no Caesars. Constantine (r. A.D. 306–337), who began the confusion, was responsible for ending it. In A.D. 324, he defeated his last opponent and made himself sole emperor. He continued Diocletian's policies—with one exception. Where Diocletian had tried to stamp out Christianity, Constantine became the patron of the church.

The Triumph of Christianity

As classical culture declined, the pagan religions lost much of their appeal. People still took comfort in the traditional rites of family, field, hearth, storehouse, and craft, but the deities worshiped in these cults seemed too petty to deal with the problems of the fourth and fifth centuries. People wanted powerful, personal gods who could offer them safety and prosperity in this world and immortality in the next. Consequently, new religions appeared and old ones were combined and interpreted in new ways.

Manichaeism, named for Mani, a Persian prophet who lived in the third century A.D., was an especially potent rival of early Christianity. The Manichaeans saw human history as a war between forces of light and darkness, good and evil. Good was spiritual; evil was material. The human body was a material prison for the element of light that was the human soul. To achieve salvation, humans had to free the light by subduing all the desires of the flesh. Manichaeans led ascetic lives, practiced a simple worship, and sustained a well-organized church. They flourished in the fourth and fifth centuries, and their faith persisted into the Middle Ages.

Christianity drew much from the cults with which it competed for converts. Except for the state's religion, none of them was much of a threat to the church.

Imperial Persecution. Until the middle of the third century, Rome's emperors generally ignored the existence of Christianity. But as the problems of the empire increased and Christians became more numerous and visible, the government's policy changed. A growing sense of insecurity made rulers less willing to tolerate dissent.

Serious trouble erupted in 250, when the Emperor Decius (r. A.D. 249–251) invoked the aid of the gods in his war against the Goths. He ordered all citizens to sacrifice to the state gods. True Christians could not obey, and Decius instituted a major persecution to uphold his law. Valerian (r. A.D. 253–260) resumed the persecutions, partly in order to confiscate the wealth of rich Christians. But his successors found other matters more pressing, and let the persecution lapse until the end of the century.

By Diocletian's day the number of Christians had grown still greater—as had hostility to Christians. Diocletian, who was struggling to hold the empire together, was not tolerant of unorthodox movements. In 303, he launched the most serious persecution Rome ever inflicted on the church. The policy was self-defeating. Christians were, by then, too familiar to be seen as much of a threat by most people, and the extreme actions of the government horrified many pagans. The plight and the demeanor of Christian martyrs aroused sympathy and made new converts.

In 311, the Eastern emperor Galerius, who had been one of the most vigorous persecutors, was persuaded, perhaps by his Christian wife, to issue an edict of toleration permitting Christian worship. Constantine, who had just conquered the western half of the empire, concurred. And when Constantine emerged as sole ruler of the empire, he reversed the government's policy. Instead of trying to stamp out Christianity, he courted the church in the hope that its unity would strengthen the state.

Development of Autocracy. The mounting crises facing the government encouraged a drift toward total military mobilization. In the name of efficiency, the government stifled the individuality, freedom, and initiative of its citizens. Traditions of popular government were forgotten. More and more emperors ruled by decree, consulting only a few high officials whom they themselves appointed. They protected themselves from assassination by removing themselves from their people. They became remote figures, unapproachable at the center of elaborate courts. They lived in great palaces, and those who came before them had to prostrate themselves and kiss the hems of their purple robes. The emperor's new title, *dominus* ("lord"), expressed his claim that his authority derived not from the Roman people but from the gods.

Constantine built a new capital for the empire. He chose the district of Byzantium on the Bosporus as the location for "Constantinople" (modern Istanbul) because it was midway between the eastern and Danubian frontiers. The site was also easy to defend, for it was surrounded on three sides by water. Constantinople's dedication in A.D. 330 was the repudiation of Rome's pagan, republican traditions and the proclamation of a new era of Christian autocracy.

The Byzantine emperors of Constantinople secured their position by separating the civilian bureaucracy from the military. This reduced the chance of anyone combining the two kinds of power and mounting a coup. An elaborate administrative hierarchy was set up. It divided responsibility and prevented anyone from having very much authority. The entire system was kept under surveillance by a network of spies and secret police. The situation was an invitation to corruption and inefficiency.

The cost of a 400,000-man army, a vast civilian bureaucracy, an imperial court, and the splendid buildings the government continued to erect was more than the empire's economy could sustain. Fiscal policies were inept. In A.D. 301, Diocletian had instituted price controls to deal with inflation. But his *Edict of Maximum Prices,* which set legal limits for the costs of goods and services, simply drove commerce underground. Black marketeering could not be suppressed even by making it a capital offense. When the peasants who could not pay their taxes and officials who could not collect them tried to escape, Diocletian used force to keep them in their places. Peasants, faced with enslavement by their government, often sought protection on a *villa*, the country estate of a powerful landowner. He protected them from the tax collectors, and they served him as *coloni*. Their descendants increasingly became tied to these estates.

Division of the Empire. Constantine's death was followed by a struggle for succession among his sons. Constantius II (r. A.D. 337–361), the victor, reunited the empire and bequeathed it to his cousin Julian (r. A.D. 361–363). The new emperor, whom Christian historians dubbed "the Apostate," concluded that Constantine's pro-Christian policy had caused more strife within the empire than it had resolved, and he set about reviving Rome's traditional cults. Julian was a student of Neoplatonism, a religious philosophy devised by Plotinus (A.D. 205–270). It attempted to combine rational speculation with mysticism, and it was harshly critical of the church's lack of intellectual sophistication. Julian refrained from persecution, but he withdrew the privileges of the church, removed Christians from high offices, and introduced new forms of pagan worship. His reign, however, was too short to permit his ideas to take root. When he died in battle against Persia, the pagan renaissance died with him.

By the time that Emperor Valentinian (r. A.D. 364–375) came to the throne, there were so many trouble spots (see Map 5-3) that he concluded that he could not defend the empire alone. He appointed his brother Valens (r. A.D. 364–378) as co-ruler. Valentinian resided at Milan and spent his reign fighting, defending the West against German tribes known as Franks and Alemanni.

Valens was posted to the East, where he was confronted by a different kind of threat from another group of Germans. In A.D. 376, the Visigoths asked permission to enter the empire to escape the Huns, a fierce tribe migrating out of central Asia. Valens acquiesced, but was unable to provide for the huge number of refugees who fled into the empire. In desperation the Goths began to plunder the Balkan provinces. Valens confronted the Goths at Adrianople in Thrace in A.D. 378, and he and his army were destroyed.

Theodosius (r. A.D. 379–395), an able general, was named co-ruler in the East. He pacified the Goths, enrolling many of them in his army. After the death of his Western colleague, Theodosius united the empire for the last time. In A.D. 394, he attempted to end the confusion created by the government's vague religious policy. He forbade the celebration of pagan cults, and made Christianity the official religion of the empire. A year later he died, dividing the empire between his two sons. They fell to quarreling and worsened what was already a very bad situation.

The Rural West. The disintegration of the empire was encouraged not just by wars and politics, but by the divergence of the cultures of its Eastern and Western halves. The West, which had fewer and younger cities, grew increasingly rural. The institution of the *villa,* a fortified country estate, reorganized Western society. The *coloni* who lived on a *villa* served its owner in return for eco-

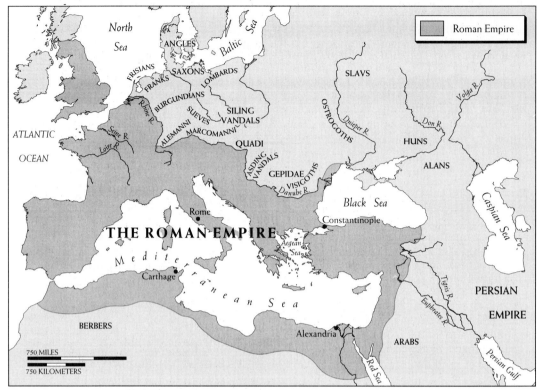

MAP 5-3 The Empire's Neighbors *In the fourth century the Roman Empire was nearly surrounded by ever more threatening neighbors. The map shows who these so-called barbarians were and where they lived before their armed contact with the Romans.*

nomic assistance and protection from both barbarian invaders and imperial officials. As the upper classes abandoned the cities and set up independent local governments on their *villae,* the central government lost its ability to provide fundamental services—like the maintenance and policing of roads. This hastened the decline of trade and communications and depressed the standard of living on the *villae,* which were forced to become self-sufficient. By the fifth century A.D., the Western empire had dissolved into isolated estates on which rural aristocrats dominated the lives of a class of dependent laborers. The Christian church alone sought to keep alive some memory of imperial unity.

The Byzantine East. In the East the situation was quite different. The loss of the West enabled Constantinople to concentrate on its own affairs. A vital and flourishing hybrid of Christian and classical culture emerged, and the East entered the "Byzantine" phase in its civilization. Because of its defensible location and the relative health of its economy, Constantinople was able to divert most of the barbarians to the West. Eastern cities continued to prosper, and the East's central government retained its power. Constantinople continued in the hands of Christian emperors until the Turks conquered it in 1453. For a thousand years it saw itself as chief heir to the cultural legacy of ancient Greece and Rome.

Emergence of Christianity as the State Religion. The emergence of Christianity as the dominant religion in both the eastern and western halves of the old Roman Empire ended some of the church's problems, but created others. As the church acquired prestige and influence, it began to attract converts for the wrong reasons and to lose its spiritual fervor. It also had to come to some understanding with the state. In the East the state was strong enough to subordinate the church. But in the West imperial power faded, and church leaders exercised remarkable independence.

Arianism and the Council of Nicaea. As Christianity spread, doctrinal disputes among Christians became a threat to social order. Governments intervened between warring factions to preserve the peace, and Christians began to persecute other Christians with as much zeal as fanatical pagans had once persecuted them.

The most disruptive of the doctrinal controversies was the fight over Arianism, an explanation of Christ advanced by a priest named Arius of Alexandria (ca. A.D. 280–336). Arius argued that Jesus was a unique being created by God the Father and through whom God created all other beings. For Arius, Jesus was neither fully man nor fully God but something in between. In Arius's opinion, proponents of the doctrine of the Trinity, which asserts that God is a unity of three persons (Father, Son, and Holy Spirit), were indistinguishable from polytheists.

Arian theology had the advantage of appearing to be simple and rational. But Athanasius (ca. A.D. 293–373), bishop of Alexandria, objected that the Arian view of Christ destroyed Christ's effectiveness as an agent of human salvation. Athanasius believed that only a fully human and fully divine Christ could have the power to turn humanity into divinity and bestow eternal life on his followers.

In A.D. 325, Constantine tried to resolve the issue by inviting all the Christian bishops to a meeting at Nicaea, not far from Constantinople. Athanasius's arguments prevailed and were enshrined in the council's Nicene Creed. Arianism, however, continued to spread. Some later emperors were Arians, and some of the most successful missionaries to the barbarians were Arians. Many of the German tribes that overran the empire were Arian Christians.

Arts and Letters in the Late Empire

The art and literature of the late empire reflect the confluence of pagan and Christian ideas and the changing tastes of the aristocracy. Much of the literature of the period is polemical, and much of its art is propagandist. The men who came to power as the empire declined were soldiers from the provinces whose roots were in the lower classes. By restoring and absorbing classical culture they hoped to stabilize their world and confirm their credentials as aristocrats.

The newly arrived ruling class's acquisition of classical culture was facilitated in several ways. Works by great authors were reproduced in many copies and were transferred from inconvenient papyrus rolls to sturdier codices, bound volumes that are the ancestors of modern books. Scholars also condensed long works into shorter versions and wrote commentaries to make them more intelligible. Grammars for the classical languages also had to be compiled as native tongues replaced Latin and Greek in many of the provinces.

Christian Writers. Original works by pagan writers of the late empire were neither numerous nor especially distinguished. But the late empire saw a great outpouring of Christian writings. Christian "apologists" (authors who explained Christian practices to pagans) produced a large amount of poetry and prose. There were also sermons, hymns, and biblical commentaries designed for use by Christians.

The church produced several important scholars in this period of its history. Jerome (A.D. 348–420), who was thoroughly trained in classical Latin literature and rhetoric as well as Hebrew, produced a Latin version of the Bible, the Vulgate ("common use"). It became the standard Bible for the Roman Catholic church. Eusebius of Caesarea (ca. A.D. 260–ca. A.D. 340) wrote an idealized biography of Constantine and an *Ecclesiastical History* that set forth a Christian view of history as a process whereby God's will was revealed. But it is the work of Augustine (A.D. 354–430), bishop of Hippo in North Africa, that best illustrates the complexity of the relationship between classical culture and Christian faith.

Augustine was born at Carthage and trained as a teacher of rhetoric. His father was a pagan, but his mother was a Christian and hers was ultimately the stronger influence. He had a difficult intellectual journey that carried him through Manichaeism, skepticism, and Neoplatonism before he was converted to Christianity. His skill in pagan rhetoric and gifts as a philosopher made him peerless among his contemporaries as a defender of Christianity. Augustine reconciled Christianity and classical culture by arguing that faith was the starting point for and liberator of human reason. Reason is the means by which people understand what is revealed by faith.

Augustine's greatest works are his *Confessions,* an autobiography describing his path to faith, and *The City of God,* a response to the pagan charge that a sack of Rome by the Goths in A.D. 410 was caused by Christianity's attack on Rome's old gods. Augustine separated the destiny of the church from that of the Roman Empire. He contrasted the evil secular world, the "City of Man," with the spiritual realm represented by the church, the "City of God." The former was fated to be destroyed on the Day of Judgment, and there was no reason to expect that its conditions would improve before that. The fall of Rome was, therefore, neither surprising nor important. All states, even a Christian Rome, were part of the City of Man and were therefore corrupt and mortal. Only the City of God was immortal, and it, consisting of all the saints on earth and in heaven, was untouched by earthly calamities.

∼ The Decline and Fall of the Empire in the West

Whether important to Augustine or not, the massive barbarian invasions of the fifth century put an end to imperial government in the West. Since that time, people have speculated about the causes of the collapse of the ancient world. Theories have been advanced that cite soil exhaustion, plague, climatic change, and even poisoning caused by lead water pipes. Some scholars blame the institution of slavery for Rome's failure to make advances in science and technology that might have solved its economic problems. Others blame excessive government interference in the economic life of the empire, and still others the destruction of the urban middle class, the carrier of classical culture.

Although all these things may have contributed something, a simpler explanation for Rome's failure can be found. The growth of Rome's empire was fueled by conquests that provided the Romans with the means to continue to expand. Ultimately, there were not enough Romans to conquer and govern any more territory. And when pressure from outsiders grew, the Romans could not find the resources to advance and defeat the enemy as they had in the past. Still, their tenacity and success in resisting invasion for so long were remarkable. To blame the ancients for their failure to end slavery and bring on industrial and economic revolutions is to blame them for not achieving what has been achieved only once in human history. The real question may not be why did Rome fall, but how did it manage to last so long.

Augustus ended the civil wars that plagued the republic and created an era of unity, peace, order, and prosperity. As a result, he was regarded with almost religious awe and attained more military and political power than any Roman before him. At his death he was able to pass on the regime to his family, the Julio-Claudians, and for almost 200 years, with a few brief interruptions, the empire was prosperous, peaceful, and well-run.

But problems were growing. The government assumed numerous responsibilities that promoted the growth of a large bureaucracy that was an increasing burden on the treasury. The costs of government also grew as pressure on the frontiers from barbarian tribes forced Rome to maintain a large standing army. Higher taxes and bureaucratic control stifled civic spirit and private enterprise.

Rome's rulers resorted to many devices for dealing with their problems. More and more, the emperors' rule and their safety depended on the loyalty of the army. When they courted the soldiers with gifts, the burden of taxes increased. The rich and powerful avoided their obligations, but the government bore down ever more heavily on ordinary people. Ultimately, even extreme measures failed, and the Roman Empire fell. But something of its culture survived to lay a foundation for the modern West.

Review Questions

1. How did Augustus alter Rome's constitution and government? How did his innovations solve the problems that had plagued the republic? Why were the Roman people willing to accept him as their head of state?

2. How was the Roman Empire organized? What enabled it to function smoothly? What role did the emperor play in the maintenance of political stability?

3. How did the literatures of Augustus's "Golden Age" and of the "Silver Age" of the first and second centuries A.D. differ? What contributions did the poetry of Vergil and Horace make to the stabilization of Augustus's imperial system of government?

4. Why were Christians at first persecuted by Roman authorities? What enabled them to acquire such enormous popularity by the fourth century A.D.?

5. What were the political, social, and economic problems that beset Rome in the third and fourth centuries A.D.? How did Diocletian and Constantine deal with them? Were these emperors effective in stemming the Roman empire's decline? What problems were they unable to solve?

6. What are the difficulties involved in explaining the fall of the Roman Empire? What sorts of theories have scholars advanced to explain Rome's decline and fall? Which explanations do you find most convincing? Why?

Suggested Readings

J. P. V. D. BALSDON, *Roman Women* (1962). A standard treatment.

T. BARNES, *The New Empire of Diocletian and Constantine* (1982). A study of the character of the late empire.

P. BROWN, *The World of Late Antiquity, A.D. 150–750* (1971). A brilliant and readable essay.

J. BURCKHARDT, *The Age of Constantine the Great* (1956). A classic work by the Swiss cultural historian.

C. M. COCHRANE, *Christianity and Classical Culture* (1957). A study of intellectual change in the late empire.

S. DILL, *Roman Society in the Last Century of the Western Empire* (1958). A classic social history.

MICHAEL GRANT, *The Fall of the Roman Empire* (1990). A lively, well-written account.

T. RICE HOLMES, *Architect of the Roman Empire*, 2 vols. (1928–1931). An account of Augustus's career in detail.

A. H. M. JONES, *The Later Roman Empire*, 3 vols. (1964). A comprehensive study of the period.

H. LIETZMANN, *History of the Early Church*, 2 vols. (1961). From the Protestant viewpoint.

R. MACMULLEN, *Enemies of the Roman Order* (1966). An original and revealing examination of opposition to the emperors.

R. MACMULLEN, *Corruption and the Decline of Rome* (1988). A study that examines the importance of changes in ethical ideas and behavior.

F. G. B. MILLAR, *The Roman Empire and Its Neighbors* (1968). An analysis of Roman foreign relations in the imperial period.

A. MOMIGLIANO (ed.), *The Conflict Between Paganism and Christianity* (1963). A valuable collection of essays.

M. I. ROSTOVTZEFF, *Social and Economic History of the Roman Empire*, 2nd ed. (1957). A masterpiece whose main thesis has been much disputed.

E. T. SALMON, *A History of the Roman World, 30 B.C. to A.D. 138* (1968). A good survey.

R. SYME, *The Roman Revolution* (1960). A brilliant study of Augustus, his supporters, and their rise to power.

L. R. TAYLOR, *The Divinity of the Roman Empire* (1931). A study of the imperial cult.

6

The Early Middle Ages (476–1000): The Birth of Europe

KEY TOPICS IN THIS CHAPTER

⌁ How the fusion of Germanic and Roman cultures laid the foundation for a distinctively European society following the collapse of the Roman Empire

⌁ The Byzantine and Islamic empires and their impact on the West

⌁ The role of the church in Western society during the early Middle Ages

⌁ Politics and economics in Europe under the Franks

⌁ The characteristics of feudal society

The collapse of Roman civilization inaugurated the Middle Ages by forcing the peoples of the Mediterranean world to experiment with new ideas and institutions. In what had been the northern and western provinces of the Roman Empire, aspects of Greco-Roman and German cultures combined with Christianity to create a uniquely European way of life. In the East, two other civilizations appeared: Byzantium and Islam.

Significant Dates from the Early Middle Ages

313	*Constantine legalizes Christianity*
325	*Council of Nicaea defines Christian doctrine*
410	*Visigoths sack the city of Rome*
476	*Last Roman emperor of the West is deposed*
529	*Benedictine monasticism originates*
533	*Justinian codifies Roman law*
622	*Muhammad's flight from Mecca (Hegira)*
732	*Charles Martel defeats Muslims at Poitiers*
751	*Pepin III "the Short" crowned king of the Franks*
755	*Pepin creates the Papal States*
768–814	*Charlemagne builds a European empire*
800	*Pope Leo III crowns Charlemagne emperor*
814–840	*Louis the Pious*
843	*Treaty of Verdun partitions the Carolingian Empire*

～ On the Eve of the Frankish Ascendancy

The attempts that were made in the late third century to save the Roman Empire influenced the way in which it fell. Diocletian (r. 284–305) dealt with simultaneous assaults on the eastern and western frontiers of the empire by sharing leadership of the empire with a colleague, Maximian. His division of the central government into eastern and western branches set the stage for the halves of the empire to evolve separately. Imperial rule gradually faded from the West, but the eastern emperors became increasingly autocratic.

Constantine the Great (r. 306–337) temporarily reunited the empire, but in 324 he moved its capital from Rome to Constantinople, a new city he built on the site of ancient Byzantium at the crossroads of the major sea and land routes that linked Europe and Asia Minor. Constantinople, the "new Rome," flourished at the expense of the empire's old capital. The city of Milan, which had more direct communications with the Rhine and Danube frontiers, became the defensive center of the western empire. When, in 402, Milan became too exposed to barbarian invasions, the seat of western government was moved to Ravenna on the Adriatic coast. By the late fourth century, the West was in political disarray, the city of Rome was no longer of much political significance, and imperial power and prestige had shifted decisively to Constantinople.

Germanic Migrations

The German tribes did not burst on the West all of a sudden (see Map 6-1). Roman and Germanic cultures had commingled peacefully for centuries as Romans "imported" barbarian domestics, slaves, and soldiers. Some barbarians rose to command posts in Roman legions.

A Contemporary Description of Attila the Hun

In 448, three years before Attila's invasion of Italy, a Roman envoy, Priscus, visited the Hun's home in a Scythian village at the base of the Danube River. Knowing Attila's reputation for savagery, he was surprised to find him a simple and cultured man.

∽ How would you account for the discrepancy between this portrait of Attila and his reputation? Has history falsely portrayed this fiercest of warriors? What does it say about the Huns' system of justice that Attila dispensed judgments on the street as he walked?

Attila's residence . . . was made of polished boards, and surrounded with wooden enclosures, designed not so much for protection as for appearance's sake. . . . I entered the enclosure of Attila's palace, bearing gifts to his wife, whose name was Kreka. . . . Having been admitted by the barbarians at the door, I found her reclining on a soft couch. The floor of the room was covered with woolen mats for walking on. . . . Having approached, saluted her, and presented the gifts, I went out and walked to the other houses. . . . Attila came forth from [one of] the house[s] with a dignified strut, looking round on this side and on that. . . . Many persons who had lawsuits with one another came up and received his judgment. Then he returned into the house and received ambassadors of barbarous peoples. . . .

[We were invited to a banquet with Attila at three o'clock.] The cupbearers gave us a cup, according to the national custom, that we might pray before we sat down. Having tasted the cup, we proceeded to take our seats, all the chairs being ranged along the walls of the room on either side. Attila sat in the middle on a couch; a second couch was set behind him, and from it steps led up to his bed, which was covered with linen sheets and wrought coverlets for ornament, such as Greeks and Romans used to deck bridal beds. The places on the right of Attila were held chief in honor; those on the left, where we sat, were only second. . . .

The attendant of Attila first entered with a dish full of meat, and behind him came the other attendants with bread and viands [plates of food], which they laid on the tables. A luxurious meal, served on silver plate, had been made ready for us and the barbarian guests, but Attila ate nothing but meat on a wooden trencher [a wooden plate]. In everything else, too, he showed himself temperate; his cup was of wood, while to the guests were given goblets of gold and silver. His dress, too, was quite simple, affecting only to be clean. The sword he carried at his side, the latchets of his . . . shoes, the bridle of his horse were not adorned with gold or gems or anything costly . . . like those of the other Scythians.

[After two courses were eaten and] evening fell, torches were lit and two barbarians, coming forward in front of Attila, sang songs they had composed, celebrating his victories and deeds of valor in war.

James Harvey Robinson (ed.), Readings in European History, *Vol. 1 (Boston: Athenaeum, 1904), pp. 47–48.*

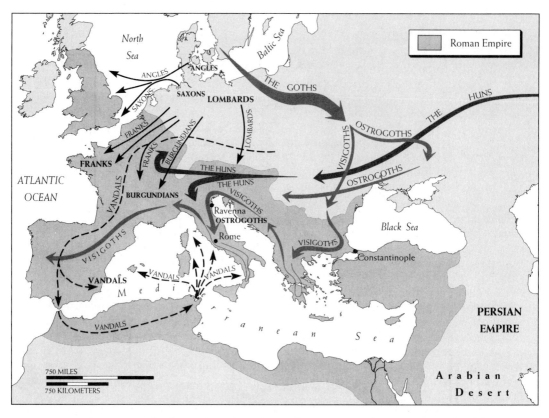

MAP 6-1 Barbarian Migrations into the West in the Fourth and Fifth Centuries *The intrusion of barbarians into the empire from the end of the fourth through the fifth centuries created a constantly shifting pattern of migration. The map shows the routes usually taken by the newcomers and the areas most affected.*

Beginning in 376, with the arrival of the Visigoths (the "West Goths"), the rate of barbarian migration increased to the point where it overwhelmed the western half of the empire. The Visigoths were pushed into the empire by a notoriously violent people, the Huns of Mongolia. The eastern emperor Valens (r. 364–378) allowed the Visigoths to enter the empire in exchange for their promise to help defend its eastern frontier. They became the first of the *foederati*, allied alien nations residing within the empire.

The Visigoths arrived in the empire an impoverished people fleeing the Huns. When some Roman profiteers exploited their misery, the Visigoths rebelled and destroyed Valens and his army (the battle of Adrianople, 378). Constantinople defended itself by persuading the Visigoths to move west. The western government responded by shifting troops from the frontiers to the defense of Italy. This cleared the way for other German tribes to enter the empire unopposed.

It may seem surprising that there was so little resistance in the West to the migration of the Germanic tribes. The largest tribe probably numbered no more than 100,000 people, a small group compared to the native Roman population. But the invaders were successful because they had come upon a badly overextended western empire divided politically by ambitious military commanders and weakened physically by decades of famine, pestilence, and overtaxation.

Fall of the Roman Empire

In the early fifth century, Italy suffered a series of devastating blows. In 410 the Visigoths, under Alaric (ca. 370–410), sacked Rome. In 452, the Huns, led by Attila—known to contemporaries as the "scourge of God"—invaded Italy. In 455, Rome was overrun yet again, this time by the Vandals.

By the mid-fifth century, power in western Europe had passed from Roman emperors to barbarian chieftains. In 476, the traditional date for the fall of the Roman Empire, the barbarian Odovacer (ca. 434–493) deposed the West's nominal emperor, Romulus Augustulus, and ruled without an imperial figurehead. In 493, in a coup manipulated by the eastern emperor, Zeno (r. 474–491), Theodoric (ca. 454–526), king of the Ostrogoths (the "East Goths"), took Odovacer's place. By that time barbarians had thoroughly overrun the western empire. The Ostrogoths settled in Italy, the Franks in northern Gaul, the Burgundians in Provence, the Visigoths in southern Gaul and Spain, the Vandals in Africa and the western Mediterranean, and the Angles and Saxons in England.

Despite the shift of power to barbarian leaders, western Europe was not transformed into a savage land. The Germans respected Roman culture and were willing to learn from the people they had conquered. Except in Britain and northern Gaul, Roman language, law, and government coexisted with the new Germanic institutions. Only the Vandals and the Anglo-Saxons—and, after 466, the Visigoths—refused to profess at least titular obedience to the emperor in Constantinople.

Religion was a potential link between the Romans and their new rulers. The Visigoths, the Ostrogoths, and the Vandals were converted to a kind of Christianity before they entered the West. Unfortunately, western Christians considered them heretics, for the missionaries who worked among them were followers of Arius, the heretical theologian who argued that Christ was a creature of God, not an equal partner in a divine Trinity. This problem was resolved about 500 by the conversion of the Franks to the orthodox or *catholic* ("universal") form of Christianity supported by the bishops of Rome. The Franks conquered and converted the Goths and other barbarians in western Europe.

Despite western military defeat, the Goths and the Franks were far more Romanized than the Romans were Germanized. Latin language, orthodox Christianity (that which professed the creed written by the Council of Nicaea in 325), and Roman law were to triumph in the West during the Middle Ages.

~ The Byzantine Empire

As western Europe succumbed to the Germanic invasions, the eastern part of the old Roman Empire became a new medieval nation, the Byzantine Empire of Constantinople. From 324, when Constantinople was founded, to 1453, when it was occupied by the Ottoman Turks, the city was the seat of a Christian government whose power waxed and waned, but endured.

The Reign of Justinian

The Byzantine Empire reached its height during the reign of the emperor Justinian (r. 527–565). Although urban institutions were quickly disappearing in the West, Justinian's empire contained more than 1,500 cities. The largest, with perhaps 350,000 inhabitants, was Constantinople, which was fast becoming the center of Western commerce and communications. The large provincial cities of the Byzantine Empire had populations of about 50,000 and sustained a flourishing economy.

Justinian's most important counselor was his brilliant wife Theodora (d. 548). If the controversial *Secret History* of Procopius, Justinian's court historian, is to be believed, Theodora, the daughter of a bear trainer in the circus, began her career as a prostitute. Her background may have given her a toughness that was useful to her husband, for she guided him through crises that threatened to overwhelm his government. She was particularly useful in dealing with the religious quarrels that troubled the peace of the empire. Whereas Justinian remained a strictly orthodox Christian, Theodora pacified a powerful faction of Christian heretics, the Monophysites, by lending them royal patronage. (The Monophysites believed that Jesus had only one nature, a composite divine-human one. The orthodox church claimed that he had two: one fully human and the other fully divine.) The Monophysites were strong enough to form a separate church in the eastern provinces of the empire. After Theodora's death, the imperial government made the mistake of attempting to stamp out their heresy. Consequently, a few years later, when Persian and Arab armies invaded their part of the empire, the resentful Monophysites offered little resistance.

Law. Byzantine policy ("one God, one empire, one religion") was to centralize government and enforce legal and doctrinal conformity throughout the empire. To this end Justinian ordered a codification of Roman law. His *Corpus Juris Civilis (Body of Civil Law)* contained four parts. The *Code,* which appeared in 533, revised imperial edicts issued since the reign of Hadrian (117–138). The *Novellae* ("New Things") was composed of the decrees issued by Justinian. (It was added to by his successors). The *Digest* was a summary of the opinions of famous legal experts. The *Institutes* was a textbook for young lawyers. It spelled out the principles of law implied by the *Code* and the *Digest.* These works had little immediate effect on medieval common law, but during the Renaissance they became the foundation for most subsequent European law down to the nineteenth century.

Religion. Religion, as well as law, was expected to promote the centralization of the Byzantine Empire. In 380, Christianity was proclaimed the official religion of the eastern empire, and the chief bishop ("patriarch") of Constantinople began to preside over the crowning of its emperors. From the fourth through the sixth centuries, the churches of Constantinople, Alexandria, Antioch, and Jerusalem acquired enormous wealth and functioned as the state's welfare agency.

Persecution and absorption into popular Christianity served to curtail many pagan religious practices. But orthodox Christianity never succeeded in stamping out the heresies that continually sprang up in the empire. Large numbers of Jews also resided in the empire. Under Roman law Jews had legal protection so long as they did not proselytize among Christians, build new synagogues, or attempt to enter sensitive public offices or professions. Justinian developed a program to persuade Jews to convert. Later emperors both ordered Jews to be baptized and granted tax breaks to those who voluntarily complied. Neither policy—persuasion nor coercion—was very successful.

Eastern Influences

Justinian was the last Byzantine emperor to try to regain control of the West and to reestablish the old Roman Empire. He failed, and his successors were too preoccupied by developments in the East to devote much attention to the West. During the reign of Heraclius (610–641) the Byzantine Empire acquired a decidedly Eastern, as opposed to Roman, look. Heraclius spoke Greek, not Latin, and spent his entire reign resisting Persian and Islamic invasions. The Persians were fought to a draw but, after 632, Islamic armies relentlessly advanced into imperial territory. They overran Asia Minor and besieged Constantinople for the first time in 677. Not until the reign of Leo III (717–740) of the Isaurian dynasty were they driven back and Asia Minor recovered.

Leo's relations with western Christians worsened when he forbade the use of images in eastern churches and tried to impose the same ban on the West. Islamic theology, which condemned image veneration as idolatry, may have inspired Leo and his immediate successors to pursue this policy. Be that as it may, *iconoclasm* was an affront to western Christianity, which had carefully nurtured the adoration of Jesus, Mary, and the saints in images and icons. Leo's attempt to legislate for the church was also an example of eastern Caesaro-papism—the emperor's claim to be both a secular ruler and the head of the church—which, as we will see, the Western church always resisted. Until it was reversed in the late eighth century, the ban on images worsened the divisions in Christendom and doomed much religious art to destruction.

At Manzikert in 1071, the Byzantine Empire was defeated by the Muslim Seljuk Turks, who rapidly overran the eastern provinces of the empire. Although Constantinople was to remain in Christian hands for another four centuries, this was the beginning of the end for the Byzantine Empire. In 1092, after two decades of steady Turkish advance, the eastern emperor Alexius I Comnenus (r. 1081–1118) appealed to the West for help. Three years later the West responded with the first of the great Crusades. The First Crusade enabled Constantinople to recover some territory, but a century later (1204) the Fourth Crusade attacked Constantinople itself and did more damage to the city than all previous non-Christian invaders.

Despite its vicissitudes, until 1453 the Byzantine Empire maintained a protective barrier between Europe and the Persian, Arab, and Turkish armies of the East. The Byzantines were also the most advanced Christian civilization of the early Middle Ages and the source of much of the classical learning that filtered through to the West during the medieval period.

⁓ Islam and the Islamic World

In the sixth century a new religion appeared in Arabia to spark the creation of a third medieval civilization: Islam. By the time its founder, the Prophet Muhammad, died in 632, Islamic armies had become the chief concern of the emperors of Constantinople and of Europe's German kings.

Muslims are enjoined to live by the divine law, or Shari'a, and have a right to have disputes settled by an arbiter of the Shari'a. Here we see a husband complaining about his wife before the state-appointed judge, or qadi. The wife, backed up by two other women, points an accusing finger at the husband. In such cases, the first duty of the qadi, who should be a learned person of faith, is to try to effect a reconciliation before the husband divorces his wife, or the wife herself seeks a divorce. [Bibliothèque Nationale, Paris]

Muhammad's Religion

Muhammad (570–632), an orphan, was raised by a family of modest means that lived near the ancient Arab shrine at Mecca. As a youth, he worked as a merchant's assistant, traveling the major trade routes. At the age of twenty-five, he married a wealthy Meccan widow and with her support became a kind of social activist. He opposed the materialism of Meccan society and some of his people's pagan practices. When he was about forty, he had a deep religious experience that commenced a stream of revelations mediated by the angel Gabriel. The revelations, which Muhammad continued to receive throughout his life, are believed by his followers literally to be the words of God. Between 650 and 651, they were collected in a sacred book, the Qur'ān ("reciting"). Muhammad's message was fundamentally a call for all Arabs to submit to God's will as it was revealed through "the Prophet." Consequently, Muhammad's religion came to be known as *Islam* and his followers as *Muslims.* Both terms indicate "submission" or "surrender."

Muhammad did not claim that his message was new—only that it was final and definitive. He taught what a long line of Jewish prophets—from Noah to Jesus Christ—had taught. But he was unique in that he was the last of the prophets that God would send. Islam, like Judaism, was a strictly monotheistic and theocentric religion. And both faiths rejected Christianity's Trinitarian view of God and the concept of God's incarnation as a human being in the Christ.

Mecca, Muhammad's birthplace, had long been one of Arabia's most sacred places. Its Ka'ba—a simple, rectangular stone structure containing a sacred black meteorite and various other holy objects—was the Arab world's holiest shrine. By attacking idolatry, Muhammad threatened the pagan faith that drew Arabs to the Ka'ba and made Mecca a center for trade. In 622, the Meccan authorities turned on Muhammad and forced him and his followers to flee to Medina, 240 miles to the north. This event, the *Hegira* ("flight"), marks the beginning of the Islamic calendar, for it prompted Muhammad to create the community that evolved into the Islamic state.

Muhammad had great success in Medina. He organized raids on caravans going to and from Mecca. He made throngs of converts, and by 624 his army was powerful enough to persuade Mecca to submit to his authority. He returned in triumph, cleansed the Ka'ba of its idols, and designated it the chief shrine for his new religion. Islam, like Christianity, developed by assimilating popular pagan religious customs.

Muhammad stressed practice more than doctrine, and Islam gradually evolved a set of rules for its faithful: (1) to be honest and modest in all dealings and behavior; (2) to be unquestionably loyal to the Islamic community; (3) to abstain from pork and alcohol; (4) to pray facing Mecca five times a day; (5) to contribute to the support of the poor and needy; (6) to fast during daylight hours for one month each year; and (7) to make a pilgrimage to the Ka'ba at least once in a lifetime. Muslim men were permitted to have up to four wives—provided they treated them all justly and equally—and as many concubines as they wished. A man could divorce a wife with a simple declaration of his intent. A wife could initiate divorce, but the procedure was more involved for her. She was expected to be totally loyal and devoted to her husband, and only her husband was to be allowed to see her face.

Islam made no rigid distinction between the clergy and the laity. In place of a priesthood, it developed a scholarly elite of laymen, the *ulema* ("persons with correct knowledge"). Its members were men whose authority derived from their reputations for great piety and learning. Their opinions had the force of law in Muslim society. They also kept a critical eye on Muslim rulers to ensure that they adhered to the letter of the Qur'ān.

Islamic Diversity

Islam was very successful in unifying the Arab tribes and various pagan peoples, for it appealed to the pride of groups that had been marginalized in a world dominated by Judaism and Christianity. Islam proclaimed Muhammad to be history's major religious figure and his followers to be God's chosen people.

As early as the seventh century, however, divisions began to appear within the Islamic community. Disagreement about who had the best right to the caliphate—the office held by the successor to Muhammad's political authority—was one source of discord. Another was disagreement on doctrinal issues involving the extent to which Islam was meant to be a religion only for Arabs.

Several groups emerged from these disputes. The Kharijites were the most radical. Their leaders seceded from the camp of the fourth caliph, Ali (r. 656–661), when he sought political advantage by compromising on a matter of principle. The Kharijites were "Puritans" who wanted to exclude from Islam all but rigorously virtuous Muslims. In 661, one of their members assassinated Ali.

More influential were the Shi'a, or "partisans of Ali" (*Shi'at Ali*). The Shi'a looked on Ali and his descendants as the rightful successors of Muhammad not only by virtue of kinship, but also by the expressed will of the Prophet. To the Shi'a, Ali's assassination revealed the basic truth of a devout Muslim life: a true *imam* ("ruler") must expect to suffer unjustly even unto death. So too must his followers. A theology of martyrdom is the mark of Shi'a teaching, and the Shi'a are still an embattled minority within mainstream Islamic society.

A third group, which has been dominant for most of Islamic history, was the majority centrist Sunnis (followers of *sunna*, "tradition"). Sunnis put loyalty to the community of Islam above all else and reject the exclusivism and purism of the Kharijites and the Shi'a.

Islamic Empires

Under Muhammad's first three successors—the caliphs Abu Bakr (r. 632–634), Umar (r. 634–644), and Uthman (r. 644–656)—Muslim armies spread along the southern and eastern coasts of the Mediterranean, acquiring territory that is still mostly held by Islamic states (see Map 6-2). By the eighth century, the Muslims had built a vast empire stretching from Spain to India. The capital of this empire moved from Mecca to the more centrally located Damascus. Then, in 750, the Abbasid family unseated the Umayyad caliphs of Damascus in a civil war and established Baghdad as their dynasty's seat. Shortly thereafter, the huge Muslim empire began to break up into separate states, and rival caliphs appeared to claim Muhammad's legacy.

The Muslim advance was rapid and thorough because the Byzantine and Persian empires that bordered Arabia had exhausted themselves in a long war. The Muslims struck just as the Byzantine emperor Heraclius drove his Persian opponent out of Egypt, Palestine, Syria, and Asia Minor. Before Heraclius died in 641, Arab armies had taken all but Asia Minor from him, and by 643 they had overrun most of the Persian Empire. By the end of the century the last Byzantine territory in North Africa had come under Muslim control.

Most of the inhabitants of the Byzantine lands the Muslims occupied were Christians, but, as Semitic peoples, they also had links with the Arabs. The Christian communities of Egypt and Syria were strongly influenced by the Monophysites, and Heraclius's efforts to stamp out their heresy and im-

MAP 6-2 Muslim Conquests and Domination of the Mediterranean to About 750 *Islam spread rapidly, as both a religion and an empire. The most alarming development from the Western point of view was the Muslim conquest of Spain and the southern Mediterranean in the 125 years that followed Muhammad's rise to power.*

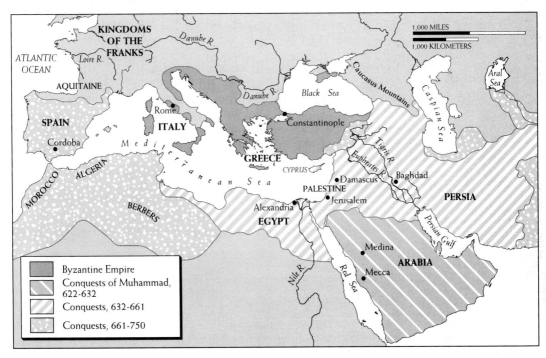

pose Greek orthodoxy led many of them to welcome the Islamic invaders as liberators from Byzantine oppression.

Islam gained Christian converts in North Africa and Spain, but its thrust into the European heart of Christendom was rebuffed by Charles Martel, ruler of the Franks. His defeat of an Arab raiding party at Poitiers (in central France) in 732 ended Arab attempts to enter Europe by way of Spain. The Isaurian dynasty, which Leo III (r. 717–740) established in Constantinople at that time, defended Asia Minor from Islamic aggression and kept the Muslims out of eastern Europe. It was not until Constantinople fell to the Ottoman Turks in the fifteenth century that Europe was again seriously threatened by Muslim expansion.

The Western Debt to Islamic Culture

The Christian West was very hostile to Islam, but it profited a great deal from contact with the Muslims. Arab cultures of the early medieval period were far superior to those of Christian Europe. Europe learned important technologies from the Muslims, and Muslim scholars made major works of Greek science and philosophy available to the West in Latin translation. As late as the sixteenth century, in addition to the works of the ancient world's Hippocrates and Galen, the basic gynecological and child-care manuals used by Western midwives and physicians were compilations by a Baghdad physician, Al-Razi or Rhazes, and the philosophers ibn-Sina or Avicenna (980–1037) and Averröes (1126–1198), Islam's greatest authority on Aristotle. The works of multilingual Jewish scholars also helped create bridges between the Muslim and Christian worlds.

～ Western Society and the Developing Christian Church

Europe, overrun by barbarians from the north and east and threatened in the south by a vigorous and expansive Islam, declined during the fifth and sixth centuries. Trade waned, and the West lost the urban centers where exchanges of goods and ideas promoted cultural growth.

No help could be expected from the East. The Byzantine emperors of the seventh century, who had all they could do to cope with the Islamic threat to their domains, maintained little contact with Europe. As the Muslims conquered Mediterranean islands and ports and strangled Christian shipping, Europe's communications with the East declined further. Forced by these developments to rely on their own resources, westerners drew on their Germanic and Greco-Roman heritages to create distinctive new cultures.

As western cities and governments declined, people sought employment and protection on the self-sufficient estates of the great landholders. Peasants made up 90 percent of the population of medieval Europe. Some were free and owned their own land. Some surrendered their land to a more powerful man in exchange for assistance in time of dire need. They became *serfs*. Serfs were bound to the land they worked. They were not free to leave it, but, on the other hand, tradition protected them from being separated from it and sold as slaves.

As trade declined, the farming belts became regionally insular and self-contained. Barter sufficed for any exchange of goods that took place among the domains of the great landholders, which were the basic political and economic units of medieval society. Producers adjusted their output to the needs of their local markets. Since there was no way to turn excess goods into profit, there was little incentive for experimentation or expansion. This was the social background for the evolution of the characteristic medieval institutions: an economic system called *manorialism,* and a political system called *feudalism.*

In its struggle to survive, the Christian church kept some of medieval Europe's fading urban centers alive. During the period of the late empire the church had modeled itself on Rome's imperial government. It had located its administrative offices near the empire's centers of power—in cities. As the western empire crumbled and secular magistrates disappeared, people turned to bishops, the only Roman "officials" remaining, to fill the vacuum of authority. The local *cathedral* (a church served by a bishop) became the center of urban life and its bishop the effective governor of his city. The church thus took over some of the duties of the state and preserved some of the skills and procedures of Roman government.

The church was compelled by Rome's decline and the loss of the state as its protector to become involved in politics. The struggle to survive the period of the German and Islamic invasions cost the church some of its spiritual integrity, but it emerged a potent civilizing and unifying force. Its message of trust in God's providence and the worth of each individual was a source of solace in difficult times. Its rituals and creeds united people across barriers of social class, education, and gender. And the church's unique hierarchical administration was staffed by the best-educated minds in Europe—men who had experience that was needed by the German kings who were trying to set up national government.

Monastic Culture

The early medieval church was bolstered by the surging popularity of a unique religious institution: the monastery. The first monks were hermits who, in the fourth century, responded to Constantine's popularization of Christianity by fleeing to remote areas. Free from the temptations of ordinary life, they practiced the extreme ascetic disciplines that many believed were the mark of true Christians. The suffering the monks willingly embraced make them the Christian heroes of their age—replacing the martyrs that the Roman government was no longer producing.

Medieval Christians viewed monastic life—embracing, as it did, the biblical "counsels of perfection" (chastity, poverty, and obedience)—as the highest calling. Monks and the secular clergy, who gradually adopted some monas-

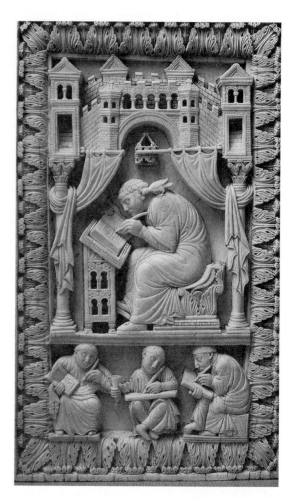

Saint Gregory the Great, shown in a monastic scriptorium, or study, receiving the divine word from a dove perched on his shoulder. Below him three monks are writing. The middle monk holds an inkwell in his left hand. [Kunsthistorisches Museum, Vienna]

tic disciplines, met a more demanding spiritual standard than that expected of ordinary believers. Consequently, the clergy came to be respected as superior to the laity, a belief that served the papacy in struggles with secular rulers.

The hermit monasticism pioneered by men like Anthony of Egypt (ca. 251–356) soon evolved into communal monasticism. In the first quarter of the fourth century, Pachomius (ca. 286–346), another Egyptian, set up a highly regimented community in which hundreds of monks shared a life of labor, order, and discipline—enforced by a strict penal code. Such monastic communities strived to become little "cities of God," isolating themselves from the collapsing Roman Empire and its nominally Christian society. Basil the Great (329–379) invented the style of communal monasticism that came to dominate the East. It lessened the asceticism of Pachomius and advised monks to care for the needy outside their communities: orphans, widows, and the infirm.

Athanasius (ca. 293–373) and Martin of Tours (ca. 315–ca. 399) introduced the West to Eastern monastic practices. But, in 529, Benedict of Nursia (ca. 480–547) wrote a *Rule* (a constitution) for a monastery he established at Monte Cassino near Naples in Italy. The uniquely Western style of monasticism it defined became standard throughout Europe. Benedict's *Rule* governed a monk's every activity, even explaining how he should sleep. It advised against the ascetic severities of Eastern monasticism. Benedict insisted that monks have good food, some wine, adequate clothing, and proper amounts of sleep and relaxation. Periods of time were set aside each day for prayers, liturgical activities, and study—as well as manual labor (farming). The program was designed to create autonomous religious communities that were economically, spiritually, and intellectually self-sufficient. Benedictine monks were chiefly responsible for the missionary work that, at the start of the Middle Ages, converted England and Germany to Christianity. Their disciplined organization and devotion to hard work made them an economic and political power, as well as a spiritual force, wherever they went.

The Doctrine of Papal Primacy

Constantine and the eastern emperors looked on the church as a department of the state. They even intervened in its theological debates and legislated its doctrine. The state was, however, less successful in controlling the Western than the Eastern church. The bishops of Rome took advantage of the decline of imperial power in the West to develop the doctrine of "papal primacy," a claim to the right of undisputed leadership of an independent church.

Papal primacy was a response to the decline of imperial Rome and the increasing pretensions of Constantinople. In 381, the ecumenical Council of Constantinople declared the bishop (patriarch) of Constantinople to be of first rank after the bishop of Rome. Pope Damasus I (366–384)[1] fought back by claiming that Rome had a unique "apostolic" primacy. He insisted that he and all other popes were heirs to the apostle Peter and his unique legacy as the "rock" on which Jesus had said (Matthew 16:18) that the church would be built. After the Council of Chalcedon (451) accorded the Byzantine patriarch the same primacy over the East that Rome traditionally had in the West, Pope Leo I (440–461) assumed the title *pontifex maximus* ("supreme priest") to assert his claim to supremacy over all the bishops of the church. At the end of the fifth century, Pope Gelasius I (492–496) proclaimed the authority of the church to be "more weighty" than that of the state, for the church was responsible for the means of salvation—the most serious human concern.

The Germanic and Islamic invasions prevented either emperors or eastern patriarchs from doing much to bring the popes and the Western church under their control. When the Lombard tribes invaded Italy at the end of the sixth century, Pope Gregory I, "the Great" (590–604), ignored the impotent

---

[1]Papal dates give the years of each reign.

imperial authorities and assumed the right to negotiate with the barbarians as the chief representative of the Italian people.

The Division of Christendom

By the time Gregory became pope, the patriarch of Constantinople was using the title "universal" patriarch—implying supremacy to Rome. Since the patriarch had no effective power in the West, this snub of the West was an admission that Christendom had split into separate Eastern (Byzantine) and Western (Roman Catholic) churches.

The division of the church was apparent in language, doctrine, disciplinary codes, and liturgies. The Greek Byzantine church had a mystical, otherworldly orientation that contrasted with the more practical Christianity of the West's Latin church. Eastern church organization more effectively imitated the hierarchy of the imperial government than did the Western church. But the power of the patriarch over the clergy was constrained by the power the emperor had over him. Where the Western church tried to impose monastic celibacy on all clergy, parish priests in the Eastern church were allowed to marry (bishops were not). The Eastern church used leavened bread in the Eucharist; Rome mandated unleavened bread. The Byzantines rejected the Catholic doctrine of purgatory. They also permitted divorce, and, unlike the Catholics, performed their liturgies in the vernacular of the laity.

In addition to these divergent practices, the East and the West evolved incompatible positions on the fundamental question of authority within the church. Where the Latin church looked to the Roman pope to define doctrine, the Greek church relied on the authority of the Bible and ecumenical councils. Disputes over the right to define doctrine became acute when the East mounted its ultimately unsuccessful assault on the veneration of holy images ("iconoclasm") and when the West added the word *filioque* ("also from the Son") to the Nicene Creed. (This was an attempt to subvert eastern compromises with Arianism by insisting that the Holy Spirit proceeded from the Father and the Son as equal partners in the Godhead.) The claims of Roman popes to a primacy of authority over the whole church were completely unacceptable to the East. In the East Christianity evolved not one organization, but a communion of self-governing, independent national churches. When, in the ninth century, the crucial issue of authority came to a head, Pope Nicholas I and Patriarch Photius excommunicated each other. In 1054, Pope Leo IX and Patriarch Michael Cerularius officially divided the church by repeating the mutual condemnation.

Rome's quarrels with Constantinople threatened the papacy's survival, for popes had traditionally been dependent on the eastern empire for military help against the barbarians. But as that help declined in effectiveness and Christianity spread to the invaders, the popes began to seek allies among Europe's new German rulers. The popes eventually concluded that the Franks of northern Gaul were Europe's ascendant power and the church's most promising protectors. In 754, Pope Stephen II (752–757) initiated the most fruitful political alliance of the Middle Ages. He persuaded Pepin III, ruler of the Franks, to defend Rome from the Lombards. By throwing in his lot with the Germans, the pope acknowledged the passing of the old empire and the rise of a new, independent West.

∼ The Kingdom of the Franks

Merovingians and Carolingians: From Clovis to Charlemagne

A warrior chieftain named Clovis (ca. 466?–511), who converted to orthodox Christianity around 496, founded the first Frankish dynasty, the Merovingians. (It was named for Merovich, an early leader of one branch of the Franks.) Clovis and his successors united the Salian and Ripuarian Franks; subdued the Burgundians and Visigoths; and transformed Rome's Gaul into "France," the kingdom of the Franks.

Governing the Franks. The Merovingians struggled with the perennial problem of medieval politics: the competing claims of the "one" and the "many." As kings worked to centralize governments, powerful local magnates fought to preserve their regional autonomy. The result was a battle between forces that tried to unify society and those that promoted its fragmentation.

The Merovingian kings tried to pull their nation together by making pacts with the landed nobility and by relying for help in running their domain on a new kind of royal official, the *count*. Counts were appointed to manage territories on which they had no hereditary claim. Since the people on the lands the counts governed had no tradition of loyalty to them, the king expected counts to be more obedient than landed aristocrats. But, as time passed, kings found it impossible to prevent counts from establishing hereditary claims to their offices. As they came to resemble the older nobility, they joined forces in fragmenting the Frankish kingdom into tiny independent principalities. The Frankish custom of dividing the kingdom equally among the king's legitimate male heirs also worked against the unification of a Frankish state.

By the seventh century the Merovingian king was king in title only. Real executive authority had devolved on one of his officials, the "mayor of the palace." From the ascent to that post of Pepin I of Austrasia (d. 639) until 751, one family, the Carolingians, held that office. In 751, with the enterprising connivance of the pope, they simply shoved the Merovingians aside and expropriated the Frankish crown.

Pepin II (d. 714), who had ruled the Frankish kingdom in fact if not in title, bequeathed his post to his illegitimate son, Charles "Martel" ("the Hammer"). Charles (d. 741) created a great cavalry by bestowing lands as *fiefs* or *benefices* ("provisional" grants) on powerful noblemen on condition that they equip themselves to serve in his army. His army proved its worth at Poitiers in 732, when it broke the momentum of the Muslim advance and secured the Pyrenees as the border of western Europe.

Much of the land that Martel distributed as fiefs to create his army came from the church. The church was dependent on the protection of the Franks, and it could do little to prevent the confiscation of property that funded its own defense. Eventually, however, the church was partially compensated for its losses.

The land that Martel handed out forged an alliance between the Carolingians and the landed aristocracy. Where the Merovingians had tried to weaken the aristocrats by raising landless men to power, the Carolingians staffed their government almost entirely from the ranks of the landed nobility. By playing to strength rather than challenging it, the Carolingians secured their position—at least for the short term.

The Frankish Church. The church played a large role in the Frankish government, for its monasteries were the intellectual centers of Carolingian society. Already in Merovingian times the higher clergy were employed in tandem with counts as royal agents.

The Carolingians—particularly Charles Martel and his successors, Pepin III, "the Short" (d. 768), and Charlemagne (r. 768–814)—relied on Christian missionaries to pacify the barbarian lands into which they expanded. Conversion to Nicene Christianity was an essential part of the process of assimilating conquered peoples. As the cavalry broke bodies, the clergy won hearts and minds. The confusion of the missions of the church and state increased when the king appointed Christian bishops to govern the lands they labored to convert.

An event from the career of Boniface (born Wynfrith, 680?–754), an Anglo-Saxon monk who was the most famous of the Carolingian missionaries, illustrates how deeply involved in politics the church became. In 751, Pope Zacharias (741–752) sanctioned Pepin the Short's bid for the Frankish throne. Pepin was proclaimed king by the nobility in council, and the last of the Merovingians—the puppet king Childeric III—was hustled off to a monastery, where enforced celibacy ended his line. At Pepin's coronation Boniface may have anointed the new king—a ritual traditionally associated with the ordination of priests. The church apparently intended to give the Carolingian monarchy a sacral character.

In 753, Zacharias's successor, Pope Stephen II (752–757), collected the price for the church's support. Stephen journeyed to Pepin's court to demand that the Franks drive off the Lombards, who were besieging Rome, and confirm papal claims to central Italy. In 755, the Franks defeated the Lombards and gave the pope the lands surrounding Rome—including many to which the eastern emperor laid claim. This acknowledged the pope's secular authority over a district known as the Papal States.

About this time (750–800) a document called the *Donation of Constantine* appeared. It claimed that Constantine had given the papacy title to the western half of his empire. It was intended to support the church in its dealings with the Franks, and the popes continued to use it in political struggles with kings until it was exposed as a forgery in the fifteenth century. The

Franks were overwhelming protectors for the popes. They drew almost as slight a boundary between state and church as did the eastern emperors. To prevent their absorption into the Frankish state, the popes made sweeping claims to secular rights and privileges for the church.

The Reign of Charlemagne (768–814)

In 774, Charlemagne, the son of Pepin the Short, completed his father's work by conquering Italy's Lombards and assuming their crown. On all sides he pushed out the frontiers of the kingdom he had inherited (see Map 6-3). The Saxons of northern Germany were brutally Christianized and dispersed in small groups throughout Frankish lands. The Muslims were chased beyond the Pyrenees, and the Avars (a tribe related to the Huns) were practically annihilated—bringing the Danubian plains into the Frankish orbit. By the time of his death on January 28, 814, Charlemagne's kingdom embraced modern France, Belgium, Holland, Switzerland, almost the whole of western Germany, much of Italy, a portion of Spain, and the island of Corsica—an area approximately equal to that of the modern Common Market.

The New Empire. Charlemagne believed that his huge domain entitled him to an imperial title. At Aachen (Aix-la-Chapelle), he constructed a palace city in conscious imitation of the courts of the eastern emperors. And to create a new Frankish empire, he turned to the church—which he treated with a paternalism almost as great as that of an eastern emperor—for practical help and theoretical justification.

Charlemagne's imperial pretensions were confirmed on Christmas Day, 800, when Pope Leo III (795–816) crowned him emperor. This event inaugurated what came to be known as the Holy Roman Empire, a medieval approximation of the West's old Roman Empire. The fateful ceremony was in part an effort by the pope to enhance the church's stature and to gain some leverage over a powerful king. When the emperor received the crown from the hands of the pope, a precedent was set that was useful for the church in its future dealings with the state. But the coronation was no coup d'etat for Leo. Charlemagne's power over the church did not diminish, and his international standing improved. The eastern emperors reluctantly recognized his imperial dignity—once he disclaimed any ambition to move into their lands.

The New Emperor. Charlemagne stood a majestic six feet three and one-half inches tall—a fact confirmed when his tomb was opened and exact measurements of his remains were taken in 1861. He was restless, ever ready for a hunt. Informal and gregarious, he insisted on the presence of friends even when he bathed. He was widely known for his practical jokes, lusty good humor, and warm hospitality. Aachen was a festive court to which people and gifts came from all over the world. In 802, the caliph of Baghdad, Harun-al-Rashid, even sent Charlemagne a white elephant, the transport of which across the Alps was as great a wonder as the creature itself.

MAP 6-3 The Empire of Charlemagne to 814 *Building on the successes of his predecessors, Charlemagne greatly increased the Frankish domains.*

Map legend:
- The Frankish Empire, 768
- } Charlemagne's Kingdom to 814
- Tributary Peoples, 814
- Possessions of the Byzantine Empire

Charlemagne had five official wives (in succession), many mistresses and concubines, and numerous children. This connubial variety caused some political upheavals when Pepin, his oldest son by his first marriage, grew jealous of the attention he showed the sons of his second wife. Pepin joined some nobles in an ill-fated conspiracy against Charlemagne and spent the rest of his life in confinement in a monastery.

Problems of Government. Charlemagne governed his kingdom through counts. There may have been as many as 250 of them strategically distributed throughout the administrative districts into which the kingdom was divided. A count was usually a local magnate who possessed armed might and who could be persuaded in his self-interest to enforce the will of a generous king. His duties were to maintain a local army, to collect tribute and dues, and to administer justice in the name of the king.

This last responsibility involved a district law court called the *mallus.* Its job was to hear testimony from both parties in a case and to pass judgment on the character or believability of each side. In situations where such testimony was insufficient, recourse was had to duels or to various tests or ordeals. A defendant's hand might be immersed in boiling water and his innocence determined by the way his wounds healed. Or a suspect might be bound with ropes and thrown into a river or pond that had been blessed by a priest. If the pure water rejected him and he floated, he was pronounced guilty. God was believed to render the verdict in an ordeal. The job of the *mallus* was to assess a monetary compensation to be paid to the injured party. This was a popular way to settle grievances that otherwise might have led to the outbreak of bloody vendettas.

Charlemagne never solved the problem of creating a loyal bureaucracy to govern his kingdom. The counts he appointed, like their Merovingian predecessors, tended to become little despots within their districts. Charlemagne tried to oversee these overseers by commissioning special envoys, the *missi dominici,* to visit the counts and report back on their behavior. The impact of occasional inspections by the *missi* was marginal. And when Charlemagne appointed provincial governors (prefects, dukes, and margraves) to keep permanent watch over the counts, they proved to be no more trustworthy than the counts. The situation was not improved by appointing churchmen to political office. They embraced the same secular lifestyles and aspirations as the counts and were generally indistinguishable from the lay nobility. "Capitularies" (royal decrees) discouraged the more outrageous behavior of the clergy. But Charlemagne made little distinction between bishops and counts. Both were vassals—that is, upper-class "servants" who took an oath of homage to the king.

To be a Christian at this difficult period in the history of Europe was largely a matter of submitting to rituals like baptism and assenting to the creeds endorsed by the state. Both clergy and laity were too preoccupied with the struggle to survive to worry much about elevated ethical issues.

Alcuin and the Carolingian Renaissance. One of Charlemagne's strategies for improving the government of his empire was an intensive effort to elevate the educations of the clerics and officials who staffed the royal bureaucracy. By providing better training for the sons of the nobility who filled the religious and secular offices of the realm, court scholarship served to strengthen the state.

Charlemagne accumulated a great deal of wealth in the form of loot and land from conquered tribes. He used some of this booty to attract Europe's best scholars to Aachen—men like Theodulf of Orleans, Angilbert, Einhard (Charlemagne's biographer), and Alcuin of York (735–804), a famous Anglo-Saxon educator who became director of the king's palace school. The school provided basic instruction in the seven liberal arts, with special concentration on grammar, logic, rhetoric, and simple mathematics.

The curriculum was designed to give bureaucrats the simple tools of their trade, but it accomplished more than that. It improved the accuracy of Latin used in official documents, and it made a new, clear style of handwriting standard throughout the empire. Carolingian "minuscule" was far more legible than Merovingian script. By making reading both easier and more pleasurable, it encouraged subsequent Latin scholarship and lay literacy. A modest renaissance or rebirth of antiquity also occurred in the palace school as its scholars collected and preserved ancient manuscripts. Alcuin worked on the text of the Bible and made editions of the works of Gregory the Great and the *Rule* of Saint Benedict. These scholarly projects aimed at concrete reforms and served official efforts to bring uniformity to church law and liturgy, to educate the clergy, and to improve moral life within the monasteries.

The Carolingian Manor. Early medieval Europe's chief economic institution was a kind of communal farm called a *manor*. Medieval farmers usually preferred to cluster in villages rather than to live on individual farms. They shared labor and expensive agricultural implements like plows and oxen. But instead of dividing their manor's harvest equally among all its workers, each family had its own strips of land and lived from the products of its own fields.

The status of peasants was determined by the size of their holdings. A freeman who had his own allodial or hereditary property (land free from the claims of an overlord) became a serf by surrendering his property to an overlord in exchange for protection. Such a person received his land back from his lord with a new set of rights and obligations. Although the land was no longer his property, he had full use of it and could not be separated from it. His chief duty to his lord was to work his lord's *demesne,* the fields on the manor that produced the crops meant for the lord's table. Peasants who entered the service of a lord with little real property (perhaps only a few farm implements and animals) became unfree serfs. Such serfs were much more vulnerable to the lord's demands, often spending up to three days a week working the lord's fields. Truly impoverished peasants, those who had nothing to offer a lord except their hands, had the lowest status and were the least protected from excessive demands on their labor.

By Charlemagne's day, a plow with a moldboard and a three-field system of cultivation were greatly improving agricultural productivity. Unlike the ancient "scratch" plow (a pointed stick), the moldboard plow cut deep into the soil and turned it over to utilize more of its fertility. This new type of plow was able to break up the dense, waterlogged soils of northern Europe and open to cultivation lands that had defeated Roman farmers.

To maintain the fertility of their fields, ancient farmers used a two-field system of crop rotation—simply alternating fallow and planted fields annually. A fallow field was plowed to keep down weeds and permit the land to "rest," but not planted. The medieval three-field system left only one-third of a farm fallow in a given year and thus decreased the amount of unproductive land that had to be plowed. In fall, one field was planted with winter crops of wheat or rye to be harvested in early summer. In late spring, a second field was planted with summer crops of oats, barley, lentils, and legumes, which were harvested in August or September. The third field was fallow.

Religion and the Clergy. Religion had an intrinsic appeal to the masses of ordinary men and women who found themselves burdened, fearful, and with little hope of material betterment this side of eternity. The same was true of the upper classes. Charlemagne, who frequented the Church of Saint Mary in Aachen several times a day, decreed on his deathbed that all but a fraction of his great treasure be spent to endow masses and prayers for his soul.

The priests who served the people—the lower clergy—were poorly prepared to provide spiritual leadership. They were recruited from the ranks of the serfs and fared no better than other peasants. Lords owned the churches on their lands and were free to staff them with their own serfs. The Church expected a lord to liberate a serf who entered the clergy, but many "serf priests" said mass on Sunday and toiled as peasants for the rest of the week.

Because priests on most manors were no better educated than their congregations, religious instruction barely existed. For most people religion was more a matter of practice than doctrine. They baptized their children, attended mass, tried to learn the Lord's Prayer and the Apostles' Creed, and received the last rites when death approached. They were in awe of sacred relics and devoted to an army of saints who they hoped would intercede for them with their divine overlord in the court of heaven. Simple faith depended little on understanding.

Breakup of the Carolingian Kingdom

As Charlemagne aged, he discovered that his empire was becoming ungovernable, for there was no way to prevent his vassals from doing what they wanted with the lands they held. In feudal society the intensity of one's loyalty to a lord depended on how far away that lord was. Local people obeyed local leaders more readily than distant kings. Charlemagne had to appoint powerful men to control the far-flung regions of his empire, but their power was always at the cost of his own. In the Carolingian as in the Merovingian kingdom, the noble tail came increasingly to wag the royal dog.

Louis the Pious. The Carolingians did not give up easily. Charlemagne's successor was his only surviving son, Louis "the Pious" (r. 814–840). Before his death Charlemagne designated Louis "co-emperor." The imperial title symbolized the Carolingian policy of unifying the kingdom by persuading its subjects to transcend regional and tribal loyalties.

Louis's fertility impeded the unification of the empire. He had three sons by his first wife, and, according to Salic (Salian Frankish) law, each was entitled to a share of his kingdom. Louis tried to break this legal tradition by making his eldest son, Lothar (d. 855), co-regent and sole imperial heir (817). In 823, Louis's second wife bore him a fourth son, Charles "the Bald" (d. 877). In the interest of securing an inheritance for her son, the queen incited her step-sons, Pepin and Louis "the German," to rebellion. Supported by the pope, they joined forces and defeated their father in a battle near Colmar (833).

The Treaty of Verdun and Its Aftermath. Pepin's death in 838 and Louis's in 840 helped clear the field of contenders. In 843, by the terms of the Treaty of Verdun, the surviving Carolingians agreed to partition the empire into three equal parts. Lothar, who retained the now meaningless imperial title, received the middle section, called Lotharingia (Holland, Belgium, Switzerland, Alsace-Lorraine, and Italy). Charles the Bald got the equivalent of modern France, and Louis the German, Germany.

The Treaty of Verdun was only the start of the fragmentation of the Carolingian lands. When Lothar died in 855, his middle kingdom was divided among his three sons. This partition of the partition changed the balance of power. Henceforth, the eastern and western Frankish kingdoms—Germany and France—would squabble endlessly over portions of the fractionalized middle kingdom.

In Italy the decline of the Carolingian Empire created a political vacuum the popes hoped to fill. But both popes and kings became pawns in the hands of the nobles of Italy and Germany. It is especially at this juncture in European history—the last quarter of the ninth and the first half of the tenth century—that one may speak accurately of a "dark age," for the political breakdown of the empire and the papacy coincided with renewed barbarian attacks. Successive waves of Normans ("North-men" from Scandinavia, commonly called Vikings), Magyars (Hungarians from the plains of Russia), and Muslims (from Sicily and Africa) simultaneously attacked Europe on every border.

The Vikings were the most serious threat. Thanks to their unique skills as seamen, they were able to raid Europe's coasts and penetrate up its rivers—reaching lands from Gibraltar to Novgorod. Since they moved rapidly and randomly, there was little defense against them. The Franks built fortified towns and castles to serve as refuges. Sometimes they bought off the invaders with silver or grants of land (France's duchy of "Normandy," for example). Since there was little that the central governments of kings could do against myriad bands of raiders, each district of a kingdom turned for protection to its resident local strongman.

∼ Feudal Society

In the absence of effective central governments that could protect them, medieval people evolved feudal societies. The weaker submitted to the stronger, and those who could guarantee security from rapine and starvation ruled.

Medieval feudalism emerged from a society dominated by warlords. Feudal society was held together by the oaths that individuals made—commitments to provide personal protection or maintenance in exchange for service. Men who pledged their services as soldiers became vassals, a professional military class with its own code of knightly conduct. Networks of personal relationships among members of this class created military organizations in each district. The leaders of these armies, whether or not they had a legal basis for their actions, assumed most of the responsibilities for governing the people who lived under their protection.

Origins

The roots of feudal government go back to the sixth and seventh centuries, when the weakness of the West's governments made it necessary for freemen whose families or groups were unable to fend for themselves to seek alliances with more powerful individuals. Freemen, who entered into various kinds of contractual relations of dependence on superiors, came to be described as *vassi* ("those who serve"). *Vassalage* denotes the placement of oneself in the personal service of an individual who promises one protection.

Owners of large estates tried to acquire as many vassals as they could, for these men could be equipped as soldiers for their private armies. At first these men were maintained in their lord's own household, but, as numbers grew, this became impractical. Since the collapsing economy was taking money out of circulation, vassals could not be paid a salary. Hence, the practice evolved of granting them a *benefice* or a *fief* (the right to use a piece of the lord's land to maintain themselves in his service). Vassals lived on their fiefs and were responsible for the peasants who tilled the land for them.

Vassalage and the Fief

A vassal swore *fealty* to his lord: that is, he promised to serve his lord and to refrain from actions contrary to his lord's interests. His chief obligation was military—duty as a mounted knight. Bargaining might take place over terms of service, but custom limited the number of days a lord could keep a vassal in the field. (In France in the eleventh century, about forty days was standard.) In addition to military duty the vassal was expected to attend his lord's court or council when summoned and to render his lord financial assistance at times of special need: to ransom him from his enemies, to outfit him for a major military campaign, or to defray the costs of the festivities at the marriage of a daughter or the knighting of a son.

Louis the Pious extended this arrangement beyond the lay nobility to the higher clergy. He required bishops and abbots to swear fealty and to hold their offices from him as benefices. He formally "invested" clerics with the rings and staffs that were the symbols of their spiritual offices. The practice of lay investiture of clergy was offensive to the church, for it implied the subservience of the church to the state. In the late tenth and eleventh centuries, reform-minded clergy rebelled against the ceremonies of vassalage, but the reformers had no intention of surrendering the grants of land that were the rewards for oaths of homage.

A lord's obligations to his vassals were very specific. He had to protect the vassal from physical harm, to stand as his advocate in court, and to provide for his maintenance by giving him a fief. In Carolingian times a fief varied in size from one or more small villas to several *mansi* (a unit of twenty-five to forty-eight acres). Royal vassals are known to have received fiefs composed of from 30 to 200 *mansi*. With prizes like this in the offing, vassalage was sought by the highest classes of Carolingian society. In the short run, the policy marshalled the nobility behind the king, but in the long run, the granting of fiefs undercut royal power. Kings found it difficult or impossible to reclaim land once it was granted to vassals. And the vassals of a king, enriched by his donations, created vassals of their own. Since it was possible for a vassal to accept fiefs from more than one lord, all kinds of conflicts of interest could arise. The ninth century developed the concept of the "liege lord," the master to whom a vassal owed primary duty, but this did little to halt the continuing fragmentation of both land and loyalty.

Kings were further weakened by the fact that the fiefs they granted tended to become the real property of their vassals. Although title to a fief remained with the lord who granted it, it was hard for him to prevent his vassal from passing the fief on to an heir. In the ninth century, hereditary possession became a legally recognized principle and laid the basis for claims to real ownership. This process enabled the nobility to appropriate much of the royal domain.

Since lay society was illiterate, the feudal era relied on symbols and ceremonies to seal the contracts that established rights to land and obligations to serve. A freeman originally became a vassal by a secular act of "commendation." In the mid-eighth century, a religious "oath of fealty" increased the solemnity of the ceremony. A vassal reinforced his promise of fidelity to a lord by swearing an oath with his hand on a sacred relic or the Bible. In the tenth and eleventh centuries, paying homage to the lord involved not only the swearing of such an oath but also the placement of the vassal's hands between the lord's and the sealing of the ceremony with a kiss.

Despite feudalism's obvious vulnerability to abuse and confusion, it created social stability in early medieval Europe and helped restore political centralization during the High Middle Ages. The genius of feudal government lay in its adaptability. Contracts of different kinds could be made with almost anybody to serve almost any purpose. The foundations of the modern nation-state were laid in France and England as kings compromised with their vassals and fine-tuned feudal arrangements to construct some sort of centralized government.

The centuries between 476 and 1000 saw the decline of classical civilization and the birth of new medieval civilizations. The eastern and western halves of the old Roman Empire lost contact with each other and developed in different directions.

In the East the Byzantine Empire, with its capital at Constantinople, preserved classical literature, but used it to guide the development of a passionately Christian culture. Religion also provided the means for uniting the Arabs and sending them forth to conquer an empire that soon stretched from Spain to China. Islamic culture, as well as the Islamic state, reached its creative peak during the early medieval centuries. Although the Muslims treasured classical literature and traced their religion to the same root as Christianity, Muslims and Christians remained estranged and suspicious of one another.

In the West the barbarian invasions and a collapsing economy rapidly distanced people from classical culture. Cities faded, and society became largely agrarian. Although the Latin church preserved some classical literature and some memories of Roman institutions, the West was to be many centuries in recovering its classical heritage. Its "renaissances" began with the reign of the Frankish emperor Charlemagne and continued through the sixteenth century. The mixture of barbarian customs, Christian faith, and remnants of classical culture slowly created a distinct identity for the West. But the early medieval era was not a time of great cultural ambition in Europe, for its society was primitive and fragmented. Western people were concerned with finding ways to satisfy the basic needs of food (manorialism) and public order (feudalism). Aspirations to a civilization as elaborate as those of Byzantium and Islam would come later.

∾ Review Questions

1. What changes took place in Christianity between its founding and the coronation of the emperor Charlemagne in 800? What were the distinctive features of the early church? What role did the church play in the Western world after the fall of the Roman Empire?

2. What changes took place in the Frankish kingdom between its foundation and the end of Charlemagne's reign? What were the characteristics of Charlemagne's rule? Why did Charlemagne encourage learning at his court? Could the Carolingian renaissance have endangered his authority? Why did his empire break apart?

3. How and why was the history of the eastern half of the former Roman Empire so different from that of its western half? Did Justinian strengthen or weaken the Byzantine Empire? How does his reign compare to Charlemagne's?

4. What were the tenets of Islam? How were the Muslims able to build an empire so quickly? What contributions did the Muslims make to the development of Western Europe?

5. How and why did feudal society begin? What were the essential features of feudalism? Do you think that modern society could ""slip back" into a feudal pattern?

∾ Suggested Readings

G. BARRACLOUGH, *The Crucible of Europe: The Ninth and Tenth Centuries* (1976). Sweeping survey of political history.

M. BLOCH, *Feudal Society*, vols. 1 and 2, trans. by L. A. Manyon (1971). A classic on the topic and as an example of historical study.

P. Brown, *Augustine of Hippo: A Biography* (1967). Late antiquity seen through the biography of its greatest Christian thinker.

H. Chadwick, *The Early Church* (1967). Among the best treatments of early Christianity.

K. F. Drew (ed.), *The Barbarian Invasions: Catalyst of a New Order* (1970). Collection of essays that focuses the issues.

H. Fichtenau, *The Carolingian Empire: The Age of Charlemagne*, trans. by Peter Munz (1964). Strongest on political history of the era.

F. L. Ganshof, *Feudalism*, trans. by Philip Grierson (1964). The most profound brief analysis of the subject.

R. Hodges and D. Whitehouse, *Mohammed, Charlemagne and the Origins of Europe* (1982). For the social and economic history of early medieval Europe.

A. Hourani, *A History of the Arab Peoples* (1991). A comprehensive text that includes an excellent overview of the origins and early history of Islam.

J. Leclercq, *The Love of Learning and the Desire for God: A Study of Monastic Culture*, trans. by Catherine Misrahi (1962). Lucid, delightful, absorbing account of the ideals of monks.

C. Mango, *Byzantium: The Empire of New Rome* (1980). Perhaps the most readable account.

H. Pirenne, *A History of Europe, I: From the End of the Roman World in the West to the Beginnings of the Western States*, trans. by Bernhard Maill (1958). Comprehensive survey, with now-controversial views on the demise of Western trade and cities in the early Middle Ages.

S. Runciman, *Byzantine Civilization* (1970). Succinct, comprehensive account by a master.

R. W. Southern, *The Making of the Middle Ages* (1973). Originally published in 1953, but still a fresh account by an imaginative historian.

S. Wemple, *Women in Frankish Society: Marriage and the Cloister, 500–900* (1981). What marriage and the cloister meant to women in these early centuries.

L. White, Jr., *Medieval Technology and Social Change* (1962). Often-fascinating account of the way primitive technology changed life.

7

The High Middle Ages (1000–1300): The Ascendancy of the Church and the Rise of States

---

KEY TOPICS IN THIS CHAPTER

~ Germany's Saxon dynasty and the Holy Roman Empire

~ A movement to reform the church and free it from political domination by kings and emperors

~ The emergence of strong national monarchies in England and France

~ The fragmentation of Germany, the conclusion of a struggle for supremacy between the Hohenstaufen dynasty and the papacy

---

The High Middle Ages (1000–1300) was a period of political expansion and consolidation and of intellectual flowering and synthesis. With respect to the development of Western institutions, this may have been a more creative era than the Italian Renaissance or the German Reformation.

The borders of western Europe were secured against foreign invaders, and Europeans, who had long been the prey of foreign powers, mounted a military and

economic offensive against the East. The rulers of England and France established nuclei for nation-states by adapting feudal principles of government to the creation of centralized political realms. Parliaments and popular assemblies emerged in some places to enable the propertied classes to influence the development of the new monarchies. The Holy Roman Empire was, however, the great exception to the trend toward national centralization. The lands that composed it remained weak and fragmented until modern times.

The High Middle Ages also saw the establishment of the distinctive Western traditions that separated church and state. The popes prevented the church from being divided and absorbed into the new nations by making the papacy a monarchy among monarchies. Some religious reformers subsequently blamed Gregory II, the pope who led the fight against lay "investiture" of clergy, for diverting the church from its spiritual mission into the murky world of politics.

∽ Otto I and the Revival of the Empire

Unifying Germany

In 918 the duke of Saxony, Henry I ("the Fowler," d. 936), became the first non-Frankish king of Germany, the founder of its Saxon dynasty. Henry reversed the process of political fragmentation that had set in with the decline of the Carolingian Empire. He consolidated the duchies of Swabia, Bavaria, Saxony, Franconia, and Lotharingia and checked the invasions of the Hungarians and the Danes.

The German state that Henry bequeathed to his son Otto I, ("the Great," r. 936–973), was the strongest kingdom in Europe. In 951, Otto invaded Italy and proclaimed himself its king. In 955, he defeated the Hungarians at Lechfeld, an achievement that secured German borders against barbarian attack and established the frontiers of western Europe.

Embracing the Church

Otto secured the power of the throne by refusing to allow Germany's dukes to claim their duchies by the hereditary rights that the feudal nobility asserted to other fiefs. He also used the clergy to undercut the authority of lay lords. Otto appointed bishops and abbots of monasteries to administer his lands and be his agents. They were more likely than laymen to be sympathetic to his plans to restore imperial authority, and, unlike laymen, they could not marry and attempt to pass on to their sons the lands they held from the king. The church—sensing no conflict between its spiritual mission and politics—eagerly embraced the wealth and power Otto pressed on it.

In 961, Otto rescued Pope John XII (955–964) from a scuffle with the Italian nobility, and on February 2, 962, the pope bestowed the lapsed imperial title on Germany's king. Otto's intervention in Italian politics extended his control over the church. Otto appointed the higher clergy and declared him-

Significant Dates from the Period of the High Middle Ages

910	*Monastery of Cluny founded*
955	*Otto I defeats the Hungarians*
1059	*Papal elections by the College of Cardinals*
1066	*Norman Conquest of England*
1075–1122	*Investiture Controversy*
1095–1099	*First Crusade captures Jerusalem*
1144	*Islamic armies reconquer Edessa*
1152	*Hohenstaufen dynasty founded*
1154	*Plantagenet dynasty founded*
1187	*Jerusalem reconquered by Saladin*
1189–1192	*Third Crusade (Richard the Lion-Hearted)*
1202	*Fourth Crusade (Constantinople)*
1209	*Albigensian Crusade*
1214	*Battle of Bouvines*
1215	*Fourth Lateran Council; Magna Carta*
1257	*Imperial electoral college established*

self special "protector" of the Papal States. When Pope John belatedly recognized the royal web in which he had become entangled, he joined a plot against the new emperor. Otto promptly ordered an ecclesiastical synod to depose John and agree that no future pope take office without first swearing allegiance to the emperor. Otto's popes ruled at his pleasure.

The Italian interests that Otto bequeathed to his successors—Otto II (r. 973–983) and Otto III (r. 983–1002)—distracted them from events in Germany, and their German base disintegrated. It had been unwise to dream of an empire before monarchy itself was firmly in place. As the briefly revived empire began to crumble in the first quarter of the eleventh century, the papacy seized the opportunity to reclaim its independence and exact revenge for the presumption of kings.

～ The Reviving Catholic Church

The Cluny Reform Movement

In the tenth century a campaign designed to liberate the clergy from the control of the feudal nobility was launched by the monastery of Cluny in east-central France. Since the last days of the Roman Empire, monks—the least worldly of the clergy—had been the church's most popular advocates. Their educations were the best available, the relics and rituals they maintained were believed to have magical potency, and the religious ideals embodied in their way of life set the standard for Christian society.

In 910, in the midst of an unprecedented boom in the construction of monasteries, William the Pious, duke of Aquitaine, endowed Cluny. Cluny

A portion of the Romanesque abbey church of Cluny, reconstructed between 1080 and 1225. In the twelfth century it was Europe's largest church (555 feet long). [Adros Studio]

was intended to be a model Benedictine monastery, maintaining the strictest observance of the *Rule* and restoring the purest liturgical practices.

The Cluniac reformers claimed that a truly spiritual church could not be created so long as laymen had the power to appoint and dominate clerics. The secular lords who endowed Cluniac houses renounced any claim to intervene in their management, and the abbots who ran them were sincere churchmen dedicated to the maintenance of the strictest religious discipline.

Cluniac ideals soon spread from the monastery to the parish, and the reformers argued that the "secular clergy" (those serving the *saeculum*, the "world") ought to adopt the ascetic lifestyle of the "regular" clergy (those living by a *regula*, a monastic "rule"). They also insisted that bishops be freed from the authority of the feudal nobility and made accountable only to an independent papacy.

Cluny trained men who were dispatched to reform other monasteries throughout France and Italy. Aggressive abbots, like Saint Odo (926–946), acquired almost 1,500 dependent cloisters for Cluny and took the lead in various social reform movements. In the late ninth and early tenth centuries, Cluny inspired a series of church decrees called the "Peace of God." This was an attempt to ease the suffering caused by the endemic warfare of medieval society by threatening excommunication for all soldiers who attacked members of non-combatant groups: women, peasants, merchants, and clergy. A "Truce of God" was subsequently proclaimed. It ordered men to abstain from warfare during part of each week (eventually, Wednesday night to Monday morning) and in all holy seasons.

During the reign of Emperor Henry III (r. 1039–1056), Cluniac reformers reached the pinnacle of power. Pope Leo IX (1049–1054) appointed Cluniacs to key administrative posts in Rome, and they encouraged him to suppress simony (the selling of things like church offices) and to enforce celibacy on parish priests. The papacy itself, however, continued to be dominated by powerful laymen. Prior to Leo IX's reign, Henry III had deposed three popes who were the pawns of Rome's aristocratic families and installed his own candidate on the papal throne.

When Henry died, he bequeathed the empire to a son, Henry IV (r. 1056–1106), who was too young to rule. Reform-minded popes took advantage of the weakness of the boy king's regents to assert their independence. Pope Stephen IX (1057–1058) reigned without seeking imperial confirmation of his title. And in 1059, Pope Nicholas II (1059–1061) decreed that a body of high church officials, the college of cardinals, would henceforth choose the pope. This electoral procedure, which is still followed, was designed to prevent the Italian nobility and the German kings from interfering in the choice of popes. It proclaimed the papacy an independent, self-perpetuating ecclesiastical monarchy.

The Investiture Struggle: Gregory VII and Henry IV

It was not until the reign of Pope Gregory VII (1073–1085), a fierce advocate of Cluny's reforms, that the German monarchy was prompted to react to the church's new policies. In 1075, Pope Gregory condemned "lay investiture," the appointment of any clergyman to any church office by a secular ruler, as a form of simony meriting excommunication. The pope's decree attacked the foundations of imperial government. Since the days of Otto I, German kings had preferred to appoint bishops rather than lay nobles to administer state lands. By denying the king the right to appoint men to ecclesiastical office, the pope was denying him the power to choose some of the most important agents of the imperial government. Prohibition of lay investiture proclaimed the spiritual origins of episcopal office, but it did not recognize that the religious offices of the church had long since become entwined with the secular offices of the state.

Henry opposed Gregory's action as a direct challenge to a well-founded tradition on which imperial authority rested. But the pope had important allies. The German nobles were ready to seize any opportunity to undercut the authority of the king who was the chief threat to their independence. Lines of battle were quickly drawn. German bishops loyal to Henry assembled at Worms in January 1076 to repudiate Gregory. Gregory promptly excommunicated Henry and absolved his subjects from their oaths of allegiance to him. This gave the German magnates an excuse to launch a general uprising against their king. Henry had no recourse but to come to terms with Gregory. Henry crossed the Alps in mid-winter to reach Gregory's castle at Canossa. There he reportedly stood barefoot in the snow for three days until the pope agreed to absolve him.

Although the pope appeared to have won, his victory was ephemeral. Henry's absolution deprived his nobles of their excuse for continuing their rebellion. The king regrouped his forces and regained much of his power. In March 1080, Gregory excommunicated Henry once again, but this time the German nobles refused to rise to the bait. Four years later Henry drove Gregory into exile and placed his own man, Clement III, on the papal throne. Clement, however, was never recognized within the church, and Gregory's party regained power during the pontificates of Victor III (1086–1087) and Urban II (1088–1099).

The investiture controversy ended in 1122 with a compromise spelled out by the Concordat of Worms. Emperor Henry V (r. 1106–1125) formally renounced the right to invest bishops. In exchange Pope Calixtus II (1119–1124)

A twelfth-century German manuscript portrays the struggle between Emperor Henry IV and Pope Gregory VII. In the top panel, Henry installs the puppet pope Clement III and drives Gregory from Rome. Below, Gregory dies in exile. The artist was a monk; his sympathies were with Gregory, not Henry. [Thuringer Universitäts- und Landesbibliothek, Jena]

recognized the emperor's right to be present at episcopal consecrations and to invest bishops with fiefs before and after their investment by the church with the ring and staff that symbolized spiritual office. The old church-state "back scratching" continued, but now on different terms that made the church appear, at least, to be an independent organization. The pope's attempts to weaken the emperor did little, however, to guarantee the freedom of the church. The decline of the empire allowed Germany's feudal nobles to fragment their nation and to impose their will on its clergy.

The First Crusades

What the Cluny reform was to the clergy the Crusades to the Holy Land were to the laity: an outlet for the religious zeal and self-confidence that invigorated Europe in the High Middle Ages.

Late in the eleventh century, Alexius I Comnenus, emperor of Constantinople, appealed to the Christian West for help against the Seljuk Turks. At the council of Clermont in 1095, Pope Urban II answered this appeal by proclaiming the First Crusade (see Map 7-1). The Crusade was popular with different people for different reasons. The pope was pleased. By calling the Crusade, he demonstrated his power as the West's spiritual leader and gained leverage in dealing with the Eastern church. European governments were delighted. The departure of large numbers of warring nobles eased the task of maintaining the peace. Hordes of idle, restless noble youths were enthralled. Many were the younger sons of noblemen who, in an age of growing population and limited wealth, had few prospects of obtaining fiefs at home.

Although motives were mixed, the First Crusade owed more to genuine piety than the mercenary ventures organized by the later Crusaders. Popes won recruits by promising Crusaders a plenary indulgence should they die in battle—that is, complete remission of punishment for their unrepented mortal sins and from suffering for them in purgatory. The Crusaders were also driven by the passions of a Holy War, a struggle against a hated infidel for possession of the most sacred Christian shrines. The Crusade was the ultimate pilgrimage to the Holy Land, and the desire to be part of it even affected those who were not going East. It sparked the first massacres of Europe's Jews.

Initial Victory. Three great armies—perhaps 100,000 men—gathered in France, Germany, and Italy, and, by different routes, converged on Constantinople in 1097. They were not the disciplined professional force the East had hoped to enlist in the defense of Christendom. The Eastern emperor suspected their true motives, and the common people whom they pillaged hardly considered them Christian brothers. Nonetheless, these fanatical Crusaders accomplished what no Eastern army had ever been able to do. They defeated one Seljuk army after another and on July 15, 1099, captured Jerusalem. The Crusaders' success was due to the superior military technology the West had

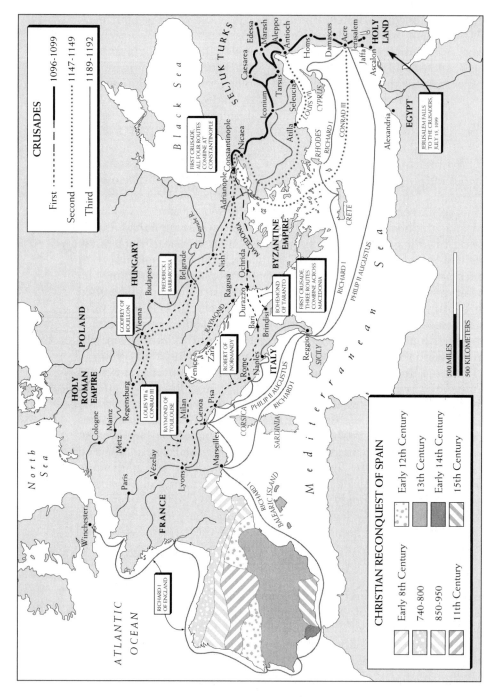

MAP 7-1 The Early Crusades *Routes taken by several leaders of the Crusades during the first century of the movement are shown.*

evolved and to the inability of the Muslim states to cooperate in mounting an effective resistance.

The Crusaders set up governments in Jerusalem, Edessa, and Antioch. Godfrey of Bouillon, leader of the French-German army (and after him his brother Baldwin), ruled over the kingdom of Jerusalem. The pretentious claims of the "Crusader States" ignored the fact that they were little more than precarious European outposts in a Muslim world. This soon became clear as the Muslims rallied and took the offensive against the "savages" who had invaded their lands. The Crusaders responded by erecting castles and hunkering down in a state of perpetual siege. The once fierce warriors became international businessmen promoting trade between East and West. Some, like the Knights Templars, built huge fortunes. The Templars were an order of soldier-monks devoted to protecting pilgrims to the Holy Land. Their services to travelers led them into the profitable fields of banking and money-lending and made their monastic order one of Europe's greatest commercial institutions.

Subsequent Defeat. After forty years, the Latin hold on the East began to weaken. When Edessa fell to Islamic armies in 1144, Bernard of Clairvaux (1091–1153), Christendom's most powerful monastic leader, attempted a rescue by sparking a Second Crusade. It was a dismal failure.

In October 1187 Saladin (r. 1138–1193), king of Egypt and Syria, conquered Jerusalem. Europe responded by declaring a Third Crusade (1189–1192) that enlisted the most powerful western rulers: Emperor Frederick Barbarossa; Richard the Lion-Hearted, king of England; and Philip Augustus, king of France. Despite its promise, the Third Crusade degenerated into a tragicomedy. Frederick Barbarossa accidentally drowned while fording a small stream in Asia Minor. Richard the Lion-Hearted and Philip Augustus reached the outskirts of Jerusalem, but their intense personal rivalry doomed the campaign. Philip Augustus quickly returned to France and preyed on Richard's continental territories. As Richard headed home, he was captured by the Emperor Henry VI. Henry was suspicious of Richard, for Richard's brother-in-law, Henry "the Lion," duke of Saxony, was the emperor's mortal enemy. England's bill for its king's Eastern adventure was greatly increased by the ransom Germany demanded for his release.

Politically and religiously, the Crusades were a failure. The Holy Land remained under Muslim control into the modern era. Economically, however, the Crusades were important. They stimulated western trade with the East. The merchants of Venice, Pisa, and Genoa, who followed in the wake of the Crusaders, successfully challenged Islamic domination of the Mediterranean. Wherever their trading centers sprang up, important cultural as well as economic exchanges were made.

The Pontificate of Innocent III (1198–1216)

The pope who inaugurated the Crusades hoped that they would help to unite Europe in support of the leader of its church. The papal policy of establishing some kind of supremacy over the nations that were emerging in Europe during the High Middle Ages reached its apogee during the reign of Pope Innocent III.

The New Papal Monarchy. Under Innocent, the papacy became a great secular power with a treasury and a bureaucracy equal to that of any king. Innocent increased ecclesiastical taxation—both in amount and in effectiveness of collection. A tax known as Peter's pence was imposed on all but the poorest laymen. The clergy paid the pope an income tax of 2.5 percent—as well as *annates* (the forfeiture to the papacy of one's income during the first year of tenure in a new benefice) and fees for the bestowal of things like the *pallium,* an archbishop's symbol of office. Innocent also reserved to the pope the right to grant absolution for many kinds of sins and religious crimes. (Monetary penalties were frequently imposed.)

Crusades. Innocent did not shrink from using the Crusade, the traditional weapon of the Church against Islam, to suppress dissent in Europe. As the church became increasingly secular and materialistic, critics, whom the church branded heretics, began to speak out. Much heresy was a layman's response to the greed and neglect of duty of the clergy.

In 1209, Innocent launched a Crusade to exterminate the Albigensians (residents of Albi in France), a people also known as the Cathars ("pure ones"). The Cathars advocated a simple, pious way of life modeled on the New Testament's description of Jesus and the apostles. But they rejected important Christian doctrines. They were dualists who denied that the wrathful deity of the Old Testament, who created the sinful material world, was the same god as the spiritual savior to whom Jesus prayed. Their opposition of spirit to flesh led them to oppose the Christian claim that God was incarnate in Jesus—and to suggest that the true church was an invisible, spiritual force, not the worldly institution headed by the pope. The more radical Cathars recommended celibacy, contraception, or abortion to prevent more immortal souls from being imprisoned in sinful matter. But the Cathars' dualism was also used to justify a certain latitude in sexual behavior. (If the flesh and the spirit were fundamentally different, it mattered little what the former did.) The Catholic church's tradition of teaching on social issues like contraception and abortion originated in this environment.

Since the Albigensian lands were wealthy, the nobility from northern France were eager to fight the pope's Crusade. The church gave them a perfect excuse to extend their power into the south. After a succession of massacres and a special campaign led by King Louis VIII of France from 1225 to 1226 utterly devastated the formerly prosperous Albigensian districts, Pope Gregory IX (1227–1241) sent in the Inquisition to root out any heretics who had survived the pogrom. An inquisition was a formal ecclesiastical tribunal for the detection and punishment of heresy. Bishops had used inquisitions since the mid-twelfth century to maintain diocesan discipline, but Innocent

III had created a centralized court of inquisition to dispatch papal legates to preside at trials and executions anywhere in Europe.

Innocent was also responsible for the fourth of the Crusades intended for the Holy Land. In 1202, some 30,000 Crusaders gathered in Venice, planning to sail for Egypt. Many of the Crusaders were poor soldiers of fortune, and they were unable to pay the price the Venetians demanded for their transport. Venice persuaded them to work off their passage by conquering Zara, a Christian city that was one of Venice's commercial rivals. To the shock of Pope Innocent III, the Crusaders obliged and, in 1204, allowed Venice to seduce them into storming the most important Christian city in the East: Constantinople.

Although the assault on Constantinople was an embarrassment to the pope, the papacy came to terms with the Venetians and shared the spoils. One of Innocent's confidants became patriarch of Constantinople and launched a mission to win the Greeks and the Slavs to the Roman church. Westerners retained control of Constantinople until 1261, when the Genoese, who envied Venice's coup, helped the exiled Eastern emperor, Michael Paleologus, recapture the city. The half-century of occupation did nothing to improve relations between East and West.

The Fourth Lateran Council. At the Fourth Lateran Council, which met in 1215, Innocent defined crucial disciplines and doctrines that the church was to enforce throughout Europe. Most significant for the development of Catholicism was the council's endorsement of the doctrine of transubstantiation as the church's explanation of the Mass. Transubstantiation is the belief that, at the moment of priestly consecration, the bread and wine of the Lord's Supper become the body and blood of Christ. This idea was consistent with the popular piety of the twelfth century. But since the power to perform this miracle was reserved to priests, it also contributed to Innocent's campaign to extend the clergy's control over the laity. The latter goal was reflected, as well, in the council's formalization of the sacrament of Penance and its order that, henceforth, every adult Christian was to confess and take communion at least once a year—at Easter.

Franciscans and Dominicans. The interest of the laity in religious devotion was particularly intense at the turn of the twelfth century. It helped fuel heretical movements—particularly those, like the Waldensians, Beguines, and Beghards, that preached a life of poverty in imitation of Christ. This idea was not necessarily heretical, but it could promote criticism of the established church, and it caused Innocent deep concern.

By licensing two new religious orders, the Franciscans and the Dominicans, Innocent fought fire with fire. Unlike the regular monks, these orders of *friars* ("brothers") were *mendicants* ("beggars"). Refusing to accept land and endowments, they stayed in the world, preaching and caring for the poor and supporting themselves by begging and working. Their saintly behavior did much to refute the heretics who argued that Christian unworldliness was incompatible with obedience to the orthodox church. These *tertiaries,* or "Third Orders," provided refuges for pious laymen and laywomen whose desire to live according to high religious ideals might otherwise have tempted them into heresies.

The Franciscan Order was founded in 1210 by Saint Francis of Assisi (1182–1226), the son of a rich cloth merchant. The Dominican Order, the Order of Preachers, was founded in 1216 by Saint Dominic (1170–1221), a well-educated Spanish cleric. Both orders reported directly to the pope, not to any local bishop. They thus provided the central government of the church with an army of dedicated servants who could be dispatched on all kinds of missions.

Pope Gregory IX (1227–1241) canonized Saint Francis only two years after Francis's death. But the pope also turned the Franciscans from the path their founder had marked out for them. The pope declared that a nomadic life of strict poverty and extreme asceticism was both impractical and unbiblical. Most Franciscans accepted the pope's modification of their order's rule, but a radical branch, the Spiritual Franciscans, resisted and drifted into heresy.

The Dominicans dedicated themselves to combating heresy. They preached, staffed the offices of the Inquisition, and taught at the universities. The man who did the most to further their mission was the great theologian, Saint Thomas Aquinas (d. 1274). His synthesis of faith and reason has been embraced by the Catholic Church as the definitive statement of its beliefs.

~ England and France: Hastings (1066) to Bouvines (1214)

While Germany and Italy were engaged in struggles between popes and emperors, new dynasties were establishing themselves in England and France. They laid the foundations for medieval Europe's strongest nations.

As the Roman Empire fell, German tribes known as Anglo-Saxons took possession of the old Roman province of Britain. England ("Anglo-land") was named for them. The last of the Anglo-Saxon kings of England, Edward the Confessor, died childless in 1066. Because Edward had a Norman mother and owed a personal debt of gratitude to the Norman ducal house, he favored William, duke of Normandy (d. 1087), as his successor. But the Anglo-Saxon assembly—which, in accordance with the ancient traditions of the German tribes, had the right to enthrone kings—preferred a native son. It chose Harold Godwinsson. This prompted William to invade England, and at Hastings on October 14, 1066, he destroyed Harold and decimated the Anglo-Saxon nobility.

William the Conqueror

By judiciously combining continental feudalism and Anglo-Saxon custom, William constructed the most effective monarchy in Europe. He assessed the value of his realm by commissioning a county-by-county survey of its people, animals, and implements—a detailed accounting known as the *Domesday*

William the Conqueror on horseback urging his troops into combat with the English at the Battle of Hastings (October 14, 1066). From the Bayeux Tapestry, about 1073–1083. [Giraudon/Art Resource, N.Y.]

Book (1080–1086). He compelled every man of property to become his vassal. (Legal title to land required that it be held as a fief from the king.) Since the Norman nobles who replaced the Anglo-Saxon magnates had no following among their subjects and had to stick together to survive, they seldom asserted their independence. William kept unique Anglo-Saxon tax and court systems that contributed to the centralization of political authority. And he honored the Anglo-Saxon tradition of "parleying"—that is, of holding conferences between the king and the people who had vested interests in royal policies. By consulting with his nobles on affairs of state, William kept England on track toward the creation of the parliamentary traditions that have shaped the constitutions of so many modern nations.

Henry II

The English monarchy continued strong under William's sons and heirs, William Rufus (r. 1087–1100), and Henry I (r. 1100–1135). When Henry died without a male heir, a civil war erupted that threatened to undo the Conqueror's work. But a compromise between the factions resulted in the accession of Henry II (r. 1154–1189), son of the duke of Anjou and Matilda, daughter of Henry I. Henry II established the Plantagenet dynasty, the family name of the Angevin (or Anjouan) kings who ruled England until the death of Richard III in 1485. Henry, by his own rights of inheritance and those of his wife, Eleanor of Aquitaine (ca. 1122–1204), brought virtually the entire west coast of France under control of the English king.

In addition to ruling much of France (as a nominal vassal of the king of France), Henry conquered a part of Ireland and made the king of Scotland take an oath of homage to him. The French king, Louis VII, who had good reason to fear these developments, tried to contain the English or drive them from the continent. This policy was finally successful—but not until the mid-fifteenth century and the end of the Hundred Years' War.

Eleanor of Aquitaine and Court Culture

Eleanor of Aquitaine, who divorced King Louis VII of France shortly before she married King Henry II of England in 1152, was a powerful influence on the politics and culture of both nations. Women of Eleanor's generation were beginning to venture into the masculine fields of politics and business, and she set them an example. She insisted on accompanying her first husband on the Second Crusade, and she stirred up so much trouble for her second that from 1179 until his death in 1189 he kept her under house arrest.

After marrying Henry, Eleanor settled in Angers, the chief town of Anjou. There, her court became a center of patronage for musicians and poets. The troubadour Bernart de Ventadorn composed many of the most popular love songs of the period in her honor. From 1154 to 1170, the queen resided in England, but then she separated from Henry and moved to Poitiers to live with her daughter Marie, the countess of Champagne. Poitiers popularized a new fad among the aristocracy: "courtly love." The troubadours who developed the art composed erotic stories that satirized carnal love or depicted it with tragic irony. Carnal love was contrasted with "courteous" love, a passion for a lady that ennobled her lover. Chrétien de Troyes's stories of King Arthur and the Knights of the Round Table—of Sir Lancelot's secret and illicit love for Arthur's wife, Guinevere—are the most famous products of the movement.

Popular Rebellion and Magna Carta

Henry II was a strong king who believed in autocratic monarchy. He insisted that the church operate within parameters set by the state and spelled out his expectations in the *Constitutions of Clarendon* (1164). The *Constitutions* limited the right to appeal cases from England to the papal court, subjected clergy to the king's courts, and gave the king control over the election of bishops. The archbishop of Canterbury, Thomas à Becket (1118?–1170), who was once Henry's compliant chancellor, fled England rather than accept the *Constitutions*. He was induced to return in 1170; that year his continued resistance to the king prompted some of Henry's men to assassinate him. The church leapt at the opportunity to canonize Becket (1172) and to use his martyrdom to bolster its case for freedom from state control.

Henry was followed on the throne by two of his sons: Richard the Lion-Hearted (r. 1189–1199) and John (r. 1199–1216). Neither was a success. Richard imposed ruinous taxation to fund the disastrous Third Crusade and died fighting to recover lands he had lost to the French while he was in the East. In 1209, Pope Innocent III excommunicated his successor, John, in a dispute over the appointment of an archbishop for Canterbury. To extricate himself from a mess of his own making and to win support for a war with France, John gave

The English Nobility Imposes Restraints on King John

The construction of a sound constitutional monarchy for England in the Middle Ages required the king's willingness to share power. He had to be strong but could not act as a despot or rule by fiat. When the danger of despotism became acute in England during the reign of King John, the English nobility forced him to endorse Magna Carta—a reaffirmation of traditional rights and personal liberties, principles still enshrined in English law.

⌇ Does Magna Carta protect basic rights, or does it grant special privileges? Do the rights that it outlines indicate that a common sense of what was "fair" shaped the political thinking of medieval people? Would the granting of the rights mentioned here have strengthened or weakened the king?

A free man shall not be fined for a small offense, except in proportion to the gravity of the offense; and for a great offense he shall be fined in proportion to the magnitude of the offense, saving his freehold [property]; and a merchant in the same way, saving his merchandise; and the villein [a free serf, bound only to his lord] shall be fined in the same way, saving his wainage [wagon], if he shall be at [the king's] mercy. And none of the above fines shall be imposed except by the oaths of honest men of the neighborhood. . . .

No constable or other bailiff of [the king's] shall take anyone's grain or other chattels without immediately paying for them in money, unless he is able to obtain a postponement at the good will of the seller.

No constable shall require any knight to give money in place of his ward of a castle [i.e., standing guard], if he is willing to furnish that ward in his own person, or through another honest man, if he himself is not able to do it for a reasonable cause; and if we shall lead or send him into the army, he shall be free from ward in proportion to the amount of time which he has been in the army through us.

No sheriff or bailiff of [the king], or any one else, shall take horses or wagons of any free man, for carrying purposes, except on the permission of that free man.

Neither we nor our bailiffs will take the wood of another man for castles, or for anything else which we are doing, except by the permission of him to whom the wood belongs. . . .

No free man shall be taken, or imprisoned, or dispossessed, or outlawed, or banished, or in any way injured, nor will we go upon him, nor send upon him, except by the legal judgment of his peers, or by the law of the land.

To no one will we sell, to no one will we deny or delay, right or justice.

James Harvey Robinson (ed.), Readings in European History, Vol. I (Boston: Athenaeum, 1904), pp. 236–237.

in to the pope—even declaring his kingdom a papal fief. John's efforts to restore his father's Angevin empire foundered, however, when his armies were defeated by the French at Bouvines in 1214. John's disillusioned barons rebelled and forced him to agree to limitations on royal authority.

A document called simply Magna Carta ("Great Charter") spelled out the terms that John and his subjects agreed to in 1215. Among other things, the king promised not to arrest and hold people without giving his reasons, and he acknowledged the necessity of consulting with representatives of the propertied classes before imposing new taxes. Magna Carta intended to put some constraints on monarchy, but not to weaken it fatally. In the short run, it had little effect, for John's successors largely ignored it. But Magna Carta helped keep alive the traditions that undergird modern English law.

Philip II Augustus

In England during the High Middle Ages, the propertied classes had to fight a strong monarchy to secure their rights. In France the shoe was on the other foot. There, weak kings were confronted by powerful subjects who opposed the development of a strong monarchy.

In 987, when the Carolingian line came to an end in France, the French nobles chose Hugh Capet, count of Paris, to be king. Although his descendants managed to hang on to the title—and to create a Capetian dynasty—for the next two centuries the great feudal princes were France's real rulers. The early Capetian kings even had to struggle to win effective control of the royal domain, the area around Paris and the Île-de-France to the northeast. But by the reign of Philip II (1180–1223), Paris had become the center of French government and culture; the Capetians had secure hereditary rights to the crown; and it was possible for the kings of France to begin to impose their will on their vassals, the French nobles.

In a way the Norman conquest of England in 1066 helped the Capetian kings to unify France and build a true national monarchy. As the Plantagenet dynasty extended its control over French territory, the Capetian kings were able to enlist support from powerful nobles who considered the English king the greater threat to their independence. The Capetians also won the support of the wealthy merchant class that had begun to develop in France's reviving cities.

The king of England was at some disadvantage in dealing with the king of France, for, as duke of Normandy, he was a vassal of the French king. A skillful politician, like Philip II Augustus, was able to exploit the ambiguity of that relationship. By accusing his English rival of violating the duties of vassalage, Philip could enlist his other vassals in efforts to reclaim the English king's French fiefs. During the reigns of kings Richard the Lion-Hearted and John, France's armies seized all the territories the English had occupied on the French coast (with the exception of Aquitaine).

King John of England enlisted the help of the Holy Roman Emperor Otto IV (r. 1198–1215) against France in what became Europe's first multinational war. The French decisively won the crucial battle at Bouvines in Flanders on July 27, 1214. The victory encouraged the people of France to unite in support of their king. The defeat so weakened Otto IV that he fell from power in

Germany. And John's subjects welcomed him home with the rebellion that culminated in Magna Carta.

～ France in the Thirteenth Century: The Reign of Louis IX

The growth of Capetian royal power under Philip Augustus seemed to receive divine confirmation during the reign of his grandson Louis IX (r. 1226–1270). Louis, who was canonized shortly after his death, embodied the medieval view of the perfect ruler. The saintly king was an ascetic whose moral character was far superior to the ethics of his royal and papal contemporaries. But he was also what his generation expected a king to be, a decisive leader and an enthusiastic soldier.

Generosity Abroad

Some of Louis's decisions suggest naiveté or an overly scrupulous conscience. In 1259, he negotiated the Treaty of Paris to end the long-simmering dispute between England and France. Although he could have driven the English off the continent, he refused to take advantage of King Henry III's weakness. Had he ruthlessly confiscated English territories on the French coast, he might have prevented the resumption of hostilities between the two nations and spared Europe the bloodshed of the Hundred Years' War.

Louis earned the gratitude of the papacy by remaining officially aloof during its struggle with Frederick II, an emperor from Germany's Hohenstaufen dynasty. But Louis's brother, Charles of Anjou, did the pope a great service by attacking imperial lands in Italy and Sicily. Charles was crowned king of Sicily in Rome, and his subsequent defeat of the son and grandson of Frederick II ended the Hohenstaufen dynasty. For such service to the church, by both action and inaction, the Capetian kings of the thirteenth century received many papal favors.

Order and Excellence at Home

Louis's greatest achievement was to improve the government of France. Louis used the efficient bureaucracy that his predecessors had developed to exploit their subjects to promote order and justice. He commissioned auditors (*enquêteurs*) to monitor royal officials—especially the *baillis* and *prévôts* whom Philip Augustus had appointed to run the government's grass-roots offices. He abolished private wars and serfdom within the royal domain. He gave his subjects the judicial right of appeal from local to higher courts, and he made the tax system more equitable. The services the French people received from their king generated enthusiasm for the monarchy and for the nationhood it symbolized.

French national identity was strengthened by other developments that took place during Louis's reign. His was the golden age of Scholasticism, when thinkers like Thomas Aquinas and the Franciscan scholar Bonaventure made the University of Paris the intellectual center of Europe. France became the showcase for monastic reform, chivalry, and the new Gothic style in art and architecture that had been popularized by Suger, abbot of St. Denis and advisor to Louis VII (d. 1180). French culture began to set the standard for Europe, a pattern that continued into the modern era.

Louis's virtues reflected medieval ideals of kingship. He was something of a religious fanatic. He supported the work of the Inquisition in France. And he personally sponsored and led the last two of the great Crusades for the Holy Land. Both were failures. But Louis's death of a fever during the second of his holy wars only enhanced his reputation as a saintly king. His successors pointed to him to confirm their claim that God had bestowed on their house a divine right to rule.

∼ The Hohenstaufen Empire (1152–1272)

During the twelfth and thirteenth centuries, stable governments developed in both England and France. The situation within the Holy Roman Empire (Germany, Burgundy, and northern Italy) was very different. There (see Map 7-2), disunity and blood feuding created a legacy of political fragmentation that endured into modern times.

Frederick I Barbarossa

The Investiture Controversy, in which the popes had challenged the right of emperors to appoint the higher clergy, had weakened Germany's kings and strengthened its barons. After the Concordat of Worms, the German princes dominated episcopal appointments and exploited their rich endowments.

Imperial authority revived, however, with the accession to the throne of Frederick I Barbarossa (r. 1152–1190), founder of the Hohenstaufen dynasty. There were some developments that helped Frederick lay a strong foundation for a new empire. Disaffection with the incessant squabbling of the feudal princes was widespread. There was growing resentment of the theocratic pretensions of the papacy. And at the University of Bologna a scholar named Irnerius (d. 1125) was reviving the study of Roman law (Justinian's *Code*). Roman law promoted the centralization of states, and it provided a secular foundation for imperial power that minimized the significance of coronation by the pope.

Frederick's base of operation was in Switzerland, the bridge between Germany and Italy. He was relatively successful in regaining control over the German nobility. In 1180 his strongest rival, Henry the Lion (d. 1195), duke of Saxony, fell from power and was exiled to Normandy. Although Frederick was not strong enough to intervene in the internal affairs of Germany's great duchies, he was vigilant in enforcing his rights as their feudal overlord. This

MAP 7-2 Germany and Italy in the Middle Ages
The Holy Roman Empire embraced hundreds of independent territories that the emperor ruled only in name. The papacy controlled the area around Rome and tried to enforce its will on Romagna. Under the Hohenstaufens (mid-twelfth to mid-thirteenth centuries), German rulers briefly extended their power to southern Italy and Sicily.

strategy was designed to keep memories of royal authority alive until the king was strong enough to confront his greater vassals.

Italy proved to be the great obstacle to fulfillment of Frederick's imperial plans. In 1155, Frederick restored Pope Adrian IV (1154–1159) to power in Rome after a religious revolutionary, Arnold of Brescia (d. 1155), had wrested the city away from him. Frederick's reward was a papal coronation, which he believed gave him the right to rule Italy. Although the imperial Diet of Roncaglia in 1158 gave official sanction to Frederick's Italian claims, the Italian people, particularly those of Lombardy, refused to accept the governors he appointed.

As this challenge to royal authority was occurring, one of Europe's most skilled lawyers, Cardinal Roland, was elected Pope Alexander III (1159–1181). Frederick soon found himself at war with the pope, the city of Milan, and the kingdom of Sicily. In 1167, the combined forces of the northern Italian cities drove him back into Germany, and a decade later (1176) Italian forces soundly defeated him at Legnano. In the Peace of Constance in 1183 Frederick at last recognized the claims of the Lombard cities to rights of self-rule.

Henry VI and the Sicilian Connection

Frederick's reign ended with stalemate in Germany and defeat in Italy. But in the last years of his life, he discovered a new opportunity for his dynasty. The Norman ruler of the kingdom of Sicily, William II (r. 1166–1189), who wanted to be free to mount a campaign for the conquest of Constantinople, asked Frederick for an alliance. In 1186, the treaty was sealed by a marriage between Frederick's son, the future Henry VI (r. 1190–1197), and Constance, heiress to Sicily.

Sicily was a fatal acquisition for the Hohenstaufen kings. It tempted them to sacrifice their traditional territorial base in northern Europe for projects in Italy, and it inflamed resistance to them in Italy. By encircling Rome the Hohenstaufens convinced the popes that the survival of the church hinged on the destruction of the empire.

When Henry VI came to the throne in 1190, he faced a multitude of enemies: a hostile papacy; supremely independent German princes; and an England whose adventurous king, Richard the Lion-Hearted, was encouraged to plot against Henry by the exiled duke of Saxony, Henry the Lion. In 1194, Constance bore her husband a son, the future Frederick II. To strengthen his dynasty, Henry campaigned vigorously for recognition of the boy's hereditary right to the imperial throne. The German princes were reluctant to abandon the custom of electing emperors, but what Henry could offer them in exchange was recognition of full hereditary rights to their own fiefs. The encircled papacy was determined to prevent this and anything else that might secure Hohenstaufen power.

Otto IV and the Welf Interregnum

Henry died in September 1197, after arranging for young Frederick to become a ward of the papacy. Henry's brother, Philip of Swabia, claimed the title of

German king, but the Welf family, enemies of the Hohenstaufens, backed a rival, Otto of Brunswick—the son of the troublesome Henry the Lion. Richard of England supported Otto; the French supported the Hohenstaufens; and the papacy switched its allegiance back and forth to prevent anyone from surrounding Rome. The result was anarchy and civil war.

Otto outlasted Philip and won general recognition in Germany and coronation as emperor by Pope Innocent III (1198–1215). Within four months of his coronation (October 1209), the wind changed. An attack on Sicily convinced Innocent that Otto was trying to surround Rome. The pope promptly excommunicated him and raised up a rival claimant to his throne.

Frederick II

Pope Innocent's ward, the Hohenstaufen prince Frederick, was now of age, and unlike Otto he had a hereditary claim to the throne. In December 1212 the pope, Philip Augustus of France, and Otto's German enemies arranged for Frederick to be crowned king of the Romans in Mainz. When Philip Augustus defeated the armies of Otto and John of England at the battle of Bouvines in 1214, the way was cleared for Emperor Frederick II to mount the throne in Charlemagne's imperial city of Aachen (1215). The young ruler's allies probably expected him to be their puppet, but he quickly demonstrated an independent streak.

Frederick, who had grown up in Sicily, disliked Germany. He spent only nine of the thirty-eight years of his reign in Germany, and he wanted only one thing from the German princes: the imperial title for himself and his sons. To secure it, he was willing to allow Germany's feudal nobility to become the undisputed lords of their domains. Frederick's lack of interest in building a centralized monarchy for Germany halted the development of the nation and condemned it to six centuries of chaotic disunity.

Frederick's policy with respect to the papacy was equally disastrous. The popes, who excommunicated Frederick four times, came to view him as the Antichrist, the biblical beast of the Apocalypse whose persecution of the faithful signaled the end of the world. Although Frederick abandoned Germany, he was determined to unite Lombardy with his Sicilian kingdom and surround Rome. This the popes were determined to prevent.

The popes won the fight with the Hohenstaufens, but their victory was Pyrrhic. The contest led Pope Innocent IV (1243–1254) to launch the church into European politics on a massive scale. Wholesale secularization increased criticism of the church by religious reformers and the royal advocates of nationalism. Innocent organized and led the German princes against Frederick, and German and Italian resistance kept Frederick on the defensive throughout his last years.

When Frederick died in 1250, the German monarchy died with him. The German nobility repudiated the idea of hereditary succession to the German monarchy and, in 1257, established an electoral college with power to bestow the title "king of the Romans." This ensured that their king would be their puppet.

Manfred, Frederick's illegitimate son, fought hard to save something of the Hohenstaufen legacy, but he was defeated in 1266. In 1286 Charles of Anjou, the adventurous brother of the sainted French king Louis IX, destroyed the last of the Hohenstaufens, Frederick's grandson Conradin. With their disappearance, Germany temporarily ceased to meddle in Italy's affairs. But the field was not left to the papal monarchy and the Italian magnates. France and, to a lesser extent, England aspired to the role Germany had tried to play in Italy.

～ Medieval Russia

According to legend, Prince Vladimir (972–1015) of Kiev, early Russia's greatest city, decided to modernize his people by converting them to one of the world's great religions. After receiving delegations from Muslims, Roman Catholics, Jews, and Greek Orthodox Christians, Vladimir chose Greek Orthodoxy. Given Kiev's proximity to Constantinople and Russia's commercial ties with the Byzantine Empire, the choice must have been a foregone conclusion.

Politics and Society

Vladimir's successor, Yaroslav the Wise (1016–1054), developed Kiev into a magnificent political and cultural center with buildings rivaling those of Constantinople. After his death, however, rivalry among the Russian princes split their people into three groups: the Great Russians, the White Russians, and the Little Russians (Ukrainians). Kiev became simply one principality among many.

The governments of the Russian principalities combined monarchy (a prince), aristocracy (a council of noblemen), and democracy (a popular assembly of all adult males). The broadest social division was between freemen and slaves. Freemen included clergy, army officers, boyars (wealthy landowners), townsmen, and peasants. Slaves were mostly prisoners of war. There was also a large semi-free group composed of debtors working off their obligations.

Mongol Rule (1243–1480)

In the thirteenth century, Mongol (or Tatar) armies swept over China, much of the Islamic world, and Russia. Ghengis Khan (1155–1227) invaded Russia in 1223, and Kiev fell to Batu Khan in 1240. When the Mongols divided their empire, a group called the *Golden Horde* (a name derived from the Tatar words for the color of Batu Khan's tent) exacted tribute from the Russian cities. The Golden Horde established its capital at Sarai on the lower Volga and ruled the steppe region of what is now southern Russia. Its agents were stationed in all the principal Russian towns to oversee taxation and the conscription of soldiers.

Mongol rule distanced the Russians from Western culture. The Mongols intermarried with the Russians, and the Russian women who were influenced by Islam, the religion adopted by the Golden Horde, began to wear veils and to lead more secluded lives. The Mongols, however, left Russian political institutions and religion largely intact. They maintained peace, and their far-flung trade contacts brought most Russians greater prosperity than they had enjoyed before.

Russian Liberation

The princes of Moscow, who assisted the Mongols with the collection of tribute, grew wealthy in the service of their masters. When Mongol rule began to weaken, the princes started to add to the territory controlled by Moscow. In a process that has come to be known as "the gathering of the Russian Land," they expanded the principality of Moscow by purchase, colonization, and conquest.

In 1380, Grand Duke Dimitri of Moscow (1350–1389) defeated Tatar forces at Kulikov Meadow. His victory marked the beginning of the decline of Mongol hegemony. Another century passed before Ivan III, ("the Great," d. 1505), brought all of northern Russia under Moscow's control and ended Mongol rule (1480). By the last quarter of the fourteenth century, Moscow had become the political and religious center of Russia. And in 1453, when Constantinople fell to the Turks, Moscow proclaimed itself the "third Rome," the guardian of Orthodox civilization.

With its borders finally secured at the start of the High Middle Ages, western Europe was free to develop its characteristic cultural and political institutions. The map of Europe as it appears today began to take shape. England and France developed centralized monarchies that unified them as modern nation-states. But Germany and Italy failed to coalesce.

The dream of creating a Holy Roman Empire tempted German rulers into Italy, *where they made enemies of the popes and the rising commercial cities. The result was an unprecedented contest between church and state that drove the church to establish a powerful papal monarchy. The church's involvement with politics alienated kings, secularized the papacy, and increased the church's vulnerability to the attacks of religious reformers.*

⌒ Review Questions

1. How did the Saxon king Otto I rebuild the German Empire? How did he establish control over the various German duchies? How did he use the church to achieve his political goals? Does he deserve to be called "the Great"?

2. What were the main reasons for the Cluny reform movement? How do you account for its success? What was the impact

of the reform on the subsequent history of the medieval church?

3. In the dispute between Pope Gregory VII and King Henry IV over the issue of lay investiture, what were the causes of the controversy, the actions of the contending parties, and the outcome of the struggle? What was at stake for each of the disputants, and what were the ramifications of the confict?

4. What did Voltaire, the eighteenth-century French intellectual, mean when he said that the Holy Roman Empire was neither holy nor Roman? Do you agree with him?

5. What developments in western and eastern Europe promoted the crusading movement? Why did the Crusaders fail to establish lasting political and religious control over the Holy Land? What impact did the Crusaders have on the West's politics, religion, and economics? Which of its outcomes do you consider most important? Why?

6. Why does Hohenstaufen rule deserve to be remembered as a disaster for Germany? What factors prevented German consolidation during the Hohenstaufen era? If France and England could coalesce into reasonably strong states, why was Germany not able to do the same?

∼ Suggested Readings

J. W. BALDWIN, *The Government of Philip Augustus* (1986). An important scholarly work.

G. BARRACLOUGH, *The Origins of Modern Germany* (1946). Dated but penetrating political narrative setting modern Germany in the perspective of the Middle Ages.

G. BARRACLOUGH, *The Medieval Papacy* (1968). Brief survey with pictures.

H. E. J. COWDREY, *Popes, Monks, and Crusaders* (1984). Re-creation of the atmosphere that gave birth to the Crusades.

R. H. C. DAVIS, *A History of Medieval Europe: From Constantine to St. Louis*, part 2 (1972). Succinct, lucid survey.

E. H. KANTOROWICZ, *The King's Two Bodies* (1957). Controversial analysis of political concepts in the High Middle Ages.

H. LEYSER, *Hermits and the New Monasticism: A Study of Religious Communities in Western Europe, 1000–1150* (1984). The new power and influence of reformed monasticism.

H. E. MAYER, *The Crusades*, trans. by John Gilligham (1972). Extremely detailed; the best one-volume account.

J. B. MORRALL, *Political Thought in Medieval Times* (1962). Readable and illuminating account.

C. PETIT-DUTAILLIS, *The Feudal Monarchy in France and England from the Tenth to the Thirteenth Century*, trans. by E. D. Hunt (1964). Political narrative in great detail.

I. SPECTOR, *Russia: A New History* (1935). Admirable simplicity.

B. TIERNEY, *The Crisis of Church and State* (1964). Extremely useful collection of key documents.

G. VERNADSKY, *A History of Russia*, I–IV (1946–1963). A graspable magisterial survey.

S. WILLIAMS (ed.), *The Gregorian Epoch: Reformation, Revolution, Reaction* (1964). Scholarly debate over Gregory's reign.

8

The High Middle Ages(1000–1300): People,Towns, and Universities

The Traditional Order of Life
Nobles
Clergy
Peasants

Towns and Townspeople
The Chartering of Towns
The Rise of Merchants
Challenging the Old Lords
Problems of Self-Government
Towns and Kings

Schools and Universities
University of Bologna
Cathedral Schools
University of Paris
The Curriculum

Gender and Family
Women
Children

KEY TOPICS IN THIS CHAPTER
~ The major groups composing medieval society
~ The rise of towns and a new merchant class
~ The founding of universities and educational curriculum
~ How women and children fared in the Middle Ages

From the tenth to the twelfth centuries, the effects of increasing political stability were felt in Europe. Agricultural production increased, population exploded, and trade and urban life revived. The contacts with foreign lands promoted by the Crusades stimulated both economic and cultural development. A new merchant class, the ancestors of modern capitalists, evolved to serve the West's growing markets, and an urban proletariat appeared.

Guided by Muslim intellectuals, Western scholars began once again to study classical literature. Schools and universities opened. Literacy increased among the laity, and the twelfth century witnessed a true renaissance. The creative vigor of the new European civilization was proclaimed by the awesome Gothic churches that were the supreme products of its art and science.

⌇ The Traditional Order of Life

Medieval political theorists identified three services that were essential for society's functioning. Each was assigned to a separate class: protection (the knights and landed nobility), prayer (clergy), and production (peasants and village artisans). The revival of towns in the eleventh century created a fourth class: traders and merchants. They were thought of as a "middle" class, for they combined features of both the laboring and the propertied classes. Like the peasantry, they were economically productive, but they did not work the land. Like the nobility and clergy, they were rich, but they were not associated with the institutions of feudal government. Their appearance produced a crack in the old social order that ultimately led to its collapse.

Nobles

As medieval culture evolved, a landed aristocracy, with special social and legal status, evolved from the ranks of feudal vassals or warrior knights. In the late Middle Ages the aristocratic class was composed of a higher and lower nobility. The higher were the great landowners and territorial magnates; the lower were petty knights with fiefs, newly rich merchants who bought country estates, and wealthy farmers whose prosperity raised them from serfdom. Land was important, for it was the special mark of the nobility that they lived off the labor of others. Nobles were lords of manors who neither tilled the soil nor engaged in commerce—activities considered beneath the dignity of aristocrats.

Warriors. In the eighth century, European warfare changed dramatically. The appearance of the stirrup enabled cavalry to rout the infantry that had dominated ancient battlefields. The stirrup gave a rider a firm mount so that he could charge an enemy and strike a blow without lofting himself off his horse. Cavalry equipment and training was expensive, so lords divided their lands up into fiefs to support the vassals who staffed their armies. Arms thus became the nobleman's profession and war the justification for his way of life.

The code by which the nobility lived exalted strength, honor, and aggression. Nobles welcomed war as an opportunity for enhancing their fortunes by plunder and their reputations by acts of courage. Peace meant economic stagnation and boredom. Peasants and townspeople, on the other hand, needed peace in order to prosper. Consequently, the interests of the classes conflicted, and the nobility looked down on the commoners as cowards.

The quasi-sacramental ceremony of dubbing marked entrance into the noble class. A candidate for knighthood took a bath of ritual purification, confessed, communed, and maintained a night-long prayer vigil. A priest then blessed his standard, lance, and sword and girded him with the weapons he was to use in the defense of the church and the service of his lord. Dubbing on the shoulders with the sword by a senior knight raised the candidate to a state as sacred in his sphere as clerical ordination made the priest in his.

In the twelfth century, knighthood was legally restricted to men of high birth. The closing of the ranks of the nobility was a reaction to the growing wealth and power of the social-climbing commercial classes. Kings, however, preserved some social mobility by elevating anyone they wanted to knighthood. The sale of titles to wealthy merchants was an important source of revenue.

Way of Life. When not at war, noblemen honed their military skills at hunts and tournaments. Their passion for hunting was so great that they forbade commoners to take game from the forests. The peasantry greatly resented being deprived of a source of free food, and resentment of the nobility's monopoly of the forests contributed to the peasant uprisings of the late medieval period.

Tournaments sowed different seeds of social disruption. Mock battles, intended as military training, tended to get out of hand—resulting in serious bloodshed and animosity among the combatants. The church opposed tournaments as occasions for pagan revelry and senseless violence. Kings and princes also finally concluded that they were a danger to public order. Henry II of England proscribed them in the twelfth century, but they continued in France until the mid-sixteenth century.

During the twelfth century, distinctive standards for conduct at court ("courtesy") began to be imposed on vassals when they attended their lords. Thanks to the influence of powerful women like Henry II's queen, Eleanor of Aquitaine, court etiquette became almost as important as battlefield expertise.

Knights were expected to be literate gentlemen, capable of praising ladies in lyric poetry. Although the poetry of courtly love was sprinkled with frank eroticism and courtly poets wrote rapturously of women married to other men, the love that ennobled them was usually not said to be the kind consummated by sexual intercourse. Court poets condemned illicit carnal love as a source of suffering as much as joy, and the courtly love movement may have been an attempt to curtail the notorious philandering of the noble classes.

Social Divisions. The noble class was composed of many different kinds of noblemen, and some were superior to others. Status within the nobility was a function of how much authority one had over others; a chief with many vassals obviously far outranked the small country nobleman who was lord over none but himself.

The social hierarchy that existed within the nobility affected the ranking of their servants. Chief stewards, charged to oversee a lord's manor and the education of his children, became powerful "lords" within their delegated "domains." In time the social superiority of the higher ranks of domestic servants was legally recognized, for medieval law acknowledged the privileges of wealth and power wherever they appeared.

In the late Middle Ages there were shifts in wealth and power that sent the landed nobility into a decline from which it never recovered. Climatic changes depressed the agricultural economy that was the source of its wealth, and famines and plagues caused massive demographic dislocations. Changing military tactics rendered noble cavalry nearly obsolete. And wealthy towns helped kings curtail the power of the nobles in local government. After the fourteenth century, possession of land and wealth counted far more than family tree as a qualification for entrance into the highest social class.

Clergy

Unlike the nobility and the peasantry, the rank of clergy was acquired by training and ordination, not by birth. Consequently, people of talent could climb the clerical hierarchy, a ladder of social mobility for gifted individuals.

Secular and Regular Clerics. There were two clerical vocations: secular and regular. The *secular* clergy lived and worked among the laity in the world *(saeculum).* The most prestigious of them were wealthy cardinals, archbishops, and bishops, recruited almost exclusively from the nobility. Below them in rank were the urban priests, the cathedral canons, and the court clerks. At the bottom of the clerical hierarchy was the great mass of poor parish priests, who were neither financially nor intellectually superior to the lay people they served. Until the eleventh century, parish priests routinely lived with women in a relationship akin to marriage, and stretched their meager incomes by "moonlighting" as teachers, artisans, or farmers. This practice was accepted and even admired by their parishioners.

Regular clergy were monks who lived under the rule *(regula)* of a cloister. By retreating from the world and adopting rigorous ascetic disciplines, monks attempted to emulate the suffering of Christ. Since they practiced what their contemporaries believed to be the ideal Christian way of life, they were respected, influential persons. The regular clergy (including nuns who, as women, were not strictly entitled to clerical rank) were never completely cut off from the secular world. They maintained contact with the laity through charitable activities (such as feeding the destitute and tending the sick), as instructors in monastic schools, and as supplemental preachers and confessors in parish churches. Some monks of great learning and rhetorical skill rose to prominence as secretaries and private confessors to kings and queens, and monasticism inspired many of the religious and social reform movements of the medieval era.

The Benedictine rule had been adopted by most Western monasteries by the end of the Carolingian era, but during the High Middle Ages numerous new orders appeared. Saint Benedict had emphasized hard work and self-sufficiency more than rigorous ascetic discipline. Thanks to generations of bequests and careful husbandry of resources, many Benedictine houses, like the famous Cluny, grew wealthy and self-preoccupied—devoting much of their time to creating ever more elaborate liturgies for their elegantly appointed sanctuaries. The new orders rejected Benedictine "luxury." They modeled their rules on the example of poverty and self-sacrifice set by Christ and the apostles in the New Testament.

The Carthusians, who were founded in 1084, were the strictest of the new orders. Carthusian monks lived in isolation, fasted three days a week, observed long periods of silence, and employed self-flagellation to discipline their bodies.

The Cistercians, who were founded in 1098 at Cîteaux in Burgundy, claimed to restore what they believed was the original intent of the Benedictine rule before it was corrupted by materialistic influences. They stressed cultivation of the inner life and the spiritual goals of monasticism. And to avoid contamination by the secular world, they located their houses in remote areas where there were few worldly comforts.

The monastic ideal was so popular in the eleventh century that many secular clergy (and some lay persons) chose to live as Canons Regular. These people stayed in the world to serve the laity, but lived according to a rule that was credited to Saint Augustine. They merged the spiritual disciplines of the cloister with traditional pastoral duties. Early in the thirteenth century, the desire to combine the virtues of the secular and regular clerical professions inspired another innovation: the mendicant friars (the Dominicans and Franciscans). And during the late thirteenth and fourteenth centuries, laymen and laywomen set up satellite convents known as *beguine* houses. These were religious communes formed by people who worked in the world but lived together under a quasi-monastic rule. The church was uncomfortable with the beguines, for their religious enthusiasm sometimes blossomed into heresy. The Franciscans and Dominicans assumed responsibility for many of these establishments.

Prominence of the Clergy. The clergy were far more numerous in medieval than in modern society. Estimates suggest that 1.5 percent of fourteenth-century Europe was in clerical garb. The clergy as a whole, like the nobility, lived on the labor of others. Their income came from tithes, church taxes, and endowments. The church was a major landowner that collected huge sums in rents and fees. Monastic communities and high prelates acquired great fortunes and immense secular power.

Respect for clergy as members of society's "first estate" derived in large part from their role as mediators between God and humanity. When the priest celebrated the Eucharist, he brought the very Son of God down to earth in tangible form. The priest alone had the power to extend God's forgiveness to sinners. His threat of excommunication—cutting a sinner off from the sacraments that were the only avenue to salvation—was a powerful weapon for intimidating the laity.

Since the priest was the agent of an authority far superior to any earthly magistrate, it was considered inappropriate for him to be subservient to the laymen who ran the state. Clergy, therefore, were granted special privileges and immunities. They were not to be taxed by secular governments without approval from the church. Clerical crimes were under the jurisdiction of special ecclesiastical courts, not the secular courts. The churches and monasteries where clergy worked were also deemed to be outside the legal jurisdiction of the state. People who took refuge in them received asylum and could not be apprehended by the officials of the secular government.

By the late Middle Ages lay people came increasingly to resent the special privileges of the clergy. The anti-clerical sentiments that developed during the medieval era contributed to the success of the Reformation of the sixteenth century. The Protestant theologians insisted that clergy and laity had equal spiritual standing before God.

Peasants

The largest and lowest class in medieval society was the one on whose labor the welfare of all the others depended: the agrarian peasantry. Many peasants lived and worked on manors, the primitive cells of rural social life. When the Frankish tribes moved into Europe at the start of the Middle Ages, individuals divided up the lands belonging to farming villages. They became the lords of these estates or "manors," and those who lived on them became their property. A manor was, therefore, a small, self-sufficient community within a larger village community.

The Duties of Tenancy. Since the lord of the manor was a soldier, not a farmer, the peasants who lived on his land worked it for him. They were free to divide the labor as they wished, and any products they raised above and beyond what they owed their lord they could keep for themselves. No set rules governed the size of manors—nor how many might belong to a single lord.

There were both servile and free manors. The tenants of the free manors had once been freemen *(coloni)*—the original owners of the land, who swapped it for a guarantee of security from a powerful lord. Tenancy obligations on free manors were limited, for their tenants had had some leverage in negotiating terms. Tenants of servile manors were, by comparison, far more vulnerable to the whims of their landlords. As time passed, however, the two types of manor merged, and tenants of greater and lesser degrees of servitude came to dwell on the same manor. Free, self-governing peasant communities that acknowledged no lords also survived in many regions.

The lord was both judge and policeman on his manor. Cultivation of his *demesne,* the plots of land producing his income, took precedence over those of his tenants. He could impress his tenants into labor gangs for special projects or lead them out as footsoldiers when he went to war. He owned and leased to his peasants many of the machines they used to raise and process the food. His income was fattened by petty taxes and monopolies called *banalities:* the requirement, for instance, that all his tenants grind their grain in his mill or bake their bread in his oven. The lord also collected an inheritance tax—usually the best animal from a deceased serf's estate. And without a lord's permission—obtained by purchase—a serf could neither travel nor marry outside his manor.

The Life of a Serf. Burdened as a serf's life was, it was superior to chattel slavery. Serfs had their own dwellings and modest strips of land. They managed their own labor. They were permitted to market surpluses for their own profit. They were free to choose spouses from the local village community. Their marriages were protected by the church. They could pass on property to their children. And they could not be sold away from their lands.

Serfs seldom ventured far beyond the villages where they were born. Since the church was the only show in town, life on the manor was organized around religion. But poverty of religious instruction meant that beliefs and practices were by no means unambiguously Christian. Although there were social and economic distinctions among the peasants, common dependence on the soil forced them to work together to survive. The ratio of seed to grain yield was poor; about two bushels of seed were required to produce six to ten bushels of grain in good times. There was rarely an abundance of bread and ale, the staple peasant foods. Two crops on which the modern West depends, potatoes and corn (maize), were unknown in Europe until the sixteenth century. Pork was the major source of animal protein, for pigs, unlike cattle, could forage for themselves in the forests. Excess plow teams were also slaughtered when winter set in. Survival hinged on the grain crops. When they failed or fell short, famine threatened.

Changes in the Manor. As the medieval era waned, the manor and serfdom gave way to the free single-family farm. Many things contributed to the change. Technological advances such as the collar harness (ca. 800), the horseshoe (ca. 900), and the three-field system of crop rotation improved agricultural productivity. To meet the demand of the new markets created by the towns that sprang up during the High Middle Ages, peasants brought more fields into production. The surplus income they produced could be used to buy their freedom from the obligation of labor services. As the towns revived trade and brought back a money-based economy, lords found it more profitable to lease their *demesnes* to tenant farmers than to work them with serfs. Although tenants thereby gained greater personal freedom, they were not necessarily better off materially. In hard times serfs might elicit assistance from landlords, who looked on them as a personal investment. But since rent-paying workers insisted on their independence, their landlords felt that they should take care of themselves.

As the medieval economy expanded and costs of living rose, the landed aristocracy, which lived on a fixed income of traditional rents, found it hard to keep up. In the mid-fourteenth century the nobles in England and France tried to increase taxes on the peasants and limit their freedom of movement. The result was armed revolts in the countryside. Although these uprisings were brutally crushed, they are vivid testimony to the breakup of medieval society.

⌁ Towns and Townspeople

In the eleventh and twelfth centuries, only about 5 percent of western Europe's population lived in towns. Urban communities were not very large. Of Germany's 3,000 towns, for example, 2,800 had populations under 1,000. Only 15 towns exceeded 10,000, and the largest, Cologne, had a mere 30,000. London was the only English city larger than 10,000. Paris was larger than London, but not by much. Europe's most populous towns were in Italy. Florence and Milan approached 100,000.

The Chartering of Towns

Despite their comparatively small size, towns were where the action was. Towns were originally dominated by the feudal lords who granted the land on which they were built, but most acquired political independence. The charter that a lord issued to the residents of a town gave them much greater freedom than rural workers enjoyed. Freedom was a requirement of life for men and women who lived by invention and audacious commercial enterprise. Towns were meant to attract the skilled laborers who manufactured things desired by lords and bishops and to serve as markets for the merchants who roamed about in search of valuable items from faraway places.

Towns promoted the disintegration of feudal society by providing serfs with options. A serf who fled his manor could find refuge in a town and a chance to better himself. Industry could lift a skilled craftsman into a higher social class. The mere threat of migration of serfs to towns forced lords to offer them more favorable terms of tenure to keep them on the land. The growth of towns thus improved the lot of the peasantry—both those who stayed in the countryside and those who left.

The Rise of Merchants

The first merchants were probably enterprising serfs or outcasts who found no place in the feudal system. Only men who had nothing to lose and everything to gain would have been tempted by the enormous risks and dangers of foreign trade. They traveled together in armed caravans and convoys, buying goods and products as cheaply as possible at the source, and selling them elsewhere for all they could get. The greed and daring of these rough-hewn men, more than anything else, created our modern urban lifestyle.

Merchants were considered an oddity, for they did not fit into any of the three classes that made up feudal society: the nobility, the clergy, and the peasantry. As late as the fifteenth century, the nobility were still snubbing the urban "patriciate" (the hereditary ruling class that arose in some cities). Over time, however, the powerful grew to respect the merchants, and the weak always tried to imitate them, because wherever the merchants went, they left a trail of wealth behind.

Challenging the Old Lords

As the traders established themselves in towns and grew in wealth and numbers, they organized to challenge the older feudal authorities. They wanted to end the tolls and tariffs demanded by the myriad of nobles through whose domains their caravans had to travel. Wherever merchants settled they opposed the tolls, tariffs, and other petty restrictions that hampered the flow of trade. Merchant *guilds* (unions, or protective associations) sprang up in the eleventh century, followed in the twelfth by guilds of craftsmen. Together these groups worked to change the rules of what the other classes believed to be a natural, static social order.

Townspeople wanted simple, uniform laws that were valid over large areas. They objected to the fortress mentality that caused feudal lords to divide the countryside into tiny jurisdictions. City-dwellers set up independent communes to wrest control of their towns from the nobles, and they began to fight against the disintegrative effects of feudalism. Both the church and the king were eager, for reasons of their own, to join the townspeople in a fight to weaken the local magnates.

Problems of Self-Government

By 1100, in many cities the old urban nobility and the new *burgher* upper class had merged. By working together, the wealthiest citizens created town councils that became the chief organ of municipal government.

Small artisans and craftsmen developed their own protective associations or guilds and won political recognition on the town councils. Townspeople thought of themselves as citizens with basic rights, not as subjects liable to a master's whim. The urban poor certainly knew economic hardship and political exploitation, but so long as there was some social mobility, they had a stake in the system that gave them a reason to cooperate with it.

Social Tensions. Despite urban democratic tendencies, class distinctions were prominent in towns. The wealthiest urban groups aped the lifestyle of the old landed nobility. They wanted coats of arms, castles, and country estates. Once businesses had set up lines of communication and worked out banking procedures for shifting funds around, their managers left most traveling to underlings. Investors were able to settle down on their country manors and still run their companies. The departure of the social-climbing entrepreneurs was an economic loss for the towns that gave them their starts.

A need to be socially distinguished and distinct was not confined to the rich. Towns tried to restrain competition by defining grades of luxury in dress and residence for each social group and vocation. Overly conspicuous consumption was a kind of indecent exposure punishable by "sumptuary" laws—regulations restricting the types and amount of clothing one might wear or the decoration of one's home. These rules were meant to maintain order by keeping everyone clearly and peacefully in place.

The need for laws to limit competition among classes suggests that medieval towns were not internally harmonious social units. They were collections of self-centered groups, each seeking to advance its own interests. Conflict between haves and have-nots was inevitable. The poorest workers in the export trades (usually the weavers and woolcombers) were distinct from the economically better off and socially ascending independent artisans and small shopkeepers. These latter had differences with the merchants who brought competitive foreign goods into the city. Theoretically, poor men could work their way up this hierarchy from its lower social and vocational levels. Some lucky ones succeeded, but until they did they were excluded from the city council. Only property-owning families of long standing had full rights of citizenship. Urban self-government, in other words, tended to become inbred and aristocratic.

Shrinking Opportunities. Artisans formed guilds to gain the clout needed to win a direct voice in government. This pleased some urban residents, but it alienated others, for guilds curtailed the social mobility of the poorer laborers.

The guilds' representatives on city councils worked to discourage imports and to protect the local market. They ensured that the local businesses that served the market maintained quality standards and fair pricing. But so protective of their markets did the guilds become that they discouraged the invention of new techniques of production and refused to license new producers. This infuriated the journeymen trained in guild shops, for it prevented them from winning guild membership and setting up in business for themselves. These politically disenfranchised workers, who had no hope of advancement, formed a true urban proletariat. And the protectionism practiced by the guild-dominated urban governments ultimately depressed the economy for everyone.

Towns and Kings

A natural alliance developed between the governments of towns and the centralized nation-states that medieval kings struggled to establish. Towns supplied royal governments with experienced bureaucrats and lawyers who knew Roman law, the tool for designing kingdoms and empires. Towns provided the money that kings needed to hire professional armies and free themselves from dependence on the feudal nobility. Towns, in short, had the human, financial, and technological resources to empower kings.

Towns wanted strong monarchs, for national governments provided the best support for commerce. A powerful king could control the local despots, whose tolls and petty wars disrupted trade. Unlike a local magnate, kings also tended to remain at a distance and to allow towns to exercise their precious autonomy. Kings could provide protection over long distances, create standardized currencies to ease buying and selling, and simplify the payment of dues and taxes.

The relationship between kings and towns fluctuated with the fate of monarchy in various nations. In France, where the Capetian dynasty flourished, towns were integrated into royal government. In England, towns supported the barons against unpopular kings like John, but cooperated with more effective monarchs in subduing the nobility. In Germany, where the feudal magnates triumphed over their kings, towns came under the control of territorial princes. In Italy, towns had unique opportunities. Italy had no native royal family for towns to support. And since both townsmen and feudal aristocrats were united in opposition to the political ambitions of German kings and Roman popes, they tended to cooperate. As the two classes fused, town governments extended their authority into the countryside, reviving the ancient institution of the city-state.

Between the eleventh and fourteenth centuries, towns enjoyed considerable autonomy and once again became the centers of Western civilization. But after the fourteenth century, as true nations began to appear, the towns and the church were steadily bent to the will of kings. By the seventeenth century, few had escaped integration into the larger purposes of the "state."

∼ Schools and Universities

In the twelfth century, European scholars became acquainted with Aristotle's treatises on logic, the writings of Euclid and Ptolemy, Roman law, and the basic works of Greek physicians and Arab mathematicians. Islamic scholars living in Spain were chiefly responsible for the translations and commentaries that made these ancient texts accessible to Westerners. The result was a cultural renaissance and the birth of Europe's universities.

University of Bologna

When the term *university* first began to be used, it meant simply a corporation of individuals who "united" for mutual protection. Since schools attracted students and teachers from great distances, many were foreigners who had no civil rights in the towns where they worked. Unless they organized to protect themselves—like the members of an urban trade guild—they were exploited by the townspeople on whom they were dependent for food and lodging.

The first of the great medieval universities was chartered in Bologna, Italy, by Emperor Frederick Barbarossa in 1158. Bologna, which became a model for schools in Italy, Spain, and southern France, was directed by its students. Its students "unionized" to guarantee fair rents and prices and high-quality teaching from their masters. They hired their teachers, set pay scales, and assigned lecture topics. Masters who did not live up to student expectations were boycotted, and price-gouging by townspeople was countered by threats to take the university and its profitable business to another town.

Bologna was most famous for the courses in law it offered advanced students. In the late eleventh century, Western scholars discovered the *Corpus*

Juris Civilis, the collection of ancient Roman law made by the Emperor Justinian in the sixth century. In the early twelfth century, Irnerius of Bologna took the lead in the field by using the *Corpus Juris* to create commentaries (glosses) on current laws. Around 1140, another resident of Bologna, a monk named Gratian, wrote the standard legal text in church (canon) law, the *Concordance of Discordant Canons* (or, simply, the *Decretum*).

Masters, as well as students, formed protective associations, and their guilds dominated the universities of northern Europe. Masters' guilds had a monopoly on teaching, and their tests for admission set standards for certification of teachers. The first academic degree evolved as a license to teach *(licentia docendi).*

Cathedral Schools

The basic course of study at all medieval universities was the liberal arts program. It consisted of the *trivium* (grammar, rhetoric, and logic) and the *quadrivium* (arithmetic, geometry, astronomy, and music). This amounted to instruction in reading, writing, and computation. University study normally began between the ages of twelve and fifteen. Since all books and all instruction were in Latin, matriculating students were expected to arrive with a good knowledge of that language. The first four years of their course of study were devoted primarily to the *trivium*—the polishing of their Latin. This earned them a bachelor of arts degree. A master's degree entailed an additional three or four years of work on the *quadrivium,* the study of classical texts dealing with mathematics, natural science, and philosophy. Doctoral degrees were available in a few fields like law, medicine, and theology. A degree in theology at the University of Paris might take twenty years or more to earn.

The liberal arts curriculum evolved in the cathedral and monastery schools that trained clergy. In the early Middle Ages these were the only schools that existed, and the clergy were the only literate class. But by the late eleventh century, students who had no interest in clerical vocations, but who needed Latin and related intellectual disciplines for careers as notaries or merchants, began to frequent the church's schools. In 1179, a papal decree obliged cathedrals to provide teachers gratis for laity who wanted to learn. By the thirteenth century, the demand for literate men to staff the growing urban and territorial governments and expanding merchant firms gave rise to schools offering secular vocational education.

University of Paris

The University of Paris, which provided the model for the schools of northern Europe, was founded in part on the cathedral school of Notre Dame. King Philip Augustus and Pope Innocent III chartered Paris in 1200 and gave its students protections and privileges denied ordinary citizens. Only in self-defense might a citizen strike a student. All citizens were obligated to testify

The architecture of the early Middle Ages is known as Romanesque because it is closely related to the style of the late Roman Empire. It is characterized by thick stone walls and rounded arches that support the roof. The few windows are often very small, mere slits, giving Romanesque buildings a fortresslike appearance. Shown here is the Abbey of Germigny-des-Prés in northern France. [Giraudon/Art Resource, N.Y.]

Beginning in the mid-twelfth century, the Gothic style evolved from Romanesque architecture. The word gothic at first meant "barbaric," and was applied to the new style by its critics. Its most distinctive visible features are its ribbed, criss-crossing vaulting; its pointed rather than rounded arches; and its prominent exterior "flying" buttresses. The vaulting, the exterior flying buttresses, and the increased height they made possible gave prominence to the strong vertical aspect of Gothic buildings. The buttresses, by shifting much of the structural weight of the buildings off the walls, also made possible wide expanses of windows—hence the extensive use of stained glass and the characteristic colored light that often floods Gothic cathedrals. Use of the windows to show stories from the Bible, saints' lives, and local events was similar to earlier use of mosaics. Shown here is an example of French Gothic, Reims Cathedral, where the kings of France were crowned. [Scala/Art Resource, N.Y.]

Student Life at the University of Paris

As the following account by Jacques de Vitry makes clear, not all students at the University of Paris in the thirteenth century were preoccupied by their studies. They fought constantly and subjected each other to ethnic insults and slurs.

~ Why were students from different lands so prejudiced against one another? Does the rivalry of faculty members appear to have been as intense as that among students? What criticisms did students have of the faculty? Do they sound credible?

Almost all the students at Paris, foreigners and natives, did absolutely nothing except learn or hear something new. Some studied merely to acquire knowledge, which is curiosity; others to acquire fame, which is vanity; others still for the sake of gain, which is cupidity and the vice of simony. Very few studied for their own edification, or that of others. They wrangled and disputed not merely about the various sects or about some discussions; but the differences between the countries also caused dissensions, hatreds and virulent animosities among them, and they impudently uttered all kinds of affronts and insults against one another.

They affirmed that the English were drunkards and had tails; the sons of France proud, effeminate and carefully adorned like women. They said that the Germans were furious and obscene at their feasts; the Normans, vain and boastful; the Poitevins, traitors and always adventurers. The Burgundians they considered vulgar and stupid. The Bretons were reputed to be fickle and changeable, and were often reproached for the death of Arthur. The Lombards were called avaricious, vicious and cowardly; the Romans, seditious, turbulent and slanderous; the Sicilians, tyrannical and cruel; the inhabitants of Brabant, men of blood, incendiaries, brigands and ravishers; the Flemish, fickle, prodigal, gluttonous, yielding as butter, and slothful. After such insults from words they often came to blows.

I will not speak of those logicians [professors of logic and dialectic] before whose eyes flitted constantly "the lice of Egypt," that is to say, all the sophistical subtleties, so that no one could comprehend their eloquent discourses in which, as says Isaiah, "there is no wisdom." As to the doctors of theology, "seated in Moses' seat," they were swollen with learning, but their charity was not edifying. Teaching and not practicing, they have "become as sounding brass or a tinkling cymbal," or like a canal of stone, always dry, which ought to carry water to "the bed of spices." They not only hated one another, but by their flatteries they enticed away the students of others; each one seeking his own glory, but caring not a whit about the welfare of souls.

Translations and Reprints from the Original Sources of European History, Vol. 2 (Philadelphia: Department of History, University of Pennsylvania, 1902), pp. 19–20.

against anyone seen abusing a student. And university laws required teachers to be carefully examined before being licensed to teach Parisian students. Students were thus recognized in law to be both a valuable and a vulnerable resource.

Paris originated the college or house system. The first colleges were charitable hospices providing room and board for poor students who could not afford to study otherwise. The university soon discovered that these institutions were useful for overseeing students, and it encouraged all students to enroll in them. The most famous of the Parisian colleges was the Sorbonne, founded around 1257 by Robert de Sorbon, the royal chaplain. Early universities were mobile associations of students and teachers that used rented or borrowed space. But endowed colleges provided buildings that rooted a university to a particular spot. This reduced the university's leverage in negotiating with townspeople, for it could no longer threaten to move to another location.

The Curriculum

The education provided by cathedral and monastery schools was limited to grammar, rhetoric, and some elementary geometry and astronomy. The standard texts were the Latin grammars of Donatus and Priscian, Saint Augustine's *On Christian Doctrine*, Cassiodorus's *On Divine and Secular Learning*, Boethius's treatises on arithmetic and music, and a few of Aristotle's logical works. The books that entered Europe from Muslim lands in the early twelfth century vastly expanded libraries and made possible the more elaborate curricula of universities. The most revolutionary of the new texts were the complete works of Aristotle, which were in general circulation by the mid-thirteenth century. They shaped the dominant intellectual movement of the day: Scholasticism.

In the High Middle Ages scholars assumed that truth was not something one had to go out and find for oneself. It was already enshrined in the works of the great authorities of the past—men like Aristotle and the fathers of the church. It had only to be apprehended and absorbed. Teachers did not encourage students to strive independently for undiscovered truth. They taught them rather to use logic and dialectic to organize and harmonize the accepted truths of tradition. Dialectic, the art of discovering a truth by finding the contradictions in arguments against it, reigned supreme in all disciplines. Instead of observing phenomena for themselves, students read the traditional authorities in their fields, made short summaries of their teaching, disputed interpretations by elaborating arguments pro and con, and then took positions based on logical cogency.

Because printing with movable type did not yet exist, only a few expensive, hand-copied books were available. Few students could afford texts for quiet, private study. Most had to learn from discussions, lectures, and debates. They memorized the information with which they worked, and they were required to think on their feet. Rhetorical skill, the ability to make an eloquent defense of the knowledge one had clarified by logic and dialectic, was the goal of an education. In order to succeed in debate, students had to become walking encyclopedias. They were filled with information they could regurgitate as needed.

The Summa. The *summa,* a summary of all that was known about a particular subject, was the characteristic intellectual product of the High Middle Ages. The summa's chief purpose was to heap up clarified truth by reconciling apparent contradictions among authorities.

Medieval scholars labored to produce universal summaries for all disciplines, but the most influential were those that appeared in theology, the "queen of the sciences." About 1122, Peter Abelard (1079–1142) published *Sic et Non,* a book that facilitated scholastic debate by juxtaposing seemingly contradictory statements from the works of sacred authorities. A few years later (1155–1157), Peter Lombard (1100–1169) worked this material into his *Four Books of Sentences,* which became the standard theological textbook of the Middle Ages. About 1265, Thomas Aquinas entered the field with the *Summa Theologica.* His achievement, in the opinion of Catholic theologians, is the epitome of what the summa aspired to be: the last word.

Critics of Scholasticism. Even in its heyday, Scholasticism had strong critics. Some complained that the regimen of the schools was heartless and potentially damaging to Christian faith. The *dictatores,* the professional grammarians and rhetoricians who taught good writing and speaking rather than the highly abstract dialectic of Scholasticism, urged students to go directly to sources (in their original languages) and draw their own conclusions. Their point of view was championed by the humanists of the sixteenth-century Renaissance, and it still informs modern liberal arts curricula.

The church was also not completely at ease with Scholasticism. Scholastic thinkers relied heavily on Aristotelian logic to develop their arguments, and there were obvious conflicts between Christian doctrine and ideas that Aristotle defended. For example, since logic cannot account for why there is something rather than nothing or deal with an infinite regression of causes, Aristotle believed in the eternality of the world. He taught that the world was a "given" that had always been. But Christianity affirmed the Jewish concept of creation described in the book of Genesis. Aristotle also taught that since logic was the same in all minds, intellect or mind was ultimately the same in all people. This obliterated individuality and threatened Christian teaching about individual responsibility and personal immortality.

Some of the early Scholastics were inclined to question Christian doctrines that could not be reconciled with Aristotle's teachings. Berengar of Tours (d. 1088), for example, concluded that the church's claim that the bread and wine of the Eucharist became the body and blood of Christ was logically indefensible. Peter Abelard attempted a reinterpretation of the Trinity that preserved a premise of Aristotle's logic; namely, that three could not be one and one could not be three. The boldness of the new logicians shocked conservatives, who concluded that the love of learning at the universities had clearly got in the way of the love of God.

A century of suspicion that Aristotle was undermining Christian theology culminated in 1277, when the bishop of Paris condemned 219 philosophical propositions. The condemnation was a warning to scholars who were more interested in secular philosophy than in Christian truth, and it chilled the relationship between learning and religion. Thinkers ceased to look for ways to reconcile reason and revelation. William of Ockham (d. 1349), for instance, denied that theological truths could be studied in the same way as natural phenomena. Knowledge of God was available only through biblical revelation.

~ Gender and Family

Women

The concept of femininity developed by medieval scholars was at odds with the lives of the real women of the era. Christian theologians concluded from the evidence contained in Greco-Roman medical, philosophical, and legal texts—and the Bible itself—that women were physically, mentally, and morally inferior to men. The Bible clearly taught that a woman was a "weaker vessel" who required protection and discipline from a man. Wives were to submit to their husbands and accept corrective beatings from them. The celibate Christian clergy felt that women were debased by marriage and that virgins and celibate widows were more to be honored than wives.

There were contrary forces at work shaping roles for women in medieval society. The church reinforced many traditional negative assumptions about women, but it condemned bawdy literature that denigrated women and insisted on the female's spiritual equality with the male. The learned churchman Peter Lombard argued, for instance, that God took Eve from Adam's side because he wanted woman neither to rule over nor to be enslaved by man. She was to stand with him as his companion and partner in a marriage characterized by mutual aid and trust. In chivalric romances, in courtly love literature, and in the cult of the Virgin Mary that swept Europe in the twelfth and thirteenth centuries, female traits of gentleness, compassion, and grace were exalted over the rougher male virtues. In these traditions, women were put on pedestals and praised as superior to men in the delicate arts of self-control and civilized life.

Germanic traditions moderated Roman customs and gave medieval women basic rights that prevented their being treated as mere chattel. Roman women in their teens married men much older than themselves, but German women married later in life and took husbands of their own age. In German lands a groom provided a dowry for his bride to hold as her own property, and all the Germanic law codes granted women economic freedom. They could inherit, administer, dispose of, and confer on their children family property and personal possessions. They could also prosecute men in court for bodily injury and rape.

In the ninth century, the Carolingians, who had tolerated polygyny, concubinage, and divorce, were influenced by Christianity to make monogamous marriage official policy. The result was both a gain and a loss for women. On the one hand, the choice of a wife became a very serious matter, and wives gained greater dignity and legal security. But on the other hand, a woman's burden as household manager and bearer of children greatly increased. Where previously several women may have shared the tasks of running a nobleman's estate and providing heirs to continue his line, now all these duties rested on the shoulders of one woman. After the ninth century, mortality rates for Frankish women rose and their longevity decreased.

The demands placed on wives explain the cloister's appeal as a refuge for women. But few women were able to choose the celibate life. (There may, for instance, have been no more than 3,500 nuns in all of England at the end of the Middle Ages.) Entrance into a nunnery was contingent on one's ability to bring the house a sizable donation (a "dowry"), and only a few upper-class women could afford the price of admission. But those who did could acquire educations, rise to positions of leadership, and enjoy economic and political power beyond the reach of their sisters in secular life.

Most medieval women were neither aristocratic housewives nor nuns. They were laboring family women who were as prominent and as creative a part of a community's work force as its men. They could not attend the universities and were excluded from the learned professions of scholarship, medicine, and law, but they were admitted to the blue-collar trades. Between the ages of ten and fifteen, girls, like boys, held apprenticeships, and many learned to be skilled workers. When they married, they might continue their trades, operating their bake shops or dress shops next to a husband's business, or they might become assistants and partners in a husband's line of work. Women held virtually every job from butcher to goldsmith, although they were especially prominent in the food and clothing industries and as domestic servants. Women, as well as men, earned membership in guilds and were accorded the rank of "master," but they often found their freedom of movement within a profession more carefully regulated than a man's. Usually women performed the same work as men for a 25 percent lower wage. Townswomen increasingly had opportunities to go to school and acquire literacy in the vernacular. Peasant women, who tilled the fields, had no such chance for self-improvement.

Children

The image of medieval children and the reality of their lives seem, like those of women, to have diverged. In medieval art children are rarely portrayed as different from adults. Some historians have wondered, therefore, if people in the Middle Ages thought of childhood as a distinct period of life requiring special treatment. They have also noted that infant and child mortality was extremely high during the Middle Ages, and speculated that a parent could not have risked becoming emotionally attached to a child who had a 30 to 50 percent chance of dying before the age of five.

The practice of infanticide, which continued despite its condemnation by the church, suggests that children were held in low esteem in ancient and early medieval society. The Romans regulated family size by exposing unwanted children, but showered attention and affection on the offspring they chose to raise. The Germans, by contrast, had large families, but tended to neglect their children. Among the German tribes one paid a much lower *wergild,* or compensatory fine, for injury to a child than for injury to an adult.

It is possible that instead of distancing parents from children, high rates of infant and child mortality increased their attachment. Evidence of special attention being paid to children is found in the great variety of children's toys and child-rearing equipment, like walkers and potty chairs, that existed in the Middle Ages. Medieval medical authorities also offered advice on postnatal care and childhood diseases—cautioning against abuse and recommending moderation in discipline. The church urged parents to love children as Mary loved Jesus. And evidence from medieval art and literature suggests that when infants and children died in the Middle Ages, parents grieved as pitiably then as now.

The medievals who recognized childhood understood it to be brief. Medieval children assumed adult responsibilities at early ages. Young peasants joined their parents in the fields as soon as they could physically manage the labor. The urban working class sent children as young as eight away from home for apprenticeship training. And the church permitted boys to marry at fourteen and girls at twelve. The pressure put on children to mature and learn may have been a sign of concern for them, for no parental responsibility was deemed greater than that of equipping a child for useful employment.

The economic expansion of the High Middle Ages revived urban life in Europe. As cities grew, new social groups, the merchant-artisan classes, rose to prominence. They successfully challenged the old feudal nobility and brought European communities the blessings and problems of nascent capitalism. The seeds of social conflict and class struggle were sown, but a potentially significant alliance was also struck between the urban classes and the kings who were struggling to end the fragmenting influences of feudalism. The re- *sult was to be the defeat of feudalism and the formation of Europe's nations.*

The new wealth of towns provided patronage for education and culture. The first universities appeared in the eleventh century and, with them, a new way of thinking (Scholasticism) and a revival of art and science. The creativity of the era testifies to the intensity of the human vitality of the rising "middle" class and its determination to reshape the social and political institutions of the Western world.

⁓ Review Questions

1. How did the responsibilities of the nobility differ from those of the clergy and peasantry during the High Middle Ages? In what ways did each social class contribute to the stability of society?

2. What led to the revival of trade and the growth of towns in the twelfth century? What political and social conditions were essential for a revival of trade? How did towns change medieval society?

3. What were the strengths and weaknesses of the educations provided by medieval universities? How would you evaluate the standard curriculum?

4. How would you define Scholasticism? What was the Scholastic program and method of study? Who were the main critics of Scholasticism? What were their complaints?

5. Do Germanic law and Roman law reflect different understandings of the position of women in society? How did options and responsibilities differ for women in each of the social classes? What are the theories concerning the concept of childhood in the Middle Ages?

∼ Suggested Readings

P. Ariès, *Centuries of Childhood: A Social History of Family Life* (1962). Pioneer effort on the subject.

J. W. Baldwin, *The Scholastic Culture of the Middle Ages: 1000–1300* (1971). Best brief synthesis available.

M. Bloch, *French Rural History,* trans. by J. Sondheimer (1966). A classic by a great modern historian.

B. A. Hanawalt, *The Ties That Bound: Peasant Families in Medieval England* (1986). Elucidating demographic and economic study of rural life.

C. H. Haskins, *The Renaissance of the Twelfth Century* (1927). Still the standard account.

C. H. Haskins, *The Rise of Universities* (1972). A short, minor classic.

D. Herlihy, *Medieval Households* (1985). Bread-and-butter account of household structure in antiquity and the Middle Ages.

G. Künstler, *Romanesque Art in Europe* (1973). Standard survey.

E. Mâle, *The Gothic Image: Religious Art in France in the Thirteenth Century* (1913). An enduring classic.

K. Mertes, *The English Noble Household, 1250–1600* (1988). Good background for the debate over the structure and quality of English family life.

A. Murray, *Reason and Society in the Middle Ages* (1978). A view of the Middle Ages as an age of reason as well as of faith.

E. Panofsky, *Gothic Architecture and Scholasticism* (1951). A controversial classic.

H. Pirenne, *Medieval Cities: Their Origins and the Revival of Trade,* trans. by Frank D. Halsey (1970). A minor classic.

H. Rashdall, *The Universities of Europe in the Middle Ages,* vols. 1–3 (1936). Dated but still extremely useful for documents of the period.

S. Shahar, *The Fourth Estate: A History of Women in the Middle Ages* (1983). A comprehensive survey, making clear the great variety of women's work.

B. Stock, *The Implications of Literacy* (1983). How the ability to read changed medieval society.

9

The Late Middle Ages (1300–1527): Centuries of Crisis

Political and Social Breakdown

*The Hundred Years' War
and the Rise of National
Sentiment
Progress of the War*

The Black Death

*Preconditions and Causes
Social and Economic Consequences*

**Ecclesiastical Breakdown and Revival:
The Late Medieval Church**

*The Thirteenth-Century Papacy
Boniface VIII and Philip the Fair
The Avignon Papacy (1309–1377)
The Great Schism (1378–1417)
and the Conciliar Movement
to 1449*

KEY TOPICS IN THIS CHAPTER

~ The Hundred Years' War between England and France

~ The effects of the bubonic plague on population and society

~ The growing power of secular rulers over the papacy

~ Schism, heresy, and reform of the church

During the late Middle Ages, Europeans endured so many calamities that Western civilization seemed in imminent danger of collapse. From 1337 to 1453, France and England waged an increasingly bloody conflict known as the Hundred Years' War. Between 1348 and 1350, the first wave of the bubonic plague (the Black Death) swept over Europe, carrying off a third of its population. In 1378, a quarrel between competing candidates for the papacy tore the church apart and inaugurated a schism that endured for thirty-seven years. And in 1453, the Turks overran Constantinople and charged up the Danube Valley toward the heart of Europe.

These crises were accompanied by intellectual developments that undercut assumptions about God, mankind, and the social order that had given comfort to earlier generations. Some philosophers came to the conclusion that human reason was much more limited in scope than the scholastics had imagined. Feudal institutions, which had been assumed to be divinely ordained, were assaulted by kings who aspired to absolute monarchy. Claims to absolute authority, by both kings and popes, were challenged by political theorists who argued that rulers were accountable to their subjects for the way in which they governed.

Significant Dates from the Period of the Late Middle Ages

1309–1377	*Avignon Papacy*
1340	*Sluys: First Major Battle of Hundred Years' War*
1346	*Battle of Crécy and seizure of Calais*
1347	*Black Death strikes*
1356	*Battle of Poitiers*
1358	*Jacquerie disrupts France*
1360	*Peace of Brétigny*
1378–1417	*Great Schism*
1381	*English Peasants' Revolt*
1414–1417	*Council of Constance*
1415	*Battle of Agincourt*
1422	*Treaty of Troyes*
1431	*Joan of Arc executed as a heretic*
1431–1449	*Council of Basel*
1453	*End of Hundred Years' War*

∾ Political and Social Breakdown

The Hundred Years' War and the Rise of National Sentiment

Late medieval rulers practiced the art of feudal government, but on a grander scale and with greater sophistication than their predecessors. They governed by carefully negotiating alliances with powerful factions within their domains: the feudal nobility, the church, and the towns. The Norman kings of England and the Capetian kings of France fine-tuned feudal relationships, stressing the duties of lesser magnates to greater ones—and the unquestioning loyalty of all vassals to the king. The result was a centralization of royal power and the creation of a "national" consciousness that equipped both kingdoms for war on an unprecedented scale.

The Causes of the War. The Hundred Years' War began in May 1337, when a fight broke out over the right of succession to the French throne. In 1328, Charles IV died without male issue, and the direct line of the Capetian royal house came to an end. Edward III (r. 1327–1377), king of England, claimed the throne of France by right of his mother, Charles IV's sister. But the French barons had no intention of turning themselves over to the young king of England. They offered their allegiance to a cadet branch of the Capetian house: to Charles IV's cousin, Philip VI, duke of Valois (1328–1350). Philip inaugurated the Valois dynasty that ruled France into the sixteenth century.

The English king's assertion of a claim to the French throne was more a justification than a cause for war, for England and France had long been on a collision course. Since the days of the Norman conquest, the king of England had held fiefs on the continent as a vassal of the king of France. English possession of French land stood in the way of attempts by the French kings to centralize the government of their nation. England and France also had competing economic interests in neighboring Flanders and on the high seas. The Hundred Years' War was, in light of its many causes, a struggle for national identity as well as for control of territory.

French Weakness. France should have had no difficulty in winning the war. It had three times the population of England, far greater resources, and the advantage of fighting on its own soil. Yet, until 1415, the major battles were stunning victories for the English.

Internal disunity prevented France from marshalling all its forces against the English, and powerful feudal traditions slowed France's adaptation to new military technologies employed by the English. England's infantry was more disciplined than France's, and English archers wielded a formidable weapon, the longbow, capable of firing six arrows a minute that could pierce the armor of a knight at 200 yards.

Progress of the War

The Conflict During the Reign of Edward III. In the first of the three stages (see Map 9-1) into which the war can be divided, Edward sparked rebellions against France in the cities of Flanders by placing an embargo on the English wool that fed Flemish mills. In 1340, the Flemish cities decided that their economic interests lay with England and acknowledged Edward's claim to be king of France and legitimate overlord of Flanders. On June 23 of that same year, Edward defeated the French fleet in the Bay of Sluys, the first great battle of the war.

In 1346 Edward attacked Normandy. After a series of easy victories that culminated at the battle of Crécy, he seized the port of Calais. Exhaustion and the onset of the Black Death forced a truce in late 1347. There was no further action until 1356, when the English won their greatest victory. Near Poitiers, they routed France's feudal nobles and captured the French king, John II, "the Good" (1350–1364). The loss of king and vassals led to a breakdown of political order in France.

Power in France shifted momentarily to the *Estates General*, a body somewhat like the English Parliament that represented the propertied classes. The powerful merchants of Paris, led by Étienne Marcel, demanded rights similar to those granted the English privileged classes by Magna Carta. But unlike the English Parliament, which represented the interests of a comparatively unified island people, the French Estates General was too divided to be an instrument for effective government. It took time for the leaders of the far-flung regions of a large nation like France to come to know and trust each other.

The French privileged classes were able to avoid taxation by foisting the costs of the war onto the backs of the peasantry. Beginning in 1358, the desperate peasants rose up in bloody rebellions called the *Jacquerie* (from "Jacques

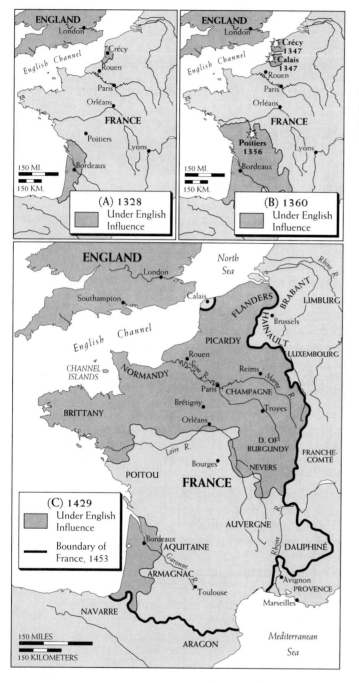

MAP 9-1 The Hundred Years' War *The Hundred Years' War went on intermittently from the late 1330s until 1453. These maps show the remarkable English territorial gains up to the point when Joan of Arc suddenly and decisively turned the tide of battle in favor of the French in 1429.*

Bonhomme," a peasant caricature). The nobility restored order by matching the rebels atrocity for atrocity.

On May 9, 1360, England compelled France to accept terms spelled out in the Peace of Brétigny. Edward renounced his claim to the French throne, but he demanded an end to his vassalage to the king of France and confirmation of his sovereignty over the lands he held in France (including Gascony, Guyenne, Poitou, and Calais). France was also required to pay a ransom of 3 million gold crowns for King John the Good. The treaty was completely unrealistic, and sober observers on both sides knew that the peace it brought could not last long. Within a few years France had reopened hostilities, and by the time of Edward's death in 1377, the English possessed only a few coastal enclaves and the territory around Bordeaux.

French Defeat and the Treaty of Troyes.

After Edward's death, domestic problems caused England to lose interest in war with France. During the reign of Edward's grandson and successor, Richard II (r. 1377–1399), England experienced its own version of the *Jacquerie*. In June 1381, John Ball, a secular priest, and Wat Tyler, a journeyman, led a mob of peasants and artisans in an assault on London. The revolt was quickly put down, but it left scars that took decades to heal.

Richard II was deposed by his cousin, Henry IV, who spent his reign confirming his hold on England. Henry's son and heir, Henry V (r. 1413–1422), revived the war with France as a strategy for uniting his people behind their king.

Henry's moment was well chosen, for powerful, antagonistic factions had developed within the French nobility. When Henry V invaded Normandy, the duke of Burgundy's party refused to assist its enemies, the Armagnacs, in defending France. After Henry routed the Armagnacs at Agincourt on October 25, 1415, the Burgundians came to terms with the Armagnacs. But their fragile alliance was shattered in September 1419, when the duke of Burgundy was assassinated by an Armagnac. Burgundy's son and heir determined to avenge his father's death by assisting the English in an invasion of Armagnac territory.

With Burgundian assistance Henry V took Paris, captured the French king (Charles VI), and married his daughter. In 1420, the Treaty of Troyes disinherited the French king's son and proclaimed Henry V heir to the French throne. When Henry and Charles died within months of one another in 1422, Henry's infant son, Henry VI, was proclaimed king of both France and England. But an effective union of the two nations was never attempted.

Joan of Arc and the War's Conclusion.

Charles VI's son, Charles VII, escaped the English and asserted his right to his father's throne. But the success of the unprecedented campaign that rallied the people of France to his side was due less to him than to a remarkable woman called Joan of Arc (1412–1431). Joan was a peasant from Domrémy who informed Charles VII, in March 1429, that God had commissioned her to deliver Orléans from the English armies that

A contemporary portrait of Joan of Arc (1412–1431) in the National Archives in Paris. [Giraudon/Art Resource, N.Y.]

besieged it. The king was skeptical, but he was willing to try anything to reverse French fortunes.

Circumstances worked to Joan's advantage. The siege of Orléans had gone on for six months, and the exhausted English troops were at the point of withdrawal when Joan arrived with a fresh French army. The English retreat from Orléans was followed by a succession of victories popularly attributed to Joan. She deserved credit, but not for military leadership. Joan's talent lay in inspiring her men with self-confidence and a sense of commitment to a nation. Within a few months of the liberation of Orléans, Charles VII was able to be crowned in France's coronation church at Rheims.

Charles showed little gratitude to his unconventional ally. When the Burgundians captured Joan in May 1430, he abandoned her. The Burgundians and the English, hoping to demoralize their opponents by discrediting Joan, accused her of heresy and turned her over to the Inquisition. After ten weeks of interrogation, the "Maid of Orléans" was executed as a relapsed heretic (May 30, 1431). Twenty-five years later (1456), Charles reopened her trial and had her cleared of all charges. But it was not until 1920 that she became Saint Joan.

In 1435, the duke of Burgundy recognized the inevitable and came to terms with Charles. Once France was unified, the English had no hope of clinging to their continental possessions. When the war ended in 1453, the English occupied only a little territory around the port of Calais.

England and France had finally separated, and both nations now had to adjust to the new situation. The war awakened French nationalism and hastened France's transition from a feudal monarchy to a centralized state. The loss of their continental empire disillusioned the English people with their government and set them on the path to a civil war that ended the medieval phase in the history of England's monarchy.

∽ The Black Death

Preconditions and Causes

In the late Middle Ages, nine-tenths of the population worked the land. The three-field system of seasonal planting and crop rotation increased food production. But population growth kept pace with the food supply. Europe's population doubled between the years 1000 and 1300, and by 1300 there were more mouths than could be fed. A European probably faced extreme hunger at least once during a life span that averaged thirty-five years.

Between 1315 and 1317, crop failures contributed to the worst famines of the Middle Ages. Starvation undermined health and increased vulnerability to a virulent bubonic plague that struck in 1348. This "Black Death," so called by contemporaries because of the way it discolored the bodies of its victims, followed the trade routes from Asia into Europe. Appearing first in Sicily, it entered Europe through the ports of Venice, Genoa, and Pisa. Areas like Bohemia, which lay outside the major trade routes, were virtually unaffected. By the early fifteenth century, the plague may have reduced the population of western Europe by two-fifths.

The plague was transmitted to the bloodstream by flea bites. Pneumonic infection—from a victim's sneezing—was also possible. Medieval physicians had no understanding of these processes and could offer no explanation, defense, or cure.

The plague inspired an obsession with death and dying, deep pessimism, and panicky superstition. Amulets and folk remedies abounded. Some people recommended a temperate, disciplined regimen. Others rushed to enjoy all of life's pleasures before it was too late. Troops of flagellants, religious fanatics who whipped themselves in ritual penance, paraded through the countryside, contributing to the general alarm. Sometimes unpopular minorities, like the Jews, were accused of spreading the disease and were murdered.

Social and Economic Consequences

Farms Decline. The plague was most virulent in places where people lived close together. Whole villages and urban districts were sometimes wiped out. As the number of laborers decreased, the wages of those who survived increased. Many serfs abandoned farming and sought more rewarding jobs in urban industries. Agricultural prices fell because of lowered demand, and the price of luxury and manufactured goods—the work of scarce, skilled artisans—rose. These economic developments caused the nobility a significant loss of

Boccaccio Describes the Ravages of the Black Death in Florence

The Black Death provided an excuse for the poet, humanist, and story-teller Giovanni Boccaccio (1313–1375) to assemble a great collection of tales, the Decameron. *Ten congenial men and women flee Florence to escape the plague and while away the time telling stories. In one of these, Boccaccio embedded a fine clinical description of plague symptoms as seen in Florence in 1348—and noted the powerlessness of physicians and the lack of remedies.*

~ What did people of the Middle Ages do to escape the plague? Would any of their actions be judged sound according to modern concepts of medicine? What can the study of calamities like the Black Death tell us about the people of the past?

In Florence, despite all that human wisdom and forethought could devise to avert it, even as the cleansing of the city from many impurities by officials appointed for the purpose, the refusal of entrance to all sick folk, and the adoption of many precautions for the preservation of health; despite also humble supplications addressed to God, and often repeated both in public procession and otherwise, by the devout; towards the beginning of the spring of the said year [1348] the doleful effects of the pestilence began to be horribly apparent by symptoms that [appeared] as if miraculous.

Not such were these symptoms as in the east, where an issue of blood from the nose was a manifest sign of inevitable death; but in men and women alike it first betrayed itself by the emergence of certain tumours in the groin or the armpits, some of which grew as large as a common apple, others as an egg, some more, some less, which the common folk called *gavoccioli*. From the two said parts of the body this deadly *gavoccioli* soon began to propagate and spread itself in all directions indifferently; after which the form of the malady began to change, spots black or livid making their appearance in many cases on the arm or the thigh or elsewhere, now few and large, now minute and numerous. And as the *gavoccioli* had been and still were an infallible token of approaching death, such also were these spots on whomsoever they shewed themselves. Which maladies seemed to set entirely at naught both the art of the physician and the virtues of physic; indeed, whether it was that the disorder was of a nature to defy such treatment, or that the physicians were at fault . . . and, being in ignorance of its source, failed to apply the proper remedies; in either case, not merely were those that recovered few, but almost all died within three days of the appearance of the said symptoms . . . and in most cases without any fever or other attendant malady.

The Decameron of Giovanni Boccaccio, *trans. by J. M. Rigg (London: J. M. Dent & Sons, 1930), p. 5.*

power. Without workers, the value of estates declined, and in order to keep workers on those estates, landowners had to moderate demands on them. As a result, rents everywhere declined steadily after the plague.

The church was insulated from some of the problems that afflicted the nobility. As a great landholder, it suffered economic losses. But these were off-set by an increased demand for masses for the dead and by a flood of gifts and bequests.

To recoup their losses, some landowners converted arable land to sheep pasture. (Herding required far fewer expensive laborers than the cultivation of grain.) The nobility also sought to use their monopoly of political power to reverse their declining fortunes. They passed laws that ordered peasants to stay on the land and that froze wages at low levels. Resentment of such legislation helped fuel the French *Jacquerie* and the English Peasants' Revolt.

Cities Rebound. Although the plague hit urban populations especially hard, the cities ultimately prospered from its effects. The decline of the rural no-bility made it easier for the cities to extend their influence into the country-side. They controlled immigration, limited competition in their markets, and absorbed the rural gentry into the ranks of the urban patriciate.

The omnipresence of death whetted the appetite for pleasure and for the luxuries produced by cities. Initially the demand for manufactured goods could not be met. Craft guilds had purposely kept the numbers of masters and ap-prentices low. The first wave of plague drastically reduced an already restricted supply of artisans. As a result, the prices of manufactured and luxury items rose to new heights. The forces that impoverished the landed nobility enriched townspeople. For as the rising prices of manufactured goods caused wealth to pour into cities, reduced demand for agricultural products depressed their worth and lowered the cost of living for urban dwellers.

The rapidly changing economic conditions created by the plague were not an unmixed blessing for towns. They increased some of the tensions that had long seethed in urban governments. The merchant classes found it diffi-cult to maintain their traditional dominance over the prospering artisans' guilds. The guilds used their increasing political clout to enact restrictive leg-islation designed to protect local industries. Master artisans kept demand for their products high by restricting the number of shops licensed to share their market. This frustrated many trained journeymen who were eager to set up in business for themselves and created strife within the guilds.

⌒ Ecclesiastical Breakdown and Revival: The Late Medieval Church

Kings took full advantage of the rising power of the towns and the declining status of the feudal nobility to centralize governments and economies. The church, which might have resisted the royal drift toward nationalism, faltered just as the new monarchies began to flex their muscles. The plague had weak-ened the church by killing large numbers of clergy, but the church's most se-rious problems were created by the popes themselves.

The Thirteenth-Century Papacy

In the latter half of the thirteenth century the papacy appeared to be in a strong position. Frederick II had been vanquished. Imperial pressure on Rome had been removed. The saintly French king, Louis IX, was an enthusiastic supporter of the church. The Eastern orthodox clergy even accepted reunion with Rome in 1274 in an attempt to persuade the West to send Constantinople help against the Turks.

But as early as the reign of Pope Innocent III (1198–1216), when papal power was at its height, there were signs of trouble. Innocent created a centralized papal monarchy with a clearly political mission. What the church gained in secular power, it lost in spiritual authority. His successors continued down the path he blazed, and the thirteenth-century papacy became a powerful political institution. It was governed by its own law and courts, serviced by an efficient international bureaucracy, and preoccupied with finances and secular goals. Rome's interests, not local needs, determined church appointments, policies, and discipline.

Many observers commented on the popes' departure from the simplicity and other-worldliness of the New Testament apostolic community. They began to draw a dangerous distinction between the papal monarchy and the "true" church of faithful Christians.

Political Fragmentation. The papacy of the thirteenth century was undermined by its own success. The demise of imperial power meant that the popes lost their position as the leaders of Italian resistance to German kings. Italy erupted in political intrigue, and the papacy became just another of the prizes up for grabs.

Pope Gregory X (1271–1276) tried to guarantee the independence of the cardinals by ordering their sequestration immediately following the death of a pope. He hoped that physical isolation would prevent outsiders from influencing papal elections, but the college of cardinals was already too politicized for this to have much effect.

Political infighting was so great that from 1292 to 1294 the college was unable to elect a pope. Finally, in frustration, the cardinals chose a compromise candidate—a saintly but inept Calabrian hermit, Celestine V. Celestine shocked Europe by abdicating under suspicious circumstances after only a few weeks in office. His death, which soon followed, led to rumors that he had been murdered to guarantee that his successor had a clear title to office. The new pope, Boniface VIII (1294–1303), was as worldly wise as Celestine had been naively innocent.

Boniface VIII and Philip the Fair

Boniface came to the throne just as England and France were maturing as nation-states. France's Philip IV, "the Fair" (r. 1285–1314), was no saintly monarch like his grandfather Louis IX. He was a ruthless politician who was to teach Boniface that what the pope had inherited from Innocent III was only an illusion of power. The papal monarchy was no match for the kings who were emerging, in the late thirteenth century, at the head of Europe's new nations.

The Royal Challenge to Papal Authority. If Edward I (r. 1272–1307) of England had been able to resolve problems with Scotland, the Hundred Years' War might have been underway by the time Boniface came to the papal throne. France and England were both mobilizing resources for a war they considered inevitable. And since one of their strategies was to levy extraordinary taxes on their clergy, Boniface found himself involved. In 1215, Pope Innocent III had decreed that the clergy were to pay no taxes to rulers without prior papal consent. Boniface, therefore, had to take a strong stand in defense of papal prerogatives. On February 5, 1296, he issued a bull, *Clericis Laicos*, that forbade lay taxation of the clergy without papal approval.

Edward I retaliated by denying the clergy the protection of the state's laws and courts. Philip the Fair cunningly deprived the papacy of the bulk of its income by forbidding the exportation of money from France to Rome. Boniface had no choice but to come to terms with Philip, and he issued a second bull, conceding the right of a king to tax clergy "during an emergency."

For much of his reign Boniface was under siege by powerful enemies in Italy. The Colonnas—rivals of Boniface's family, the Gaetani—joined with the Spiritual Franciscans in a campaign to invalidate Boniface's election. They alleged that Boniface had forced his predecessor, Celestine V, from office, murdered him, and won the papal election by bribing the cardinals. Boniface hung on, and his fortunes slowly improved. In 1300, Rome celebrated a Jubilee, an occasion on which pilgrims to Rome received an especially generous indulgence (remission of sin). Tens of thousands flocked to Rome in apparent support of the papacy.

Boniface was emboldened by the experience to reassert the papacy's claim to leadership in international politics. He infuriated Edward by supporting the Scots against the English. But his most serious confrontation was with Philip. Philip had arrested Boniface's Parisian legate, Bernard Saisset, the bishop of Pamiers, and convicted him in the royal courts of heresy and treason. Philip demanded that Boniface recognize the legitimacy of the proceedings, but to do so would have been to relinquish the pope's jurisdiction over the French clergy. Boniface demanded Saisset's unconditional release and revoked his previous concessions on the matter of clerical taxation. In December 1301, Boniface sent Philip the bull *Ausculta Fili* (*Listen, My Son*). It pointedly informed the king that "God has set popes over kings and kingdoms."

Philip unleashed a ruthless anti-papal campaign, and Boniface was forced to take a stand against his argument that the state should control the churches within its national boundaries. On November 18, 1302, the bull *Unam Sanctam* declared that temporal authority was "subject" to the spiritual power of the church. The French received the pope's letter as a declaration of war.

Guillaume de Nogaret, Philip's chief minister, denounced Boniface to the French clergy and led an army into Italy to take the pope prisoner. In mid-

The Palace of the Popes in Avignon, France. In 1311, Pope Clement V made the city his permanent residence, and the popes remained there until 1377. [Fritz Henle/Photo Researchers, Inc.]

August of 1303, Nogaret surprised Boniface in his retreat at Anagni. The pope was badly beaten and almost executed before the people of Anagni rallied to his defense. He returned to Rome, but the ordeal was too much for an aged man. He died in October 1303.

Boniface's successor, Benedict XI (1303–1304), excommunicated Nogaret, but he was in no position to retaliate against the French government. His successor, Clement V (1305–1314), a Frenchman and former archbishop of Bordeaux, completely capitulated. He released Nogaret from excommunication and explained that *Unam Sanctam* was not intended in any way to diminish royal authority. He also gave in to Philip's demand that the Crusading order, the Knights Templars, be condemned for heresy and dissolved—so that the state could confiscate its wealth. France's victory seemed complete in 1309, when Clement, pleading safety and convenience, moved the papal court to Avignon. Avignon was an independent city situated on land that belonged to the pope, but it was in the southeast corner of territory that was culturally French. The papacy was to remain in Avignon for almost seventy years (until 1377), and no pope was ever again seriously to threaten a king.

The Avignon Papacy (1309–1377)

The Avignon popes were in appearance, although not always in fact, dominated by the French king, and during Clement V's pontificate Frenchmen flooded into the college of cardinals. Cut off from their Roman estates, the popes at Avignon had to find new sources of income. Their ingenuity and success quickly earned them unfortunate reputations as greedy materialists. Clement V expanded papal taxes on the clergy. Clement VI (1342–1352) began selling *indulgences,* releases from penance for sin. The doctrine of purgatory—a place of punishment where souls ultimately destined for heaven atoned for venial sins—developed as part of this campaign. By the fifteenth century, the church was encouraging the living to buy reduced sentences in purgatory for deceased loved ones.

Pope John XXII. By the time Pope John XXII (1316–1334) ascended the throne, the popes were strongly enough established in Avignon to re-enter the field of international politics. The result was a quarrel with the German emperor, Louis IV, that inspired an important debate about the nature of legitimate authority.

John backed a candidate who lost to Louis in the imperial election of 1314 and obstinately—and without legal justification—refused to confirm Louis's title. Louis retaliated by accusing John of heresy and declaring him deposed in favor of an antipope. Two outstanding pamphleteers made the case for the king: William of Ockham, whom John excommunicated in 1328, and Marsilius of Padua (ca. 1290–1342), whose teaching John declared heretical in 1327.

William of Ockham (d. 1349) was a brilliant logician and critic of the "realist" philosophers who claimed that general terms, like "church," corresponded to transcendent realities that actually existed. Ockham, a "nominalist," insisted that such words were only names the human mind gave to abstract ideas it invented. This position led Ockham to conclude that the real church was the historical human community, not some supernatural entity. The pope was only one of its members, and, as such, had no special powers that made him infallible. The church was best guided not by popes, but by scripture and by councils that represented the whole body.

In *Defender of Peace* (1324), Marsilius of Padua argued that clergy were limited to purely spiritual functions and had no right to coerce laity. The spiritual crimes over which the pope had jurisdiction would be punished in the next life, not in this one. An exception might be made if a secular ruler declared a divine law also a law of the state, for God had given the state exclusive authority to maintain secular order by force. A true pope lived according to the strictest apostolic ideals and presumed to lead only by spiritual example.

National Opposition to the Avignon Papacy. John's successor, Benedict XII (1334–1342), began construction of a great palace at Avignon, and his high-living French successor, Clement VI (1342–1352), presided over a splendid, worldly court. The cardinals became lobbyists for various secular patrons, and Avignon's fiscal tentacles spread farther and farther afield.

Secular governments responded by passing legislation restricting papal jurisdiction and taxation in France, England, and Germany. The English had no intention of supporting a papacy that they believed was the puppet of their French enemy. The French monarchy insisted upon its "Gallican liberties," a well-founded tradition that granted the king control of ecclesiastical appointments and taxation. The governments of German and Swiss cities also took the initiative to limit and even to overturn traditional clerical privileges and immunities.

John Wycliffe and John Huss. Discontent with the worldly clergy and politicized papacy found expression in popular lay religious movements as well as in government legislation. The most significant were the Lollards in England and the Hussites in Bohemia. The Lollards drew their ideas from the writings of John Wycliffe (d. 1384)—as did John Huss (d. 1415), the martyr of the Hussite movement. Neither man would have approved, however, of all that his alleged followers did in his name.

Wycliffe was an Oxford theologian and a major intellectual spokesman for the rights of royalty against the secular pretensions of popes. Wycliffe strongly supported the actions English kings took from 1350 on to reduce the power of the Avignon papacy over the church in England. Wycliffe, like the Franciscans, believed that clergy "ought to be content with food and clothing." His arguments for clerical poverty provided justification for confiscations of ecclesiastical property by the state.

Wycliffe maintained that since all authority came from God, only leaders who lived pious lives could lay claim to legitimacy. This argument empowered faithful laypeople to pass judgment on corrupt ecclesiastics and undertake the reform of the church. The argument could also be used to justify resistance to secular rulers whose immoral lives proved that they held no mandate from God. Wycliffe, in some ways, anticipated positions that later Protestants would take—challenging papal infallibility, the dogma of transubstantiation that gave the priesthood power over the laity, and policies that restricted the laity's access to the Scriptures.

The Lollards, English advocates of Wycliffe's teaching, preached in the vernacular, disseminated translations of Holy Scripture, and championed clerical poverty. So long as they restricted their attention to religious matters, the English government tolerated them. But after the Peasants' Revolt of 1381 popularized egalitarian notions that could be linked to Wycliffe's works, the state decided that Lollardy was subversive. In 1401, it was declared a capital offense.

Heresy was not so easily dealt with in Bohemia, where governments were weak. The University of Prague, founded in 1348, was the center for a Czech nationalistic movement that opposed German encroachments on Bohemia. The leader of the movement was John Huss, who in 1403 became rector of the university. Religious reform was an instrument he used to help the Czechs build a national identity.

The Czech reformers advocated vernacular translations of the Bible and rejected practices they labeled superstitions (particularly some customs associated with the Eucharist). They repudiated the Catholic rubric that reserved the cup at communion to the priest, and they offered both the wine and the bread to the laity. This removed any suggestion that the clergy were spiritually superior to the people. Hussites also denied the validity of the doctrine of transubstantiation. They believed that bread and wine remained bread and wine after priestly consecration. And like the Lollards, they doubted that a priest guilty of mortal sin could perform a valid sacrament.

Wycliffe's teaching was responsible, in part, for the Hussite movement. After Anne of Bohemia married King Richard II of England in 1381, Czech students enrolled at Oxford and sent copies of Wycliffe's works home. Huss became the leader of the Wycliffe faction at the University of Prague.

Huss was excommunicated in 1410, and in 1414 he successfully petitioned for a hearing before an international church council that was assembling at Constance, Switzerland. Although he was guaranteed safe conduct by Emperor Sigismund, he was imprisoned and executed for heresy on July 6, 1415. The reaction in Bohemia to his execution and that of his colleague, Jerome of Prague, a few months later was fierce. The Taborites, a militant branch of the Hussites, took up arms under John Ziska to transform Bohemia into a religious and social paradise. Within a decade, they had won control of the Bohemian church.

The Great Schism (1378–1417) and the Conciliar Movement to 1449

Urban VI and Clement VII. In January 1377, Pope Gregory XI (1370–1378) yielded to international pressure and took the papacy back to Rome. Europe rejoiced—prematurely, as it turned out—at the end of the church's "Babylonian Captivity" in Avignon (a reference to the exile of the ancient Israelites from their homeland).

Gregory died soon after returning to Rome, and the cardinals elected an Italian archbishop, Pope Urban VI (1378–1389). When Urban announced his intention to reform the Curia (the church's central administration), the cardinals, most of whom were French, sensed a challenge to their power and insisted on returning the papal court to their base of operation in Avignon. Five months after Urban's enthronement, a group of thirteen cardinals announced that Urban's election was invalid because it had been forced on them by the Roman mob. They proceeded to elect a "true" pope, Clement VII (1378–1397), a cousin of the French king. Urban denied their allegations and appointed cardinals to replace them in his college.

Europe, confronted with two papal courts, distributed its support along political lines: England and its allies (the Holy Roman Empire, Hungary, Bohemia, and Poland) acknowledged Urban VI, whereas France and those in its orbit (Naples, Scotland, Castile, and Aragon) supported Clement VII. (The Roman Catholic Church has subsequently decided that the Roman line of popes was the legitimate one.)

Since the schism threatened the survival of the church in its traditional form, responsible leaders hoped to end it quickly. The easiest solution would have been for one or both of the popes to resign for the good of all, but neither was willing to sacrifice himself. In 1409, thirty-one years after the schism began, cardinals from both sides attempted to resolve the problem by deposing both popes and electing a new one. To their consternation, neither Rome nor Avignon accepted their action, and Christendom was presented with a third pope (resident in Pisa).

Conciliar Theory of Church Government. Europe's leaders, seeing no other option, began to listen to scholars who believed that an ecumenical church council could end the schism. There were problems: only a pope could convene a legitimate council, and none of the popes wanted to summon a council that would depose him. Also, since a pope's authority derived directly from God and not from his people, it was not at all certain that a council could depose a pope.

The supporters of the council, the conciliarists, were moved to examine medieval assumptions about authority. In the process they developed a rationale for democratic government. The conciliarists defined the church as the whole body of the faithful. Ultimate authority rested, therefore, with the people. Popes were chosen to care for the people's church, and they served at the people's pleasure.

The Council of Constance (1414–1417). Emperor Sigismund finally prevailed on John XXIII, the Pisan pope, to summon a council in Constance in 1414. Without the hope of support from any quarter, the competing popes were forced to come to terms. The cardinals at the council then proceeded to elect a new pope, Martin V (1417–1431). Before the council disbanded, it passed a resolution *(Sacrosancta)* that stated that the council was the true government of the church and supreme over popes. Provisions were also made for meetings of councils at regular intervals.

Conciliar government of the church peaked at the Council of Basel (1431–1449), when the council presumed to negotiate church doctrine with the heretic Hussites of Bohemia. In November 1433, an agreement was reached giving the Bohemians jurisdiction over their church (similar to that held by the French and the English), a unique liturgy, and an exalted role for the laity.

The exercise of such power by a council did not please the pope, and in 1438 he upstaged the council by negotiating reunion with the Eastern church. The agreement, signed in Florence in 1439, was short-lived, but it restored papal prestige. And when Basel asserted its authority by threatening the pope with deposition, the kings of Europe, fearing a return to schism, withdrew their support for the conciliar movement. A decade later the papal bull *Execrabilis* (1460) condemned conciliarism. The movement had, however, achieved something. It had planted the thought that the role of the leader of an institution was to provide for the well-being of its members. This idea had ramifications for the state as well as the church.

War, plague, and schism convulsed Europe in the late Middle Ages. Even God's house became a shambles as competing popes fought over it. William of Ockham, the leading intellectual of the day, advocated philosophical skepticism—acknowledgment of the limits of human reason. And as the leadership of traditional institutions failed, ordinary men and women rose up to lay claim to the mantle of authority.

But there was more to the age than loss and doubt. The fourteenth century saw the birth of humanism and an explosion of lay education. The artistic and cultural movements abroad in the fifteenth century heralded Italy's great Renaissance.

⌇ Review Questions

1. What were the underlying and precipitating causes of the Hundred Years' War? What advantages did each side have? Why were the French finally able to drive the English almost entirely out of France?

2. What were the causes of the Black Death, and why did it spread so quickly throughout western Europe? Where was it most virulent? What were its effects on European society? How important do you think disease is in changing the course of history?

3. What was at issue in the struggle between Pope Boniface VIII and King Philip the Fair? Why was Boniface unable to put up a stronger fight? How had political conditions changed since the reign of Pope Innocent III? What did the changes mean for the future of the papacy?

4. What changes took place in the church and in its relationship to secular society between 1200 and 1450? How did it respond to political threats from increasingly powerful monarchs? How great an influence did the church have on secular events?

5. What is meant by the term *Avignon Papacy*? How did this period in the church's history shape the development of the papacy? What caused the Great Schism? How was it resolved? Why was the Conciliar Movement a threat to the papacy?

6. Why did kings in the late thirteenth and early fourteenth centuries have more power over the church than it had over them? What had changed to make this era different from earlier ones, in which popes dominated rulers? What did kings hope to achieve through their struggles with the church?

⌇ Suggested Readings

R. BARBER (ed.), *The Pastons: Letters of a Family in the War of the Roses* (1984). Revelations of English family life in an age of crisis.

J. HUIZINGA, *The Waning of the Middle Ages: A Study of the Forms of Life, Thought, and Art in France and the Netherlands in the Dawn of the Renaissance* (1924). A classic study of "mentality" at the end of the Middle Ages. Exaggerated, but engrossing.

G. LEFF, *Heresy in the Later Middle Ages*, vols. 1–2 (1967). Magisterial survey of all the major heretical movements.

W. H. MCNEILL, *Plagues and Peoples* (1976). The Black Death in a broader context.

F. OAKLEY, *The Western Church in the Later Middle Ages* (1979). Eloquent, sympathetic survey.

E. PERROY, *The Hundred Years' War*, trans. by W. B. Wells (1965). Still the most comprehensive one-volume account.

Y. RENOVARD, *The Avignon Papacy 1305–1403*, trans. by D. Bethell (1970). The standard narrative account.

B. TIERNEY, *Foundations of the Conciliar Theory* (1955). Important study showing the origins of conciliar theory in canon law.

W. ULLMANN, *Origins of the Great Schism* (1948). A basic study by a controversial interpreter of medieval political thought.

P. ZIEGLER, *The Black Death* (1969). Highly readable account.

10

Renaissance and Discovery

KEY TOPICS IN THIS CHAPTER

～ The politics, culture, and art of the Italian Renaissance

～ Political struggle and foreign intervention in Italy

～ The powerful new monarchies of northern Europe

～ The thought and culture of the northern Renaissance

The late medieval period was an era of creative breaking up. The social order that had persisted in Europe for a thousand years failed, but Europe did not decline; it merely changed direction.

By the late fifteenth century, Europe's population was recovering from the losses inflicted by the plagues, famines, and wars of the fourteenth century. In many places, able rulers were establishing stable, centralized governments. The city-states of Italy were doing especially well. Italy's strategic location permitted it to dominate world trade, which still centered on the Mediterranean. The great wealth trade brought Italy's rulers and merchants allowed them to become patrons of government, education, and the arts. The result was a cultural Renaissance led by Italians.

Renaissance Humanists revived the study of Greek and Latin and recovered the classical literary heritage. They reformed education and, thanks to the invention of the printing press, became the first scholars able to reach out to the general public. In their eagerness to educate ordinary men and women, they championed the development of vernacular languages as vehicles for art and serious thought.

In western Europe, in particular, powerful nations began to appear and to inspire passionate patriotism. During the late fifteenth and sixteenth centuries, these nations entered an era of unprecedented territorial expansion. The colonies they established around the world produced a flood of gold and exotic new products that transformed Western civilization.

∽ The Renaissance in Italy (1375–1527)

The Renaissance was a time of transition from the medieval to the modern world. Medieval Europe, especially before the twelfth century, was a fragmented feudal society with a marginal agrarian economy. Intellectually, it was dominated by the church. Renaissance Europe, especially after the fourteenth century, was characterized by growing national consciousness and political centralization, an urban economy based on commerce and capitalism, and an increasingly secular culture. Italy, between 1375 and 1527, led in the creation of the most striking features of the Renaissance way of life.

The Italian City-State

Italy had always had a cultural advantage over the rest of Europe, for its geography made it the natural gateway between East and West. Its trade with the Middle East, which continued uninterrupted throughout the Middle Ages, supported a vibrant urban culture. During the thirteenth and fourteenth centuries, Italy's trade-rich cities became powerful city-states, ruling the countryside (see Map 10-1). And, by the fifteenth century, the great Italian cities were home to the banks that dominated Europe's economy.

The growth of Italy's cities and urban culture was promoted by the endemic warfare between Guelf (pro-papal) and Ghibelline (pro-imperial) factions in Italian politics. Either the pope or the emperor might have brought the cities under control if either had been free to concentrate on the task. Instead, each tried to weaken the other, and the merchant oligarchies who governed the cities were the winners. Free from dominance by kings or territorial princes, the Italian cities expanded into the surrounding countryside, assimilated the rural nobility, and grew into city-states. The five greatest were the duchy of Milan, the republics of Florence and Venice, the Papal States, and the kingdom of Naples.

Social Class and Conflict. Social strife and competition for power were intense within Italy's city-states. By the fifteenth century, most had concluded that they could preserve order only by turning themselves over to despots. (Venice was a notable exception, remaining an oligarchic republic under the control of a small group of merchant families.)

Legend:
- Duchy of Milan
- Republic of Genoa
- Republic of Florence
- Republic of Venice
- Papal States
- Kingdom of Naples

D. OF SAVOY
Milan
Turin
SALUZZO
MANTUA
Venice
FERRARA
Genoa
MODENA
ROMAGNA
LUCCA
Florence
Siena
SIENA
CORSICA (GENOA)
Rome
SARDINIA (ARAGON)
Naples
Tyrrhenian Sea
Adriatic Sea
Palermo
SICILY
Syracuse
Mediterranean Sea

200 MILES
200 KILOMETERS

MAP 10-1 Renaissance Italy *The city-states of Renaissance Italy were self-contained principalities whose internal strife was monitored by despots and whose external aggression was controlled by treaty.*

The history of Florence best illustrates the forces that contended within Italian city governments. There were four politically active groups in Florence: the old rich (the *grandi,* the nobles and merchants who were traditional leaders), an emergent newly rich merchant class (capitalists and bankers known as the *popolo grosso* or "fat people"), the middle-burgher ranks (guildmasters, shop owners, and professionals), and the *popolo minuto* (the "little people" of the lower middle classes). In 1457, about 30,000 Florentines, one-third of the population, were listed as paupers.

In 1378, following the economic dislocation of the Black Death, there was a great uprising of the poor in Florence, the Ciompi Revolt. It established a chaotic four-year reign of power for the lower classes. Stability was not achieved until Cosimo dé Medici (1389–1464) took over in 1434.

Cosimo dé Medici, in addition to being the richest man in Florence, was an astute statesman. He controlled the city from behind the scenes, skillfully

Significant Dates from the Italian Renaissance (1375–1527)

1434	*Medici rule established in Florence*
1454–1455	*Treaty of Lodi*
1494	*Charles VIII of France invades Italy*
1495	*League of Venice*
1499	*Louis XII invades Italy*
1500	*The Borgias conquer Romagna*
1512–1513	*The Holy League defeats the French*
1515	*Francis I invades Italy*
1527	*Sack of Rome by imperial soldiers*

manipulating the constitution and influencing elections. Florence was governed by a council of six (later, eight) men, the *Signoria,* elected from the most powerful guilds. Through informal, cordial relations with the electoral committee, Cosimo saw to it that the members of the *Signoria* were his men. His grandson, Lorenzo the Magnificent (1449–1492), had virtual totalitarian control over Florence. The assassination of Lorenzo's brother in 1478, by the pope and a rival Florentine family, the Pazzi, led Lorenzo to rule with a firm hand. But he was careful to court popular support.

Despotism was less subtle elsewhere. When internal fighting and foreign intrigue got so bad that city governments lapsed into paralysis, dominant groups agreed to call in a hired strongman, a *podestà.* He was a neutral outsider empowered to do whatever was necessary to maintain law and order and foster a good climate for business. Because a despot could not depend on the warring factions of his city to cooperate, he policed and protected his town with a mercenary army. This was hired from military brokers called *condottieri.*

The job of a *podestà* was hazardous. He could be dismissed by the oligarchy that hired him, or he could be assassinated by those whom he offended. However, the spoils of a successful career were very great, for a *podestà* might establish a dynasty. The Visconti family that came to power in Milan in 1278 and the Sforza family that followed them in 1450 both had such roots.

Be it the comparatively tranquil republic of Venice, the strong-arm democracy of Florence, or the undisguised despotism of Milan, a disciplined Italian city provided a congenial climate for intellectual and artistic pursuits. Despots were as vigorous as republicans in promoting Renaissance culture. Spiritually minded popes were no less enthusiastic than more worldly vicars of Christ. All had what it took to be great patrons: great wealth.

Humanism

The Florentine Leonardo Bruni (1374–1444) was the first to describe the scholarship of the Renaissance as the study of *humanitas* ("humanity"). Modern authorities have proposed different definitions of the term. Some have seen Humanism as an un-Christian philosophy emphasizing human dignity, individualism, and secular values. Others have pointed to Humanists who were the champions of Catholic Christianity against the pagan teaching of Aristotle. Still others have suggested that Humanism took no particular philosophical position and was simply an educational program concentrating on rhetoric and sound scholarship.

There is truth in each of these observations. Humanism was the scholarly study of the Latin and Greek classics and the church fathers—pursued as an end in itself and as a guide to reforming society. Humanists advocated the *studia humanitatis,* a liberal arts curriculum composed of grammar, rhetoric, poetry, history, politics, and moral philosophy. These subjects were considered innately worth pursuing and also useful in preparing people for lives of virtuous action. The first Humanists were orators and poets. Some taught rhetoric within the universities, but many were employed as secretaries, speech writers, and diplomats in princely and papal courts.

Manuel Chrysoloras, a Byzantine scholar, taught at Florence from 1397 to 1403 and opened the world of Greek scholarship to a generation of young Italian Humanists. But the study of classical and Christian antiquities had begun long before he arrived. There was a Carolingian renaissance in the ninth century. Another was led by the cathedral school of Chartres in the twelfth century. The University of Paris in the thirteenth century was transformed by the study of Aristotle. The works of Saint Augustine had a comparable effect on the early fourteenth century. These scholarly revivals pale, however, in comparison with the achievements of Italy's late medieval Renaissance.

Humanists did not use the techniques of debate that the Scholastic movement had popularized in the medieval universities. Instead of summarizing and reconciling the views of respected commentators on a topic, they went directly to the original sources. Avidly searching out manuscript collections, Italian Humanists recovered all that remained of Greek and Latin literature and made it generally available to scholars during the fourteenth and fifteenth centuries. They so assimilated the classics and identified with the ancients that they came to think of the previous centuries as a hiatus, a "dark middle age" separating ancient civilization from its rebirth in their day.

Petrarch, Dante, and Boccaccio. Francesco Petrarch (1304–1374), called "the father of Humanism," abandoned the practice of law to pursue a love of letters. His highest aspiration was to equal the literary productions of the ancients. His *Letters to the Ancient Dead* was an imagined correspondence with Cicero, Livy, Vergil, and Horace. His Latin epic poem *Africa* (a tribute to the Roman general Scipio Africanus) was intended to continue the work of Vergil. His biographies of famous Romans, *Lives of Illustrious Men,* was homage to Plutarch. But Petrarch's most famous work was original and vernacular: a collection of highly introspective love sonnets addressed to a married woman named Laura, whom he admired in the courtly love tradition—from a safe distance.

Classical and Christian values coexist, but not always harmoniously, in Petrarch's work. He rejected Scholastic learning as sterile and useless, but published tracts refuting Aristotelian arguments that undercut faith in personal immortality. His imagined dialogues with Saint Augustine bear witness to his acceptance of many other traditional medieval Christian beliefs.

Petrarch had a far more secular point of view than his famous near-contemporary, Dante Alighieri (1265–1321). Dante's *Vita Nuova* and *Divine Comedy*, which rank with Petrarch's sonnets as cornerstones of Italian vernacular literature, are moving reflections of medieval piety. Petrarch's student, Giovanni Boccaccio (1313–1375), also created bridges between medieval literature and Humanism. His *Decameron* consists of 100 often bawdy tales—many retold from medieval sources. It is a stinging exposé of sexual and economic misconduct and a sympathetic look at human nature.

Educational Reforms and Goals. Humanists were activists who refused to be slaves to tradition. They treated the magnificent manuscript collections they assembled as if books were potent medicines for the ills of contemporary society. The goal of their studies was to discover the good and to practice virtue. Humanist learning was intended to ennoble people by fitting them for the free use of their gifts of mind and body.

Traditional methods of education had to be reformed to create the kind of useful schooling, nurturing well-rounded people, that the Humanists favored. The rediscovery in 1416 of the complete text of Quintilian's *Education of the Orator* provided Humanists with a classical guide for the revision of curricula. Mentors, such as Vittorino da Feltre (d. 1446), articulated the goals and methods of the reform. Vittorino required his students to master difficult works by Pliny, Ptolemy, Terence, Plautus, Livy, and Plutarch, and to take vigorous physical training.

Humanist learning was not confined to the classroom. Baldassare Castiglione's (1478–1529) influential *Book of the Courtier* was written as a practical guide for the nobility at the court of Urbino. It urged them to combine the study of ancient languages and history with the practice of athletic, military, and musical skills. In addition to these accomplishments, a courtier was to practice good manners and maintain an exemplary moral character.

Women, most notably Christine de Pisan (1363?–1434), helped shape and profit from educational reform. Christine's father was physician and astrologer to the court of King Charles V of France. At the French court she received as fine an education as any man and became an expert in classical, French, and Italian languages and literature. Married at fifteen and widowed with three children at twenty-seven, she turned to writing lyric poetry to support herself. Her works were soon being read at all the European courts. Her most famous book, *The City of Ladies*, chronicles the accomplishments of the great women of history.

The Florentine "Academy." The revival of the study of ancient Greek literature, particularly the works of Plato, was the most important of the Renaissance's renewed contacts with the past. Interest in Greek led Florence, in 1397, to invite the Byzantine scholar Manuel Chrysoloras to immigrate and open a

Pico della Mirandola States the Renaissance Image of Man

One of the most eloquent statements of the Renaissance's aspirations for human beings comes from the Italian Humanist Pico della Mirandola (1463–1494). His Oration on the Dignity of Man *(ca. 1486) claims that humans are free to become whatever they choose.*

⤳ How much freedom of choice is really described here? Are human options limited? Does this statement differ from what the church traditionally had outlined as life's possibilities? Is the concept of freedom in this passage a modern one?

The best of artisans [God] ordained that that creature (man) to whom He had been able to give nothing proper to himself should have joint possession of whatever had been peculiar to each of the different kinds of being. He therefore took man as a creature of indeterminate nature and, assigning him a place in the middle of the world, addressed him thus: "Neither a fixed abode nor a form that is thine alone nor any function peculiar to thyself have we given thee, Adam, to the end that according to thy longing and according to thy judgment thou mayest have and possess what abode, what form, and what functions thou thyself shalt desire. The nature of all other beings is limited and constrained within the bounds of laws prescribed by Us. Thou, constrained by no limits, in accordance with thine own free will, in whose hand We have placed thee, shalt ordain for thyself the limits of thy nature. We have set thee at the world's center that thou mayest from thence more easily observe whatever is in the world. We have made thee neither of heaven nor of earth, neither mortal nor immortal, so that with freedom of choice and with honor, as though the maker and molder of thyself, thou mayest fashion thyself in whatever shape thou shalt prefer. Thou shalt have the power to degenerate into the lower forms of life, which are brutish. Thou shalt have the power, out of thy soul's judgment, to be reborn into the higher forms, which are divine." O supreme generosity of God the Father, O highest and most marvelous felicity of man! To him it is granted to have whatever he chooses, to be whatever he wills.

Giovanni Pico della Mirandola, Oration on the Dignity of Man, *in* The Renaissance Philosophy of Man, *ed. by E. Cassirer et al. (Chicago: Phoenix Books, 1961), pp. 224–225.*

school. The ecumenical Council of Ferrara-Florence, which met in 1439 to negotiate the reunion of the Eastern and Western churches, brought more Greek scholars and manuscripts to Italy. Their numbers increased greatly when Constantinople fell to the Turks in 1453.

Medieval Scholastics were preoccupied with Aristotle's logic and science, but Renaissance thinkers were enthralled by Plato's poetry and mysticism. Platonism's appeal lay in its flattering view of human nature and its apparent congruence with Christianity. Platonism posited the existence of a realm of eternal ideas that were the prototypes for the imperfect, perishable things of the world in which humans lived. Plato argued that the presence in the human mind of an innate knowledge of mathematical truths and moral standards proved that a part of a human being was rooted in the eternal.

Cosimo dé Medici (1389–1464) encouraged the study of Plato and the Neoplatonic philosophers by funding a Platonic Academy, a gathering of influential Florentine Humanists headed first by Marsilio Ficino (1433–1499) and later by Pico della Mirandola (1463–1494). From Florence the complete works of Plato began to circulate in the West and to change the West's view of human nature. Pico's *Oration on the Dignity of Man* succinctly articulated the new faith in human potential. Published in Rome in December 1486, the *Oration* was a preface to a collection of 900 theses proposed for a public debate on all of life's important issues. It declared humans to be the only creatures in the world possessed of the freedom to become whatever they chose to be—angels or pigs.

Civic Humanism. Although some Humanists were clubbish snobs—an intellectual elite with narrow, antiquarian interests—others preached a "civil Humanism," an education that promoted virtue and equipped one for public service. They entered politics, produced an art and literature to celebrate the cities in which they lived, promoted the use of vernacular languages, and wrote histories of contemporary events. On occasion, their scholarship contributed to political upheaval.

The Humanists' careful study of classical languages equipped them to carry out scientific, critical analyses of important historical documents. Some Humanists, like Lorenzo Valla (1406–1457), author of the standard Renaissance text on Latin philology *(Elegances of the Latin Language)*, made discoveries that shook the foundations of medieval institutions. Valla demonstrated that the *Donation of Constantine,* a document which the church had cited since the eighth century to bolster its claim to secular power, was a fraud. Valla pointed out that the *Donation* was filled with anachronistic terms (e.g., fief) and references that would have been meaningless to a man of Emperor Constantine's day. Valla also publicized errors in the Latin Vulgate, the version of the Bible authorized for use in the Western church.

Intentionally or unintentionally, Humanism provided ammunition for critics of traditional medieval organizations. Young Humanists were among the earliest supporters of Martin Luther and the Protestant Reformation.

Renaissance Art

In Renaissance Italy—and in Reformation Europe—the interests of the laity triumphed over those of the clergy. As people began to appreciate the secular world, secular learning, and purely human pursuits as ends in themselves, medieval Christian values adjusted to a more this-worldly spirit.

This development stemmed in part from the crises within the papacy that cost the late medieval church much of its power and prestige. But it also

Florentine women doing needlework, spinning, and weaving. These activities took up much of a woman's time and contributed to the elegance of dress for which Florentine men and women were famed. [Alinari/Art Resource]

owed much to the rise of national sentiment, the creation of competent governmental bureaucracies staffed by laypersons rather than clerics, and the rapid growth of lay education during the fourteenth and fifteenth centuries.

The new perspective on life can be perceived in the painting and sculpture of the "High" or mature Renaissance (the late fifteenth and early sixteenth centuries). Whereas medieval art was abstract and formulaic, Renaissance art was concerned with the observation of the natural world and the communication of human emotions. Renaissance art displayed a rational (chiefly mathematical) order, a symmetry and proportionality that reflected a Humanistic faith in the harmony and intelligibility of the universe.

During the fifteenth century, artists developed new technical skills. Slow-drying oil-based paints were invented, and new methods of drafting appeared. *Chiaroscuro*, the use of shading, and linear perspective, the adjustment of the size of figures to create the illusion of depth, permitted artists to paint a more natural world. Whereas flat Byzantine and Gothic paintings were intended to be read like pages in a book, Renaissance paintings were windows on a three-dimensional world filled with life.

Giotto (1266–1336), the father of Renaissance painting, was the first to intuit what could be done with the new techniques. Though still filled with religious seriousness, his work was less abstract and more naturalistic than that of a medieval painter. The Black Death of 1340 slowed the development of art, but ideas like Giotto's emerged again in the fifteenth century in the work of the painter Masaccio (1401–1428) and the sculptor Donatello (1386–1466). The heights were reached by the great masters of the High Renaissance: Leonardo da Vinci (1452–1519), Raphael (1483–1520), and Michelangelo Buonarroti (1475–1564).

Leonardo came closer than anyone to achieving the Renaissance ideal of universal competence. He was one of the greatest painters of all time—as is demonstrated by his famous portrait, *Mona Lisa.* Kings and dukes employed him as a military engineer. An early advocate of scientific experimentation, he defied the church by dissecting corpses to learn human anatomy. He also did significant descriptive work in botany. Leonardo's sketch books were filled with designs for such modern machines as airplanes and submarines. He had so many ideas that it was difficult for him to concentrate long on any one of them.

Raphael, an unusually sensitive man, was loved for both his work and his kindly personality. He is famous for his tender madonnas, the best known of which graced the monastery of San Sisto in Piacenza and is now in Dresden. Art historians consider his fresco *The School of Athens*, a group portrait of the great Western philosophers, a perfect example of Renaissance technique.

Michelangelo, a more melancholy genius, also excelled in a variety of arts and crafts. His *David*, an eighteen-foot-high sculpture of a biblical hero in the guise of a Greek god, splendidly illustrates the Renaissance artist's devotion to harmony, symmetry, and proportion—and to the glorification of the human form. Four different popes commissioned works by Michelangelo. The most famous are the frescoes for the Sistine Chapel, painted during the pontificate of Pope Julius II (1503–1513). The Sistine frescoes originally covered 10,000 square feet and involved 343 figures—most of which Michelangelo insisted on executing with minimal help from his assistants. It took him four years to complete the extraordinarily original and moving images that have become the best-known icons of the Christian faith.

Michelangelo lived to be almost ninety, and his later works illustrate the passing of the High Renaissance and the advent of a new style known as *Mannerism*. Mannerism was a reaction against the simplicity and symmetry of High Renaissance art. It made room for the strange, even the abnormal, and gave freer reign to the subjectivity of the artist. The name reflects an increased tendency by artists to express individual perceptions and feelings—to paint, compose, or write in a "mannered" or "affected" way. The Venetian Tintoretto (d. 1594) and the Spanish El Greco (d. 1614) are Mannerism's best representatives.

Slavery in the Renaissance

The vision of innate human nobility that inspired the Renaissance was marred by what modern observers might consider a significant blind spot. Slavery flourished in Italy as extravagantly as did art and culture. The slave market developed as early as the twelfth century, when Spaniards began to sell Muslim war captives to wealthy Italians. Many of these people were employed as household or domestic slaves, but collective plantation slavery also evolved during the High Middle Ages in the eastern Mediterranean. The Venetians set up sugar cane plantations that were models for later west Mediterranean and New World slavery.

This portrait of Katharina, by Albrecht Dürer, provides evidence of African slavery in Europe during the sixteenth century. Katharina was in the service of one João Bradao, a Portuguese economic minister living in Antwerp, then the financial center of Europe. Dürer became friends with Bradao during his stay in the Low Countries in the winter of 1520–1521. [Bildarchiv Foto Marburg/Art Resource, N.Y.]

The demand for slaves soared after the Black Death (1348–1350) reduced the supply of laborers everywhere in western Europe. Slaves of all races were imported from Africa, the Balkans, Constantinople, Cyprus, Crete, and the lands surrounding the Black Sea. Most well-to-do Italian households had slaves; even the clergy owned them. Owners could dispose of them like any piece of property. A strong young slave cost the equivalent of the wages paid a free servant over several years. But given the prospect of a lifetime of free service, slaves were very good bargains.

As in ancient Greece and Rome, slaves of the Renaissance era were often integrated into households like family members. Some female slaves became mothers of their masters' children, and quite a few of these children were adopted and raised as legitimate heirs of their fathers. It was clearly in the self-interest of owners to protect their investments by keeping slaves healthy and happy, but slaves remained an uprooted and resentful people—a threat to social stability.

∾ Italy's Political Decline: French Invasions (1494–1527)

The Treaty of Lodi

The protection of Italy from foreign invasion depended on the ability of its independent city-states to cooperate. During the last half of the fifteenth century, the Treaty of Lodi (1454–1455) brought Milan and Naples, traditional enemies, into alliance with Florence against Venice and the Papal States. This created a balance of power within Italy and a united front against external enemies.

The peace established by the Treaty of Lodi ended in 1494, when Naples, Florence, and Pope Alexander VI prepared to attack Milan. Ludovico il Moro, the despot of Milan, turned to France for help. Ludovico suggested that the French revive their claim to Naples, which they had ruled from 1266 to 1435. He did not pause to consider that France also had a claim on Milan.

Charles VIII's March Through Italy

Charles VIII (r. 1483–1498), an eager youth in his twenties, responded to Ludovico's call with lightning speed. Within five months, he had crossed the Alps (August 1495) and marched through Florentine territory and the Papal States to Naples. Piero dé Medici, ruler of Florence, tried to placate the French by handing over Pisa and other Florentine possessions. His people, incited to revolution by the radical preacher Girolamo Savonarola (1452–1498), promptly drove him into exile. Savonarola persuaded the Florentines that France's invasion was God's punishment for their immorality and paid Charles a large ransom to persuade him to spare the city. Savonarola remained in power for four years—until the Florentines tired of his puritanical tyranny and pro-French policy and executed him in May 1498.

Charles's lightning march through Italy alarmed Ferdinand of Aragon, who believed that a French-Italian axis was a danger to his homeland. Ferdinand proposed an alliance (the League of Venice of March 1495) uniting Aragon, Venice, the Papal States, and the Emperor Maximilian I against the French. When Milan, which regretted inviting the French into Italy, joined the League, Charles was forced to retreat.

Pope Alexander VI and the Borgia Family

Louis XII (r. 1498–1515), Charles's successor, was able to return to Italy, for he made an ally of Pope Alexander VI (1492–1503). Alexander, a member of the infamous Borgia family, was probably the church's most corrupt pope.

Alexander's goal was to use the power of the papacy to create a hereditary duchy in Romagna for his children, Cesare and Lucrezia Borgia. Romagna, on the Adriatic coast northeast of Rome, had broken free from the Papal States during the Avignon papacy. When Venice opposed Alexander's efforts to reclaim the region, Alexander broke with the League of Venice and allied with France. The dissolution of the league enabled the French to reconquer Milan, and the pope's reward was the hand of the sister of the king of Navarre for his son—and the promise of French military aid in Romagna. In 1500, Louis and Ferdinand of Aragon partitioned Naples, while the pope and Cesare completed the conquest of Romagna. Alexander then declared his son "duke of Romagna."

Pope Julius II

When Cardinal Giuliano della Rovere became Pope Julius II (1503–1513), he suppressed the Borgias and placed Romagna under papal jurisdiction. Julius, the "warrior pope," brought the Renaissance papacy to a peak of military prowess and diplomatic intrigue. Once he had driven the Venetians out of Romagna (1509) and fully secured the Papal States, he set about ridding Italy of his former allies, the French. Julius, Ferdinand of Aragon, and Venice formed a second Holy League in October 1511. Emperor Maximilian I and the Swiss joined them, and by 1512 the French were in full retreat.

The French were nothing if not persistent. Louis's successor, Francis I (r. 1515–1547), led yet another assault on Italy. When French armies massacred the Swiss at Marignano in September 1515, the Holy League weakened, but the Habsburg emperor took up the cause. The result was four Habsburg-Valois wars that ended in defeat for France.

Francis had greater success in dealing with the pope. The Concordat of Bologna (August 1516) gave the French king control over the French clergy in exchange for French recognition of the pope's authority over church councils and his right to collect money in France. By in effect nationalizing the French Catholic church, this agreement undercut the appeal of the Reformation to France's kings and kept France Catholic.

Niccolò Machiavelli

As the armies of France, Spain, and Germany made a shambles of Italy, Niccolò Machiavelli (1469–1527), a Florentine scholar, struggled to make sense of the tragedy that was befalling his homeland. The lesson it taught him was that political ends—the maintenance of peace and order—are justified by any means.

Machiavelli's Humanist education had included a close study of the history of ancient Rome that had given him a somewhat romanticized, idealized view of the past. Machiavelli was impressed by the apparent ability of the Romans to act decisively and heroically for the good of their country, and he lamented the absence of such traits among his compatriots. He believed that if the Italians could cease their internal feuding and unite in defense of their nation, they could drive out the invaders.

Although Machiavelli was devoted to republican ideals, the realities of political life in Italy convinced him that a strongman was needed to rescue the Italians from the consequences of their own short-sighted selfishness. The salvation of Italy required, for the present, a cunning dictator who was willing to use "Machiavellian" techniques to manipulate his people.

It is possible that Machiavelli intended *The Prince,* which he wrote in 1513, as a satire on politics, not as a serious plea for despotism. But Machiavelli seems to have been in earnest when he advised rulers to consider the usefulness of fraud and brutality as means to the higher end of unifying Italy.

Machiavelli hoped that the Medici family might produce the leader Italy needed. In 1513, one of its members, Leo X (1513–1521), captured the papacy, and his kin dominated the powerful territorial state of Florence. *The Prince* was dedicated to Lorenzo dé Medici, duke of Urbino and grandson of Lorenzo the Magnificent. The Medicis, however, failed to meet the challenge Machiavelli set them. In the year of Machiavelli's death (1527), the second Medici pope, Clement VII (1523–1534), watched helplessly as Rome was sacked by the army of Emperor Charles V.

⌒ Revival of Monarchy: Nation Building in the Fifteenth Century

The feudal monarchy of the High Middle Ages was characterized by the division of the basic powers of government between the king and his vassals. The nobility and the towns acted through representative assemblies (such as the English Parliament, the French Estates General, and the Spanish Cortes) to thwart the centralization of royal power. But, by 1450, territorial princes in many parts of Europe were being brought under the control of centralized national monarchies. The old problem of the one and the many was clearly being decided in favor of the king.

Towns were the crucial factor in this political transition. Where townspeople could be persuaded to ally with kings, they broke the bonds of feudal society by taking the place of the nobility and the clergy as royal officials and advisors. They helped the king reclaim the powers of taxation, war making, and law enforcement that under the feudal system had been exercised by semi-autonomous vassals. As the vassals ceded their rights to a centralized government, the regions they had ruled combined to form a true nation. Unlike the nobility, who were identified with certain districts, professional civil servants—the Spanish *corregidores,* the English justices of the peace, and the French bailiffs—found that their careers were best advanced by focusing on national, not regional, issues.

As kings acquired the bureaucratic machinery needed to enforce their decrees, they were able to bypass feudal councils and representative assemblies. Ferdinand and Isabella of Spain rarely called the Cortes into session. The French Estates General did not meet from 1484 to 1560. And after 1485, when England's Parliament granted Henry VII (r. 1485–1509) the right to collect the customs revenues he needed to cover the costs of government, the king summoned no more parliaments.

By the fifteenth century, monarchies had also begun to create standing national armies that ended the nobles' traditional monopoly of the military. Changing technologies—such as artillery—enhanced the importance of the common man's infantry and diminished the significance of the noble cavalry. Professional soldiers—even foreign mercenaries—who fought for pay and booty were far more efficient than feudal vassals who fought for honor's sake.

Since the strength of infantry is dependent upon numbers, monarchs needed large armies. Those who failed to meet the payrolls of professional soldiers ran the risk of mutiny. Consequently, the growing cost of warfare in the fifteenth and sixteenth centuries increased government's need for new sources of income. Efforts to expand royal revenues were hampered by the stubborn insistence by the highest classes on immunity from taxation. The nobles believed that the king should live as they did, from the income of his estates, and they considered taxation insulting. Kings, therefore, found it easier to increase revenues at the expense of those least able to resist and least able to pay.

Monarchs had several options when it came to raising money. As feudal lords, they could collect rents from the royal domain. They could levy national taxes on basic food and clothing. (France, for instance, had a tax on salt, the *gabelle*, and Spain had the *alcabala*, a 10 percent sales tax.) Rulers could also, with the assistance of parliamentary bodies that did not represent the peasantry, levy direct taxes on the peasantry. (In France the king relied heavily on such a tax, the *taille*.) Some governments sold public offices and issued high-interest bonds, but they did not tax the nobility. Instead, they turned to the nobles and the bankers for loans. A king's most powerful subjects were often also his creditors.

France

Charles VII (r. 1422–1461) was a king made great by those who served him. His ministers created a permanent professional army, which—thanks to the inspiration of Joan of Arc—drove the English out of France. An enterprising merchant banker, Jacques Coeur, devised policies for Charles that strengthened France's economy, diplomatic corps, and national administration. These tools helped the ruthless Louis XI (r. 1461–1483), Charles's son, make France a great power.

The rise of France in the fifteenth century depended on the defeat of two opponents: the king of England and the duke of Burgundy. The Hundred Years' War cost England its continental possessions. But Burgundy, England's sometime ally in that war, emerged in the mid-fifteenth century as Europe's strongest state. Burgundy's duke, Charles the Bold, hoped to link his scattered family domains to create a new "middle" kingdom between France and Germany. It required a coalition of continental powers to stop him.

When Charles the Bold died in a battle at Nancy in 1477, the dream of Burgundian empire died with him. Louis XI and the Habsburg emperor, Maximilian I, divided up Burgundy's lands. The Habsburgs got the better parts, but the dissolution of Burgundy freed Louis XI to concentrate on France's internal affairs. Louis harnessed France's nobility, fostered its trade and industry, and ended his reign with a kingdom almost twice the size of that with which he had started.

Louis's successors failed to build on the excellent foundation he laid. Their invasions of Italy in the 1490s and the long series of losing wars with the Habsburgs that resulted left France, by the mid-sixteenth century, almost as divided internally as it was during the Hundred Years' War.

Spain

In 1469, the marriage of Isabella of Castile (r. 1474–1504) and Ferdinand of Aragon (r. 1479–1516) greatly accelerated the process of creating a unified

Spanish monarchy. Castile was the richer and more populous of the two states, having about 5 million inhabitants to Aragon's 1 million. Castile also had a lucrative, centrally managed sheep-farming industry managed by a state organization called the *Mesta*. Although the two kingdoms shared a common dynasty, the family of Ferdinand and Isabella, each retained its own government agencies—separate laws, armies, coinage, taxation, and cultural traditions.

Together, Ferdinand and Isabella could do what neither could accomplish alone: bring the nobility under control, secure the borders of their realms, launch wars of conquest, and enforce a common Christian faith among all their subjects. In 1492, they conquered the last Muslim state on the Iberian peninsula, Granada. Naples became a Spanish possession in 1504. And by 1512, Ferdinand had acquired the kingdom of Navarre.

Ferdinand and Isabella relied on the Hermandad, a league of cities and towns, for help in subduing the powerful landowners who dominated the countryside. Townspeople replaced the nobility within the royal administration, and the monarchy circumscribed the power of the nobility by extending its authority over wealthy chivalric orders.

Spain had long been remarkable among European lands as a place where three religions—Islam, Judaism, and Christianity—coexisted with a certain degree of toleration. Ferdinand and Isabella reversed this policy and made Spanish Christianity the prime example of state-controlled religion. The monarchs ran the church and used it to advance the cause of national unity. Of particular utility was the ecclesiastical court that tried cases of heresy, the Inquisition. In 1479 the Inquisition, run by Tomás de Torquemada (d. 1498), Isabella's confessor, was assigned the task of monitoring the activities of the converted Spanish Jews *(conversos)* and Muslims *(Moriscos)*. In 1492, the Jews who refused to convert were exiled and their properties were confiscated. In 1502, the same fate befell the Moors of Granada. The state's rigorous enforcement of orthodoxy kept Spain a loyal Catholic country and made it a base of operation for the Counter-Reformation, the Catholic response to the Protestant Reformation of the sixteenth century.

The marriage alliances arranged by Ferdinand and Isabella were part of a grand plan to contain France, and they set the stage for Europe's politics in the sixteenth century. In 1496, their eldest daughter and heir, Joanna (later known as "the Mad") wed Archduke Philip, the son of Emperor Maximilian I. Charles, the child of this union, inherited a united Spain from his grandparents. This, augmented by his Habsburg patrimony and election as emperor in 1519, created a European kingdom almost as large as Charlemagne's. Ferdinand and Isabella's second daughter, Catherine of Aragon, married Arthur, the son of England's King Henry VII. After Arthur's premature death, Catherine was betrothed to his brother, the future King Henry VIII. Henry's ultimate decision to end this marriage led him to break with the papacy and declare England a Protestant nation.

Spain's power was also enhanced by the success of the overseas explorations that Ferdinand and Isabella sponsored. The discoveries made in their names by the Genoese adventurer Christopher Columbus (1451–1506) led to the creation of Spain's empire in Mexico and Peru. Gold and silver from this "new world" enabled Spain to dominate Europe during the sixteenth century.

England

The last half of the fifteenth century was an especially difficult period for the English. While they were adjusting to their loss of the Hundred Years' War, a fight broke out between branches of their royal family, the House of York and the House of Lancaster. For thirty years (1455–1485) a dynastic struggle, known today as the Wars of the Roses (York's heraldic emblem was a white rose and Lancaster's a red rose), kept England in a state of turmoil.

Henry VI (r. 1422–1461), a weak king from the Lancastrian house, was challenged by his cousin, the duke of York, who had supporters in England's prosperous southern towns. In 1461, the duke of York's son seized power as Edward IV (r. 1461–1483). Although his reign was briefly interrupted in 1470–1471, by a short-lived restoration of Henry VI, Edward maintained the upper hand and greatly increased the power and wealth of the monarchy.

Edward's brother, Richard III (r. 1483–1485), usurped the throne from Edward's son. He was, in turn, challenged by Henry Tudor, a distant royal relation who had inherited the leadership of the Lancastrian faction. In 1485, at the battle of Bosworth Field, Henry killed Richard and established England's Tudor dynasty. The new dynasty portrayed Richard as an unprincipled villain, the murderer of Edward's sons. This Tudor propaganda, which may or may not be true, is reflected in Shakespeare's popular and powerful play *Richard III*.

Henry Tudor, Henry VII (r. 1485–1509), married Edward IV's daughter, Elizabeth of York. By uniting the rival branches of the royal family, he created an uncontestable claim to the throne for their offspring. Henry also brought the English nobility under control by means of something called the Court of Star Chamber. Created with the sanction of Parliament in 1487, the court was charged with responsibility for cases involving the nobility. Since it was staffed by the king's chief councillors, the nobles could not use the tactics of intimidation and bribery that had enabled them to make a mockery of lesser courts.

The Court of Star Chamber enhanced the power of the monarchy. Henry construed legal precedents to the advantage of the crown, and he confiscated so much property from the nobility that he did not have to convene Parliament to raise the money he needed to govern. Henry began to shape a monarchy that during the reign of his granddaughter, Elizabeth I, became one of early modern Europe's most exemplary administrations.

The Holy Roman Empire

Germany and Italy were exceptions to the general trend toward political centralization seen in the histories of other European nations during the last half of the fifteenth century. Germany's rulers maintained the ancient practice of partitioning lands among all their sons. As a result, by the end of the Middle Ages Germany was divided into some 300 autonomous entities, and its fragmented authorities were powerless to halt the development of revolutionary movements like the Reformation.

German princes and cities worked together to maintain law and order, if not unity, within the Holy Roman Empire. In 1356, the emperor and the major German territorial rulers issued the *Golden Bull.* It allotted choice of an emperor to a seven-member electoral college: the archbishops of Mainz, Trier, and Cologne; the duke of Saxony; the margrave of Brandenburg; the count Palatine; and the king of Bohemia. The college was also intended to encourage cooperation among regions of the empire.

The emperor more often reigned than ruled, for the extent of his powers, especially over the seven electors, was renegotiated with every imperial election. But in the fifteenth century an effort was made to create some unity of purpose among the principalities. A regular national meeting—the imperial diet or *Reichstag,* composed of the seven electors, the nonelectoral princes, and the sixty-five imperial free cities—began to be held.

In 1495, the diet won concessions from Maximilian I (r. 1493–1519) that were intended to promote order in the nation. Private warfare was banned. A court (the *Reichskammergericht*) was established to enforce internal peace. An imperial Council of Regency (the *Reichsregiment*) was appointed to coordinate the development of policy. Although these reforms were important, they fell far short of the creation of a centralized state. During the sixteenth and seventeenth centuries, the territorial princes were virtually sovereign rulers in their domains.

∾ The Northern Renaissance

The Humanist scholars of the Renaissance were responsible for the development of a climate in Europe favorable to religious and educational reform. Humanism spread to northern Europe from Italy through such intermediaries as students who studied in Italy and merchants who traded there. Reform was also promoted by the Brothers of the Common Life, an influential lay religious movement that began in the Netherlands and permitted men and women to live a shared religious life without making formal vows of poverty, chastity, and obedience.

The northern Humanists developed a distinctive culture. They tended to come from more diverse social backgrounds and to be more interested in religious reform than their Italian counterparts. They were also more willing to write for lay audiences. This latter was a crucial factor, for the invention of printing with movable type was about to create a world in which intellectual elites would argue their cases before the public—and spark mass movements.

The Printing Press

Since the days of Charlemagne, kings and princes had encouraged literacy. Without people who could read, think critically, and write reliable reports, no kingdom, large or small, could be properly governed. During the late Middle Ages, the number of Europe's universities tripled from twenty to sixty, and new schools spread literacy far beyond the ranks of the clergy.

The invention of a process of cheap paper manufacture brought down the price of books and made them more common. Previously, books had been inscribed on expensive sheets of leather called vellum. Since it required 170 calfskins or 300 sheepskins to make a single vellum Bible, few people could afford the complete text. Whole pages were sometimes carved on wooden blocks and printed, but the production of such blocks was difficult.

In the mid-fifteenth century, Johann Gutenberg (d. 1468) of Mainz was stimulated by the growing market for books to invent printing with movable type. Books priced for all budgets, treating all subjects from theology to farming and child-rearing, quickly followed. The new technology was enormously profitable for printers, and their numbers exploded. By 1500, about fifty years after Gutenberg opened his shop, printing presses were operating in over 200 European cities.

Literacy deeply affected people everywhere, nurturing self-esteem and a

An early printing press. Between 1435 and 1455, Johann Gutenberg worked out the complete technology of casting individual letters into rectangular metal type, composing the type into pages held together by pressure, and printing those pages on an adaptation of the wooden standing press using ink made of lampblack mixed with oil varnish. This new technology made it possible for the first time in the West to manufacture numerous identical copies of written works. [Huntington Library]

critical frame of mind. By standardizing texts and opening up discussions, the print revolution made anyone who could read an authority. As a result, ordinary men and women became less credulous and docile than their ancestors. But print also gave rulers a powerful tool for the political and religious manipulation of subjects.

Erasmus

The career of Desiderius Erasmus (1466?–1536), the most famous of the northern Humanists, illustrates the impact of the printing press. Erasmus was both an educational and a religious reformer. His example proves that many loyal Catholics advocated religious reform long before the Reformation erupted.

Erasmus earned part of his living by tutoring. The short Latin dialogues he prepared for his students were intended to teach them how to live as well as how to speak. These pieces, published under the title *Colloquies*, came in consecutive editions to include extensive prods to reform—anticlerical dialogues and satires of religious superstitions. Erasmus also published a collection of proverbs. His *Adages* grew from a first edition of 800 examples to a final edition of over 5,000. It popularized such common modern expressions as "to leave no stone unturned" and "where there is smoke, there is fire."

Erasmus aspired to unite the classical ideals of humanity and civic virtue with the Christian virtues of love and piety. He believed that disciplined study of the classics and the Bible offered the best hope for the reformation of individuals and society. The phrase *philosophia Christi* describes his program: a simple, ethical piety in imitation of Christ. He saw this as the opposite of the dogmatic, ceremonial, and factious religious practices of the later Middle Ages. Erasmus was the enemy of anyone, Catholic or Protestant, who let doctrine and disputation overshadow humble piety and Christian practice.

Erasmus used his knowledge of classical languages to produce an improved version of the Bible based on the best manuscript sources available at the time. He believed that only as people drank from the pure, unadulterated sources could moral and religious health result. His Greek edition of the New Testament in 1516 made possible a new, more accurate Latin translation in 1519.

The church authorities were unhappy with Erasmus's "improvements" on their traditional Bible, the Latin Vulgate, and his widely read anticlerical satires. At one point in the mid-sixteenth century all of Erasmus's works were placed on the Catholic church's *Index of Forbidden Books.* Luther, the Protestant leader, also condemned some of Erasmus's views. But friends and foes in both camps used the scholarly tools that Erasmus had created to promote the cause of reform.

Humanism and Reform

In Germany, England, France, and Spain, Humanism stirred both educational and religious reform.

Germany. Rudolf Agricola (1443–1485) introduced Italian learning to Germany. Conrad Celtis (d. 1508), the first German poet laureate, and Ulrich von Hutten (1488–1523), a knight, promoted a nationalistic version of Humanism that was hostile to non-German cultures—especially that of papal Rome. Hutten, who attacked indulgences and published an edition of Valla's exposé of the *Donation of Constantine,* died in 1523 fighting in a hopeless revolt of the German knights against their princes.

A *cause célèbre* helped to unite reform-minded German Humanists. About 1506, a converted Jew named Pfefferkorn, assisted by the Dominican friars of Cologne, launched a campaign to suppress Jewish literature. Johann Reuchlin (1455–1522) was, at the time, Europe's foremost Christian authority on Hebrew and Jewish learning. He was the first Christian scholar to compile a reliable Hebrew grammar, and he was personally attracted to Jewish mysticism. When Pfefferkorn attacked Reuchlin, many German Humanists (motivated by a love of academic freedom rather than Judaism) rushed to Reuchlin's defense. The controversy produced one of the great books of the period, the *Letters of Obscure Men* (1515), a merciless satire of monks and Scholastics. It also predisposed the Humanists to rally around Martin Luther in 1517, when some of the same people attacked him for his famous ninety-five theses against indulgences.

England. English scholars and merchants and touring Italian prelates brought Italy's learning to England. Erasmus lectured at Cambridge, and his close friend, Thomas More (1478–1535), became the most famous of the English Humanists. More's *Utopia* (1516), a critique of contemporary society, rivals the plays of Shakespeare as the most-read sixteenth-century English work. *Utopia* described an imaginary society that overcame social and political injustice by holding all property and goods in common and requiring all persons to earn their bread by their own work.

Humanism in England, as in Germany, paved the way for the Reformation, but some Humanists, like More and Erasmus, remained steadfastly loyal to the Roman Catholic Church. When More, one of Henry VIII's chief councillors, refused to accept the king's divorce of Catherine of Aragon and England's break with the papacy, Henry ordered his execution (July 1535).

France. When France invaded Italy, Italian learning penetrated France. Guillaume Budé (1468–1540), an accomplished Greek scholar, and Jacques Lefèvre d'Étaples (1454–1536), a biblical authority, were the leaders of French Humanism. Lefèvre's scholarly works exemplified the new critical scholarship that was to stimulate Martin Luther's thinking and bring on the Reformation. Marguerite d'Angoulême (1492–1549), sister of King Francis I, queen of Navarre, and a noted spiritual writer, was patron to a generation of young reform-minded Humanists that numbered among its members the Protestant reformer John Calvin.

Spain. In Spain Humanism was enlisted in the defense of the Catholic faith, not in the cause of reform. Francisco Jiménez de Cisneros (1437–1517), a confessor to Queen Isabella and (after 1508) the Grand Inquisitor and chief defender of orthodoxy, was the country's leading Humanist. In 1509, he founded the University of Alcalá near Madrid. He printed a Greek edition of the New Testament, and he translated many religious tracts that were used to reform clerical life and improve the clergy's direction of the piety of the laity. His greatest achievement was the *Complutensian Polyglot Bible,* a six-volume edition of the Hebrew, Greek, and Latin texts of the Bible in parallel columns.

～ Voyages of Discovery and the New Empire in the West

The intellectual restlessness that marked the Renaissance and the Reformation was accompanied by a literal restlessness. In the fifteenth century, the Atlantic ceased to be regarded as a wall closing Europe in and began to be explored as a highway leading to global adventures (see Map 10-2). Henry the Navigator (r. 1394–1460), prince of Portugal, led the way by sponsoring exploration of the African coast. By the last decades of the fifteenth century, the Portuguese were transporting gold from Guinea by sea and competing with the land routes controlled by Arab traders.

The rush for Africa's gold expanded into a search for India's spices. Spices, especially pepper and cloves, were in great demand in Europe. They were used to preserve food as well as to enhance its taste. In 1487, Bartholomew Dias (d. 1500) rounded the Cape of Good Hope at the tip of Africa. In 1498, Vasco da Gama (d. 1524) reached the coast of India. The cargo he brought back to Portugal was worth sixty times the cost of his voyage. The Portuguese quickly built an empire in the East that gave them control of the European spice trade.

While Portugal explored the Indian Ocean, Spain attacked the Atlantic. Christopher Columbus (1451–1506) dreamed of finding a short route to the spice islands of the East Indies, but he blundered on something much greater. On October 12, 1492, after a thirty-three-day voyage from the Canary Islands, he landed in San Salvador (Watlings Island) in the eastern Bahamas. He thought he was near Japan. Not until his third voyage to the Caribbean did Columbus realize that the island of Cuba was not Japan and that the South American continent beyond it was not China. Amerigo Vespucci (1451–1512) and Ferdinand Magellan (1480–1521) proved that the lands Columbus found were not, as he died believing, the edge of the Orient. They were a new continent separated from the East by an ocean even greater than the Atlantic. Magellan ventured onto this Pacific Ocean and died in the Philippines.

A Conquered World

Columbus's voyage in 1492 began more than three centuries of Spanish exploitation of a vast American empire. That empire transformed cultures on both sides of the Atlantic. As Europeans and their technologies entered the Americas, American goods and bullion flooded Europe's markets. In neither place was life ever again the same. In parts of both South and North America,

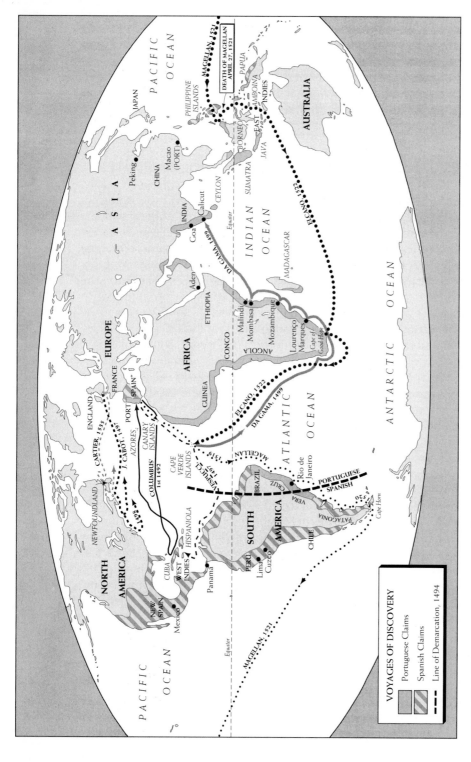

MAP 10-2 European Voyages of Discovery and the Colonial Claims of Spain and Portugal in the Fifteenth and Sixteenth Centuries

Spain established a kind of Roman Catholicism, a system of economic dependence, and a hierarchical social structure that has endured to the present day.

Since Columbus was convinced that he had landed in the East Indies, he called the peoples he encountered "Indians." The name persisted even after it was clear that America was not the Indies. The ancestors of the Native Americans had migrated across the Bering Strait from Asia many thousands of years before the European voyages of discovery. As early as the first millennium B.C., those who lived in Mesoamerica (from central Mexico to the Yucatan and Guatemala) and the Andean region (Peru and Bolivia) were pioneering advanced civilizations.

The earliest of the Mesoamerican civilizations was the Olmec, which dates from about 1200 B.C. By the first millennium A.D., its city of Teotihuacán was one of the largest urban centers in the world. The first millennium A.D. also saw the flowering of the civilization of the Mayas in the Yucatan region. The Mayans acquired considerable knowledge of mathematics and astronomy and built great cities centered on huge pyramids.

The first great interregional civilization in Andean South America, the Chavín, emerged during the first millennium B.C. From A.D. 100 to A.D. 600, regional cultures, the Nazca on the southern coast of Peru and the Moche on the northern coast, appeared. The Huari-Tiahuanco culture again imposed interregional conformity from 600 to 1000, and the Chimu Empire flourished on Peru's northern coast from 800 to 1400. These early Andean societies built great ceremonial centers throughout the Andes; constructed elaborate irrigation systems, canals, and highways; and created exquisite pottery, textiles, and metalwork.

The Aztecs. When the Spanish explorers arrived, Mesoamerica was dominated by the Aztecs and Andean America by the Incas. The forebears of the Aztecs

A sixteenth-century Aztec drawing depicts the Spanish conquest of Mexico. [The Bettmann Archive]

entered the Valley of Mexico early in the twelfth century. In 1428, a chief named Itzcoatl inaugurated an era of Aztec conquest that reached its climax just after 1500. The Aztec state, which centered on Tenochtitlán (modern-day Mexico City), was a collection of enslaved and terrorized tribes. Aztec religion involved the sacrifice of thousands of people a year to the gods of the sun and the soil. By extorting this grim tribute, the Aztecs nourished resentment among their subjects and caused them to dream of liberation.

In 1519, Hernán Cortés landed on the coast of Mexico with a mere 600 men. Montezuma, the Aztec ruler, initially believed Cortés to be a god, for an Aztec legend claimed that a priest (Quetzalcoatl) who had been driven into exile four centuries earlier would return about the time that Cortés appeared. Montezuma tried to appease Cortés with gold, for the Aztecs, who had recently been ravaged by epidemics of European origin (principally smallpox), were in no condition to fight. Gold only stimulated the Spaniards' appetites. Cortés's forces marched on Tenochtitlán and captured Montezuma, who died under unexplained circumstances. The Aztecs rose up to defend themselves. But by 1521, they were defeated, and Cortés had proclaimed the former Aztec Empire to be New Spain.

The Incas. The Incas of the highlands of Peru, like the Aztecs, had conquered many tribes. By the early sixteenth century they ruled harshly over several million subjects—using impressed labor to build roads and cities, to farm, and to fight.

In 1531, Francisco Pizarro, inspired by Cortés's example, invaded the Inca Empire. His army of 200 men was equipped with guns, swords, and horses—the military potential of which escaped the Incas. Pizarro lured the Inca chief Atahualpa to a conference, where he captured him and killed several thousand Indians. Atahualpa raised a huge ransom in gold, but in 1533, Pizarro executed him. Division within the ranks of the Spaniards prevented them from establishing control of the sprawling Inca territories until the late 1560s.

The conquests of Mexico and Peru are among the most brutal episodes in modern Western history. In addition to loss of life, they prevented the Indian civilizations from having significant impact on Western civilization. The Spaniards and the Indians made some accommodations to each other, but in the end European values, religion, economic goals, and language dominated. South America was transformed into Latin America.

The Economy of Exploitation

The native peoples of America and their lands were immediately drawn into the Atlantic economy and the world of competitive European commercialism. For the Indians of Latin America—and later the blacks of Africa—that meant various forms of forced labor. The colonial economy of Latin America had three components: mining, agriculture, and shipping.

The early *conquistadores* ("conquerors") were primarily interested in gold, but by the middle of the sixteenth century, silver mining had become more profitable. The chief mining centers were Potosí in Peru and various smaller sites in northern Mexico. The Spanish crown received one-fifth (the *quinto*) of all mining revenues and monopolized the production and sale of the mercury that was required in the silver-mining process. Mining by native forced labor for the benefit of Spaniards epitomized the extractive economy that was fundamental to colonial life.

The West Indies (Cuba, Hispaniola, Puerto Rico, and other islands) evolved a plantation system that used the labor of black slaves from Africa to produce sugar for the European market. But the agricultural institution that characterized most of the Spanish colonies was the *hacienda,* a large landed estate owned by persons born in Spain *(peninsulares)* or persons of Spanish descent born in America *(creoles).* The hacienda economy was subordinate to the mining economy, for its major products—food and leather—were consumed by American mining communities. Laborers on the hacienda were usually bound to the land and prevented from moving from the service of one landowner to another.

The Spaniards very quickly decided that the Indian population would supply the labor needed for mining and agriculture in the New World. Various means were developed to utilize the labor of Indians. An *encomienda* was a grant of the right to the labor of a specific number of Indians for a particular period of time. Spain's monarchs opposed this arrangement, for they feared that the holders of *encomienda* might become a powerful independent nobility in the New World. The *repartimiento* required adult male Indians to devote a certain number of days of labor annually to Spanish economic enterprises. Although this sounded more humane, *repartimiento* service was often extremely harsh. The term limitation for laborers led some Spanish managers to work them to death on the assumption that new men were always scheduled to replace those currently employed.

Eventually a shortage of workers and the crown's opposition to extreme kinds of forced labor promoted the use of free labor. But the freedom of Indian workers was more apparent than real. They had to purchase the goods they needed from the landowners or mine owners for whom they worked. This created debts that bound them to their employers, a form of exploitation known as *debt peonage.*

The enslavement of Africans was introduced to the New World on the sugar plantations of the West Indies. It was an extension of a system of forced labor that the Spanish and the Portuguese had previously used in Europe.

The Impact

Deaths in combat, by forced labor, and from European diseases had devastating demographic consequences for the Indian population. Europeans lived in a far more complex human and animal environment than did Native Americans. Their interaction, over a long period, with different ethnic groups and animal species helped them develop strong immune systems that enabled them to survive the ravages of measles, smallpox, and typhoid. Native Americans evolved in a simpler, more sterile environment. They were defenseless against Europe's diseases. Within a generation of the conquest, the Indian population of New Spain (Mexico) was reduced by 92 percent, from 25 million to 2 million.

The loss of life and destruction of cultures in the New World resulted in mixed blessings for the Old World. The bullion that flowed into Europe through Spain vastly increased the amount of money in circulation and created an inflation rate of 2 percent a year. Prices doubled in Spain by 1550 and quadrupled by 1600. In Luther's Wittenberg, the cost of basic food and clothing increased almost 100 percent between 1519 and 1540. Wages and rents, on the other hand, lagged well behind the rise in prices.

The new money enabled governments and private entrepreneurs to sponsor basic research and industrial expansion and to promote the growth of capitalism. The economic thinking of the age favored the creation of monopolies, the charging of high interest for loans, and the free and efficient accumulation of wealth. The late fifteenth and the sixteenth centuries saw the maturation of this type of capitalism and its attendant social problems. Those who owned the means of production were ever more clearly separated from the workers who operated them. The new wealth raised the expectations of the poor and encouraged reactionary behavior by the rich. The social distinctions that became ever more visible in the new economic system prepared the way for the upheaval of the Reformation by making many people critical of traditional institutions and eager for new ideas—especially those that promised freedom and a chance at a better life.

During the late Middle Ages, previously divided lands came together as nations, and the foundations of modern France, Spain, England, Germany, and Italy were laid. Byzantine and Islamic scholars made ancient Greek science and scholarship available to the West, and Europeans reclaimed a classical cultural heritage from which they had been separated for almost eight centuries. This prompted renaissances of intellectual and artistic activity in both southern and northern Europe.

The new political unity spurred national ambition, and by the late fifteenth century Europeans were venturing far afield—to the shores of Africa, to the southern and eastern coasts of Asia, and to the New World of the Americas. For the first time, they confronted truly non-European civilizations. The savage exploitation of the peoples and lands of the New World revealed the dark side of Europe's culture. And the influx of New World gold and silver exacerbated Europe's economic and social problems. Some Europeans were driven by what they saw to question their civilization's traditional values.

∼ Review Questions

1. How would you define the term *Renaissance* as it is used to explain what happened in fifteenth- and sixteenth-century Italy?

2. How would you define *Renaissance Hu-* manism? In what ways was the Renaissance a break with the Middle Ages? In what ways did it owe its existence to medieval civilization?

3. Who were the leading, or most characteristic, literary and artistic figures of the Italian Renaissance? What was "the spirit of the Renaissance" that they all shared?

4. Why did the French invade Italy in 1494? How did this event trigger Italy's political decline? In what ways do the actions of Pope Julius II and the ideas of Niccolò Machiavelli signify the start of a new era in Italian civlization?

5. Does the history of Renaissance Italy support or refute the common assumption that creative work proceeds best in periods of calm and peace?

6. How did the northern Renaissance differ from the Italian Renaissance? In what ways was Erasmus the embodiment of the northern Renaissance?

7. What prompted the voyages of discovery? How did the Spanish establish their empire in the Americas? What did native peoples experience during and after the conquest?

∽ Suggested Readings

H. BARON, *The Crisis of the Early Italian Renaissance*, vols. 1 and 2 (1966). A major work, setting forth the civic dimension of Italian Humanism.

B. BERENSON, *Italian Painters of the Renaissance* (1957). Eloquent and authoritative.

C. BOXER, *Four Centuries of Portuguese Expansion, 1415-1825* (1961). Comprehensive survey by the leading authority.

G. A. BRUCKER, *Renaissance Florence* (1969). Comprehensive survey of all facets of Florentine life.

J. BURCKHARDT, *The Civilization of the Renaissance in Italy* (1867). The old classic that still has as many defenders as detractors.

R. E. CONRAD, *Children of God's Fire: A Documentary History of Black Slavery in Brazil* (1983).

A. W. CROSBY, *The Columbian Exchange: Biological and Cultural Consequences of 1492* (1973). A study of the epidemiological disaster that Columbus visited upon Native Americans.

E. L. EISENSTEIN, *The Printing Press as an Agent of Change: Communications and Cultural Transformations in Early Modern Europe*, 2 vols. (1979). Bold, stimulating account of the centrality of printing to all progress in the period.

W. K. FERGUSON, *Europe in Transition, 1300–1520* (1962). A major survey that deals with the transition from medieval society to Renaissance society.

C. GIBSON, *Spain in America* (1956). A splendidly clear and balanced narrative.

M. GILMORE, *The World of Humanism, 1453–1517* (1952). A comprehensive survey, especially strong in intellectual and cultural history.

D. HERLIHY, *The Family in Renaissance Italy* (1974). Excellent on family structure and general features.

F. KATZ, *The Ancient American Civilizations* (1972). An excellent introduction.

P. O. KRISTELLER, *Renaissance Thought: The Classic, Scholastic, and Humanist Strains* (1961). A master shows the many sides of Renaissance thought.

I. MACLEAN, *The Renaissance Notion of Women* (1980). An account of the views of Renaissance intellectuals and their sources in antiquity.

L. MARTINES, *Power and Imagination: City States in Renaissance Italy* (1980). Stimulating account of cultural and political history.

H. A. MISKIMIN, *The Economy of Early Renaissance Europe, 1300–1460* (1975). Shows interaction of social, political, economic, and cultural change.

E. PANOFSKY, *Meaning in the Visual Arts* (1955). Eloquent treatment of Renaissance art.

J. H. PARRY, *The Age of Reconnaissance* (1964). A comprehensive account of exploration in the years 1450 to 1650.

M. MANN PHILLIPS, *Erasmus and the Northern Renaissance* (1956). A learned, rewarding account of the man and the movement.

11

The Age of Reformation

KEY TOPICS IN THIS CHAPTER

~ The social and religious background to the Reformation

~ Martin Luther's challenge to the church and the course of the Reformation in Germany

~ The Reformation in Switzerland, France, and England

~ Transitions in family life between medieval and modern times

---

In the second decade of the sixteenth century, a powerful religious movement began in northern Germany. Protestant reformers, attacking what they believed to be burdensome superstitions that robbed people of money and peace of mind, led a revolt against the medieval church.

The Protestant Reformation op-

posed aspects of the Renaissance, especially the optimistic view of human nature that Humanist scholars derived from classical literature. But the Reformation embraced some Renaissance ideas—particularly educational reform and a train- *ing in ancient languages that permitted scholars to go to original sources. Protestant challenges to Catholic practices originated in the study of the Bible's Hebrew and Greek texts.*

～ Society and Religion

A struggle between two political foes set the stage for the Reformation: the monarchies that were centralizing governments of nation-states, and the towns and regions that were defending their traditional autonomy against them. Since the fourteenth century, the king's law and custom had been superseding local law and custom almost everywhere. Many townspeople and village folk viewed religious revolt as a part of a wider fight for political independence.

The Reformation began in the free cities of Germany and Switzerland. There were about sixty-five of them, most of which developed Protestant movements even if they did not ultimately come under Protestant control. These cities were troubled by more than a desire to defend themselves against intervention by princely authorities. They suffered deep internal social and political divisions, and some of their factions favored the Reformation more than others. Guilds whose members were prospering and rising in social status were often in the forefront of the Reformation, but less distinguished groups were also attracted to the Protestant revolt. People who felt pushed around by either local or distant authorities tended, at least initially, to find in the Protestant movement an ally. The peasants on the land responded as

The Reformation broke out against a background of deep social and political divisions that bred resentment against authority. This early-sixteenth-century woodcut by Georg Pencz presents a warning against tyranny. It shows a world turned upside down, with the hunted becoming the hunters. The message: tryanny eventually begets rebellion. [Hacker Art Books]

Significant Dates from the Period of the Protestant Reformation

1517	*Luther posts ninety-five theses against indulgences*
1519	*Charles V becomes Holy Roman Emperor*
1521	*Diet of Worms condemns Luther*
1524–1525	*Peasants' Revolt in Germany*
1527	*The Schleitheim Confession of the Anabaptists*
1529	*Marburg Colloquy between Luther and Zwingli*
1529	*England's Reformation Parliament convenes*
1531	*Formation of Protestant Schmalkaldic League*
1533	*Henry VIII weds Anne Boleyn*
1534–1535	*Anabaptists take over Münster*
1534	*England's Act of Supremacy*
1536	*Calvin arrives in Geneva*
1540	*Jesuits, founded by Ignatius of Loyola, recognized as order by pope*
1546	*Luther dies*
1547	*Armies of Charles V crush Schmalkaldic League*
1547–1553	*Edward VI, king of England*
1555	*Peace of Augsburg*
1553–1558	*Mary Tudor, queen of England*
1545–1563	*Council of Trent*
1558–1603	*Elizabeth I, queen of England; the Anglican settlement*

much as the townsfolk, for they, too, were finding their freedoms eroded by princely governments.

For many converts to Protestantism, religion and politics seemed to be sides of the same coin. When Protestant preachers scorned the authority of ecclesiastical landlords and ridiculed papal laws as arbitrary human inventions, they raised issues of political as well as religious liberty. An attack on the legitimacy of the one kind of authority translated immediately into a critique of the other.

Popular Religious Movements and Criticism of the Church

The Protestant Reformation was also, in part, a response to the crises that afflicted the late medieval church: the papacy's "exile" in Avignon, the Great Schism, the conciliar movement, and the flagrant worldliness of the Renaissance popes. These things led many clergy and laity to become increasingly critical of the traditional teaching and spiritual practice of the church. The late Middle Ages were marked by calls for reform and by widespread experimentation with new religious practices.

The laypeople of the late medieval period were less subservient to the clergy than their ancestors. The residents of cities had grown increasingly knowledgeable about the world and politics. As soldiers, pilgrims, explorers, and traders, they traveled widely. The establishment of postal systems and printing presses increased the information at their disposal. Improved access to books and libraries raised the rate of literacy among them and heightened their curiosity. Education equipped them to take the initiative in shaping the cultural lives of their communities.

The lay religious movements that preceded the Reformation all advocated religious simplicity in imitation of Jesus. They were inspired by an ideal of apostolic poverty which they saw in the Gospels' descriptions of the lives of Jesus and his disciples. They wanted a more egalitarian church that gave its members, as well as its head, a voice. They wanted a more spiritual church, one that emulated the New Testament model.

The Modern Devotion. One of the most constructive lay religious movements of the period was the "Modern Devotion," led by the Brothers of the Common Life. The brothers advocated the practice of monastic disciplines by ordinary men and women. They took no formal vows, held no church offices, and supported themselves by working at secular jobs.

After Gerard Groote (1340–1384) began the movement in the Netherlands, the brother and (less numerous) sister houses spread rapidly throughout northern Europe, influencing parts of southern Europe as well. The Modern Devotion brought clerics and laity together to share a common life that stressed individual piety and practical religion. Thomas à Kempis (d. 1471) summarized the philosophy of the movement in what became the most popular religious book of the period, the *Imitation of Christ.* This guide to the inner life was intended primarily for monks and nuns, but it spoke also to the many laity who sought spiritual growth through the practice of ascetic disciplines.

The brothers were active in education. Their movement appeared at a time when the laity were demanding good preaching in the vernacular and were even taking the initiative to endow special preacherships to ensure it. Brothers worked as copyists, sponsored publications, ran hospices for poor students, and conducted schools for the young. Some famous scholars, such as Erasmus and Reuchlin, began their training with the brothers.

The Modern Devotion has been seen as the source of Humanist, Protestant, and Catholic reform movements in the sixteenth century. But it was actually a very conservative movement. By integrating traditional clerical doctrines and values with an active common life, the brothers met the need of late medieval people for a more personal piety and a better-informed faith. The Modern Devotion helped laypersons develop full religious lives without surrendering involvement with the world.

Lay Control over Religious Life. The medieval papacy's successful campaign to win control over the appointment of candidates to church offices did not improve the administration of the church. The popes sold ecclesiastical posts to the highest bidders. The purchasers were entitled to the income of their offices, but they were not required personally to carry out the duties of the posts they purchased. They hired inexpensive, often poorly trained and motivated substitutes to do their work, and they lived elsewhere—often in Rome. Rare was the late medieval German town that did not complain about clerical malfeasance or dereliction of duty.

City governments sometimes took the initiative in trying to improve religious life by endowing preacherships. These positions provided for well-trained, dedicated pastors who could provide regular preaching and pastoral care that went beyond the perfunctory services offered by other clergy. In many instances these preacherships became platforms for Protestant preachers.

Because medieval churches and monasteries were holy places, they had been exempted from secular taxes and laws. It was also considered inappropriate for holy persons (clergy) to do "dirty jobs" like military service, compulsory labor, standing watch at city gates, and other obligations of citizenship. Nor was it thought right that the laity, of whatever rank, should sit in judgment over God's priestly intermediaries. On the eve of the Reformation, however, secular governments had had enough, and they were taking steps to curtail these privileges.

Long before 1520, when Luther published his famous summary of economic grievances *(Address to the Christian Nobility of the German Nation)*, communities were loudly protesting the financial abuses of the medieval church. Prominent among these was the sale of *indulgences*, papal letters that guaranteed sinners released time from purgatory. If rulers and magistrates were given a share of the profits, they usually did not object. But it was a different matter if local revenues were siphoned off for projects far from home. The state did not join the campaign against financial exactions like indulgences until rulers found new ways to profit from religion. The financial appeal of Protestantism lay in its rationale for the state's dissolution of monasteries and confiscation of ecclesiastical properties.

∽ Martin Luther and German Reformation to 1525

The kings of France and England were able to limit ecclesiastical taxation and papal jurisdiction over their churches. But Germany lacked the political unity needed to enforce "national" religious reforms. What happened on a universal level in England and France occurred locally and piecemeal in Germany. But popular resentment of ecclesiastical abuses did spread through Germany, and by 1517 it was pervasive enough to win Martin Luther a widespread, sympathetic audience.

Luther (1483–1546) was the son of a successful Thüringian miner. He received his early education in a school run by the Brothers of the Common Life. Between 1501 and 1505, he attended the University of Erfurt, where the nominalist teachings of William of Ockham and Gabriel Biel (d. 1495) prevailed. After receiving his master of arts degree in 1505, Luther obeyed his parents and registered with the law faculty. But he never began the study of law. To the disappointment of his family, he entered the Order of the Hermits of Saint Augustine in Erfurt on July 17, 1505. This decision was an attempt to resolve a long-standing spiritual struggle. It came to a head during a lightning storm in which a terrified Luther promised Saint Anne, the patron of travelers in distress, that he would enter a monastery if he escaped death.

Luther, who was ordained in 1507, led a conventional monastic life. In 1510, he journeyed to Rome on business for his order and saw firsthand some of the things that were raising doubts about the church. In 1511, he moved to the Augustinian monastery in Wittenberg. A year later, he earned his doctorate in theology from Wittenberg's university and joined its faculty.

Justification by Faith Alone

Reformation theology was a response to the failure of traditional medieval religion to provide many laypeople and clergy with personal or intellectual satisfaction. Luther was especially plagued by his inability to achieve the perfect righteousness that medieval theology taught that God required for salvation. The church's teachings and sacrament of penance failed to console Luther and give him hope. The church seemed to demand of him a perfection he knew neither he nor any other human being could achieve.

The study of St. Paul's letters eventually brought Luther an insight into the process of salvation that quieted his fears. Luther concluded from his reading of the Scriptures that the righteousness that God demanded was not the product of religious works and ceremonies. It was a gift God gives to those who believe and trust in Jesus Christ, who alone is perfectly righteous. To believe in Christ meant to stand before God clothed in Christ's righteousness— to be justified by faith in him alone, not by confidence in one's record of good works.

The doctrine of justification by faith was incompatible with the church's practice of issuing indulgences, which remitted the obligation to perform a "work of satisfaction" for one's sins. According to medieval theology, after the priest absolved a penitent of guilt for his sins, the penitent still had to pay the penalty for those sins. The penitent could discharge the penalty here and now by prayers, fasting, almsgiving, retreats, and pilgrimages. But penitents whose works of satisfaction were inadequate could expect to suffer for them in purgatory.

Indulgences had originally been given to Crusaders whose penances were incomplete when they fell in battle with the enemies of the church. But indulgences also became available to laypeople who were anxious about the consequences of neglected penances or unrepented sins. In 1343, Pope Clement VI (1342–1352) declared the existence of the church's "treasury of merit," an infinite reservoir of excess good works earned by the saints and available for the pope to assign to others. "Letters of indulgence" were drafts on this treasury to cover the works of satisfaction owed by penitents. In 1476, Pope Sixtus IV (1471–1484) greatly expanded the market for these letters by proclaiming the church's power to grant indulgences not only to the living, but to souls in purgatory.

Martin Luther Discovers Justification by Faith Alone

Many years after the fact, Martin Luther described his famous discovery that God's righteousness was not active and punishing but passive and transforming. It made those who believed in Christ as holy in God's eyes as Christ was holy.

∽ Why did Luther find the monastic life so unsatisfying? Did he misunderstand the church's teaching about God's love and mercy? How does his discovery of God's "passive righteousness" give him peace of mind?

Though I lived as a monk without reproach, I felt that I was a sinner before God with an extremely disturbed conscience. I could not believe that he was placated by my satisfaction. I did not love, yes, I hated the righteous God who punishes sinners, and secretly, if not blasphemously, certainly murmuring greatly, I was angry with God, and said, "As if, indeed, it is not enough, that miserable sinners, eternally lost through original sin, are crushed by every kind of calamity by the law of the decalogue, without having God add pain to pain by the gospel and also by the gospel threatening us with his righteousness and wrath!" Thus I raged with a fierce and troubled conscience. Nevertheless, I beat importunately upon Paul at that place, most ardently desiring to know what St. Paul wanted.

At last, by the mercy of God, meditating day and night, I gave heed to the context of the words, namely, "In it the righteousness of God is revealed, as it is written, 'He who through faith is righteous shall live' " [Romans 1:17]. There I began to understand that the righteousness of God is that by which the right-eous [man] lives by a gift of God, namely by faith. And this is the meaning: the righteousness of God is revealed by the gospel, namely, the passive righteousness with which merciful God justifies us by faith, as it is written, "He who through faith is righteous shall live." Here I felt that I was altogether born again and had entered paradise itself through open gates. There a totally other face of the entire Scripture showed itself to me. Thereupon I ran through the Scriptures from memory. I also found in other terms an analogy, as, the work of God, that is, what God does in us, the power of God, with which he makes us strong, the wisdom of God, with which he makes us wise, the strength of God, the salvation of God, the glory of God.

And I extolled my sweetest word with a love as great as the hatred with which I had before hated the word "righteousness of God." Thus that place in Paul was for me truly the gate to paradise.

Preface to the Complete Edition of Luther's Latin Writings *(1545), in* Luther's Works, *Vol. 34, ed. by Lewis W. Spitz (Philadelphia: Muhlenberg Press, 1960) pp. 336–337.*

Indulgences had been granted, at first, only for significant services to the church, but by Luther's day their price had been significantly discounted to permit mass marketing. Pope Julius II (1503–1513) excited considerable interest by declaring a special Jubilee indulgence, to be sold in 1517, to raise funds for the rebuilding of Saint Peter's in Rome. In 1517, Archbishop Al-

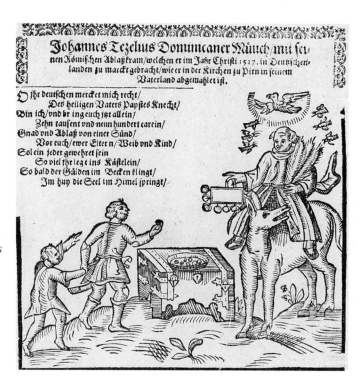

Johannes Tezelius Dominicaner Münch, mit seinen Römischen Ablaßkram, welchen er im Jahr Christi 1517. in Deutschlanden zu marckt gebracht, wie er in der Kirchen zu Pirn in seinem Vaterland abgemahlet ist.

O ihr deutschen mercket mich recht,
Des heiligen Vaters Papstes Knecht,
Bin ich, vnd br ing euch jtzt allein,
Zehn tausent vnd neun hundert carein,
Gnad vnd Ablaß von einer Sünd,
Vor euch, ewer Eltern, Weib vnd Kind,
Sol ein jeder gewehret sein
So viel ihr legt ins Kästelein,
So bald der Gülden im Becken klingt,
Im huy die Seel im Himel springt,

A contemporary caricature depicts John Tetzel, the famous indulgence preacher. The last lines of the jingle read: "As soon as gold in the basin rings, right then the soul to Heaven springs." It was Tetzel's preaching that spurred Luther to publish his ninety-five theses. [Staatliche Lutherhalle, Wittenberg]

brecht of Mainz was in debt to the Fugger bank of Augsburg. He had taken out a loan to pay the pope for permission to ignore church law and simultaneously hold three profitable ecclesiastical offices: the archbishoprics of Mainz and Magdeburg and the bishopric of Halberstadt. In exchange for Albrecht's help in promoting the sale, Pope Leo X agreed to share the proceeds, and a famous preacher, John Tetzel (d. 1519), was employed to drum up business in Luther's neighborhood.

According to tradition, Luther posted his ninety-five theses opposing the sale of indulgences on the door of Castle Church in Wittenberg on October 31, 1517. Luther especially protested Tetzel's insinuation that indulgences remitted sins and released the dead from punishment in purgatory. Luther believed Tetzel's claims went far beyond traditional practice and made salvation something that could be bought and sold.

Election of Charles V

The ninety-five theses made Luther famous overnight and prompted official proceedings against him. In April 1518, he was summoned to appear before the general chapter of his order in Heidelberg, and the following October he was called to Augsburg to be examined by the papal legate and general of the Dominican Order, Cardinal Cajetan. The death of the Holy Roman Emperor Maximilian I on January 12, 1519, however, diverted attention from Luther's case to the contest for a new emperor.

MAP 11-1 The Empire of Charles V *Dynastic marriages and simple chance concentrated into Charles's hands rule over the lands shown here, plus Spain's overseas possessions. Crowns and titles rained in on him; election in 1519 as emperor gave him new burdens and responsibilities.*

Charles I of Spain, a youth of nineteen, succeeded his grandfather to become Emperor Charles V (see Map 11-1). But there was a price. The electors, who traditionally enhanced their power at every opportunity, forced him to agree to consult with a diet of the empire on all major domestic and foreign issues. This ruled out unilateral imperial action in Germany—something for which Luther was to be thankful.

Luther's Excommunication and the Diet of Worms

While the imperial election was being held, Luther was in Leipzig (June 27, 1519) to debate an Ingolstadt professor, John Eck. This contest led Luther to question the infallibility of the pope and the inerrancy of church councils and, for the first time, to appeal to the Scripture as the sole authority governing faith.

In 1520, Luther described his position in three famous pamphlets. *The Address to the Christian Nobility of the German Nation* urged the German princes forcefully to reform the Roman Catholic church and to curtail its political and economic power. The *Babylonian Captivity of the Church* examined the sacraments, arguing that only two of the church's seven (Baptism and the Eucharist) were authentic. The pamphlet also claimed that the Scriptures, decrees of church councils, and decisions of secular princes were superior to the authority of a pope. The eloquent *Freedom of a Christian* summarized Luther's key theological doctrine, salvation by faith alone.

On June 15, 1520, a papal bull, *Exsurge Domine*, condemned Luther for heresy and gave him sixty days to retract. The final bull of excommunication, *Decet Pontificem Romanum*, was issued on January 3, 1521. In April of that year, Luther appeared before a diet of the empire in Worms, at which the newly elected Charles V presided. Ordered to recant, Luther refused, for such an act, he claimed, would violate Scripture, reason, and conscience. On May 26, 1521, Luther was placed under the imperial ban. This meant that his heresy became a crime punishable by the state. Friends protected Luther by hiding him in Wartburg Castle. The year (April 1521 to March 1522) he spent in seclusion was put to good use. At Wartburg Luther created one of the indispensable tools of the Reformation: a German translation of Erasmus's Greek text of the New Testament.

Imperial Distractions: France and the Turks

Charles V was too preoccupied with military ventures to pay much attention to the Reformation that erupted in Wittenberg following Luther's trial. France wanted to move into Italy to drive a wedge through Charles's empire, and the Ottoman Turks were advancing on eastern Europe. Charles needed friendly relations with the German princes in order to recruit German troops for his armies.

In 1526, the Turks overran Hungary at the Battle of Mohacs, and in western Europe the French organized the League of Cognac in preparation for the second of four wars between the Habsburg and Valois dynasties (1521–1559). Thus preoccupied, the emperor, at the Diet of Speyer (1526), granted each German prince the right to deal as he saw fit with the situation Luther had created. This cleared the way for the Reformation to put down deep roots in places where the princes sympathized with it, and it inaugurated a tradition of princely control over religion that was to be enshrined in law by the Peace of Augsburg in 1555.

The Peasants' Revolt

In its first decade the Protestant movement suffered more from internal division than from imperial interference. By 1525, Luther had become as controversial a figure in Germany as the pope, and many of his early supporters had broken with him. Germany's peasants, who had welcomed Luther as an ally, had a particular reason for losing faith in him. Since the late fifteenth century, their leaders had been struggling to prevent the territorial princes from ignoring traditional restraints and imposing new regulations and taxes. Many peasants saw Luther's proclamation of Christian freedom and criticism of monastic landowners as a declaration of support for their cause.

Luther and his followers sympathized with the peasants, but Lutherans were not social revolutionaries. Luther's freedom of the Christian individual was an inner release from guilt and anxiety, not a restructuring of society by violent revolution. When the peasants rebelled against their masters in 1524–1525, Luther condemned them in the strongest possible terms and urged the princes to crush their revolt without mercy. Tens of thousands of peasants (possibly 100,000) died in the struggle. Had Luther supported the Peasants' Revolt, he would have contradicted his own teaching. He would also probably have ended any chance of the survival of his reform beyond the 1520s.

⌒ The Reformation Elsewhere

Zwingli and the Swiss Reformation

Switzerland's political environment was as favorable to the success of a religious revolt as Germany's. Switzerland was a loose confederacy of thirteen autonomous cantons (states) and allied areas. Some (e.g., Zurich, Bern, Basel, and Schaffhausen) became Protestant, some (especially in the heartland around Lucerne) remained Catholic, and a few effected a compromise. Two developments prepared the ground for the Swiss Reformation: (1) a growth of national sentiment created by opposition to the practice of impressing Swiss soldiers into mercenary service outside the homeland; and (2) an interest in church reform that had been stimulated by the convocation of famous church councils in the Swiss cities of Constance (1414–1417) and Basel (1431–1449).

The Reformation in Zurich. Ulrich Zwingli (1484–1531), the leader of the Swiss Reformation, received a Humanist education, and he gave Erasmus credit for sparking his interest in reform. He served as a chaplain with Swiss mercenaries in Italy in 1515, and his experiences at a disastrous battle at Marignano prompted him to become an ardent critic of mercenary service. By 1518, he was also widely known for opposing the sale of indulgences and for denouncing religious superstitions.

In 1519, Zwingli applied for the post of people's priest in Zurich's main church. His fitness was questioned because of his acknowledged fornication with a barber's daughter. Many of his contemporaries, however, sympathized with the plight of celibate clergy, and Zwingli defended himself forcefully. Later he led the fight to abolish clerical celibacy and to establish the right of clergy, in all Protestant countries, to marry.

As the people's priest in Zurich, Zwingli had a pulpit from which to campaign for reform. Zwingli's program for reform was simple: whatever lacked literal support in Scripture was to be neither believed nor practiced. Application of that standard led him, as it did Luther, to question many traditional teachings and practices: fasting, transubstantiation, the worship of saints, pilgrimages, purgatory, clerical celibacy, and some of the sacraments. A public debate, held on January 29, 1523, ended with the city government endorsing Zwingli's ideas. Zurich took the lead in the Swiss Reformation and pioneered the kind of Protestantism that came to be called "puritanical."

The Marburg Colloquy. Landgrave Philip of Hesse (1504–1567), who believed that Protestants had to cooperate in order to fend off attacks from Catholics, tried to unite the Swiss and German reformations. He brought Luther and Zwingli together in his castle in Marburg in early October 1529. But theological disagreements—over the nature of Christ's presence in the Eucharist—prevented the two leaders from endorsing a political alliance. Luther concluded that Zwingli was a dangerous fanatic, and Zwingli believed that Luther was irrationally in thrall to medieval ideas.

The disagreement splintered the Protestant movement. Separate defense leagues were formed, and separate credal statements were proposed. Semi-Zwinglian views were embodied in the *Confessio Tetrapolitana* prepared by the Strasbourg reformers Martin Bucer and Caspar Hedio. In 1530, it was presented to the Diet of Augsburg as an alternative to the *Augsburg Confession*, which the Lutherans had proposed as a basis for unity.

Swiss Civil Wars. As Protestants and Catholics divided up the Swiss cantons, civil wars began. There were two major battles, both at Kappel: one in June 1529, the second in October 1531. The first was a clear victory for the Protestants. The Catholic cantons were forced to repudiate their foreign alliances and recognize the rights of Protestants. The second battle cost Zwingli his life. He was wounded on the battlefield, captured, and executed, but the treaty that ended the fighting confirmed the right of each canton to determine its own religion.

Thereafter, things settled down. Heinrich Bullinger (1504–1575), Zwingli's protégé, assumed leadership of the Swiss Reformation and guided its evolution as an established religion.

Anabaptists and Radical Protestants

The moderate pace and seeming failure of the Lutheran and Zwinglian reformations to elevate standards of ethical conduct discontented many people. Those who wanted a more rapid and thorough implementation of "primitive Christianity" (the church described in the New Testament) accused the reformers of going only halfway. These people were attracted to radical Protestant movements, chief among which were the Anabaptists (ancestors of the Mennonites and Amish). The Anabaptists ("rebaptizers") took their name from their rejection of infant baptism and their insistence on adult baptism.

Conrad Grebel (1498–1526) symbolically inaugurated Anabaptism by performing the first adult rebaptism in Zurich in January 1525. In October 1523,

Grebel's passion for biblical literalism had caused him to break with his mentor, Zwingli, when Zwingli supported the government's plea for a gradual removal of traditional religious practices. In 1527, Grebel's followers, the Swiss Brethren, published a statement of their principles, the *Schleitheim Confession*. They practiced adult baptism and opposed the swearing of oaths. They committed themselves to pacifism and refused to take part in secular governments. Anabaptists literally withdrew from society to be free to live as they believed the first Christians had lived. State authorities viewed their behavior as an attack on society's bonds.

The Anabaptist Reign in Münster. Lutherans and Zwinglians joined Catholics in persecuting the Anabaptists. In 1529, rebaptism became a capital offense throughout the Holy Roman Empire, and from 1525 to 1618 somewhere between 1,000 and 5,000 people were executed for undergoing rebaptism. Brutal punishments for nonconformists increased after state authorities witnessed the behavior of a group of Anabaptist extremists who took over the German city of Münster in 1534–1535.

Anabaptists converted the majority of the citizens of Münster and established a town government that forced Lutherans and Catholics to convert or emigrate. Münster became an Old Testament theocracy, replete with charismatic leaders and the practice of polygamy. The latter was an attempt to provide for the women, recently widowed or deserted, who greatly outnumbered the men of the city.

The outside world was deeply shocked, and Protestant and Catholic armies united to crush the radicals. After this bloody episode, Anabaptism reasserted its commitment to pacifism, and the movement spread largely among rural populations. Subsequent Anabaptist leaders were moderates like Menno Simons (1496–1561), founder of the Mennonites.

Other Nonconformists. The Anabaptists were not the only Protestant radicals. The Spiritualists were extreme individualists who believed that the only religious authority one ought to obey was the voice of God's spirit in one's heart. Thomas Müntzer (d. 1525), an early convert to Lutheranism and a leader of a peasants' revolt, belonged to this camp—as did Sebastian Franck (d. 1541), a freelance critic of all dogmatic religion, and Caspar Schwenckfeld (d. 1561), a prolific author for whom the tiny Schwenckfeldian denomination is named.

The Reformation's critique of religious superstition encouraged some people to become extreme rationalists. The Antitrinitarians were the most prominent exponents of commonsense, rational, ethical religion. In 1553, the Spaniard Michael Servetus (1511–1553) was executed by the Protestant government of Geneva for rejecting the doctrine of the Trinity. Italian reformers, Lelio (d. 1562) and Faustus Sozzini (d. 1604), founded Socinianism, a Humanistic faith that opposed emerging Protestant orthodoxies and advocated religious toleration.

John Calvin

In the second half of the sixteenth century, Calvinism replaced Lutheranism as the dominant Protestant force in Europe. Although Calvinists believed strongly in divine predestination, they also believed that Christians ought to reorder society according to God's plan. They were zealous reformers who used the machinery of government to compel men and women to live according to codes of conduct that they believed were set forth in the Scriptures.

The founder of Calvinism, John Calvin (1509–1564), was the son of a well-to-do secretary to the bishop of Noyon in Picardy. The church benefices the boy received at age twelve paid for the excellent education he received at Parisian colleges and the law school at Orléans. Young Calvin associated with a group of Catholic Humanists (led by Jacques Lefèvre d'Étaples and Marguerite d'Angoulême, the queen of Navarre after 1527) who advocated reform. Calvin eventually concluded that these people were ineffectual, but they helped awaken his interest in the Reformation.

It was probably in the spring of 1534 that Calvin converted to Protestantism, an experience he describes as God's making his "long stubborn heart . . . teachable." In May 1534, he dramatically surrendered the benefices that had long supported him and joined the Reformation.

Geneva. In Luther's Saxony, religious reform paved the way for political revolution. In Calvin's Geneva, political revolution awakened an appetite for religious reform. In 1527, the Genevans, with the assistance of the city-states of Fribourg and Bern, won their independence from the House of Savoy and drove out their resident prince-bishop. The city councils assumed his legal and political powers.

Late in 1533, Bern sent the Protestant reformers Guillaume Farel (1489–1565) and Antoine Froment (1508–1581) to Geneva. In the summer of 1535, after much internal turmoil, the Genevans discontinued the traditional Mass and other Catholic religious practices. On May 21, 1536, the city officially endorsed the Reformation.

Calvin arrived in Geneva in July 1536. He had been forced to flee France to avoid persecution for his religious beliefs, and he was intending to seek refuge in Strasbourg. The third Habsburg-Valois war forced him to detour to Geneva, where Farel persuaded him to stay. Before a year had passed, Calvin had drawn up articles for the governance of Geneva's new church as well as a catechism to guide its people. Both were presented for approval to the city councils in early 1537. Because of the strong measures they proposed for governing Geneva's moral life, the reformers were accused of creating a "new papacy." Both within Geneva and outside it, opponents attacked the new orthodoxy. Bern, which had adopted a more moderate Protestant reform, pressured Geneva to restore ceremonies and holidays that Calvin and Farel opposed. In February 1538, the four syndics (the leading city magistrates) turned against the reformers and drove them out.

Calvin went to Strasbourg to became pastor to a group of French exiles. During his long stay in Strasbourg, he wrote a second edition of his masterful *Institutes of the Christian Religion.* Many scholars consider this work to be the definitive theological explication of Protestant faith. Calvin married, took part in ecumenical discussions, and learned important lessons in practical politics from the Strasbourg reformer Martin Bucer.

In 1540, Geneva elected syndics who wanted to establish the city's independence from Bern. They believed that Calvin would be a valuable ally and invited him to return. Within months of his return in September 1540, the city implemented new ecclesiastical ordinances. Civil magistrates were pledged to work with the clergy in maintaining discipline within the city.

The church Calvin designed was administered by four kinds of officials: (1) five presiding pastors; (2) various teachers or doctors who handled religious instruction; (3) twelve elders, laymen chosen by and from the Genevan councils to "oversee the life of everybody"; and (4) deacons, also laymen, who managed the church's charitable disbursements.

Calvin believed that a strong church government was needed to maintain the highest moral standards for the community, for no Christian city could tolerate conduct that was not pleasing to God. The consistory, a committee composed of the elders and the pastors of the church and presided over by one of the four syndics, was given this responsibility. It meted out punishments for a broad range of moral and religious transgressions—from missing church services (a fine of 3 sous) to fornication (six days on bread and water and a fine of 60 sous). Among the sins it punished were statements critical of Calvin and the consistory.

Calvin branded his opponents wanton "Libertines" and showed them little mercy. His most prominent victim was the Spanish physician and amateur theologian Michael Servetus. Servetus fled to Geneva in 1553, seeking refuge from the Inquisition—only to be burned at the stake for having written a book that denied the doctrine of the Trinity.

After 1555, the city's syndics were all solidly behind Calvin, and he began to attract followers from across Europe. Geneva welcomed the thousands of Protestants who were driven out of France, England, and Scotland, and at one point more than a third of the population of the city consisted of refugees (over 5,000 of them). They were utterly loyal to Calvin, for in their experience Geneva was Europe's only "free" city. Whenever they were allowed to return to their homes, they ardently championed Calvinistic reforms.

∾ The English Reformation to 1553

The king of England was the only major European monarch to break with the papacy, but England's Reformation owed more to nationalism than to sympathy with Lutheran or Calvinistic theology. England had a long history of maintaining the rights of the crown against the pope. Edward I (d. 1307) defeated Pope Boniface VIII's attempt to deny kings the right to tax their clergy. In the mid-fourteenth century, the English Parliament passed the first Statutes of Provisors and *Praemunire*. These curtailed the right of the pope to appoint candidates to church offices in England, limited the amount of money that could be sent out of England to Rome, and restricted the number of court cases that could be appealed to Rome from English jurisdiction.

In the late Middle Ages, Wycliffe and the Lollards fanned anticlerical sentiment among the English of all classes, and by the early 1520s advocates of reform were smuggling Lutheran writings into England. In 1524–1525, William Tyndale (ca. 1492–1536) translated the New Testament into English. Published in Cologne and Worms, it began to circulate in England in 1526. Access to a Bible in the language of the people became the centerpiece of the English Reformation.

The King's Affair

Henry VIII (r. 1509–1547), the king who severed England's ties with the papacy, initially opposed the Reformation. When Luther's ideas began to circulate, Henry's chief ministers, Cardinal Thomas Wolsey (ca. 1475–1530) and, later, Sir Thomas More (1478–1535), encouraged him to rush to the pope's defense. Henry declared his Catholic convictions by publishing a treatise justifying the seven sacraments. It earned him a contemptuous response from Luther and the grant of a title, "Defender of the Faith," from Pope Leo X.

It was the king's unhappy marriage, not his doubts about theology, that allowed the seeds of reform to take root in English soil. Henry had married Catherine of Aragon (d. 1536), daughter of Ferdinand and Isabella of Spain and the aunt of Emperor Charles V. By 1527, the union had produced only one surviving child, a daughter, Mary. Since the precedent for women rulers was weak and the practice controversial, Henry feared that civil war would break out if he left his throne to a daughter.

Henry had wed Catherine in 1509, under unusual circumstances that had required a papal dispensation. Catherine had been the wife of Henry's elder brother, Arthur, the heir to their father's throne. When Arthur died, Catherine was betrothed to Henry, the new heir, in order to preserve England's alliance with Spain. Catherine's numerous miscarriages and stillbirths convinced Henry that their union, despite papal permission, had been a sin and had violated God's laws against incest (see Leviticus 18:16, 20:21).

By 1527, Henry was thoroughly enamored of Anne Boleyn, one of the aging Catherine's young ladies in waiting. In order to wed Anne, who he believed would be a more fruitful mate, he needed a papal annulment of his marriage to Catherine. Legally, it would have been difficult for the pope to justify an annulment of a marriage that had been approved by a papal dispensation. But in practical terms, it was impossible. The soldiers of the Holy Roman Empire had just mutinied and sacked Rome, and the pope, Clement VII, was a prisoner of Catherine's nephew, Charles V.

Cardinal Wolsey, Henry's Lord Chancellor and a papal legate who had aspirations to become pope, was given the job of securing the annulment. After two years of profitless diplomatic maneuvering, Henry concluded that Wolsey had failed and dismissed him in disgrace (1529). Thomas Cranmer (1489–1556) and Thomas Cromwell (1485–1540), both of whom harbored Lutheran sympathies, then became the king's chief advisers. They struck a different course: Why not simply declare the king supreme in England's spiritual affairs as he was in England's temporal government? Then the king would need no foreign permission to settle the king's affair.

The Reformation

In 1529, Parliament convened for a seven-year session, and began to issue a flood of legislation that established the king's authority over the clergy. In January 1531, Convocation (a legislative assembly representing the English clergy) recognized Henry as head of the church in England "as far as the law of Christ allows." In 1532, Parliament passed a decree (Submission of the Clergy) that gave the king control over canon law and jurisdiction over clergy. Another act (Conditional Restraint of Annates) recognized the king's power to withhold from Rome the payment of dues traditionally owed the pope.

In January 1533, Thomas Cranmer secretly wed Henry to the pregnant Anne Boleyn. In February 1533, Parliament's Act for the Restraint of Appeals forbade appeals from the king's courts to those of the pope. In March 1533, Cranmer became archbishop of Canterbury, England's primate—or highest ranking clergyman—and declared that the king had never been validly married to Catherine. In 1534, Parliament ended all payments by the English clergy and laity to Rome and gave Henry sole jurisdiction over high ecclesiastical appointments. The Act of Succession in the same year declared Anne Boleyn's children legitimate heirs to the throne, and the Act of Supremacy proclaimed Henry "the only supreme head in earth of the Church of England." In 1536, the first Act for Dissolution of Monasteries closed the smaller houses, and three years later all English monasteries were shut and their endowments confiscated by the king.

Not all of Henry's subjects approved of the nationalization of their church, but Henry encouraged compliance by making examples of two of his most prominent critics. When Thomas More and John Fisher, bishop of Rochester, refused to accept the Act of Succession and the Act of Supremacy, Henry had them executed.

Henry was far bolder in politics than in piety. Except for his break with Rome and his approval of the use of English Bibles in English churches, Henry opposed changes in doctrine and practice. The Ten Articles of 1536, a program for England's nationalized church, made only mild concessions to Protestant tenets. In 1539, the king issued the Six Articles, which were intended to stem a rising tide of enthusiasm for Protestantism. These reaffirmed transubstantiation, denied the Eucharistic cup to the laity, preserved mandatory celibacy for the clergy, authorized private masses, and ordered the continuation of auricular confession. England had to await Henry's death before it could become a genuinely Protestant country.

The King's Wives

Henry was more successful as a politician than as a husband. In 1536, Anne Boleyn, who had disappointed Henry by bearing him another daughter (Elizabeth), was executed for alleged treason and adultery. Henry married four more times. His third wife, Jane Seymour, died in 1537, shortly after giving birth to the long-desired male heir, Edward VI. Henry then wed Anne of Cleves as part of a plan that Cromwell promoted to forge an alliance among Protestant princes. Neither the alliance nor Anne—whom Henry found to have a remarkable resemblance to a horse—proved worth the trouble. The marriage was annulled by Parliament, and Cromwell was executed. Catherine Howard, Henry's fifth wife, was beheaded for adultery in 1542. And his last wife, Catherine Parr, a patron of Humanists and reformers, for whom Henry was the third husband, survived him to marry a fourth time.

The Protestant Reformation Under Edward VI

When Henry died, his son, Edward VI (r. 1547–1553), was only ten years old. The young king's regents gave him a Protestant education—enlivened by correspondence with John Calvin.

Edward's government repealed Henry's Six Articles and laws against heresy, and it sanctioned clerical marriage and lay communion with both cup and bread. In 1547, the chantries, endowments supporting priests who said masses for the dead, were dissolved. In 1549, the Act of Uniformity imposed Thomas Cranmer's *Book of Common Prayer* on all English churches, and a year later images and altars were ordered removed from churches.

The Second Act of Uniformity, passed in 1552, revised the *Book of Common Prayer* and published a forty-two-article confession of faith written by Thomas Cranmer. The confession endorsed the Protestant doctrines of justification by faith and supremacy of Holy Scripture. It recognized only two sacraments and denied transubstantiation—although it affirmed the real presence of Christ in the Eucharistic elements.

The turn toward Protestantism that took place during Edward's reign was reversed by his heir, Catherine of Aragon's fervently Catholic daughter, Mary. In 1553, Mary succeeded her teenaged half-brother and made it her mission, as queen, to restore England to the Catholic community. Despite a bloody persecution of Protestants, she was unable completely to undo the work her father and brother had begun. When she died childless in 1558, Anne Boleyn's daughter, Elizabeth (d. 1603), came to the throne and engineered a compromise. The Elizabethan "settlement" left England with a stable, moderately Protestant national church.

⟿ Political Consolidation of the Lutheran Reformation

The Expansion of the Reformation

Charles V, who spent most of his time in Spain and Italy, returned to the empire in 1530 to convene a diet at Augsburg. The purpose of the meeting was to resolve the religious conflicts that had developed within the empire since Luther's break with the papacy in 1520. Charles adjourned the meeting with a blunt order to all Lutherans to revert to Catholicism.

The Reformation was too far advanced by that time to be halted by this sort of peremptory gesture. The emperor's mandate served only to persuade Lutherans that they needed to form a defensive alliance, the Schmalkaldic League. The league issued the *Augsburg Confession,* a moderate Protestant creed—followed in 1538 by Luther's more strongly worded *Schmalkaldic Articles.* And the German Lutherans formed regional consistories, judicial bodies composed of theologians and lawyers, to replace the bishops who had formerly administered their churches.

Charles was prevented from doing much about this by the outbreak of new hostilities with France and with the Turks. Consequently, the league's leaders, Landgrave Philip of Hesse and Elector John Frederick of Saxony, were, for the time being, able to hold him at bay as Lutheranism spread.

Christian II (r. 1513–1523) introduced Lutheranism to Denmark, where it became the state religion. In Sweden in 1527, Gustavus Vasa (r. 1523–1560) persuaded a Swedish nobility that was eager to confiscate church property to embrace the reform. Poland, primarily because of the absence of a central political authority, became a model of religious pluralism and toleration. In the second half of the sixteenth century, it sheltered Lutherans, Anabaptists, Calvinists, and even Antitrinitarians.

Reaction and Resolution

In 1547, the armies of Charles V crushed the Schmalkaldic League, and the emperor issued the *Augsburg Interim.* It ordered Protestants to return to Catholic beliefs and practices. A few concessions were made to Protestant tastes. Clerical marriage was permitted in individual cases when the pope approved, and laypeople were allowed to receive both the bread and the wine at communion. Many Protestant leaders chose exile rather than comply with the terms of the *Interim,* but the Reformation was too entrenched by 1547 to be ended by imperial fiat.

Maurice of Saxony, hand-picked by Charles V to replace Elector John Frederick as ruler of Saxony, recognized the inevitable and shifted his allegiance to the Protestants. And, wearied by three decades of war, the emperor himself finally surrendered his lifelong quest for the restoration of religious unity in Europe. In 1552, Charles reinstated John Frederick and Philip of Hesse and issued the Peace of Passau (August 1552), guaranteeing religious freedom for Lutherans. The Peace of Augsburg in September 1555 made the division of Christendom permanent. It legalized a principle well established in practice: *cuius regio, eius religio*—the ruler of a land determines the religion of that land. A subject who was discontented with the religion chosen by his ruler was permitted to migrate to a district that practiced his preferred faith.

～ Catholic Reform and Counter-Reformation

Before Luther spoke out, proposals had been made for reforming the Roman Catholic Church. One of the boldest came on the eve of the last church council that met before the Reformation, the Fifth Lateran Council (1513–1517). But the pope, remembering how the councils of Constance and Basel had usurped the authority of his predecessors, squelched the initiative.

The Modern Devotion, the popular late medieval movement that promoted pious practices, inspired many of the laity and clergy who pushed for reform. And in 1517, a new kind of religious organization was founded in Rome, the Oratory of Divine Love. It encouraged cooperation among learned laity and clergy who were deeply committed to the cultivation of inner piety, the promotion of Christian living, and the reform of the church.

The fervent Catholic faith of the sixteenth century generated many new religious orders. The Theatines were founded in 1524 to groom devout, reform-minded leaders for the higher levels of the church hierarchy. The Capuchins were established in 1528 to minister to ordinary people by return-

The Ecstasy of St. Teresa of Avila, by Gianlorenzo Bernini (1598–1680). Mystics like Saint Teresa and Saint John of the Cross helped revive the traditional piety of medieval monasticism. [Scala/ Art Resource, N.Y.]

ing to the ideals of Saint Francis. The Somaschi, in the mid-1520s, and the Barnabites, in 1530, dedicated themselves to caring for the residents of war-torn areas of Italy. The Ursulines, founded in 1535, undertook the religious education of girls from all social classes. The Oratorians, established in 1575, promoted religious literature and church music—the great hymnist and musician Giovanni Palestrina (1526–1594) was one of them. And, thanks to the inspiration of the Spanish mystics, Saint Teresa of Avila (1515–1582) and Saint John of the Cross (1542–1591), older monastic orders also underwent renewal.

Ignatius of Loyola and the Jesuits

The most influential of the new orders, the Society of Jesus, was organized in the 1530s by Ignatius of Loyola (1491–1556). Ignatius, a dashing courtier and caballero, began his spiritual pilgrimage in 1521 when he was seriously wounded in battle. He passed a lengthy and painful convalescence reading Christian classics and studying the techniques developed by the church's saints for overcoming mental anguish and pain. A dramatic conversion experience determined him to do whatever was necessary to become a "soldier of Christ."

The lessons Ignatius learned from his struggles with himself became a program for the religious and moral reform of the individual. Ignatius believed that a person could create a new self through study and discipline, and his devotional guide, *Spiritual Exercises*, taught techniques for achieving spiritual self-mastery.

The Protestant reformers of Ignatius's day made a virtue of opposing the authority of the traditional church. Ignatius, however, urged Catholics to deny themselves and submit without question to the church. Perfect discipline and self-control were to be cultivated—as were enthusiasm for traditional spirituality, mystical experience, and willingness to subordinate all personal goals to those of the church. People imbued with these qualities were well equipped to counter the Reformation. Within a century the ten original "Jesuits" were joined by more than 15,000 ardent recruits, who recovered districts initially lost to Protestantism in Austria, Bavaria, and the Rhineland, and staffed missions as far afield as India, Japan, and the Americas.

The Council of Trent (1545–1563)

Pope Paul III (1534–1549), in response to pressure from Emperor Charles V, finally announced a general council to address the crisis created by the Reformation. The commission, appointed by the pope to prepare for the council, was chaired by Caspar Contarini (1483–1542), a member of the Oratory of Divine Love. Contarini was such an advocate of reform that his critics branded him a "semi-Lutheran." The report he presented to the pope in February 1537 was so blunt an indictment of the papal curia that Protestants circulated it to justify their break with the papacy.

The opening of the council, which met in Trent in northern Italy, was delayed until 1545, and its three sessions spread over eighteen years (1545–1563) (see Map 11-2). Long interruptions were caused by war, plague, and politics. Unlike the late medieval councils, Trent was strictly under papal control—and dominated by Italian clergy. Only high-ranking churchmen could vote. Theologians from the universities, the lower clergy, and laypersons did not have a voice in the council's decisions.

MAP 11-2 The Religious Situation About 1560 *By 1560 Luther, Zwingli, and Loyola were dead, Calvin near the end of his life, the English break from Rome fully accomplished, and the last session of the Council of Trent about to assemble. Here is the religious geography of Western Europe at this time.*

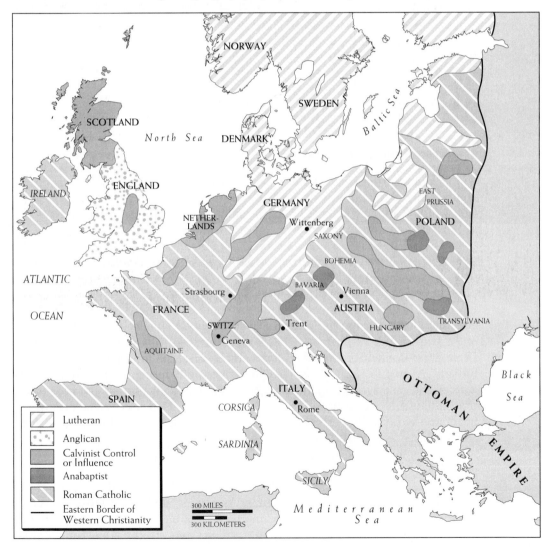

The council focused on the restoration of internal church discipline. It curtailed the selling of church offices and other religious goods. It ordered bishops who resided outside their dioceses to return home and to take steps to elevate the conduct of their charges. Bishops were enjoined to preach and to conduct frequent tours of inspection of the clergy. Trent also sought to increase respect for the parish priest by requiring him to be neatly dressed, better educated, strictly celibate, and active among his parishioners. To this end Trent called for the construction of a seminary in every diocese.

Trent made no doctrinal concessions to Protestantism. On the contrary, it ringingly affirmed most of the things to which Protestants objected: traditional Scholastic education; the role of good works in salvation; the authority of tradition; the seven sacraments; transubstantiation; the withholding of the Eucharistic cup from the laity; clerical celibacy; purgatory; indulgences; and the veneration of saints, relics, and sacred images.

Trent was not designed to heal the rifts that had developed within Christendom, but to strengthen the Roman Catholic Church in opposition to Protestantism. Some secular rulers were initially leery of Trent's assertion of papal authority, but they were reassured as the new legislation took hold and parish life revived under the guidance of a devout and better-trained clergy. The increasing religious polarization of Europe was, however, a source for anxiety.

The Church in Spanish America

The Roman Catholic priests who accompanied the expeditions that explored and conquered the Americas were imbued with the Christian Humanism that flourished in sixteenth-century Spain. They wanted to convert the Indians not only to Christianity but to European civilization as well.

The early Spanish conquerors and the mendicant friars who worked among the Indians were often at odds. Many priests believed that conquest was a necessary prerequisite for the conversion of the Indians, but they deplored exploitation of native peoples and tried to defend them. Bartolomé de Las Casas, a Dominican, contended that conquest was not necessary for conversion. The campaign he began in 1550 for royal legislation regulating conquest was successful, but his rhetoric encouraged the growth of the "Black Legend"—a condemnation of all Spanish colonists for inhumanity toward the Indians. Although the "Black Legend" contained elements of truth, it exaggerated the case against Spain. The Aztec demands for human sacrifice prove that Indian rulers could also be exceedingly cruel. Had the Aztecs discovered Spain and won the upper hand, they would have dealt with Europeans much as Spaniards dealt with Indians.

By the end of the sixteenth century, the church in Spanish America had made peace with colonialism. On numerous occasions, individual priests defended the rights of Indian tribes, but the church also profited from the growing prosperity of the Spanish colonists. As a great landowner with a stake in the colonial status quo, it did not challenge Spanish domination or any but the most extreme modes of economic exploitation. By the time the colonial era drew to a close in the late eighteenth century, the Roman Catholic Church had become one of the strongest and most conservative institutions in Latin America.

⁓ The Social Significance of the Reformation in Western Europe

Luther, Zwingli, and Calvin believed that Christians were called not to separate themselves from the world, but to take up their Christian duties as citizens of the state. Consequently, they have been called "magisterial reformers," meaning not only that they were leaders of major Protestant movements but also that they were willing to use the magistrate's sword to advance their causes.

To some modern observers this looks like a compromise of the highest religious principles, but the reformers did not see it that way. They assumed that their reforms had to conform to the realities of the societies of which they were members. The reformers were so sensitive to what they believed was politically and socially possible that some scholars claim that they actually encouraged acceptance of the status quo. But despite this political conservatism, the Reformation, in some places, contributed to radical changes in traditional religious practices and institutions.

The Revolution in Religious Practices and Institutions

Religion in Fifteenth-Century Life. On the eve of the Reformation, the clergy and the religious made up 6 to 8 percent of the total population of the central European cities that were about to become Protestant. In addition to their spiritual authority, they exercised considerable political power. They legislated, taxed, tried cases in special church courts, and enforced laws with threats of excommunication. The church calendar regulated the daily life of the city. About one-third of the year was given over to some kind of religious observance, fast, or celebration. Cloisters, which educated the children of prominent citizens and enjoyed the patronage of powerful aristocratic families, had great influence. There was booming business at religious shrines, where pilgrims gathered by the hundreds or thousands. Begging friars constantly worked the streets, and several times each year special preachers arrived to sell letters of indulgence.

The conduct of many of the religious was a source of concern. Despite the fact that clergy were sworn to celibacy and forbidden legal marriages, many had concubines and children. Society's response to these relationships was mixed, but the church tolerated them upon payment of penitential fines. Everywhere there were complaints about the clergy's exemption from taxation and immunity from prosecution in civil courts. And people grumbled about having to support church offices whose occupants lived and worked elsewhere.

Religion in Sixteenth-Century Life. The Reformation made few changes in the politics or class structures of the cities where it triumphed. The same aristocratic families governed as before, and the same people were rich and poor. The Reformation did, however, have a profound impact on the clergy. Their numbers fell by two-thirds; religious holidays shrank by one-third. Monasteries and nunneries nearly disappeared—transformed into hospices or educational institutions. Parish churches were reduced in number by at least one-third. Worship was conducted in the vernacular. In some places, particularly those influenced by the Zwinglian reform, the walls of sanctuaries were stripped bare and whitewashed.

The laity observed no obligatory fasts. Local shrines were closed down, and anyone found venerating saints, relics, and images was subject to punishment. Copies of Luther's translation of the New Testament or excerpts from it could be found in private homes. Instead of controlling access to the Scriptures, the new clergy encouraged laypersons to study them. Protestant clergy could marry, and many did. They paid taxes and were punished for their crimes in civil courts. The moral life of the community was supervised by committees composed of equal numbers of laity and clergy, and secular magistrates had the last word in resolving disputes. Not all Protestant clergy were enthusiastic about lay authority in religion. The laity complained about "new papists" among the Protestant preachers, men who sought the strict control over the lives of the laity that the Catholic clergy enjoyed.

The laity themselves were no less ambivalent about certain aspects of the Reformation, and they could be just as reactionary as some clergy. Over half of the original converts returned to the Catholic fold before the end of the sixteenth century.

The Reformation and Education

The Reformation's implementation of Humanistic educational theories in new Protestant schools and universities had significant cultural impact. Even when the Reformers' views on doctrine and human nature separated them from the Humanists, they shared the Humanists' belief in the unity of wisdom, eloquence, and action. The Humanist program of study, which emphasized language skills and a reliance on original sources, was essential for the practice of a Protestant faith that acknowledged no authority higher than that of Scripture.

When, in August 1518, Philip Melanchthon (1497–1560), a young professor of Greek, joined Luther at the University of Wittenberg, his first act was to champion Humanist curricular reforms. In his inaugural address, *On Improving the Studies of the Young,* Melanchthon defended classical studies against medieval Scholasticism, and he and Luther completely restructured the University of Wittenberg's program of study. Canon law and commentaries on Lombard's *Sentences* were dropped. Old-fashioned Scholastic lectures on Aristotle were replaced by a straightforward historical approach. Students read primary sources directly, not as interpreted by Scholastic commentators. Candidates for theological degrees relied on exegesis of the Bible, not the citation of "authorities," to defend their theses. New chairs of Greek and Hebrew were created. Luther and Melanchthon also pressed for universal compulsory education so that both boys and girls could learn to read the Bible in vernacular translation.

In Geneva, John Calvin and his successor, Theodore Beza, founded an academy that developed into the University of Geneva. Their school, which concentrated on training Calvinist ministers, developed a program similar to the one designed by Luther and Melanchthon. Calvinist refugees trained in the academy carried Protestant educational reforms to France, Scotland, England, and the New World. Thanks to them, a working knowledge of Greek and Hebrew became commonplace in educated circles in the sixteenth and seventeenth centuries.

Some contemporaries complained that the original Humanist program narrowed focus as Protestants took it over, but Humanist culture and learning profited from the Reformation. Protestant schools and universities consolidated and preserved for the modern world many of the basic pedagogical achievements of Humanism.

The Reformation and the Changing Role of Women

The Protestant reformers rejected ascetic disciplines, like celibacy, as vain attempts to earn salvation. They urged clergy to marry, in part to dispel the belief that the lives of clergy were spiritually more meritorious than those of laypersons. The development of a more positive attitude toward marriage translated into a more positive attitude toward women.

Medieval thinkers often degraded sexual women as temptresses (like Eve) and exalted virginal women as saints (like Mary). Protestants praised woman in her own right, but especially in her biblical vocation as mother and housewife. The reformers acknowledged the contribution their wives made to their ministries, and Protestants stressed as no religious movement before them the sacredness of home and family. The ideal of companionate marriage—that is, of husband and wife as co-workers in a special God-ordained community of the family—greatly improved women's legal status. Since Protestant marriage was not a sacrament, divorce was easier, and women had the right to leave husbands who flagrantly violated marriage contracts. Although from a modern perspective, Protestant women remained subject to men, new marriage laws gave them greater security and protection.

Because they wanted women to become pious housewives modeling their lives on biblical precepts, Protestants encouraged vernacular literacy for girls. Some women became authors and contributed to the literature of the Reformation. Many, in the course of their studies, pondered the significance of biblical passages that suggested they were equal to men in the presence of God. The discussion of woman's role that Protestant theology encouraged inched society marginally closer to the emancipation of women.

∼ Family Life in Early Modern Europe

Marriage

The Reformation was one factor among many that worked changes in domestic life at the end of the Middle Ages. Men and women began to delay first marriages to later ages than they had in previous centuries. Grooms tended to be in their mid- to late twenties rather than in their late teens and early twenties, and brides in their early to mid-twenties rather than in their teens. The church-sanctioned minimum age for marriage remained fourteen for men and twelve for women, and betrothal could still occur at these young ages if parents approved.

Later marriages were a reflection of the difficulty couples were encountering in amassing enough capital to establish an independent household. Family size and population increased in the fifteenth and early sixteenth centuries. That meant that property tended to be divided among more heirs, and an average couple had to work longer to prepare materially for marriage. Many—

A young couple in love (ca. 1480), by an anonymous artist. [Bildarchiv Preussischer Kulturbesitz]

possibly 20 percent of all women in the sixteenth century—never married. Single women often grew increasingly impoverished as they aged without the support of a husband or children.

Marriages tended to be "arranged" in the sense that the male heads of two families met and discussed the terms of a marriage before they informed the prospective bride and bridegroom. It was rare, however, for the two people involved not to know each other in advance or to have no prior relationship. Children had a legal right to protest and resist an unwanted marriage. A forced marriage was, by definition, invalid, and no one believed an unwanted marriage would last. The best marriage was one desired by both parties and approved by their families.

Later marriages to older partners shortened the length of the average marriage and elevated the rate of remarriage. Maternal mortality increased with late marriage and, as the rapid growth of orphanages and foundling homes between 1600 and 1800 testifies, so did out-of-wedlock pregnancies.

Family Size

The early modern family was conjugal or nuclear. It consisted of a father and a mother and an average of two to four surviving children. A wife endured a pregnancy about every two years. About one-third of the children born died by age five, and one-half were gone by age twenty. Rare was the family at any social level that did not suffer the loss of children. Martin Luther fathered six children, two of whom died—one at eight months and another at thirteen years.

Birth control methods of limited effectiveness had been available since antiquity: acidic ointments, sponges, and *coitus interruptus*. The church's growing condemnation of contraception in the thirteenth and fourteenth centuries suggests that its use was increasing. St. Thomas Aquinas defended the church's position by asserting that a natural act, like sex, was moral only when it served the end for which it was created—in this case, the production of children and their subsequent rearing to the glory of God. Christian moral teachings may, however, have increased some couples' use of contraception by encouraging husbands to empathize with the burden frequent pregnancies placed on their wives.

Infant and Child Care

Theologians and physicians joined in condemning the widespread custom of putting newborn children out to wet nurses. Wet nurses were mothers who made money by suckling other women's children. Wet nursing often exposed an infant to great risks from disease or neglect, but nursing a child was a chore some upper-class women found distasteful. Husbands also disliked it, for the church forbade sexual intercourse while a woman was lactating on the theory that sexual intercourse spoiled a woman's milk. Nursing also has a contraceptive effect, and there is evidence that some women prolonged nursing to fend off new pregnancy. For wealthy burghers and noblemen who wanted an abundance of male heirs, time spent nursing was time wasted.

In addition to wet nursing, other practices common to early modern families cause them to appear cold and unloving. A child who spent the first year of his life with a wet nurse might, between the ages of nine and fourteen, find himself sent away from home again for an apprenticeship or employment. Also, the gap in ages between husband and wife was often great, and a widower or widow sometimes remarried very quickly.

The forms love and affection take, however, are as relative to time and culture as other values. A kindness in one historical period can seem a cruelty in another, depending on the options that are available. Primitive living conditions, which made single life difficult, necessitated quick remarriages. A competitive economic environment with limited opportunities for vocational education encouraged early apprenticeships if children were to have jobs. There is no convincing evidence that people of the Reformation era were less capable of loving one another than modern people are.

The Lutheran Reformation, which made pluralism a fact of Western religious life, was the product of an age of widespread discontent. People at all levels of society had come to resent a church that failed to hold clergy accountable for their spiritual conduct while exempting them from the secular burdens imposed on the laity. Spiritual and secular grievances combined to fuel a revolution that restructured both the church and the state.

Luther's declaration that Scripture was the only authority governing faith opened a Pandora's box, for people proved to have very different ideas about what Scripture taught. Lutheran, Zwinglian, Anabaptist, Spiritualist, Calvinist, and Anglican versions of biblical religion appeared in rapid succession, and Protestants had difficulty containing their revolution.

A move to reform the Catholic church was underway long before the Reformation broke out in Germany, but, lacking papal support, it made little progress until the mid-sixteenth century. Catholic reform, when it came, was doctrinally reactionary but administratively and spiritually innovative. The church demanded strict obedience and conformity, but it also provided the laity with a better-educated and disciplined clergy. The result was a smaller but more vigorous church, prepared to fight for its place in an increasingly pluralistic culture.

Review Questions

1. What were the main problems of the church that contributed to the Protestant Reformation? Why was the church unable to suppress dissent as it had earlier?

2. On what did Luther and Zwingli agree? On what did they disagree? What about Luther and Calvin? Did differences and splits within the ranks lessen the effectiveness of the Protestant movement?

3. Why did the Reformation begin in Germany? How did the political context Germany provided for a reform movement differ from the situation in France or Italy?

4. What was the Catholic Reformation?

What were the major reforms instituted by the Council of Trent? Did the Protestant Reformation have a healthy effect on the Catholic church?

What were the major reforms instituted by the Council of Trent? Did the Protestant Reformation have a healthy effect on the Catholic church?

5. Why did Henry VIII break with the Catholic church? Did he establish a truly Protestant religion in England? What problems did his successors face as a result of his religious policies?

6. What impact did the Reformation have on women in the sixteenth and seventeenth centuries? What new factors and pressures affected relations between men and women, family size, and child care during this period?

∼ Suggested Readings

W. BOUWSMA, *John Calvin: A Sixteenth Century Portrait* (1988). Interpretation of Calvin against the background of Renaissance intellectual history.

J. DELUMEAU, *Catholicism Between Luther and Voltaire: A New View of the Counter Reformation* (1977). Programmatic essay on a social history of the Counter-Reformation.

A. G. DICKENS, *The English Reformation* (1974). The best one-volume account.

H. O. EVENNETT, *The Spirit of the Counter Reformation* (1968). Essay on the continuity of Catholic reform and its independence from the Protestant Reformation.

B. GOTTLIEB, *The Family in the Western World* (1992). Accessible overview, with up-to-date annotated bibliographies.

R. P. HSIA (ed.), *The German People and the Reformation* (1988). Substantial excerpts from the latest research.

J. L. IRWIN (ed.), *Womanhood in Radical Protestantism, 1525–1675* (1979). Sources illustrating images of women in sectarian Protestant thought.

D. L. JENSEN, *Reformation Europe: Age of Reform and Revolution* (1981). Excellent, up-to-date survey.

J. F. McNEILL, *The History and Character of Calvinism* (1954). The most comprehensive account, and very readable.

H. A. OBERMAN, *Luther: Man Between God and the Devil* (1989). Perhaps the best account of Luther's life, by a Dutch master.

J. O'MALLEY, *The First Jesuits* (1993). Extremely detailed account of the creation of the Society of Jesus and its original purposes.

S. OZMENT, *Protestants: The Birth of a Revolution* (1992). The Reformation in Germany.

S. OZMENT, *When Fathers Ruled: Family Life in Reformation Europe* (1983). A survey of sixteenth-century attitudes toward marriage and parenthood.

J. J. SCARISBRICK, *The Reformation and the English People* (1990). Eloquent argument that the Reformation changed little religiously; that it was a political, not a spiritual, triumph.

D. STARKEY, *The Reign of Henry VIII* (1985). Portrayal of the king as in control of neither his life nor his court.

J. STAYER, *Anabaptists and the Sword* (1972). The political philosophies of sectarians.

L. STONE, *The Family, Sex and Marriage in England, 1500–1800* (1977). Controversial but in many respects still reigning view of English family history.

R. H. TAWNEY, *Religion and the Rise of Capitalism* (1947). Advances beyond Weber's arguments relating Protestantism and capitalist economic behavior.

M. WEBER, *The Protestant Ethic and the Spirit of Capitalism*, trans. by Talcott Parsons (1958). First appeared in 1904–1905 and has continued to stimulate debate over the relationship between religion and society.

F. WENDEL, *Calvin: The Origins and Development of His Religious Thought*, trans. by Philip Mairet (1963). The best treatment of Calvin's theology.

G. H. WILLIAMS, *The Radical Reformation* (1962). Broad survey of the varieties of dissent within Protestantism.

12

The Age of Religious Wars

KEY TOPICS IN THIS CHAPTER
∽ The war between Calvinists and Catholics in France
∽ The Spanish occupation of the Netherlands
∽ The struggle for supremacy between England and Spain
∽ The devastation of central Europe during the Thirty Years' War

---

Political rivalries and religious conflicts combined to make the late sixteenth and the early seventeenth centuries an "age of religious wars." The era was plagued both by civil conflicts within nations and by battles among nations. In France, the Netherlands, and England, Catholic and Protestant subjects struggled against one another, and the Catholic governments of France and Spain attacked the Protestant regimes in England and the Netherlands. Germany's great Thirty Years' War (1618–1648) drew every major European nation, directly or indirectly, into its deadly net.

Renewed Religious Struggle

During the first half of the sixteenth century, religious war was confined to central Europe, to districts of the empire where Lutherans struggled for recognition. In the second half of the sixteenth century, western Europe (France, the Netherlands, England, and Scotland) became the chief arena for conflict as Calvinists fought for their cause.

The Peace of Augsburg (1555) ended the first phase of the struggle in central Europe by granting each ruler of a region of the empire the right to determine the religion of his subjects. Augsburg, however, recognized only Lutheranism. Both Lutherans and Catholics scorned Anabaptists and other sectarians, and Calvinists were not yet strong enough to demand legal standing.

The struggle for Protestant religious rights had intensified in western Europe by the time the Council of Trent adjourned in 1563. Led by the Jesuits, a reinvigorated Roman Catholic Church mounted an international counteroffensive against Protestantism. By 1564, when John Calvin died, Geneva had become a refuge for Europe's persecuted Protestants and a school to train leaders prepared to meet the Catholic challenge.

Genevan Calvinism and Tridentine Catholicism were equally dogmatic, aggressive, and irreconcilable church systems. Calvinism adopted a presbyterian organization that distributed authority among local governments. Boards of *presbyters* (elders) representing individual congregations directly shaped the policy of the church at large. The Roman Catholic Church of the Counter-Reformation was, by contrast, a centralized, hierarchical system. It stressed absolute obedience to the pope, and the pope and bishops—not synods of local churches—ruled supreme. Calvinism attracted proponents of political decentralization who opposed totalitarian rulers, whereas Catholicism was preferred by advocates of absolute monarchy who favored "one king, one church, one law."

The contrast between the two religions can be seen in the artistic styles they favored. The Baroque, a successor to Mannerism, triumphed in Catholic countries. Baroque art, a grandiose display of life and energy, is best represented by the work of people like Peter Paul Rubens (1571–1640) and Gianlorenzo Bernini (1598–1680). Protestant patrons often preferred a simpler, more rationally controlled, and less exuberantly emotional art—such as the English churches designed by Christopher Wren (1632–1723) and the gentle portraits of a Dutch Mennonite, Rembrandt van Rijn (1606–1669).

As religious wars engulfed Europe, intellectuals perceived the wisdom of religious pluralism and toleration. Skepticism, relativism, and individualism in religion increasingly came to be seen as virtues. Valentin Weigel (1533–1588), a Lutheran who surveyed a half-century of religious strife in Germany, spoke for many when he advised people to look within themselves for religious truth and not to churches and creeds.

Politicians were slower than intellectuals to see the wisdom of toleration. Religious strife and civil war were best held in check by the *politiques,*

In stark contrast to the Baroque style, this seventeenth-century Calvinist church in the Palatinate has no interior decoration to distract the worshiper from the Word of God. The intent was to create an atmosphere of quiet introspection and reflection on one's spiritual life and God's Word. [German National Museum, Nuremberg]

rulers like Elizabeth I of England who urged tolerance, moderation, and compromise—even indifference—in religious matters. Rulers like Mary I of England, Philip II of Spain, and Oliver Cromwell, who tended to take religion with the utmost seriousness, did not achieve lasting success.

⁓ The French Wars of Religion (1562–1598)

Anti-Protestant Measures and the Struggle for Political Power

Lutheran ideas began to circulate in Paris in the 1520s, and the French government quickly placed their advocates under surveillance. French Protestants came to be known as *Huguenots*—from Besançon Hugues, the leader of the revolt that liberated Geneva from the House of Savoy in the 1520s.

In 1525, when Emperor Charles V captured King Francis I of France at the Battle of Pavia, the French government launched an attack on Protestantism. It hoped that cooperation with Charles's anti-Protestant campaign would lead to favorable terms for the king's release. A second crackdown was sparked a decade later following a major Protestant publicity drive (on October 18, 1534) that plastered Paris and other cities with anti-Catholic placards. (This was the event that drove John Calvin and other members of the French reform party into exile.) Save for a few brief interludes, the French monarchy staunchly opposed Protestantism until the ascension to the throne of Henry of Navarre in 1589.

Hostilities between the French and the empire, the Habsburg-Valois wars, ended with the Treaty of Cateau-Cambrésis in 1559. The peace led to the shift of the European balance of power from France to Spain and to the outbreak of civil conflict within France. These developments began with an accident. In 1559, the French king, Henry II, was mortally wounded in a tournament and his sickly fifteen-year-old son, Francis II, ascended the throne under the regency of the queen mother, Catherine de Médicis. The weakness of this government tempted three powerful families to seek dominance over France: the Bourbons, whose power lay in the south and west; the Montmorency-Chatillons, who controlled the center of France; and the Guises, whose lands were in the east.

The Guises, the strongest, won control of the young king. Francis, duke of Guise, had been Henry II's general, and his brothers, Charles and Louis, were cardinals of the church. Francis II's wife, Mary Stuart, Queen of Scots, was their niece. Since the name of Guise was synonymous with militant, reactionary Catholicism, the Bourbon and Montmorency-Chatillon families developed Protestant sympathies. The Bourbon prince of Condé (d. 1569), Louis I, and the Montmorency-Chatillon admiral, Gaspard de Coligny (1519–1572), became the leaders of the French Protestant resistance to the Guises.

Appeal of Calvinism

Ambitious aristocrats and discontented townspeople had different reasons for joining Calvinist churches in opposing the Guise-dominated French monarchy. Although there were more than 2,000 Huguenot congregations in France by 1561, Huguenots were a majority of the population in only two regions: Dauphiné and Languedoc. Huguenots made up only about one-fifteenth of the population, but they controlled important districts and were heavily represented among the more powerful segments of French society. Over two-fifths of the French aristocracy became Huguenots. Many probably saw Protestantism as a way to strengthen their authority over their domains. They hoped to establish within France a principle of territorial sovereignty akin to that endorsed for the Holy Roman Empire by the Peace of Augsburg.

The military organization of Condé and Coligny progressively merged with the Huguenot churches, for each side had much to gain from the other. Calvinism justified and inspired political resistance, and political resistance to the Catholic monarchy was needed if Calvinism was to become a viable religion in France. However beneficial mutually, the confluence of secular and religious motives cast suspicion on the sincerity of Calvinists, for religious conviction was neither the only nor always the main reason for conversion.

Catherine de Médicis and the Guises

Francis II died in 1560, but his mother, Catherine de Médicis, continued to rule France as regent for her second son, Charles IX (r. 1560–1574). Fearing the Guises, Catherine, whose first concern was always to preserve the monarchy, sought allies among the Protestants. In 1562, after conversations with Coligny and Theodore Beza, Calvin's successor, she issued the January Edict. This granted Protestants freedom to hold synods and to worship publicly outside towns—but only privately within them. Royal efforts to promote toleration ended abruptly in March 1562, when the duke of Guise precipitated war with the Huguenots by massacring a Protestant congregation at Vassy.

Had Condé and the Huguenot armies rushed immediately to the queen's side after this attack, they might have secured an alliance with Catherine, who feared the powerful Guises. But the Protestant leaders hesitated, and the Guises won control of the young king and his mother. Cooperation with the Guises became Catherine's only alternative to capitulation to the Protestants.

The Peace of Saint-Germain-en-Laye. During the first French war of religion (April 1562 to March 1563), the duke of Guise was assassinated. A brief resumption of hostilities in 1567–1568 was followed from September 1568 to August 1570 by the bloodiest phase in the conflict. Condé was killed, and Huguenot leadership passed to Coligny, who was far the better military strategist. The Peace of Saint-Germain-en-Laye (1570), which he negotiated, won Huguenots religious freedoms within their territories and the right to fortify their cities.

Queen Catherine tried to survive by balancing the fanatical Huguenot and Guise extremes. Like the Guises, she preferred a Catholic France and tolerated Protestants only as a counter to Guise domination of the monarchy. But after the Peace of Saint-Germain-en-Laye, when the crown tilted toward the Bourbon-led Huguenot faction and Coligny became Charles IX's most trusted adviser, Catherine switched sides. She began to plot with the Guises to prevent the Protestants from winning over her son.

There was reason for Catherine to fear Coligny's hold on the king. Coligny was on the verge of persuading the young king to invade the Netherlands to help the Dutch Protestants in their struggle against their Habsburg ruler. Such a move would have placed France squarely on a collision course with Spain. Catherine knew that France stood little chance in such a contest.

The Saint Bartholomew's Day Massacre. On August 18, 1572, the French nobility gathered in Paris for the wedding of Henry of Navarre, a Huguenot leader, to the king's sister, Marguerite of Valois. Four days later Coligny was wounded by an assassin's bullet. Catherine, who had apparently been party to a plot by the Guises to eliminate Coligny, panicked. She feared both the king's reaction to her complicity with the Guises and the Huguenot response under a furious Coligny. In desperation she convinced Charles that a Huguenot coup was afoot and that only the swift execution of Protestant leaders could save the crown.

Theodore Beza Defends the Right to Resist Tyranny

One of the oldest problems in political and social theory has been that of knowing when resistance to repression in matters of conscience is justified. Since Luther's day, Protestant reformers had urged their followers to obey established political authority. After the 1572 Saint Barholomew's Day Massacre, however, Protestant pamphleteers urged Protestants to resist tyrants and persecutors with armed force. In 1574 Theodore Beza pointed out the obligation of rulers to their subjects and the latter's right to resist.

⌁ At what point does Beza believe that a ruler has gone too far and has forfeited his legitimacy? To whom may subjects appeal against a tyrant? Does Beza believe that individuals may take the law into their own hands?

It is apparent that there is a mutual obligation between the king and the officers of a kingdom; that the government of the kingdom is not in the hands of the king in its entirety, but only the sovereign degree; that each of the officers has a share in accord with his degree; and that there are definite conditions on either side. If these conditions are not observed by the inferior officers, it is the part of the sovereign to dismiss and punish them. . . . If the king, hereditary or elective, clearly goes back on the conditions without which he would not have been recognized and acknowledged, can there be any doubt that the lesser magistrates of the kingdom, of the cities, and of the provinces, the administration of which they have received from the sovereignty itself, are free of their oath, at least to the extent that they are entitled to resist flagrant oppression of the realm which they swore to defend and protect according to their office and their particular jurisdiction? . . .

We must now speak of the third class of subjects, which though admittedly subject to the sovereign in a certain respect, is, in another respect, and in cases of necessity the protector of the rights of the sovereignty itself, and is established to hold the sovereign to his duty, and even, if need be, constrain and punish him. . . . The people is prior to all the magistrates, and does not exist for them, but they for it. . . .. Whenever law and equity prevailed, nations neither created nor accepted kings except upon definite conditions. From this it follows that when kings flagrantly violate these terms, those who have the power to give them their authority have no less power to deprive them of it.

Constitutionalism and Resistance in the Sixteenth Century: Three Treatises by Hotman, Beza, and Mornay, trans. and ed. by Julian H. Franklin (New York: Pegasus, 1969), pp. 111–114.

On August 24, Saint Bartholomew's Day, 1572, Coligny and 3,000 fellow Huguenots were ambushed in Paris and butchered. Within three days an estimated 20,000 Huguenots were executed in coordinated attacks throughout France. Protestants across Europe were horrified, while Pope Gregory XIII and

Philip II of Spain greeted the news of the Protestant deaths with special religious celebrations.

Catholics were to regret the slaughter of the French Protestants, for Saint Bartholomew's Day changed the nature of the struggle between Protestants and Catholics everywhere. The disastrous outcome of France's internal squabbling over political power and religious freedom convinced Protestants in many lands that they were engaged in an international war for survival—a struggle to the death with an adversary whose cruelty justified any means of resistance.

Protestant Resistance Theory. At the start of the Reformation, Protestants tried to honor the biblical mandate (Romans 13:1) that directed subjects to obey the rulers God placed over them. Luther only grudgingly approved resistance to Charles V after the emperor, at the Diet of Augsburg in 1530, ordered Protestants to return to Catholicism. Calvin, secure in his control of Geneva, had always condemned willful disobedience and rebellion against lawfully constituted governments. But he also taught that lower magistrates, as part of lawfully constituted governments, had the duty to oppose higher authorities if these became tyrannical.

An early Calvinist rationale for revolution was developed by John Knox, a Scot driven into exile by the Catholic regent for Scotland, Mary of Guise. Knox's *Blast of the Trumpet Against the Terrible Regiment of Women* (1558) declared that the removal of a heathen (i.e., Catholic) tyrant was not only permissible, but a Christian duty. The Saint Bartholomew's Day massacre persuaded other Calvinists to a similar point of view. François Hotman's *Franco-Gallia* (1573) argued that France's representative assembly, the Estates General, was an authority superior to the crown. Theodore Beza's *On the Right of Magistrates over Their Subjects* (1574) justified the overthrow of tyrants by lower authorities. And Philippe du Plessis Mornay's *Defense of Liberty Against Tyrants* (1579) urged princes, nobles, and magistrates to cooperate in rooting out tyranny in any land where it appeared.

The Rise to Power of Henry of Navarre

Henry III (r. 1574–1589), the last of Henry II's sons to wear the French crown, was caught between the vengeful Huguenots and a radical Catholic League formed in 1576 by Henry of Guise. Like his mother, Catherine, Henry sought a middle course—appealing to the neutral Catholics and Huguenots who put the political survival of France above its religious unity.

In May 1576, Henry, in the Peace of Beaulieu, promised the Huguenots almost complete religious and civil freedom. The move was premature, for the Catholic League was able to force Henry to reverse himself. In October 1577, the Edict of Poitiers once again restricted Huguenots to limited areas.

By the mid-1580s, the Catholic League, with Spanish help, was supreme in Paris. In 1588, Henry III launched a surprise attack to rout the league—the "Day of the Barricades." The coup failed, and the king had to flee. News of the English victory over the Spanish Armada in 1588 emboldened Henry to order the assassinations of both the duke and the cardinal of Guise. These murders enraged the Catholic League, now led by another Guise brother, Charles, duke of Mayenne. By April 1589, the king was left with no choice but to seek an alliance with the Protestant leader, Henry of Navarre, the Bourbon heir to the Valois throne.

As the two Henrys prepared to attack the Guise stronghold in Paris, a fanatical Jacobin friar assassinated Henry III and cleared the way for Henry of Navarre to become King Henry IV (r. 1589–1610) of France. The pope, Sixtus V, and the king of Spain, Philip II, were aghast at the prospect of France suddenly becoming a Protestant nation. Philip dispatched troops to support the Catholic League and to claim the throne of France for his daughter, Isabella, Henry II's granddaughter.

The threat of Spanish intervention in the affairs of France rallied the people of France to Henry IV's side and strengthened his hold on the crown. Henry was a popular man who had the wit and charm to neutralize any enemy in a face-to-face meeting. He was also a *politique*, a leader who considered religion less important than peace. Henry concluded that since most of his subjects were Catholics, he could best rule as a Catholic who was committed to protecting Protestants. Consequently, on July 25, 1593, he embraced Catholicism—reputedly claiming that "Paris is worth a mass." The Huguenots were horrified, and Pope Clement VIII remained skeptical. But the majority of the French people, clergy and laity, were relieved. They had had enough of war.

The Edict of Nantes

On April 13, 1598, Henry issued the Edict of Nantes, which ended the civil wars of religion, and the following month (May 2, 1598) the Treaty of Vervins made peace between France and Spain.

The Edict of Nantes made good on a promise of toleration that Henry IV had made the Huguenots at the start of his reign. By granting some religious rights to a dissenting Protestant minority within what was to remain an officially Catholic country, Nantes came close to creating a state within a state. It designated certain towns and territories as places where Huguenots, who by this time numbered well over a million, could openly conduct worship, hold public offices, enter universities, and maintain forts. Nantes was a truce more than a peace. It turned a hot war into a cold one that claimed Henry IV as a victim. In May 1610, he was assassinated by a Catholic fanatic.

∼ Imperial Spain and the Reign of Philip II (1556–1598)

Pillars of Spanish Power

Philip II of Spain dominated international politics for much of the latter half of the sixteenth century. Bitter experience had led his father, Charles V, to the conclusion that the Habsburg family lands were too large to be governed by

A view of the Escorial, Philip II's massive palace-monastery-mausoleum northwest of Madrid. Built between 1563 and 1584, it was a monument to the piety and power of the king. Philip vowed to build the complex after the Spanish defeated the French at Saint-Quentin on St. Lawrence's Day in 1577. The floor plan of the Escorial resembles a grill, the symbol of St. Lawrence (who, according to legend, was martyred by being roasted alive on a grill). [Odyssey Productions]

one man. Consequently, Charles divided them between his son and his brother. Philip inherited the intensely Catholic and militarily supreme western half. The eastern portion (Austria, Bohemia, and Hungary) went to Philip's uncle, Emperor Ferdinand I. The imperial title, thereafter, remained with the Austrian Habsburgs.

Philip was a reclusive man who preferred to rule as the remote executive manager of a great national bureaucracy. His character is reflected in the unique residence he built outside Madrid, the Escorial. A combination palace, church, tomb, and monastery, it was a home for a monkish king. Philip was a learned and pious Catholic, a regal ascetic with a powerful sense of duty to his office. He may even have arranged the death of his son Don Carlos (1568), when he concluded that the boy was too mad and treacherous to be entrusted with the power of the crown.

New World Riches. Philip's home base was Spain, the populous and prosperous district of Castile. The wealth of the New World flowed through the port of Seville, giving Philip great sums with which to pay armies and underwrite international intrigues. Despite the flood of bullion, Philip's expenses exceeded his income. Near the end of his life he destroyed one of Europe's great banks, the house founded by the Fuggers of Augsburg, by defaulting on his loans.

The American wealth that entered Europe through Spain caused dramatic social change. Increased prosperity led to increased population. By the early seventeenth century, the towns of France, England, and the Netherlands had tripled and quadrupled in size, and Europe's population had reached an estimated 100 million. Growth in wealth and population triggered inflation—a steady 2 percent a year rise in prices. More people with more currency to spend meant increased competition for food and jobs. Consequently, prices doubled and tripled while wages stagnated.

This was especially the case in Spain, where the new wealth was concentrated in the hands of a few. Nowhere did the underprivileged suffer more than in Spain. The Castilian peasantry, the backbone of Philip II's great empire, were the most heavily taxed people in Europe.

Supremacy in the Mediterranean. At the start of Philip's reign, his attention focused almost exclusively on a struggle with the Turks in the Mediterranean. During the 1560s, the Turks had advanced deep into Austria, and their fleets had spread out across the Mediterranean.

Between 1568 and 1570, armies under Philip's half-brother, Don John of Austria, the illegitimate son of Charles V, suppressed and dispersed the Moors in Granada. In May 1571, Spain, Venice, and the pope formed the Holy League—again under Don John's command—to counter Turkish acts in the Mediterranean. On October 7, 1571, Don John's fleet engaged the Ottoman navy under Ali Pasha off Lepanto in the Gulf of Corinth. The result was the largest naval battle of the sixteenth century and a clear victory for the Christians. Thirty thousand Turks died and over one-third of the Turkish fleet was sunk or captured. The Mediterranean for the moment belonged to Spain.

In 1580, Philip confirmed his dominance of the south by annexing Portugal. This augmented Spanish seapower and brought the magnificent Portuguese overseas empire in Africa, India, and the Americas into the Spanish orbit.

The Revolt in the Netherlands

Philip was far less successful in northern Europe than he was in the Mediterranean. A rebellion in the Netherlands set in motion a chain of events that ended Spain's dreams of world empire.

The Netherlands, the richest district in Europe, were governed for Philip by his half-sister, Margaret of Parma. She was assisted by a council headed by Cardinal Granvelle (1517–1586). Granvelle hoped to check the advance of Protestantism in the Netherlands by promoting church reform. He also planned to reduce the autonomy of the seventeen Netherlands provinces and to create a centralized royal government directed from Madrid. The merchant towns of the Netherlands were, however, accustomed to their independence, and many, like magnificent Antwerp, had become Calvinist strongholds. Two members of the royal council opposed their Spanish overlords: the Count of Egmont (1522–1568) and William of Nassau, the Prince of Orange (1533–1584)—known as "the Silent" because of his small circle of confidants.

William of Orange was a *politique* who placed the Netherlands' political autonomy and well-being above religious creeds. In 1561, he married Anne of Saxony, the daughter of the Lutheran Elector Maurice and the granddaughter of the late Landgrave Philip of Hesse, but he remained a Catholic until 1567, when he turned Lutheran. After the Saint Bartholomew's Day massacre in 1572, Orange became a Calvinist.

In 1561, Cardinal Granvelle began an ecclesiastical reorganization of the Netherlands that was intended to tighten the control of the Catholic hierarchy over the country and to accelerate its consolidation as a Spanish ward. Orange and Egmont, with the support of the Dutch nobility, succeeded in gaining Granvelle's removal from office in 1564. But aristocratic control of the country after Granvelle's departure proved woefully inefficient, and popular unrest grew.

In 1564, Philip unwisely insisted that the decrees of the Council of Trent be enforced throughout the Netherlands. Opposition materialized under the leadership of William of Orange's younger brother, Louis of Nassau, who had been raised a Lutheran. The Calvinist-inclined lesser nobility and townspeople joined him in a national covenant, the *Compromise,* a solemn pledge to resist Trent and the Inquisition. In 1566, when Margaret's government spurned the protesters as "beggars," Calvinists rioted, and Louis called for help from French Huguenots and German Lutherans. A full-scale rebellion against the Spanish regency seemed about to erupt.

The Duke of Alba. A revolt failed to materialize, however, for the Netherlands' higher nobility, who were repelled by the behavior of Calvinist extremists, would not support it. And Philip dispatched the duke of Alba to restore order and make an example of the would-be rebels.

In 1567, an army of 10,000 was transferred from Milan, and responsibility for the Netherlands was delegated to a special tribunal, the Council of Troubles (as Spain called it) or the Council of Blood (as it came to be known in the Netherlands). The new government inaugurated a reign of terror. It executed the counts of Egmont and Horn and several thousand suspected heretics, and it imposed high taxes to force the Netherlanders to pay the costs for the suppression of their revolt. Persecution and taxation drove tens of thousands of refugees from the Netherlands during Alba's cruel six-year rule, and the duke came to be more hated than Granvelle or the radical Calvinists.

Resistance and Unification. William of Orange, who was an exile in Germany during these turbulent years, now emerged as the leader of an independence movement in the Netherlands. The northern, Calvinist-inclined provinces of Holland, Zeeland, and Utrecht, of which Orange was the *stadholder,* or governor, became his base. Here, as elsewhere, a fight for political independence was combined with a struggle for religious liberty.

The uprising in the Netherlands was a true popular revolt that enlisted all kinds of people. William even endorsed the raids of the "Sea Beggars," an international group of anti-Spanish exiles and criminals who were brazen pirates. In 1572, the Beggars captured Brill and other seaports in Zeeland and Holland. They incited the native population to join the rebellion, and resistance spread steadily southward. In 1574, the people of Leiden heroically resisted a long Spanish siege, and the Dutch opened the dikes and flooded their country to repulse the hated Spanish. The faltering Alba had by that time ceded power to Don Luis de Requesens, who replaced him as commander of Spanish forces in the Netherlands in November 1573.

The greatest atrocity of the war followed Requesens's death in 1576. Spanish mercenaries, leaderless and unpaid, ran amok in Antwerp on November 4, 1576. Seven thousand people lay dead in the streets as a result of what came to be called "the Spanish Fury." This brief event did more to unify the Netherlanders than all previous appeals to religion and patriotism. The ten largely Catholic southern provinces (approximating modern Belgium) joined the seven largely Protestant northern provinces (roughly the modern Netherlands) in opposing Spain.

The Pacification of Ghent declared the unification of the Netherlands on November 8, 1576. The Netherlanders resolved religious differences by agreeing on a territorial settlement like the one the Peace of Augsburg had defined for the Holy Roman Empire in 1555. In January 1577, the last four provinces joined the all-embracing Union of Brussels, and for the next two years the Spanish faced a unified and determined Netherlands.

In November 1576, Don John, the victor over the Turks at Lepanto, took command of Spain's land forces and promptly experienced his first defeat. In February 1577, he signed the Perpetual Edict, a humiliating treaty that promised the removal of all Spanish troops from the Netherlands within twenty days.

The Spanish, however, were nothing if not persistent. The nobility's fear of Calvinist extremism caused a break-up of the Union of Brussels, and Don John and Alessandro Farnese of Parma, the regent Margaret's son, re-established Spanish control in the southern provinces. In January 1579, the southern provinces formed the Union of Arras and made peace with Spain. The northern provinces responded by organizing the Union of Utrecht.

Netherlands' Independence. Seizing the opportunity to break the back of Netherlands' resistance, Philip II declared William of Orange an outlaw and placed a bounty of 25,000 crowns on his head. This stiffened the resistance of the northern provinces, and in a famous speech to the Estates General of Holland in December 1580 (the Apology), Orange denounced Philip as a heathen tyrant whom the Netherlands need no longer obey.

On July 22, 1581, most of the northern provinces belonging to the Union of Utrecht formally repudiated Philip's authority and pledged themselves to the French duke of Alençon, Catherine de Médicis's youngest son. Alençon was seen as a compromise between the extremes of Spanish Catholicism and Calvinism, and he was expected to aspire to nothing more than titular authority over the provinces. When he rashly attempted to impose his will on them in 1583, he was deposed and sent back to France.

William of Orange was assassinated in July 1584, and his son, Maurice (1567–1625), became leader of the Dutch resistance. Fortunately for him and his cause, Philip II overextended himself by meddling in the affairs of France and England. Things built to a climax in 1588, when Philip's great Armada was defeated in the English Channel. By 1593, the northern provinces had driven out all Spanish soldiers, and in 1596 France and England formally recognized the independence of these provinces. Peace with Spain was concluded in 1609, and full international recognition came in the Peace of Westphalia in 1648.

∿ England and Spain (1553–1603)

Mary I

In an effort to protect England's Reformation, Edward VI (d. 1553) sought to disinherit his Catholic half-sister, Mary Tudor (r. 1553–1558), by designating as heir to the throne his cousin, Lady Jane Grey, a granddaughter of Henry VIII's younger sister Mary. The people of England, however, believed that Mary was clearly the rightful heir and rioted on her behalf. In short order, Jane Grey lost both the crown and her head.

As queen, Mary exceeded the worst fears of the Protestants. Her Parliaments repealed the Protestant statutes of Edward and reverted to the strict Catholic religious practice of her father, Henry VIII. She executed as heretics the great Protestant leaders who had served her brother: John Hooper, Hugh Latimer, and Thomas Cranmer. The names of 282 Protestants whom she burned at the stake are recorded. Many others avoided martyrdom by fleeing to the continent. The "Marian exiles" settled in Germany and Switzerland, where they established communities of worship, wrote tracts justifying armed resistance, and waited for the time when a Protestant counteroffensive could be launched in their homelands. Many absorbed religious beliefs that were much more radical than those they had brought from England.

In 1554, Mary chose a highly unpopular husband, Prince Philip (later Philip II) of Spain. She favored him because he was the leader of the militant Catholicism that Mary hoped to establish in England, but many of Mary's subjects feared that the marriage would lead to Spain's dominance of England. The politically troublesome marriage was childless, and Mary died knowing that her half-sister, Elizabeth, the daughter of her father's first Protestant marriage, would follow her to the throne.

Elizabeth I

Elizabeth I (r. 1558–1603), the daughter of Henry VIII and Anne Boleyn, was perhaps the most astute politician of the sixteenth century. Assisted by a shrewd adviser, Sir William Cecil (1520–1598), she built a true kingdom on the ruins of Mary's reign. Between 1559 and 1563, she and Cecil guided a religious settlement through Parliament. It merged a centralized episcopal system, which the queen controlled, with broadly defined Protestant doctrine and traditional Catholic ritual. The resulting Anglican church avoided inflexible religious extremes and spared England the religious conflicts that were bloodying continental nations.

Catholic and Protestant Extremists. Religious compromises were unacceptable to zealots of both persuasions, and subversive groups worked to undermine Elizabeth. When she ascended the throne, most of her subjects were Catholics. The extremists among them, encouraged by the Jesuits, plotted to replace her with Mary Stuart, Queen of Scots. Unlike Elizabeth, whose father had declared her illegitimate, Mary Stuart had an unblemished claim to the throne inherited from her grandmother Margaret, sister of Henry VIII. Elizabeth responded swiftly to Catholic assassination plots, but rarely let emotion override her political instincts. Despite proven cases of Catholic treason and even attempted regicide, she executed fewer Catholics during her forty-five years on the throne than Mary Tudor had executed Protestants during her brief five-year reign.

Elizabeth dealt cautiously with the extreme Protestants—the "Puritans" who wanted to "purify" the national church of every vestige of "popery." The Puritans had two major grievances: (1) the retention of Catholic ceremony and vestments within the Church of England, which made it appear to the casual observer that no Reformation had occurred, and (2) the continuation of the episcopal system of governance, which enabled the queen to take the pope's place in dominating the church.

The more extreme Puritans, the Congregationalists, wanted every congregation to be autonomous, a law unto itself, with neither higher episcopal nor presbyterian control. But most sixteenth-century Puritans were not separatists. They campaigned in Parliament for an alternative national church of semiautonomous congregations governed by representative presbyteries (hence, Presbyterians), following the model of Calvin and Geneva. Elizabeth conceded nothing that lessened the hierarchical unity of the Church of England and her control over it. The Conventicle Act of 1593 gave separatists the option of either conforming to the practices of the Church of England or facing exile or death.

Deterioration of Relations with Spain. Despite the sincerest desires on the part of both Philip II and Elizabeth to avoid a direct confrontation, events led inexorably to war between England and Spain. In 1567, when the Spanish duke of Alba marched his army into the Netherlands, many in England feared that Spain intended to use the Netherlands as a base for an invasion of England. In 1570, Pope Pius V (1566–1572), who openly favored a military expedition to recover England for Catholicism, branded Elizabeth a heretic. His mischievous act only complicated a difficult situation.

Following Don John's demonstration of Spain's awesome seapower at the battle of Lepanto in 1571, England signed a mutual defense pact with France.

Throughout the 1570s, Elizabeth's famous seamen, John Hawkins (1532–1595) and Sir Francis Drake (1545?–1596), preyed on Spanish shipping in the Americas. Drake's circumnavigation of the globe, between 1577 and 1580, was one in a series of dramatic demonstrations of England's growing ascendancy on the high seas.

The Saint Bartholomew's Day massacre forced a change in Elizabeth's foreign policy. Protestants in France and the Netherlands appealed to Elizabeth as their only protector. In 1585 she signed the Treaty of Nonsuch, which sent English soldiers to the Netherlands. And funds that had previously been funneled covertly to Henry of Navarre's army in France now flowed openly. These developments strained relations between England and Spain, but the event that brought on war was Elizabeth's decision to execute Mary, Queen of Scots (1542–1587).

Mary, Queen of Scots. Mary Stuart, the daughter of King James V of Scotland and Mary of Guise, had resided in France from the time she was six years old—training for her role as the future wife of King Francis II. The death of her young husband in 1561 sent Mary back to Scotland to rule a land she barely knew. A year earlier, a fervent Protestant Reformation had won legal recognition in the Treaty of Edinburgh, and Mary, raised a Catholic, had no sympathy with it or with its dour morality. She determined to introduce the Scots nobles to the gaiety and sophistication of French court life.

John Knox, the leader of the Scottish Reformation, railed openly about the queen's private Mass and Catholic practices (which Scottish law made a capital offense for everyone else). Although Queen Elizabeth personally despised Knox, she recognized that his defense of Protestantism served her foreign policy. It limited Mary's ability to persuade the Scots to cooperate with France against England.

In 1568, a scandal cost Mary her throne. In 1565, Mary had married Lord Darnley, a youth with connections to the royal houses of both England and Scotland. Although she succeeded in having a son by him (the James who was someday to inherit both Scotland and England), Darnley proved an impossible husband. Mary reputedly took the earl of Bothwell as her lover, and he, allegedly, murdered Darnley. Acquitted of this crime, Bothwell abducted Mary and married her. This amounted to usurpation of the throne, and outraged Protestant nobles forced Mary to abdicate in favor of her infant son and to flee Scotland.

Mary unwisely entered England seeking refuge from her cousin Elizabeth. Elizabeth distrusted Mary, for in the opinion of Catholics, Mary had the superior claim to the English throne. Elizabeth, therefore, held Mary under house arrest—for nineteen years. In 1583, Elizabeth's vigilant secretary, Sir Francis Walsingham, uncovered a plot against Elizabeth involving the Spanish ambassador Bernardino de Mendoza. In 1586, Walsingham exposed still another Spanish scheme to unseat Elizabeth, and this time he had proof of Mary's involvement. Elizabeth was loath to execute Mary. She feared that such an act would diminish the aura of divine right that was one of the props of monarchy, and she knew that it would raise a storm of protest among Catholics. But Elizabeth finally concluded that she had no choice, and Mary was beheaded on February 18, 1587. Mary's death dashed Catholic hopes for a bloodless reconversion of England and persuaded Philip II that the time had come for a military assault on the Protestant nation.

The Armada. Spain's preparations for war were interrupted in the spring of 1587 by successful raids Sir Francis Drake led on the port city of Cadiz and the coast of Portugal. These strikes forced Philip to postpone his invasion of England until the spring of 1588.

On May 30, 1588, the ill-fated Armada of 130 ships, bearing 25,000 sailors and soldiers under the command of the duke of Medina-Sidonia, set to sea. The barges that were to transport Spanish soldiers from their galleons onto England's shores were prevented from leaving Calais and Dunkirk to rendezvous with the fleet. While the Spanish vessels waited, an "English wind" sprang up and helped the swifter English and Dutch ships in routing the Spanish forces.

Spain never fully recovered from this defeat. By the time Philip died on September 13, 1598, his forces had suffered reversals on all fronts. His successors, Philip III (r. 1598–1621), Philip IV (r. 1621–1665), and Charles II (r. 1665–1700), were all inferior leaders. They allowed the French to emerge as the leading continental power and the Dutch and English to whittle away at Spain's overseas empire.

By contrast, when Elizabeth died on March 23, 1603, she left behind a strong nation poised to expand into a global empire. Since Elizabeth had never married—choosing instead to use the hope of winning her hand as a tool for English diplomacy—her death ended the Tudor dynasty. Ironically, her heir, James I of England, was Mary's son, James VI of Scotland.

∾ The Thirty Years' War (1618–1648)

The Thirty Years' War in the Holy Roman Empire was the last and most destructive of the wars of religion, and it was unusually devastating. Religious passions escalated entrenched hatreds on all sides, and virtually every major European land was drawn into the conflict. When the hostilities ended in 1648, the agreements among the victorious nations shaped the map of northern Europe as we know it today.

Preconditions for War

Fragmented Germany. In the second half of the sixteenth century, Germany was a collection of about 360 autonomous political entities: secular principalities (duchies, landgraviates, and marches), ecclesiastical principalities (archbishoprics, bishoprics, and abbeys), free cities, and regions dominated by knights with castles. The Peace of Augsburg (1555) had given each a degree of sovereignty within its borders. Since each levied its own tolls and tariffs and coined its own money, travel and trade were difficult. And many little states had pretensions that exceeded their powers.

During the Thirty Years' War, Germany, Europe's crossroads, became Europe's stomping ground. The great conflict had many causes—most relating in some way to a fear of German unification. The Council of Trent raised Protestant suspicions about an imperial-papal conspiracy to use the Holy Roman Empire to restore Catholic dominance throughout Europe. The imperial diet, which was controlled by the German magnates, was leery of any attempt to consolidate the empire at the expense of the liberties of the territorial princes. It countered every move by the emperor to impose his will in the empire, and individual German rulers called on allies outside of Germany for help in defending their rights. Allies were eager to help, for even the Catholic nations of Europe feared what might happen to the balance of power if Germany was brought under control by the Catholic emperor.

Religious Division. Religious differences accentuated political divisions among states both internationally and within Germany (see Map 12-1). By 1600, there may have been slightly more Protestants than Catholics in the Holy Roman Empire. The territorial principle proclaimed by the Peace of Augsburg in 1555 was designed to freeze Lutherans and Catholics in place by forcing each territory to declare its faith. But as time passed, there were troublesome shifts of opinion. Lutherans gained control in some Catholic areas— and Catholics in a few places designated as Lutheran.

Lutherans were more successful in securing rights to worship in Catholic lands than Catholics were in securing such rights from Lutherans. Catholic rulers, weakened by the Reformation, had no choice but to make concessions to Protestant communities within their territories, and these Protestant enclaves were continuing sources of tension. Protestants were also reluctant to enforce the "Ecclesiastical Reservation" provision of the Peace of Augsburg, which called for the restoration to Catholic control of ecclesiastical principalities when their rulers converted to Protestantism.

Protestant and Catholic antipathies were not the only sources of religious strife. Warring factions emerged among Protestants in the second half of the sixteenth century. Liberal and conservative branches of Lutheranism opposed each other, and Calvinists failed to come to terms with either of these.

Calvinism loosened the bonds of the Holy Roman Empire. Although not recognized as a legal religion by the Peace of Augsburg, Calvinism won a foothold in the empire when Frederick III (r. 1559–1576), Elector Palatine (ruler within the Palatinate), made it the official religion of his domain. His royal city of Heidelberg became a German Geneva, an intellectual center for Calvinism and a staging area for Calvinist penetration into the empire.

The Lutherans came to fear the Calvinists almost as much as they did the Catholics, for the bold missionary forays of the Palatine Calvinists threatened to overturn the arrangements that had been agreed to in the Peace of Augsburg for the stabilization of the empire. Some Lutherans were also

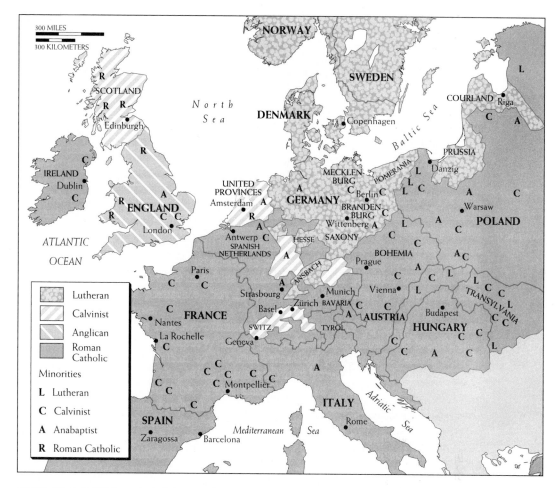

MAP 12-1 Religious Divisions About 1600 *By 1600 few could seriously expect Christians to return to a uniform religious allegiance. In Spain and southern Italy, Catholicism remained relatively unchallenged, but note the existence elsewhere of large religious minorities, both Catholic and Protestant.*

shocked by outspoken Calvinist criticism of their doctrines, such as faith in Christ's real presence in the Eucharist.

Like the Calvinists, the Jesuits also actively undermined the terms of the Peace of Augsburg. Catholic Bavaria, supported by Spain, became for the Counter-Reformation what the Palatinate was for Calvinism. Jesuit missionaries, operating from Bavaria, won major cities (e.g., Strasbourg and Osnabrück) back to the Catholic fold. In 1609, Maximilian, duke of Bavaria, organized a Catholic League to counter a Protestant alliance formed in the same year by the Calvinist Elector Palatine, Frederick IV (r. 1583–1610). The army the league assembled under the command of Count Johann von Tilly tipped Germany into war (see Map 12-2).

MAP 12-2 The Holy Roman Empire About 1618 *On the eve of the Thirty Years' War, the empire was politically and religiously fragmented, as this somewhat simplified map reveals. Lutherans dominated the north and Catholics the south, while Calvinists controlled the United Provinces and the Palatinate and were important in Switzerland and Brandenburg.*

Four Periods of War

The Bohemian Period (1618–1625). The war broke out in Bohemia after the ascent to the Bohemian throne in 1618 of Ferdinand, Habsburg archduke of

Styria and heir to the empire. Ferdinand, who had been educated by Jesuits, was determined to restore Catholicism to the Habsburg lands. No sooner had he become king of Bohemia than he revoked the religious freedoms of Bohemia's Protestants. The Protestant nobility responded in May 1618 by literally throwing his regents out a window—the "defenestration of Prague." A year later, when Ferdinand (II) became Holy Roman Emperor, the Bohemians refused to recognize his jurisdiction and declared their allegiance to the Calvinist Elector Palatine, Frederick V (r. 1616–1623).

The Bohemian revolt escalated into an international war. Spain, Maximilian of Bavaria, and the Lutheran Elector John George I of Saxony (r. 1611–1656)—who saw a chance to weaken the Elector Palatine—sided with Ferdinand. Tilly, the empire's general, routed Frederick V's troops at the Battle of White Mountain in 1620. By 1622, Ferdinand had subdued Bohemia and conquered the Palatinate. As the remnants of Frederick's army retreated north, the duke of Bavaria followed—claiming land as he went.

The Danish Period (1625–1629). Maximilian's forays into northwestern Germany raised fears of a Catholic consolidation of the empire. Christian IV (r. 1588–1648), king of Lutheran Denmark and duke of German Holstein, was encouraged by the English, French, and Dutch to undertake the defense of Protestantism. He invaded Germany in 1626, but was quickly forced to retreat.

Ferdinand II, who worried about his ability to control the victorious Maximilian, hired a mercenary, Albrecht of Wallenstein (1583–1634), to continue the war. A brilliant and ruthless military strategist, Wallenstein succeeded, by 1628, in becoming a law unto himself, but he so effectively broke the back of Protestant resistance that Ferdinand was able to issue the Edict of Restitution in 1629. It ordered the return of all church lands acquired by the Lutherans since 1552. Compliance would have meant Protestant concession of sixteen bishoprics and twenty-eight cities and towns to Catholic governors. The edict struck panic in the hearts of the Habsburgs' opponents and reignited resistance.

The Swedish Period (1630–1635). Gustavus Adolphus of Sweden (r. 1611–1632), a deeply pious Lutheran monarch and a military genius, emerged as the new Protestant champion. He was handsomely bankrolled by two very interested bystanders: Cardinal Richelieu, the minister of the Catholic king of France, who wanted to prevent a powerful Habsburg empire from materializing on his border; and the Habsburgs' Protestant opponents of long standing, the Dutch. The Swedish king won a smashing victory at Breitenfeld in 1630 that suddenly reversed the course of the war. The battle was decisive, but far from final.

Gustavus Adolphus died fighting Wallenstein's forces at the Battle of Lützen in November 1632, and in 1634 Ferdinand had Wallenstein, who had outlived his usefulness, assassinated. In the Peace of Prague of 1635, the German Protestant states reached a compromise agreement with Ferdinand. But the Swedes, with encouragement from France and the Netherlands, refused to join them, and the war continued.

MAP 12-3 Europe In 1648 *At the end of the Thirty Years' War, Spain still had extensive possessions. Austria and Brandenburg-Prussia were prominent, the independence of the United Provinces and Switzerland was recognized, and Sweden held important river mouths in north Germany.*

The Swedish-French Period (1635–1648). The French openly entered the war in 1635 and prolonged it for thirteen more years. French, Swedish, and Spanish soldiers looted the length and breadth of Germany. The Germans, who were too disunited to repulse the foreign armies, simply watched and suffered. By the time peace talks began in the Westphalian cities of Münster and Osnabrück in 1644, an estimated one-third of the German population had died. It was the worst catastrophe in Europe since the Black Death of the fourteenth century.

The Treaty of Westphalia

The Treaty of Westphalia ended hostilities in 1648 by ensuring the continued fragmentation of Germany (see Map 12-3). The territorial principle proclaimed by the Peace of Augsburg in 1555 was reasserted to confirm rulers in their right to determine the religions of their subjects. Calvinism was added to the list of legal religious options, and the German princes were acknowledged supreme over their principalities. Bavaria was elevated to the rank of an elector state, and Brandenburg-Prussia began to evolve as the most powerful north German principality. The independence of the Swiss Confederacy and of the United Provinces of Holland, long a fact, was proclaimed in law. And France emerged with considerable territorial gain.

War between France and Spain continued outside the empire until 1659, when the French forced the Spanish to accept the humiliating Treaty of the Pyrenees. Germany's fragmentation and Spain's humbling left victorious France the dominant power in Europe. The competitive nationalisms of the modern world are rooted in these religious conflicts of the seventeenth century.

Religion and politics both played major roles in each of the great conflicts of the Age of Religious Wars: France's civil strife, Spain's struggle with the Netherlands, England's resistance to Spain, and the devastation of Germany by a consortium of European powers. But neither religion nor politics alone explains the course of the wars. The religious differences that were occasions for war were sometimes ignored in pursuit of political objectives shared by Catholics and Protestants. The wars ended with an agreement to disagree—with the recognition of minority religious rights and a guarantee of the traditional boundaries of political sovereignty. Europe at mid-century had real, if brief, peace.

◆ Review Questions

1. What part did politics play in the religious positions adopted by France's leaders? How did the French king (or his regent) decide which side to favor? What led to the infamous Saint Bartholomew's Day Massacre? What did it achieve?

2. How did Spain acquire the dominant position in Europe in the sixteenth century? What were its strengths and weaknesses as a nation? What were Philip II's goals? Which did he fail to achieve? Why?

3. Define the term *politique*. How does it apply as a description of Henry of Navarre (Henry IV of France), Elizabeth I, and William of Orange?

4. What changes occurred in the religious policies of England's government in the process of establishing the Anglican church? What were Mary I's political objectives? What was Elizabeth I's "settlement"? How was it imposed on England? Who were her opponents? What were their criticisms of her?

5. Why was the Thirty Years' War fought? Could matters have been resolved without war? To what extent did politics determine the outcome of the war? What were the terms and objectives of the Treaty of Westphalia?

6. Was, as some have claimed, the Thirty Years' War "the outstanding example in European history of meaningless conflict"?

◆ Suggested Readings

F. BRAUDEL, *The Mediterranean and the Mediterranean World in the Age of Philip the Second*, vols. 1 and 2 (1976). Widely acclaimed work of a French master historian.

R. DUNN, *The Age of Religious Wars, 1559–1689* (1979). Excellent brief survey of every major conflict.

G. R. ELTON, *England Under the Tudors* (1955). Masterly account.

P. GEYL, *The Revolt of the Netherlands, 1555–1609* (1958). The authoritative survey.

J. GUY, *Tudor England* (1990). A standard history and good synthesis of recent scholarship.

J. LYNCH, *Spain under the Hapsburg I: 1516–1598* (1964). Political narrative.

J. NEALE, *Queen Elizabeth I* (1934). Superb biography.

G. PARKER, *Philip II* (1978). Readable, admiring account.

J. H. M. SALMON (ed.), *The French Wars of Religion: How Important Were the Religious Factors?* (1967). Scholarly debate over the relation between politics and religion.

K. THOMAS, *Religion and the Decline of Magic* (1971). Provocative, much-acclaimed work focused on popular culture.

C. V. WEDGWOOD, *The Thirty Years' War* (1939). Extremely detailed account that downplays the war's achievements.

J. WORMALD, *Mary, Queen of Scots: A Study in Failure* (1991). Mary portrayed as a queen who did not understand her country and was out of touch with the times.

The first efforts by people to draw images to describe their vision of the world were Paleolithic cave paintings. This depiction of bulls and horses is found in the Dordogne valley of southern France.
[Ancient Art and Architecture Collection/Ronald Sheridan's Photo Library]

This painting from a royal Egyptian tomb shows a noble family hunting birds. Its artist has rendered details from nature accurately, but has arranged individual figures of different sizes in two-dimensional space. The painting resembles more a page to be read than a window through which to view a scene.
[Courtesy of the Trustees of the British Museum]

Greek vase paintings are both works of art and invaluable sources of information for historians. This picture of a fight between a lapith and a centaur (a scene from mythology) is found on a red figure vase from the fifth century B.C. Only the figures' black background has been painted. The red areas are the natural color of the vase's fired clay.
[Firenze Museo Archaeologico. (Art Resource)]

This cameo shows profiles of the Emperor Claudius and his wife, Agrippina the younger, superimposed over profiles of Germanicus, the nephew of the Emperor Tiberius, and his wife, Agrippina the elder.
[Kunsthistorisches Museum, Vienna]

This mosaic depicts the Empress Theodora and her attendants at a church service. Its rich, but abstract, style marks a break with the naturalism of classical art. The change probably reflects the other-worldly values of early medieval Christianity.
[Scala/Art Resource, NY]

This page from the Lindisfarne Gospel (ca. 700 A.D.) illustrates the artistic vision of northern Europeans, who were little influenced by Greece and Rome. It uses plant and animal shapes from nature to create wildly energetic abstract patterns.
[Lindisfarne Gospels: Decorated initial to the Gospel according to St. Matthew manuscripts. Courtesy of the British Library, London. (Superstock)]

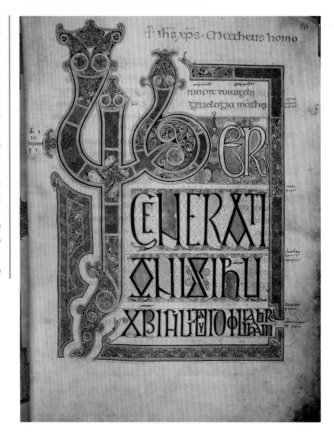

This portrayal of the funeral of St. Francis of Assisi was created by Giotto (1266–1336), a Florentine painter whose work heralded the Italian Renaissance. Giotto and most later painters thought of pictures not as pages to be read, but as windows offering views of a coherently organized world. [Scala/Art Resource, NY]

These scenes, representing events in the story of Adam and Eve, are from the frescoes that Michelangelo Buonarroti painted for the ceiling of the Vatican's Sistine Chapel (1503–1513). They illustrate how the Renaissance adapted ideals from classical pagan art for use by a Christian culture. [The Vatican, Rome. (Superstock)]

13

Paths to Constitutionalism and Absolutism: England and France in the Seventeenth Century

Two Models of European Political Development

Constitutional Crisis and Settlement in Stuart England
James I
Charles I
Oliver Cromwell and the Puritan Republic
Charles II and the Restoration of the Monarchy
James II and Renewed Fears of a Catholic England
The "Glorious Revolution"

Rise of Absolute Monarchy in France
Henry IV and Sully
Louis XIII and Richelieu
Young Louis XIV and Mazarin

The Years of Louis's Personal Rule
King by Divine Right
Versailles
Suppression of the Jansenists
Louis's Early Wars
Revocation of the Edict of Nantes
Louis's Later Wars
Louis XIV's Legacy

KEY TOPICS IN THIS CHAPTER

~ The factors behind the divergent political paths taken by England and France in the seventeenth century

~ The conflict between Parliament and the king over taxation and religion in early Stuart England, the English Civil War, and the abolition of the monarchy

~ The Restoration of the English monarchy and the development of Parliament's supremacy over the throne after the "Glorious Revolution"

~ The establishment of an absolutist monarchy in France under Louis XIV

~ The wars of Louis XIV

During the seventeenth century, England and France evolved contrasting political systems. England became a parliamentary monarchy with a policy of religious toleration. France developed an absolutist, highly centralized monarchy that demanded religious conformity. Both systems defy simple description. English monarchs did not share all power with Parliament, and the kings of France were not free of all institutional or customary restraint on their authority.

Significant Dates from the Seventeenth Century

1603	*James I, king of England*
1611	*Authorized, or King James, Version of the Bible*
1625	*Charles I, king of England*
1642	*Outbreak of the English Civil War*
1643	*Louis XIV, king of France*
1648	*Treaty of Westphalia*
1649	*Charles I executed*
1649–1652	*The Fronde*
1649–1660	*England, Puritan Commonwealth*
1660	*Charles II restores the English monarchy*
1667–1668	*War of Devolution*
1685	*James II, king of England*
1685	*Louis XIV revokes Edict of Nantes*
1688	*England's "Glorious Revolution"*
1689	*William and Mary rule England*
1689–1697	*Nine Years' War*
1701	*Act of Settlement, the Hanoverian Succession*
1702–1714	*War of the Spanish Succession*
1702	*Queen Anne, the last of the Stuarts*
1715	*Deaths of Louis XIV and Anne, queen of England*

∼ Two Models of European Political Development

In the second half of the sixteenth century, changes in military technology sharply increased the cost of warfare and forced governments to look for new sources of revenue. Monarchs who, like the French, developed incomes that were not controlled by nobles or by assemblies representing their wealthy subjects achieved what was called absolute power. In places like England, where rulers had insufficient funds and limited powers of taxation, royal authority was constrained by the necessity of cooperating with other agents of government.

The contrast between the French and English political systems that was visible at the end of the seventeenth century was not apparent in 1600. The much revered Queen Elizabeth had broad support in England and summoned its Parliament only as needed to provide taxes. The Stuart kings who followed Elizabeth to the throne of England pursued fiscal and religious policies that united their nation's propertied classes in opposition to the crown.

Elizabeth's contemporary, Henry IV (r. 1589–1610) of France, on the other hand, struggled with a divided nation emerging from the turmoil of religious war. Under his successor, Louis XIII (r. 1610–1643), the French crown began to assert new authority. In the second half of the seventeenth century, Louis XIV brought the French nobles under tight control. The aristocratic *Parlement* of Paris won the right to register royal decrees before they became law, and the king allowed regional *parlements* considerable authority over local administration. But when the nobles discovered that a strong king was a source of patronage and a guardian of their privileged place in society, they lost interest in developing anything like England's Parliament. An Estates General had appeared in the late Middle Ages. But once the monarchy won control over taxation, it had no reason to call the Estates into session. No meetings were held from 1614 until the eve of the French Revolution in 1789.

~ Constitutional Crisis and Settlement in Stuart England

James I

When the childless Elizabeth died in 1603, no one contested the right of James VI of Scotland (the son of Mary Stuart, Queen of Scots) to claim the throne of England as James I. But a formidable task lay ahead of him. As a Scot, James was an outsider who had no native constituency to help him deal with England's religious factions and substantial national debt. James's advocacy of the divine right of kings, a subject on which he had written a book (*A Trew Law of Free Monarchies*) in 1598, also set him on a collision course with English tradition.

England's Parliament, its chief check on royal power, met only when summoned by the monarch to authorize certain tax levies. James planned to develop alternative resources that would enable him to operate without calling Parliament. Relying on the authority of ill-defined privileges claimed to be attached to the office of king, James created new customs duties known as *impositions*. Members of Parliament resented these, but they preferred to wrangle and negotiate behind the scenes rather than risk serious confrontation.

Religious problems added to political tensions during James's reign. Puritans within the Church of England had hoped that James's upbringing as a Scottish Presbyterian would incline him to further the reformation of the English church. They wanted to eliminate both elaborate religious ceremonies and the bishops who presided over them—creating in their places a simple church governed by presbyters elected by the people. James, however, had no intention of using his national church to foster a tradition of representative government that he believed was an insult to the divine right of kings.

In January 1604, James responded to a list of Puritan grievances (the so-called Millenary Petition) by pledging himself to maintain and even enhance the Anglican episcopacy. As he explained: "A Scottish presbytery agreeth as well with monarchy as God and the devil. No bishops, no king." James did, however, accept the Protestant demand for the use of vernacular Scriptures, and in 1611, the royal commission he appointed issued an eloquent new translation of the Bible. For generations the Authorized, or King James, Version remained the standard English text.

James had no sympathy with the moral agenda implicit in English Puritanism. The recreations and sports of which the Puritans disapproved were, to the king, innocent activities that were good for people. James also believed that Puritan rigidity about such things discouraged Roman Catholics from converting to the Church of England. Consequently, in 1618 James tried to force a change by ordering the clergy to read his *Book of Sports*, which legalized games on Sunday, from their pulpits. When they refused, he backed down.

James's lifestyle seemed designed to give offense to the Puritans, for the royal court was a center of scandal and corruption. James governed by favorites, the most influential of whom, the duke of Buckingham, was rumored to be the king's homosexual lover. Buckingham controlled royal patronage and openly sold peerages and titles to the highest bidders. There had always been court favorites, but never before had a single person controlled access to the monarch.

Disappointed and disgusted by James, some Puritans began voluntarily to leave England for the New World. In 1620, Puritan separatists founded Plymouth Colony in Cape Cod Bay. Later in the same decade, a larger, better-financed group of Puritans founded the Massachusetts Bay Colony.

In addition to his domestic policy, James's conduct of foreign affairs also roused opposition. James made peace and avoided war, for he feared that wars could generate debts that would force him to beg assistance from Parliament. The treaty he signed with Spain in 1604, although long overdue, was interpreted by some of his subjects as confirmation of his pro-Catholic sentiment. Their suspicions increased when James tried unsuccessfully to relax the penal laws against Catholics. The situation further deteriorated when, in 1618, James wisely hesitated to rush English troops to the aid of German Protestants involved in the Thirty Years' War and when he suggested that his son Charles marry the Spanish Infanta, the daughter of the king of Spain.

As James aged and his health failed, the reins of government passed to Charles and to Buckingham, and parliamentary opposition and Protestant sentiment combined to undo his pro-Spanish foreign policy. A marriage alliance was rejected, and in 1624, shortly before James's death, Parliament pushed England into a continental war against Spain.

Charles I

Although it approved of war with Spain, Parliament was unwilling to finance the venture. Therefore, Charles I (r. 1625–1649), with the assistance of the unpopular Buckingham, followed his father's example. Without parliamentary approval, he imposed new tariffs and duties, collected discontinued taxes, and subjected people of property (under threat of imprisonment) to the "forced loayn"—a tax that, theoretically, was to be repaid. Soldiers in transit to war zones were also quartered in English homes.

When Parliament met in 1628, its members were furious. They refused to acquiesce to the king's request for funds unless he agreed to abide by terms they set forth in a Petition of Right: (1) no more forced loans or taxation without the consent of Parliament, (2) no imprisonment of citizens without due cause, and (3) an end to billeting troops in private homes. Though Charles promised what was demanded, Parliament had little confidence that he would keep his word.

Years of Personal Rule. In August 1628, Buckingham, Charles's chief minister, was assassinated. Although his death led some to rejoice, it was not enough to reconcile king and Parliament. In January 1629, Parliament issued more decrees critical of the king. The levying of taxes without parliamentary consent and Charles's high-church policies were declared acts of treason. Charles responded by dissolving Parliament, which did not reconvene until a war with Scotland created a fiscal crisis in 1640.

Without funds from Parliament, Charles could not continue his foreign wars. But when he made peace with France in 1629 and Spain in 1630, some of his subjects accused him of wanting to strengthen his ties with Roman Catholic nations. Many Protestant leaders feared that Catholics were establishing ascendancy over the king. Charles had wed a French princess, whose marriage contract gave her the right to hear Mass daily at the English court. Charles also supported a group within the Church of England (the Arminians) that opposed some Puritan doctrines and advocated elaborate services of worship.

To allow Charles to rule without having to compromise with Parliament to win financial support, his chief minister, Thomas Wentworth, earl of Stafford (after 1640), instituted what came to be known as a policy of *thorough*. By promoting strict efficiency and administrative centralization in government, the monarchy hoped to establish absolute royal control over England. Toward this end, Charles's men exploited every legal fundraising device. They enforced previously neglected laws and extended existing taxes into new areas. Charles won challenges to his policies in the courts, but at the cost of alienating the propertied men who would sit in any future Parliament he might be forced to call.

During these years of personal rule, Charles lived expensively. He surrounded himself with an elaborate court and patronized some of the greatest artists of the day. Like his father, he sold titles of nobility to raise money— and to diminish the prestige of the aristocracy. Nobles and great landowners saw their fortunes and their local influence and social standing diminishing, and they began to fear that Charles might actually succeed in ruling without ever calling another Parliament.

Charles might have ruled indefinitely without Parliament had he not departed from the tolerant example set by his father and tried to impose religious conformity within England and Scotland. William Laud (1573–1645), Charles's religious advisor and archbishop of Canterbury (after 1633), encouraged the king's preference for high-church Anglicanism (or Anglo-Catholicism), a religious establishment characterized by a powerful episcopacy, elaborate liturgy, and the practice of pious devotions in place of the preaching-centered worship favored by Puritans. In 1637, Charles and Laud, over objections by English Puritans and the Scots, attempted to impose the English episcopal system and prayerbook on Scotland. The Scots rebelled, and Charles, having insufficient resources for a war, was forced to call Parliament.

The members of Parliament were in the peculiar position of wanting to oppose their king's policies while crushing the rebellion against him. Led by John Pym (1584–1643), they refused to consider granting funds for war until Charles agreed to redress their list of grievances. The king responded by dissolving what came, for obvious reasons, to be known as the Short Parliament (April–May 1640). When the Presbyterian Scots invaded England and defeated an English army at the Battle of Newburn in the summer of 1640, Charles was forced to reconvene Parliament—on its own terms—for a long, fateful session.

The Long Parliament. The landowners and the merchant classes whom Parliament represented resented the king's financial measures and paternalistic rule. Those who were Puritans also resented his religious policies. The Long Parliament (1640–1660), therefore, enjoyed support from many important factions.

The House of Commons began by impeaching the king's chief advisors, the earl of Stafford and Archbishop Laud. (Stafford was executed for treason in 1641 and Laud in 1645.) Parliament then abolished the instruments the king used to implement the political and religious policy of "thorough," the Court of Star Chamber and the Court of High Commission. The levying of new taxes without consent of Parliament became illegal, and Parliament established itself as a permanent branch of England's government. It decreed that it could not be dissolved without its own consent and that no more than three years could elapse between its meetings.

Members of Parliament were united in their desire to trim the powers of the monarchy, but religious reform was a divisive issue. Moderate Puritans (Presbyterians) and extreme Puritans (Independents) wanted to abolish the episcopal system and the *Book of Common Prayer.* But the Presbyterian majority hoped to reshape the English church along Calvinist lines, with local congregations subject to higher representative bodies (the presbyteries), while the Independents wanted a decentralized church in which each congregation had responsibility for itself. In addition, a considerable number of conservatives in both houses of Parliament were determined to preserve the English church as currently constituted.

These divisions intensified in October 1641, when a rebellion erupted in Ireland and Parliament was asked to raise funds for a royal army to suppress it. Pym and his followers argued that Charles could not be trusted with an army and that Parliament should take command of England's armed forces. Conservatives in Parliament were appalled by Pym's proposed departure from tradition.

Eruption of Civil War. Charles saw the division within Parliament as a chance to reassert his power. On December 1, 1641, Parliament presented him with the "Grand Remonstrance", a summary of over 200 grievances against the crown. In January 1642, he sent soldiers into Parliament to arrest Pym and other leaders. Forewarned, they managed to escape, but Charles withdrew from

London and began to raise an army against Parliament. Shocked by this action, the House of Commons passed the Militia Ordinance, which gave Parliament authority to raise its own army. For the next four years (1642–1646), civil war engulfed England.

Charles assembled his forces at Nottingham, and the war began in August. The royal army, the Cavaliers, was based in the northwestern half of England. It fought to establish a strong monarchy and an Anglican, episcopal church. The parliamentary opposition, called "Roundheads" because of its members' preference for close-cropped hair, had its stronghold in the southeastern half of the country. It fought for parliamentary government and a decentralized, Presbyterian church.

Oliver Cromwell and the Puritan Republic

Two things contributed to Parliament's victory. The first was an alliance struck between Parliament and Scotland in 1643. It was made possible by Parliament's acceptance of the Scots' Presbyterian system of church govern-

Oliver Cromwell's New Model Army defeated the royalists in the English Civil War. After the execution of Charles I in 1649, Cromwell dominated the short-lived English republic, conquered Ireland and Scotland, and ruled as Lord Protector from 1653 until his death in 1658. [Historical Pictures/Stock Montage, Inc.]

ment. The second was the reorganization of the parliamentary army under Oliver Cromwell (1599–1658), a middle-aged country squire who favored the Independents. Cromwell and his "godly men" wanted neither the king's episcopal system nor the Presbyterian organization endorsed by Parliament's Solemn League and Covenant with Scotland. The only established state church they would accept was one that granted freedom of worship to Protestant dissenters.

In 1644, Parliament won the largest engagement of the war, the Battle of Marston Moor, and in June 1645, Cromwell's newly reorganized and fanatical forces, the New Model Army, were victorious over the king at Naseby. Charles tried to exploit the divisions within Parliament by winning the Presbyterians and the Scots over to his side, but Cromwell foiled him. In December 1648, Colonel Thomas Pride used Cromwell's soldiers to prevent the Presbyterians, who had a majority in Parliament, from taking their seats. After "Pride's Purge," only a "rump" of fewer than fifty members remained. This Rump Parliament dominated by Independents did not hesitate to use its power. On January 30, 1649, after trial by a special court, the Rump Parliament executed the king and abolished the monarchy, the House of Lords, and the Anglican church. Civil war had become revolution.

From 1649 to 1660, England was officially a Puritan republic, although in reality it was dominated by Cromwell. Cromwell's military achievements were impressive. His army conquered Ireland and Scotland, creating the political entity known today as Great Britain. But Cromwell was less successful as a politician, for he was easily frustrated by the necessity of working with the dawdling members of Parliament. When in 1653 the House of Commons entertained a motion to disband his expensive army of 50,000, Cromwell marched in and disbanded Parliament.

Calling himself "Lord Protector," Cromwell established a military dictatorship that had only modest support in the country. Cromwell's great army and foreign adventures cost three times as much as Charles's government, but the Protector was unable to prevent near chaos from erupting in many parts of England. Commerce suffered throughout the land, and people chafed under Cromwell's rigorous enforcement of Puritan codes of conduct. Cromwell was as intolerant of Anglicans as Charles had been of Puritans.

Cromwell failed to build a political system that provided a workable alternative to the monarchy and Parliament. He tried various arrangements, none of which worked. By the time he died in 1658, a majority of the English were ready to end the Puritan republican experiments and return to traditional institutions of government. In 1660, the exiled Charles II (r. 1660–1685), son of Charles I, was invited home to restore the Stuart monarchy.

Charles II and the Restoration of the Monarchy

Charles II, a man of considerable charm and political skill, was restored to the throne amid great rejoicing, and England returned to the institutions it had abandoned in 1642: a hereditary monarchy with no obligation to summon Parliament regularly, and an Anglican church with bishops and prayerbook established as the state religion. Charles had secret Catholic sympathies and favored a policy of religious toleration, but few in Parliament believed that patriotism and religion could be separated. Between 1661 and 1665, Parliament enacted the Clarendon Code to exclude Roman Catholics, Presbyterians, and Independents from the religious and political life of the nation. Penalties were imposed for attending non-Anglican worship services. Adherence to the *Book of Common Prayer* and the *Thirty-Nine Articles* (the Anglican church's statement of faith) was demanded, and oaths of allegiance to the Church of England were required of persons who wished to serve in local government. Charles also tried to tighten his grip on the rich English colonies in North America and the Caribbean, many of which had been developed by separatists who wanted independence from English rule.

Charles's foreign policy was dominated by a series of naval wars with Holland caused by England's Navigation Acts. These acts required imports to be carried either in English ships or in ships registered to the country from which their cargo originated. Since Dutch vessels carried goods from many nations, this was a direct attack on Holland's shipping industry. In 1670, Charles allied with the French, who were also at war with Holland, and received French aid to underwrite the cost of the campaign. In exchange for the promise of a substantial subsidy from Louis XIV of France, Charles also secretly pledged to announce, at some propitious moment, his conversion to Catholicism. The time to fulfill that pledge never came.

To unite the English people behind the war with Holland and to show good faith with Louis XIV, Charles issued a Declaration of Indulgence (1672) that suspended all laws against Roman Catholics and Protestant nonconformists. But again, Parliament blocked the king's efforts to promote religious tolerance by refusing to grant money for the war until Charles rescinded the Declaration. Parliament then passed the Test Act, which excluded Roman Catholics from public office by requiring all royal officials to swear an oath repudiating the doctrine of transubstantiation.

The Test Act was aimed in large measure at the king's brother, James, duke of York, heir to the throne and a recent, devout convert to Catholicism. In 1678 a notorious liar, Titus Oates, accused Charles's Catholic wife of plotting with Jesuits and Irishmen to kill her husband and bring his Catholic brother to the throne. Parliament, caught up in the hysteria of Oates's "Popish Plot," executed several people, and a faction in Parliament, the Whigs, nearly won passage for a bill excluding James from the succession.

Chronically short of money and having little hope of adequate grants from Parliament, Charles II increased customs duties and won financial aid from Louis XIV. These resources enabled him to suppress much of his opposition and to avoid recalling Parliament from 1681 to 1685. When Charles died in 1685 (after a deathbed conversion to Catholicism), he left James in position to call a Parliament filled with royal friends.

James II and Renewed Fears of a Catholic England

James II (r. 1685–1688) did not know how to exploit his opportunities. He alienated Parliament by insisting on the repeal of the Test Act. When Parliament balked, he dissolved it and flaunted the Test Act by openly appointing known Catholics to high offices. In 1687, he issued a Declaration of Indulgence that suspended all religious tests and permitted free worship. Candidates for Parliament who opposed the Declaration were removed from office by the king's soldiers and replaced by Catholics. In June 1688, James imprisoned seven Anglican bishops who had refused to publicize his suspension of laws against Catholics.

Under the guise of a policy of enlightened toleration, James tried to subject all English institutions to the power of the monarchy. His goal was absolutism, and even conservative, loyalist "Tories," as the royal supporters were called, could not abide this. The English feared, with reason, that once James had the power, he would imitate Louis XIV, who in the year James came to the throne had revoked the Edict of Nantes and used soldiers to suppress Protestant worship in France.

A birth galvanized James's enemies into action against him. The English had hoped that James would die without a male heir and the throne would pass to Mary, his eldest daughter. She was a Protestant—the wife of William III of Orange, who was stadtholder of the Netherlands, great-grandson of William the Silent, and leader of the resistance in Europe to Louis XIV's imperial designs. But on June 20, 1688, James's Catholic second wife gave birth to a son, a Catholic heir to the throne. Within days of the boy's birth, Whig and Tory members of Parliament had agreed to invite Orange to invade England to preserve "traditional liberties."

The "Glorious Revolution"

When the English people failed to oppose the landing of William of Orange's army in November 1688, James accepted defeat and fled to France. Parliament completed the bloodless "Glorious Revolution" by declaring the throne vacant and proclaiming William and Mary its legal heirs. William and Mary, in turn, issued a Bill of Rights that limited the powers of the monarchy and guaranteed the civil liberties of the English privileged classes. Henceforth, England's monarchs would be subject to law and would rule by the consent of a Parliament that was to be called into session every three years. The Bill of Rights also prohibited Roman Catholics from occupying the English throne. The Toleration Act of 1689 legalized all forms of Protestantism—save those that denied the Trinity—and outlawed Roman Catholicism.

In 1701 the Act of Settlement closed the century of strife, as the seventeenth century came to be known in England, by providing for the English crown to go to the Protestant House of Hanover in Germany if none of the children of Queen Anne (r. 1702–1714), the second daughter of James II and the last of the Stuart monarchs, survived her. Since she outlived her children, the Elector of Hanover became King George I of England—the third foreigner to occupy the English throne in just over a century.

Although the "Glorious Revolution" of 1688 was not a popular revolution like those that occurred in America and France a hundred years later, it established a framework of government by and for the governed, a permanent check on monarchical power by the classes represented in Parliament. English philosopher John Locke's *Second Treatise of Government* (1690), written prior to the revolution, came to be read by some as a justification for it. Locke claimed that the relationship of a king and his people was a bilateral contract. If the king broke that contract, the people (by whom Locke meant those with property) had the right to depose him. Locke's political theory and England's parliamentary monarchy were destined to have wide appeal.

∼ Rise of Absolute Monarchy in France

In seventeenth-century France, unlike England, the independence of the nobility and religious pluralism were smothered by absolute monarchy. The dictum of Louis XIV (r. 1643–1715) was "one king, one law, one faith."

Louis's predecessors had provoked a rebellion among the nobility by trying to impose direct rule on the nation at all levels. Rather than destroying existing social and political institutions, Louis worked through them. His genius lay in his ability to make the monarchy the most powerful political institution in France while assuring the nobles and other wealthy groups of the security of their standing and influence on the local level. Once nobles understood that the king would protect their local authority, they supported his central authority. The king and the nobles thus came to recognize that they needed each other, but that Louis XIV was the senior partner in the relationship.

Henry IV and Sully

Louis XIV learned much from his predecessors. Henry IV (r. 1589–1610), who came to the throne at the end of the French wars of religion, sought to rein in the French nobility—particularly the provincial governors, the regional *parlements,* and the powerful *Parlement* of Paris. These groups were divisive elements within the state, whose chief interest was the protection of their privileges.

Since the war-weary French were eager for the restoration of order, Henry and his finance minister, the duke of Sully (1560–1641), were able to increase government regulation of the economy. They established monopolies on gunpowder, mines, and salt. They began construction of a canal system which, by linking France's rivers, created a waterway from the Atlantic to the Mediterranean. They introduced the *corvée,* a labor tax that drafted workers to build and maintain roads. Sully even dreamed of joining the whole of Europe in a kind of common market.

Louis XIII and Richelieu

Henry IV was assassinated in 1610, and the following year Sully retired. Louis XIII (r. 1610–1643), Henry's son, was only nine years old at the time, so the task of governing fell to the queen mother, Marie de Médicis (d. 1642). Sensing a lack of support from the French nobility, Marie sought to make a friend of France's arch-rival, Spain. In 1611, she negotiated the Treaty of Fontainebleau. It provided for a ten-year mutual defense pact and marriage alliances between the royal houses of the two nations. Louis XIII was to wed the Spanish Infanta, and his sister, Elizabeth, was engaged to the heir to the Spanish throne. The queen's most propitious move was to appoint Cardinal Richelieu (1585–1642) as the king's chief adviser. Richelieu, loyal and shrewd, was the architect of the successes of the French monarchy in the first half of the seventeenth century.

Richelieu was a devout Catholic, but he believed that his nation's interests were best served by curbing the Catholic Habsburgs. Although he endorsed the queen's treaty with Catholic Spain and encouraged conformity to Catholic practices in France, Richelieu was determined to contain Spain—even when that meant aiding Protestants. In the Thirty Years' War, Richelieu contributed money to the Protestant army of Gustavus Adolphus, but he also insisted that Catholic Bavaria be spared from attack and that Catholics in conquered countries be permitted to practice their religion. Thanks to Richelieu, France emerged from the war with substantial gains in land and political influence.

At home, Richelieu pursued centralizing policies utterly without qualm. Supported by the king, who let his chief minister make most decisions of state, Richelieu stepped up the campaign Henry IV had begun against separatist provincial governors and *parlements*. He created royal civil servants, known as *intendants*, to guard against abuses in the sale of royal privileges, such as the right to collect taxes or sell licenses. (Such things were essential to the power of the nobility.) Richelieu made it clear to everyone that there was only one law in France. If noblemen disobeyed the king's edicts, they were imprisoned or executed. Such treatment of the nobility won Richelieu much enmity—even from his patron, the queen mother.

Richelieu began a campaign against the Huguenots that was to end in 1685 with Louis XIV's revocation of the Edict of Nantes. In 1629, royal armies occupied important Huguenot cities and imposed the Peace of Alais. It truncated the Edict of Nantes by denying Protestants the right to maintain garrisoned cities, separate political organizations, and independent law courts. Richelieu was prevented from moving farther down the road to a policy of extreme intolerance only by France's alliances with Protestant powers in the Thirty Years' War.

Richelieu was a modern politician in the sense that he understood the use of propaganda and the importance of mobilizing popular support for government policies. He employed the arts and the printing press to defend his actions and to persuade the French people to accept things done for *raisons d'état* ("reasons of state"). Louis XIV's masterful use of propaganda to develop royal power was a tribute to Richelieu's example.

Young Louis XIV and Mazarin

Louis XIII survived Richelieu by only five months. Since his heir, Louis XIV (r. 1643–1715), was five years old, the son's reign began, as the father's had, with a regency government. The queen mother, Anne of Austria (d. 1666), placed the reins of government in the hands of Cardinal Mazarin (1602–1661), Richelieu's protégé.

Many among the aristocracy and the wealthy commercial classes deeply resented Richelieu's efforts to build a strong, centralized monarchy, and Mazarin was confronted by a violent political backlash. From 1649 to 1652, there were widespread rebellions, known collectively as the *Fronde* (after the slingshot used by street boys). The uprisings were exploited by nobles and townspeople who wanted to reverse the drift toward absolute monarchy and to preserve local autonomy.

The *Parlement* of Paris initiated the revolt in 1649, and the many (the nobles) briefly triumphed over the one (the monarchy). Mazarin released some aristocratic prisoners in February 1651, and he and Louis XIV departed for brief exiles. (Mazarin left France, and Louis fled Paris.) When the nobles failed to establish order and near anarchy ensued, support for the young king materialized. Louis and Mazarin returned in October 1652. The Fronde convinced most French people that the rule of one strong king was preferable to the rule of many competing regional powers. On the other hand, Louis XIV and his later advisers concluded that heavy-handed policies, like those of Richelieu and Mazarin, could endanger the monarchy.

∾ The Years of Louis's Personal Rule

On the death of Mazarin in 1661, Louis XIV assumed personal control of the government. Unlike his royal predecessors, he appointed no single chief minister. This had the advantage of making revolt more difficult to rationalize; rebellious nobles could no longer claim that they were opposing their king's wicked minister, but not the king himself. Mazarin had prepared Louis well for the duties of government, and the young king's experiences during the Fronde had stiffened his resolve to be a strong ruler. Louis wrote in his memoirs that the Fronde caused him to loathe "kings of straw."

Louis devised two successful strategies for enhancing the power of the monarchy. First, he became a master of propaganda and political image creation. Louis never missed an opportunity to indoctrinate the French people with a strong sense of the grandeur of his crown. Second, Louis made sure the French nobles and other major social groups benefited from the growth of his

Bishop Bossuet Defends the Divine Right of Kings

The revolutions of the seventeenth century caused many to fear anarchy far more than tyranny, among them the influential French bishop Jacques-Bénigne Bossuet (1627–1704), the leader of French Catholicism in the second half of the seventeenth century. Louis XIV made him court preacher and tutor to his son, for whom Bossuet wrote a celebrated Universal History. *In the following excerpt, Bossuet defends the divine right and absolute power of kings. He depicts kings as embracing in their person the whole body of the state and the will of the people they govern and, as such, as being immune from judgment by any mere mortal.*

∽ Why might Bossuet have wished to make such extravagant claims for absolute royal power? How might these claims be transferred to any form of government? What are the religious bases for Bossuet's argument? Does his argument for absolute royal authority entail the necessity of enforcing a single uniform religion throughout France?

The royal power is absolute.... The prince need render account of his acts to no one. "I counsel thee to keep the king's commandment, and that in regard of the oath of God. Be not hasty to go out of his sight; stand not on an evil thing for he doeth whatsoever pleaseth him. Where the word of a king is, there is power; and who may say unto him, What doest thou? Whoso keepeth the commandment shall feel no evil thing" [Eccles. 8:2–5]. Without this absolute authority the king could neither do good nor repress evil. It is necessary that his power be such that no one can hope to escape him, and finally, the only protection of individuals against the public authority should be their innocence. This confirms the teaching of St. Paul: "Wilt thou then not be afraid of the power? Do that which is good" [Rom. 13:3].

God is infinite, God is all. The prince, as prince, is not regarded as a private person: he is a public personage, all the state is in him; the will of all the people is included in his. As all perfection and all strength are united in God, so all the power of individuals is united in the person of the prince. What grandeur that a single man should embody so much! ...

Behold an immense people united in a single person; behold this holy power, paternal and absolute; behold the secret cause which governs the whole body of the state, contained in a single head: you see the image of God in the king, and you have the idea of royal majesty. God is holiness itself, goodness itself, and power itself. In these things lies the majesty of God. In the image of these things lies the majesty of the prince.

From "Politics Drawn from the Very Words of Holy Scripture," as quoted in James Harvey Robinson (ed.), Readings in European History, vol. 2 (Boston: Athenaeum, 1906), pp. 275–276.

authority. Although he maintained control over foreign affairs, he usually conferred informally with regional *parlements* before making rulings that would affect them. Likewise, he rarely enacted economic regulations without consulting local opinion, and local *parlements* were given considerable latitude in regional matters.

King by Divine Right

Reverence for the king, the personification of government, had been nurtured in France since Capetian times, and it was widely accepted that the king's wish was the law of the land. Louis XIV transformed this traditional reverence for the crown into a belief in the king's divine right to absolute authority.

Bishop Jacques-Bénigne Bossuet (1627–1704), the king's tutor, provided the theoretical rationale for Louis's concept of royal authority. Bossuet was an ardent champion of the so-called "Gallican liberties," traditional exemptions the French clergy claimed from interference in their affairs by the papacy. Bossuet's theory of the "divine right of kings" gave kings spiritual legitimacy as caretakers of the churches of their nations. Bossuet drew his evidence from the Old Testament, whose rulers were divinely appointed by and answerable only to God. Just as medieval popes had insisted that only God could judge a pope, so Bossuet argued that none save God could judge the king. Kings may have remained duty-bound to reflect God's will in their rule, but as God's regents on earth they could not be made accountable to mere princes and parliaments. This argument justified Louis XIV's alleged declaration, *"L'état, c'est moi"* ("I am the state").

Versailles

One of Louis XIV's most successful instruments of propaganda was the splendid court he housed in the palace he built on the outskirts of Paris at Versailles (1682). Versailles was a temple to royalty—a proclamation of the glory of its "Sun King." It was also home to Louis and thousands of his subjects: France's more important nobles and numerous royal officials and servants. The maintenance of Versailles and its elaboration, which continued throughout Louis's lifetime, consumed over half his annual revenues, but the palace paid political dividends well worth the investment.

Louis demonstrated that he alone was the sole source of power and privilege in France by organizing life at court around his personal routine. Nobles scrambled for the honor of being present at intimate moments in the king's day—his rising, dressing, or retiring—in hopes of having a chance to whisper special requests in his ear. Like menial servants, the most distinguished of aristocrats fought for the privilege of holding the king's candle or assisting him with the left sleeve of his nightshirt. These duties were choreographed by an extraordinarily elaborate court etiquette.

Court life was carefully planned to domesticate and trivialize the nobility. Barred by law from high government positions, the nobles were kept busy and dependent with ritual and play so that they had little time to plot revolt. Luxurious dress codes and high-stakes gambling drove them into debt and dependency on the king. Members of the court spent the afternoons hunting, riding, or strolling about the lush gardens of Versailles. Evenings were given over to plays, concerts, gambling, and the like, followed by supper at 10:00 P.M.

The real business of government was handled by Louis and members of

Versailles, as painted in 1668 by Pierre Patel the Elder (1605–1676). The central building is the hunting lodge built for Louis XIII earlier in the century. The wings that appear here were some of Louis XIV's first expansions. [Giraudon/Art Resource, N.Y.]

councils charged with responsibility for foreign affairs, domestic relations, and the economy. The chief ministers of these councils were talented self-made men or members of families with long histories of loyal service to the crown. Louis trusted them with power, for, unlike the nobility, they had no power bases in the provinces and depended solely on the king for their standing in government and society.

Suppression of the Jansenists

Like Richelieu before him, Louis believed that political stability required religious conformity. The first deviant religious group to attract his attention was composed of Roman Catholics called Jansenists.

Catherine de Médicis had prevented the Jesuits from working in France because of their close connections to Spain, but following Henry IV's conversion to Catholicism, the ban was lifted (1603). Jesuits who swore an oath of allegiance to the king and acquired special licenses were permitted to establish a limited number of colleges and conduct various public activities. The

Jesuits were not, however, easily harnessed. They became the royal confessors. They dominated the education of the upper classes, and they promoted the religious reforms and doctrine of the Council of Trent throughout France.

Jansenism, which appeared in the 1630s, was a Catholic movement named for a Flemish theologian and bishop, Cornelius Jansen (d. 1638), who was a critic of the Jesuits. Jansenists were advocates of the teachings of Saint Augustine, who emphasized the role divine grace played in human salvation. They objected to the Jesuits' emphasis on free will, for they believed with Saint Augustine that original sin so corrupted humankind that individuals could do nothing good nor secure their own salvation without divine grace. Jansenist emphasis on salvation by grace led the Jesuits to charge that Jansenists were crypto-Protestants.

The fight between the Jansenists and the Jesuits had political as well as theological dimensions. Jansen had ties with a prominent Parisian family, the Arnaulds, who, like many others in France, believed that the Jesuits had arranged the assassination of Henry IV in 1610. The Arnaulds dominated Jansenist communities at Port-Royal and Paris during the 1640s, and, in 1643, a book by Antoine Arnauld *(On Frequent Communion)* attracted attention by charging that the Jesuits' confessional practices permitted the easy redress of almost any sin.

On May 31, 1653, Pope Innocent X declared that five Jansenist theological propositions concerning grace and salvation were heresies. In 1656, the pope banned a book by Cornelius Jansen (*Augustinus*, 1640), and the Sorbonne censured Antoine Arnauld. In the same year Antoine's friend, Blaise Pascal (d. 1662), published a defense of Jansenism, the first of his *Provincial Letters*. A deeply religious man, Pascal objected to Jesuit moral theology not only because it was lax, but also because its rationalism failed to do justice to religious experience.

In 1660, Louis banned Jansenism and closed down the Port-Royal community. This drove Jansenism underground, where it apparently continued to thrive; in 1710 Louis found it necessary to order a more thorough purge of Jansenist sentiment. By suppressing Jansenism, a kind of Catholicism broad enough to appeal to France's Huguenots, Louis eliminated the best hope for peacefully unifying the religions of his country.

Louis's Early Wars

Governing for Warfare. The economy of France was overwhelmingly agrarian, as was true of other nations in Louis's day. But Jean-Baptiste Colbert (1619–1683), Louis's brilliant financial adviser, managed it so skillfully that France was able to support a huge standing army.

Colbert centralized France's economy as Louis centralized France's government. The kind of economic policy Colbert recommended was called *mercantilism* by later commentators. Its aim was to maximize exports and the internal reserves of bullion they earn. Colbert advocated state supervision of industries and tariffs to regulate the flow of imports and exports. He sponsored new national industries and developed a tight regimen of work and ideology for state-run factories. He simplified the administrative bureaucracy; reduced the number of tax-exempt nobles; and increased the *taille*, the direct tax on the peasantry that provided much of the king's income.

Thanks to Colbert, France became one of the world's commercial powers, and Louis was able to finance ambitious military ventures. An army of about 250,000 men was created for him by a father-son team of war ministers: Michel Le Tellier (minister to 1666) and Tellier's son, the marquis of Louvois (minister from 1667 to his death in 1691).

Before Louvois, the French army had been an amalgam of local companies of recruits and mercenaries who, without regular pay to sustain them, often lived by pillage. Louvois made soldiering a respectable profession: discipline was improved; a system of promotion by merit was introduced; enlistment, for terms of four years, was restricted to single men; pay was good; and military conduct at all levels was monitored by civil servants. New technology was also provided for Louvois's new army by a brilliant military engineer, Sebastien Vauban (1633–1707). He perfected the arts of fortifying and besieging towns. He devised the system of trench warfare, and he developed the concept of defensive frontiers that remained basic to military tactics through World War I.

The War of Devolution. Louis's first great foreign adventure was the War of Devolution (1667–1668). Like the later War of the Spanish Succession, it was fought to press a claim Louis's wife, Marie Thérèse (1638–1683), had to Spain's Belgian provinces. In 1659, Marie had surrendered her place in the line of succession to the Spanish throne in exchange for a 500,000-crown dowry to be paid to Louis. The dowry was never paid, and Philip IV of Spain, who died in September 1665, left a will disinheriting Marie in favor of a sickly four-year old son by a second marriage, Charles II (r. 1665–1700). Louis decided to contest the will, and the legal grounds he chose gave the war its name. Louis argued that in certain regions of Brabant and Flanders, which were part of Philip's estate, property "devolved" to the children of a first marriage rather than to those of a second. Therefore, Marie's claim to these districts took precedence over that of Charles.

In 1667, when Louis sent his armies into Flanders and the Franche-Comté, England, Sweden, and the United Provinces of Holland responded by forming the Triple Alliance. In 1668, Louis signed the Treaty of Aix-la-Chapelle and agreed to a peace that won him control of some towns bordering the Spanish Netherlands (see Map 13-1).

Invasion of the Netherlands. In 1670, France persuaded England to join an alliance against the Dutch, and the Triple Alliance crumbled. In 1672, Louis struck directly at Holland, the power that had organized the Triple Alliance. Unless Holland was neutralized, Louis knew he could make no progress in the Spanish Netherlands—nor could he fulfill dreams of European hegemony.

MAP 13-1 The Wars of Louis XIV *This map shows the territorial changes resulting from Louis XIV's first three major wars. The War of the Spanish Succession was yet to come.*

Louis's attack on the United Provinces of Holland was countered by the young Prince of Orange, the future William III of England. Orange was the great-grandson of William the Silent, the native leader who had repulsed Philip II and established the independence of Holland. Orange persuaded the Holy

Roman Emperor, Spain, Lorraine, and Brandenburg to join him in opposing the "Christian Turk," the voracious king of France who was beginning to be seen as a menace to the whole of western Europe. In 1676, a victory over the Dutch fleet gave France control of the Mediterranean. The United Netherlands retained all of its territory, but the war ended in 1679 with no clear winner.

Revocation of the Edict of Nantes

Following the Peace of Nijmwegen, which ended the war in the Netherlands and halted for the moment Louis's aggression in Europe, Louis launched a campaign to unify France religiously. The Edict of Nantes of 1598 had established a legal Protestant minority in France, but the Huguenots' relations with the Catholic majority (nine-tenths of the French population) were never good. The French Catholic church denounced Calvinists as heretics and traitors and declared their persecution a pious, patriotic duty.

Louis hounded the Huguenots out of public life by banning them from government office and excluding them from the professions. He raised their taxes, and quartered his troops in their towns. And in October 1685, he outlawed their faith by revoking the Edict of Nantes. Protestant churches and schools closed. Protestant clergy went into exile. Nonconverting laity were enslaved on the galleys, and Protestant children were baptized by Catholic priests.

In 1685, Louis XIV revoked the Edict of Nantes, *thus ending religious toleration in France. [Robert Harding Picture Library, London]*

Louis's flaunting of religious intolerance was a major blunder, for it persuaded Protestant countries that he had to be resisted at all costs. More than a quarter-million French people fled their homeland to stiffen opposition to France in England, Germany, Holland, and the New World. Many of the Huguenots who remained in France joined guerilla resistance to the king. But Louis, to his death, was persuaded that the revocation of Nantes was his most pious act, one that placed God in his debt.

Louis's Later Wars

The League of Augsburg and the Nine Years' War. In 1681, Louis's forces conquered the free city of Strasbourg, prompting new defensive coalitions to form against him. One of these, the League of Augsburg, grew to include England, Spain, Sweden, the United Provinces, and the electorates of Bavaria, Saxony, and the Palatinate—with the support of Emperor Leopold. From 1689 to 1697, the league and France fought the Nine Years' War, while in North America England and France fought King William's War, a struggle for dominance of the colonies.

In 1697, mutual exhaustion led to an interim settlement, the Peace of Ryswick. The treaty was a triumph for William of Orange, now William III of England, and the Emperor Leopold. It secured Holland's borders and thwarted Louis's expansion into Germany.

War of the Spanish Succession. Louis had a fourth chance to win dominance over Europe. On November 1, 1700, Charles II of Spain, known as "the Sufferer" because of his genetic deformities and lingering illnesses, died. Louis and the Austrian Emperor Leopold each claimed the Spanish inheritance for a grandson. Louis's grandson, Philip of Anjou, had the better claim, for his grandmother, Marie Thérèse was the older sister of the Spanish princess, Margaret Thérèse, who had married Leopold. But Marie Thérèse had renounced her right to the Spanish throne when she married Louis.

Louis feared that the Habsburgs would dominate Europe if they controlled both Spain and the Holy Roman Empire. Most of the nations of Europe, however, feared France more than the Habsburgs. As a result, even before Charles II died, international negotiations were underway to partition his inheritance in a way that would preserve the balance of power.

Charles II upset these negotiations by bequeathing his estate to Philip of Anjou. Louis, finding himself the unexpected winner, ignored partition agreements, sent his grandson to Madrid to become Philip V of Spain, and invaded Flanders. In September 1701, England, Holland, and the Holy Roman Empire formed the Grand Alliance. They hoped to secure Flanders as a neutral barrier between Holland and France and to gain a share of the Spanish inheritance for the Habsburgs. The result was the War of the Spanish Succession (1702–1714), another total war enveloping all of western Europe.

The French army was poorly financed, poorly equipped, and poorly led. England, on the other hand, had advanced weaponry, superior tactics, and a splendid general, John Churchill, the duke of Marlborough. Marlborough routed French armies in two decisive engagements: Blenheim in August 1704, and Ramillies in 1706. In 1708–1709, famine and excessive taxation caused revolts that tore France apart, and Louis wondered aloud how God could forsake one who had done so much for Him.

MAP 13-2 Europe in 1714 *The War of the Spanish Succession ended in the year before the death of the aged Louis XIV. By then France and Spain, although not united, were both ruled by members of the Bourbon family, and Spain had lost its non-Iberian possessions.*

Louis could not bring himself to accept the stiff terms the alliance demanded for peace, and hostilities continued. A clash at Malplaquet (September 1709) created carnage unsurpassed until modern times. France and England finally declared an armistice at Utrecht (July 1712) and came to terms with Holland and the emperor in the Treaty of Rastadt in March 1714. Philip V remained king of Spain, but England won Gibraltar and became a Mediterranean power (see Map 13-2). The eighteenth century would belong to England as the sixteenth had belonged to Spain and the seventeenth to France.

Louis XIV's Legacy

Louis XIV left France a mixed legacy. Although the monarchy was still strong at the time of his death, it was more feared than admired. Its finances were insecure, and its debts great. Its tightly centralized control of political and economic life had suppressed the development of representative institutions. And its use of Versailles to trivialize the lives of aristocrats had diminished their capacity to provide the nation with effective leadership.

On the positive side, Louis erected magnificent buildings, provided patronage for important artists, and brought a new majesty to France. He skillfully handled the fractious French aristocracy and bourgeoisie. He appointed talented ministers, councillors, and *intendants*. And he created a new French empire by expanding trade into Asia and colonizing North America.

The Sun King's rule was not so absolute as to oppress the daily lives of his subjects. Louis's France was not a modern police state. His interests were those that traditionally had been assumed to be the responsibilities of rulers: the making of war and peace, the regulation of religion, and the oversight of economic activity. Even at the height of his power, local elites enjoyed considerable independence so long as they did not interfere with his authority on the national level. The French people showed little interest in representative government before a severe financial crisis demonstrated the impotency of their monarchy at the end of the eighteenth century.

In the seventeenth century, England and France developed divergent forms of government. England became the model for parliamentary monarchy, France for absolute monarchy. The politically active nobility and wealthy commercial classes of England struggled throughout the century to limit the authority of rulers. They advocated neither democracy nor religious freedom in a modern sense, but they firmly established representative government in England and extended legal recognition to a variety of religious beliefs.

In France, the monarchy remained supreme. Although the king had to mollify local elites, France developed no national institution like the English Parliament. Louis XIV was able, on his own authority, to fund the largest army in Europe, and he could and did crush religious dissent. His reign provided later continental rulers with a model of effective centralized monarchy.

⁓ Review Questions

1. What similarities and differences do you see between the systems of government and religious policies in place in England and France at the end of the seventeenth century? What accounts for the path each nation took?

2. Why did the English king and Parliament come into conflict in the 1640's? Does one of them bear more responsibility than the other for the war that broke out? What role did religion play in the struggle?

3. What was the Glorious Revolution? Why did it take place? What were James II's mistakes? What were the issues involved in the events of 1688? What kind of settlement emerged from the revolution? How did England in 1700 differ from England in 1600?

4. By what stages did absolutism develop in France? How did the policies of Henry IV and Louis XIII contribute to the creation of absolute monarchy?

5. How did Louis XIV consolidate his monarchy? What limits were there on his authority? What was Louis's religious policy?

6. How successful was Louis XIV's foreign policy? What were its aims? Were they realistic? To what extent were they attained?

⁓Suggested Readings

W. Beik, *Absolutism and Society in Seventeenth-Century France* (1985). An important study that questions the extent of royal power.

R. Bonney, *Political Change in France Under Richelieu and Mazarin, 1624–1661* (1978). A careful examination of the manner in which these two cardinals laid the foundation for Louis XIV's absolutism.

P. Burke, *The Fabrication of Louis XIV* (1992). Examines the manner in which the public image of Louis XIV was forged in art.

P. Collinson, *The Religion of Protestants: The Church in English Society, 1559–1625* (1982). The best recent introduction to Puritanism.

R. S. Dunn, *The Age of Religious Wars, 1559–1715* (1979). Lucid survey setting the conflicting political systems of France and England in larger perspective.

R. Hutton, *Charles the Second, King of England, Scotland, and Ireland* (1989). Replaces all previous biographies.

W. H. Lewis, *The Splendid Century* (1953). Focuses on society, especially in the age of Louis XIV.

C. Russell, *The Causes of the English Civil War* (1990). A major revisionist account, which should be read with Stone below.

L. Stone, *The Causes of the English Revolution, 1529–1642* (1972). Brief survey stressing social history and ruminating over historians and historical method.

V. Tapié, *France in the Age of Louis XIII and Richelieu* (1984). A narrative account.

D. Underdown, *Revel, Riot, and Rebellion* (1985). On popular culture and the English civil war.

C. V. Wedgwood, *Richelieu and the French Monarchy* (1950). Fine biography.

J. B. Wolf, *Louis XIV* (1968). Very detailed political biography.

14

New Directions in Thought and Culture in the Sixteenth and Seventeenth Centuries

KEY TOPICS IN THIS CHAPTER

~ The astronomical theories of Copernicus, Brahe, Kepler, Galileo, and Newton, and the emergence of the scientific worldview

~ Witchcraft and witch hunts

~ The literary imagination in a changing world

~ The philosophical foundations of modern thought

During the sixteenth and seventeenth centuries, science created a new view of the universe that challenged many previously held beliefs. The earth moved from the center of things to become only one of several planets orbiting a sun that was only one of millions of stars. The new cosmology forced people to rethink humanity's place in the larger scheme of things. Traditional religion and the new science came into apparent conflict, and the grounds for faith and morality had to be reconsidered.

The achievements of science were so impressive that the scientific method was heralded as the method for productive human thought in general. In the West, philosophers, theologians, and politicians—as well as students of nature—came to believe that all truth ought to resemble the truths verifiable by science.

Major Works of the Seventeenth Century

1543	*On the Revolutions of the Heavenly Spheres* (Copernicus)
1605	*The Advancement of Learning* (Bacon)
	King Lear (Shakespeare)
	Don Quixote, Part I (Cervantes)
1609	*On the Motion of Mars* (Kepler)
1620	*Novum Organum* (Bacon)
1632	*Dialogues on the Two Chief Systems of the World* (Galileo)
1637	*Discourse on Method* (Descartes)
1651	*Leviathan* (Hobbes)
1656–1657	*Provincial Letters* (Pascal)
1667	*Paradise Lost* (Milton)
1677	*Ethics* (Spinoza)
1678	*The Pilgrim's Progress* (Bunyan)
1687	*Principia Mathematica* (Newton)
1690	*Treatises of Government* (Locke)
	An Essay Concerning Human Understanding (Locke)

∼ The Scientific Revolution

For a thousand years, medieval European high culture had rested on a nearly universal consensus: one Christian church teaching one worldview. But during the sixteenth century, the Reformation and the religious wars shattered confidence in the correctness of that consensus. The result was a skepticism that motivated thinkers to reconsider what they had been taught about nature and humanity.

The developments that took place in the sixteenth and seventeenth centuries have been described as a *Scientific Revolution*. The metaphor is misleading if it is assumed to imply a rapid, widespread transformation of culture. The development of scientific attitudes was a slow process that never involved more than a few hundred people.

Rejection of the Earth-Centered Universe

Less than revolutionary methods were sometimes employed to achieve the Scientific Revolution. Such was the case with Nicolaus Copernicus (1473–1543), an Italian-educated Polish astronomer with an international reputation. Copernicus was assumed to be a fairly conventional thinker until, in the year of his death (1543), he published *On the Revolutions of the Heavenly Spheres*. The book provided Copernicus's successors with an intellectual springboard for a criticism of the previously accepted view of the position of the earth in the universe.

The maps of the universe commonly accepted in Copernicus's day were variants of one found in the ancient Greek astronomer Ptolemy's *Almagest*

(A.D. 150). They assumed that the earth was the center point of a ball-shaped universe composed of concentric, rotating crystalline spheres to which the heavenly bodies were attached. At the outer regions of these spheres lay the realm of God and the angels.

The laws of physics that the Greek philosopher Aristotle had described lay behind Ptolemy's model. The earth was at the center because it was the heaviest of objects. It did not move, for motionlessness was the natural state of physical things. The heavenly bodies moved because they were attached to spheres that transferred motion down from the highest level where a "prime mover" imparted movement to the system. Christians, of course, identified Aristotle's "prime mover" with God.

Medieval astronomers were aware of problems with Ptolemy's system. Ptolemy claimed that planets were attached to spheres, but planets actually seemed to move in non-circular patterns around the earth. (At times, planets actually seemed to go backward!) Defenders of Ptolemy credited these strange motions to *epicycles*—orbits attached to orbits. Like spinning jewels on rings, planets were said to revolve in orbits connected to their primary orbits around the earth. This was plausible, but in practice it produced a very cluttered model for the universe.

Copernicus's *On the Revolutions of the Heavenly Spheres* was meant not to destroy Ptolemy's theory, but to propose a correction that would provide a more elegant solution to the mathematical problems it raised. Copernicus suggested that if the earth were assumed to move about the sun in a circle, the epicycles could be, if not eliminated, at least reduced in number. The movement of the earth also explained what astronomers thought they saw. By distorting their perspective on the circular orbits of the planets, it made the planets appear to move elliptically.

Except for modifying the position of the earth, Copernicus maintained most of the other assumptions of Ptolemaic astronomy: circular orbits, epicycles, etc. His system was, therefore, no better than the earlier ones at predicting the location of the planets, and he uncovered no new data. The importance of his work was its illustration of a new approach to solving scientific problems. By focusing attention on the relationship between mathematics and the observed behavior of planets, Copernicus illustrated the methods of the new science—the fusion of mathematics with empirical data and observation. Mathematics provided the models for the new scientific thinking; but empirical evidence helped persuade the learned public of its validity.

Scientific Empiricism

Tycho Brahe (1546–1601), a Danish astronomer, spent most of his life opposing Copernicus and advocating a revised version of Ptolemy's earth-centered model for the universe. (Brahe suggested that the moon and the sun revolved around the earth and that the other planets revolved around the sun.) To make his case, Brahe collected the most accurate astronomical data that had ever been acquired by observation with the naked eye.

When Brahe died, his astronomical tables passed to Johannes Kepler (1571–1630), a German astronomer and a convinced Copernican. After much work, Kepler discovered that Brahe's data could be reconciled with the theory that the sun was at the center of things if the Copernican concept of circular orbits was abandoned. Brahe's observations suggested that the orbits of the planets were elliptical. Kepler published his views in 1609 (*On the Motion of Mars*), but their acceptance was hampered by the fact that no one could explain why planets would revolve in ellipses. The solution to that puzzle appeared eighty years later when Isaac Newton proposed the theory of gravity. Newton's insights were the result of new data and a new way of thinking about nature provided by another astronomer, Galileo.

A Universe of Mathematical Laws

Ptolemy could have known most of the astronomical data available to Kepler, for it had all been gathered with the naked eye. But in the year that Kepler published his theories, an Italian scientist, Galileo Galilei (1564–1642), first

ceed alike from the divine Word, the former as the dictate of the Holy Ghost and the latter as the observant executrix of God's commands. It is necessary for the Bible, in order to be accommodated to the understanding of every man, to speak many things which appear to differ from the absolute truth so far as the bare meaning of the words is concerned. But Nature, on the other hand, is inexorable and immutable; she never transgresses the laws imposed upon her, or cares a whit whether her abstruse reasons and methods of operation are understandable to men. For that reason it appears that nothing physical which sense-experience sets before our eyes, or which necessary demonstrations prove to us, ought to be called in question (much less condemned) upon the testimony of biblical passages which may have some different meaning beneath their words. For the Bible is not chained in every expression to conditions as strict as those which govern all physical effects; nor is God any less excellently revealed in Nature's actions than in the sacred statements of the Bible. . . .

From this I do not mean to infer that we need not have an extraordinary esteem for the passages of holy Scripture. On the contrary, having arrived at any certainties in physics, we ought to utilize these as the most appropriate aids in the true exposition of the Bible and in the investigation of those meanings which are necessarily contained therein for these must be concordant with demonstrated truths. I should judge the authority of the Bible was designed to persuade men of those articles and propositions which, surpassing all human reasoning, could not be made credible by science, or by any other means than through the very mouth of the Holy Spirit. . . .

But I do not feel obliged to believe that the same God who has endowed us with senses, reason, and intellect has intended to forgo their use and by some other means to give us knowledge which we can attain by them.

From Discoveries and Opinions of Galileo by Galileo Galilei. Copyright © 1957 by Stillman Drake. Used by permission of Doubleday, a division of Bantam Doubleday Dell Publishing Group, Inc.

turned a telescope on the heavens. He saw stars where none had been known to exist, mountains on the moon, spots moving across the sun, and moons orbiting Jupiter. He discovered that the heavens were far more complex than anyone had formerly suspected—far too complex to be explained by any revision of the Ptolemaic model.

Galileo's *Dialogues on the Two Chief Systems of the World* (1632) published his findings and his arguments for the Copernican view. The Roman Catholic church responded to Galileo's work by indicting him for heresy, and Galileo recanted his opinions to avoid punishment. Following his formal capitulation to the church, he allegedly muttered under his breath; "It [the earth] still moves."

Galileo's most important achievement was to articulate the concept of a universe that obeyed laws that could be described by mathematics. The mathematical regularity that Copernicus saw in the heavens, Galileo believed, was characteristic of all physical nature. The smallest atom behaved with the same mathematical precision as the largest heavenly sphere. This insight led scientists to focus on phenomena that could be quantified to explain everything

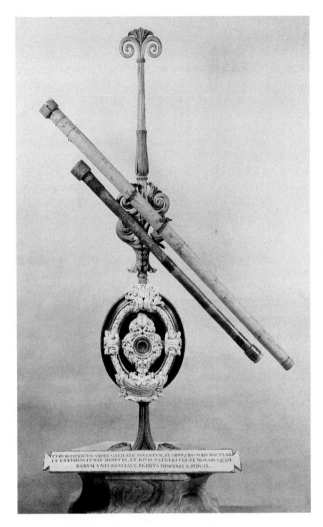

The telescope with which Galileo worked after 1609. He observed earth's moon and the cyclical phases of the planet Venus and discovered the most prominent moons of Jupiter. These observations had revolutionary intellectual and theological implications in the seventeenth century. [Instituto e Museo de Storia della Scienza, Scala/Art Resource, N.Y.]

else. Qualities, such as color, beauty, taste, etc., were assumed to be secondary functions of things that could be quantified. Attempts were even made to develop mathematical models to explain social relationships and political systems.

The new science promoted a new concept of reality. The real was what could be measured by mathematics. Nature was not a living thing with will, understanding, and intention. It was a cold, rational, mechanistic system. What was real and lasting was what was mathematically measurable.

Newtonian Physics

Isaac Newton (1642–1727), an English mathematician, established a basis for physics that endured for over two centuries. His thinking was prodded by the search for a solution to a question that plagued the scientists who accepted the Copernican model for the universe: What force kept the heavenly bodies moving in an orderly fashion? Aristotelian physics had solved this problem for Ptolemy by suggesting that the universe was a system of concentric spheres arranged according to their weights—from the material earth at the center outward to the ethereal realms of the highest heavens.

In 1687, Newton published *The Mathematical Principles of Natural Philosophy* (in Latin, *Principia Mathematica*). The work was permeated by Galileo's mathematical bias and inspired by Galileo's suggestion that inertia applied to bodies both at rest and in motion. That is, what the physicist needs to explain is not why there is motion instead of rest, but why there is a change in an existing state—be it rest or motion.

Newton theorized that the paths traveled by the heavenly bodies were determined by gravity, an attraction each physical thing has for everything around it. Since the strength of this attraction is proportional to the mass and proximity of each object, the order that exists among the planets can be explained as the balance they have achieved among their mutual forces. Newton demonstrated the effects of gravity mathematically, but he made no attempt to explain what gravity was in itself.

Newton believed that mathematics held the key to understanding nature, but, like the other advocates of the new science, he also believed that the ultimate test of a theory was its ability to explain empirical data and observation. The final test of any hypothesis was whether it described what could be observed. Science began and ended with empirical observation of what was actually in nature, not with a rational argument about what ought to be there. Consequently, religious dogma could not dictate conclusions to science.

Science and Faith

After Newton, spirits and divinities were no longer needed to explain the operation of the universe. Newton demonstrated that natural phenomena were not chaotic expressions of arbitrary decisions made by supernatural beings. They were predictable functions of regular laws that could be explained mathematically.

Newton and most scientists of his day were very devout. They knew that by altering the picture of the created world they were changing the image of its Creator. They concluded that the Creator of a universe ruled by reason must be rational and that the study of the world the Creator made must lead to a better understanding of the Creator. Science and religious faith were, therefore, not only compatible but mutually supporting. The search for the explanation for natural phenomena led a scientist to reconstruct a series of causes that led in the end to the assertion of faith in a first, or ultimate, divine cause.

At the very time when Europeans were tiring of the wars of religion and of irresolvable disputes over dogma, the new science offered them a peaceful means for arriving at a common view of God. Faith in science's rational deity also promoted faith in the rationality of human beings and in their capacity to progress—once science liberated them from dogma and superstition. The Scientific Revolution thus made virtues out of the pursuit of change and the criticism of inherited views—activities that earlier generations had opposed as leading to dangerous, destabilizing heresies. But it remained to be seen whether the God of reason could take the place of the personal deity traditionally worshiped in the West.

∼ Continuing Superstitions: Witchcraft and Witch Hunts

Loss of faith in traditional certainties drove some thinkers to seek a new grounding for truth in reason and science. But there was a darker alternative. Many people responded to the intellectual challenges of the age with fear and suspicion. In their desperate search for security, they crossed the line that divides religion from magic and the occult. This was as true for the learned as for the less educated.

The centuries that fostered the growth of Western science also nurtured superstition. Witch hunts and panics erupted almost everywhere. Between 1400 and 1700, an estimated 70,000 to 100,000 people were sentenced to death for practicing harmful magic (*malificium*) and diabolical witchcraft. Belief in demons was virtually universal, and witches were said to fly to *sabbats*, sexual orgies with the Devil where they practiced every indecency imaginable. These beliefs had roots in both popular and elite cultures—especially in clerical culture.

Village Origins

Village societies deal with the threats and terrors of life by acknowledging certain people as "cunning folk." These people are believed to have special powers to help with problems caused by disease and infertility, and sometimes they are called on to avert or mitigate natural disasters. The witch cultures of village societies may have perpetuated ancient, pre-Christian religious practices and may also have been a form of rural rebellion. They were part of a system of beliefs that empowered peasants who felt oppressed by the wealthy, urbanized classes.

Influence of the Clergy

Widespread belief in magic was the essential precondition for the great witch hunts of the sixteenth and seventeenth centuries. Such belief was not limited to ordinary people. It was shared by intellectuals and the Christian clergy. Exorcism of demons had been one of the traditional functions of the clergy, who encouraged fear of demons and the Devil as a strategy for persuading people to accept the discipline of the church. Many Christians would have been hard pressed to distinguish between magic and the sacramental rituals performed by the clergy.

In the late thirteenth century, the church declared that its priests were the only possessors of legitimate magical power. Inasmuch as such power was not human, theologians reasoned that it had to come either from God or from the Devil. If it came from God, it was properly confined to the church. Those who practiced magic outside the realm of the church evidently derived their power from pacts they had made with the Devil to destroy Christendom. The church's campaign to defend Christian society against witchcraft served to expand the church's authority. Since the "cunning folk" were revered local spiritual leaders who were outside the control of the church, they were the priests' competitors. Their removal was necessary for ecclesiastical dominance of village society.

Role of Women

Since a reputation for magical powers enhanced one's standing in a village society, claims to such powers were made by the people most in need of security and influence: the old and the impoverished—especially single or widowed women. A good 80 percent of the victims of witch hunts were women, most of whom were single and between forty-five and sixty years of age.

Persecution of witches may have been a way a male-dominated society destroyed unconventional women who were not under male control. But older single women may simply have been perceived, along with other poor people, as burdens that society need not tolerate. Some women's professions, such as midwifery, linked women with the unexplained deaths of beloved wives and infants and exposed them to accusations of malfeasance.

Witch Panics

The great witch panics occurred in the second half of the sixteenth and early seventeenth centuries. They were, in part, a response to the suffering caused by the religious divisions and wars of the era. Increasing levels of violence exacerbated fear and hatred, and these emotions were vented on scapegoats. Witch hunts also helped church and state enforce conformity and eliminate competition for the loyalty of their subjects.

Some argue that the Reformation was responsible for the witch panics. By challenging the legitimacy of many of the traditional Catholic practices that had previously provided protection against demons and the Devil, the Reformation may have encouraged people to take things into their own hands. But the Reformation may also have helped to end the witch craze. By ridiculing the sacramental magic of the old church and preaching faith in a God who was absolutely sovereign over his creation, Protestantism subordinated the Devil to God's divine plan. Ultimately, for Protestants, God was the only significant spiritual force in the universe, and his freely offered grace, not magic, was the only defense against the power of evil. This faith, the growing influence of science, and stronger governments that opposed mob actions helped end the pursuit of witches.

ᕀ Literary Imagination in Transition

The world of the seventeenth century was no longer medieval, but not yet modern. It was the interplay of both points of view that made the intellectual life of the period so rich and vital. The great literary figures of the era produced both critiques and defenses of traditional values and explored the implications of popular new ideas that encouraged people to believe that they had a significant degree of control over their own lives.

Miguel de Cervantes Saavedra: Rejection of Idealism

Spain's unique Catholic religion shaped its literature. There was religious reform in Spain, but no Protestant Reformation. The Spanish state empowered the Inquisition to enforce uniformity of opinion in Spain, and the religion of which the state approved was the mystical, ascetic piety of the early Middle Ages.

For centuries Spain had been a nation of crusaders, and the interplay between Catholic piety and political power, which is characteristic of a crusade, promoted respect for the virtues of medieval chivalry—in particular, the pursuit of honor and the demonstration of loyalty. The novels and plays of the period are almost all devoted to stories in which the honor and loyalty of characters is tested.

Miguel de Cervantes Saavedra (1547–1616), who is generally acknowledged to be the greatest writer Spain has produced, was preoccupied with the exploration of the strengths and weaknesses of religious idealism. Cervantes educated himself by wide reading and immersion in the "school of life." In his youth he worked in Rome for a Spanish cardinal. He entered the army and was decorated for gallantry in the Battle of Lepanto (1571). He also spent five years as a slave in Algiers after his ship was pirated (1575). Later, while working as a tax collector, he was imprisoned for padding his accounts. It was in prison in 1603 that he began to write his most famous work, *Don Quixote.*

Cervantes set out to satirize the chivalric romances popular in Spain in his day, but he developed a deep affection for Don Quixote, the deluded knight whose adventures he narrates. *Don Quixote* is satire only on the surface. The work raises serious questions about the things that give meaning to human lives.

Cervantes's Don Quixote is a none-too-stable, middle-aged man who is driven mad by reading too many chivalric romances. He aspires to become the knight of his own imagination and sets out to prove his worthiness by brave deeds. He dedicates himself as a courtly lover to the service of Dulcinea, a quite unworthy peasant girl whom he imagines to be a refined and noble lady. Sancho Panza, a clever, worldly-wise peasant, accompanies him as his squire and watches with bemused skepticism as the Don repeatedly makes a fool of himself. The story ends tragically when a well-meaning friend tries to restore Don Quixote's reason by defeating him in battle and forcing him to renounce his quest for knighthood. Stripped of the delusion that gave meaning to his life, the Don returns to his village to die a shamed and broken-hearted old man.

Don Quixote examines side by side the modern realism of Sancho Panza and the old-fashioned religious idealism of his Don. It comes to the conclusion that both are respectable and both are necessary for human fulfillment.

William Shakespeare: Dramatist of the Age

Little is known about William Shakespeare (1564–1616), the greatest playwright in the English language. He married at the early age of eighteen, and by 1585 he and his wife, Anne Hathaway, were the parents of three children. He may have worked for a time as a schoolteacher. His plays demonstrate a broad, but erratic, knowledge of history and classical literature that suggests that he was not a formally trained professional scholar.

Once he could afford it, Shakespeare chose to live the life of a country gentleman. He entered eagerly into the commercialism and the bawdy pleasures of the Elizabethan Age, and his work shows no trace of Puritan anxiety about worldliness. He was radical in neither politics nor religion, and his few allusions to Puritans are more critical than complimentary. By modern standards he was a political conservative, accepting the social rankings and the power structure of his day and demonstrating unquestioned patriotism.

Shakespeare experienced every aspect of life in the theater—as playwright, actor, and owner-producer. He wrote and performed for a famous company of actors, the King's Men, and, from 1590 to 1610, many of his plays were staged at Elizabeth's court. Although the French drama of the period was dominated by classical models, the Elizabethan audience that Shakespeare wanted to please welcomed a mixture of styles: classical comedies and tragedies, medieval morality plays, and contemporary Italian short stories.

Shakespeare wrote all kinds of plays that synthesized the best from the past and from the work of his contemporaries. The most original of Shakespeare's tragedies may be *Romeo and Juliet* (1597), but four of his greatest were the products of one short period in his career: *Hamlet* (1603), *Othello* (1604), *King Lear* (1605), and *Macbeth* (1606). Shakespeare also wrote comedies and plays based on real historical events. The later were strongly colored by the propaganda that served the Tudor monarchy, but almost all of Shakespeare's plays have demonstrated a remarkable ability to transcend the limits of the world for which they were written. Their keen analyses of human motivation and stirring evocations of human emotion keep them alive and capable of drawing crowds to theaters.

John Milton: Puritan Poet

John Milton (1608–1674) was a devout Puritan with a deep appreciation for classical literature and the Italian Renaissance. Youthful travels in Italy shaped his thinking, but it was England's political and religious crises that motivated him to take up his pen. Like his Catholic contemporaries in Spain, the Protestant Milton believed that standing a test of character was the most important thing in a person's life. This theme runs through much of his work, and his strong sense of commitment to principle infused him with a desire to create a body of work that would influence the course of public events in England.

In 1639, Milton spoke out against Charles I and Archbishop Laud in defense of the Presbyterian form of church government and various Puritan reforms. In 1642, a brief failed marriage, which was later reconciled, led him to publish several tracts defending the right to divorce. After Parliament had subjected these pamphlets to censorship, Milton wrote an eloquent defense of freedom of the press, *Areopagitica* (1644). Until the upheavals of the civil war moderated his views, Milton believed that government should have the least possible control over the private lives of individuals. He supported the Independents in Parliament who wanted to dissolve the national church and grant autonomy to individual congregations, and he defended the decision to execute Charles I (*On the Tenure of Kings and Magistrates*).

Milton's eyesight began to fail in the 1650s, and he was blind by the time he composed the great poems that are his masterpieces. *Paradise Lost* (1667), which tells the story of Satan's revolt in heaven and Adam's fall on earth, is a study of the destructive qualities of pride and the redeeming possibilities of humility. The Satan of *Paradise Lost* is a proud but tragic figure who prefers to reign in hell than to serve in heaven. He epitomizes the corruption of the virtues that, if preserved, give a person a potential for greatness.

Milton hoped that *Paradise Lost* would become England's *Iliad* or *Aeneid*. Just as those great works articulated the values that underlay Greek and Roman civilization, Milton sought to capture the theological ideals that were fundamental to the culture of Puritan England. Unlike the extreme Calvinists, Milton did not believe that all earthly events, among which he included Adam's first sin, were part of a divinely predestined plan. Like the Dutch theologian Jacob Arminius (d. 1609), who accused the Calvinists of determinism, Milton defended human free will. Milton shared the Arminian belief that human beings had to take responsibility for their fates and that their efforts to improve their characters could, with God's grace, bring salvation.

The failure of the Puritan revolution led Milton to contemplate the nobility of those who do the best they can in the face of certain defeat. This was the theme of his last works: *Samson Agonistes* (1671), the biblical tale of Samson, and *Paradise Regained* (1671), the story of Christ's temptation in the wilderness.

John Bunyan: Visions of Christian Piety

A more extreme Puritan point of view than that espoused by Milton is found in the works of John Bunyan (1628–1688). Bunyan does not approach Milton in poetic artistry, but he movingly defends the popular religious culture of England's ordinary people. Bunyan, who had only the most basic education and who earned his living as a tinker, became the great spokesman for a fading cause: radical Puritanism in Restoration England.

Bunyan served in Oliver Cromwell's revolutionary army, and after the restoration of the monarchy in 1660, his fiery preaching landed him in prison. During an incarceration that lasted for twelve years, he wrote his famous autobiography, *Grace Abounding*. Many Puritans kept diaries and wrote autobiographies, for their conviction that individuals could do nothing to earn God's gift of grace made them anxious and introspective. They believed that they could never know for sure that God had elected them for salvation. But those who were confident that their daily lives revealed the effects of God's grace had good grounds for hope. Although their struggle against the flesh and the world did not earn them salvation, so long as it was successful they had reason to believe that they were already saved.

The anxious quest for salvation is the subject of Bunyan's *The Pilgrim's Progress*, a work unique in its contribution to Western religious symbolism and imagery. It is a huge allegory, a story of the journey of Christian and his friends Hopeful and Faithful to the Celestial City. It teaches that one must give up all earthly distractions to search for "Life, life, eternal life."

∾ Philosophy in the Wake of Changing Science

The intellectual revolution that launched modern science and created a theology based on reason also transformed Western philosophy. The new methods of science—empirical observation and mathematical description—appealed to philosophers who were disillusioned by the logic chopping of medieval Scholasticism. They hoped that better answers to questions about matters of faith, morality, and political authority might be found if these subjects were analyzed scientifically.

Francis Bacon: Empirical Method

Francis Bacon (1561–1626), the English lawyer, statesman, and author who is often honored as the father of scientific methods of research, was not himself a scientist. His contribution to science was to help create an intellectual climate conducive to its growth.

In books such as *The Advancement of Learning* (1605), the *Novum Organum* (1620), and the *New Atlantis* (1627), Bacon attacked medieval Scholasticism's reverence for authority: the belief that most truth had already been discovered and only needed to be explicated. He urged his contemporaries to strike out on their own in search of a new understanding of nature. Bacon was a leader among the early European writers who defended the desirability of innovation and change.

Bacon believed that knowledge was not just an end in itself. It should produce useful results. It should improve the human condition. He claimed that Scholasticism had nothing more to contribute toward this end, for its practitioners did nothing but rearrange old ideas. If progress were to be made,

The microscope of Robert Hooke (1535–1703). The microscope became the telescope's companion as a major optical instrument in the seventeenth century. Several scientists, including Galileo, had a hand in its development, but the Englishman Hooke and the Dutchman Anton von Leeuwenhoek (1632–1723) did the most to perfect it. [Historical Collections, National Museum of Health and Medicine, Armed Forces Institute of Pathology]

philosophers had to examine the foundations of their thought. And if they relied on empirical observation more than logical speculation, Bacon promised that they would discover new information that would create new capabilities for humankind.

Bacon's rejection of the past was not motivated by a kind of adolescent rebellion against his elders. It sprang from a clear understanding that the world was becoming much more complicated than it had been for his medieval forebears. Like Columbus, and partially because of him, Bacon claimed that he had to chart a new route to intellectual discovery. The new worlds that were emerging on the globe were opening new worlds for the mind. Most people in Bacon's day assumed that the best era in human history lay in antiquity, but Bacon disagreed. He looked to a future of material improvement achieved through the empirical examination of nature.

René Descartes: The Method of Rational Deduction

René Descartes (1596–1650), the gifted French mathematician who invented analytic geometry, popularized a scientific method that relied more on deduction than empirical observation and induction. Thinkers all over Europe eagerly applied his techniques to all kinds of subject matters.

Descartes's *Discourse on Method* (1637) tried to put all human thought on a secure mathematical footing. In order to arrive at truth, Descartes said that it was necessary to question all ideas except those that were clear and distinct. The only idea worthy of trust was not one vouched for by some authority, but an idea that persuaded one's own reason of its truth. Descartes began his search for truth by seeing if he had any ideas he could not doubt— ideas that were self-substantiating. He discovered that he could not doubt his own act of thinking and, therefore, his own existence. To doubt doubting, one had to accept the existence of the doubter. With this clear and distinct idea as a premise, Descartes was able to construct arguments deducing the existence of God and a real world external to the human mind.

Descartes divided existing things into two basic categories: things thought and things occupying space. Thinking was characteristic of the mind, and extension (things occupying space), of the body. Since space was measurable by mathematical means, mathematical laws governed the world of extension. These can be grasped by reason, for mathematical truths have the capacity to form a coherent system in which each part is deduced from some other part. Spirits, divinities, or immaterial things have no place in the world of extension. It belongs to the scientist who uses mathematical reason to comprehend the mechanical properties of matter.

In the natural sciences, Descartes's deductive methodology eventually lost favor to induction, the process by which a scientist arrives at a hypothesis by generalizing from discrete bits of empirical data. But his approach remained popular with people who pondered subjects for which little empirical data was available—political theory, psychology, ethics, and theology.

Blaise Pascal: Reason and Faith

Blaise Pascal (1623–1662), a French mathematician and physical scientist, warned against what he believed to be a false optimism promoted by the new rationalism and science. Pascal was a deeply religious man who surrendered his wealth to pursue a life of austerity. The seriousness with which he took human sinfulness made him distrustful of those who claimed that science could perfect human nature.

Pascal opposed both dogmatism and skepticism. His dream was to find some middle ground that would avoid the Jesuits' dogmatic *casuistry* (clever argumentation that minimizes the paradoxes of faith) and the skepticism that led to either atheism or *deism* (a philosophy that substituted a rational "prime mover" for the Bible's personal God). Pascal never completed this project, but

Pascal invented this adding machine, the ancestor of mechanical calculators, around 1644. It has eight wheels with ten cogs each, corresponding to the numbers 0–9. The wheels move forward for addition, backward for subtraction. [Bildarchiv Preussischer Kulturbesitz]

he did produce a provocative collection of reflections on faith, his posthumously published *Pensées*.

Pascal's sister was a member of the Jansenist community of Port-Royal, and Pascal wrote his *Provincial Letters* to defend the Jansenists against their Jesuit enemies. Jansenism was a kind of Catholicism based on Saint Augustine's claim that original sin robbed humanity of the ability to do good and made it completely dependent on God's grace for salvation. Pascal agreed that human endeavors, like reason and science, were of no avail in matters of religion. They could not establish the two essential truths of the Christian religion: (1) that a loving God exists, and (2) that human beings, who are corrupt by nature, are utterly unworthy of God. Pascal argued that rational analysis of the human condition revealed humanity's utter corruption and demonstrated that reason itself was inadequate to the challenge of resolving the problems of human nature and destiny. Reason was no substitute for faith, but, when its limits were grasped, reason proved the need for faith and divine grace.

Pascal constructed an ingenious argument (a "wager") to demonstrate the unreasonableness of skepticism. He pointed out that it is a better bet to believe that God exists than not to do so. If God does exist, the believer will gain everything. If it should turn out that God does not exist, the believer will not have lost much by believing. Pascal was convinced that religious faith was valuable whether or not God exists, for it provided motivation for discipline and helped one maintain an important perspective on life. Pascal promised his readers self-understanding through "learned ignorance" (i.e., through contemplation of the significance of human limitations).

Baruch Spinoza: The World as Divine Substance

Where Pascal claimed that reason could do little to establish faith, the most controversial thinker of the seventeenth century, Baruch Spinoza (1632–1677), tried to reduce faith to reason. During his lifetime, his ideas caused both Jews and Protestants to attack him as an atheist. When his *Ethics* appeared following his death in 1677, religious leaders universally condemned it as an espousal of *pantheism* (a doctrine equating God and nature).

The *Ethics* was written, in the spirit of the new science, as a geometrical system of definitions, axioms, and propositions. The most controversial part of the book deals with the nature of substance and of God. According to Spinoza, a true substance must be self-caused, free, and infinite. Its description, therefore, corresponds to the traditional description of God. If substance and God are the same, everything that exists is contained in God. Spinoza's doctrine is not literally pantheistic, for God could be assumed to be greater than the created world that He, as primal substance, embraces. But if Spinoza is correct, everything that is true of the natural world is also true of God. Mind and matter are fundamentally the same, for both are extensions of the substance of God. And everything that transpires in the world is an expression of God.

Since Spinoza seemed to imply that the world was eternal and human actions were unfree and inevitable, Jews and Christians rejected him. For them, the world was created by God in time, and human beings were given enough freedom to enable them to be held responsible for their actions. Spinoza found his most enthusiastic followers among nineteenth-century thinkers who rejected revelation and theism and sought a purely rational religion.

Thomas Hobbes: Apologist for Absolutism

Thomas Hobbes (1588–1679), the most original political philosopher of the seventeenth century, turned to reason and empirical observation for an explanation of social institutions. Hobbes was an urbane and much-traveled man who enthusiastically supported the new scientific movement. He visited Paris and came to know Descartes. He spent time in Italy with Galileo. He took an interest in the research of William Harvey (1578–1657), the man who discovered that blood circulated through the human body. Hobbes was also a superb classicist. His translation of Thucydides' *History of the Peloponnesian War*, the first in English, is still reprinted today.

The English Civil War made Hobbes a political philosopher and inspired his *Leviathan* (1651). In this work Hobbes developed a thoroughly materialistic and mechanical explanation for human conduct. He theorized that all psychological processes derive from bare sensation—that, therefore, all motivations are egoistical. They are intended to increase pleasure and minimize pain. The human power of reasoning is only a process of adding and subtracting the consequences of the general names people agree to give to things.

Despite his mechanistic view of human nature, Hobbes believed that people could make progress by using scientific reasoning. Progress, however, was contingent on their prior correct use of the greatest of human creations, the commonwealth. It created the conditions essential for rational, civilized life.

The key to Hobbes's political philosophy is found in a brilliant myth he created to explain humanity's original state. Hobbes claimed that nature inclines people to a "perpetual and restless desire" for power. Because all people want, and in the state of nature possess, a right to everything, their equality breeds enmity, competition, diffidence, and perpetual quarreling—"a way of every man against every man." Whereas earlier and later philosophers saw the original human state as a paradise from which humankind had fallen, Hobbes saw it as a corruption from which only a politically organized society could deliver people. Unlike Aristotle and Christian thinkers like Thomas Aquinas, Hobbes did not believe human beings were naturally sociable; they were self-centered beasts and utterly without a master until one was imposed by force.

People escape the terrible state of nature by entering a social contract; that is, by agreeing to live in a commonwealth tightly ruled by law. A desire for "commodious living" and a fear of death drives them to accept the constraints of communal life. The social contract obliges every person, for the sake of peace and self-defense, to agree to set aside his or her right to all things and be content with as much liberty against others as he or she would allow others against himself or herself. Because words and promises are insufficient to guarantee this agreement, the social contract also authorizes the coercive use of force to compel compliance.

Believing the dangers of anarchy to be greater than those of tyranny, Hobbes thought that rulers should have unlimited power. There is little room in Hobbes's political philosophy for protest in the name of individual conscience, nor for resistance to legitimate authority by private individuals. Contemporary Catholics and Puritans alike criticized these features of the *Leviathan*, but Hobbes insisted that loss of rights for some individuals was clearly preferable to the suffering everyone experienced in a civil war. It mattered little to Hobbes whether his ruler was Charles I, Oliver Cromwell, or Charles II (each of whom Hobbes supported), so long as he kept his subjects from reverting to the chaos that was their natural condition.

John Locke: Defender of Moderate Liberty

John Locke (1632–1704) studied the works of Francis Bacon, René Descartes, and Isaac Newton, and he tried to synthesize the rationalism of Descartes and the experimental science advocated by Bacon and Newton. Although he was not as original as Hobbes, he had a greater impact on events. His ideas assisted opponents of absolutist monarchies in organizing both the American and the French revolutions.

Locke's sympathies were with the leaders of popular revolutions. His father fought with the parliamentary army during the English Civil War. In 1682, Locke himself joined a rebellion against Charles II led by Anthony Ashley Cooper, the earl of Shaftesbury. Its failure forced him to seek asylum in Holland.

Locke's *Essay Concerning Human Understanding* (1690) developed a scientific explanation for the human thinking process. Locke claimed that the mind of a newborn was a blank tablet that contained no innate ideas. It acquired all its knowledge subsequently from sensory experience. What people knew, therefore, was not the external world in itself, but the impression interaction with that world left on the mind.

If there were no innate ideas, there could be no innate moral norms. Morals, consequently, were the products of a person's rational decision to subordinate self-love to a concern for others. Such a decision was rational, for it enhanced the pleasures of human social life. Locke believed that the moral precepts taught by Christianity were identical to the ideals that uncorrupted reason would embrace without the aide of revelation. Reason and religion were but two guides to the same path.

During the reign of Charles II, Locke wrote *Two Treatises of Government,* which was designed to counter those who argued that the power of a ruler is absolute. Sir Robert Filmer, the author of *Patriarcha, or the Natural Power of Kings* (1680), had compared the rights of kings over their subjects to those of fathers over their children. Locke disputed this by maintaining that both fathers and rulers are bound by the law of nature, which creates everyone equal and independent. People enter into social contracts that empower legislatures and monarchs to "umpire" their disputes, but they do this to preserve their natural rights. They do not surrender these rights by giving rulers absolute authority over them. The job of a ruler is to preserve the law of nature.

Locke's differences with Hobbes stemmed from the latter's negative views of human nature. Locke believed that the natural human state was not Hobbes's jungle of selfish egomaniacs, but a community of perfect freedom and equality in which everyone enjoyed the rights of life, liberty, and property. The warfare that Hobbes feared emerged for Locke only when rulers failed to preserve people's natural freedom and tried to enslave them.

The Scientific Revolution and the thought of writers whose work was contemporaneous with it mark a major turning point in history. During the seventeenth century, many of the fundamental premises of the medieval worldview were abandoned. The earth moved from the center of the universe, and the universe became much larger and more complex than had previously been imagined. New knowledge of the physical universe called into question dogmas that rested on the authority of the church and Scripture. Theology and metaphysics yielded to mathematics as the preferred instrument for exploring nature. Political thought became much less concerned with religious issues and much less in awe of traditional authorities. Arguments were developed to promote greater freedom of religious and political expression. People became aware of the influence of environment on human character and action. Life on earth became the chief preoccupation of Western intellectuals, and they demonstrated greater self-confidence in their capacity to control the world and themselves.

Review Questions

1. What contributions to the Scientific Revolution were made by Copernicus, Brahe, Kepler, Galileo, and Newton? What did Bacon contribute to the foundation of scientific thought? Who do you think made the most important contribution? Why?

2. Was the Scientific Revolution truly a revolution? Which has a greater impact on history: a political or an intellectual revolution?

3. How did Newton reconcile his scientific discoveries with his faith in God? How did his efforts compare with those of Galileo and Pascal? Are reason and faith compatible?

4. How do the political philosophies of Hobbes and Locke compare? How did each view human nature? Would you rather live under a government designed by Hobbes or by Locke? Why?

5. How do you explain the fact that witchcraft and witch hunts flourished during an age of scientific enlightenment? Were there unique aspects of life in the late sixteenth and early seventeenth centuries that encouraged witch panics? Might the Reformation have contributed to them?

6. What concerns about the adequacy of past values were raised by Cervantes, Shakespeare, and Milton? What new worldview did they shape for their generation?

Suggested Readings

R. ASHCRAFT, *Revolutionary Politics and Locke's Two Treatises of Government* (1986). The most important study of Locke to appear in recent years.

V. M. BRITTAIN, *Valiant Pilgrim: The Story of John Bunyan and Puritan England* (1950). Illustrated historical biography.

H. BUTTERFIELD, *The Origins of Modern Science, 1300–1800* (1949). An authoritative survey.

I. B. COHEN, *Revolution in Science* (1985). A general consideration of the concept and of historical examples of change in scientific thought.

M. DURAN, *Cervantes* (1974). Detailed biography.

M. A. FINOCCHIARO, *The Galileo Affair: A Documentary History* (1989). A collection of all the relevant documents and introductory commentary.

A. R. HALL, *The Scientific Revolution, 1500–1800: The Formation of the Modern Scientific Attitude* (1966). Traces undermining of traditional science and rise of new sciences.

C. HILL, *Milton and the English Revolution* (1977). A major biography.

M. HUNTER, *Science and Society in Restoration England* (1981). Examines the social relations of scientists and scientific societies.

M. JACOB, *The Newtonians and the English Revolution* (1976). A controversial book that attempts to relate science and politics.

R. KIECKHEFER, *European Witch Trials: Their Foundations in Popular and Learned Culture, 1300–1500* (1976). Excellent background for understanding the great witch panic.

T. S. KUHN, *The Copernican Revolution* (1957). A scholarly treatment.

B. LEVACK, *The Witch Hunt in Early Modern Europe* (1986). Lucid up-to-date survey of research.

D. LINDBERG AND R. L. NUMBERS (eds.), *God and Nature: Historical Essays on the Encounter Between Christianity and Science* (1986). The best collection of essays on the subject.

K. THOMAS, *Religion and the Decline of Magic* (1971). Provocative, much-acclaimed work focused on popular culture.

R. S. WESTFALL, *Never at Rest: A Biography of Isaac Newton* (1981). An important major study.

15

Successful and Unsuccessful Paths to Power (1686–1740)

The Maritime Powers
> *Spain*
> *The Netherlands*
> *France After Louis XIV*
> *Great Britain: The Age of Walpole*

Central and Eastern Europe
> *Sweden: The Ambitions of*
> *Charles XII*
> *The Ottoman Empire*

> *Poland: Absence of Strong Central*
> *Authority*
> *The Habsburg Empire and the*
> *Pragmatic Sanction*
> *Prussia and the Hohenzollerns*

The Entry of Russia into the European Political Arena
> *Birth of the Romanov Dynasty*
> *Peter the Great*

KEY TOPICS IN THIS CHAPTER

- ◇ The decline of Spain and the Netherlands, as maritime powers, relative to France and England
- ◇ Opposition to the French monarchy from the nation's aristocrats
- ◇ The political stability of Britain in the early eighteenth century
- ◇ The efforts of the Habsburgs to secure their holdings
- ◇ The emergence of Prussia as a major power under the Hohenzollerns
- ◇ The efforts of Peter the Great to transform Russia into a powerful, centralized nation along Western lines

---

The late seventeenth and early eighteenth centuries witnessed significant shifts of power and influence among the states of Europe, Great Britain, France, Austria, Russia, and Prussia emerged as the dominant powers, as Spain, the United Netherlands, Poland, Sweden, and the Holy Roman and Ottoman empires declined.

The most successful states were those that developed strong central political authorities. The turmoil of seventeenth-century English civil wars and the Fronde in France had impressed people with the value of the monarch as a guarantor of domestic tranquility and had created on the continent support for the kind of absolutist government pioneered by France's Louis XIV. More often than not, a nation's power reflected the character, personality, and energy of its ruler.

Events and Reigns

1533–1584	*Ivan the Terrible*
1584–1613	*Time of Troubles*
1613	*Michael Romanov becomes tsar*
1640–1688	*Frederick William, the Great Elector*
1682–1725	*Peter the Great*
1683	*Turkish siege of Vienna*
1688–1713	*Frederick I of Prussia*
1697	*Peter the Great's European tour*
1700–1721	*The Great Northern War*
1703	*Saint Petersburg founded*
1711–1740	*Charles VI, the Pragmatic Sanction*
1713	*War of the Spanish Succession ends*
1713–1740	*Frederick William I of Prussia*
1714	*George I founds the Hanoverian dynasty*
1715	*Louis XV becomes King of France*
1720–1742	*Robert Walpole dominates British politics*
1726–1743	*Cardinal Fleury*
1727	*George II*
1740	*Maria Theresa succeeds to the Habsburg throne*
1740	*Frederick II invades Silesia*

～ The Maritime Powers

Spain

At the end of the seventeenth century, Spain yielded its position as the dominant power in western Europe to Britain and France. Spain's political decline was linked to the failure of an economy that had never been healthy. Spain developed few industries and wool remained virtually its only export. The Spanish government financed imports by using the gold and silver mined in its New World empire, but this income was often imperiled by raids on Spain's treasure fleet carried out by pirates and hostile navies.

Spain also had serious internal problems. The monarchy had never been strong. It relied on the cooperation of the local nobility and the church to control Castile, Aragon, Navarre, the Basque provinces, and other districts. Beginning with the defeat of the Spanish Armada in 1588, whatever prestige the crown had earned began to fade. From 1665 to 1700, the royal government was headed by the physically malformed, dull-witted, and sexually impotent Charles II. And on his death, foreign powers intervened (the War of the Spanish Succession) to place their candidates on Spain's throne.

The Treaty of Utrecht (1713) recognized Philip V (r. 1700–1746), the grandson of Louis XIV, as Spain's king. The new Bourbon dynasty should have attempted to consolidate its internal power and to protect Spain's overseas trade. Instead, Philip's wife, Elizabeth Farnese, persuaded him to use his resources to advance her family's ambitions in Italy. Not until Charles III (r.

1759–1788) ascended the throne did Spain have a king who was concerned with domestic administration and the management of the empire. He was able to improve Spain's internal government, but it was too late for him to claim a hand in Europe's game of power politics.

The Netherlands

Like Spain, the United Provinces of the Netherlands ceased to be a great power during the eighteenth century. Wars with Louis XIV and England permitted the British to establish naval supremacy. After the death of William III of England in 1702, the provinces blocked the emergence of another strong stadtholder who could provide unified political leadership. The Dutch fishing industry declined. The Dutch lost their technological superiority in shipbuilding. Countries that had relied on Dutch ships to transport their goods began to trade directly with each other. And Dutch domestic industries stagnated. Only in the area of international finance did the United Provinces retain significant influence.

France After Louis XIV

France, although less strong in 1715 than in 1680, remained a great power. France had a large population, an advanced economy, and a highly developed administrative structure. France's resources were drained by the last of Louis XIV's wars, but the other major states of Europe were similarly debilitated by the conflicts. All that France needed to recover economically was wiser political leadership and a less ambitious foreign policy.

France did enjoy a period of recovery, but the quality of its leadership was at best indifferent. The prestige of the monarchy was already faltering when Louis XIV was succeeded by his five-year-old great-grandson Louis XV (r. 1715–1774). The young king's regent—his uncle, the duke of Orléans—made matters worse.

Orléans was a gambler who turned over the financial management of the kingdom to a Scottish speculator, John Law (1671–1729). Law believed that an increase in the money supply would stimulate postwar economic recovery, so he established a bank to issue paper money. Law transferred responsibility for management of the national debt to the "Mississippi Company," a corporation with a monopoly on trading privileges with the French colony of Louisiana in North America. The company issued shares of its stock in exchange for government bonds and relied on the profits of stock speculation to redeem those bonds. Initially the price of the stock rose handsomely, but smart investors took their profits and demanded to exchange the currency of Law's bank for gold. That institution lacked sufficient bullion to back up its printed money, and in February 1720, the government was forced to halt gold trading in France. Law fled the country, and the "Mississippi Bubble," as the affair was called, burst. The fiasco brought disgrace on the government and cast a shadow over French economic life for the rest of the century.

***Renewed Authority of the* Parlements.** The duke of Orléans further weakened the monarchy by attempting to restore a role for the French nobility in the decision-making processes of the government. Louis XIV had filled governmental offices with commoners and kept aristocrats busy competing for symbolic honors at Versailles. The regent, who was pressured by the aristocrats to restore a balance of power, set up a system of councils on which the nobles were to serve with the bureaucrats. The experiment failed, for the nobles, who had been thoroughly domesticated, lacked both the talent and the desire to govern.

The great French families were not, however, prepared to surrender their ancient claims to a free hand in the management of their domains. Their chief preoccupation was with limiting the power of the monarchy. Their most effective weapons were the *parlements*, the aristocratically dominated courts.

The French *parlements* were different from the English Parliament. They did not have the power to legislate, but, as courts that enforced the law, their formal approval was required to make a royal law valid. Louis XIV had curtailed the authority of stubborn, uncooperative *parlements*, but the duke of Orléans reinstated their power to allow or disallow laws. For the rest of the century, until the revolution that overthrew the monarchy in 1790, the aristocrats used the *parlements* to resist royal authority.

Cardinal Fleury and Louis XV. After 1726, things briefly improved for the monarchy. A seventy-three-year-old churchman, Cardinal Fleury (1653–1743), became the king's chief minister. Like his seventeenth-century predecessors, the cardinals Richelieu and Mazarin, Fleury was a political realist who understood the political ambition—and incapacity—of the nobility. He was determined to give France a period of peace in which to recover economically. He repudiated part of the national debt, built new roads and bridges, and encouraged the growth of new industries. Fleury was never able, however, to impose sufficient taxes on the nobles or the church to put the state on a stable financial footing.

Following Fleury's death in 1743, his work was speedily undone. Despite the cardinal's best efforts to train Louis XV for the responsibilities of office, the king possessed the vices but not the virtues of his great-grandfather. He wanted absolute power but would not work the long hours required to use it. He became a pawn of the intrigues of his court, and his personal life was scandalous. Louis XV was too mediocre a man to be evil, but in a monarch mediocrity could be a greater fault than vice.

Despite political drift, France remained a great power. At mid-century, its army was still the largest and strongest on the continent. Its commerce and production were expanding. Its colonies were producing wealth and spurring the growth of domestic industries. France had great potential, but it lacked the political leadership needed to integrate its forces.

Great Britain: The Age of Walpole

The British monarchy was not as degraded as the French, but it was not entirely stable. In 1714 the Hanoverian dynasty, which Parliament had acknowledged in the Act of Settlement of 1701, came to the throne. George I

Cardinal Fleury (1653–1743) was the tutor and chief minister of Louis XV from 1726 to 1743. Fleury gave France a period of peace and prosperity, but was unable to solve the state's long-term financial problems. This portrait is by Hyacinthe Rigaud (1659–1743). [Photographie Bulloz]

(r. 1714–1727) was immediately confronted by a challenger. In December 1715, James II's son, James Edward, the "Stuart pretender" (1688–1766), landed in Scotland. The men who rallied to his side were dispersed less than two months later, but the experience alerted the new dynasty to the necessity of consolidating its position.

Whigs and Tories. During the seventeenth century, England had been one of the most politically restive countries in Europe, and as Queen Anne's reign (1702–1714) grew to a close, there were sharp clashes between political factions called Whigs and Tories. Neither group was organized like a modern political party. Each was a network of politicians who worked on the local level, and each also had a few national spokesmen who articulated positions and principles. The Tories favored a strong monarchy, low taxes for landowners, and the Anglican church. The Whigs believed that the monarchy should acknowledge the final sovereignty of Parliament. They defended urban commercial interests as well as the prosperity of rural landowners. And they advocated religious toleration for Protestant nonconformists. Both groups were conservative in that they defended the status quo.

The Tories wanted peace with France, but the Elector of Hanover, who as George I was to succeed Queen Anne, believed that it was in Hanover's interest to keep France at war. The Whigs sought his support, and in the final months of Anne's reign, some Tories opened channels of communication with the Stuart pretender. Under these circumstances, it was little wonder that the Whigs won the confidence of the new king. For the forty years following his succession, the chief difference between Whigs and Tories was that the former had access to public office and patronage and the latter did not.

The Leadership of Robert Walpole. English politics remained in a state of flux until Robert Walpole (1676–1745) persuaded the king to redesign the nation's government. Walpole, a Norfolk squire, had been active in the House of Commons and had served as a cabinet minister. A British financial scandal similar to the French Mississippi Bubble brought him to the king's attention.

Management of Britain's national debt had been assigned to the South Sea Company. It exchanged government bonds for its stock. And, as in the French case, the price of its stock soared until speculators began to sell their holdings in 1720. Parliament intervened to prevent a crash and, under Walpole's leadership, adopted measures to honor the national debt. Walpole's contemporaries credited him with saving the financial integrity of their nation.

Walpole has often been regarded as the first prime minister of Great Britain. He originated England's system of administration by cabinet ministers, each of whom is assigned responsibility for a separate branch of government. But unlike a modern prime minister, he was not chosen by the House of Commons. His power depended on his ability to manipulate the House while retaining the favor of his kings, George I and George II (r. 1727–1760).

Walpole's slogan, "Let sleeping dogs lie," summarized his policy of maintaining peace abroad while promoting the status quo at home. Corruption was the glue that held his government together, for politicians quickly learned that to oppose him was to risk the almost certain loss of government patronage for self, family, and friends.

The Structure of Parliament. The eighteenth-century British House of Commons was neither a democratic nor a representative body. Members of Parliament were chosen by property owners and expected to protect their economic and social interests. Each county elected two members. But if the more powerful landed families in a county agreed on the candidates, there was no contest. Other members were chosen by units called boroughs. A few boroughs were large enough to hold truly democratic elections, but most boroughs had a very small number of electors. A rich family could buy up most of the property to which the votes of a borough were attached and, in effect, "own" a seat in Parliament.

Members of Parliament did not pretend to represent the people at large, but they did provide England with unified government. Owners of property were suspicious of the bureaucrats who worked for the crown and preferred themselves to undertake the duties of local administration (e.g., as judges, militia commanders, tax collectors). In this sense the British nobles and substantial landowners governed the nation. And since they accepted the sover-

One of a series of Hogarth etchings satirizing the notoriously corrupt English electoral system. Hogarth shows the voters going to the polls after having been bribed and intoxicated with free gin. Voting was then in public. The secret ballot was not introduced in England until 1872. [Metropolitan Museum of Art, Harris Brisbane Dick Fund, 1932. Acc. #32.35.(124)]

eignty of the Parliament that represented their interests, they acknowledged a central political authority. Parliament thus provided Britain with the kind of unity that elsewhere in Europe was possible only under an absolutist monarchy.

Parliament also accounted in part for the strong financial position of the British government. Continental kings could impose taxes unilaterally, but the British monarch could do so only with the consent of Parliament. Since the property owners represented in Parliament levied taxes on themselves, in England, unlike France, there were virtually no exemptions from taxation. Consequently, vast sums could be raised to fight the wars Parliament supported. By 1693, when the Bank of England was set up to regulate credit, all the financial policies were in place to permit Britain to become a great power.

The British people enjoyed more political freedom than the citizens of continental states. Patronage did not stifle divergent points of view among

Lady Mary Wortley Montagu Gives Advice on Election to Parliament

In this letter of 1714, Lady Mary Wortley Montagu discussed with her husband the various paths that he might follow to gain election to the British House of Commons. Note the emphasis she placed on knowing the right people and on having large amounts of money to spend on voters. Eventually her husband was elected to Parliament in a borough that was controlled through government patronage.

 ✑ What are the various ways in which candidates and their supporters used money to campaign? What role did friendships play in the campaigning? How important do the political ideas or positions of the candidates seem to be? Women could not vote in eighteenth-century parliamentary elections, but what kind of influence do they seem to exert?

You seem not to have received my letters, or not to have understood them: you had been chose undoubtedly at York, if you had declared in time; but there is not any gentleman or tradesman disengaged at this time; they are treating every night. Lord Carlisle and the Thompsons have given their interest to Mr. Jenkins. I agree with you of the necessity of your standing this Parliament, which, perhaps, may be more considerable than any that are to follow it; but, as you proceed, 'tis my opinion, you will spend your money and not be chose. I believe there is hardly a borough unengaged. I expect every letter should tell me you are sure of some place; and, as far as I can perceive you are sure of none. As it has been managed, perhaps it will be the best way to deposit a certain sum in some friend's hands, and buy some little Cornish borough: it would, undoubtedly, look better to be chose for a considerable town; but I take it to be now too late. If you have any thoughts of Newark, it will be absolutely necessary for you to enquire after Lord Lexington's interest; and your best way to apply yourself to Lord Holdernesse, who is both a Whig and an honest man. He is now in town, and you may enquire of him if Brigadier Sutton stands there; and if not, try to engage him for you. Lord Lexington is so ill at the Bath, that it is a doubt if he will live 'till the elections; and if he dies, one of his heiresses, and the whole interest of his estate, will probably fall on Lord Holdernesse.

'Tis a surprize to me, that you cannot make sure of some borough, when a number of your friends bring in so many Parliament-men without trouble or expense. 'Tis too late to mention it now, but you might have applied to Lady Winchester, as Sir Joseph Jekyl did last year, and by her interest the Duke of Bolton brought him in for nothing; I am sure she would be more zealous to serve me, than Lady Jekyl.

Lord Wharncliffe (ed.), Letters and Works of Lady Mary Wortley Montagu, *3rd ed., vol. 1 (London, 1861), p. 211.*

members of the government. Newspapers and public debate flourished. Free speech and freedom of association were possible. And there was no standing army to intimidate the populace.

Rights that the English regarded as traditional raised a real barrier to the government's arbitrary use of power. If public outcry was loud enough, Parliament would rescind unpopular measures or allow itself to be persuaded to begin or end wars. Despite manifest corruption, Britain became a European power of the first order with a form of government and an economy that provided a model for all progressive Europeans.

～ Central and Eastern Europe

The maritime nations of western Europe had well-defined borders and strong central governments. Conflicts among them occurred less in Europe than on the high seas and in their overseas empires.

East of the Elbe River, political organization was "soft." Economies were largely agrarian. Serfdom persisted. Cities were few. And since no states had overseas empires, military conflicts were fought out at home rather than abroad. The wars of the seventeenth century accustomed people to frequently shifting political loyalties, and the rulers of the region's numerous small states and principalities resisted the development of any centralized monarchy.

In the last half of the seventeenth century, the political and social institutions that were to characterize eastern and central Europe for the next 200 years emerged. Following the Peace of Westphalia, the Austrian Habsburgs accepted the weakness of Germany's Holy Roman Empire and turned their attention to developing a base of power farther east. At the same time in northern Germany, Prussia evolved as a challenger to Habsburg domination. And by the start of the eighteenth century, Russia was becoming a major military power. Austria, Prussia, and Russia rose as Sweden, Poland, and the Ottoman Empire declined.

Sweden: The Ambitions of Charles XII

Sweden had seized the opportunity of the Thirty Years' War to make a bid for empire. During the seventeenth century, it won control of the Baltic—permitting Russia and Germany access to the sea only on its terms. Sweden's economy, however, was not strong enough to sustain continued political success.

In 1697, a headstrong (possibly insane) king, Charles XII (r. 1697–1718), ascended Sweden's throne. Three years later Russia launched the Great Northern War (1700–1721) to win a foothold on the Baltic. Charles XII fought vigorously and often brilliantly, but he mismanaged the campaign. After an initial victory and a distracting foray into Poland, Charles invaded Russia. His army bogged down in the brutal winter weather and suffered decisive defeat at Poltava in 1709. The war ended in 1721, when Sweden ran out of resources. Russia occupied a large section of the eastern Baltic coast and broke Sweden's monopoly of the sea. After Charles XII's death, the Swedish nobles curtailed the power of the monarchy, and Sweden abandoned foreign adventures.

The Ottoman Empire

The Ottoman Empire was the chief barrier to expansion of Europe's south-eastern states: the Austrian Habsburgs and Russia. Late in the seventeenth century, the Ottomans still controlled most of the Balkan peninsula and the entire coastline of the Black Sea.

Although officially Islamic, the Ottoman Empire contained an ethnically and religiously diverse population. Its government was based on religiously defined units called *millets*. Laws and regulations applied to people according to the *millets* to which they belonged rather than to the districts in which they lived. The non-Islamic residents of the empire were known as *zimmis*. They could practice their faiths, but they were second-class citizens who could not rise in the service of the empire. This arrangement limited interaction and integration of people of different religions.

From its beginnings in the fifteenth century, the Ottoman Empire had been an aggressive power pressing westward from Istanbul (Constantinople) into Europe. By 1683, it was besieging the city of Vienna and forcing Christians in the Balkan peninsula and on the islands of the eastern Mediterranean to convert to Islam. Many of these people had previously been forced to convert to Roman Catholicism by the Venetians, and they welcomed the Turks as liberators.

By the end of the seventeenth century, the Ottomans were overextending themselves. Since military campaigns left Ottoman sultans little time to attend to civilian affairs, political factions in the capital became accustomed to independence. They resisted attempts to strengthen the central government, and rivalries among them weakened the effectiveness of the empire's administration. Control of distant provinces came to depend on the goodwill of local rulers, and commercial agents representing foreign nations won dominance over the empire's trade and its economy.

By the early eighteenth century, the weakness of the Ottoman Empire was creating a political vacuum on the southeastern perimeter of Europe. For the next two centuries, European states probed and appropriated parts of the empire. In 1699, the Turks surrendered Hungary, Transylvania, Croatia, and Slavonia to the Habsburgs. Russia also moved into Ottoman territory, and early in the nineteenth century many of the peoples who lived in the Balkans and around the Black Sea launched campaigns to establish independent states. The result was political and ethnic turmoil that still continues.

Poland: Absence of Strong Central Authority

In no other part of Europe was the failure to maintain a competitive political position so complete as in Poland. The fault lay with the Polish nobility, who defeated all attempts to establish an effective central government—even one of their own making.

The Polish monarchy was elective, and divisions among the noble families prevented them from choosing one of their own to be king. Most of

Poland's monarchs were outsiders, the tools of foreign powers. The Polish nobles belonged to a central legislative body called the *Sejm* (Diet). It was an aristocratic assembly that excluded representatives from corporate bodies, such as towns. The Diet was virtually powerless. Its rule of *liberum veto* permitted any one of its members unilaterally to disband its meetings—a practice known as "exploding" the Diet. The need to achieve unanimity on every issue made it extremely difficult for the Diet to exercise its authority. Government as it was developing elsewhere in Europe simply was not tolerated in Poland. Consequently, during the last half of the eighteenth century, Poland disappeared from the map of Europe.

The Habsburg Empire and the Pragmatic Sanction

The Thirty Years' War was a turning point for the Austrian Habsburgs. It ended their dreams of dominating Germany and returning the region to the Catholic fold. The subsequent decline of the Spanish branch of the Habsburg family led the Austrians to strike out in a new direction on their own.

The Treaty of Westphalia legalized Protestantism and recognized the autonomy of more than 300 political entities within the Holy Roman Empire. The Habsburg family retained a firm hold on the imperial title, but the effectiveness of the title depended on the emperor's ability to elicit cooperation from the members of the empire's Diet. Although the post-Westphalian Holy Roman Empire resembled Poland in its lack of central authority, the Diet, which met at Regensburg from 1663 until its dissolution in 1806, provided some regulation for daily economic and political life. The Habsburgs' domains and the emerging Prussian state also helped stabilize Germany.

Consolidation of Austrian Power. The Habsburgs began by consolidating their power within their hereditary possessions (see Map 15-1). These included the Crown of Saint Wenceslas (encompassing the kingdom of Bohemia in what was until recently Czechoslovakia and the duchies of Moravia and Silesia) and the Crown of Saint Stephen (Hungary, Croatia, and Transylvania). In the early eighteenth century, the family acquired the former Spanish (thereafter Austrian) Netherlands, Lombardy (northern Italy), and, for a brief time, the Kingdom of Naples (southern Italy). For most of the eighteenth and nineteenth centuries, the Habsburgs' power derived from lands located outside Germany.

The Habsburgs' possessions were extremely difficult to rule. The various lands that composed their empire were held by different titles, and in most areas they could govern only with the cooperation of the local nobles. Geographical barriers and differences of language and custom prevented the Habsburgs' subjects from developing a common identity. Even the Habsburg zeal for Roman Catholicism was no bond for unity, for many of the Magyar nobles of Hungary were zealous Calvinists. The Habsburgs tried to chart common policies for their far-flung domains, but they repeatedly found it necessary to bargain with nobles in one part of Europe to maintain their position in another.

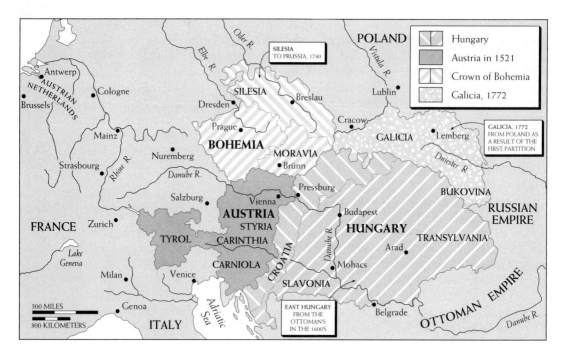

MAP 15-1 The Austrian Habsburg Empire, 1521–1772 *The empire had three main units: Austria, Bohemia, Hungary. Expansion was mainly eastward: east Hungary from the Ottomans (seventeenth century) and Galicia from Poland (1772). Meantime, Silesia was lost, but Habsburgs retained German influence as Holy Roman Emperors.*

Despite these difficulties, Leopold I (r. 1657–1705) rallied his people to fight off the Turks and France's Louis XIV. In 1699, the Ottomans recognized his sovereignty over Hungary, and Leopold's increasing strength in the East enhanced his political leverage in Germany. He began to bring his Magyar subjects under control and to extend his reach into the Balkan peninsula and western Romania. These new possessions made it possible for him to develop the port of Trieste as a base for Habsburg power in the Mediterranean.

The Dynastic Problem of Charles VI. Leopold was succeeded by Joseph I (r. 1705–1711) and Charles VI (r. 1711–1740). Charles, who had no male heir, feared that after his death the European powers would intervene in the Austrian Habsburg lands just as they had in the Spanish Habsburgs' domains in 1700. To prevent this and to provide his realm with a semblance of legal unity, he devoted most of his reign to winning the approval of his family, the estates representing his subjects, and Europe's chief nations for a document called the Pragmatic Sanction. It recognized a single line of inheritance for the Habsburg dynasty through Charles VI's daughter Maria Theresa (r. 1740–1780).

Charles succeeded in establishing the line of succession and the basis for future legal bonds within the Habsburg holdings, but he was unable to prevent other nations from attacking his daughter. Less than two months after his death, the fragility of his foreign agreements was revealed. In December 1740, Frederick II of Prussia invaded the Habsburg province of Silesia, and Maria Theresa had to fight to defend her inheritance.

Prussia and the Hohenzollerns

Like the Habsburgs, the Hohenzollerns of Prussia acquired a collection of lands held by different feudal titles. But the Hohenzollerns were more successful than the Habsburgs in forging their diverse holdings into a centrally administered state. Although their possessions were geographically scattered and poor in economic resources, a powerful bureaucratic machine enabled them to mobilize every social class and most economic pursuits to support the institution that united their far-flung realm: the army. As a result, "Prussian" has become synonymous with administrative rigor and military discipline.

A State of Disconnected Territories. The Hohenzollern family rose to prominence in 1417, as rulers of the German territory of Brandenburg (see Map 15-2). To this they added the duchy of Cleves and the counties of Mark and Ravensburg in 1609, the duchy of East Prussia in 1618, and the duchy of Pomerania in 1637. At Westphalia in 1648, the Hohenzollerns lost part of Pomerania to Sweden but were compensated by the grant of three bishoprics and the promise of the archbishopric of Magdeburg (1680). By the late seventeenth century, the scattered Hohenzollern holdings constituted a block of territory within the Holy Roman Empire second in size only to that of the Habsburgs.

Despite its size, the Hohenzollern conglomerate was weak. Except for Pomerania, none of the new acquisitions was contiguous with the home base in Brandenburg. All were exposed to foreign aggression. All were poor in natural resources. Many had been devastated during the Thirty Years' War. Each was dominated by a native aristocracy that limited the power of the Hohenzollern ruler. They shared no single concern that might encourage their unification.

Frederick William, the Great Elector. Frederick William (r. 1640–1688), "the Great Elector," transformed this unlikely conglomerate into a powerful modern state. His instruments were a tightly centralized bureaucracy and a rigorously disciplined army. Threats of invasion by Sweden and Poland inspired their creation.

The army with which Frederick William began his reign was too small to intimidate his neighbors. But in 1655, the Brandenburg estates refused his request for taxes to finance a larger force. In desperation, he used the soldiers at his disposal to collect the money he needed to employ more.

The elector skillfully co-opted potential opponents into his service. In exchange for supporting the Hohenzollerns, the Prussian nobles—the Junkers—were granted complete control over the serfs on their estates. Fred-

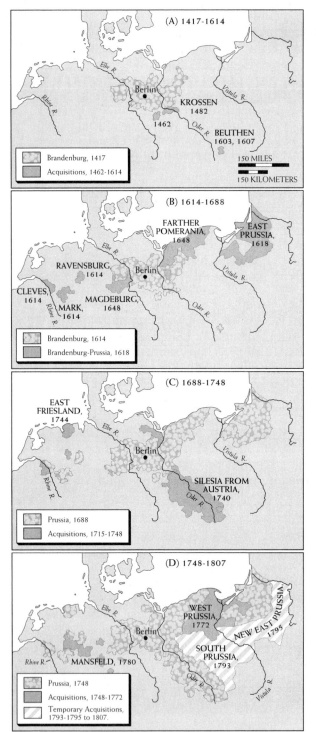

MAP 15-2 Expansion of Brandenburg-Prussia *Seventeenth-century Brandenburg-Prussia expanded mainly by acquiring dynastic titles in geographically separated lands. Eighteenth-century expansion occurred through aggression to the east: Silesia seized in 1740 and various parts of Poland in 1772, 1793, and 1795.*

erick William also used the Junkers to collect his taxes, which fell most heavily on the peasants and the urban classes. And the privilege of joining the army officer corps was largely reserved to the nobles.

Since the army was the one institution that drew members from all the Hohenzollern territories and all its soldiers and civilian personnel took an oath of loyalty to the elector, the army defined the state. Total mobilization of the state's resources enabled Frederick William to build a military machine far larger than that usually sustained by a small country. Prussia thus became a power with which other nations had to reckon.

Frederick William I, King of Prussia. The house of Hohenzollern had created a nation, but it did not yet possess a crown. The acquisition of a royal title was the achievement of the Great Elector's son, Frederick I (r. 1688–1713). Frederick was the least "Prussian" member of his family. He built palaces, founded Halle University (1694), supported the arts, and lived luxuriously. In 1700, when the War of the Spanish Succession broke out, he made a deal with the Holy Roman Emperor. In exchange for the use of the Prussian army, the emperor permitted Frederick to assume the title of "King in Prussia."

Frederick's heir, Frederick William I (r. 1713–1740), was both the most eccentric and the most effective of the Hohenzollern monarchs. After giving his father a funeral that would have pleased the luxury-loving Frederick I, Frederick William I imposed policies of strict austerity. He increased the size of the army and consolidated an obedient, compliant bureaucracy. He ruled alone without the assistance of ministers. His officials submitted reports in writing to him in his office, or *Kabinett.* Then he alone examined the papers, made decisions, and issued orders.

Frederick William's civilian bureaucrats observed military discipline. All departments were centrally managed by a General Directory *(General-Ober Finanz-Kriegs-und-Domänen-Direktorium).* The nobility were subjected to taxation, and most remaining feudal dues were transformed into money payments. Service to the state and the monarch was to become impersonal—a mechanical and unquestioning recognition of a duty to an office, not of a loyalty engendered by respect for the unique qualities of the individual who held that office.

The Prussian Army. Frederick William was a near fanatic where his army was concerned. He required each district in his kingdom to provide him with a certain number of men. They were trained with rigorous discipline. A show regiment composed of the tallest men in Europe was recruited. There were different laws for soldiers and for civilians, and royal patronage made the officer corps society's highest class. Frederick William merged the army, the Junker nobility, and the monarchy into a single political entity, which he symbolized, in 1725, by beginning the practice of always appearing in military uniform.

Frederick William's military force grew from about 39,000 in 1713 to over 80,000 in 1740. Prussia was only the thirteenth most populous nation in Europe, but it fielded Europe's third or fourth largest army. Military priorities and values dominated Prussian government, society, and daily life as in no other state of Europe. Other nations possessed armies, but Prussia was possessed by its army.

Having built the best army in Europe, Frederick William avoided using it. He enjoyed drilling his soldiers but not sending them into battle. Although he terrorized his family and associates—occasionally knocking out teeth with his walking stick—he did not pursue aggressive foreign policies. He regarded the army as a symbol of Prussian power and unity, not an instrument to be used for foreign adventures.

Frederick II, "the Great" (r. 1740–1786) inherited his father's superb military machine, but not his father's self-restraint. Frederick celebrated his ascension to the throne by invading Silesia and beginning a contest between Austria and Prussia for control of Germany. The struggle dominated central European affairs for over a century.

∼ The Entry of Russia into the European Political Arena

The rise of Prussia and the consolidation of the Austrian Habsburg domains doubtless seemed to many at the time only one more shift in the ancient game of German politics. But the entrance of Russia into European affairs was something wholly new. Russia had long been considered a part of Europe only by courtesy. Hemmed in by Sweden on the Baltic and by the Ottoman Empire on the Black Sea, it had no warm-water ports. Archangel, a port on the White Sea, was its chief outlet to the West, but it was closed by ice during part of the year. Russia was a land of vast, but unfocused, potential.

Birth of the Romanov Dynasty

The reign of Ivan IV, "the Terrible" (1533–1584), the first Muscovite prince to use the title "Tsar of Russia," was followed by a period of anarchy and civil war. In 1613, an assembly of nobles who hoped to end the confusion of the "Time of Troubles" agreed to recognize a seventeen-year-old boy as their tsar: Michael Romanov (r. 1613–1654). He founded the dynasty that ruled Russia until 1917.

Michael Romanov and his two successors, Alexis I (r. 1654–1676) and Theodore III (r. 1676–1682), stabilized Russia's government, but their nation remained weak and poor. Russia's administrative bureaucracy was controlled by the old nobility, the *boyars*. It was only barely capable of maintaining order. The chief threats to peace were peasant revolts and raids by *cossacks*, horsemen who lived on the steppe frontier. There was also the danger of mutiny by the *streltsy*, Moscow's garrison.

Peter the Great

In 1682, two boys ascended the fragile Russian throne: Peter I, "the Great" (r. 1682–1725), and Ivan V. The succession had been bloodily disputed, and the

Peter the Great (r. 1682–1725) seeking to make Russia a major military power, reorganized the country's political and economic structures. His reign saw Russia enter fully into European power politics. [The Bettmann Archive]

weapons of the streltsy had decided the outcome. Sophia, the boys' sister, served as regent until Peter's followers overthrew her in 1689. Peter then ruled personally, although in theory he shared the crown with the sickly Ivan until Ivan's death in 1696.

Like Louis XIV of France, whose youthful development had also been shaped by social upheavals, Peter resolved to establish a strong central monarchy. For ideas about how this could be done, he turned to the West. Products and workers from the West had filtered into Russia, and Europe's culture, particularly its military science, intrigued Peter.

In 1697, Peter made a famous tour of Europe. For convenience, he traveled officially incognito rather than as a head of state. The European leaders whom he visited found their almost seven-foot-tall guest both crude and rude. But Peter was thoroughly at home in their shipyards and munitions factories. There he discovered the sources of power for which he was looking.

Peter returned to Moscow determined to Westernize his nation. He set himself four objectives which he pursued ruthlessly: taming the boyars and the streltsy, achieving secular control of the church, reorganizing the internal administration, and developing the economy. Policy in each area was intended to strengthen the military power of the nation and the authority of the monarchy.

Taming the Boyars and Streltsy. In 1698, immediately on his return from abroad, Peter launched an attack on the boyars. He personally shaved their long beards and sheared off the dangling sleeves of their shirts and coats—Russian peculiarities that Western Europeans had mocked. More important, he pressed the boyars into the service of the state.

In 1722, Peter published a Table of Ranks. It tied a person's social status to his rank in the bureaucracy or the army rather than the nobility. This enabled Peter to enhance the standing of boyars who submitted to the central state, but the Russian nobility was never as thoroughly domesticated as the Prussian aristocracy. They retained control over the serfs and local government.

The streltsy fared less well than the boyars. They rebelled while Peter was on his European tour. When he returned, he brutally suppressed their revolt and executed about 1,200 of them. Their corpses were publicly displayed to demonstrate the consequences of disloyalty to the tsar.

Achieving Secular Control of the Church. Peter was similarly ruthless in his dealings with the Russian Orthodox Church, which was firmly opposed to Westernization. In 1667, Patriarch Nikon had attempted to reform the church by introducing some changes into its texts and rituals. Since the Russian church had always claimed to be the protector of the most ancient and authentic Christian rituals, these reforms stirred up considerable unrest. A group that came to be known as the Old Believers resisted the patriarch's mandates, and late in the century thousands of them committed suicide rather than submit to the new rituals. The tragedy discouraged the church hierarchy from making any further substantial moves toward modern thought.

Peter wanted to make sure that the clergy did not blunder into another Old Believer schism or organize to oppose Westernization. Consequently, he abolished the office of patriarch in 1721 and created a synod headed by a layman, the Procurator General, to rule the church. This subjection of the church to state control was the most radical of Peter's breaks with tradition.

Reorganizing Domestic Administration. Peter modeled his domestic administration on Sweden's government. It used "colleges" composed of several persons, rather than departments headed by a single minister, to handle the collection of taxes, foreign affairs, war, and the economy. In 1711, Peter created a central senate of nine members who were to run the government when the tsar was in the field with the army. The chief purpose of Peter's reforms, like those of Prussia's kings, was to establish a bureaucracy that could support an efficient army.

Developing the Economy and Waging War. The economic projects Peter promoted were those that served the military. To get the men needed to staff them, young Russians were sent abroad for training, and western European craftsmen were invited to immigrate. Although few of Peter's enterprises met with much success, the iron industry he began in the Ural Mountains had by mid-century made Russia the largest iron producer in Europe.

Peter believed that Russia's economic development and its future political power depended on the acquisition of warm-water ports that would allow Russia to communicate with the West. To acquire these, the tsar went to war with the Ottoman Empire and with Sweden. In 1696, his armies drove the Turks from Azov on the Black Sea, but they held their prize only until 1711.

Achievements on the Swedish front were more lasting. In 1700, Russia invaded Swedish territory on the Baltic. When Charles XII, the erratic king of Sweden, failed to follow up a victory over Peter at Narva, Peter was able to regroup. In 1709, Charles renewed the war, and Peter defeated him at the Battle of Poltava. In 1721, the Peace of Nystad ended the "Great Northern War" and confirmed Russia's conquest of Estonia, Livonia, and part of Finland. Their ports provided Russia with access to the markets and capitals of western Europe.

Peter moved the capital of Russia to a new city he built on the Gulf of Finland, Saint Petersburg. Like other monarchs of his day, he followed the example of Louis XIV and constructed a kind of Versailles. The Russian aristocrats were compelled to move to Saint Petersburg, where the tsar could keep an eye on them. The city filled with lavish buildings modeled on those that housed the courts of western Europe. It lodged Russia's claim to a place among Western nations.

Despite Peter's determination to strengthen the Russian monarchy, he could not bring himself to secure its future. He quarreled with his only son, Alexis, and the heir to the throne died mysteriously in his father's prison. Although Peter claimed the right to name a successor, he had not done so when he died in 1725. Consequently, for over thirty years soldiers and nobles were free to thrust their candidates onto the throne. Peter had made Russia a modern state, but not a stable one.

By the second quarter of the eighteenth century, the major European powers were not yet nation-states in which the citizens felt themselves united by a shared sense of community, culture, language, and history. They were still monarchies in which the cohesion of the state was a function of the personality of the ruler and the personal relationships of great noble families. Monarchs had generally grown stronger, but nobles were still able to resist or obstruct the policies of their rulers.

In foreign affairs there were two long-term conflicts. In central Europe, Austria and Prussia contested leadership of Germany. In western Europe, France and Great Britain fought on two successive fronts. During the reign of Louis XIV, the French bid for dominance in Europe was at the heart of their struggle. During the eighteenth century, they dueled for control of overseas commerce. These conflicts were accompanied by economic and social developments that, in the long run, turned out to be the more significant contributors to the transformation of life in Europe.

~ Review Questions

1. Why did Britain and France remain leading powers while Spain and the United Netherlands declined?

2. How did the structure of British government change under the political leadership of Walpole? What were the chief sources of Walpole's political strength?

3. How was the Hohenzollern family able to forge a conglomerate of diverse land holdings into the state of Prussia? Who were the major personalities involved in this process? What were their individual contributions? Why was the military so important in Prussia?

4. How do the Hohenzollerns and the Habsburgs compare with respect to their approach to dealing with the problems that confronted their domains? Which family was more successful? Why? Why were the rulers of Sweden, the Ottoman Empire, and Poland less successful?

5. How did Russia become a great power? Why? How would you describe the character of Peter the Great? What were Russia's domestic problems before he came to power? What were his methods of reform? To what extent did he succeed? How were his reforms related to his military ambitions?

6. Can you support the claim that "Peter the Great was a rational ruler, interested in the welfare of his people"? Can you make a case for Peter as a bloody tyrant, concerned only with promoting his own glory?

~ Suggested Readings

J. BLACK, *Eighteenth Century Europe, 1700–1789* (1990). An excellent survey.

J. BREWER, *The Sinews of Power: War, Money and the English State, 1688–1783* (1989). An extremely important study of the financial basis of English power.

F. L. CARSTEN, *The Origins of Prussia* (1954). Discusses the groundwork laid by the Great Elector in the seventeenth century.

J. C. D. CLARK, *English Society, 1688–1832: Social Structure and Political Practice During the Ancien Regime* (1985). An important, controversial work that emphasizes the role of religion in English political life.

A. COBBAN, *A History of Modern France*, 2nd ed., vol. 1 (1961). A lively and opinionated volume.

N. DAVIS, *God's Playground*, vol. 1 (1991). Excellent on pre-partition Poland.

P. M. G. DICKSON, *Finance and Government Under Maria Theresa* (1987). A definitive work.

W. DOYLE, *The Old European Order, 1660–1800* (1992). The most thoughtful treatment of the subject.

P. DUKES, *The Making of Russian Absolutism: 1613–1801* (1982). An overview based on recent scholarship.

R. J. W. EVANS, *The Making of the Habsburg Monarchy, 1550–1700: An Interpretation* (1979). Places much emphasis on intellectual factors and the role of religion.

F. FORD, *Robe and Sword: The Regrouping of the French Aristocracy After Louis XIV* (1953). An important book for political, social, and intellectual history.

H. HOLBORN, *A History of Modern Germany, 1648–1840* (1966). The most comprehensive survey in English.

R. A. KANN and Z. V. DAVID, *The Peoples of the Eastern Habsburg Lands 1526–1918* (1984). A helpful overview of the subject.

R. K. MASSIE, *Peter the Great: His Life and His World* (1980). A good popular biography.

D. McKAY and H. M. SCOTT, *The Rise of the Great Powers, 1648–1815* (1983). Now the standard survey.

J. H. PLUMB, *The Growth of Political Stability in England, 1675–1725* (1969). An important interpretive work.

N. V. RIASANOVSKY, *A History of Russia*, 5th ed. (1992). The best one-volume introduction.

P. F. SUGAR, *Southeastern Europe Under Ottoman Rule, 1354–1804* (1977). An extremely clear presentation.

B. H. SUMNER, *Peter the Great and the Emergence of Russia* (1951). A classic study.

E. N. WILLIAMS, *The Ancien Régime in Europe* (1972). Very high quality state-by-state survey.

16

Society and Economy Under the Old Regime in the Eighteenth Century

---

KEY TOPICS IN THIS CHAPTER

~ The varied privileges and powers of Europe's aristocracies in the Old Regime and their efforts to increase their wealth

~ The plight of rural peasants

~ Family structure and family economy

~ The transformation of Europe's economy by the agricultural and industrial revolutions

~ Urban growth and the social tensions that accompanied it

~ The strains on the institutions of the Old Regime brought about by social change

---

The French Revolution of 1789 was a turning point in European history. The era that led up to it—which afterwards came to be called the ancien régime *("Old Regime")—was characterized by absolutist monarchies and an agrarian econ-* *omy that struggled to provide adequately for the general population.*

Tradition, hierarchy, corporateness, and privilege were the chief social characteristics of the Old Regime. Men and women saw themselves less as individu-

als than as members of groups, but society was not so rigid as to prevent all change. Both population and standards of living increased. Farming slowly became commercialized, more food was produced, and the Industrial Revolution began to make consumer goods more plentiful. The spirit of rationality that had fostered the Scientific Revolution of the seventeenth century thrived in the eighteenth—the "Age of Reason" or the "Enlightenment." On many fronts, the Old Regime nourished changes that brought its way of life to an end.

Major Features of Life in the Old Regime

Prerevolutionary Europe was dominated by aristocratic elites that possessed numerous inherited privileges and by established churches that were closely linked to the aristocracy and the state. At the other end of the social scale there was an urban labor force, usually organized by guilds, and a rural peasantry that labored under high taxes and feudal dues.

For most of these people, the past weighed more heavily on their minds than the future. Few persons considered innovation desirable—especially if it altered social relationships. When there was trouble, both nobles and peasants claimed only to be seeking the restoration of their traditional rights. The nobles tried to defend their autonomy in local government from intrusion by monarchical bureaucracies. The peasants wanted the maintenance or revival of customary manorial privileges (such as access to common lands, courts, or grievance procedures).

The traditional view of society that everyone claimed to be defending was a hierarchy of classes inherited from the Middle Ages, and during the eighteenth century medieval distinctions of rank and degree not only persisted but became more rigid. States or societies were seen as constructs composed of "communities," not as unions established by individual citizens. People had few rights as individuals. Their rights were generally those of the communities to which they belonged—groups such as villages, municipalities, noble families, clergy, guilds, universities, and parishes. Each of these had its own set of privileges—such as licenses to practice trades, opportunities to educate children for a particular occupation, entitlements to certain kinds of income, or exemptions from taxation or some especially humiliating punishment for crime.

With the exception of Britain, where there was some early industrial development, the economies of all eighteenth-century nations remained as tradition-bound as their social systems. The quality and quantity of the grain harvest was the single most important fact of life for everyone.

The Aristocracy

The eighteenth century was the great age for aristocracy. In most nations, aristocrats accounted for only 1 to 5 percent of the population, but they were the wealthiest and most influential of the social classes. Land was considered to be the most respectable investment for their money. But, over the century, aristocrats' investments became more diversified. Local governments and running their estates were their chief occupations, and in most countries they had their own house in a parliament, estate, or diet. Their conduct at royal courts defined high culture and set standards of artistic taste and polite behavior for the rest of society.

Although there were differences among the nobilities of various nations, aristocratic status everywhere was a matter of birth and inherited privilege. During the eighteenth century, nobles across Europe concluded that the growth of national monarchies threatened the privileges that defined their caste. The steps they took to defend themselves led to the "aristocratic resurgence." They protected their exclusiveness by making it more difficult to become a noble. They monopolized appointments to positions of power: the officer corps of the armies, the bureaucracies, the government ministries, and the church. They used aristocratically controlled institutions (the British Parliament, the French *parlements,* and the diets of Germany and the Habsburg Empire) to limit royal power. And they improved their financial position by expanding their exemption from taxation and by increasing their exploitation of the peasantry.

British Nobility

Great Britain had the smallest, wealthiest, best-defined, and most socially responsible aristocracy. It numbered about 400 families, the male heads of which constituted Parliament's House of Lords. Through use of patronage and local influence, aristocrats also dominated elections to the Commons. British nobles, however, had few exemptions or legal privileges, so the landowners who levied the taxes in Parliament also paid them.

Direct or indirect control of local government gave noble families immense influence, which they augmented by participating in commerce and the professions. Estates from which aristocrats drew rents ranged from a few thousand to 50,000 acres and accounted for about one-fourth of Britain's arable land. Nobles also invested in commerce, canals, urban real estate, mines, and industries. Since the eldest sons of aristocratic families inherited their titles and lands, younger sons had to find other careers. They went into commerce, the army, the professions, and the church. Thus most positions of leadership in society were claimed by men with noble connections.

French Nobility

The class structures of large continental nations like France were more complex than those of Britain. France had approximately 400,000 nobles. They were divided into two groups: nobles of the sword and nobles of the robe. The former derived their status from military service; the latter purchased their titles or earned them by serving in the bureaucracy. Nobles were further distinguished between those that belonged to the royal court at Versailles and those that did not. The court nobility reaped immense wealth from high office and came to monopolize appointments to the church, the army, and the bureaucracy. The provincial nobility (the *hobereaux*) could not compete. They were often little better off than wealthy peasants.

Despite these differences, hereditary privileges set all aristocrats off from everyone else in French society. There were many feudal dues that nobles could collect from their tenants, and nobles enjoyed exclusive hunting and fishing privileges. The nobles were liable for payment of a kind of income tax, the *vingtième* (the "twentieth"), but they were exempt from many other duties. They did not pay the *taille* (the levy on land that was the basic tax of the Old Regime), and they could not be called up for the royal *corvées* (the forced labor on public works required of peasants).

Eastern European Nobilities

East of the Elbe River, the customs associated with nobility were more complicated and more repressive. Here, aristocracy was linked with the military. In Poland, there were thousands of nobles *(szlachta)*. Most of them were relatively poor, but after 1741 they were exempt from taxes and until 1768 they had the right of life and death over their serfs. Political power was the prerogative of a few rich nobles who had immense estates.

In Austria and Hungary, the nobles, through their manorial courts, exercised judicial authority over the peasantry. They enjoyed various degrees of exemption from taxation, and a few—like the Hungarian Prince Esterhazy, who owned 10 million acres of land—were immensely rich.

In Prussia, Frederick the Great aided the status of the Junker nobles. Frederick drew his officers almost wholly from the Junker class, and he needed their enthusiastic support for his wars. The nation's bureaucracy was, like its army, managed by nobles. And in Prussia, as elsewhere in eastern Europe, nobles had extensive power over the serfs who lived on their states.

In eighteenth-century Russia, nobility was reinvented. Peter the Great (r. 1682–1725) tried to create a new and unified sense of identity among Russia's nobles by linking their status to state service. The nobles, however, resisted royal demands for compulsory service, and in 1736 Empress Anna (r. 1730–1740) reduced such service to twenty-five years. In 1762, Peter III (r. 1762) granted complete exemption to the greater nobles. And in 1785, Catherine the Great (r. 1762–1796) legally defined the privileges of the nobility in exchange for the assurance that nobles would serve the state voluntarily. These privileges included the right to transmit noble status to one's wife and children, judicial protection of noble rights and property, power over serfs, and exemption from personal taxes.

∾ The Land and Its Tillers

Land was the economic basis of eighteenth-century life. Well over three-fourths of all Europeans lived in the country, and few people ever traveled more than a few miles from their birthplaces. Except for the wealthier landowners, most people who lived on the land were poor and vulnerable to exploitation.

Europe's rural classes were subject to different degrees of social dependency. English tenants and most French cultivators were free persons. The serfs of Germany, Austria, and Russia, who were legally bound to particular plots of land and particular lords, were not. Everywhere, by controlling local government and courts, the class that owned the land dominated the class that tilled it.

Obligations of Peasants

The power of landlords increased as one moved across Europe from west to east. Although there were some serfs in eastern France, most French peasants owned a bit of land. Few possessed enough to support their families, and most had to rent land from a lord. This obligated them to render feudal dues. Nearly all French peasants were subject to *banalités*—which included such obligations as renting their lord's mill to grind their grain and his oven to bake their bread. Their lord could also requisition a number of days of their labor each year.

In Prussia and the Habsburg Empire, despite attempts by the monarchies late in the century to enact reforms, landlords exercised almost complete control over serfs.

In parts of southeastern Europe dominated by the Ottoman Empire, peasants were technically free, but were, in practice, dependent on their lords. An estate's owner was often an absentee whose property was managed by an overseer. During the seventeenth and eighteenth centuries, these estates began more and more to be run as commercial enterprises specializing in cash crops. Scarcity of labor more than legal rights gave peasants some independence, for oppressed peasants could always migrate from one landlord to another who offered them better conditions. When, however, political disorder began to spread from the capital at Istanbul into the Balkan peninsula in the seventeenth century, peasants had to turn to their landlords for protection from bandits and rebels. As in medieval times, the manor house of the local landowner became the peasants' refuge. Landlords also controlled the housing and tools peasants needed and furnished their seed grain. Thus, despite their legal freedoms, Balkan peasants became increasingly dependent on their landlords.

Serfs were worst off in Russia. Russian nobles reckoned their wealth by the number of "souls" (that is, male serfs) they owned rather than by the acreage they possessed. Serfs were mere economic commodities. Landlords could demand as many as six days a week of labor from them, and lords had the right to punish serfs as they saw fit. Serfs had no legal recourse against the whims of lords, and there was little to distinguish Russian serfdom from slavery.

Peasant Rebellions

The czars contributed to the degradation of Russia's serfs. Peter the Great gave whole villages to favored nobles, and Catherine the Great confirmed the authority of the nobles over their serfs in exchange for the nobles' political cooperation. Between 1762 and 1769, abuse of serfs spawned over fifty peasant revolts. The brutal suppression of the greatest of these uprisings, Pugachev's Rebellion—a conflict (1773–1775) named for its instigator, Emelyan Pugachev (1726–1775)—doomed for a generation any attempt to improve the condition of the serfs. Pugachev's was the largest peasant uprising of the century, but smaller disturbances took place in Bohemia in 1775, in Transylvania in 1784, in Moravia in 1786, and in Austria in 1789. There were almost no revolts in western Europe, but England experienced numerous rural riots.

The goals of the peasant uprisings were fundamentally conservative. Rural laborers directed their wrath more against property than persons, and they fought to defend traditional customs against practices they considered innovations—things such as unfair pricing, new or increased feudal dues, changes in methods of payment or land use, unjust officials, or brutal overseers and landlords. No one advocated a radical restructuring of society to abolish traditional class structures.

~ Family Structures and the Family Economy

Households

In preindustrial Europe, the family household was the basic unit of production and consumption. Few shops or farms employed more than a handful of people who did not belong to the families of their owners. Therefore, the structure of the family determined the structure of the economy.

Northwestern Europe. Different forms of family organization evolved in different parts of Europe. In northwestern Europe, the household centered on the nuclear family: a married couple, their younger children, and their servants. Except for a few wealthy families, households were small (five or six members). High mortality and late marriage meant that three generations seldom survived to share the same home. Children lived with their parents only until their early teens. Then they left home to enter the work force—usually as servants who lived and worked in another household. A child of a skilled artisan might remain with his or her parents to learn a valuable skill, but only rarely would more than one child do so. Children's labor was more remunerative outside the home.

The word "servant" in this context may be misleading. It does not refer to someone who provides personal services for the wealthy. A servant in preindustrial Europe was a person hired to work for a household in exchange for room, board, and wages. The servant was usually young and by no means socially inferior to his or her employer. Normally the servant was an integral part of the household and ate with the family. Being a servant for several years—often as many as eight or ten—made it possible for young people to acquire training in productive skills and to accumulate the savings needed to strike out on their own.

These young men and women eventually married. But instead of returning to their parental households, they set up independent establishments in new places (a marriage pattern called *neolocalism*). Since it took them some time to amass the property they needed to fund a household, they married late—men after age twenty-six; women, twenty-three. The new couple usually had children as soon after marriage as possible. Although premarital sexual relations were common and brides were often pregnant, births out of wedlock were rare.

Eastern Europe. As one moved eastward across the continent, the structure of the household and the pattern of marriage changed. Eastern European households tended to be larger (nine to twenty members) than those of the west, for young couples joined one of their parental households rather than setting up on their own. Consequently, men and women were able to marry at a much younger age—usually before twenty. It was not unusual, especially among Russian serfs, for wives to be older than their husbands and for three or perhaps four generations of family members to live together.

Landholding patterns in eastern Europe contributed to the district's characteristic family organization. Lords who wanted to ensure an adequate labor force to work their lands shaped peasant families. In Poland, for example, landlords could forbid marriage between their own serfs and those from another estate, and they could require widows and widowers to remarry. Polish landlords frowned on the hiring of free laborers (the west's "servants"). This cut off individuals from employment that might have enabled them to acquire capital to set up independent households. In Russia, landlords ordered the families of young people to arrange early marriages for them within their villages. Single-generation households were discouraged, for a death or serious illness in such a household might mean that the land assigned to it would go out of cultivation.

The Family Economy

Throughout Europe, almost everyone lived in a household, for it was virtually impossible for ordinary people to support themselves independently. People living outside a household were viewed with suspicion. Some were considered a disruptive, possibly criminal, element in society. Others were resented as potential beggars who would become drains on community resources.

Everyone in a household worked. Since frequent poor harvests and economic slumps prevented most households from accumulating a surplus to fall back on, they could not afford idle members. The income they produced was used to sustain the household, not to profit individuals. Few families in western Europe had enough land to support themselves from farming alone. One or more of their members usually worked elsewhere and sent wages home.

Priscilla Wakefield Demands More Occupations Be Opened to Women

At the end of the eighteenth century, a number of English women writers began to demand a wider life for women. Priscilla Wakefield was among such authors. She was concerned that women found themselves only able to pursue occupations that paid poorly. Often they were excluded from work on the grounds of their alleged physical weakness. She also believed that women should receive equal wages for equal work. Many of the issues she raised have yet to be adequately addressed on behalf of women.

꘏ Can you infer from this selection what arguments were used at the end of the eighteenth century to limit the fields of employment open to women? Why were women's wages lower than those of men for comparable work? What occupations traditionally filled by men does Wakefield believe women might also pursue?

Another heavy discouragement to the industry of women, is the inequality of the reward of their labor, compared with that of men; an injustice which pervades every species of employment performed by both sexes.

In employments which depend on bodily strength, the distinction is just; for it cannot be pretended that the generality of women can earn as much as men, when the produce of their labor is the result of corporeal exertion; but it is a subject of great regret, that this inequality should prevail even where an equal share of skill and application is exerted. Male stay-makers, mantua-makers, and hair-dressers, are better paid than female artists of the same professions; but surely it will never be urged as an apology for this disproportion, that women are not as

Fathers of peasant families often became migrant workers and left the burden of tilling the family farm to their wives and younger children.

A family economy also characterized life for skilled urban artisans. The father of the household was usually its chief craftsman. He might employ one or more servants, but would expect his children to work also. His eldest child was usually trained in his trade. His wife often sold his wares or opened a small shop of her own. Wives of merchants often ran their husbands' businesses, especially when their husbands were traveling. If business was poor, family members would look for outside employment, not to support themselves as individuals but to ensure the survival of the family unit.

In western Europe, the death of a father often meant disaster for his household, for its economic life usually centered on his land or skills. Sometimes a widow or children were prepared to take over a farm or business, but widows usually kept their households from foundering by remarrying quickly. High mortality rates meant that many households were composed of spouses and children who had survived the breakup of earlier families. They were the lucky ones, for households often simply dissolved. Widows who could not

capable of making stays, gowns, dressing hair, and similar arts, as men; if they are not superior to them, it can only be accounted for upon this principle, that the prices they receive for their labor are not sufficient to repay them for the expense of qualifying themselves for their business; and that they sink under the mortification of being regarded as artisans of inferior estimation . . . .

Besides these employments which are commonly performed by women, and those already shown to be suitable for such persons as are above the condition of hard labor, there are some professions and trades customarily in the hands of men, which might be conveniently exercised by either sex. Watchmaking, requiring more ingenuity than strength, seems peculiarly adapted to women; as do many parts of the business of stationer, particularly, ruling account books or making pens. The compounding of medicines in an apothecary's shop, requires no other talents than care and exactness; and if opening a vein occasionally be a indispensable requisite, a

woman may acquire the capacity of doing it, for those of her own sex at least, without any reasonable objection. . . . Pastry and confectionery appear particularly consonant to the habits of women, though generally performed by men; perhaps the heat of the ovens, and the strength requisite to fill and empty them, may render male assistants necessary; but certain women are most eligible to mix up the ingredients, and prepare the various kinds of cakes for baking. Light turnery and toy-making depend more upon dexterity and invention than force, and are therefore suitable work for women and children. . . .

Farming, as far as respects the theory, is commensurate with the powers of the female mind: nor is the practice of inspecting agricultural processes incompatible with the delicacy of their frames if their constitution be good.

Priscilla Wakefield, Reflections on the Present Condition of the Female Sex *(1798), (London: 1817), pp. 125–127; as quoted in Bridget Hill, ed.,* Eighteenth-Century Women: An Anthology *(London: George Allen & Unwin, 1984), pp. 227–228.*

remarry or support themselves became dependent on charity or on relatives. Their children entered the work force at an unusually early age or resorted to crime and begging.

The family economy of eastern Europe provided greater security. There were fewer artisan and merchant households and far less geographical mobility in the East than in the West. Also, serfdom, rural village structures, and multigenerational families created a broader base of support for households.

Women and the Family Economy

For women, marriage was an economic necessity. Other than aristocrats and members of religious orders, few women could support themselves. In order to survive, a woman helped maintain her parents' household until she devised a means of getting a household of her own. The bearing and rearing of children was a means to this end.

By the age of seven, a girl would have begun to help with household work. She would remain in her parents' home as long as her labor elsewhere was not more remunerative to her family. An artisan's daughter, who was learning and practicing a valuable skill, might stay with her parents until marriage. But a farm girl, whose tasks could be assumed by her parents and brothers, usually left home between the ages of twelve and fourteen. She might find employment on another farm, but more often she would migrate to a nearby town to become a servant.

A young woman's chief goal was to accumulate sufficient capital for a dowry. Marriage within the family economy was a joint economic undertaking. Both brides and grooms were expected to contribute capital toward the establishment of their new households. It might take a young woman ten years or more to accumulate a dowry.

Once married, a woman's chief concern was not homemaking or child rearing, but coping with economic pressures. She and her husband were engaged in a constant struggle to ensure an adequate food supply for their household. Couples practiced birth control to limit family size. (The most common method was *coitus interruptus.* Infants were often turned over to wet-nurses so that their mothers could return to work.

The work of a married woman was in many ways a function of her husband's occupation. In the few peasant households that possessed enough land to support themselves, wives were their husbands' chief assistants. In most cases, however, men had to find outside employment to supplement the income from their land, and women had to assume primary responsibility for plowing, planting, and harvesting. An artisan or merchant's wife might actively participate in her husband's trade or manufacturing enterprise. And when her husband died, she might take over the business or hire an artisan to work under her management.

Despite the essential economic contributions women made to their households, many occupations and professions were closed to them because of their gender. Women at all levels of society had fewer opportunities for education than men, and they usually received lower wages than men for the same work.

Children and the World of the Family Economy

For all women, childbirth was a time of fear and personal vulnerability. Contagious diseases endangered both mother and child, and midwives were not universally skillful. Most mothers and newborn infants faced the challenges of immense poverty and wretched housing. Some women nursed their own infants, but many surrendered them at birth to wet-nurses who took them away and kept them for months or years. Convenience encouraged this practice among the wealthy, but economic necessity dictated it for the poor. The demands of the family economy did not permit a woman to devote herself entirely to rearing a child.

The birth of a child was not always welcome. It might be born to an unwed mother, or it might represent another economic burden on an already hard-pressed household. In some places, records show a clear relationship between rising food prices and increasing numbers of abandoned children.

Unwanted births sometimes led to infanticide. But during the late seventeenth and the early eighteenth centuries, society developed an increased sense of responsibility for abandoned children. The size and number of foundling hospitals expanded. Early in the eighteenth century, for instance, an average of 1,700 children a year were being admitted to the Paris Foundling Hospital. But in 1772, the peak year, the orphanage accepted 7,676 children. There was not enough space in institutions to care for all who were in need. In some cases, hospitals were compelled to use a lottery to choose children for admission. Parents would sometimes leave personal tokens on an abandoned baby in the vain hope that they might one day be able to reclaim it. But leaving a child at a foundling hospital did not guarantee its survival. At the hospital in Paris, only about 10 percent of children lived to the age of ten.

The eighteenth century marked the beginning of the modern awareness of the importance of childhood and gave unprecedented attention to the education of children. Although the increasing demands of the job market made literacy more valuable and increased literacy rates during the century, most Europeans remained illiterate. Not until the late nineteenth century, when nations became aware of the importance of a trained citizenry, did formal schooling become a routine childhood experience.

～ The Revolution in Agriculture

The chief concern of traditional peasant society was the maintenance of stable conditions that would ensure the food supply. Across Europe, the tillers of the soil resisted change. Traditional methods of cultivation were proven to work; new means involved risks that few were prepared to take. Failure of a harvest meant not only hardship but death from either outright starvation or protracted debility. Even small increases in the cost of food could exert heavy pressure on peasant or artisan families.

During the eighteenth century, population growth slowly but steadily drove up the price of bread, the staple food of the poor. The rise in grain prices benefited landowners and the wealthier peasants who had surplus grain to sell. But inflation put serious pressure on consumers, the urban laborers, and the peasants with small farms.

Rising grain prices encouraged an Agricultural Revolution as landlords experimented with techniques to increase yields. But the new commercialized agriculture frightened the peasants by challenging the traditional means of production on which they relied. When the rural poor rose in revolt, governments, hungry for taxes and dependent on the nobility, called out armies to defend the agents of change.

New Crops and New Methods

The drive to improve agricultural production began in the Low Countries during the sixteenth and seventeenth centuries. It was inspired by the pressures of growing population and a shortage of land. Dutch agriculturalists devised better ways to build dikes and to drain land, and they experimented with new crops that would increase the supply of animal fodder and restore the soil.

English landlords led the drive for agricultural development in the eighteenth century. They originated a few new farming methods and popularized ideas developed in the Low Countries. They increased yields by promoting the use of iron plows to turn earth deeply and by planting wheat with a drill rather than by casting. They used fertilizers to make sandy soil productive. They developed crop rotation—using wheat, turnips, barley, and clover—to replace the fallow field method of cultivation. Instead of "resting" land, a field was planted with a crop that restored the soil and produced animal fodder. Additional fodder meant that more livestock could be raised and fed during the winter to ensure a year-round supply of meat. And larger numbers of animals meant increased quantities of manure available as fertilizer for production of grain.

Enclosure. Many agricultural innovations were incompatible with the way land had traditionally been used in England. Small cultivators who lived in villages did most of the farming. Each of them tilled an assortment of strips scattered about the fields belonging to a village. Much of the land was left fallow and unproductive each year in order to maintain its fertility. Animals grazed on common land in the summer and on the stubble of the harvest in the winter. Since decisions about farming were made communally, the system discouraged innovation and favored the poorer farmers who needed the common land and stubble fields for their animals. The methods of traditional production aimed at a steady but not a growing supply of food.

In 1700, approximately half the arable land in England was farmed by this method. But during the second half of the century, the rising price of wheat encouraged landlords to consolidate or "enclose" their lands to increase production. Enclosure was a more rational, commercial approach to land use. But the process involved fencing common lands, reclaiming untilled waste, and combining strips into block fields. These procedures created turmoil in the economic and social life of the countryside and prompted riots.

Because many English farmers either owned their strips or rented them with rights that amounted to ownership, the great landlords had to resort to parliamentary acts to legalize the enclosure of the land that their families had long rented to tenant farmers. Between 1761 and 1792, almost 500,000 acres were enclosed through acts of Parliament, and in 1801 a general enclosure act streamlined the process.

The enclosures permitted the expansion of both farming and innovation and thus increased food production. But they also disrupted small traditional communities. Some people were forced off the land, but enclosures did not depopulate the countryside. In some counties, where new soil came into production and services subsidiary to farming expanded, population increased.

The enclosure movement did not create the labor force needed for the British Industrial Revolution, but it did demonstrate the new entrepreneurial or capitalistic attitude that was emerging in English society. Commercialization of agriculture, which spread from Britain slowly across the continent during the next century, strained the paternal relationship that had long existed between the governing and governed classes. In the past, landlords had looked after the welfare of the lower orders—accepting price controls or waiving rents during depressed periods. But as landlords became increasingly concerned about profits, they abandoned the peasants to the mercy of the marketplace.

Eastern Europe's Response. The Agricultural Revolution had its greatest impact west of the Elbe. In Prussia, Austria, Poland, and Russia, few improvements were made in farming, for nothing in the relationship of the serfs to their lords encouraged innovation. Landlords or their agents, not village councils, directed farm management. The great landowners sought to squeeze more labor from their serfs rather than greater productivity from their soil. Their chief method of increasing production was to bring previously untilled lands under the plow. The only change in agriculture that improved nutrition was the introduction of maize and the potato.

Population Expansion

The population explosion that the world contends with today began in the eighteenth century. Previously, when Europe experienced dramatic increases in population, balance was restored by plagues, wars, or famine. But beginning in the second quarter of the eighteenth century, population began to increase despite these calamities.

In 1700 Europe's population, excluding the European provinces of the Ottoman Empire, was probably between 100 million and 120 million. By 1800, there were almost 190 million, and by 1850, 260 million. The population of England and Wales rose from 6 million in 1750 to over 10 million in 1800. France grew from 18 million in 1715, to approximately 26 million in 1789. Russia's population increased from 19 million in 1722 to 29 million in 1766. Such extraordinary sustained growth put new demands on all resources and considerable pressure on existing social organization.

Population expanded across the continent in both rural and urban districts. No one is certain what caused its growth. There was a decline in the death rate, for there were fewer wars and fewer epidemics in the eighteenth century. Hygiene and sanitation improved. But the most important factor may have been changes in the food supply. Grain production expanded, and, more important, the potato began to be cultivated. A product of the New World, the potato came into widespread European production during the eighteenth century. It was a significant new product, for a single acre of land could produce enough potatoes to feed a peasant family for an entire year. More food meant that more children survived to adulthood to rear children of their own.

The impact of the population explosion can hardly be overestimated. It increased demands for food, goods, jobs, and services. It provided a new pool of labor. It forced traditional modes of production and life to be revised. It prompted migration as economies were reorganized, and it caused more people to become socially and politically discontent. The world of the Old Regime literally outgrew its traditional bounds.

～ The Industrial Revolution of the Eighteenth Century

The industrialization of Europe's economy began in the second half of the eighteenth century. Early in the nineteenth century the movement, which was led by Britain, began to be called the *Industrial Revolution*—the economic equivalent of a great political revolution that took place in France in the 1790s.

Industrialization wrought numerous revolutionary changes. It increased humanity's control over the forces of nature and made possible the production of more goods and services than ever before. It met existing consumer demands while creating new ones. It raised standards of living, and it ended the widespread poverty that Europeans had always taken for granted. It inaugurated an era of unprecedented, sustained economic growth. Previously, periods of growth alternated with periods of stagnation. But since the late eighteenth century, the expansion of the Western economy has been relatively uninterrupted.

The Industrial Revolution exacted a high social cost. New means of production demanded new skills, new discipline in work, and a large labor force. And by the middle of the nineteenth century, it was apparent that industrialization was causing unanticipated problems with the environment.

A Revolution in Consumption

The most visible aspect of the Industrial Revolution was the invention of machinery, the establishment of factories, and the creation of a new kind of work force. But intangible changes in attitudes and expectations were behind these things. Early in the eighteenth century, an unprecedented demand for the relatively humble goods of everyday life—clothing, buttons, toys, china, furniture, rugs, kitchen utensils, candlesticks, brassware, silverware, pewterware, glassware, watches, jewelry, soap, beer, wines, and foodstuffs—sparked the ingenuity of designers and inventors. As each consumer expectation was met, a new one took its place, and the demands of the market motivated the development of an ever more productive industrialized economy.

Numerous factors contributed to the growth of a new, consumer-oriented economy. During the seventeenth century, the Dutch had enjoyed enormous prosperity that enabled them to pioneer a society centered on consumption. In the eighteenth century, increasing numbers of people came to have more

Consumption of all forms of goods increased greatly in the eighteenth century. This engraving illustrates a shop, probably in Paris. Here women, working apparently for a woman manager, are making dresses and hats to meet the demands of the fashion trade. [Bildarchiv Preussischer Kulturbesitz]

disposable income—possibly because of the improvements taking place in agriculture. This enabled them to buy more consumer goods than previous generations. As a result, an economy was created that grew by expanding domestic markets in Europe, not by exporting things to foreign markets.

These changes were not entirely spontaneous. People had to be persuaded that they needed or wanted new consumer goods, and entrepreneurs did this by developing new methods of marketing. The career of the porcelain manufacturer Josiah Wedgwood (1730–1795) illustrates how this was done. He first produced luxury goods that attracted the royal family and the aristocracy. Once he had gained their business, he produced a less expensive version of his chinaware for middle-class customers. He used advertising. He opened showrooms. He sent out traveling salesmen with samples and catalogues of his wares. There seemed to be no limit to the markets for different kinds of consumer goods that could be stimulated when advertising pandered to the desire to emulate one's social superiors. Manufacturers also discovered that by changing styles they could increase demand. The desire to have the latest in fashions and inventions led people to return to the market again and again.

Increasing consumption quietly, but steadily, blurred the edges of social distinctions. As more people saw others consuming, human nature led them to seek to imitate that new consumption. Fashion publications made all levels of society aware of new styles, which could be quickly and inexpensively copied. Even servants began to dress well if not luxuriously. New foods and beverages created a demand for new kinds of dishware for the home. New modes of leisure appeared that required new things for their enjoyment. New standards for polite living were described in print and quickly disseminated to all parts of a nation, and its people were encouraged to define their status by the quality and quantity of the goods they consumed.

The consumer economy has always had its critics. Yet ever-increasing consumption has become a hallmark of modern life. It would be difficult to overestimate the importance of the desire for consumer goods and an increasing material standard of living in modern communities. Availability of consumer goods has become the hallmark of a nation's prosperity, and the lack of these things—as much as the absence of civil liberties—lies behind increasing social tensions in many societies.

Industrial Leadership of Great Britain

Great Britain inaugurated the Industrial Revolution and maintained industrial leadership in Europe into the middle of the nineteenth century. Its industrialization, which was promoted by increasing domestic demand for goods and by the markets that existed in its North American colonies, was made possible by a fortunate combination of factors.

England took the lead in inventing the consumer society. The newspapers that thrived in Britain facilitated the advertising that created consumer demand. Eighteenth-century London, the largest city in Europe, established the dominant standards for fashion and taste, and the structure of British society allowed people to imitate the lifestyles of their superiors. As a result, the British were the first to develop the love affair with fads and fashions that creates insatiable appetites for new goods.

Britain, the single largest free-trade area in Europe, had an excellent infrastructure: good roads and waterways without internal tolls or other trade barriers. The country was endowed with natural resources: agriculture, coal, and iron ore. It was politically stable. The property rights of its citizens were secure. Sound systems of banking and credit created a stable climate for investment. Taxes were high, but collection was efficient and fair. Parliament regulated taxation so that all social classes and regions of the nation paid the same dues. British society was also relatively mobile. The aristocracy accepted into its ranks entrepreneurs who amassed large fortunes. Even persons of wealth who were not admitted to the aristocracy enjoyed social prominence and political influence.

New Methods of Textile Production.   Textile manufacturers pioneered the Industrial Revolution. Their enterprise evolved in the country, not in cities. Eighteenth-century society was primarily agricultural, and the peasant family was the basic unit of economic production. Although peasants were agricultural workers, they could participate in other kinds of industries while they farmed. They tilled the land in spring and summer and spun thread or wove textiles in the winter. Under what is termed the "domestic" or "putting-out" system, urban textile merchants bought wool or other unfinished fibers and sent it to the homes of peasants to be spun into thread. Other peasants wove that thread into cloth and returned it to the merchants who marketed it. A spinning wheel or handloom was standard equipment in thousands of peasant cottages from Ireland to Austria. Sometimes peasants owned wheels and looms, but by the middle of the century the merchant capitalist usually provided the machinery as well as the raw material.

Textile production remained part of the family economy in Britain and on the continent well into the nineteenth century. By the middle of the eighteenth century, however, the demand for cotton textiles was outstripping home production and prompting the invention of machines that transformed the industry.

Thanks to the invention of the flying shuttle in the 1730s, weavers had the technical capacity to produce the quantity of cotton fabric demanded. Spinners, however, could not provide them with enough thread until 1765, when James Hargreaves (d. 1778) invented the spinning jenny. This device originally allowed 16 spindles of thread to be spun simultaneously. By the close of the century its capacity had been increased to 120 spindles.

The spinning jenny broke the bottleneck between the productive capacity of spinners and weavers, but it was still a machine intended for use in a cottage. The invention that took cotton textile manufacture out of the home and put it into the factory was Richard Arkwright's (1732–1792) water frame, patented in 1769. This was a water-powered device that produced a 100 percent cotton fabric rather than the standard earlier blend of cotton and linen. When Arkwright lost his patent rights, other manufacturers hastened to appropriate his invention. Domestic production lessened as factories sprang up in the countryside near streams that provided the necessary waterpower. Cotton output increased by 800 percent between 1780 and 1800. By 1815, cotton composed 40 percent of the value of British domestic exports. By 1830, it was just over 50 percent.

The Industrial Revolution had commenced in earnest by the 1780s, but the full economic and social ramifications of the productive capacity it unleashed were not felt until the early nineteenth century. The expansion of industry and the incorporation of new inventions took place slowly. For example, although Edmund Cartwright (1743–1822) invented the power loom in the late 1780s, it was not until the 1830s that there were more power-loom weavers than hand-loom weavers in Britain. Nor did all of the social ramifications of industrialism appear immediately. The first cotton mills used waterpower, were located in the country, and rarely employed more than two dozen workers. Not until late in the century, after James Watt (1736–1819) perfected the steam engine (1769) and adapted it to textile machinery, could factories be located in cities. The steam engine made possible the modern combination of urbanization with industrialization.

The Steam Engine. The steam engine permitted almost all areas of production to be industrialized, because it provided a new source of energy. For the first time in history, people had at their disposal a steady and essentially unlimited source of inanimate power. Unlike engines moved by water, wind, animals, and people, the coal- or wood-fed steam engine was portable, dependable, and inexhaustible. Its potential uses were legion.

Early in the eighteenth century, Thomas Newcomen had invented the first engine using steam power. It was driven by injecting steam into a cylinder to push up a piston and then condensing the steam to allow the piston to fall back. The machine was heavy and energy inefficient, but it was widely used in Britain to pump water out of coal and tin mines.

During the 1760s James Watt, a Scottish engineer, began to experiment with the Newcomen machine. He achieved much greater efficiency by separating the condenser from the piston and the cylinder. But his design required precise metalwork in order to be realized. Matthew Boulton, a successful toy and button manufacturer, and John Wilkinson, a cannon manufacturer, helped him solve the technical problems. And in 1776, a Watt steam engine found its first commercial application: pumping water from mines in Cornwall.

Watt retained exclusive patent rights until 1800 and was reluctant to make changes in his invention. As a result, the use of the steam engine spread slowly. Boulton eventually persuaded him to make improvements that allowed the engines to be used not only for pumping but also for running cotton mills. By the early nineteenth century, the steam engine had become the prime mover in every industry and had begun to transform transportation.

Iron Production. The manufacture of high-quality iron has been basic to modern industrial development. It is the chief material used in all heavy industry and transportation. In the early eighteenth century, British iron-makers produced somewhat less than 25,000 tons annually. Technical problems limited their output. They used charcoal to smelt ore. Charcoal, which was derived from Britain's diminishing forests, was expensive and did not easily reach ideal temperatures. This was unfortunate, for it was also difficult to generate the blasts of air needed to generate the heat of a smelting furnace.

Things improved once ironmakers switched to coke, a charcoal-like derivative of coal, and once the steam engine was adapted to power blast furnaces. Coke was cheap, for Britain had large coal deposits. And the steam engine had the felicitous effect of improving iron production while increasing demand for iron.

In 1784, Henry Cort (1740–1800) introduced a new "puddling" process; that is, a new method for melting and stirring ore. Cort's technique removed more slag (the impurities that bubble to the top of a pot of molten ore) and produced better iron. Cort also developed a rolling mill that formed molten metal into continuous bars, rails, or sheets. Previously, metal had to be shaped by pounding. The result was a better, more versatile product at a lower cost. By the early nineteenth century, Britain was producing over a million tons annually.

～ Cities

Remarkable changes occurred in urban areas between 1500 and 1800. In 1500, Europe (excluding Hungary and Russia) had only 156 cities whose populations reached or exceeded 10,000. Only 4 of those cities (Paris, Milan, Venice, and Naples) were larger than 100,000. By 1800, there were about 363 cities of 10,000 or more inhabitants, and 17 had populations larger than 100,000. The percentage of Europe's people living in urban areas had risen from about 5 percent to 9 percent, and urban concentration in northern Europe had surpassed that of the south.

Patterns of Preindustrial Urbanization

Growth in towns was particularly rapid in the eighteenth century—a phenomenon not unrelated to the political and social upheavals of the era. London in 1700 had about 700,000 inhabitants. By 1800, it had almost 1 million. At the time, Paris had over 500,000 inhabitants. Berlin's population tripled during the century, reaching 170,000. Warsaw had almost 120,000 in 1794. Saint Petersburg, which did not exist until 1703, grew to over 250,000 inhabitants by the end of the century.

These raw figures conceal significant changes that took place in how cities grew and how population distributed itself. Even in France and Great Britain, probably somewhat less than 20 percent of the population lived in cities, and the town of 10,000 inhabitants was much more common than the giant urban center. From 1500 to 1750, most major urban expansion took place within established large cities. After 1750, the pattern changed. New cities were founded, and there was rapid growth of the older, smaller cities.

Growth of Capitals and Ports. The cities that grew most vigorously from 1600 to 1750 were capitals and ports. They profited from the development of the monarchical state and the burgeoning of its bureaucracies, armies, courts, and support personnel. The growth of port cities reflected the expansion of Europe's overseas trade—most especially the Atlantic routes. Except for Manchester in England and Lyons in France, the great urban conglomerates were not centers of industrial manufacture.

During this period (1600 to 1750), cities with populations of fewer than 40,000 inhabitants declined. Rural labor was cheaper than urban labor, and expansion of the putting-out system transferred to the countryside much production that had occurred in medieval cities.

Emergence of New Cities and Growth of Small Towns. In the middle of the eighteenth century, a new pattern emerged that continued into the nineteenth century. The growth of existing large cities slowed while new cities emerged and smaller cities expanded. Several factors were at work. There was the general overall population increase. The early stages of the Industrial Revolution, which was a rural phenomenon, fostered the growth of smaller towns and cities. And factory organization began to create concentrations of population in new places. Even in places where there was little industrialization, the increasing prosperity of European agriculture promoted urban development.

Urban Classes

The urban rich and poor were visibly segregated. The moneyed classes lived in fashionable townhouses arranged around parks. The poorest town dwellers usually congregated along the rivers. Small merchants and craftsmen lived above their shops, and whole families might share a single room. There was little pure water. Sanitary facilities that are now taken for granted were still unknown. Cattle, pigs, goats, and other animals wandered the streets. All the contemporary descriptions of Europe's eighteenth-century cities emphasize the grace and beauty of the homes of the wealthy and the dirt and stench that prevailed elsewhere. It did not require the factories of the Industrial Revolution to make cities into hellholes for the poor and the dispossessed.

Poverty was usually worse in the countryside, but its effects—crime, prostitution, vagrancy, begging, and alcoholism—were more visible in cities. So were its punishments. Public tortures and executions of criminals were frequent spectacles in all of Europe's cities. Many a young person from the countryside migrated to a city in search of a better life, only to find degradation and death. The harsh reality of the drama of London's streets at mid-century has been graphically depicted by a keen observer, the artist William Hogarth (1697–1764).

The Upper Classes. At the top of the urban social scale stood a small group of nobles, great merchants, bankers, financiers, clergy, and government officials. These men (and they were always men) controlled the town. Rights of self-government enshrined in a royal charter usually gave a city corporation or town council authority to select its own members. In a few cities on the continent, artisan guilds controlled town councils, but it was more common for city governments to be run by self-perpetuating oligarchies, the nobles and the wealthiest commercial families.

The Middle Class. A city's most dynamic residents were the persons traditionally regarded as middle class (the *bourgeoisie*): the smaller merchants, tradesmen, bankers, and professional people. The middle class was much less clearly defined than the nobility, for it was not a single, cohesive entity. Several diverse "middling" groups occupied the middle, and some were at odds with others. Professionals, for instance, might resent those who drew their incomes from commerce. Less wealthy bourgeoisie envied richer colleagues who aspired to mix with the nobility.

Middle-class people did not draw their incomes from the land. As merchants, lawyers, or small factory owners, they were the beneficiaries of their era's expanding trade and commerce. They concentrated on amassing capital and using it to improve their social standing. They saw themselves as energetic, productive workers who supported reform, change, and legislation that fostered economic growth. They were both contemptuous and envious of the "idle" aristocracy whose manners they imitated.

The middle class led the revolution in consumption. As owners of factories and of wholesale and retail businesses, they produced and sold goods for a consumer market in which they were the chief customers. They might not enjoy the titles and social prestige of the nobility, but they could emulate the material comfort and prosperity of the aristocratic lifestyle.

The relationship between the middle class and the aristocracy was complicated. Nobles, especially in England and France, augmented their inherited wealth by embracing the commercial spirit. Like good business persons, they improved the cultivation of their lands and invested in entrepreneurial ventures. Wealthy members of the middle class, on the other hand, imitated the early customs of the nobility by putting their money into landed estates. However, there was much tension between the two groups. What was at issue between them was not a clash over values or social ideals, but a quarrel over sharing power. The upward social mobility of the bourgeoisie threatened the exclusive privileges of the nobles. They defended themselves by using their control of government bureaucracies and government patronage to frustrate the schemes of traders, bankers, manufacturers, and lawyers.

If the urban middle class envied the nobility, it feared the lower orders. The poor were a potentially violent element in society; a threat to property; and, as objects of charity, a drain on community resources.

Artisans. The lower classes were much more varied than either the aristocracy or the middle class cared to admit. Shopkeepers, artisans, and wage earners composed the single largest group in any city. They had their own culture, values, and institutions, and, like the peasants, they were in many respects conservative. Their economic position was very vulnerable, but they also contributed to the revolution in consumption. They could buy more goods than the poor of earlier generations, and many of them tried to copy the domestic consumption of the middle class.

The lives of artisans and shopkeepers centered on their work and their neighborhoods. They usually lived near or at their places of employment—shops with fewer than a half-dozen laborers. The medieval guild system still existed, but it had lost much of its power. Guilds endorsed conservative policies. Rather than promoting economic growth or innovation, they tried to preserve the jobs of their members by reducing competition and preventing too many people from learning a particular trade. The guilds were artisans' chief protection against the operation of the commercial market. They were particularly strong in central Europe.

The Urban Riot

The conservative outlook of the artisan class shaped its understanding of social and economic justice. The poor accepted grim conditions that appeared to be established and inevitable. They objected to changes that might increase their burdens and reduce their already scant opportunities. Often the only means they had to make their voices heard by town governments was to riot in the streets.

Changes in the price of bread, the staple food of the poor, were most likely to spark urban disorder. Since fear of riots restrained the greed of merchants, riots were a collective method for imposing a socially acceptable "just price" in place of the price that might be set by a free market. Bread riots were not the irrational acts of desperate people, but highly ritualized aspects of the Old Regime's economy of scarcity.

Since the riot was a way in which people who were excluded from the political processes could make their wills known, riots of all kinds were com-

The Gordon Riots of 1780, in London, triggered by anti-Catholic bigotry, were among the most destructive civil disturbances in the history of Europe. [The Bettmann Archive]

mon in the eighteenth century. Frequently, uprisings were incited by religious bigotry, but violence was normally directed against property rather than people. The rioters were usually not "riff-raff" but small shopkeepers, freeholders, craftsmen, and wage earners. They demanded what they perceived to be the restoration of a traditional right or practice, not the total overthrow of a social order.

During the last half of the century, urban riots were often used by politicians to achieve private ends. The angry crowds that tore up the streets of eighteenth-century towns could become tools of factions within the upper classes. In Paris, the aristocratic *Parlement* often urged people to riot in support of its disputes with the monarchy. In Great Britain in 1792, the government incited mobs to attack people who sympathized with the French Revolution.

～ The Jews in the Age of the Ghetto

There were Jewish communities that produced famous intellectuals in Amsterdam and other Western cities, but in the eighteenth century the vast majority of Europe's Jews lived in eastern Europe. About 3 million resided in Poland, Lithuania, and the Ukraine. Fewer than 100,000 lived in Germany, approximately 40,000 in France, and only about 10,000 in either England or Holland.

In most nations, unless rights were specifically granted to Jews, they did not enjoy the same privileges as a monarch's Christian subjects. Jews were treated as resident aliens whose right to remain might be revoked at any moment. They lived apart from Christians in separate communities—"ghettos," distinct districts in cities or whole villages in the countryside. In Poland for much of the century, they were virtually self-governing. In other areas, they lived under the burden of discriminatory legislation.

Since Jews were often prevented from owning land, many were driven into trade and commerce. Some became very successful bankers, and during the seventeenth century a few of them helped nations finance wars. The loans they made to monarchs were often not repaid, but the "court Jews" became famous for their financial acumen and influence. They formed a tiny network of closely intermarried, exclusive families which were hardly characteristic.

Most of Europe's Jews lived in poverty. They occupied the most undesirable sections of cities or poor rural villages. They worked at the lowest occupations. Their religious beliefs, rituals, and the laws of most communities kept them apart from their Christian neighbors in situations of social inferiority. Those who converted to Christianity were welcomed, even if not always warmly, into gentile society. But until the last two decades of the eighteenth century, those who remained loyal to their faith were subject to discrimination and persecution. They were barred from some professions, restricted in their freedom of movement, deprived of political representation and protection under the law, subject to confiscation of their property and to exile, and generally regarded as inferiors. Sometimes force was used to persuade them to convert or their children were taken away from them and given Christian instruction.

At the close of the eighteenth century, European society was on the brink of a new era. The commercial spirit, although not new, began to have freer play than ever before. It encouraged human beings to operate as individuals rather than as members of communities struggling for survival in an economy of scarcity. Agricultural and industrial revolutions, motivated by a desire for greater consumption, overcame scarcity. The accompanying changes in landholding and production transformed society.

Population expanded. Cities grew. Birth became less significant than wealth in determining social relationships. Class structures and hierarchies remained, but their boundaries blurred. The diverse middle class, which was growing wealthier from trade, commerce, and the practice of the professions, wanted social prestige and influence equal to its wealth. In pursuit of this goal, it was willing to innovate and challenge tradition. This helped close one era in European history and bring on quite a different one.

⌒ Review Questions

1. How did the lives of English aristocrats change during the course of the eighteenth century? How did the situation of the English aristocracy differ from that of the French? What kind of privileges distinguished European aristocrats from other social groups?

2. How would you define *family economy*? How did the northwestern European household differ from the households common to eastern Europe? In what ways were the lives of women in preindustrial Europe constrained by the family economy?

3. How did technological innovations transform European agriculture? To what extent did the English aristocracy contribute to the Agricultural Revolution? What were some of the reasons for peasant revolts in Europe in the eighteenth century?

4. What factors explain the increase in Europe's population in the eighteenth century? What were the effects of the population explosion? How did population growth contribute to changes in consumption?

5. What caused the Industrial Revolution of the eighteenth century? What were its major technological innovations? What impacts did these innovations have? Why did Great Britain take the lead in the Industrial Revolution? How did the consumer contribute to the Industrial Revolution?

6. What was city life like during the eighteenth century? Were all European cities fundamentally the same? What changes took place during the century in the distribution of population in cities and towns? How did the lifestyle of the upper class differ from that of the middle and lower classes? What were some of the causes of urban riots?

～ Suggested Readings

J. Blum, *The End of the Old Order in Rural Europe* (1978). The most comprehensive treatment of life in rural Europe, especially central and eastern, from the early eighteenth through the mid-nineteenth centuries.

F. Braudel, *Capitalism and Material Life, 1400–1800* (1974). An investigation of the physical resources and human organization of preindustrial Europe.

J. Cannon, *Aristocratic Century: The Peerage of Eighteenth-Century England* (1985). A useful treatment based on the most recent research

P. Deane, *The First Industrial Revolution*, 2nd ed. (1979). A well-balanced and systematic treatment.

J. De Vries, *The Economy of Europe in an Age of Crisis, 1600–1750* (1976). An excellent overview that sets forth the main issues.

J. De Vries, *European Urbanization, 1500–1800* (1984). The most important and far-ranging recent treatment of the subject.

M. W. Flinn, *The European Demographic System, 1500–1820* (1981). A major summary.

R. Forster and O. Ranum, *Medicine and Society in France* (1980).

D. V. Glass and D. E. C. Eversley (eds.), *Population in History: Essays in Historical Demography* (1965). Fundamental for understanding the eighteenth-century increase in population.

A. Goodwin (ed.), *The European Nobility in the Eighteenth Century* (1953). Essays on the nobility in each state.

P. Goubert, *The Ancien Régime: French Society, 1600–1750*, trans. by Steve Cox (1974). A superb account of the peasant social order.

O. H. Hufton, *The Poor of Eighteenth-Century France, 1750–1789* (1975). A brilliant study of poverty and the family economy.

E. L. Jones, *Agriculture and Economic Growth in England, 1650–1815* (1968). A good introduction to an important subject.

H. Kamen, *European Society, 1500–1700* (1985). The best one-volume treatment.

N. McKendrick (ed.), *The Birth of a Consumer Society: The Commercialization of Eighteenth-Century England* (1982). Deals with several aspects of the impact of commercialization.

M. A. Meyer, *The Origins of the Modern Jew: Jewish Identity and European Culture in Germany, 1749–1824* (1967). A general introduction organized around individual case studies.

S. Pollard, *The Genesis of Modern Management: A Study of the Industrial Revolution in Great Britain* (1965). Treats the issue of industrialization from the standpoint of factory owners.

G. Rudé, *The Crowd in History, 1730–1848* (1964). A pioneering study.

S. Schama, *The Embarrassment of Riches: An Interpretation of Dutch Culture in the Golden Age* (1987). A broad examination of the impact of wealth on the Dutch.

R. Wall (ed.), *Family Forms in Historic Europe* (1983). Essays that cover the entire continent.

E. A. Wrigley, *Continuity, Chance and Change: The Character of the Industrial Revolution in England* (1988). A major conceptual reassessment.

17

Empire, War, and Colonial Rebellion

Periods of European Overseas Empires

Eighteenth-Century Empires
Mercantile Empires
The Spanish Colonial System
African Slavery, the Plantation System, and the Atlantic Economy

Mid-Eighteenth-Century Wars
The War of Jenkins's Ear
The War of the Austrian Succession (1740–1748)

The "Diplomatic Revolution" of 1756
The Seven Years' War (1756–1763)

The American Revolution and Europe
Resistance to the Imperial Search for Revenue
The Crisis and Independence
American Political Ideas
Events in Great Britain
The American Example

KEY TOPICS IN THIS CHAPTER

~ Europe's mercantilist empires

~ Spain's vast colonial empire in the Americas

~ The wars of the mid-eighteenth century in Europe and the colonies

~ The struggle for independence in Britain's North American colonies

---

During the eighteenth century, Europeans began to make war on a global scale. Austria and Prussia fought for dominance in central Europe while Great Britain and France dueled for commercial and colonial supremacy. The result was a new balance of power: Great Britain built a world empire, and Prussia became one of Europe's leading nations.

After the Peace of Paris of 1763, every European state subordinated financial planning to military policy. The resulting fiscal programs had far-reaching political consequences: the American Revolution, enlightened absolutism, a financial crisis for the French monarchy, and reform of Spain's American empire.

Significant Dates from the Eighteenth Century

1713	*Treaty of Utrecht*
1739	*War of Jenkins's Ear*
1740–1748	*War of the Austrian Succession*
1756–1763	*Seven Years' War*
1759	*British conquest of Quebec*
1763	*John Wilkes challenges the British monarchy*
1764	*Sugar Act*
1765	*Stamp Act*
1770	*Boston Massacre*
1773	*Boston Tea Party*
1774	*First Continental Congress*
1776–1783	*War of the American Revolution*

Periods of European Overseas Empires

Europe's relations with the world beyond its shores have gone through several stages. The first—an age of exploration, conquest, and settlement—was over by the end of the seventeenth century. The second, which ended about 1820, was dominated by colonial rivalry among Spain, France, and Great Britain. During this period, both the British colonies of North America and the Spanish colonies of Central and South America emancipated themselves. In the nineteenth century, European nations built new empires in Africa and Asia. Europeans also settled in Australia, New Zealand, and South Africa. These nineteenth-century empires were dismantled in the mid-twentieth century by a process of "decolonization" that granted political independence to former colonies.

For four-and-a-half centuries, Europe—a relatively small continent—dominated much of the rest of the world, and Europeans treated other peoples as inferiors. Europeans owed their ability to dominate the world not to any innate cultural superiority, but to technological advances that gave them superior military power: ships and guns.

Eighteenth-Century Empires

The empires European nations built in the eighteenth century were designed for purposes of trade. They were intended to bring wealth to nations rather than to provide areas for settlement. Extensive trade rivalries sprang up among the European colonial powers, and the need to protect their empires forced the European nations to build large navies. Spain led the way in developing the elaborate machinery needed to exploit foreign possessions. Slave labor was used to develop these possessions, and the Atlantic slave trade was itself a major source of European wealth. That trade also made the peoples of Africa part of the history of the New World.

Mercantile Empires

In 1713, in the Treaty of Utrecht, the nations of Europe agreed on the boundaries of their empires. Except for Brazil, which was Portuguese, Spain claimed all of mainland South America; the islands of Cuba, Puerto Rico, and half of Hispaniola; and the North American territories of Florida, Mexico, California, and the Southwest. The British held the North Atlantic seaboard, Nova Scotia, Newfoundland, Jamaica, Barbados, and a few trading stations on the Indian subcontinent. The French occupied the valleys of the Saint Lawrence, the Ohio, and the Mississippi rivers; the West Indian islands of Saint Domingue, Guadeloupe, and Martinique; and stations in India. The Dutch controlled Surinam (Dutch Guiana) in South America, various posts in Ceylon and Bengal, and trade with Java (Indonesia). All of these powers also possessed numerous smaller islands in the Caribbean.

Mercantilist Goals. *Mercantilism,* a name given by its later critics to a system whereby governments regulate trade and commerce to increase national wealth, was the economic policy that characterized the administration of Europe's empires. Mercantilists believed that bullion was the measure of a country's wealth, and they advocated courses of action that would maintain an excess of exports over imports. A favorable trade balance enabled a state to siphon gold and silver away from its rivals.

The economic well-being of the home country was the primary goal of the mercantilist system. Colonies existed to provide markets and natural resources for the industries of the home country. The home country furnished their military security and political administration, and it was taken for granted that the colonies were the inferior partner in the relationship.

Mercantilists assumed that the world's resources were limited and that one nation's economy could grow only at the expense of others. The home country and its colonies were to trade exclusively with each other. Navigation laws, tariffs, and regulations prohibiting trade with the subjects of other monarchs created national commercial monopolies.

Mercantilism existed more in theory than in practice, for the policy was at odds with economic reality—and perhaps with human nature. Colonial and home markets simply failed to mesh. Spain could not produce sufficient goods for all of South America, and manufacturing in Britain's North American colonies competed with factories in England. Also, colonists of different countries wanted to trade with each other. English colonists could buy sugar more cheaply from the French West Indies than from English suppliers. Since governments could not control the activities of all their subjects, smuggling flourished. When governments tried to halt it, colonists organized to resist.

French-British Rivalry. The French and British colonists of North America quarreled endlessly with each other. Both groups coveted the lower Saint Lawrence River valley, upper New England, and the Ohio River valley. They competed over fishing rights, fur trade, and alliances with Native American tribes. The two nations also struggled on the Indian subcontinent.

Both France and Britain granted exclusive rights to trade in India to monopolistic companies: England's East India Company and France's *Compagnie des Indes.* The volume of trade with India and Asia was marginal to the economics of empire, but India had the potential to become a huge market and to provide Westerners entry to China. The European bases in India were trading posts *(factories)* licensed by various Indian governments.

In the middle of the eighteenth century, the situation in India changed. The governments of several Indian states declined, and the leaders of the French and English trading companies—Joseph Dupleix (1697–1763) and Robert Clive (1725–1774), respectively—seized the opportunity to expand their privileges. Each company began, in effect, to take political control of parts of India and to try to check the growth of the other.

The Spanish Colonial System

Colonial Government. Because Queen Isabella of Castile (r. 1474–1504) had commissioned Columbus, the crown of Castile was the link between the New World and Spain. Its powers, both at home and in America, were subject to few limitations. Spain governed America through a Council of the Indies, which, in conjunction with the monarch, legislated for the colonies and nominated the viceroys of New Spain (Mexico) and Peru. Virtually all political power flowed from the top down.

Each of the viceroyalties was divided into judicial councils or *audiencias.* There were also various kinds of local officers, the most important of whom were the *corregidores* who presided over municipal councils. The system provided the monarchy with vast opportunities for patronage—which was usually bestowed on persons born in Spain.

Trade Regulation. The government of Spain's colonies was designed to serve Spain's commercial interests. The *Casa de Contratación* (House of Trade) in Seville regulated all trade with the New World, and Cadiz was the only port authorized for use by ships trading with America.

A complicated system of fleets organized from Seville guarded Spain's trade monopoly. Each year, a fleet of commercial vessels (the *flota*), belonging to Seville merchants and escorted by warships, carried merchandise from Spain to a few specified ports in America. After selling their wares, the ships were loaded with silver and gold bullion, wintered in heavily fortified Caribbean ports, and then sailed back to Spain. Spanish colonists were prohibited from establishing direct trade with each other and from developing their own shipping and commerce. Foreign merchants were also forbidden access to Spain's colonies.

Colonial Reform Under the Spanish Bourbon Monarchs. A crucial change in the Spanish colonial system occurred after the War of the Spanish Succession (1701–1714) brought a French Bourbon prince to Spain's throne. Philip V (r. 1700–1746) and his successors tried to improve Spain's economy and its international prestige by developing the empire's trade monopoly. The *flota* system had never worked perfectly, and it had been allowed to decay under the last of Spain's Habsburg kings.

Philip V sent coastal patrol vessels to suppress smuggling in American waters. The ensuing conflicts with English vessels led to war with England in 1739. In that year, Philip tried to strengthen his hold over the Americas by establishing the viceroyalty of New Granada, a district that today includes Venezuela, Colombia, and Ecuador.

The European wars that raged during the reign of Ferdinand VI (1746–1759) revealed the vulnerability of Spain's empire to naval penetration. When Spain accepted defeat in 1763, its rulers concluded that administrative reforms were needed if the empire was to survive.

Charles III (r. 1759–1788) enacted the most significant reforms. Under him the power of royal ministers increased, and that of the Council of the Indies and the Casa de Contratación declined. In 1765, he abolished the monopolies of Seville and Cadiz and permitted other Spanish cities to trade with America. He also opened more South American and Caribbean ports to trade and authorized some commerce between colonial ports. In 1776, he organized a fourth viceroyalty in the region of Rio de la Plata—modern Argentina, Uruguay, Paraguay, and Bolivia (see Map 17-1).

While relaxing control over trade, Charles III tried to increase the efficiency of tax collection and to eliminate bureaucratic corruption. To this end, he added the office of *intendent* to the administration of his empire. The *intendent* was a loyal, royal bureaucrat resembling the French *intendant*, the effective instrument of Louis XIV's absolutism.

Thanks to the Bourbon reforms, Spain's trade expanded and became more varied. But the reforms, by bringing the colonies more directly under the control of *peninsulares* (persons born in Spain), hastened the end of the empire. Spaniards were sent to the New World to fill the new governmental offices, more Spanish merchants entered Latin America, and the economy remained organized for the benefit of Spain. As a result, the *creoles* (persons of European descent born in the colonies) came to feel that they were second-class subjects. In the early nineteenth century, their resentment spawned wars of independence.

African Slavery, the Plantation System, and the Atlantic Economy

Eighteenth-century colonial rivalries centered on the American islands of the West Indies, which produced tobacco, cotton, indigo, coffee, and sugar. The

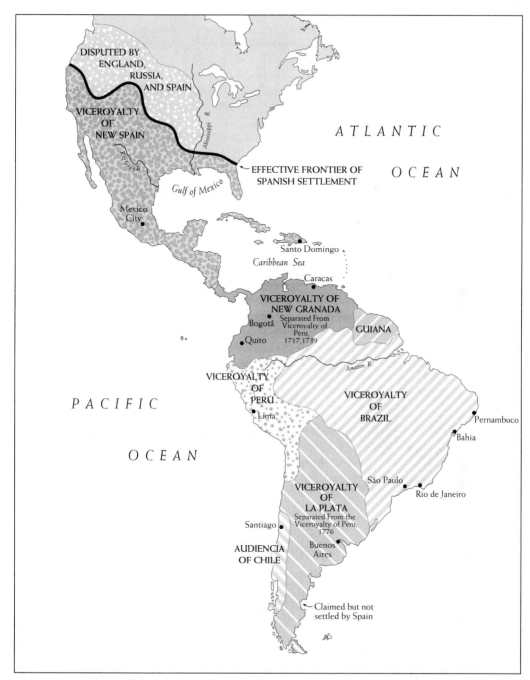

MAP 17-1 Viceroyalties in Latin America in 1780 *The late-eighteenth-century viceroyalties in Latin America display the effort of the Spanish Bourbon monarchy to establish more direct control of the continent. They sought this through the introduction of a larger number of royal officials and by establishing more governmental districts.*

market for these commodities was growing, for Europe was coming to regard them as staples, not luxuries.

Since slave labor was used to raise these crops in the West Indies, in the Spanish and Portuguese settlements in South America, and in the British colonies on the south Atlantic seaboard of North America, their production stimulated another kind of commerce: a trade in black West Africans.

Slavery had existed in Western societies since the beginning of civilization. Before the eighteenth century, the only moral scruples associated with it affected opinions about appropriate sources of slaves. In the mid-fifteenth century, the Ottoman Empire ceased to export white slaves. At the same time, the Portuguese began to import black Africans into the Iberian peninsula. Black slaves were not uncommon in other parts of the Mediterranean, and a few—because of the novelty of their color—found their way into wealthy households in northern Europe.

The Plantation System. The Spanish and Portuguese who developed the New World faced a severe labor shortage. European settlers were neither inclined nor numerous enough to undertake the manual work themselves, and the diseases they spread among the Native Americans soon reduced that pool of potential laborers. Consequently, the Spanish and Portuguese began to import African slaves. By the late sixteenth century, black slaves equaled or surpassed the numbers of white European settlers in the islands of the West Indies and the cities of South America.

Although the numbers of slaves declined at the end of the seventeenth century in the Spanish districts of South America, slavery prospered in Brazil and the Caribbean and spread to the British North American colonies. The first slaves were brought to Jamestown, Virginia, in 1619, and at one time or another slavery existed in all the English colonies. The wealthiest New World colonies were those that exploited slave labor to produce staples such as sugar, rice, tobacco, and cotton. Sugar led the field.

By the close of the seventeenth century, the world was developing an insatiable appetite for sugar, and the Caribbean Islands were its chief suppliers. The commercial production of sugar required a large investment in land and equipment, and only slave labor could provide enough workers to make a great sugar plantation profitable. As the production of sugar increased, so did the demand for slaves. By 1725, almost 90 percent of the residents of Jamaica were black slaves. The situation was similar throughout the West Indies.

Colonial trade moved by a triangular route. European goods were taken to Africa to be exchanged for slaves. Slaves were then shipped to the West Indies to be traded for sugar and other agricultural products that could be sold in Europe. Another trade route connected New England and the West Indies and involved the exchange of New England's fish or the goods it imported from Europe for sugar.

The plantations worked by slaves were isolated in rural settings, but they were part of a huge transatlantic economic system. Their agricultural products were intended for overseas markets, not for domestic consumption. And virtually all of the manufactured goods they consumed were imported from Europe. The prosperity of cities such as Newport, Rhode Island; Liverpool, England; and Nantes, France, derived from a vast trade network based on slavery. Even if they had no direct contact with slaves, all of the shippers who handled cotton, tobacco, and sugar depended on slavery—as did all the manufacturers and merchants who produced the finished products for the consumer market.

Slave Experience. The slave trade was as profitable as it was inhumane. The Spanish, Portuguese, Dutch, French, and English all took part in the forcible transport of perhaps as many as 9 million black Africans to the New World. During the first four centuries of settlement, far more black slaves came involuntarily to the New World than did free European settlers. The conditions under which they crossed the Atlantic were unspeakably wretched. They were packed into the holds of vessels like goods, not passengers. Their food was bad. Disease ran rampant among them, and huge numbers died on the crossing. But the trade thrived, for it was cheaper to import new slaves than to rear slave children to adulthood. Also, the mortality rate of slaves on plantations was very high, and more and more Africans had to be enslaved simply to keep the labor force at a consistent level.

Conditions of life for slaves on plantations differed from colony to colony. Slaves in Portuguese areas had the least legal protection. In the Spanish colonies, the church tried to provide some help to black slaves, but it paid more attention to Native Americans. In the seventeenth century, laws governing slavery were developed in the British and the French colonies, but they provided only the most limited protection. Their chief purpose was to head off the slave revolts that virtually all slaveowners feared. Slave masters could whip slaves and inflict exceedingly harsh corporal punishment. Slaves were forbidden to gather in large groups lest they plot against their masters. The marriages of slaves were usually not recognized, and the children of slaves inherited the servile status of their parents. Slave families could be separated by their owners. And investment in their welfare—in their food and housing—was a function of the market value of their labor. Usually it was cheaper to replace them than to maintain them. Although some scholars have argued that slaves lived better in some areas than others, all slaves led difficult lives under conditions that did not vary significantly.

The Africans who were transported to the Americas were, like the Native Americans, converted to Christianity. In the Spanish, French, and Portuguese domains, they became Roman Catholics; in the English colonies, Protestants. Although some aspects of African cultures survived in muted forms, religious conversion was part of a process that imposed a crushing set of European values on the non-European residents of the colonies.

Many Europeans considered Africans savages and looked down on them because they were slaves. Many Western cultures attached negative connotations to blackness that encouraged people to use racism to justify slavery. Al-

A Slave Trader Describes the Atlantic Passage

During 1693 and 1694, Captain Thomas Phillips carried slaves from Africa to Barbados on the ship Hannibal. *The financial backer of the voyage was the Royal African Company of London, which held an English crown monopoly on slave trading. Phillips sailed to the west coast of Africa, where he purchased the Africans who were sold into slavery by an African king. Then he set sail westward.*

∾ Who are the various people described in this document who in one way or another were involved in or profited from the slave trade? What dangers did the Africans face on the voyage? What attitudes, common to his generation, could have led this ship captain to treat and think of his human cargo simply as goods to be transported? What arguments does the captain use to justify the self-pity in which he indulges?

Having bought my complement of 700 slaves, 480 men and 220 women, and finish'd all my business at Whidaw [on the Gold Coast of Africa], I took my leave of the old king and his cappasheirs [attendants], and parted, with many affectionate expressions on both sides, being forced to promise him that I would return again the next year, with several things he desired me to bring from England. . . . I set sail the 27th of July in the morning, accompany'd with the East-India Merchant, who had bought 650 slaves, for the Island of St. Thomas . . . from which we took our departure on August 25th and set sail for Barbadoes.

We spent in our passage from St. Thomas to Barbadoes two months eleven days, from the 25th of August to the 4th of November following: in which time there happened such sickness and mortality among my poor men and Negroes.

though racial arguments became more insistent in the nineteenth century, the fact that slaves could be differentiated physically from the rest of the population was fundamental to the maintenance of slavery and to the creation of the racial prejudices that plague the modern West. A society like that of the American colonies—one totally dependent on slave labor and racial differences—was novel in both European and world history. It endured from the sixteenth century through the second half of the nineteenth century, and today every nation where this form of plantation slavery existed contends with the long-term effects of that institution.

∾ Mid-Eighteenth-Century Wars

The War of Jenkins's Ear

The challenge that English smugglers, shippers, and pirates mounted to Spain's monopoly of West Indian trade came to a head in the late 1730s. The Treaty

Of the first we buried 14, and of the last 320, which was a great detriment to our voyage, the Royal African Company losing ten pounds by every slave that died, and the owners of the ship ten pounds ten shillings, being the freight agreed on to be paid by the charter-party for every Negro delivered alive ashore to the African Company's agents at Barbadoes. . . . The loss in all amounted to near 6500 pounds sterling.

The distemper which my men as well as the blacks mostly died of was the white flux, which was so violent and inveterate that no medicine would in the least check it, so that when any of our men were seized with it, we esteemed him a dead man, as he generally proved. . . .

The Negroes are so incident to the small-pox that few ships that carry them escape without it, and sometimes it makes vast havock and destruction among them. But tho' we had 100 at a time sick of it, and that it went thro' the ship, yet we lost not above a dozen by it. All the assistance we gave the diseased was only as much water as they desir'd to drink, and some palm-oil to annoint their sores, and they would generally recover without any other helps but what kind nature gave them. . . .

But what the small pox spar'd, the flux swept off, to our great regret, after all our pains and care to give them their messes in due order and season, keeping their lodgings as clean and sweet as possible, and enduring so much misery and stench so long among a parcel of creatures nastier than swine, and after all our expectations to be defeated by their mortality. . . .

No gold-finders can endure so much noisome slavery as they do who carry Negroes; for those have some respite and satisfaction, but we endure twice the misery; and yet by their mortality our voyages are ruin'd, and we pine and fret ourselves to death, and take so much pains to so little purpose.

Thomas Phillips, "Journal," A Collection of Voyages and Travels, *vol. VI, ed. by Awnsham and John Churchill (London, 1746) as quoted in Thomas Howard, ed.,* Black Voyage: Eyewitness Accounts of the Atlantic Slave Trade *(Boston: Little, Brown and Company, 1971), pp. 85–87.*

of Utrecht (1713) granted Great Britain two privileges that gave its traders and smugglers entry to the markets of the Spanish Empire: a thirty-year *asiento* (contract) to furnish slaves to the Spanish, and the right to send one ship each year to the trading fair at Portobello, a major Caribbean seaport on the Panamanian coast. The British took advantage of the arrangement by sending additional vessels to resupply, under cover of darkness, the one ship authorized to trade in Portobello. The Spanish government tried to prevent this by boarding English vessels to search for contraband.

During one such boarding operation in 1731, there was a fight, and a Spaniard cut off the ear of an English captain named Robert Jenkins. He preserved his severed ear in a jar of brandy, and in 1738, he exhibited it to the British Parliament to illustrate the atrocities that British merchants in the West Indies alleged to suffer at the hands of the Spanish. Sir Robert Walpole (1676–1745), the British prime minister, succumbed to the demands of powerful commercial interests and, late in 1739, declared war on Spain. Because of developments in continental European politics, what might have been a minor skirmish started a series of wars that lasted until 1815.

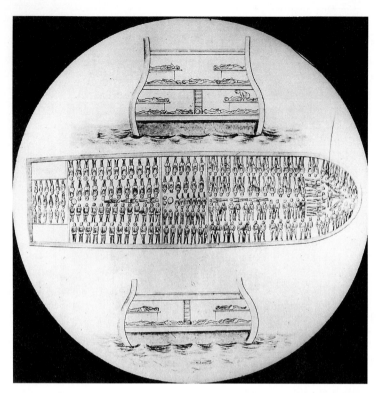

African captives imported into the Americas were carried across the Atlantic in unspeakable conditions on ships designed to maximize the number of human beings carried as cargo. This cross-section illustrates how the human cargo was arranged. [Bildarchiv Preussischer Kulturbesitz]

The War of the Austrian Succession (1740–1748)

In December 1740, Frederick II, the new ruler of Prussia, took advantage of the death of the Habsburg emperor, Charles VI, to annex the Austrian province of Silesia. His move upset the continental balance of power as established by the Treaty of Utrecht, and it could have triggered the collapse of the Habsburg Empire. The great achievement of Maria Theresa, the twenty-three-year-old woman who inherited Charles's throne, was not the reconquest of Silesia, which eluded her, but the preservation of the empire.

Maria Theresa's youth and heroism helped her win the support of some of her subjects, but so did the privileges she granted the nobility. She saved her empire by sacrificing the power of its central government. Hungary, for instance, remained loyal, because its Magyars were promised considerable local autonomy—a promise that was often made in times of weakness and ignored when the monarchy recovered its strength.

France Draws Great Britain into the War. The war between Prussia and Austria would not have involved Britain and Spain had France not intervened. France's traditional hatred for the Habsburgs led a group of aristocrats at the French court to pressure Louis XV's elderly first minister, Cardinal Fleury

(1653–1743), into supporting Prussia against Austria. This was one of the more fateful decisions in French history. France's aid to Prussia helped consolidate a new, powerful German state (with the potential to threaten France), and it forced Great Britain to enter the war to prevent France from taking the Low Countries away from Austria.

In 1744, France backed Spain against Britain in the New World, and the war spread beyond the continent. The expanding conflict taxed everyone's resources and led, in 1748, to the proclamation of a stalemate. The Treaty of Aix-la-Chapelle brought peace to Europe, but not to America. Clashes between French and English settlers in the Ohio River valley and upper New England escalated into America's French and Indian War.

The "Diplomatic Revolution" of 1756

Before the war resumed, a dramatic shift of alliances took place. Frederick II, fearing invasions from Russia and France, opened negotiations with Great Britain. In 1756, the two powers signed the Convention of Westminster, an alliance designed to prevent foreign troops from entering the Germanies.

Maria Theresa was despondent when Great Britain, Austria's ally since the days of Louis XIV, joined forces with Austria's chief enemy. However, her foreign minister, Prince Wenzel Anton Kaunitz (1711–1794), saw an opportunity for Austria in the new situation. Since France did not want to be caught between Prussia and Britain, Kaunitz persuaded it to join Austria in dismembering Prussia. The foreign policy France had followed since the sixteenth century reversed, and France committed itself to the restoration of Austrian supremacy in central Europe.

The Seven Years' War (1756–1763)

Frederick the Great Opens Hostilities. In August 1756, Frederick II invaded Saxony to prevent it from joining the Franco-Austrian alliance against Prussia. His attack hastened the very thing it was intended to prevent. Within a few months, France and Austria had persuaded Sweden, Russia, and many small German states to oppose Prussia, and the Seven Years' War was underway.

Frederick's stubborn defense of his kingdom earned him the title "the Great," but fortitude alone did not save Prussia. Britain furnished considerable financial aid, and Russia withdrew from the conflict following the death of Empress Elizabeth in 1762. The Treaty of Hubertusburg (1763) ended the continental conflict with no significant changes in prewar borders.

William Pitt's Strategy for Winning North America. While Frederick the Great was establishing Prussia as a major power, William Pitt the Elder (1708–1778) was plotting a victorious strategy for Prussia's ally, Great Britain. Although Pitt early in his career had opposed British involvement with the continent, he reversed himself in 1757 and sent huge financial subsidies to Frederick the Great. His hope was to use the German conflict to divert French resources and attention from the colonial struggle. He later boasted of having won America on the plains of Germany.

North America was Pitt's real concern. Thanks to him, the English took control of everything east of the Mississippi. Pitt engineered unprecedented cooperation among the American colonies and attacked French Canada with an army of 40,000 men, a greater force than had ever been deployed in colonial warfare. The French were unable to equal the English resources, and in September 1759, the British army under General James Wolfe defeated the French under Lieutenant General Louis Joseph de Montcalm on the Plains of Abraham at Quebec City.

Pitt aspired to more than the conquest of French Canada. British fleets won control of islands in the French West Indies—and of sugar production that was used to finance the British war effort. The British also replaced the French in the slave trade. (As a consequence, from 1755 to 1760, the value of French colonial trade fell by over 80 percent.) In India, the victory the British commander Robert Clive won over the French at the Battle of Plassey (1757) opened the way for the conquest of Bengal and then of all India. Never had a European power experienced such military success on a global scale.

The Treaty of Paris of 1763. By 1763, when the Treaty of Paris ended the war, Pitt was no longer secretary of state. George III (r. 1760–1820) had replaced him with the Earl of Bute (1713–1792), who offered the French generous terms for peace. Britain took all of Canada, the Ohio River valley, and the eastern half of the Mississippi River valley, but it returned Pondicherry and Chandernagore in India and the West Indian sugar islands of Guadeloupe and Martinique.

The battles of the Seven Years' War had been scattered about the globe and had transformed relations among nations. Prussia kept Silesia and reduced the Habsburg Holy Roman Empire to an empty shell depending largely on Hungary. France ceased to be a great colonial power. The Spanish Empire, although intact, was being infiltrated by the British. The British East India Company was imposing its authority on the decaying indigenous governments of India, and in North America the English were reorganizing the former French territories.

The war had launched Great Britain on its long career as a world power, but the financial burdens of the campaign astounded contemporaries. The search for revenue to pay off war debts and to rebuild armies was to have far-ranging consequences—particularly in the British colonies of North America.

◆ The American Revolution and Europe

Resistance to the Imperial Search for Revenue

The Treaty of Paris ratified the existence of a British empire that, in 1763, had yet to be organized administratively. In order to win the war that built the empire, the citizens of Britain had accepted a high rate of domestic taxation and a huge national debt. Since the American colonies (see Map 17-2) had been the chief beneficiaries of the war, the British believed that they should bear a greater share of its costs.

The British drive for revenue commenced in 1764, when the ministry of George Grenville (1712–1770) passed the Sugar Act. It hoped to increase revenue from imports into the colonies by more rigorously collecting what was actually a lower tax. A year later, Parliament passed the Stamp Act, a tax on legal documents and things like newspapers. From the British point of view, these taxes were legal because they were approved by Parliament, and they were just because the money they raised was to be spent in the colonies. Americans, however, argued that since they were not represented in Parliament, only their colonial legislatures had the right to tax them. They also objected to British control of colonial finances, for this imperiled the freedom of colonial governments.

In October 1765, a Stamp Act Congress met in America to draw up a protest to the crown, and groups with names like the "Sons of Liberty" organized active resistance. When the colonists threatened to boycott British im-

MAP 17-2 North America in 1763 *In the year of the victory over France, the English colonies lay along the Atlantic seaboard. The difficulties of organizing authority over the previous French territory in Canada and west of the Appalachian Mountains would contribute to the coming of the American Revolution.*

ports, Parliament repealed the Stamp Act (1766). But it also passed the Declaratory Act affirming its power to legislate for the colonies.

The Stamp Act crisis set the pattern for the next ten years: Parliament would approve legislation; the Americans would resist it by reasoned argument, economic pressure, and violence; the British would repeal the legislation, and the process would begin again. Each time, tempers became more frayed and positions more irreconcilable.

The Crisis and Independence

In 1767, Charles Townshend (1725–1767), the British finance minister, led Parliament to pass a series of revenue acts relating to colonial imports. When the colonists again resisted, the ministry sent over its own customs agents to collect the taxes—and it protected those stationed in Boston with British troops. Tensions escalated, and in March 1770, the soldiers fired on a mob. Five people died in the "Boston Massacre." In the same year, Parliament repealed all of the Townshend duties except for one on tea.

George III (r. 1760–1820) succeeded to the English throne near the end of the Seven Years' War and presided over policies that led to the revolt and loss of the American colonies. Although he tried to reassert some of the monarchical influence on Britain's politics that had eroded under George I and George II, the first two Hanoverian kings, George III never sought to make himself a tyrant, as his critics charged. This portrait is by American-born painter Benjamin West (1728–1820). [Royal Collection Enterprises]

In May 1773, Parliament passed a new law relating to the sale of tea. By permitting the direct importation of tea into the American colonies by the East India Company, it lowered the price of tea. But it also included a tax on tea imposed without the colonists' consent. In some cities, the colonists refused to permit the unloading of the tea; in Boston, a shipload of tea was thrown into the harbor.

The British ministry of Lord North (1732–1792) then embarked on a program designed to establish once and for all Parliament's authority over the colonies. During 1774, Parliament passed a series of laws that Americans dubbed the "Intolerable Acts." Parliament closed the port of Boston, reorganized the government of Massachusetts, quartered soldiers in private homes, and transferred trials of royal customs officials to England. The Quebec Act (also 1774) was viewed as an additional provocation. By extending the boundaries of Quebec to include the Ohio River valley, the act appeared to be an attempt to stop the spread of American concepts of liberty at the Appalachian Mountains.

Citizens critical of British policy formed committees and established lines of communication throughout the colonies. These committees increased awareness of common problems and made united action possible. In September 1774, the First Continental Congress was convened in Philadelphia. It hoped to persuade Parliament to abandon attempts at direct supervision of colonial affairs, but that proved impossible. By April 1775, the battles of Lexington and Concord had been fought, and by June, the colonists had suffered defeat at Bunker Hill.

A Second Continental Congress gathered in May 1775. Although it still hoped to conciliate Britain, necessity forced it to organize a government for the colonies. By August 1775, George III had declared the colonies in rebellion, and the circulation during the following winter of Thomas Paine's (1737–1809) pamphlet *Common Sense* created a consensus in the colonies in favor of separation from Great Britain.

A colonial army and navy were set up. In April 1776, the Continental Congress opened American ports to trade with all nations, and on July 4, 1776, the Continental Congress adopted the Declaration of Independence. Early in 1778, Benjamin Franklin (1706–1790) persuaded the French government to support the rebellion, and in 1779, the Spanish came to the aid of the colonies. The American Revolution, which had widened into a European conflict, continued until 1781, when George Washington defeated Lord Cornwallis at Yorktown. The Treaty of Paris, which concluded the conflict in 1783, recognized the independence of the thirteen former colonies as the United States of America.

American Political Ideas

The political reasoning that led up to the American Revolution had its roots in the arguments that seventeenth-century English aristocrats used to oppose the absolutism of the Stuart monarchs. The colonists believed that the English Revolution of 1688 had established fundamental liberties that belonged to all English people—in the homeland and in the colonies.

This "Whig" political philosophy owed much to the writings of John Locke, but Locke was only one part of colonial America's English ideological heritage. Throughout the eighteenth century, a series of British political writers called the *Commonwealthmen* had championed radical republican concepts derived from the Puritan revolution. These writers—especially John Trenchard and Thomas Gordon, author of *Cato's Letters* (1720–1723)—were motivated by their opposition to the governments of Sir Robert Walpole and his successors. They regarded much parliamentary taxation as simply a means of financing political corruption, and they considered standing armies to be instruments of tyranny.

In Great Britain, the Commonwealthmen were largely ignored, for most Britons believed themselves to be subjects of the freest government in the world. Three thousand miles away in the colonies, however, the security of British liberty was less certain. Events that coincided with the accession of George III to the throne convinced many colonists that the worst fears of the Commonwealthmen were coming true.

Events in Great Britain

George III (r. 1760–1820) believed that his two predecessors had been dominated by a few powerful Whig families and the ministries they controlled. He was determined to choose his own ministers and to create a Parliament led by the king, not the aristocracy. George used royal patronage to buy influence with the House of Commons, and between 1761 and 1770, he tried one minister after another. Each in turn failed to gain sufficient support from the factions in the House of Commons. In 1770, the king finally found in Lord North a first minister who could manage the reins of government. North remained in office until 1782.

George's efforts to curb the power of particular aristocrats were denounced by the Whigs as tyranny. George III certainly wanted to enhance the power of the monarch in the government of Great Britain, but he was not a tyrant.

The Challenge of John Wilkes. In 1763, the various factions that opposed the king were given a center around which to coalesce. John Wilkes (1725–1797), a London political radical, member of Parliament, and publisher of a newspaper called *The North Briton*, used his paper to attack Lord Bute, the king's first minister, for his handling of peace negotiations with France. Bute had him arrested, but Wilkes appealed to his privileges as a member of Parliament and was released. The courts ruled that the vague kind of general warrant by which he had been arrested was illegal, but the House of Commons concluded that he was guilty of libel and expelled him. Wilkes fled the country and was outlawed, but many hailed him as a victim of political persecution.

In 1768, Wilkes returned to England and was re-elected to Parliament. The House of Commons, bowing to the wishes of the king, refused to seat him. Although he won three subsequent elections, the House ignored the verdict and seated a rival government-supported candidate. Shopkeepers, artisans, and small property owners demonstrated in the streets in support of Wilkes. Aristocrats who wanted to humiliate the king also gave him aid. Wilkes contended that his was the cause of English liberty, and the government's opponents took as their slogan: "Wilkes and Liberty." Wilkes became lord mayor of London and was finally seated by Parliament in 1774.

The American colonists followed these developments closely, for they seemed to confirm the colonists' suspicion that the king and Parliament were conspiring against English liberty. The Wilkes affair displayed the arbitrary power of the monarch, the corruption of the House of Commons, and the contempt of both for popular electors. These same aspects of tyranny seemed, to the colonists, to be at the heart of their struggles with England.

Movement for Parliamentary Reform. The British ministry was fully aware that its troubles in America were related to political problems at home. Like the colonists, most residents of the British Isles could object to taxation without representation, for most Britons were no more directly represented in the House of Commons than were Americans. John Wilkes proved that many in England were ready to challenge the king and the power of a largely self-selected aristocratic Parliament. Wilkes's use of popular demonstrations and his appeal to public opinion against the legally constituted political authorities even showed how a popular reform movement might be organized.

This satirical portrait of John Wilkes is by William Hogarth. It depicts Wilkes with unattractive personal characteristics and questions the sincerity of his calls for liberty. [Charles Farrell Collection]

The American colonists further demonstrated to Europe how a politically restive people could fight tyranny. The Americans created revolutionary, but orderly, political bodies that functioned outside the existing political framework. They based the legitimacy of their congresses and conventions not on ancient political traditions, but on a new idea: the alleged consent of the governed.

The Yorkshire Association Movement. The American Revolution led to calls for parliamentary reform in Britain, and the method proposed for changing the system was the American strategy of working through extralegal associations. In northern England in 1778, Christopher Wyvil (1740–1822), a landowner and retired clergyman, organized the Yorkshire Association Movement. Yorkshire's men of property held a mass meeting to demand moderate changes in the corrupt system of parliamentary elections. Similar groups soon appeared elsewhere—proposing reforms that affected the entire government. The movement faded in the early 1780s, for its leaders were unwilling to follow the example of Wilkes and the American rebels and to appeal to the masses for support.

Parliament was, however, affected by the Association Movement. In April 1780, the Commons advocated a reduction in the power of the crown. In 1782, Parliament adopted an "economical" reform, which abolished some sources of royal patronage. And in 1783, Parliament obliged Lord North to form a ministry with Charles James Fox (1749–1806), a longtime critic of George III.

In 1783, the king enlisted William Pitt the Younger (1759–1806), son of the victorious war minister, in a campaign to create a more pliable House of Commons. During the election of 1784, Pitt used immense amounts of royal patronage to fill the House of Commons with men friendly to the king. Pitt abandoned efforts at parliamentary reform, and by the mid-1780s, the monarchy's influence in political affairs was reasserted. Its resurgence was, however, short-lived, for George III succumbed to mental illness, and the regency that assumed responsibility for his crown could not wage an aggressive campaign to enhance its power.

The American Example

As the crisis with Britain unfolded during the 1760s and 1770s, the American colonists first believed that they were fighting to preserve traditional English liberties against a tyrannical king and corrupt Parliament. But, in the end, they developed a new concept of liberty. The state constitutions, Articles of Confederation, and federal Constitution (1788) they produced showed Europe that there could be government without kings and nobles. Americans created a nation in which popular consent—or sovereignty—rather than divine law, natural law, tradition, or the will of kings, was the highest legal authority. The political novelty of their system was not to be ignored.

Americans embraced democratic ideals, but they did not immediately create a perfectly democratic society. The franchise remained limited. The equality of white male citizens not only before the law, but in ordinary social relations, was asserted. All of them were urged to improve their social standing and economic lot by engaging in free commercial activity. But slaves were not emancipated, nor was the issue of the rights of women or of Native Americans addressed. Still, the American colonists of the eighteenth century produced a society more free than any the world had seen. The American Revolution was a genuinely radical movement, the influence of which would expand as Americans moved across the continent and as it encouraged Europeans to question their traditional modes of government.

Throughout the eighteenth century, European nations fought their wars on two fronts: in their commercial empires overseas and in central Europe. These wars had enormous implications for the evolution of the European monarchies, for they required them to raise vast amounts of money and improve administrative efficiency. The financial crisis that developed for the kings of France unleashed the French Revolution. In *preparation for future wars, the rulers of Prussia, Austria, and Russia developed an activist form of government called enlightened absolutism. When Britain attempted to tax the North American colonies, they rebelled and won their independence. The new American democracy became a permanent witness to the viability of political alternatives that Europeans had not previously considered.*

⌒ Review Questions

1. What were the fundamental ideas associated with mercantile theory? Did they work? Which European country was most successful in establishing a mercantile empire? Which was least successful? Why?

2. What were the main points of conflict between Britain and France in North America, the West Indies, and India? How did the triangles of trade function between the Americas, Europe, and Africa?

3. How was the Spanish colonial empire in the Americas organized and managed? What changes did the Bourbon monarchs institute in the Spanish Empire?

4. What was the nature of slavery in the Americas? How was it linked to the economies of the Americas, Europe, and Africa? What was the plantation system? How did it contribute to the inhumane treatment of slaves?

5. What were the results of the Seven Years' War? Which countries emerged in a stronger position? Why?

6. To what extent were the colonists who began the American Revolution influenced by European ideas and political developments? What influence did their actions and arguments have on Europe?

⌒ Suggested Readings

B. Bailyn, *The Ideological Origins of the American Revolution* (1967). An important work illustrating the role of English radical thought in the perceptions of the American colonists.

B. Bailyn, *The Peopling of British North America: An Introduction* (1988). A study of the immigrants to the British colonies on the eve of the American Revolution.

L. Bethell (ed.), *The Cambridge History of Latin America*, vols. 1 and 2 (1984). Excellent essays on the colonial era.

D. Brading, *The First America* (1991). A major study of colonial Latin America.

J. Brooke, *King George III* (1972). The best biography.

K. N. Chaudhuri, *The Trading World of Asia and the English East India Company* (1978). Examines the impact of trade on both Asians and Europeans.

P. Curtin, *The Atlantic Slave Trade* (1969). The best work on the subject.

D. B. Davis, *The Problem of Slavery in the Age of Revolution, 1770–1823* (1975). A major work for both European and American history.

R. Davis, *The Rise of the Atlantic Economies* (1973). A major synthesis.

C. Gibson, *Spain in America* (1966). A splendidly clear and balanced discussion.

J. Lockhardt and S. B. Schwartz, *Early Latin America: A History of Colonial Spanish America and Brazil* (1983). The new standard work.

J. R. McNeil, *Atlantic Empires of France and Spain: Louisbourg and Havana, 1700–1763* (1985). An examination of imperial policies in terms of two key overseas outposts.

R. Middleton, *The Bells of Victory: The Pitt-Newcastle Ministry and the Conduct of the Seven Years' War, 1757–1762* (1985). A careful study of the intricacies of eighteenth-century cabinet government that questions the centrality of Pitt's role in the British victory.

S. W. Mintz, *Sweetness and Power: The Place of Sugar in Modern History* (1985). Traces the role of sugar in the world economy and the manner in which sugar has had an impact on world culture.

J. C. Riley, *The Seven Years' War and the Old Regime in France: The Economic and Financial Toll* (1986). A useful analysis of pressures that would undermine the French monarchy.

K. W. Schweizer, *Frederick the Great, William Pitt, and Lord Bute: The Anglo-Prussian Alliance, 1756–1763* (1991). The most recent study of this complex diplomacy.

G. S. Wood, *The Creation of the American Republic, 1776–1787* (1969). A far-ranging work dealing with Anglo-American political thought.

G. S. Wood, *The Radicalism of the American Revolution* (1991). A major interpretation.

18

The Age of Enlightenment: Eighteenth-Century Thought

KEY TOPICS IN THIS CHAPTER

∼ The intellectual and social background of the Enlightenment

∼ The *philosophes* of the Enlightenment and their agenda of intellectual and political reform

∼ Efforts of "enlightened" monarchs in central and eastern Europe to increase the economic and military strength of their domains

∼ The partition of Poland by Prussia, Russia, and Austria

The modern world's faith in the possibility and desirability of change is one of its key intellectual inheritances from the eighteenth century, the self-proclaimed Age of Enlightenment. The leaders of the Enlightenment were convinced that human reason could comprehend the processes of nature and manipulate them to create a better world. They believed that the rational order that the Scientific Revolution had discovered to pervade the physical universe should also exist in human societies. They assumed that reason provided them with the means to conduct a radical critique of all traditional beliefs and institutions and that this critique would inevitably inspire innovation and improvement. The monarchs of the era who caught its spirit and who centralized political authority in order to hasten a process of reform created a kind of government called enlightened absolutism.

∽ Formative Influences

Ideas of Newton and Locke

Two Englishmen, Isaac Newton (1642–1727) and John Locke (1632–1704), were the forerunners of the Enlightenment. The theory of gravitation that Newton developed solved the puzzles and integrated the insights of Copernicus, Kepler, and Galileo. Newton thus brought a long scientific search to a triumphant conclusion, producing a coherent, unified explanation for the behavior of all astronomical bodies. Although Newton was a Christian, his work demonstrated that the human mind, unaided by revelation, was equipped to discover truth about nature. All that was necessary, he stated, was the use of reason to formulate theories that could be confirmed by empirical observation.

Newton's suggestion that the universe operated like a rationally designed machine caused his contemporaries to speculate that human nature and human society might also be explained mechanistically. In *An Essay Concerning Human Understanding* (1690), John Locke argued that every human being is born with a mind that is a *tabula rasa,* a blank page. Personality is created when an individual's senses expose his or her formless mind to experiences of the external world. Human nature is, thus, the product of an environment, and it can be changed by changing the environment in which it develops. Locke's psychology rejected the Christian doctrine that humans are permanently flawed by sin and in need of divine grace to improve their lives. He insisted that the means were at hand for people to redesign themselves.

The Example of British Toleration and Stability

Newton and Locke created a rationale for a reformist approach to society, and their stable homeland, Great Britain (after the Glorious Revolution of 1688), furnished a test case for reformers: a society in which enlightened programs seemed to benefit everyone. England tolerated all religions except for Unitarianism and Roman Catholicism. (Even they were not actually persecuted.) The press and speech were relatively free in England. The authority of the monarchy was limited, for political sovereignty resided in Parliament. Courts protected the citizens from arbitrary action by government officials, and the army was small. England was freer than any other European nation of the day, and far from producing disorder, its liberal policies had nurtured a loyal, prosperous citizenry.

Major Enlightenment Texts

Need for Reform in France

If Great Britain illustrated the potential for social reform, France demonstrated its necessity. Louis XIV's policies—an absolute monarchy, a large standing army, heavy taxation, and religious persecution—rendered his people so miserable that many celebrated when he died. His successors further curtailed freedoms. Critics of their regimes were subject to arbitrary arrest. State regulation hampered economic growth. And aristocrats glorified militarism. The manifest need for change in France stimulated the French intellectuals who made their homeland the Enlightenment's intellectual center.

The Emergence of a Print Culture

Although printed materials contributed greatly to the success of the Protestant Reformation, the Enlightenment was the first major movement in Europe's history to flourish in a cultural environment created by the printed word. The volume of printed material increased dramatically during the eighteenth century, and print became the chief vehicle for the communication of ideas until the invention of the electronic media of our own day.

Books were costly, but the information they contained was widely disseminated. More private and public libraries were founded, and thinkers spread their ideas through inexpensive newspapers and journals.

The growing audience for the printed word affected the issues discussed in print. During the Middle Ages, when the clergy were the dominant literate class, literature dealt mostly with religion. But as ordinary men and women acquired the ability to read, the secular and material concerns of their lives began to be explored in print. In the seventeenth century, half the books published in Paris had religious themes; only 10 percent of them did by the 1780s.

Increasingly, members of the aristocracy and middle class were expected to be familiar with books and secular ideas. Periodicals such as Joseph Addison and Richard Steele's *The Spectator* (founded in 1711) provided vehicles for communicating with a wide public. People gathered in private homes or met in places like coffeehouses for serious discussions. Secret societies, such as the movement of Freemasons that began in Britain at this time, promoted reading and debate.

The expanding market for printed matter made it possible for writers to earn a living from their work. For the first time, authorship became an occupation and authors celebrities. Parisian ladies sought out popular writers as honored guests for parties in their fashionable salons, and some writers (notably Alexander Pope and Voltaire) earned fortunes.

A division soon emerged between high and low literary culture. The most successful authors addressed themselves to, and were accepted into, the upper levels of society. Other writers survived more precariously—writing for whatever newspaper or journal would pay for their pages. Many of these people were hacks who blamed their lack of success on society. They often carried Enlightenment ideas to radical extremes and transmitted them in this embittered form to a lower-class audience.

The spread of secular printed materials created a new and increasingly influential social force: public opinion. Such a phenomenon seems not to have existed before the middle of the eighteenth century. A book or newspaper could reach thousands of readers and persuade them to a single point of view. Authors were accountable only to the readers to whom they marketed their works, and the information they channeled to the public meant that governments could no longer operate in secret or with disregard to the opinions of their subjects. They, as well as their critics, had to explain and discuss policies openly.

Continental European governments sensed the political power of the new print culture and saw that it threatened their traditional authority. Consequently, they censored books and newspapers and imprisoned offending authors. The spread of the print culture revealed the importance of the freedom of the press as an instrument for maintaining political accountability.

The *Philosophes*

The writers and critics who championed reform and flourished in the emerging print culture were called *philosophes.* They included Voltaire, Montesquieu, Diderot, Rousseau, Hume, Gibbon, Smith, Bentham, Lessing, Kant, and many lesser figures. These men were activist philosophers who advocated the use of reason and common sense to reform the major institutions and social practices of their day.

The *philosophes* were not part of an organized movement and did not all advocate the same things. The chief bond among them was a common desire to reform thought, society, and government for the sake of human liberty. During the Reformation and the religious wars, writers used the printed word to debate the proper mode of faith in God. The *philosophes* of the Enlightenment employed print to proclaim a new faith in the capacity of humankind to improve itself without the aid of God.

Many of the *philosophes* were born into the middle class, whence they drew the bulk of their readership. Members of the middle class had sufficient income and leisure to buy, read, and discuss the *philosophes'* works. Although the writers of the Enlightenment did not consciously champion the goals or causes of the middle class, they did create an intellectual ferment that undermined traditional institutions that the middle class found restrictive. They taught middle-class readers how to pose pointed, critical questions. And they supported the things that contributed to the economic growth that was transforming Europe in the eighteenth century and enlarging its middle class.

The earliest exponents of the Enlightenment were individuals who worked alone to popularize the rationalism and scientific ideas of the seventeenth century. By mid-century, they had succeeded in awakening widespread interest in reform and in creating a kind of intellectual community. They began to correspond with each other, to write for each other (as well as for the general public), and to defend each other against political and religious authorities. During the second half of the century, the *philosophes* were sufficiently safe to quarrel among themselves, and their attention switched from the general and theoretical to the specialized and practical. Having convinced Europeans that change was a good idea, they began to suggest exactly what changes were most desirable.

Voltaire's Agenda of Intellectual Reform

One of the earliest and most influential of the *philosophes* was François Marie Arouet, known simply as Voltaire (1694–1778). During the 1720s, some of Voltaire's writings offended the French authorities, and he was briefly imprisoned. In 1733, after a visit to England, he indicted French society by publishing *Letters on the English,* a book lauding England's intellectual openness and political freedoms. In 1738, his *Elements of the Philosophy of Newton* popularized the thought of the great English scientist and established Voltaire's reputation as an important writer. Thereafter, he lived either in France or just across the French border near Geneva, where the royal authorities could not bother him.

Voltaire's essays, histories, plays, stories, and letters made him the literary arbiter of Europe. Using wit and sarcasm, he assaulted the evils of his day. His most famous satire, *Candide* (1759), ridiculed war, religious perse-cution, and sentimental confidence in the goodness of human nature. Like most *philosophes*, Voltaire believed that improvement of human society was necessary, but he was doubtful that reform could be permanent. The optimism of the Enlightenment was a tempered hopefulness, not a glib certainty. An undercurrent of pessimism characterized most of the works of the period.

The *Encyclopedia*

At mid-century, one of the greatest monuments of the Enlightenment began to appear: the *Encyclopedia* edited by Denis Diderot (1713–1784) and Jean le Rond d'Alembert (1717–1783). The first of its seventeen volumes of text and eleven of plates (illustrations) was issued in 1751; the last, in 1772. About 16,000 copies of various editions were sold before 1789.

All the major French *philosophes* were invited to contribute to the *Encyclopedia*, and it was the product of the collective effort of more than 100 authors. Since it brought together the most advanced ideas of its day (critiques of religion, government, and philosophy), it served as a collective plea for reform. This annoyed the French government, which made many attempts to censor it and to halt its publication. But contributors to the *Encyclopedia* learned to avoid censure by hiding controversial ideas in obscure articles or by cloaking them with irony.

The project was designed to secularize learning and undermine the in-tellectual assumptions that lingered from the Middle Ages and the Reforma-tion. Articles on politics, ethics, and society ignored divine law and concen-trated on issues affecting human well-being. Classical antiquity had more influence than Christianity in shaping the ideas expressed in the *Encyclope-dia.* The good life was a life on earth characterized by the application of rea-son to human relationships. The *Encyclopedia* diffused this Enlightenment faith across the continent, drawing in German and Russian thinkers.

❧ The Enlightenment and Religion

Many *philosophes* believed that Europe's churches were the chief impediment to the improvement and happiness of its people. They condemned almost all varieties of Christianity (especially Roman Catholicism), for they believed that piety hindered the scientific study of nature and the pursuit of a life guided by reason. Both Protestant and Catholic versions of the doctrine of original sin stated that human nature was fundamentally flawed and could not be im-proved. Both faiths taught that people could not better themselves unless God chose to bestow the gifts of grace on them. Both diverted attention from re-forming this world to preparing for the world to come. The *philosophes* also found plenty of historical evidence to support their argument that churches promoted intolerance and bigotry, that quarrels over obscure points of doc-trine drove them to torture and make war.

The *philosophes'* critique of religion was not just an attack on a set of ideas. It was an assault on some of Europe's most significant institutions. The churches were essential to the power structure of the old regime. They owned large amounts of land. The upper clergy were usually sons of aristocratic families who took an active part in politics. Membership in a nation's predominant denomination was often a requirement for admission to its political life or for full protection under its laws. Clergymen condemned political disobedience as a sin against God and provided intellectual justification for the social and political status quo.

Deism

The *philosophes* were not opposed to all religion. What they wanted was a religion without fanaticism and intolerance, a faith that would not substitute the authority of tradition for the authority of human reason. The models of nature produced by Newtonian physics suggested that the universe was a rational structure. This persuaded the *philosophes* that the God who had made the universe was a rational being who was best worshiped by honoring reason. The religion of reason is called *deism* to distinguish it from theism, a religion based on revelation.

Deists claimed that authentic religious faith was a product of reason and ordinary experience, not of supernatural or mystical communications. It described God as a kind of divine watchmaker who created the mechanism of nature, set it in motion, and then ceased to interfere with it. Deists were not atheists. They believed that the existence of God could be empirically established by the study of nature: an ordered universe implied the existence of a rational Creator. Further, because nature provided evidence that God was rational, it justified the assumption that the deity wanted human beings to behave rationally. A rational code of ethics required that good be rewarded and evil punished. Since this was not always seen to happen on earth, the deists argued that belief in a life after death, when rewards and punishments were meted out, was rational.

Deism was empirical, tolerant, reasonable, and capable of encouraging virtuous living, and deists hoped that the spread of their faith in place of traditional Christianity would end fanaticism, persecution, and rivalry among sects. Since each rational person could on his or her own arrive at the essentials of religion (the arguments for God's existence and for the necessity of moral conduct), there was no need for clergy. The deists hoped that by abolishing clergy they could eliminate a profession that had been responsible for fomenting much of the strife that had plagued European history.

Radical Enlightenment Criticism of Religion

Some *philosophes* were not content with proposing a rational religion as an alternative to faith based on revelation. They went on the offensive against traditional beliefs. Voltaire's *Philosophical Dictionary* (1764) pointed out inconsistencies in the biblical texts and humorously described the immoral acts of biblical heroes. The Scottish philosopher David Hume (1711–1776), in a chapter of his *Inquiry into Human Nature* (1748), argued that there was no empirical evidence for the belief in divine miracles that was central to much of Christianity. In *The Decline and Fall of the Roman Empire* (1776), the English historian Edward Gibbon (1737–1794) credited the rise of Christianity to natural causes, not divine intervention.

Some *philosophes* argued that religious toleration ought to extend to all faiths, not just varieties of Christianity. In 1779, Gotthold Lessing wrote *Nathan the Wise,* an influential play that used a Jewish character to make a case for toleration. But the contempt that some *philosophes* had for the colorful legends contained in the Hebrew scriptures led them to heap ridicule on Judaism as a more primitive faith than Christianity. Despite advocating toleration, the Enlightenment further stigmatized Jews.

The Enlightenment and Society

The *philosophes* believed that a rational examination of society would reveal that there were laws for human relationships similar to those that governed physical nature. Although the term did not appear until later, the idea of *social science* originated with the Enlightenment. *Philosophes* hoped to end human cruelty by discovering the laws that made societies function. But like most people, the *philosophes* had blind spots. When they contemplated social reforms, they assumed a male world and thought mostly about men. With few exceptions, they had little interest in increasing social or intellectual opportunities for women.

Reform of Criminal Law

In 1764, Cesare Beccaria (1738–1794) published *On Crimes and Punishments.* It argued that the intent of punishment should be to deter further crime, and it rigorously and eloquently opposed both torture and capital punishment. The purpose of law, Beccaria maintained, was not to impose a divinely mandated standard of conduct, but to secure the greatest happiness for the greatest number of people. A utilitarian philosophy based on happiness in this life permeated most of Enlightenment thought about reform.

Economic Reform

Mercantilist thinking—the use of legislation to protect a country's trade from foreign competition—was the economic policy pursued by most European nations in the eighteenth century. Many *philosophes* opposed it.

In France, the reform-minded economists were called *physiocrats.* Their leaders, François Quesnay (1694–1774) and Pierre Dupont de Nemours

(1739–1817), argued that government intervention in the economy should be limited to protecting property and permitting its owners to use it freely. They did not, however, advocate radical individualism. They believed that small peasant holdings should, for efficiency, be consolidated into large, scientifically managed farms.

Adam Smith's *Inquiry into the Nature and Causes of the Wealth of Nations* (1776) was the Enlightenment's most important contribution to the field of economics. Smith believed that freedom was essential to a natural economic system, and he urged the abolition of mercantilism's navigation acts, bounties, tariffs, trade monopolies, and laws regulating labor and manufacture. These policies were designed to increase the wealth of one nation by confiscating the riches of others, but Smith insisted that their effect was to hinder economic growth for all.

The mercantilists assumed that the earth's resources were limited and that one nation could acquire wealth only at the expense of others. Smith challenged this dogma. He claimed that the resources of nature were boundless and that they existed to be exploited for the enrichment of humankind. Poverty could be abolished, he maintained, if individuals were unleashed to pursue their self-interest. To enrich themselves, individuals would have to meet the needs of others in the marketplace, and their labor would expand the economy for everyone. Although Smith is often labeled a *laissez-faire* economist, he was not opposed to all government intervention. The state, he argued, should provide schools, armies, navies, and roads, and it should undertake commercial ventures that were desirable but beyond the means of private enterprise.

When Smith wrote, the population of the world was smaller, its people poorer, and the quantity of undeveloped resources per capita much greater than it is now. For people of the eighteenth century, improvement of the human condition seemed both to demand and to justify the uninhibited exploitation of nature. Not until recently has concern for the environment forced a rethinking of this position.

Political Reform

The most important political debates of the Enlightenment took place in France, but they produced no consensus. *Philosophes* advocated everything from a reformed aristocracy, to a democracy, to an absolute monarchy.

***Montesquieu and* The Spirit of the Laws.** Charles Louis de Secondat, Baron de Montesquieu (1689–1755), was a lawyer, noble of the robe, member of a provincial *parlement*, and fellow of the Bordeaux Academy of Science. Although he was comfortably ensconced within the bosom of French society, he believed that reform was needed. In 1721, he denounced the cruelty and irrationality of European society in *The Persian Letters*, satirical epistles purportedly written by two Persian tourists to explain European behavior to their friends at home.

In 1748, he published *The Spirit of the Laws*, perhaps the single most influential book of the century. To research it, Montesquieu used the empirical method advocated by the Enlightenment. He analyzed the political institutions of both ancient and modern nations. From these he concluded that there could be no single set of laws that applied to all peoples at all times and in all places. Numerous variables had to be taken into account to determine the best political system for a particular country. Size, population, social and religious customs, economic structures, traditions, and climate all helped determine whether a land should have a monarchy or a republic or something else. Montesquieu anticipated by a century the discipline which is now known as sociology.

Montesquieu believed that France would be served best by a limited monarchy, a government in which groups of citizens had rights that curtailed the power of their ruler. Montesquieu pointed to the *parlements*, the aristocratic courts, as an example of the kind of political associations he thought could do the best job of protecting the rights of Frenchmen. In championing these aristocratic bodies, he endorsed political conservativism—but as an instrument to reform a monarchy whose oppressive and inefficient absolutism, he believed, had degraded life in France.

One of Montesquieu's most influential ideas was that power ought to be divided among branches of a government. The British constitution provided him with his model: executive power in the king, legislative power in the Parliament, and judicial power in the courts. Montesquieu thought that any two of these branches could check the actions of the third. He failed, however, to understand how patronage and electoral corruption allowed a handful of powerful aristocrats to dominate the government of Great Britain. And he was unaware of the emerging cabinet system that subordinated the British executive to Parliament.

Rousseau: A Radical Critique of Modern Society. Jean-Jacques Rousseau (1712–1778) was a troubled genius who was at odds with the other *philosophes.* They believed that life would improve if people produced more goods and consumed more of the fruits of the earth. But Rousseau had contempt for societies in which commerce and industry were regarded as the most important human activities. In his *Discourse on the Moral Effects of the Arts and Sciences* (1750), he declared that Europe's materialistic civilization had corrupted human nature. And in his *Discourse on the Origin of Inequality* (1755), he traced society's problems to the effects of commerce: the uneven distribution of property.

In politics as well as economics, Rousseau's thought was a radical assault on the popular ideas of his day. Most eighteenth-century political theorists assumed that society was merely a collection of individuals pursuing personal, selfish goals. The reforms the *philosophes* suggested aimed at liberating individuals from undue restraint by government. Rousseau picked up the stick from the other end. In *The Social Contract* (1762), he suggested that society is more important than its individual members, for it determines their options. Only a relationship to a larger community creates the moral environment in which individuals are capable of significant action. The true task of a reformer, therefore, is to create the kind of community that allows people to achieve the highest morality.

Contemporary European society—an aggregate of competing individuals whose chief goal was selfish independence—was not, in Rousseau's opinion, an ideal community. He envisioned a world in which each person found personal freedom by serving the interests of the group. He tried to reconcile the ends of the individual and the group by defining freedom as obedience to democratically enacted laws representing the general will. Rousseau believed that the will of the majority of informed citizens was always right and always marked the path of true freedom. This argument led him to the notorious conclusion that some people might have to be forced to be free. Rousseau's ideal state was a direct democracy that took collective action against dissidents.

Because Rousseau rejected the eighteenth-century cult of the individual and the fruits of selfishness, his impact on his contemporaries was slight. Too many people were either making or hoping to make money to appreciate his criticism of commercial values. Rousseau proved, however, to be a figure to whom later generations returned. Many leaders of the French Revolution were inspired by him, and he influenced most of the writers of the nineteenth and twentieth centuries who were critical of the general tenor and direction of Western culture.

The writings of Jean-Jacques Rousseau (1712–1778) raised some of the most profound social and ethical questions of the Enlightenment. This portrait by Maurice Quentin was made around 1740. [Bildarchiv Preussischer Kulturbesitz]

Rousseau Argues for Separate Spheres for Men and Women

Jean-Jacques Rousseau published Émile, *a novel about education, in 1762. In it he made one of the strongest and most influential arguments of the eighteenth century in favor of distinct social roles for men and women. Furthermore, he portrayed women as fundamentally subordinate to men.*

~ How does Rousseau move from a description of the physical differences between men and women to the conclusion that they should have distinct social roles and spheres? What kinds of social activities are considered proper for women by Rousseau? What kind of education would he think appropriate for women?

There is not parity between the two sexes in regard to the consequences of sex. The male is male only at certain moments. The female is female her whole life or at least during her whole youth. Everything constantly recalls her sex to her; and, to fulfill its functions well, she needs a constitution which corresponds to it. She needs care during her pregnancy; she needs rest at the time of childbirth; she needs a soft and sedentary life to suckle her children; she needs patience and gentleness, a zeal and an affection that noth-ing can rebuff in order to raise her children. She serves as the link between them and their father; she alone makes him love them and gives him the confidence to call them his own. How much tenderness and care is required to maintain the union of the whole family! And, finally, all this must come not from virtues but from tastes, or else the human species would soon be extinguished.

The strictness of the relative duties of the two sexes is not and cannot be the same. When woman complains on this

Women in the Thought and Practice of the Enlightenment. Aristocratic women, especially in France, arranged gatherings in their salons (drawing rooms) that were crucial to the careers of *philosophes*. Politically well-connected women, like Madame Geoffrin, Mademoiselle de Lespinasse, and Madame Tencin, helped *philosophes* make useful contacts. Association with a fashionable salon brought a *philosophe* social status that added luster to his ideas and sales to his books. And sometimes his patroness provided him with money or protection from persecution. Madame de Pompadour, the mistress of Louis XV, countered attacks on *philosophes* and helped defeat efforts to censor the *Encyclopedia.*

Despite their ties with learned women, few *philosophes* were feminists. Many advocated broader educations for women and rejected the ascetic views of sexuality that were part of the traditional religious training given girls. Montesquieu's *The Persian Letters* devoted considerable space to condemning by implication the restrictions European society placed on women. Montesquieu believed that women were in no way naturally inferior to men and should have a wider role in society. But in *The Spirit of the Laws,* while supporting

score about unjust man-made inequality, she is wrong. This inequality is not a human institution—or, at least, it is the work not of prejudice but of reason. It is up to the sex that nature has charged with the bearing of children to be responsible for them to the other sex. Doubtless it is not permitted to any one to violate his faith, and every unfaithful husband who deprives his wife of the only reward of the austere duties of her sex is an unjust and barbarous man. But the unfaithful woman does more; she dissolves the family and breaks all the bonds of nature. . . .

Once it is demonstrated that man and woman are not and ought not be constituted in the same way in either character or temperament, it follows that they ought not to have the same education. In following nature's directions, man and woman ought to act in concert, but they ought not to do the same things. The goal of their labors is common, but their labors themselves are different, and consequently so are the tastes directing them. . . .

The good constitution of children initially depends on that of their mothers. The first education of men depends on the care of women. Men's morals, their passions, their tastes, their pleasures, their very happiness also depend on women. Thus the whole education of women ought to relate to men. To please men, to be useful to them, to make herself loved and honored by them, to raise them when young, to care for them when grown, to counsel them, to console them, to make their lives agreeable and sweet— these are the duties of women at all times, and they ought to be taught from childhood. So long as one does not return to this principle, one will deviate from the goal, and all the precepts taught to women will be of no use for their happiness or ours.

Jean-Jacques Rousseau, Émile; or, On Education, *trans. by Allan Bloom (New York: Basic Books, Inc., 1979), pp. 361, 363, 365.*

the right of divorce and opposing laws that directly oppressed women, he still recommended a dominant role for the husband in marriage and firmly upheld the ideal of chastity for women.

Although the *Encyclopedia* suggested some ways to improve women's lives, women's issues did not feature on the agenda of its reforms. The encyclopedists were almost all male, and most of the articles that discussed women emphasized their physical weakness and inferiority—liabilities usually attributed to menstruation or child bearing. Women were viewed primarily in a family context—as daughters, wives, and mothers—and child rearing was represented as their chief occupation. The sexual double standard was never questioned, and some contributors opposed granting women social equality.

The *Encyclopedia*'s articles convey a general sense that women were reared to be frivolous and unconcerned with important issues. But the *Encyclopedia*'s illustrations show many women engaged in vital economic activities. Many of these were working-class women, a group largely ignored in the articles.

Rousseau, the most radical of the Enlightenment political theorists, took a very conservative position on gender relations. His novel *Émile* (1762) stressed the differences between males and females and recommended that women's educations center on duties relating to the bearing and rearing of children. Rousseau excluded women from public affairs and confined them to the home. He considered women to be inferior to men in all respects except their capacity for feeling and loving, and he argued that their chief duty was to make themselves pleasing to men.

Paradoxically, in spite of these views and in spite of his own ill treatment of the many women who bore his many children, Rousseau won a vast female following. Women responded to his appreciation of their feelings and his proclamation of the importance of their vocations as wives and mothers. He accorded them a degree of dignity in the domestic sphere that they were denied in public life.

In 1792, *A Vindication of the Rights of Woman*, by Mary Wollstonecraft (1759–1797), indicted Rousseau and the *philosophes* for their failure to follow through on the Enlightenment's commitment to the rational reform of society. Wollstonecraft (who, like so many women of her day, died of puerperal fever) argued that to confine women to the home because of their supposed physical limitations was to condemn them to sexual slavery and make them victims of male tyranny. She insisted that the progress of all humanity was impeded when women were denied good educations. By demanding for women the liberty that *philosophes* had been claiming for men for more than a century, Wollstonecraft broadened the agenda of the Enlightenment to include the rights of women as well as those of men.

∼ Enlightened Absolutism

Most of the *philosophes* rejected Montesquieu's reformed aristocracy and Rousseau's direct democracy as unrealistic. Voltaire, Diderot, and others were monarchists who, rather than limiting the power of rulers, wanted to redirect it to rationalize economic and political structures and liberate intellectual life. *Philosophes* were not opposed to power if they could harness it for their own use. They hailed the *enlightened absolutism* practiced at the courts of Frederick II of Prussia, Joseph II of Austria, and Catherine II of Russia as an ideal form of government—a monarchy devoted to centralizing its power in order to enact reforms efficiently.

The Enlightenment's intellectuals often had less influence in shaping public policy than they realized. Monarchs like Frederick II and Catherine II corresponded with the *philosophes*, hosted them at court, and made a show of referring to their ideas. But enlightened absolutists were motivated by more than a *philosophe*'s zeal for humanitarian reform. They were engaged in struggles with competing nations and pursued the rational economic and social integration of their realms because it increased their military strength. They used reason in the service of a militarism that the *philosophes* considered irrational.

Frederick the Great of Prussia

Frederick II, "the Great" (r. 1740–1786), was prepared to do whatever was necessary to make his small country a leading European power. To that end he was eager to "rationalize" his government, no matter what the human costs. Frederick liked to describe himself as "the first servant of the State," a phrase that suggested that the medieval concept of personal monarchy was fading and the modern definition of the state as an impersonal governmental apparatus independent of the monarch was taking its place.

The impetus for Prussia's economic development came from the state, for the state enjoyed most of the benefits. High taxes siphoned off much of the income of the productive classes, the peasants and townspeople. Silesia, which Frederick seized from Austria in 1740, was developed as a manufacturing district, while Prussia itself was reorganized to improve agricultural production. Under state supervision, swamps were drained, new crops (potatoes and turnips) introduced, and peasants compelled to migrate where they were needed. Economic reality also encouraged Frederick, a Lutheran, to practice religious toleration. Prussia needed manpower and had to attract immigration.

Joseph II of Austria

No eighteenth-century ruler so embodied rational, impersonal force as Joseph II of Austria (r. 1765–1790), Maria Theresa's son and co-ruler with her from 1765 to 1780. He was an austere, humorless person who prided himself on an ascetic lifestyle and a passionless, rational approach to life. Despite his cold personality, Joseph II sincerely wanted to improve the lot of his people and was, unlike colleagues who ruled Prussia and Russia, neither a political opportunist nor a cynic. His well-intentioned efforts, however, spawned rebellions among both the aristocracy and the peasantry across the Habsburg domains.

Centralization of Authority. The empire led by the Austrian Habsburgs was the most diverse of the great European states of the eighteenth century. Its subjects spoke many languages and had few ties in common. The throne could not even depend on the aristocracy for support. In order to preserve the monarchy during the War of the Austrian Succession (1740–1748), Maria Theresa had granted the aristocrats, especially in Hungary, extensive freedom.

Maria Theresa strengthened the power of the crown outside of Hungary by increasing the size of the empire's administrative bureaucracy. Her efficient system of tax collection compelled even the clergy and the nobles of Austria and Bohemia to pay. She established "central councils" to handle various kinds of problems. And she brought education under state control to ensure her government a sufficient supply of trained officials. Her concern for schools extended to increasing opportunities for primary education at the local level.

Maria Theresa tried to protect peasants and serfs by using the royal bureaucracy to enforce limits on the amount of labor *(robot)* noble landowners could demand from their tenants. Her concern was not solely humanitarian; it helped her maintain a large pool from which to draw military recruits.

Joseph II followed the path blazed by his mother. But he was even more determined to have his way, and his projected reforms were more wide-ranging. Although he wanted to add territory belonging to Poland, Bavaria, and the Ottoman Empire to the Habsburg domain, his strongest desire was to increase his authority over his various realms. His strategy was to reduce the pluralism of the Habsburg holdings by imposing central authority in places that Maria Theresa had wisely chosen to ignore.

In particular, Joseph sought to rein in the nobility of Hungary. To avoid having to guarantee their existing privileges or promise them new ones at the time of his coronation, he refused to have himself crowned king of Hungary. He reorganized local governments in Hungary to increase the authority of his officials and required the use of German in all transactions. The Magyar nobility protested, and in 1790 Joseph backed down.

Ecclesiastical Policies. The church, too, was subject to Joseph's program for establishing royal absolutism. Since the Reformation of the sixteenth century, the Habsburgs had been the single most important dynasty championing Roman Catholicism. Maria Theresa had adamantly opposed religious toleration, but refused to allow the church to limit her authority. She also adopted the enlightened policy of discouraging the more extreme forms of Roman Catholic popular piety—things like public flagellation.

Joseph II was a practicing Catholic, but both enlightenment and pragmatic politics urged him to a policy of toleration. In October 1781, Joseph issued a Toleration Patent (decree) that extended freedom of worship to Lutherans, Calvinists, and the Greek Orthodox. They were permitted to have places of worship, to sponsor schools, to enter skilled trades, and to hold academic appointments and positions in public service. Later, Joseph relieved the Jews of certain taxes and signs of personal degradation and extended to them the right of private worship. These actions benefited the Jews, but fell short of granting them full equality with other Habsburg subjects.

Joseph brought various Roman Catholic institutions directly under royal control. He forbade direct communication between his bishops and the pope. Viewing religious orders as unproductive, he dissolved and confiscated the endowments of the more than 600 monasteries that did not contribute to society by running schools or hospitals. He used funds confiscated from the monasteries to create new parishes in places where there was a shortage of priests. He closed the established seminaries, accusing them of instilling in priests too great a loyalty to the papacy and too little concern for their parishioners. He replaced these schools with eight new seminaries where training emphasized parish duties. *Josephinism*, the emperor's ecclesiastical policy, subjected the Roman Catholic Church to state control and made its priests state employees.

Economic and Agrarian Reform. Like Frederick of Prussia, Joseph tried to expand the economy by using the powers of government. He abolished many internal tariffs, encouraged road building and the improvement of river transport, and personally inspected farms and factories. He reconstructed the judicial system to make laws more uniform and rational. National courts with power over the local courts of landlords were established. All of these things were intended to unify the state and increase the taxes paid to the imperial treasury.

Over the course of Joseph's reign, he introduced a series of reforms relating to serfdom that altered the structure of rural society. He did not abolish the authority of landlords over their peasants, but he did try to lessen it and make it accountable to royal officials. He ended serfdom as a legally sanctioned servile condition. He granted peasants a wide array of personal freedoms—including rights to marry, to engage in skilled work, and to have their children trained for skilled work without the permission of their landlord. He reformed the procedures of the manorial courts and created avenues for appeal to royal officials. He encouraged landlords to change land leases so that it would be easier for peasants to inherit them or to transfer them to other tenants. The intent of his reforms was to make the peasants more productive, industrious farmers by reducing their traditional burdens.

In 1789, near the end of his reign, Joseph proposed a new and daring system of land taxation. He ended aristocratic immunity from taxation and decreed that all proprietors of the land be taxed regardless of social status. No longer were the peasants alone to bear the burden of taxation. The *robot* was commuted to a monetary tax, part of which was to go to the landlord and part to the state.

Although the nobility blocked the implementation of Joseph's tax reforms, and his death in 1790 ended efforts to enforce them, they and earlier measures created turmoil throughout the Habsburg realms. Disagreements about the interpretation of newly granted rights sparked peasant uprisings, and nobles protested the taxation scheme. The Hungarian Magyars forced Joseph to rescind his centralization measures.

Joseph's brother, Leopold II (r. 1790–1792), inherited his crown. Although generally sympathetic to reform, Leopold had to repeal many of the most controversial of Joseph's decrees, some of which he himself had opposed. Expediency drove him to return much political and administrative authority to local nobles, whom he thought should have a voice in government.

Catherine the Great of Russia

Joseph II never grasped the practical necessity of forging political constituencies to support his reforms. Catherine II (r. 1762–1796), a German princess who became empress of Russia, understood only too well the fragility of her Romanov dynasty's base of power.

Tsar Peter the Great (d. 1725) had exercised vast power, but after his death the court nobility and the army, who determined the succession to the throne, chose rulers who dissipated the authority of the monarchy. Peter was followed by his wife, Catherine I (r. 1725–1727), and then his grandson, Peter

Catherine the Great, here portrayed as a young princess, ascended to the Russian throne after the murder of her husband. She tried initially to enact major reforms, but she never intended to abandon absolutism. She assured the nobility of their rights and by the end of her reign had imposed press censorship. [The Bettmann Archive]

II (r. 1727–1730). The crown then devolved on Ann, his niece. Ivan VI, who was less than a year old, became nominal tsar in 1740, until Peter's daughter, Elizabeth, took control in 1741. Political and romantic intrigues made a shambles of her court, and at her death in 1762, she was succeeded by a nephew, Peter III. His mental stability was in question. He exempted the nobles from compulsory military service and precipitously reversed Russia's foreign policy in the Seven Years' War. Inspired by adolescent hero worship for Frederick the Great, Peter refused to continue to cooperate with Austria and France in containing Prussia. That decision may have saved Prussia, but it was of no benefit to Russia. The one achievement of Peter's life was his marriage in 1745 to a young German princess born in Anhalt Zerbst, the future Catherine the Great.

For almost twenty years Catherine endured a precarious, miserable life at Elizabeth's court. But she was a shrewd woman who honed her survival skills by studying a palace seething with rumors, intrigue, and conspiracy. She befriended important nobles and read widely in the works of the *philosophes*. Her demented husband inspired neither affection nor respect. A few months after his accession as tsar, she acquiesced to his murder and seized his throne (1762).

Catherine's study of the Enlightenment and the culture of western Europe taught her how backward Russia was, and it suggested to her the reforms that were needed to sustain her nation as a great power. She understood that reform would not succeed unless it had widespread support and that she—a foreign woman who had acquired the throne in a palace coup—was not secure enough to act unilaterally.

In 1767, Catherine convened a Legislative Commission representing all sectors of Russian society to propose changes in Russia's laws and government, and the empress gave it a set of *Instructions* drawn from the political works of the *philosophes*. A year later, Catherine dismissed the commission before several of its key committees had reported. Although a revision of Russian law was not to be carried out for more than half a century, the commission was not a useless exercise. It gathered vast amounts of information about local administration and economic life, and the debates of its delegates suggested that most Russians saw no alternative to an autocratic monarchy. This consensus created support for Catherine's exercise of enlightened absolutism.

Limited Administrative Reform. Catherine's reforms made a virtue of necessity. She knew that the Moscow nobles and army who had given her the throne could take it away. She also knew that she had too few educated subjects to staff an independent bureaucracy and that her treasury could not on its own sustain the cost of an army. Catherine, therefore, had no choice but to rely on the nobles for help in running and defending her empire. Rather than create a royal bureaucracy, she appointed nobles to most of the offices responsible for local affairs. In 1785, she issued a Charter of the Nobility that secured many of the rights and privileges of the aristocracy.

Economic Growth. Catherine followed the example of Peter the Great in promoting economic development. She removed internal barriers to trade. Exports of grain, flax, furs, and naval stores were greatly increased. The small Russian urban middle class, which was vital to trade, was protected. And Catherine promoted Russia's image as a progressive nation by befriending and corresponding with *philosophes*.

Territorial Expansion. Catherine's program for the development of Russia, like Peter the Great's, called for the acquisition of warm-water ports through which Russia could maintain contact with Europe (see Map 18-1). The ports she wanted were in the hands of the Turks.

In 1769, the Ottoman Empire declared war on Russia, and Russia occupied the Ottoman provinces on the Danube River and the Crimean coast of the Black Sea. The Treaty of Kuchuk-Kainardji ended hostilities in 1774 by granting Russia a direct outlet on the Black Sea, free navigation rights in its waters, and free access through the Bosporus. The province of the Crimea became an independent state, which Catherine painlessly annexed in 1783.

The Partition of Poland

Russia's victories along the Danube River were most unwelcome to Austria, for Austria hoped to expand on that front. The Ottoman Empire was also

MAP 18-1 Expansion of Russia, 1689–1796 *The overriding territorial aim of Peter the Great in the first quarter and of Catherine the Great in the second half of the eighteenth century was to secure year-round navigable outlets to the sea for the vast Russian Empire, hence Peter's push to the Baltic Sea and Catherine's to the Black Sea. Catherine also managed to acquire large areas of Poland through the partitions of that country.*

alarmed by Russia's aggression, and it pressed Frederick the Great of Prussia for help. He saw a way to exploit the situation and restore peace among the central European powers. He suggested that Russia agree to abandon the conquered Danubian provinces if Austria and Prussia compensated it by helping it annex a large part of Poland. Prussia claimed for itself a stretch of Polish land between East Prussia and Prussia proper that would link together some of Frederick's scattered territories. And Austria was to be given Galicia and other parts of Poland (see Map 18-2).

The Polish aristocracy, who had prevented the development of a strong centralized monarchy for Poland, were helpless to defend themselves. In September 1772, they ratified the loss of nearly a third of their territory. This humiliation inspired a revival of national feeling and an attempt to create a stronger government in what was left of Poland. But this was too little, too

MAP 18-2 Partitions of Poland, 1772–1793–1795
The callous eradication of Poland from the map displayed eighteenth-century power politics at its most extreme. Poland, without strong central governmental institutions, fell victim to those states in central and eastern Europe that had developed such institutions.

late. The partition of Poland proved that a nation that had not established a strong monarchy, bureaucracy, and army could not compete as a European state.

Russia and Prussia partitioned Poland again in 1793, and Russia, Prussia, and Austria partitioned it a third time in 1795. On that occasion it disappeared from the map of Europe for more than a century.

The End of the Eighteenth Century in Central and Eastern Europe

As the eighteenth century waned, enlightened absolutism became increasingly conservative and repressive. Frederick the Great grew remote during his old age, allowing the Prussian aristocracy the freedom to abuse their military and administrative offices. A reaction to Enlightenment ideas also set in among Prussia's Lutheran intellectuals. Joseph II's plans to restructure his realms provoked unrest. When the nobility called for an end to innovation, the Austrian government resorted increasingly to censorship and intimidation by a secret police. In Russia, the Pugachev peasant rebellion (1771–1775) raised fears of social upheaval that Catherine the Great never fully laid to rest. When the French Revolution broke out in 1789, the nervous empress censored books based on Enlightenment thought and sent offensive authors into Siberian exile.

By the close of the century, fear of and hostility to change permeated the ruling classes of central and eastern Europe, and monarchs who had pursued enlightened absolutism increasingly repudiated the humanity and liberalism of the Enlightenment. From 1763 to 1789, however, the rulers of both western and eastern Europe had been the major agents of institutional change. In every case, their attempts at reform had provoked resistance and resentment from some of their subjects. George III of Britain fought for years with Parliament and lost the colonies of North America. Frederick II of Prussia succeeded with his reforms only because he allowed his nobles increased authority. Catherine II of Russia had to come to terms with Russia's nobility. And Joseph II, who did not compromise with his nobles, threw his domains into turmoil. In France, as elsewhere, the drive toward royal absolutism occasioned aristocratic rebellion, but in France the monarchy and aristocracy lost control of the forces their quarrel unleashed.

The philosophes *who promoted the Enlightenment charted a new path for Western nations. They prospered in a print culture that mobilized a new form of popular power: public opinion. Brilliant advances in the physical sciences by men like Newton encouraged them to apply rational, scientific methods of analysis to social problems. They were not extreme rationalists. They accepted passions and feelings as essential parts of human nature and recommended moderation in the conduct of life. Most of them advocated religious toleration and opposed dogmatic faiths—particularly Roman Catholicism. They hoped to create a science of society with the means to discover ways to maximize human productivity and material happiness. Rousseau went further than most philosophes. He insisted that enhanced consumption was not enough, that true social reform required the promotion of virtue.*

Dramatically different implications were drawn from these ideas by political leaders. The founding fathers of the American republic found inspiration in them, as did liberal reformers throughout Europe (especially within royal bureaucracies). The revolutionaries in France honored them. And the autocratic monarchs of eastern Europe believed that Enlightenment ideas would help them rule more efficiently. This diverse response to the Enlightenment suggests that its thought cannot be reduced to a simple formula. It was an outlook that championed change and reform and focused on human beings and their welfare on earth, rather than on God and the hereafter. But it dictated no single path to, or vision of, the world it was determined to perfect.

⌇ Review Questions

1. How did the Enlightenment change basic Western attitudes toward reform, faith, and reason? What were the major formative influences on the *philosophes*? How important were the contributions of Voltaire and the *Encyclopedia* to the success of the Enlightenment?

2. Why did the *philosophes* consider organized religion to be their greatest enemy? What were the basic tenets of deism? What criticism might a deist direct at traditional Christianity? What would a deist do to improve on Christianity?

3. What were the attitudes of the *philosophes* toward women? What was Rousseau's view of women? What were the separate spheres he imagined men and women occupying? What were Mary Wollstonecraft's criticisms of Rousseau's view?

4. How did the arguments of the mercantilists differ from the theories developed by Adam Smith in *The Wealth of Nations*? How did each side in this debate view the earth's resources? Why might Smith be regarded as an advocate of the consumer?

5. What political views were held, respectively, by Montesquieu and Rousseau? Was Montesquieu's description of the political situation in England accurate? Was Rousseau a child of the Enlightenment—or was he its enemy? Which did Rousseau value more, the individual or society?

6. Were the enlightened monarchs true believers in the ideals of the *philosophes* or was their "enlightenment" merely a pose or veneer? Was their power really absolute? What motivated their reforms? What does the partition of Poland indicate about the true nature of enlightened absolutism?

⌇ Suggested Readings

C. Becker, *The Heavenly City of the Eighteenth Century Philosophers* (1932). An influential but very contoversial discussion.

C. B. A. Behrens, *Society, Government, and the Enlightenment: The Experiences of Eighteenth-Century France and Prussia* (1985). A wide-ranging comparative study.

T. Bestermann, *Voltaire* (1969). A biography by the editor of Voltaire's letters.

E. Cassirer, *The Philosophy of the Enlightenment* (1951). A brilliant but difficult work by one of the great philosophers of the twentieth century.

H. Chisick, *The Limits of Reform in the Enlightenment: Attitudes Toward the Education of the Lower Classes in Eighteenth-Century France* (1981). An attempt to examine the impact of the Enlightenment on non-elite classes.

G. R. Cragg, *The Church and the Age of Reason* (1961). A general survey of eighteenth-century religious life.

J. Gagliardo, *Enlightened Despotism* (1967). A discussion of the subject in its European context.

P. Gay, *The Enlightenment: An Interpretation*, 2 vols. (1966, 1969). The most important and far-reaching treatment.

M. C. Jacob, *The Radical Enlightenment: Pantheists, Freemasons, and Republicans* (1981). A treatment of frequently ignored figures in the age of the Enlightenment.

C. A. Macartney, *The Habsburg Empire, 1790–1918* (1971). Provides useful coverage of major mid-eighteenth-century developments.

I. de Madariaga, *Russia in the Age of Catherine the Great* (1981). The best discussion in English.

F. Manuel, *The Eighteenth Century Confronts the Gods* (1959). A broad examination of the *philosophes'* treatment of Christian and pagan religion.

G. Ritter, *Frederick the Great* (trans. 1968). A useful biography.

R. O. Rockwood (ed), *Carl Becker's Heavenly City Revisited* (1958). Important essays qualifying Becker's thesis.

J. Schwartz, *The Sexual Politics of Jean-Jacques Rousseau* (1984). A controversial reading of Rousseau's political thought, organized around gender issues.

J. N. Shklar, *Men and Citizens, A Study of Rousseau's Social Theory* (1969). A thoughtful and provocative overview of Rousseau's political thought.

S. I. Spencer, *French Women and the Age of Enlightenment* (1984). An outstanding collection of essays that cover the political, economic, and cultural roles of women.

A. M. Wilson, *Diderot* (1972). A splendid biography of the person behind the *Encyclopedia* and other major Enlightenment publications.

19

The French Revolution

KEY TOPICS IN THIS CHAPTER

~ The financial crisis that persuaded the French monarchy to convene a meeting of the Estates General

~ The transformation of the Estates General into the National Assembly, the *Declaration of the Rights of Man and Citizen,* and the reconstuction of the political and ecclesiastical institutions of France

~ The second revolution, the end of the monarchy, and the turn to more radical reforms

~ The war of France against Europe

~ The Reign of Terror, the Thermidorian Reaction, and the establishment of the Directory

By the late 1780s, the French monarchy was confronting a major financial crisis. It could not collect adequate taxes and the nobility refused to make contributions. In the spring of 1789, the struggle between the king and the nobles of France precipitated a political crisis. Unlike earlier disputes at the top of society, this one spread and produced universal social upheaval. The resulting French Revolution changed France and Europe forever.

∽ The Crisis of the French Monarchy

The tensions and problems that produced revolution in France were common to most late-eighteenth-century states. France emerged from the Seven Years' War (1756–1763) deeply in debt. Its decision to continue to try to weaken Great Britain, its traditional enemy, by sending aid to England's rebellious American colonies worsened its financial situation. Given the economic vitality of France, its national debt was neither overly large nor disproportionate to the debts of other European powers. But the French monarchy was unable to tap the wealth of the nation through taxes to service and repay the debt. France was a paradox: a rich nation with an impoverished government.

The Monarchy Seeks New Taxes

To resolve its financial difficulties, the French monarchy would have had to bring the aristocracy under tighter control. But following the Seven Years' War, each royal minister who tried to devise a tax scheme to tap the wealth of the nobility was blocked by opposition from the aristocratic courts, the *parlements*. Both Louis XV (r. 1715–1774) and Louis XVI (r. 1774–1792) lacked the strength of character needed to wage a determined campaign. They hesitated, retreated, and tried deception.

In 1770 Louis XV's chancellor, René Maupeou (1714–1792), persuaded him to drastic action. Maupeou abolished the *parlements*, exiled their members to different parts of the country, and began to reorganize government to increase efficiency. Louis's death in 1774, not aristocratic resistance, doomed Maupeou's program. Louis XVI, in a bid for what he conceived to be popular support, restored the *parlements*.

France's plan to humiliate Great Britain by underwriting the American Revolution was a political triumph. But the policy was a fiscal disaster. In 1781, Jacques Necker (1732–1804), a Swiss banker who became France's director-general of finances, published a budget that was intended to quiet the nation's fears. He argued that if the expenditures for the American war were removed, the budget was in surplus. He also revealed that a large portion of royal expenditures went to pensions for aristocrats and court favorites. This exposé mobilized the court against him, and he was soon driven from office. His questionable budget survived, however, to make it difficult for later government officials to claim a need to raise taxes.

This late-eighteenth-century cartoon satirizes the French social structure. It shows a poor man in chains, who represents the vast majority of the population, supporting an aristocrat, a bishop, and a noble of the robe. The aristocrat is claiming feudal rights, the bishop holds papers associating the church with religious persecution and clerical privileges, and the noble of the robe holds a document listing the rights of the noble-dominated parlements. [The Bettmann Archive]

In 1786, Charles Alexandre de Calonne (1734–1802), the minister of finance, proposed another reform. He hoped to promote growth of the economy by encouraging internal trade, lowering some taxes, and transforming peasants' services to money payments. Calonne's most significant proposal was a new tax on land to be paid by all landowners, regardless of social class. Calonne intended to establish local assemblies to approve the land taxes. In these assemblies, voting power was to depend on the amount of land one owned rather than on one's social status. The new assemblies were designed to undermine the *parlements*, the bases for the political power of the French aristocracy.

The Aristocracy and the Clergy Resist Taxation

In 1787, Calonne convened an "Assembly of Notables" (the higher-ranking aristocrats and clergy) to seek support for his plan. Although the creditors were at the door and the treasury was nearly empty, the assembly adamantly refused to cooperate. Instead, it called for the reappointment of the optimistic Necker and insisted that it had no right to consent to new taxes. That right was said to be vested in a medieval institution that had not met since 1614: the Estates General.

The French Revolution

1789

May 5	*The Estates General opens at Versailles*
June 17	*The National Assembly is declared*
June 20	*The Tennis Court Oath*
July 14	*Fall of the Bastille*
August 4	*Surrender of feudal rights*
August 27	Declaration of the Rights of Man and Citizen
October 5	*Parisian women march on Versailles*

1790

July 14	*Louis XVI accepts constitutional monarchy*

1791

June 20	*The royal family attempts to flee*
October 1	*Formation of the Legislative Assembly*

1792

April 20	*France declares war on Austria*
September 2	*The September Massacres*
September 21	*The Convention meets; monarchy is abolished*

1793

January 21	*Louis XVI is executed*
February 1	*France declares war on Great Britain*
April	*Formation of the Committee of Public Safety*
June 22	*Adoption of the Constitution of 1793*
August 23	Levée en masse *proclaimed*
October 16	Marie Antoinette is executed
November 10	*The Cult of Reason and the revolutionary calendar*

1794

March 24	*Execution of* sans-culottes *leaders*
May 7	*Cult of the Supreme Being proclaimed*
June 10	*The* Law of 22 Prairial *is adopted*
July 27	*Ninth of Thermidor, the fall of Robespierre*

1795

August 22	Constitution of the Year III *and the Directory*

Since aristocrats and clergy had always dominated the Estates General, the king was not willing to risk convening such a meeting. Instead, Louis XVI replaced Calonne with Étienne Charles Loménie de Brienne (1727–1794), archbishop of Toulouse and Calonne's chief opponent at the Assembly of Notables. In office, Brienne found, to his astonishment, that the situation was as bad as Calonne had said it was, and Brienne became a convert to the idea of a land tax. The *Parlement* of Paris blocked action by insisting that only the Estates General had the authority to approve such an innovation. In desperation, Brienne appealed to the Assembly of the Clergy for extra help in meeting a payment on the national debt. The clergy not only refused; they reduced the contributions they had been making to the government.

As pressures on the government mounted, from both the Notables and the *parlements* and estates of the provinces, the king agreed that an Estates General would meet in 1789. Brienne resigned, and Necker was returned to office. In the country of its origin, royal absolutism had been defeated.

～ The Revolutions of 1789

Historians have proposed many explanations for what happened as the meeting of the Estates General in 1789 escalated into revolution. Some believe that the revolution was the culmination of an old class conflict—a struggle between the bourgeoisie and the aristocracy. Others claim that there was a great deal of social mobility that blurred the lines between aristocratic and bourgeois families. Both opposed the clumsy absolutism of the monarchy, and many simply wanted the government of France to better represent the wealthy, no matter what their social origin. When disagreements divided the propertied classes, some of the bourgeoisie turned to the tradespeople and working classes for support. But when the revolution became too radical, the upper and middle classes united to protect rights to private property. Class conflict was not, some historians believe, the cause of the revolution, but a strategy that its leaders occasionally used.

The power vacuum created by the faltering monarchy created an unprecedented opportunity for new kinds of leaders to emerge. The development earlier in the century of the print culture had produced a reading public and troops of hungry authors seeking audiences to sustain them. This encouraged political debate on a wider scale than ever before in Europe's history, and it produced a new political culture. Print communication enabled the concerns of articulate individuals to prevail over those of groups.

To some extent, explanations for the French Revolution reflect the years—or even months—of its history one considers. No single theory may adequately explain the whole event. Different groups opposed and cooperated with each other at different times. Individual leaders shifted their positions frequently. There was enormous confusion, and political situations varied from city to city and region to region.

The Estates General Becomes the National Assembly

Three groups (estates) were represented in the Estates General: the First was the clergy; the Second, the nobility; and the Third, everyone else. In reality, the Third Estate represented members of the commercial and professional middle classes. The fact that the Estates General was an assembly of men of property did not ensure cooperation among its members. The Estates had different interests over which they clashed from the start.

Debate over Organization and Voting. A debate about the organization of the Estates General split the aristocracy and the Third Estate before the meeting convened. The aristocrats demanded an equal number of representatives for each estate, and in September 1788, the *Parlement* of Paris ruled that each estate, not each delegate, should have one vote. This ensured that the aristocratic First and Second Estates could always outvote the Third. Spokesmen for the Third Estate charged the aristocrats with hypocrisy for accusing the crown of transgressing on the liberties of French citizens while pursuing a similar course of action.

The royal council decided that the Third Estate would be its best ally in the fight for fiscal reform. In December 1788, the council granted the Third Estate twice as many representatives as the nobles and clergy. This meant that the Third Estate could dominate the Estates General if voting were allowed by head rather than by order. It was correctly assumed that some liberal nobles and clergy would support the Third Estate, for the Estates shared some interests. The king did not decree the method of voting until the Estates General had gathered at Versailles.

The Cahiers de Doléances.   The men who assembled at Versailles in May 1789 brought the king *cahiers de doléances*, lists of grievances compiled by the citizens who had elected them to the Estates General. The voters were upset about government waste, indirect taxes, church taxes, corrupt clergy, and the hunting rights of the aristocracy. They wanted periodic meetings of the Estates General, more equitable taxes, more local control of administration, unified weights and measures, a free press, and equality of rights among all the king's subjects.

Unresolved procedural problems prevented the Estates General from immediately taking up issues of substance, and things ground to a halt when the Third Estate refused to obey the king and sit as a separate order. On June 1, the Third Estate took things into its own hands. It invited the clergy and the nobles to join it in dissolving the Estates General and setting up a new legislative body. On June 17 the Third Estate, with the support of some of the lower clergy, declared itself the National Assembly.

The Tennis Court Oath.   Three days later, members of the National Assembly took an oath not to disperse until they had given France a constitution. (Since they had accidentally been locked out of their usual meeting place and moved to a nearby tennis court, this came to be known as the Tennis Court Oath.) Although Louis XVI ordered the assembly to desist, within a few days it had recruited a majority of the clergy and a large group of nobles. On June 27, the king capitulated and formally requested the First and Second Estates to meet with the National Assembly and to vote by head rather than by order.

The National Assembly, which renamed itself the National Constituent Assembly, was composed of men from all three orders who shared liberal hopes for the reform of France. They succeeded in their campaign to end government by privileged hereditary orders, but at the cost of a revolution extending over a century.

Fall of the Bastille

Many members of the National Constituent Assembly wanted to create a constitutional monarchy, but Louis's refusal to cooperate thwarted them. By choosing to oppose the diverse groups that were converging against him, the king helped unite them. His efforts to nip the revolution in the bud only spurred it to flower.

His wife Marie Antoinette, Louis's brothers, and the most conservative nobles urged him to use force to break up the National Constituent Assembly, and he attempted to intimidate it by mustering royal troops in the vicinity of Versailles and Paris. On July 11, he demonstrated his intent to ignore the assembly by abruptly dismissing Necker, his minister of finance, without informing the assembly.

The mustering of royal troops created anxiety in Paris, where there had recently been bread riots. The Parisians who had met to elect representatives to the Third Estate continued to meet after the elections. By June they were organizing a citizen militia, and by July, when Louis dismissed Necker, they were convinced that the king intended an offensive against Paris and the National Constituent Assembly.

On July 14, about 800 people—mostly simple working folk—marched to the Bastille, a fortress in Paris, to demand weapons for the city's militia. The governor of the Bastille lost control of the situation, and his troops fired into the crowd. Ninety-eight people died, and many others were wounded. The enraged crowd stormed the fortress, gained entrance, released seven prisoners, and killed the governor and some of his soldiers. They found no weapons.

On July 15, the militia of Paris—calling itself the National Guard—offered its command to a hero of the American Revolution, the marquis de Lafayette. He suggested the guard's insignia: red and blue stripes, the colors of Paris, separated by a white stripe, the emblem of the king. This design became the cockade (badge) of the revolution and eventually the flag of France.

The attack on the Bastille was the first of many acts by the people of Paris that determined the course of the revolution. It revealed that the National Constituent Assembly was not in control of all the forces that were to determine the destiny of France. As word of the Bastille's fall spread, mobs in the provincial cities took to the streets to assault other governmental institutions. In an effort to gain the upper hand, Louis XVI decided to court the allegiance of the Parisian rioters. He donned a revolutionary cockade and went to Paris to authorize the National Guard and to recognize the electors' organization as the city's legitimate government.

The Great Fear and the Surrender of Feudal Privileges

The urban disturbances spawned a rumor that royal troops were to be sent to occupy the countryside. As a result, a few scattered peasant revolts, which had erupted that spring, blossomed and spread. As the "Great Fear" swept the countryside, chateaux were burned, public records and documents destroyed, and feudal dues repudiated. The peasants took possession of scarce food supplies and of land that they had lost through the aristocratic resurgence of the last quarter-century.

On the night of August 4, 1789, aristocrats in the National Constituent Assembly carried out a maneuver designed to undercut the motivation of the rebellious peasants and restore order to the countryside. Several liberal nobles and churchmen rose in the assembly to renounce their feudal rights, dues, and tithes. Their emotional speeches led other members of the assembly to divest themselves of their privileges. In a sense, these men gave up what they had already lost and what they could not have regained without civil war. Most also had enough political influence to see to it that they were compensated. Nonetheless, their act of renunciation meant that henceforth all French citizens were subject to the same and equal laws. That dramatic session of the assembly paved the way for the legal and social reconstruction of France.

The rioters who stormed through city streets and roamed the countryside had more on their minds than the political issues being debated at Versailles. Harvests in 1787 and 1788 had been poor, and food prices in 1789 were higher than they had been for almost a century. Wages had not kept up with rising prices. The winter of 1788–1789 had been unusually cold, and many people had suffered severely from hunger. Political, social, and economic grievances combined in sections of the nation to make the revolution cataclysmic.

The National Constituent Assembly exploited the fear created by the popular uprisings to intimidate the king and the conservative aristocrats. And when the various elements of the assembly began to quarrel among themselves, political factions turned for support to the masses. The shopkeeping and artisan classes were best organized to respond, and they knew the price they wanted for their cooperation.

The *Declaration of the Rights of Man and Citizen*

On August 27, 1789, the National Constituent Assembly approved the *Declaration of the Rights of Man and Citizen*, a statement of the political principles that would guide its writing of a new constitution. It affirmed that all men were born free and equal with inalienable rights to their liberty, their property, and their personal safety. Governments were said to exist to protect those rights, and all citizens were guaranteed equal protection before the law and equal opportunity of admission to public office—commensurate with their natural abilities and characters. Due process of law, presumption of innocence until proof of guilt, and freedom of religion were affirmed. Taxation was to be apportioned according to ability to pay, and property was declared a right ordained by God. The declaration was an indictment of the abuses of the absolutist monarchy, and it served as the death certificate of the old regime.

It was not accidental that the declaration focused on the rights of men and made no mention of women. Many of the Enlightenment's political theorists assigned men and women separate spheres. Men were said to be suited for public life (citizenship); women for domestic life (motherhood and homemaking). Nonetheless, in the charged atmosphere of the summer of 1789, many French women hoped that a new constitution would improve their legal situation—particularly with respect to property, inheritance, family, and divorce. Some believed that the declaration might eventually extend full citizenship to women.

The Royal Family Forced to Return to Paris

Since Louis XVI delayed ratification of both the declaration and the aristocrats' renunciation of feudalism, suspicion grew that he was again contemplating military action. On October 5, a crowd of about 7,000 Parisian women (armed with pikes, guns, swords, and knives) marched to Versailles, demanding relief from a bread shortage. Intimidated, the king agreed to sanction the decrees of the assembly, but the Parisians were deeply suspicious of him. They demanded that the royal family move to Paris, where its conduct could be monitored. Louis had no option, and on October 6, 1789, his carriage followed the crowd into the city to the palace of the Tuileries. The women's march was the first popular insurrection to use the language of popular sovereignty against a monarch.

∼ The Reconstruction of France

The National Constituent Assembly followed the royal family to Paris, and the situation remained relatively peaceful until the summer of 1792. In Paris, the assembly set about reorganizing France. The government it proposed was a constitutional monarchy. For the economy, it endorsed a policy of unregulated free trade. Its religious views were anticlerical, and it was devoted to the protection of property. On all these issues, the aristocracy and the middle-class elite stood united. Although championing civic equality before the law, the assembly spurned social equality and radical democracy. It intended to leave control of the nation in the hands of propertied men.

Political Reorganization

The Constitution, which the assembly issued in 1791, recognized a unicameral Legislative Assembly as the chief political authority for the nation. The monarch was granted a veto that could delay, but not halt, legislation.

An elaborate system of indirect election was created to diminish pressure on the government from the masses. For the purpose of allocating political privileges, France's citizens were divided into two categories: active and passive. Active citizens were men who paid annual taxes equal to three days of local labor wages. Only they could vote to chose the electors who chose the members of the legislature. Since there were higher property qualifications for service as an elector or a member of the legislature, only about 50,000 of France's 25 million people could hold office. No women were enfranchised.

These constitutional arrangements made wealth rather than birth the basis of political power, and they made no distinctions among forms of wealth—aristocratic estates or commercial property. They recognized the changes that were taking place in French society by allowing the newly emerging economic interests to have a voice in governing the nation.

Some women tried to fight the laws that deprived them of the right to vote and hold office. In 1791, Olympe de Gouges, a butcher's daughter from Montauban, published a *Declaration of the Rights of Woman.* By revising the *Declaration of the Rights of Man and Citizen* to include the word *woman* in each clause relating to men, it demanded that a woman be regarded as a citizen in her own right, not as a dependent of a citizen family. Olympe de Gouges also wanted property rights for women, men to be required to recognize the paternity of their children, equality for husbands and wives in marriage, and improved education for women.

By campaigning for a list of rights for men, the National Assembly established a set of values against which its own conduct could be measured. It prompted those to whom it had not extended full liberties to ask why they had been shut out and to claim that the revolution would not be complete until they were included.

Departments Replace Provinces. The National Constituent Assembly used the rational methods of Enlightenment science to reorganize local government and the judiciary. It replaced the provinces that had evolved as part of medieval France's feudal system with eighty-three departments (*départements*) of approximately equal size, named for rivers, mountains, or other geographical features (see Map 19–1). The departments were subdivided into districts, cantons, and communes. The system still exists.

The various seigneurial courts and *parlements* were replaced by a uniform court system staffed by elected judges and prosecutors. Court procedures were simplified, and the most degrading punishments were removed from the books.

Economic Policy

The National Constituent Assembly continued the economic policies advocated by Louis XVI's reformist ministers. These usually involved removing restraints on commerce by doing such things as suppressing guilds and liberating the grain trade. An enthusiasm for the rationalism of the Enlightenment also inspired the assembly to endorse the metric system as a uniform national standard for weights and measures.

The assembly's determination to create a "natural" economy freed from all restraints meant that it was unsympathetic to any attempt by workers to organize for their own protection. The *Chapelier Law*, which was enacted on June 14, 1791, forbade workers' associations (unions). Peasants and workers were to be left to the mercy of a largely unregulated marketplace.

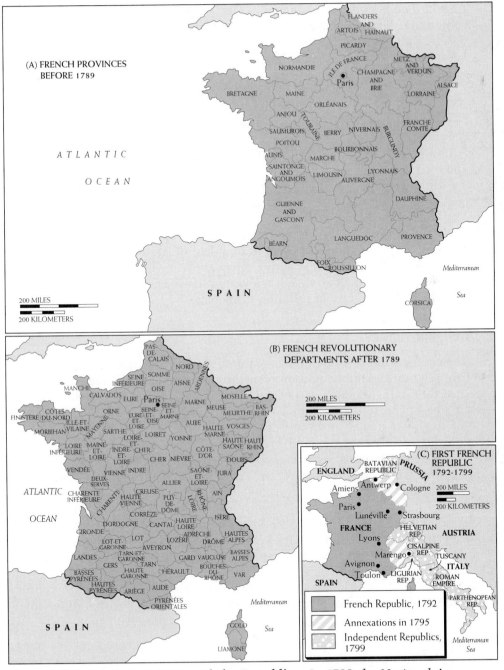

MAP 19-1 French Provinces and the Republic *In 1789 the National Assembly redrew the map of France. The ancient provinces (A) were replaced with a larger number of new, smaller departments (B). This redrawing of the map was part of the Assembly's effort to impose greater administrative rationality in France. The borders of the republic (C) changed as the French army conquered new territory.*

Church Lands and the Assignats. The assembly inherited the job of doing something about the financial crisis that had forced Louis XVI to call its predecessor, the Estates General. The assembly did not repudiate the royal debt, because it was owed to the bankers, the merchants, and the commercial traders who had powerful voices in the assembly.

Old and much-resented indirect taxes were replaced by new land taxes. But when these proved insufficient, the assembly took what may well have been, for the future of France, its most decisive action. It confiscated and sold the property of the nation's Roman Catholic Church. This step increased inflation by putting more wealth in circulation, and it invited religious schism and civil war.

In December 1789, the assembly authorized the issuance of *assignats* (government bonds) whose value was guaranteed by the revenue to be generated from the sale of church property. Initially a limit was set on the number of *assignats* to be sold, but the public's eagerness to buy them tempted the assembly to print enough of them to liquidate the national debt. This created a large body of bond holders with a direct stake in the survival of the revolutionary government, but within a few months the value of the *assignats* began to fall and the rate of inflation to increase.

Religious Policy

The confiscation of church lands required an ecclesiastical reconstruction. In July 1790 the assembly, without consulting the pope or the French clergy, issued the Civil Constitution of the Clergy. This declared the Roman Catholic Church in France to be a branch of the state. Its bishoprics were reduced from 135 to 83—to make the dioceses of religious administrators conform with the new *départements* of the civil government. Priests and bishops, who were to be salaried employees of the state, were also to be elected like other officials.

The Civil Constitution of the Clergy was a major blunder. Vigorous opposition from the French clergy provoked the assembly unwisely to demand that all clergy take an oath of loyalty to the state. Only seven bishops and about half the clergy complied. Those who did not were removed from their ecclesiastical offices. In February 1791, the pope condemned not only the Civil Constitution of the Clergy but also the Declaration of the Rights of Man and Citizen, and the Roman Catholic Church began an offensive against liberalism and the revolution that continued throughout the nineteenth century. Many French people suddenly found themselves in the position of having to choose between their religion and their loyalty to the revolution.

Counterrevolutionary Activity

The revolution had other enemies besides the pope and devout Catholics. Many aristocrats, the *émigrés*, fled to countries on France's borders and set up bases for counterrevolutionaries. The king's younger brother, the count of Artois (1757–1836), was among them. In 1791, he and the queen persuaded Louis XVI to attempt to flee France.

On the night of June 20, 1791, Louis and his immediate family, disguised as servants, left Paris hoping to reach Metz. At Varennes the king was recognized and prevented from going farther. On June 24, a company of soldiers brought the royal family back to Paris. The leaders of the National Constituent Assembly, who wanted to save the constitutional monarchy, announced that the king had not fled but been abducted. This public fiction failed to cloak the fact that the nation's most prominent counterrevolutionary was now seated on its throne.

Two months later, Marie Antoinette's brother, Leopold II of Austria, and Prussia's King Frederick William II issued the Declaration of Pillnitz. The two monarchs promised to intervene in France's affairs to protect the royal family and to preserve the monarchy—if the major European nations supported them. This provision rendered their threat meaningless, for Great Britain would not have endorsed a move on their part that would have upset the continental balance of power. France's revolutionaries, however, concluded that they were surrounded by hostile monarchists. Consequently, the precariousness of the royal family's position increased.

∾ A Second Revolution

The National Constituent Assembly dissolved itself in September 1791. One of its last acts forbade any of its members election to the Legislative Assembly that took its place.

The new assembly, which convened on October 1, faced immense problems. Louis XVI had reluctantly accepted the establishment of a constitutional monarchy, but many French aristocrats resented their loss of position and plotted against the new government. In the west of France, peasants resisted the revolutionary changes, especially as they affected the church. Radical members of the assembly sided with groups of Parisian workers and women who believed the revolution had not gone far enough. Other nations were concluding that the French Revolution was a threat to their interests. By the spring of 1792, these pressures had begun to unravel the first revolutionary settlement and promote a second series of revolutionary changes that were far more radical than the first.

End of the Monarchy

Factionalism plagued the Legislative Assembly throughout its short life (1791–1792). During meetings of the Estates General, deputies from the Third Estate had evolved clubs to bring together persons with similar political philosophies. The Jacobins, who took their name from the Dominican (Jacobin) monastery in Paris where they met, were the best organized of these groups. They were converts to the most radical of the Enlightenment's political theories. In the National Constituent Assembly, they pressed for a republic rather than a constitutional monarchy, and the events of the summer of 1791 increased their following.

A group of Jacobins called Girondists (from the department of the Gironde, which many of them represented) or Brissotins (from their spokesman in 1792, Jacques-Pierre Brissot), took a leadership role in the Legislative Assembly. They were determined to defeat the forces of counterrevolution and passed measures confiscating the property of *émigrés* who refused to return and depriving refractory clergy of state pensions. The king vetoed these laws, but he did not oppose all Girondist legislation.

On April 20, 1792, the Girondists persuaded the Legislative Assembly to declare war on Austria, now governed by Francis II (r. 1792–1835), and on Prussia. The Girondists believed that the war would solidify domestic support for the revolution and encourage its radical evolution. Paradoxically, Louis XVI favored the war, for a need for military leadership usually strengthens a nation's executive. (Louis may also have believed that he had nothing to lose, for defeat of the revolutionary armies could have hastened restoration of the old regime.)

The king was to be disappointed and the Girondists delighted. The war radicalized the revolution—leading to a second revolution that overthrew the constitutional monarchy and established a republic. To defend the nation, the government was eager to mobilize all its resources. Its need for support led it to lend a sympathetic ear to appeals for rights from patriotic groups that had previously been excluded from politics. As early as March 1792, a group of women led by Pauline Léon petitioned the Legislative Assembly for the right to bear arms and to fight for the revolution. Once the war began, a number of French women enlisted in the army and served with distinction.

The war went badly, and efforts by the Prussians to protect Louis by threatening dire consequences if the royal family was harmed increased suspicion of the king's loyalty. On August 10, 1792, a large crowd of Parisians invaded the Tuileries palace and forced Louis XVI and Marie Antoinette to take refuge in the Legislative Assembly. The crowd fought with the king's Swiss guards, and several hundred of them and a large number of Parisians died. The royal family was imprisoned in comfortable quarters, and the king was denied his political functions. The constitutional monarchy began to ignore its monarch.

The Convention and the Role of the *Sans-Culottes*

In July, radicals from the working class had established a commune, a committee of representatives from the municipal wards, to govern Paris. In September, the Paris Commune cleared the city jails by ordering the "September Massacres." Many of the approximately 1,200 people who were executed were aristocrats or priests, but the majority were simply common criminals who, because they were prisoners, were assumed to be counterrevolutionaries.

A Pamphleteer Describes a *Sans-Culotte*

This pamphlet is a 1793 description of a sans-culotte *written either by one or by a sympathizer. It describes the* sans-culotte *as a hard-working, useful, patriotic citizen who bravely sacrifices himself to the war effort. It contrasts those virtues to the lazy and unproductive luxury of the noble and the personally self-interested plottings of the politician.*

~ What resentments of social class are revealed in this document? How might these resentments have been used to unite the *sans-culottes* in support of the revolution? How is civic virtue linked with work? Where does this document suggest the *sans-culottes* will find the enemies from whom they must defend the republic?

A *sans-culotte* you rogues? He is someone who always goes on foot, who has no millions as you would all like to have, no chateaux, no valets to serve him, and who lives simply with his wife and children, if he has any, on a fourth or fifth story.

He is useful, because he knows how to work in the field, to forge iron, to use a saw, to use a file, to roof a house, to make shoes, and to shed his last drop of blood for the safety of the Republic.

And because he works, you are sure not to meet his person in the Café de Chartres, or in the gaming houses where others conspire and game; nor at the National theatre . . . nor in the literary clubs. . . .

In the evening he goes to his section, not powdered or perfumed, or smartly booted in the hope of catching the eye of the citizenesses in the galleries, but ready to support good proposals with all his might, and to crush those which come from the abominable faction of politicians.

Finally, a *sans-culotte* always has his sabre sharp, to cut off the ears of all enemies of the Revolution; sometimes he even goes out with his pike; but at the first sound of the drum he is ready to leave for the Vendée, for the army of the Alps or for the army of the North. . . .

"Reply to an Impertinent Question: What is a Sans-Culotte?" April 1793. Reprinted in Walter Markov and Albert Soboul (eds.), Die Sansculotten von Paris, *and republished and trans. by Clive Emsley in Merryn Williams (ed.),* Revolutions: 1775–1830 *(Baltimore: Penguin Books, in association with the Open University, 1971), pp. 100–101.*

The Paris Commune then compelled the Legislative Assembly to call an election—by universal male suffrage—for a new assembly to write a democratic constitution. The Convention, which was named for the American Constitutional Convention of 1787, met on September 21, 1792, a day after the French army halted the Prussian advance at the Battle of Valmy in eastern France. The victory of democratic forces at home was confirmed by victory on the battlefield, and the Convention's first act was to declare France a republic—a nation governed by an elected assembly without a king.

The* Sans-Culottes *and the Jacobins. The second revolution was the work of two groups: Jacobins who were more radical than the Girondists, and

Parisians called *sans-culottes* ("without breeches"—working-class men wore long trousers instead of the knee breeches aristocrats wore at court). The *sans-culottes* were shopkeepers, artisans, wage earners, and factory workers who had been ignored by the old regime and victimized by the economic policies of the National Constituent Assembly. To win the war, however, the revolutionary government needed their cooperation. Between the summers of 1792 and 1794, they were the dominant force determining the course of the revolution.

The *sans-culottes* knew what they wanted: immediate relief from food shortages and rising prices through price controls, and an end to social inequality. They were intensely hostile to aristocrats and suspected the original leaders of the revolution of aspiring to be a new aristocracy. Their hatred of inequality did not lead them to call for the abolition of private property, but they envisioned a nation of small property owners who were fully enfranchised. They were anti-monarchical and strongly republican, while distrustful of representative government. The *sans-culottes'* political experience had been gained in meetings of the Paris wards that, like New England town meetings, were run as direct democracies. The economic hardship of their lives made them impatient and unwilling to trust their fates to anyone but themselves.

The goals of the *sans-culottes* were not wholly compatible with those of the Jacobins, for Jacobins wanted representative government and favored an unregulated economy. But after Louis XVI's flight to Varennes, the more ex-

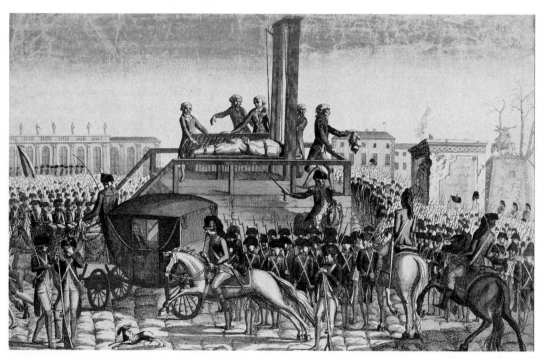

Louis XVI was executed on January 21, 1793. [Giraudon/Art Resource, N.Y.]

treme Jacobins (called "the Mountain," from their seats at the top of the assembly hall) sided with leaders of the Parisian *sans-culottes* in an effort to win the war and end the monarchy.

Execution of Louis XVI. In December 1792, Louis XVI, now stripped of his title and called "Citizen Capet" (Capet being the name given the French dynasty), was put on trial for conspiring against the liberty of the people and the security of the state. The Girondists tried to spare his life, but the Mountain won his conviction and beheaded him on January 21, 1793.

The execution of the king increased pressure on the government. The Prussians renewed their offensive and drove the French out of Belgium. Every major European power declared its opposition to the revolution, and the Convention declared war on Great Britain, Holland, and Spain. In March 1793, a royalist revolt erupted in western France and began to spread. In light of all this, the Mountain concluded that the Girondists, who had led the country into the war, were incapable of defending the nation from either its foreign or its domestic enemies.

Europe at War with the Revolution

Not all Europeans were initially opposed to the French Revolution. Some reformers hoped that the revolution would rationally reorganize a corrupt and inefficient government. Some nations were pleased that the revolution would prevent France from taking much part in European affairs for several years. But by 1792, the European monarchies were alert to the danger of both the ideas and the aggression of revolutionary France. The Declaration of the Rights of Man and Citizen was a highly exportable document applicable to the rest of Europe. To prevent the spread of revolutionary ideas, one government after another instituted repressive domestic policies.

Suppression of Reform in Britain

In 1790, *Reflections on the Revolution in France* by Edmund Burke (1729–1799), a British statesman, outlined the position that was to be taken by Europe's emerging conservative political parties. He rejected Enlightenment rationalism as an effective strategy for reform and insisted that historical realities of political development and the complexities of social relations had to be taken into account. He forecast turmoil as inexperienced people tried to lead France, and things developed much as he predicted.

Prime Minister William Pitt the Younger (1759–1806), who had supported moderate reform of Parliament during the 1780s, turned against both reform and popular movements. His government suppressed the London Corresponding Society, a working-class reform group, and drove the chemist Joseph

Priestley (1733–1804), a radical political thinker, out of the country. Early in 1793, Pitt secured parliamentary approval for acts that suspended *habeas corpus* and broadened the definition of treason to include actions that never went beyond writing. Pitt had less success curbing freedom of the press, but all political groups that opposed his government risked being indicted for sedition.

The End of Enlightened Absolutism in Eastern Europe

By sullying the idea of reform, the revolution brought an end to enlightened absolutism's experiments in eastern Europe. Francis II (r. 1792–1835), second heir to Joseph II's Habsburg empire, was a major leader of the counterrevolution. In Prussia, Frederick the Great's nephew and successor, Frederick William II (r. 1786–1797), used the Lutheran Church and the aristocracy to suppress popular uprisings. Catherine the Great burned the works of Voltaire. In 1793 and 1795, the eastern powers announced that a constitutional monarchy that had been established in Poland in 1791 was dangerously revolutionary, and they used fear of disorder to justify annexing sections of the country. Poland disappeared from the map of Europe until after World War I.

War with Europe

In general, the success of France's revolution set back reform movements in the rest of Europe. In November 1792, after French armies occupied the Austrian Netherlands, the Convention alarmed Europe's heads of state by declaring that it would aid all peoples who wished to cast off the burdens of aristocratic and monarchical oppression. The British, whose commerce was directly threatened, were on the point of declaring war on France when the Convention beat them to it (February 1793). By the time the Mountain took charge of France's government in April 1793, France was at war with Austria, Prussia, Great Britain, Spain, Sardinia, and Holland.

～ The Reign of Terror

The Republic Defended

The task of mobilizing for war in 1793 changed the way the French revolutionaries thought about themselves. They were engaged, they believed, not in a struggle over national borders, but in the defense of a bold new ideology: a republican political and social order that the world was determined to destroy. To protect the revolution, the government considered it appropriate to resort to extreme measures.

In April 1793, the Convention increased its efficiency by creating some powerful committees to serve as a collective executive. The Committee of General Security and a Committee of Public Safety handled most duties of government. The latter acquired almost dictatorial power. It was led by Jacques

Danton (1759–1794), Maximilien Robespierre (1758–1794), and Lazare Carnot (1753–1823). Each of these men was a strong republican and an opponent of the Girondists. They believed they were responsible for saving the revolution from mortal enemies at home and abroad. In that fight, they found it expedient to court the *sans-culottes* of Paris and to suppress many of the rights the revolution claimed to protect. Chief among these was the right to life. The precarious situation raised the level of anxiety and prompted a rigorous search for internal enemies that quickly got out of hand.

The Levée en Masse. In early June 1793, the Parisian *sans-culottes* invaded the Convention, expelled the Girondists, and established the radical Mountain in control. On June 22, the Convention approved a fully democratic constitution—to be implemented only at the end of the war. On August 23, Carnot issued a *levée en masse*, an order for the total military mobilization of the nation—both its men and its goods. On September 17, the ceiling on prices the *sans-culottes* demanded was instituted. Never before had Europe seen a nation organized in this way—nor one defended by a citizen army.

The Reign of Terror that the new republic promptly inflicted on itself did nothing to persuade the nations of Europe that they could risk reform and revolution. The spate of quasi-judicial bloodletting that began in the autumn of 1793 and extended into midsummer 1794 was the most infamous episode in the French Revolution. It can be understood only in context: a foreign war on one hand, and the expectations of the Convention and the *sans-culottes* for internal transformation on the other.

The Republic of Virtue

The threat of foreign armies closing in on France made it easy to dispense with legal due process, but the revolution's leaders did not see their actions simply as expedients required by war. They believed they had created something new in world history, a "republic of virtue" where concern for the common good would replace aristocratic corruption.

Every aspect of society was to be transformed for the benefit of the masses. Streets were renamed to memorialize the egalitarian vocabulary of the revolution. A republican style of dress imitated the ordinary clothing of the *sans-culottes* or the imagined garb of the Roman republic. Plays whose themes were not sufficiently republican were suppressed. Special efforts were made to fight crimes, like prostitution, that were supposedly characteristic of aristocratic societies.

The Society of Revolutionary Republican Women. During these impassioned months, women organized to fight the internal enemies of the revolution. In May 1793, Pauline Léon and Claire Lacombe founded the Society of Revolutionary Republican Women. It filled the galleries of the Convention with women who came to hear the debates and cheer their favorite speakers. It also developed a radical political agenda: stricter controls on the price of food and other commodities, persecution of food hoarders, and the indictment of working women who were insufficiently revolutionary.

By October 1793, the Convention had begun to fear the turmoil the society was causing, and a campaign to suppress women began. The deputies used Rousseau's argument that nature intended separate spheres of activity for men and women to ban all women's clubs. Olympe de Gouges, author of the *Declaration of the Rights of Woman,* who opposed the Terror and accused certain Jacobins of corruption, was guillotined in November 1793. That year women were excluded from serving in the army and shut out of the galleries of the Convention. In the republic of virtue, men were to handle duties of citizenship while women cared for the home.

De-Christianization. The most dramatic sign of the republic of virtue's determination to break with a past it regarded as corrupt was its attempt to de-Christianize France. In October 1793, the Convention decreed a new dating system that chose the first day of the French Republic, not the birth of Christ, as its point of reference. The calendar year was to consist of twelve months of thirty days with names—like Thermidor and Floreal—derived from the seasons. Every tenth day, rather than every seventh, was a holiday. In November 1793, the Convention declared the Cathedral of Notre Dame in Paris a "Temple of Reason." Its agents toured the provinces, closing churches, persecuting believers, and forcing priests to marry. This policy roused much opposition and drove a wedge between the provinces and the revolutionary government in Paris.

In May 1794, the government abandoned the worship of Reason as too abstract for most people and endorsed the "Cult of the Supreme Being." This was Rousseau's vision of a deistic civic religion that existed to promote public morality.

Robespierre. During the crucial months of late 1793 and early 1794, the chief figure on the Committee of Public Safety was Robespierre. He and those who supported his policies heralded a succession of secular ideologues of the left and the right who, in the name of humanity, were to occasion much suffering over the next two centuries. He was a complex, controversial figure—utterly selfless and committed to a republic, but also a shrewd politician. He had opposed the war in 1792 because he feared it might aid the monarchy, and he argued against de-Christianization as a political blunder. For him, the republic of virtue meant the renunciation of selfish gains from political life. This was a noble thought, but confidence in his selflessness enabled him to accept the Terror as nothing more than the instrument of swift, republican justice.

Progress of the Terror

During the summer of 1793, the Convention established tribunals to search out the enemies of the republic. Much hinged on the definition of "enemy,"

On the way to her execution in 1793, Marie Antoinette was sketched from life by the painter Jacques-Louis David as she passed his window. [Giraudon/Art Resource, N.Y.]

which shifted as the months passed. Ultimately, it applied to good republicans who opposed the policies of the dominant faction of the government.

In October 1793, the tribunals began by executing Marie Antoinette, other members of the royal family, and some aristocrats. Certain Girondist politicians then followed. By the early months of 1794, the search for enemies of the revolution had spread to the provinces and had begun to involve members of every social class—including the *sans-culottes*. Thousands died.

Late in the winter of 1794, Robespierre began to manipulate the Terror to remove political figures, on both the left and the right, who threatened his position. On March 24, he executed some leaders of the *enragés, sans-culottes* extremists who were pressing for more price regulation, social equalization, and de-Christianization. Robespierre then accused some conservative republicans of a lack of commitment to the war, of profiteering, and of rejecting the link between politics and moral virtue. On June 10, he secured passage of the Law of 22 Prairial. This increased the murderous efficiency of the tribunals by permitting them to convict suspects without hearing substantial evidence.

On July 26, Robespierre made an ill-tempered speech in the Convention, declaring that unnamed leaders of the government were conspiring against the revolution. This vague but potent threat caused the members of the Convention, who feared becoming his next victims, to act on their instinct for self-preservation. The next day (the Ninth of Thermidor), they shouted him down when he rose to make another speech. That night they arrested him, and the next day he was executed. Robespierre had destroyed rival leaders without creating his own followers.

∼ The Thermidorian Reaction

The End of the Terror

By the late summer of 1794, uprisings in the provinces had been crushed, and the foreign war was also going well. A growing sense of security persuaded the revolutionaries to end the Terror. The largest number of its over 25,000 victims had been peasants and *sans-culottes*, but the events that followed it suggest that the public believed that the *sans-culottes* were too powerful.

The Thermidorian Reaction, which began in July 1794, inaugurated a new constitutional regime sensitive to the widespread feeling that the revolution had become too radical. Wealthy middle-class and professional people soon replaced the *sans-culottes* as the voice the government heeded. The Convention allowed the Girondists who had been in prison or hiding to return to their seats. There was a general amnesty for political prisoners. The power of the Committee of Public Safety was greatly reduced, and the notorious Law of 22 Prairial was repealed. Some of the people responsible for the Terror were removed from public life. Some leaders of the Paris Commune and certain deputies were executed. The Paris Commune itself was outlawed, and the Paris Jacobin Club was closed. There was also a bloody reaction known as the "white terror." People who had been involved in the Terror were attacked and often murdered. Jacobins were executed with little more due process than they had extended to their victims. Some of this was spontaneous mob action; some was approved by the Convention.

The republic of virtue yielded, if not to vice, at least to pleasure. Well-to-do people gave up the affectation of dressing like the poor. Theaters presented new plays. Prostitutes returned to the streets. Families of victims of the Terror gave parties in which they appeared with shaved necks (like prisoners prepared for the guillotine) banded by blood-red ribbons. The Convention allowed Catholic services to be held. Priests returned, and there was a marked resurgence of Catholic piety.

The Thermidorians and their successors had seen enough of proposals for political and social reform. The stability of traditional institutions attracted them. Among other things, they wanted to return family life to what it had been before the revolution. As a result, French women may have had somewhat less freedom after 1795.

Establishment of the Directory

The fully democratic constitution adopted in 1793 had never gone into effect. The Convention replaced it with the Constitution of the Year III. This provided for a bicameral legislature: a Council of Elders—married or widowed men over forty years of age; and a Council of Five Hundred—men, married or single, and thirty or more years old. The executive was a five-person Directory chosen by the Elders from a list submitted by the Council of Five Hundred. Property qualifications limited the franchise for civilians, but all soldiers could vote.

The Directory moderated, but did not try to reverse, the revolution. By 1795, permanent changes had taken place in France. Assumptions of civic equality had replaced traditional distinctions of rank and birth, and social status was determined by property ownership. Some people who had never been allowed any political power had, to some degree, been granted it. Representation had been established as a principle of government. Henceforth France, and soon all Europe, would have to decide which new groups would be permitted representation. The post-Thermidorian course of the French Revolution was a victory for holders of property. The property that won the day was not industrial wealth, but the middle-class wealth stemming from commerce, the professions, and land. The largest new propertied class to emerge from the revolutionary turmoil was the peasantry.

Removal of the *Sans-Culottes* from Political Life

With the war effort succeeding, the Convention severed its ties with the *sans-culottes*. The Thermidorians repealed price controls and returned to an unregulated economy. As a result, the winter of 1794–1795 brought the worst food shortages of the period. Royalist agents tried to take advantage of the discontent, and on October 5, 1795 (13 Vendémiaire), they inspired riots in Paris against the Convention. A general named Napoleon Bonaparte (1769–1821) commanded the cannon that dispersed the crowd.

In March 1795, the Convention concluded peace with Prussia and Spain and took steps to prevent extreme democrats and royalists from winning seats in the Council of Five Hundred. The next year the Directory again beat back the radicals by executing a Gracchus Babeuf (1760–1797), the leader of a "Conspiracy of Equals" that advocated radical democracy and greater equality of property.

The Directory lacked a broad base of political support. It survived because France was still at war with Austria and Great Britain, and the army sustained it. The instability of the Directory and the deepening involvement of the army in its politics held profound consequences not only for France but for the entire Western world.

The French Revolution, the central political event of modern European history, unleashed forces that determined the course taken by Europe—and much of the rest of the world—for the next two centuries. The revolution started as a clash between the monarchy and the nobility. But once the Estates General gathered, the Third Estate, in all of its diversity, acquired control of the government. At first, the middle-class dominated, but quite soon the people of Paris and the peasants of the countryside made their voices heard.

The revolution transformed the social as well as the political life of France.

The nation soon found itself at war with itself, in the Reign of Terror, and at war with virtually all of the rest of Europe. Nobles surrendered social privileges. The church's property was confiscated. Vast amounts of land changed hands, and France became a nation of peasant landowners.

A desire for stability and a determination to defeat the foreign enemies of the revolution finally helped France to reorganize itself and eventually to export revolutionary ideals. This worked to the advantage of the army and, particularly, a brilliant young officer named Napoleon Bonaparte.

⟳ Review Questions

1. What is meant by this statement: "Paradoxically, France was a rich nation with an impoverished government"? How did the financial weaknesses of the French monarchy pave the way for the revolution of 1789?

2. What role did Louis XVI play in the French Revolution? What were his most serious mistakes? Had Louis been a more able ruler, could the revolution have been avoided? Would a constitutional monarchy have succeeded? Or did the revolution ultimately have little to do with the competence of the monarch?

3. How was the Estates General transformed into the National Assembly? Which social and political values associated with the Enlightenment are reflected in the *Declaration of the Rights of Man and Citizen?* How were France and its government reorganized in the early years of the revolution? Why has the Civil Constitution of the Clergy been called the greatest blunder of the National Assembly?

4. Why were some political factions dissatisfied with the constitutional settlement of 1791? What was the revolution of 1792? Why did it take place? Who were the *sans-culottes*? How did they acquire political influence? How influential were they, particularly during the Reign of Terror? What initially drew the *sans-culottes* and the Jacobins together? What ended their cooperation?

5. Why did France go to war with Austria in 1792? What were the benefits and drawbacks for France of fighting an external war while in the midst of a domestic political revolution? What were the causes of the Terror? How did the rest of Europe react to the French Revolution and the Terror?

6. In what ways did the French Revolution both live up to and betray its motto: "equality, liberty and fraternity"? Did French women benefit from the revolution? Did French peasants benefit from it?

Suggested Readings

K. M. BAKER and C. LUCAS (eds.), *The French Revolution and the Creation of Modern Political Culture*, 3 vols. (1987). A splendid collection of important original articles on all aspects of politics during the revolution.

K. M. BAKER, *Inventing the French Revolution: Essays on French Political Culture in the Eighteenth Century* (1990). Important essays on political thought before and during the revolution.

C. BLUM, *Rousseau and the Republic of Virtue: The Language of Politics in the French Revolution* (1986). An exploration of the role of Rousseau's political ideals in the debates of the French Revolution.

R. COBB, *The People's Armies* (1987). The best treatment in English of the revolutionary army.

W. DOYLE, *Origins of the French Revolution* (1980). An outstanding summary of historiographical interpretations.

J. EGRET, *The French Pre-Revolution, 1787–88* (1978) A useful survey of the coming crisis for the monarchy.

F. FEHÉR, *The French Revolution and the Birth of Modernity* (1990). A wide-ranging collection of essays on political and cultural facets of the revolution.

M. FREEMAN, *Edmund Burke and the Critique of Political Radicalism* (1980). A study of Burke's thought in the general context of modern political theory.

J. GODECHOT, *The Counter-Revolution: Doctrine and Action, 1789–1803* (1971). An examination of opposition to the revolution.

D. JOHNSON (ed.), *French Society and the Revolution* (1976). A useful collection of important essays on the social history of the revolution.

E. KENNEDY, *A Cultural History of the French Revolution* (1989). An important examination of the role of the arts, schools, clubs, and intellectual institutions.

D. G. LEVY, H. B. APPLEWHITE, and M. D. JOHNSON (eds. and trans.), *Women in Revolutionary Paris, 1789–1795* (1979). A remarkable collection of documents on the subject.

M. LYONS, *France Under the Directory* (1975). A brief survey of the post-Thermidorian governmental experiment.

M. OZOUF, *Festivals and the French Revolution* (1988). A pioneering study of the role of the public festivals in the revolution.

R. R. PALMER, *The Age of Democratic Revolution: A Political History of Europe and America, 1760–1800*, 2 vols. (1941). An impressive survey of the political turmoil in the transatlantic world.

R. R. PALMER, *Twelve Who Ruled: The Committee of Public Safety During the Terror* (1959, 1964). A clear narrative and analysis of the policies and problems of the committee.

C. PROCTOR, *Women, Equality, and the French Revolution* (1990). An examination of the manner in which ideas of the Enlightenment and the attitudes of revolutionaries affected the legal status of women.

A. SOBOUL, *The Parisian Sans-Culottes and the French Revolution, 1793–94* (1964). The best work on the subject.

D. G. SUTHERLAND, *France, 1789–1815: Revolution and Counterrevolution* (1986). A major synthesis based on recent scholarship in social history.

J. M. THOMPSON, *Robespierre*, 2 vols. (1935). The best biography.

20

The Age of Napoleon and the Triumph of Romanticism

KEY TOPICS IN THIS CHAPTER

~ Napoleon's rise, his coronation as emperor, and his administrative reforms

~ Napoleon's conquests, the creation of a French Empire, and Britain's enduring resistance

~ The invasion of Russia and Napoleon's decline

~ Romanticism and the reaction to the Enlightenment

By the late 1790s, large numbers of French citizens across the social spectrum were losing confidence in the ability of the unstable Directory to protect the gains they had made. The citizens' army, which had successfully defended the revolution, seemed better able to secure order and republican values. The most politically astute of the army generals was Napoleon Bonaparte. Ultimately, he overthrew the republic and declared himself emperor. Bonaparte overturned Europe's old political and social order and provoked a fierce new nationalism. The Napoleonic era also saw the culmination of a new phase in the history of European culture: the Romantic movement.

Significant Dates from the the Era of Napoleonic Europe

1797	*The Treaty of Campo Formio*
1798	*Nelson defeats the French navy*
1799	*Consulate established in France*
1801	*Concordat between France and the papacy*
1802	*Treaty of Amiens*
1803	*War renewed between France and Britain*
1804	*Execution of the Duke of Enghien*
	Napoleonic Civil Code issued
	Napoleon crowned as emperor
1805	*Nelson wins at Trafalgar (October 21)*
	Austerlitz (December 2)
1806	*Jena*
	Napoleon imposes the Continental System (November 21)
1807	*Treaty of Tilsit*
1808	*Spain revolts against Napoleon*
1809	*Wagram*
	Napoleon marries Marie Louise of Austria
1810	*Russia withdraws from the Continental System*
1812	*Invasion of Russia, battle at Borodino*
1813	*Leipzig (Battle of the Nations)*
1814	*Treaty of Chaumont and the Quadruple Alliance*
	Congress of Vienna convenes (September)
1815	*Napoleon returns from Elba (March 1)*
	Waterloo (June 18)
	Holy Alliance formed (September 26)
	Quadruple Alliance renewed (November 20)
1821	*Napoleon dies on Saint Helena*

∽ The Rise of Napoleon Bonaparte

The chief danger to the Directory came from royalists who believed that the restoration of the Bourbon monarchy offered the best hope for restoring stability to France. In the spring elections of 1797, constitutional monarchists and their sympathizers won the majority of offices. To preserve the republic, the Directory staged a coup d'état on 18 Fructidor (September 4, 1797). Men loyal to the Directory took control of the legislature; imposed censorship; exiled some of their enemies; and asked Napoleon Bonaparte, the officer who had put down the disturbances at the time of the Thermidorian Reaction (1795), to protect the government once again.

In this early-nineteenth-century cartoon England, personified by a caricature of William Pitt, and France, personified by a caricature of Napoleon, are carving out their areas of interest around the globe. [Bettman Archives]

Napoleon Bonaparte was born in 1769, on the Mediterranean island of Corsica. France's annexation of Corsica a year earlier made it possible for him to go to French schools and obtain a commission as a French artillery officer (1785). Although his family was impoverished minor nobility, he was a fiery Jacobin who strongly supported the revolution. During the Thermidorian Reaction, this radical background threatened his career, but his successful defense of the Directory from attack by the Parisian mob on October 5, 1795, won him a promotion and a command in Italy.

Early Military Victories

Prussia and Spain made peace with France in 1795, but Britain and Austria were unwilling to accept France's annexation of Belgium. France, therefore, invaded Italy to take the provinces of Lombardy and Venetia from Austria. Bonaparte quickly crushed his opponents. On his own initiative, he concluded the Treaty of Campo Formio (October 1797), which took Austria out of the war. All of Italy and Switzerland came under French domination.

Bonaparte judged it impossible to cross the channel and invade the British Isles. Instead, he proposed to threaten Britain's empire by capturing Egypt from the Ottomans. This would enable France to drive the British fleet from the Mediterranean and cut Britain's communications with India.

The French overran Egypt, but Bonaparte's plan failed. On August 1, 1798, Admiral Horatio Nelson (1758–1805) destroyed the French fleet at Abukir and stranded Bonaparte in Egypt. Alarmed by the Egyptian invasion, Russia, Austria, and the Ottomans joined Britain in forming the Second Coalition against France. By 1799, Russian and Austrian armies were on the verge of invading France.

The Constitution of the Year VIII

As confidence in the Directory faded, one of the Directors, the Abbé Siéyès, plotted a coup d'état. He wanted to create a new government with an executive strong enough to ignore the whims of the electorate. To carry this off, he needed military support.

Bonaparte deserted his doomed army in Egypt and returned to France in October 1799. Although some people thought that he deserved a court-martial, he was a popular figure who could offer Siéyès the military help he wanted. On 19 Brumaire (November 10, 1799), troops commanded by Bonaparte dispersed the legislature and cleared the way for Siéyès' faction to propose a new constitution.

Siéyès wanted to vest executive authority in three consuls, a title borrowed from the Roman Republic. But Bonaparte quickly swept him aside and, in December 1799, issued the Constitution of the Year VIII. Behind a screen of democratic and republican gestures, this document vested full authority in a First Consul—Bonaparte. Bonaparte anticipated the dictators of the twentieth century. He was the first modern leader to use military force and the rhetoric of revolution and nationalism to realize imperial ambitions.

∿ The Consulate in France (1799–1804)

The French Revolution ended with Bonaparte's Consulate. Most members of the Third Estate had achieved their goals. Hereditary privilege was abolished. Paths were open for professionals and merchants to win wealth and status. The peasants were satisfied with the land they had acquired and the termination of their feudal duties. These politically influential classes were profoundly conservative. They did not want to imperil their new privileges or share them with the lower social orders. Since they believed that Bonaparte would provide the best defense for the status quo, they overwhelmingly approved his constitution in a national plebiscite.

Suppressing Foreign Enemies and Domestic Opposition

Bonaparte pleased his supporters by making peace with France's enemies. Russia had already left the Second Coalition, and a French victory at Marengo, Italy, in 1800 induced Austria to end hostilities. Britain, abandoned by its allies, came to terms with Bonaparte in 1802 (the Treaty of Amiens).

Bonaparte also restored France's domestic peace. He courted his enemies, issued a general amnesty, and found employment for people of all political persuasions. High offices were shared among those who led the Reign of Terror, those who fled it, those who favored constitutional monarchy, and those who had served the old regime.

Bonaparte did, however, demand loyalty to his person, and he was ruthless and efficient in suppressing opposition. He created a highly centralized administration. He employed secret police. He stamped out the royalist rebellion in the west and, for the first time in years, brought Brittany and the Vendée under the control of the central government. He also seized or made opportunities to destroy threats to his regime. In 1804, his soldiers violated the sovereignty of the German state of Baden and arrested the Bourbon duke of Enghien. The duke was put to death, even though Bonaparte knew him to be innocent of the charges brought against him. Charles Maurice de Talleyrand-Périgord (1754–1838), France's foreign minister, later termed this act "worse than a crime—a blunder," because it turned other nations against France. But the execution seems to have ended any threat to Bonaparte from a royalist plot.

Concordat with the Roman Catholic Church

Religious tensions were a major threat to order in France. Some Roman Catholic clergy advocated counterrevolution, and many pious laypeople were unhappy with the secular state the revolution had created. Bonaparte approved of religion as an instrument of social control, but he did not want it to become a power independent of the state.

In 1801, Bonaparte shocked his anticlerical supporters by concluding a concordat with Pope Pius VII. The concordat declared that "Catholicism is the religion of the great majority of French citizens." This was merely a statement of fact. Bonaparte did not concede religious dominance of France to the Roman Catholic Church. The clergy had to swear an oath of loyalty to the state. The state named the bishops, paid their salaries, and provided the salary for one priest in each parish. The church also gave up claims to property lost to the revolution. In 1802, the Organic Articles declared the supremacy of state over church, and privileges extended to Protestant and Jewish groups also limited the influence of the Roman Catholic Church.

The Napoleonic Code

In 1802, a plebiscite granted Bonaparte the office of consul for life. He then revised the constitution to give himself supreme power and further centralized authority by creating a reformed code of French law. A single law replaced the former patchwork of legal customs that had differed from region to region.

The Civil Code of 1804—the Napoleonic Code—safeguarded property and the established social order. All privileges based on birth remained abolished. State offices were no longer sold, but appointments were made on the basis of merit. Conservative regulations affecting labor and women were endorsed. Workers' organizations were forbidden. Fathers were granted extensive control over their children and men over their wives. Laws of primogeniture were rejected in favor of a system that distributed an estate among all a decedent's children—including the females. But married women could only dispose of their property with the consent of their husbands. Divorce remained more difficult for women than for men, and the universality of the Napoleonic

Code made it impossible for women to protect their interests, as they had in the past, by exploiting confusions within the law.

Establishing a Dynasty

In 1804, a failed assassination attempt gave Bonaparte an excuse to end the republic and declare himself emperor. He argued that the establishment of a dynasty would, by creating a recognized heir, secure the future of the government and make attempts on his life pointless. Yet another constitution was promulgated and overwhelmingly ratified in a plebiscite. Bonaparte invited the pope to Notre Dame to witness his coronation, but Napoleon I placed the crown on his own head. He had no intention of allowing anyone to think that his authority depended on the church.

⁓ Napoleon's Empire (1804–1814)

Between his coronation as emperor and his defeat at Waterloo, Napoleon conquered most of Europe. His campaigns changed the map of Europe and unleashed the powerful force of nationalism. His weapon was a French nation that had been mobilized militarily by the revolution. He could muster as many as 700,000 soldiers at a time, risk as many as 100,000 in a single battle, endure heavy losses, and return to fight again. No single enemy could match his resources. Even coalitions failed—until Napoleon made mistakes that led to his own defeat.

Conquering an Empire

The Peace of Amiens (1802) between France and Great Britain was merely a truce, for Napoleon's ambition convinced his neighbors that they could not live with him. When he sent an army to recover Haiti from rebels, the British assumed that he was planning to renew France's American empire. (Spain had restored Louisiana to France in 1800.) Interventions in the Dutch Republic, Italy, and Switzerland, and Napoleon's role in the reorganization of Germany following the terms of the Treaty of Campo Formio (1797) created even greater anxiety. Austria's influence in Germany declined, and several augmented states were created in western Germany—all dependent on Napoleon.

British Naval Supremacy. In May 1803, Britain declared war. William Pitt the Younger returned as prime minister (1804) and negotiated the Third Coalition. By August 1805, he had persuaded Russia and Austria again to oppose French aggression. On October 21, 1805, a great naval victory raised the allies' hopes. The British admiral, Horatio, Lord Nelson, destroyed the combined French and Spanish fleets at the Battle of Trafalgar. The victory, which cost Nelson his life, ended the fear of a French invasion of Britain and guaranteed British control of the sea for the rest of the war.

Napoleonic Victories in Central Europe. On land the story was different. Before Trafalgar, Napoleon had marched down the Danube River to attack his continental enemies. In mid-October, at Ulm, he forced a large Austrian army to surrender, and he moved on to occupy Vienna. On December 2, 1805, in perhaps his greatest victory, he defeated a combined Austrian and Russian army at Austerlitz. The Treaty of Pressburg that followed won major concessions from Austria. Austria withdrew from Italy and left Napoleon in control of everything north of Rome. In July 1806, Napoleon organized a Confederation of the Rhine, which removed most of the western German princes from the Holy Roman Empire. Francis II of Austria dissolved that ancient body and took the title Emperor of Austria.

When Prussia, which had remained neutral up to this point, declared war, Napoleon crushed its famous army at the battles of Jena and Auerstädt (October 14, 1806). Two weeks later he was in Berlin. On June 13, 1807, he defeated the Russians at Friedland and moved on to Königsberg, the capital of East Prussia. The emperor of France had become the master of Germany and was able to threaten Britain's economy by closing continental ports to British traders.

Treaty of Tilsit. Unable to fight another battle, Tsar Alexander I (r. 1801–1825) made peace. On July 7, 1807, he signed the Treaty of Tilsit, which confirmed France's gains. Alexander saved Prussia from extinction, but at the cost of the loss of half its territory.

Napoleon disposed of the lands he conquered as if they were the domain of a Corsican family. He, as head of the clan, ruled the great French Empire. Along its borders he carved out a number of satellite states for his relatives. His step-son ruled Italy. Three of his brothers and his brother-in-law became kings. Only his brother Lucien, whose wife Napoleon disliked, was denied a kingdom. The establishment of the Napoleonic family as the collective sovereigns of Europe was unpopular, and it created the potential for serious resistance.

The Continental System

The Treaty of Tilsit isolated Britain as the only major power still opposed to Napoleon. Unable to compete with the British navy, Napoleon resorted to economic warfare. By cutting off Europe's trade with Britain, he planned to cripple that nation's economy, cause domestic unrest, and foment revolution. In 1807, he issued the Milan Decree to intimidate neutral nations into joining France's boycott of British goods.

Napoleon's Continental System hurt the European economies more than Britain's, for Britain had access to the growing markets of North and South America and the eastern Mediterranean. Napoleon refused to help things by establishing free trade within his empire and endorsed tariffs that favored France. This reduced the willingness of merchants to cooperate with the British boycott and encouraged smuggling. It was in part to prevent smuggling that Napoleon invaded Spain in 1808 and began the campaign that led to his ruin.

∽ Europe's Response to the Empire

Napoleon's policies were intended first and foremost for his own glory and that of France, but his conquests spread the reforms of the Enlightenment and France's revolution. Wherever he ruled, the Napoleonic Code was imposed, hereditary social distinctions were abolished, feudal dues disappeared, peasants were freed from serfdom, the guilds and oligarchies that had long dominated urban life were deprived of power, churches were subordinated to the state, and policies of religious toleration replaced church monopolies. These reforms did not disappear after Napoleon's fall from power. Along with the demand for representative, constitutional government, they became the program of later generations of European liberal reformers.

German Nationalism and Prussian Reform

German nationalism began simply as a celebration of the uniqueness of German culture, but Napoleon's humiliation of Prussia at Jena in 1806 politicized the movement. Nationalists warned that conquest by France endangered the independence and achievements of the German-speaking peoples, and they argued that these peoples had to unite if they hoped to survive the French onslaught. France had become powerful by appealing to the patriotism of all its people. The nationalists believed that by unifying Germany, Germans could do the same.

After Tilsit, only Prussia was in a position to indulge such patriotic feelings. Other German states were either under Napoleon's thumb or actively collaborating with him. German nationalists from other states fled to Prussia, where they called for unification and reform—ideas that were anathema to Frederick William III and the Junker nobility. Prussia, however, had no choice but to reform and reorganize.

The reform of Prussia was the work of Baron von Stein (1757–1831) and Count von Hardenberg (1750–1822). Neither man wanted to reduce the autocratic power of the Prussian monarch or to weaken the Junkers, who staffed the state bureaucracy and the army officer corps. Their hope was to fight France with their own version of France's weapon: a democracy led by a strong monarchy.

Stein ended the Junker monopoly of landholding and abolished serfdom. But the Junkers did not permit as clean a sweep of medieval customs as was occurring in the western principalities of Germany. Prussian peasants were allowed to leave the land if they chose, but those who stayed continued to owe manorial labor. Peasants could establish title to the land they worked if they forfeited a third of it to their lord, but this only increased Junker holdings. Some peasants moved to cities to find work; others became agricultural laborers; some acquired small freehold farms. The end of serfdom was not enough, however, to solve their problems, for a population explosion continued to enlarge the landless labor force.

Prussia's loss at Jena had shown that its army of serfs and mercenaries commanded by incompetent nobles was not the equal of France's companies of free patriots led by officers chosen for merit rather than birth. To remedy the situation, Prussia's reformers abolished inhumane punishments, nurtured patriotism, gave merit promotions, admitted commoners to the officer corps, and organized war colleges to modernize strategy and tactics. These measures began to restore Prussia's standing as a military power, but Napoleon forced Prussia to agree to limit the size of its army to 42,000 men. The Prussians evaded the limit by training a group of recruits each year, assigning them to the reserves, and then training another new group. In 1813, after Napoleon's retreat, Prussia introduced universal conscription; by 1814, it had an army of 270,000.

The Wars of Liberation

Spain. Resentment of French occupation was stronger in Spain than elsewhere in Europe. In 1807, a French army entered the Iberian Peninsula to force Portugal to renounce its traditional alliance with Britain. The army stayed in Spain to protect lines of supply, and a year later (1808) Napoleon used a revolt in Madrid as an excuse to depose the Spanish Bourbons and make his brother Joseph king of Spain. Subsequent attacks on the privileges of the church increased public outrage, and the peasants, urged on by the lower clergy and the monks, rose in a general rebellion.

Napoleon faced a new kind of warfare in Spain. Guerilla bands cut communications, killed stragglers, destroyed isolated units, and then disappeared into the mountains. The British landed an army—under the future duke of Wellington, Sir Arthur Wellesley (1769–1852)—to aid the insurgents. This began a long campaign that drained French strength from elsewhere in Europe and contributed to Napoleon's eventual defeat.

Austria. France's troubles in Spain tempted Austria, which wanted revenge for Austerlitz, to renew the war (1809). This was a miscalculation. The help Austria counted on from German princes did not materialize, and Napoleon's difficulties elsewhere were not as great as had been assumed.

The Peace of Schönbrunn that followed France's victory over Austria at the battle of Wagram cost Austria territory containing over 3.5 million people. Among the spoils Napoleon claimed was Marie Louise, the emperor's daughter. Napoleon's wife, Josephine de Beauharnais, was forty-six and had borne him no children. His desire to found a dynasty linked with Europe's most regal lines prompted him to divorce Josephine and marry the eighteen-year-old Austrian princess.

The Invasion of Russia

The Franco-Russian alliance concluded at Tilsit was unpopular with Russia's nobles because of France's liberal politics and the Continental System's interference with their timber sales to Britain. Russia got no help from France in its struggles with the Ottoman Empire, and the creation and enlargement—after the Battle of Wagram—of a Napoleonic satellite (the Grand Duchy of Warsaw) on Russia's doorstep angered Alexander I. The tsar was further disturbed when Napoleon annexed Holland in violation of the Treaty of Tilsit, when Napoleon recognized the French Marshal Bernadotte as King Charles XIV of Sweden, and when Napoleon married Marie Louise of Austria. At the end of 1810, Russia withdrew from the Continental System and prepared for war (see Map 20-1).

Napoleon assembled a mighty force to crush Russia's army of 160,000 men: 600,000 soldiers. His preferred strategy was a short campaign determined by a decisive battle, but the Russians deprived him of that option. Knowing that it was foolish to risk confronting his superior numbers, they retreated and "scorched the earth"—destroying all food and supplies. Not enough remained to enable Napoleon's so-called Grand Army to live off the land, and supply lines could not be maintained across Russia's huge expanse. Napoleon's advisers urged him to abandon the venture. Fearing that failure would undermine his hold on his empire, however, he gambled that the Russians would give him battle rather than abandon Moscow.

In September 1812, public opinion forced the Russian army—despite the wish of its canny commander General Kutuzov (1745–1813)—to try to stop Napoleon. At Borodino, not far west of Moscow, Napoleon fought his bloodiest engagement. The French lost 30,000 men, and the Russians almost 60,000. Yet since the Russian army was not destroyed and Napoleon gained nothing substantial, his victory was the equivalent of a defeat. The Russians set fire to Moscow and left Napoleon to face a fierce winter far from home with a badly diminished army and inadequate supplies.

Napoleon made several offers of peace to Alexander, but the tsar ignored him. By October, what was left of the Grand Army had to retreat, and by December it was clear that the Russian fiasco was raising plots against Napoleon at home. He left the remnants of his army to struggle westward, and he hastened to Paris. Only 100,000 men may have lived to describe their terrible ordeal.

European Coalition

Napoleon weathered the crisis created by the disaster. He put down his opponents in Paris and raised another 350,000 soldiers. Neither the Prussians, the Austrians, nor the Russians were eager to continue fighting, and Prince Klemens von Metternich (1773–1859), Austria's foreign minister, wanted Napoleon to survive with enough power to prevent Russia from dominating Europe. Napoleon, however, refused to negotiate, for he felt that his self-made dynasty, which lacked the support of history and tradition, would not survive if it showed any sign of weakness.

The last and most powerful coalition against Napoleon formed in 1813. Assisted by British money, the Russians drove westward to join Prussia and

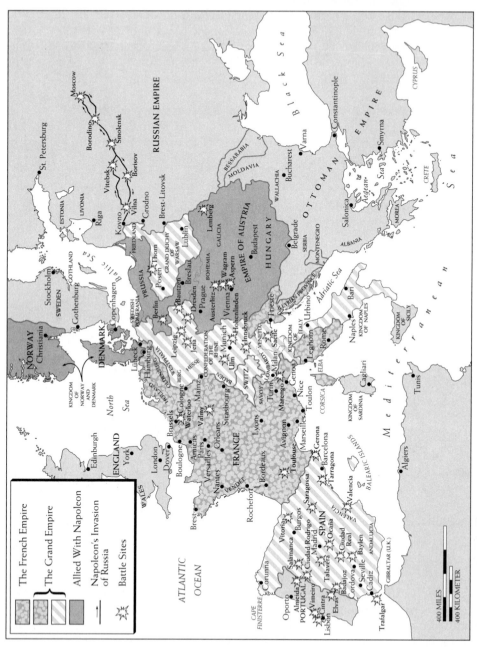

MAP 20-1 Napoleonic Europe in Late 1812 *By mid-1812 the areas shown in speckled background were incorporated into France, and most of the rest of Europe was directly controlled by or allied with Napoleon. But Russia had withdrawn from the failing Continental System, and the decline of Napoleon was about to begin.*

Austria, and Wellington attacked France from Spain. Napoleon's new army was inexperienced and poorly equipped. His generals had lost confidence and were tired. Napoleon himself was worn out and sick. Still, he defeated the allies at Dresden. In October, however, he was decisively beaten by the allied forces at Leipzig (the Battle of the Nations), and by the end of March 1814, Paris had fallen. Napoleon abdicated and went into exile on the island of Elba off the coast of northern Italy.

~ The Congress of Vienna and the European Settlement

Fear of Napoleon had held the victorious coalition together, and differences developed as soon as he was gone. Before Paris fell, the British foreign secretary—Robert Stewart, Viscount Castlereagh (1769–1822)—had negotiated a preliminary agreement: the Treaty of Chaumont (March 9, 1814). It restored the Bourbons to the throne of a France that returned to the borders it had had in 1792. Britain, Austria, Russia, and Prussia committed themselves for twenty

The leading statesmen of the Congress of Vienna are here portrayed in a single group. Metternich, in white breeches, is standing on the left; Lord Castlereagh is sitting in the center with his legs crossed. Talleyrand is seated on the right with his arm on the table. [Royal Library, Windsor Castle]

years to a Quadruple Alliance charged with keeping the peace. Remaining problems—and there were many—were to be ironed out at a conference to be held in Vienna.

Territorial Adjustments

The Congress of Vienna met from September 1814 until November 1815. The great powers found it easy to agree on what should be done about France. None wanted any single state to dominate Europe, and all were determined that France should not attempt to do so again. The restoration of the Bourbon monarchy, which was temporarily popular with the French, and a fair boundary settlement succeeded in keeping France calm and satisfied.

The powers also established border states to block future French expansion: a kingdom of the Netherlands (including Belgium) in the north, and a combined Genoa and Piedmont in the south (see Map 20-2). To the west, Prussia, which had already expanded in eastern Europe, was given new territories along the Rhine River. Austria took control of northern Italy to prevent a repetition of Napoleon's conquests there. In the rest of Germany, most of Napoleon's arrangements were left untouched. The congress endorsed rule by legitimate monarchs and rejected any hint of the French Revolution's republican and democratic politics.

Most difficult for the congress was the reorganization of eastern Europe. Alexander I of Russia wanted all of Poland. Prussia was willing to give it to him if it received all of Saxony. But Austria was unwilling to surrender its share of Poland, to see Prussia grow, and to allow Russia to penetrate deeper into central Europe. The congress came to a standstill, and a new war might have developed had France not provided a way out. Talleyrand, who represented France at Vienna, suggested that an agreement supported by France, Britain, and Austria might intimidate Alexander. When news of a secret treaty among them leaked out, the tsar accepted a smaller share of Poland and Frederick William III of Prussia only a part of Saxony. France had reclaimed for itself recognition as one of the great powers.

The Hundred Days and the Quadruple Alliance

News that the allies in Vienna were fighting among themselves encouraged Napoleon to escape from Elba and return to France (March 1, 1815). The French army had remained loyal to him, and many French people believed him to be a stronger protector than the Bourbon monarchy. Napoleon was quickly returned to power, promising a liberal constitution and a peaceful foreign policy. The allies were not convinced. They declared Napoleon an outlaw (a new device under international law) and sent armies to crush him. On June 18, 1815, Wellington, aided by the Prussians under Field Marshal von Blücher, defeated Napoleon at Waterloo, Belgium. Napoleon again abdicated and was exiled to Saint Helena, a tiny Atlantic island off the coast of Africa. He died there in 1821.

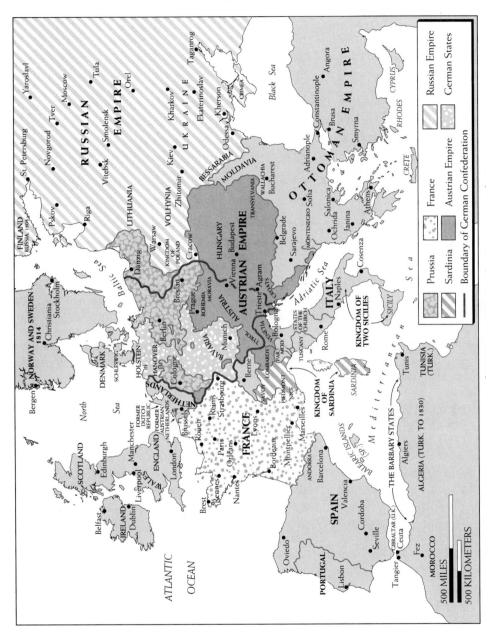

MAP 20-2 Europe After the Congress of Vienna, 1815 *The Congress of Vienna achieved the post-Napoleonic territorial adjustments shown on the map. The most notable arrangements dealt with areas along France's borders (Netherlands, Prussia, Switzerland, and Piedmont) and in Poland and northern Italy.*

The Hundred Days, as the period of Napoleon's return is called, frightened the great powers into imposing harsher terms on France: minor territorial losses, a war indemnity, and an army of occupation. Alexander, under the growing influence of a mystical religious faith, proposed a "Holy Alliance" of monarchs who agreed to act together in accordance with Christian principles. Austria and Prussia signed; but Castlereagh thought it absurd, and England abstained. The Quadruple Alliance (England, Austria, Prussia, and Russia) was renewed on November 20, 1815. The Holy Alliance quickly became associated with extreme political reaction. The Congress of Vienna negotiated a settlement that allowed Europe to avoid general war for a hundred years. France accepted the new situation without undue resentment, and the victorious powers established a balance of power and methods for adjusting to change. They have been criticized for failing to recognize the great nationalistic and democratic movements that would stir the nineteenth century, but they would have had to have been more than human to have anticipated future problems or to have encouraged developments of which they disapproved.

❧ The Romantic Movement

During the French Revolution and Napoleon's reign an important new intellectual movement developed in Europe: *Romanticism.* In many ways it was a hostile response to the Enlightenment. Romantic writers objected to what they considered to be the narrowness of the eighteenth-century *philosophes'* search for truth. They accused the latter of holding everything to a narrow scientific standard: geometrical and mathematical models to explain everything. Romantic thinkers rejected the idea that human nature was primarily rational. They demanded recognition of the importance of feelings and imagination—of faith, as well as reason—a means to knowledge.

During the Age of Romanticism (1780–1830) there were different and often independent Romantic movements in Germany, England, and France. Despite national differences, each reacted to the Enlightenment by championing the imagination or some other intuitive intellectual faculty. Unlike the *philosophes,* the Romantics saw value in the art, literature, and architecture of the Middle Ages, and many urged a revival of medieval Christianity. They were deeply interested in folklore and fairy tales. They were fascinated by dreams, hallucinations, sleepwalking, and all phenomena that suggested that there was a world beyond the reach of empirical observation, sensory data, and discursive reasoning.

❧ Romantic Questioning of the Supremacy of Reason

Many historical streams fed the Romantic movement: the individualism of the Renaissance and the Reformation; the pietism of the seventeenth century;

England's Methodist revival in the eighteenth century; the sentimental novels of the eighteenth century (e.g., Samuel Richardson's *Clarissa*); the so-called *Sturm und Drang* ("storm and stress") period of German literature; and German idealist philosophy. Two writers closely associated with the Enlightenment, Jean Jacques Rousseau and Immanuel Kant, also helped to lay intellectual foundations for Romanticism by casting doubt on the *philosophes'* rationalistic assumptions.

Rousseau and Education

Romantic writers were especially drawn to Rousseau's claim that society and wealth had corrupted human nature. Rousseau described the first human beings as happy, innocent creatures who lived in a state of equilibrium with nature. To become happy again, he argued, humankind had to be true to its natural being while developing the moral potential of life in society. His *Social Contract* (1762) was a prescription for a reform of political institutions that would achieve that goal.

Rousseau set forth his theories of human development in a novel, *Émile* (1762). It described stages in the human maturation process and urged that each child be allowed to grow freely and individually—learning by trial and error what reality is and how best to deal with it. Parents or teachers could help most by providing the basic necessities of life and warding off manifest harm. But beyond that, adults should stay out of the way—letting nature take its course. Rousseau believed that a child's sentiments as well as its reason should be permitted to flourish, and he claimed that his unguided method of education would lead to the establishment of a society in which nature would triumph over artifice. This idea led the Romantics to value the uniqueness of each individual and to assume that humankind, nature, and society were organically interrelated.

Kant and Reason

Immanuel Kant (1724–1804) wrote the two greatest philosophical works of the late eighteenth century: *The Critique of Pure Reason* (1781) and *The Critique of Practical Reason* (1788). In them he sought to reconcile the rationalism of the Enlightenment with belief in human freedom, immortality, and the existence of God.

Kant rejected the opinion of Locke and other philosophers that knowledge was rooted in sensory experience alone. He claimed that the human mind did not simply reflect the world around it like a passive mirror. It actively imposed itself on the world of sensory experience using tools it generated itself: "forms of sensibility" and "categories of understanding." In other words, the human mind perceives the world as it does because of its own techniques of perception. Human knowledge is a product of the mind's activity as well as of sensory experience.

Kant differentiated between "pure reason," which dealt with the phenomenal world of sensory experience, and "practical reason," which intuited a "noumenal" world of ethics and aesthetics. The sphere of reality accessible to pure reason was quite limited. It could not produce evidence for transcendental truths, such as the existence of God, eternal life, and ultimate rewards and punishments for personal conduct. These belonged to the realm of practical reason.

Kant thought that all human beings possessed an innate sense of moral duty—a *categorical imperative*—an inner command to act in every situation as one would have other people act in that situation. Kant saw our experience of this imperative (of our consciences) as proof of humankind's natural freedom and as a starting point for comprehending transcendental realities.

Whether the Romantics called it "practical reason," "fancy," "imagination," "intuition," or simply "feeling," they believed, with Kant, in the presence of a special power in the human mind that could go beyond the limits of the passive human understanding described by Hobbes, Locke, and Hume. Most of them assumed that poets and artists possessed these powers in particular abundance.

~ Romantic Literature

The term *romantic* appeared in England and France as early as the seventeenth century as a description of literature that was judged to be unreal, sentimental, or excessively fanciful. In both England and Germany, *romantic* came to be applied to all literature that failed to observe classical forms and rules and that gave free play to the imagination. Most folk tales and much of the art of medieval Europe fell into this category.

In the early nineteenth century, August Wilhelm von Schlegel (*Lectures on Dramatic Art and Literature, 1809–1811*) began to use *romantic* as a term of praise, not approbation. To him it indicated an exciting alternative to the predictable, lifeless work produced by authors who merely imitated classical models. He associated Dante, Petrarch, Boccaccio, Shakespeare, the Arthurian legends, Cervantes, and Calderón with Romanticism.

The Romantic movement had peaked in Germany and England before Madame de Staël (1766–1817) and Victor Hugo (1802–1885) made it a major force in France. So powerful was the classical tradition in France that no French writer openly claimed to be a Romantic until 1816. The first was Henri Beyle (1783–1842), who wrote very successful novels under the pseudonym Stendhal.

The English Romantic Writers

Lockean psychology, which regarded the mind as a passive receptor of sensory data, explained poetry as an exercise of "wit" mechanically guided by prescribed rules. The English Romantics disagreed. They saw poetry as proof of the mind's ability to actively create. When so conceived, poetry could not be dismissed as idle play. It became the highest of human acts, the fulfillment of humanity's unique ability to transcend the level on which other sentient creatures operated.

Blake. William Blake (1757–1827) considered the poet to be a seer and poetry a translation of visions. In the 1790s, he suffered a deep depression brought on by an inability to perceive in the world the attributes of beauty that he believed it to have. The more one studied the world with the tools of reason, the more the life of the imagination and its spiritual values seemed to recede. No innocence or beauty remained. Blake was deeply troubled by a strong sense of contradiction between a childlike vision of the world and a conception of it based on experience. He blamed the discordance on the materialism and injustice of English society.

Coleridge. Samuel Taylor Coleridge (1772–1834) contributed to the development of Romantic literary criticism and theory, but he is best remembered for his poems of the supernatural: "Christabel," "Kubla Khan," and "The Ancient Mariner." "The Ancient Mariner" tells the story of a sailor cursed for killing an albatross, an act that symbolizes crimes against nature and God. The poem explores guilt, punishment, and the redemptive possibilities of humility and penance. In the end, the mariner grasps the unity and beauty of all things, repents, and is delivered from the curse of having the dead albatross hung around his neck.

Wordsworth. Coleridge's closest friend was William Wordsworth (1770–1850), with whom in 1798 he published a manifesto *(Lyrical Ballads)* for a new poetry that rejected the rules endorsed by eighteenth-century critics. Wordsworth's "Ode on Intimations of Immortality" (1803)—written in part to console Coleridge, who was suffering a deep personal crisis—is among his most important works. It deals with the loss of poetic vision, something Wordsworth also felt. Nature, which he had worshiped, had ceased to speak to him, and he feared that it might never speak again. He had lost what he believed all human beings necessarily lost as they matured: their childlike vision, their initial closeness to spiritual reality.

For both Wordsworth and Coleridge, childhood was the bright period of creative imagination. Wordsworth believed that the soul had a preexistence in a celestial state before its appearance on earth. A child, being closer in time to this experience of the eternal and being undistracted by knowledge of the world, recollects the supernatural much more easily than an adult. Aging and urban life corrupt and deaden the imagination, making one's inner feelings and the beauty of nature seem less important. Wordsworth's book-length poem, *The Prelude* (1850), developed a long, autobiographical account of the growth of the poet's mind that illustrated this theory.

Lord Byron. Most of Britain's Romantic writers distrusted and disliked the greatest rebel their movement produced: Lord Byron (1788–1824). But outside

England, his rejection of tradition and advocacy of personal liberty caused him to be regarded as the embodiment of the new person of the French Revolution. An unconventional love life contributed to this reputation.

Byron had little sympathy for theories about imagination, and he was outrageously skeptical and mocking even of his own beliefs. His *Don Juan* (1819), for instance, described—with ribald humor—nature's cruelty as well as its beauty, and the poem expressed an unfashionable admiration for urban life.

The German Romantic Writers

Almost all the major German Romantics wrote novels in addition to poetry. These tended to be highly sentimental. Their characters were developed as symbols, not real individuals, and they avoided purely realistic description.

The first German Romantic novel was Ludwig Tieck's *William Lovell* (1793–1795), the story of a young man who lives for love and imagination and avoids the cold rationality that leads others to unbelief, misanthropy, and egoism. In the end, Lovell is ruined when two women, whom he naively loves, infect him with philosophy, materialism, and skepticism.

Schlegel. Lucinde (1799), by Friedrich Schlegel (1767–1845), demonstrates how the Romantics became involved in the social issues of their day. The novel attacked the assumption that women could be little more than lovers and domestics. Lucinde is the hero's perfect companion—as well as an unsurpassed lover. The book was considered shocking for its frank discussion of sex and its description of Lucinde as the equal of the male protagonist.

Goethe. Towering above all German writers is Johann Wolfgang von Goethe (1749–1832). He was both a Romantic and a critic of the excesses of Romanticism. A novel, *The Sorrows of Young Werther* (1774), first brought him to the public's attention. It depicted, through an exchange of letters, the sentimental emotions of a youth in love with another man's wife. When the correspondence ceases, grief drives Werther to suicide. The book was much admired because of its insistence on the importance of feeling and its call to transcend the conventions of polite society.

As Goethe aged, erotic themes yielded to ethical ones—explorations of relationships between morality and sensuality. *Faust*, a long dramatic poem, was his masterpiece. In Part I, published in 1808, Faust, a world-weary scholar, promises his soul to the Devil in exchange for knowledge. Faust seduces a young woman named Gretchen. And when she dies and enters heaven, he faces grief and guilt and the struggle to go on with life. In Part II of the poem, completed in 1832 (the year of Goethe's death), Faust has strange adventures with witches and mythological characters. When he finally dedicates his life to the improvement of humankind, commitment to an altruistic goal brings him peace and a knowledge of life's meaning that annuls his pact with the Devil. *Faust* was a criticism of the shallowness of much Romantic thought and a description of the serious spiritual problems that faced Europeans as their commitment to the values of traditional Christianity faded.

Religion in the Romantic Period

Methodism

Enlightenment writers tried to derive religion from reason, but the Romantics, like medieval mystics, saw it as an expression of deep human emotion. Methodism, a movement begun in England by John Wesley (1703–1791), an Oxford-educated Anglican priest, presented religion not as a set of concepts, but as a "method" for living. In 1735, Wesley came to America as a missionary and made the acquaintance of the Moravians, German "pietists." He concluded that their faith, based on unquestioning trust in God, was much stronger than his. In 1739, he had a conversion experience that assured him of his salvation and sent him forth to preach a message of simple trust. By the late eighteenth century Methodism had become a church with a wide following in Britain and, especially, America.

New Directions in Continental Religion

Methodism stressed inward, heartfelt religion and the duty to strive for Christian moral perfection in this life. It accepted enthusiastic emotional experience as fundamental to Christian conversion and worship. Similar religious movements also appeared on the continent. After the Thermidorian Reaction, there was a strong Roman Catholic revival in France. Viscount François René de Chateaubriand (1768–1848) argued, in *The Genius of Christianity* (1802), that the essence of religion was "passion," the emotion that doctrine and sacraments inspired in the heart of the Christian. A similar point of view was articulated by a Protestant scholar, Friedrich Schleiermacher (1768–1834). Schleiermacher's *Speeches on Religion to Its Cultured Despisers* (1799) defined religion as a feeling of absolute dependence on an infinite reality.

Romantic Views of Nationalism and History

Romanticism, in all its forms, glorified the individual person and the individual culture. German idealism provided its philosophic underpinning by explaining the world as the projection of subjective egos. J. G. Fichte (1762–1814) identified the individual human ego with the Absolute that underlies all existing things. The world is, he argued, created by human beings—particularly by people like Napoleon, the unusually strong who impose their wills on others.

Johann Gottfried Herder (1744–1803), who resented the preponderance of French culture in Germany, led Germans on a search for the roots of their identity as a "folk" or people. Herder opposed the Enlightenment's advocacy of universal, rational institutions (like the Napoleonic Code). His insistence

Throughout most of the eighteenth century, writers had harshly criticized virtually all aspects of the Middle Ages, which were then considered an unenlightened time. One of the key elements of Romanticism was a new appreciation of all things medieval. In this passage from The Genius of Christianity, *Chateaubriand praised the beauty of the Middle Ages and the strong religious feelings produced by stepping into a Gothic church. The description exemplifies the typically Romantic emphasis on feelings as the chief foundation of religion.*

∽ Why does Chateaubriand associate the invocation of religious feelings with a Gothic church's capacity to carry him back in time? What explanation does Chateaubriand find in nature for the religious character of a Gothic church? Does his vision of religion imply the authority of an organized church or sacred wriitings such as the Bible?

You could not enter a Gothic church without feeling a kind of awe and a vague sentiment of the Divinity. You were all at once carried back to those times when a fraternity of cenobites [a particular order of monks], after having meditated in the woods of their monasteries, met to prostrate themselves be-

on the importance of uniqueness revived the study of history and ultimately stimulated Europe's interest in world cultures. A flood of brilliant work in comparative literature, religions, and philology resulted.

Georg Wilhelm Friedrich Hegel (1770–1831), one of the most difficult and important philosophers in the history of Western civilization, was the most powerful Romantic influence on the writing of history. He believed that a historical period is defined by the ideas its people assume to be true. Ideas and, therefore, history evolve through conflict. The ideas that hold sway over a generation constitute a "thesis." This thesis is eventually challenged by conflicting ideas, an "antithesis." Ultimately, a "synthesis," a new consensus, emerges. It becomes the new thesis, and the process begins all over again. Because each stage in the process is necessary to the one that follows it, all periods of history are of almost equal value and all cultures are important because each contributes to the clash of ideas by which humankind evolves.

Romanticism contributed to the emergence of nationalism, one of the strongest historical forces of the nineteenth and twentieth centuries. The Enlightenment had generally promoted a cosmopolitan outlook, but Romantic thinkers assumed that each people, ethnic group, or nation *not only was, but ought to be, an independent political entity. In 1815, the Congress of Vienna could ignore popular pressure for change, but later statesmen struggled as divisive nationalistic passions swept across Europe, from Ireland to the Ukraine.*

fore the altar and to chant the praises of the Lord, amid the tranquility and the silence of the night. . . .

Everything in a Gothic church reminds you of the labyrinths of a wood; everything excites a feeling of religious awe, of mystery, and of the Divinity.

The two lofty towers erected at the entrance of the edifice overtop the elms and yew trees of the church yard, and produce the most picturesque effect on the azure of heaven. Sometimes their twin heads are illumined by the first rays of dawn; at others they appear crowned with a capital of clouds or magnified in a foggy atmosphere. The birds themselves seem to make a mistake in regard to them, and to take them for the trees of the forests; they hover over their summits, and perch upon their pinnacles. But, lo! confused noises suddenly issue from the tops of these towers and scare away the affrighted birds. The Christian architect, not content with building forests, has been desirous to retain their murmurs; and, by means of the organ and of bells, he has attached to the Gothic temple the very winds and thunders that roar in the recesses of the woods. Past ages, conjured up by these religious sounds, raise their venerable voices from the bosom of the stones, and are heard in every corner of the vast cathedral. The sanctuary reechoes like the cavern of the ancient Sibyl; loud-tongued bells swing over your head, while the vaults of death under your feet are profoundly silent.

Viscount François René de Chateaubriand, The Genius of Christianity, *trans. by C. I. White (Baltimore: J. Murphy, 1862), as quoted in Howard E. Hugo (ed.),* The Romantic Reader *(New York: Viking, 1957), pp. 341–342.*

∽ Review Questions

1. How did Napoleon rise to power? What groups supported him? What were the stages by which he eventually made himself emperor? What were his major domestic achievements? Did his rule more nearly fulfill or betray the ideals of the French Revolution?

2. What regions made up Napoleon's realm? Did each have equal status within it? How did Napoleon rule his empire? Which of his policies strengthened the empire? Which ones undermined it?

3. Why did Napoleon decide to invade Russia? Why did his campaign fail? Could you justify calling Napoleon a "military genius"? To what extent was his brillrance a reflection of the ineptitude of his enemies?

4. Who were the principal personalities at the Congress of Vienna? What were the most significant problems they addressed? What was the long-term significance of the Congress?

5. How does the role Romantic writers assigned "feelings" compare with the role Enlightenment writers claimed for reason? What questions did Rousseau and Kant raise about reason?

6. Why did poetry become important to Romantic writers? How did the Romantic concept of religion differ from Reformation Protestantism and Enlightenment deism? What significance did Romantics see in history?

Suggested Readings

M. H. Abrams, *The Mirror and the Lamp: Romantic Theory and the Critical Tradition* (1958). A standard text on Romantic literary theory that looks at English Romanticism in the context of German Romantic idealism.

M. H. Abrams, *Natural Supernaturalism: Tradition and Revolution in Romantic Literature* (1971). A brilliant survey of Romanticism across western European literature.

F. C. Beiser, *Enlightenment, Revolution, & Romanticism: The Genesis of Modern German Political thought, 1790-1800* (1992). The best recent study of the subject.

L. Bergeron, *France Under Napoleon* (1981). An in-depth examination of Napoleonic administration.

E. Cassirer, *Kant's Life and Thought* (1981). A brilliant work by one of the major philosophers of this century.

D. G. Chandler, *The Campaigns of Napoleon* (1966). A good military study.

K. Clark, *The Romantic Rebellion* (1973). A useful discussion that combines both art and literature.

O. Connelly, *Napoleon's Satellite Kingdoms* (1965). The rule of Napoleon and his family in Europe.

H. Honour, *Romanticism* (1979). The best introduction to the subject in terms of the fine arts.

G. N. Izenberg, *Impossible Individuality: Romanticism, Revolution, and the Origins of Modern Selfhood, 1787–1802* (1992). Explores the concepts of individualism in Germany, England, and France.

H. Kissinger, *A World Restored: Metternich, Castlereagh and the Problems of Peace, 1812–1822* (1957). A provocative study by an author who became an American Secretary of State.

G. Lefebvre, *Napoleon*, 2 vols., trans. by H. Stockhold (1969). The fullest and finest biography.

H. Nicolson, *The Congress of Vienna* (1946). A good, readable account.

B.M.G. Reardon, *Religion in the Age of Romanticism: Studies in Early Nineteenth-Century Thought* (1985). The best recent introduction to this important subject.

C. Taylor, *Hegel* (1975). The best one-volume introduction.

J. M. Thompson *Napoleon Bonaparte: His Rise and Fall* (1952). A sound biography.

T. Ziolkowski, *German Romanticism and Its Institutions* (1990). An exploration of the manner in which institutions of intellectual life influenced creative literature.

21

Restoration, Reaction, and Reform (1815–1832)

KEY TOPICS IN THIS CHAPTER

~ The challenge of nationalism and liberalism to the conservative order in the early nineteenth century

~ The domestic and international politics of the conservative order from the Congress of Vienna through the 1820s

~ The wars of independence in Latin America

~ The revolutions of 1830 on the continent and the passage of the Great Reform Bill in Britain

---

Reactionary forces favoring monarchies and aristocracies dominated European politics for the decade following the Congress of Vienna. But nationalism and liberalism, two new ideologies, resisted dynastic inheritance as a means for organizing states. Nationalists wanted the map of Europe redrawn to reflect boundaries among ethnic groups, and liberals sought moderate political reform and freer economic markets.

Significant Dates from the Era of Political Reaction and Reform

1814	*Louis XVIII, Bourbon monarchy restored in France*
1815	*Holy Alliance (Russia, Austria, and Prussia)*
	Quadruple Alliance (Russia, Austria, Prussia, and Britain)
1819	*Carlsbad Decrees*
	Peterloo Massacre
	The Six Acts passed in Great Britain
1820	*Spanish revolution*
1821	*Greek revolution*
1823	*France intervenes to crush the Spanish revolution*
1824	*Charles X becomes king in France*
1825	*Decembrist Revolt in Russia*
1829	*Catholic Emancipation Act passed in Great Britain*
1830	*Charles X abdicates; Louis Philippe proclaimed king*
	Belgian revolution
	Polish revolution
1832	*Great Reform Bill passed in Great Britain*

∼ The Challenges of Nationalism and Liberalism

The Emergence of Nationalism

The nineteenth century was the great age of *-isms:* liberalism, nationalism, republicanism, socialism, and communism. *Nationalism* was the most powerful of the political ideologies of the era. It challenged the traditional political assumption that had guided the Congress of Vienna; that is, that states are defined by the hereditary claims of rulers.

Nationalism reflected a belief in popular sovereignty. It held that a nation should be defined by the qualities of its people, not by loyalty to a dynasty.

Creating Nations. During the first half of the nineteenth century, small intellectual elites fostered nationalist ideals in various parts of Europe by teaching the history and language of their people to their compatriots. They created the beliefs and expectations that generated mass support for nationalism in the second half of the century. Historians and other scholars wrote a people's history and collected its literature. Schoolteachers then spread this work abroad and nurtured the development of a nation's official language.

The language used in schools and government offices was important to nationalists. In France and Italy, official versions of the national language were imposed in the schools, replacing local dialects. In parts of Scandinavia and eastern Europe, nationalists tried to revive earlier, "purer" versions of the national language. These resurrected tongues were often the inventions of modern linguists, but they served to bring people together. Standardization of speech was further aided by the increased availability of printed materials (books, journals, magazines, and newspapers) that "fixed" language in a permanent form. In many regions, a national printed language augmented local spoken dialects, establishing itself as the favored instrument for serious thought and political debate. As a result, far more linguistic uniformity developed in Europe than at any earlier time in its history. By 1850, however, less than half of the inhabitants of France spoke official French.

Meaning of Nationhood. Nationalists explained nationhood, and argued for it, in different ways. But their greatest difficulty was deciding which ethnic groups had the right to be considered nations with claims to territory and political autonomy. In practice, recognition as a nation has usually been based on possession of (1) a population large enough to support a viable economy, (2) a history of significant cultural association, (3) an educated elite that spreads a national language, and (4) a capacity to defend oneself or conquer other peoples. Much domestic unrest has been created by small ethnic groups that have tried, but failed, to fulfill these criteria.

During the nineteenth century, Europe dealt with continuing nationalistic upheavals on six fronts. By bringing Ireland under direct rule in 1800, England created an "Irish problem" that continues to complicate Britain's politics to this day. German nationalists, in an effort to unify all German-speaking peoples, challenged the Austrian Empire and pitted Prussia and Austria against each other. Italian nationalists tried to drive the Austrians out of the Italian peninsula. Polish nationalists struggled to free their land from Russian domination. A host of eastern European groups—Hungarians, Czechs, Slovenes, and others—sought either recognition within the Austrian Empire or independence from it. And in southeastern Europe, Serbs, Greeks, Albanians, Romanians, and Bulgarians fought the Ottoman and Russian empires. Since nationalist activities ebbed and flowed in each of these areas, their rulers often thought they needed only to ride things out until stability returned. But over the course of the century, nationalists changed Europe's map and political culture.

Early Nineteenth-Century Political Liberalism

The word *liberal*, as applied to political activity, entered the West's vocabulary during the nineteenth century. Its meaning has varied, and its current use in America has little or nothing to do with its significance to nineteenth-century Europeans.

Unlike conservatives, who associated constitutions with the upheaval that followed the French Revolution and who did not believe that all necessary political arrangements could be defined in writing, liberals wanted con-

Mazzini Defines Nationality

No political force in the nineteenth century was stronger than national-
ism. It replaced dynastic political loyalty with loyalty based on ethnic
considerations. In 1835, the Italian nationalist and patriot Giuseppe
Mazzini (1805–1872) explained his understanding of the concept. Note the
manner in which he combined a generally democratic view of politics
with a religious concept of the divine destiny of nations.

 What are the specific qualities of a people that Mazzini associates
with nationalism? How does Mazzini relate nationalism to divine purposes? Why does he make the connection? How does this view of
nationality relate to the goals of liberal freedom?

The essential characteristics of a nationality are common ideas, common principles and a common purpose. A nation is
an association of those who are brought
together by language, by given geographical conditions or by the role assigned
them by history, who acknowledge the
same principles and who march together
to the conquest of a single definite goal
under the rule of a uniform body of law.

The life of a nation consists in harmonious activity (that is, the employment of all individual abilities and ener-
gies comprised within the association)
towards this single goal. . . .

But nationality means even more than
this. Nationality also consists in the
share of mankind's labors which God as-

stitutional government. Their political aspirations were very limited, but in
1815 the kinds of constitutional governments the West now takes for granted
did not exist in Europe—even in Great Britain.

The liberal political platform derived from the Enlightenment, from England's customary liberties, and from the so-called principles of 1789 embodied in the French Declaration of the Rights of Man and Citizen. Liberals favored equality before the law for all citizens, religious toleration, and freedom
of the press. They wanted political machinery that would prevent governments from arbitrarily using their powers against the persons or property of
individuals. They generally believed that government derived its legitimacy
from the freely given consent of the governed as expressed through elected,
representative, or parliamentary bodies. And they insisted that ministers of
state be responsible to the representatives of the people, not to a monarch.

Those who espoused liberalism tended to be educated, prosperous people who were excluded in some way from the existing political system. They
were often academics, members of the professions, or people involved in the
expanding commercial and manufacturing segments of the economy. The
monarchical and aristocratic regimes that were restored after the Congress of
Vienna often failed to recognize the status achieved by these people and to
provide for their economic, professional, and social aspirations.

signs to a people. This mission is the task which a people must perform to the end that the Divine Idea shall be realized in this world; it is the work which gives a people its rights as a member of Mankind; it is the baptismal rite which endows a people with its own character and its rank in the brotherhood of nations. . . .

Nationality depends for its very existence upon its sacredness within and beyond its borders.

If nationality is to be inviolable for all, friends and foes alike, it must be regarded inside a country as holy, like a religion, and outside a country as a grave mission. It is necessary too that the ideas arising within a country grow steadily, as part of the general law of Humanity which is the source of all nationality. It is necessary that these ideas be shown to other lands in their beauty and purity, free from any alien mixture, from any slavish fears, from any skeptical hesitancy, strong and active, embracing in their evolution every aspect and manifestation of the life of the nation. These ideas, a necessary component in the order of universal destiny, must retain their originality even as they enter harmoniously into mankind's general progress.

The people must be the basis of nationality; its logically derived and vigorously applied principles its means; the strength of all its strength; the improvement of the life of all and the happiness of the greatest possible number its results; and the accomplishment of the task assigned to it by God its goal. This is what we mean by nationality.

Herbert H. Rown (ed.), From Absolutism to Revolution, *1648–1848, 2nd ed. (New York: The Macmillan Company; London: Collier-Macmillan Limited, 1969), pp. 277, 280.*

Although liberals wanted broader political participation, they did not advocate democracy. They favored expansion of representation for the propertied classes. Second only to their hostility for aristocrats was their general contempt for the poor. Liberals wanted to reinterpret the eighteenth century's concept of aristocratic privilege by using wealth, not birth, to determine an individual's political rights. This program drove a wedge between them and the rural and urban working classes that was to have important consequences.

The economics favored by nineteenth-century liberals also divided them from working people. The commercial classes generally accepted the theories of Adam Smith, the Enlightenment economist who advocated an end to the trade restraints enacted by mercantilists and the regulated economies managed by absolutist monarchs. Liberals wanted to manufacture and sell goods freely, and they opposed paternalistic governments or guilds that regulated wages or labor practices. For them, labor was simply a commodity to be bought and sold at the price it would bring on the free market. They believed that if people were set free to exploit whatever opportunities they had to enrich themselves, it would result in more and cheaper goods and services being produced for everyone.

The reforms associated with liberals varied according to where they lived. In Great Britain and France, the problem for liberals was to protect civil liberties, to define the respective powers of the monarch and the elected representative body, and to expand the electorate moderately while avoiding democracy. The situation in German-speaking Europe was different. There, monarchs and aristocrats offered stiffer resistance to liberal ideas, and German liberals had fewer opportunities to participate in government. The aristocratic landowning class filled the bureaucracies and officer corps and looked down on the small commercial and industrial middle class that had no role to play in government. Most German liberals wanted to unite Germany and believed that either Austria or Prussia had to become the instrument of its unification. Consequently, they were more tolerant of strong state and monarchical power than other liberals. Plans for a freer social and political order were deferred until after unification.

Relationship of Nationalism and Liberalism. There was no logical link between liberalism and nationalism. Indeed, nationalism sometimes opposed liberal reform. Some nationalists wanted their own ethnic group to dominate the others resident in their homeland. Some refused to cooperate with groups they regarded as cultural inferiors or as historical enemies. But liberalism and nationalism might complement each other, for a fight for representative government, civil liberties, and economic freedom by a group in one nation led it to identify with similar struggles elsewhere.

∼ Conservative Governments on the Domestic Scene

Conservative Outlooks

Until World War I, conservative governments, particularly in Great Britain and eastern Europe, successfully resisted both liberalism and nationalism. These governments were products of a new alliance among monarchies, landed aristocracies, and established churches. Traditionally, these groups had been competitors, but the upheavals of the French Revolution and the Napoleonic era transformed them into natural, if sometimes reluctant, allies.

The fate of Louis XVI convinced most monarchs that the only trustworthy governments were those composed of aristocrats and, possibly, the very wealthiest middleclass and professionals. Aristocrats believed that their property and influence would rarely be safe under any form of genuinely representative government. Most ecclesiastical leaders assumed that they had been entrusted with the task of supporting the social and political status quo and defending tradition against the critical rationalism unleashed by the Enlightenment.

Conservatives retained their customary arrogance but lost the confidence on which it had been grounded. They knew they could be driven from power, and they understood that revolution in one country could spill over into another. They were determined, therefore, to deal firmly with all potential sources of unrest.

Austria and the Germanies

Prince Metternich (1773–1859) of Austria epitomized conservatism more than any other early nineteenth-century statesman. A devoted servant of the Habsburg emperor, he and Britain's Viscount Castlereagh (1769–1822) were the architects of the agreements ratified at the Congress of Vienna.

The Congress of Vienna created a German Confederation to replace the defunct Holy Roman Empire. It consisted of thirty-nine states, each more or less autonomous, but recognizing Austrian leadership. Austria was determined to prevent any movement toward constitutionalism in these states, for the future of the Habsburg Empire depended on its ability to prevent the German Confederation from becoming a German national state. The Habsburg Empire was more threatened by liberalism and nationalism than most states, for it was nothing but a collection of diverse ethnic groups that recognized the emperor as their hereditary ruler. Metternich feared that any attempt at representative government would lead to internal squabbling among these groups, which would make it impossible for Austria to wield international influence.

Defeat of Reform in Prussia. Prussia joined Austria in holding the line against nationalism and liberalism. In 1815, Frederick William III (r. 1797–1840), carried away by the excitement that followed the "War of Liberation" (Germany's last battles with Napoleon), promised Prussia a constitutional government. Instead, in 1817, he created a new Council of State that improved administrative efficiency, but issued no constitution.

In 1819, a major disagreement over the organization of the army led to the resignation of the king's reform-minded ministers and their replacement with hardened conservatives. In 1823, on their advice, Frederick William III created eight provincial assemblies. These advisory bodies, dominated by the Junkers, reaffirmed the old bonds linking Prussia's monarchy, army, and landholders and created a conservative alliance opposed to German nationalism.

Student Nationalism. In bids to win broad bases of support, the rulers of three south German states—Baden, Bavaria, and Württemberg—issued constitutions after 1815. None recognized popular sovereignty, and all defined political rights as a gift of the monarch. Many young Germans, whose nationalism had been inflamed by the war against Napoleon, were unhappy with this. The best-organized youth were the university students whose *Burschenschaften*, like student groups today, served many functions. One of their effects was to diminish old provincial loyalties while generating enthusiasm for a united Germany.

In 1817, a student club in Jena organized a large celebration of the fourth anniversary of the Battle of Leipzig and the tercentenary of the posting of Luther's Ninety-five Theses. More than 500 people gathered for the bonfires, songs, and processions. Since some professed republicans were involved, the event made the government nervous. Two years later a *Burschenschaft* member, Karl Sand (d. 1820), was tried and executed for assassinating a conservative dramatist, August von Kotzebue (1761–1819). When some nationalists proclaimed Sand a martyr, Metternich decided to use the incident to suppress student clubs and other liberal groups.

In July 1819, Metternich persuaded the German states to endorse the Carlsbad Decrees. These dissolved the *Burschenschaften* and provided for university inspectors and press censors. The next year, the German Confederation promulgated the Final Act. It limited the subjects that might be discussed by the constitutional assemblies of Bavaria, Württemberg, and Baden, and affirmed the monarchs' right to oppose the constitutionalists. For many years thereafter, the secret police of the various German states harassed anyone who sought even moderate social or political change.

Great Britain

The years 1819 and 1820 were also a peak period for enacting repressive conservative policies in Britain. Two years of poor harvests and the widespread unemployment that followed the end of the Napoleonic wars created problems with which the Tory ministry of Lord Liverpool (1770–1828) was unprepared to deal. Its response was to protect the wealthy and abandon the British ruling class's paternalistic tradition of caring for the poor. The government had already outlawed labor unions (the Combination Acts of 1799), and during the war it ended protection for wages. In 1815, Parliament passed a Corn Law that maintained high prices for domestically produced grain by imposing duties on imports. The next year, Parliament replaced income taxes with sales taxes which weighed much more heavily on the poor than on the rich. Many of the well-off also called for the abolition of the poor law that provided public relief for the destitute and unemployed. It is hardly surprising that the lower social orders responded by calling for reform of Parliament. Mass meetings were held, reform clubs were organized, and radical newspapers, were founded.

Government ministers regarded the organizers of the protest as demagogues who seduced the people away from allegiance to their natural leaders. Memories of *sans-culottes* crowds hanging French aristocrats from lampposts were still vivid, and Britain's leaders had no intention of letting the rabble get out of hand. In December 1816, an unruly mass meeting at Spa Fields near London gave Parliament an excuse to pass the Coercion Act (March 1817), which temporarily suspended habeas corpus and extended existing laws against seditious gatherings.

The Six Acts. Threats of repression and an easing of socioeconomic conditions because of improved harvests produced a period of calm. But by 1819, the people were again restive. In the industrial north, well-organized mass meetings demanded reform. On August 16, 1819, a large gathering in Manchester, at Saint Peter's Fields, ended disastrously. The troops that were on hand to ensure order caused the crowd to panic. At least eleven people were killed and scores injured. The event—in a mocking reference to Wellington's victory at Waterloo—was dubbed the "Peterloo" Massacre.

The responsibility for Peterloo lay with the local Manchester officials whom Lord Liverpool's ministry felt it had to support. The cabinet also believed that the time had come for decisive action. Most of the radical leaders were incarcerated, and in December 1819, a few months after the German Carlsbad Decrees, Parliament passed the Six Acts. These (1) forbade large unauthorized, public meetings, (2) raised the fines for seditious libel, (3) speeded up the trials of political agitators, (4) increased newspaper taxes, (5) prohibited the training of armed groups, and (6) allowed local officials to search homes in certain counties.

France

Napoleon's abdication in 1814 opened the way for a restoration of the Bourbon monarchy that had been unseated by the revolution. The new king, Louis XVIII (r. 1814–1824), was Louis XVI's brother. (Louis XVI's son, whom royalists regarded as Louis XVII, had died uncrowned in prison.) Twenty years in exile had made Louis XVIII a political realist. He knew he could not turn back the clock, for France had changed irreversibly. Consequently, he agreed to a constitutional monarchy, but under a constitution of his own making.

The Charter. Louis XVIII's constitution, the Charter, combined a hereditary monarchy with a bicameral legislature. The monarch appointed the upper house; the lower house, the Chamber of Deputies, was elected. Only men with substantial property qualified to vote. The Charter guaranteed most of the rights enumerated by the Declaration of the Rights of Man and Citizen. It designated Roman Catholicism as France's official religion, while promising toleration for other faiths. Most important for many citizens of all classes, the Charter promised not to challenge the rights of current owners of land that had been confiscated from aristocrats and the church. Louis XVIII hoped this would reconcile to his regime those who had benefited from the revolution.

Ultraroyalism. Louis XVIII's conciliatory mood was not shared by many of his royalist supporters whose families had suffered from the revolution. Led by the count of Artois (1757–1836), who was more royalist than the king, they demanded revenge. Following Napoleon's defeat at Waterloo, royalists in the south and west of France launched the White Terror, an attack on the supporters of the revolution and Napoleon. The king could do little or nothing to halt the bloodshed.

The Chamber of Deputies, the elected house, was similarly extreme in its royalist sentiment. The majority elected in 1816 was so dangerously reactionary that the king dissolved the chamber and called for another election.

Years of give and take, during which liberals made moderate advances, ended in February 1820. The duke of Berri, Artois' son and—after him—heir to Louis's throne, was murdered by a lone assassin. The ultraroyalists persuaded Louis that liberal politicians were to blame, and the king responded with repressive measures. Electoral laws were revised to give wealthy men two votes. Press censorship was imposed, and rules protecting people from arbitrary arrest were relaxed. In 1821, the government turned secondary education over to the Roman Catholic bishops. The government's aura of constitutionalism faded as liberals were driven out of politics.

∽ The Conservative International Order

The Congress of Vienna closed with an understanding that the major powers—Russia, Austria, Prussia, and Great Britain—would hold postwar congresses to consult on matters affecting Europe as a whole. This agreement, called the Concert of Europe, aimed at coordinating foreign policies and preventing any nation from acting without the assent of the others. The purpose of the Concert of Europe was to defend a balance of power that was endangered by Russia's military might and the possibility of renewed French aggression.

The first Concert of Europe congress took place at Aix-la-Chapelle in 1818. The four major powers agreed to remove their troops from France and restore France's standing among European nations, but Britain rejected a proposal by Tsar Alexander I (r. 1801–1825) that the Quadruple Alliance undertake to defend the borders and the existing governments of all European countries. The dispute remained academic until a series of revolutions began in southern Europe in 1820.

Tsar Alexander I (r. 1801–1825). A mild reformer when he succeeded to the throne, Alexander became increasingly reactionary after 1815. [Bettmann Archive]

The Spanish Revolution of 1820

After Napoleon's fall, Ferdinand VII (r. 1814–1833), heir to the earlier Bourbon dynasty, ascended the Spanish throne. Once in power, he ignored a pledge he had made to issue a written constitution, dissolved Spain's parliament (the Cortes), and ruled alone. In 1820, a group of army officers, who were about to be sent to suppress revolution in Spain's Latin American colonies, rebelled and frightened Ferdinand into accepting a constitution. About the same time, a revolt in Naples forced the king of the Two Sicilies to endorse a constitution, and there were similar, but unsuccessful, uprisings elsewhere in Italy.

Metternich, who feared for the stability of Austria's empire, worried that disturbances in Italy might spread into the Habsburg lands. Britain opposed joint intervention by the major powers in either Italy or Spain. But when the Congress of Troppau met in late October 1820, Tsar Alexander persuaded Russia's colleagues in the Holy Alliance (Austria and Prussia) to issue the Protocol of Troppau. It declared that stable governments could intervene to restore order in countries experiencing revolution. The decision to authorize Austrian intervention in Italy, however, was delayed until January 1821 (the Congress of Laibach). Austrian troops then marched into Naples and restored the king and nonconstitutional government to the Two Sicilies.

The final postwar congress took place in October 1822 at Verona. Once again Britain balked at joint action to deal with the situation in Spain. Its new foreign minister, George Canning (1770–1827), in effect withdrew Britain from continental affairs. Austria, Prussia, and Russia agreed to allow the French to send an army into Spain (April 1823). The Spanish revolution was suppressed within a few months, but the purge of liberals that followed was one of the century's bloodiest expressions of reactionary politics.

George Canning advanced Britain's commercial interests by preventing the politics of European reaction from spreading to Spain's colonies in Latin America. These were in revolt, and Canning exploited their revolutions to end Spain's colonial monopoly and win Britain access to Latin American trade. For this reason, Britain accepted the Monroe Doctrine (1823) which declared the United States' opposition to further European colonization and intervention in the Americas. Canning's policy won Britain dominance over the commerce of Latin America for the rest of the century.

The Greek Revolution of 1821

While conservative restorations were occurring in Italy and Spain, a famous revolution erupted in Greece. It attracted the support of illustrious liberal literary figures who, seeing their hopes crushed across Europe, hoped that Greece's revolt heralded the return of democracy to the land that gave it birth. Philhellenic societies flourished in most countries, and Lord Byron one of the era's famous poets, went to Greece to die fighting for the cause of liberty in 1824.

The Greeks were struggling to free themselves from the Ottoman Empire, whose slow deterioration threatened the international balance of power. Most of Europe's great nations had keen interests in Ottoman holdings in the eastern Mediterranean. Russia and Austria wanted parts of the Balkans. France and Britain wanted commercial access to the empire and control of key naval posts in the Mediterranean. Christians of all nations wanted access to the shrines in the Holy Land.

The goals of the great powers often conflicted with the desire many of the Ottoman Empire's subjects had for independence. Suspicion of rebels and of nationalistic movements delayed direct intervention in Greek affairs by European nations for several years. Eventually, however, Britain, France, and Russia concluded that Greek independence would promote their strategic interests without threatening their domestic security. In 1827, they issued the Treaty of London, demanding Turkish recognition of Greek independence, and they sent a joint fleet to support the Greek revolt. In 1829, Russia conquered and annexed the Ottoman territory known today as Romania. The Treaty of Adrianople, which ended that campaign, also stipulated that the Turks would allow Britain, France, and Russia to decide Greece's future. In 1830, a second Treaty of London declared Greece an independent kingdom, and Otto I (r. 1832–1862), son of the king of Bavaria, was chosen to found a new Greek dynasty.

Serbian Independence

The year 1830 also saw the establishment of a second independent state on the Balkan peninsula. Serbia had been seeking independence from the Ottoman Empire since the late eighteenth century. From 1804 to 1813, a remarkable leader, Karageorge (1762–1817), fought a guerilla war which, although unsuccessful, helped publicize the cause and build a sense of national identity. In 1815 and 1816, a new leader, Milos (1780–1860), won increased autonomy for part of Serbian territory. But a majority of Serbs lived outside the borders of this district. In 1830, the Ottoman sultan granted independence to Serbia; by the late 1830s, the major powers had extended it recognition.

The structure of the new nation remained in doubt for many years following its birth. Milos, who became its hereditary prince, persuaded the Ottomans to extend its borders in 1833. The new boundaries pertained until 1878, but continuing agitation for land created problems with Austria. And questions about the status of minorities, particularly Muslims, increased internal tensions.

In the 1820s, Slavic Russia, although separated from Serbia by Austrian territory, declared itself the protector of the Slavs of Serbia. In 1856, the great powers established a collective protectorate, but Russia continued to claim a special relationship.

The Wars of Independence in Latin America

The Napoleonic era concluded Europe's 300 years of colonial domination of Latin America (see Map 21-1). A slave revolt—begun in 1794 by Toussaint L'Ouverture (1743–1803) and Jean-Jacques Dessalines (1758–1806)—won Haiti independence in 1804. Haiti's revolution, a popular uprising of a repressed so-

MAP 21-1 Latin America in 1830 *By 1830, Latin America had been liberated from European government. This map illustrates the early borders of the states of the region with the dates of their independence.*

cial group, was unusual. Generally speaking, the drive for liberty on the South American continent was led by the Creole elite—merchants, landowners, and professional people of Spanish descent. Very few Indians, blacks, mestizos, mulattos, or slaves became involved in the fight or benefited from it. The Haitian slave revolt haunted the Creoles, as did the memory of a revolt by Indians in the Andes in 1780 and 1781. The Creoles were determined that their struggle for independence should not diminish their privileged position in society. Many revolutionaries have seen no inconsistency in denying to others the liberties they claim for themselves.

Creole discontent had many sources. Latin American merchants wanted to trade more freely within their region and with North America and Europe. They wanted commercial regulations that would benefit them rather than a European motherland. Creoles in Spanish districts deeply resented the favoritism shown *peninsulares* (whites born in Spain) when appointments were made to colonial governments, churches, and armies.

Prepared for revolution by reading the Enlightenment *philosophes* and by observing the American Revolution, the Creoles' impetus to act came when Napoleon toppled the monarchies of Portugal in 1807 and of Spain in 1808. The Portuguese royal family fled to Brazil and established a government in exile. Spain's Bourbon monarchy, however, disappeared—leaving a political

Toussaint L'Ouverture (1743–1803) began the revolt that led to Haitian independence in 1804. [Historical Pictures/Stock Montage, Inc.]

vacuum throughout Spanish Latin America. The Creole elite feared that Napoleon's puppet monarchy in Spain would impose reforms incompatible with their interests and drain them of money to fund France's wars. Between 1808 and 1810, therefore various Creole juntas (political committees) took charge of different regions of Latin America. Spain was never able to restore its authority over the continent.

Argentina. Vast size, geographical barriers, regional differences, and the absence of an integrated economy meant that different parts of Latin America took different routes to independence. The first region to assert itself was that of the Rio de la Plata, modern Argentina. The center of revolt was Buenos Aires. In 1810, its junta not only thrust off Spanish authority but also sent armies of liberation into Paraguay and Uruguay. They were defeated, but they cost Spain control of both areas. Paraguay asserted its independence, and Brazil absorbed Uruguay.

The Buenos Aires government then set about liberating Peru, the most loyal royalist stronghold on the continent. José de San Martín (1778–1850), the dominant general of the Rio de la Plata forces, created a disciplined army and led it on a daring march over the Andes Mountains. By early 1817, he had occupied Santiago, Chile, where a local rebel, Bernardo O'Higgins (1778–1842), was established as dictator. San Martín constructed a navy at Santiago, and in 1820, launched it against Peru. A year later, he drove the royalist forces from Lima and declared himself Protector of Peru.

Venezuela. What San Martín did for the south, Simón Bolívar (1783–1830) did for the north. In 1810, Bolívar, the son of a wealthy and aristocratic family, helped organize a republican junta in Caracas, Venezuela. Civil war erupted. From 1811 to 1814, the fledgling republic was assaulted by royalists on the one hand and slaves and *llaneros* (cowboys) on the other, and Bolívar was forced into exile. In 1816, with help from the president of Haiti, he renewed his fight for a republican Venezuela. He captured Bogota, capital of New Granada (a viceroyalty that encompassed modern Colombia, Bolivia, and Ecuador), and used it as a base for war in Venezuela. By the summer of 1821, he had taken Caracas and been named president.

A year later, Bolívar and San Martín cooperated in liberating Quito, the capital of Ecuador. San Martín disagreed with Bolívar's republicanism and urged the establishment of monarchies in Latin America. But San Martín soon gave up the struggle, retiring from public life and exiling himself to Europe. Without San Martín's guidance, the political situation in Peru deteriorated, and in 1823, Bolívar sent in an army and took control. On December 9, 1824, at the battle of Ayacucho, he gave the royalist forces the defeat that ended their attempts to retain an empire in America for Spain.

New Spain (Mexico). The campaign for independence in New Spain (the viceroyalty that encompassed modern Mexico, Texas, California, and the southwestern United States) best illustrates the conservative nature of the

Latin American revolutions. The local governing junta that here, as elsewhere, was organized to lead the revolt quickly lost the initiative. A Creole priest, Miguel Hidalgo y Costilla (1753–1811), proposed a program of sweeping social reform and incited the Indians of his parish to rise up. They and other repressed groups (black and mestizo urban and rural workers) responded enthusiastically, and soon Father Hidalgo had an army of 80,000. They captured several major cities and marched on Mexico City itself. Atrocities were committed on both sides, and in July 1811, Hidalgo was captured and executed. Leadership of his movement passed to José María Morelos y Pavón (1765–1815), a mestizo priest who was far more radical than Hidalgo. He called for substantial land reforms and an end to forced labor. He kept the revolt alive for five more years until he, too, was captured and executed in 1815.

The revolt had the effect of uniting Mexico's conservatives, both Creole and Spanish. Since they opposed any reform that might diminish their privileges, they were worried when the Bourbon monarch, Ferdinand VII, was restored to the Spanish throne. He had been forced to accept a liberal constitution that conservative Mexicans feared might lead to the imposition of liberal reforms on Mexico. To defend their conservative principles, they launched a revolution. In 1821, a former royalist general, Augustín de Iturbide (1783–1824), declared Mexico's independence and took the title of emperor. His regime was short-lived, but it established persons opposed to social reform in control of an independent Mexico.

Brazil. Brazil's independence came relatively simply and peacefully. In 1807, the Portuguese royal family and several thousand government officials and members of the court took refuge from Napoleon in Brazil. Their arrival transformed Rio de Janeiro into a court city. The prince regent, João, addressed many of the local complaints and, in 1815, made Brazil a kingdom independent of Portugal. In 1820, a revolution in Portugal allowed João VI (r. 1816–1824) to return to Lisbon, and his son, Dom Pedro, became regent for Brazil. In 1822, Dom Pedro declared himself emperor of Brazil in order to block attempts by the revolutionary government in Portugal to regain control of its former colony. Thus, unlike most other Latin American nations, Brazil won its independence without an internal fight that disrupted established institutions. Elsewhere, wars of independence encouraged the abolition of slavery, but not in Brazil.

Consequences of Latin American Independence. Latin America emerged from its wars for independence economically exhausted and politically unstable. Only Brazil, which had little internal adjustment to make, prospered immediately. In other places, the fight for independence had led to civil wars in which disaffected populations challenged new governments. Economies contracted until overall production in 1830 was lower than it had been in 1800. The situation provided Britain a great opportunity, for Britain was able to offer grateful Latin American governments and businesses protection, markets, and capital investment.

～ The Conservative Order Shaken in Europe

During the first half of the 1820s, Europe's restored conservative governments successfully resisted the forces of liberalism. The only liberal advances (the Greek revolution and the Latin American Wars of Independence) occurred on the periphery of the European world.

In the middle of the 1820s, things changed, and conservative regimes were assaulted by new waves of discontent. Russia responded with suppression; France, with revolution; and Britain, with accommodation.

Russia

Many Russian aristocrats were exposed to the ideas of the French Revolution and the Enlightenment. When the Russian army pursued Napoleon across Europe and occupied France, some of its officers became aware of how backward their homeland was. They developed reformist sympathies that were not shared by their tsar. Both at home and abroad, Alexander I had taken the lead in suppressing liberalism and nationalism. While he lived, there could be no challenge to tsarist autocracy.

Some of the officers who were interested in politics formed small secret societies to discuss reform. They evolved no single, coherent program. Some advocated representative government and the abolition of serfdom. Some called for democracy and limited independence for Poland. Some favored constitutional monarchy, but wanted protection for the aristocracy. All agreed that Russia's government had to change, and sometime during 1825 they began to plan a coup d'état.

Dynastic Crises. Alexander I suddenly and unexpectedly died in late November 1825. He left no direct heir, and a peculiar dispute broke out over the succession. His brother Constantine, who would have been next in line for the throne, had disqualified himself by marrying a woman who was not of royal blood. Furthermore, Constantine did not want the crown. Alexander had left secret instructions naming a younger brother, Nicholas (r. 1825–1855), as the new tsar. But Nicholas was not confident of the legality of this arrangement. He, therefore, acknowledged Constantine as tsar, while Constantine acknowledged him. This muddle continued for about three weeks, until the army command warned Nicholas of a conspiracy in the officer corps. Much to the delight of the exasperated Constantine, Nicholas overcame his scruples and declared himself tsar.

A number of junior officers had plotted to rally the troops under their command to the cause of reform. On December 26, 1825, when the army was to take the oath of allegiance to Nicholas, the Moscow regiment—whose chief officers, surprisingly, were not secret society members—refused. They called for a constitution and the coronation of Constantine, who was personally more popular than Nicholas and politically less conservative. Nicholas ordered the cavalry and the artillery to attack the insurgents, and more than sixty people were killed. Nicholas himself then presided over a commission appointed to investigate the "Decembrist Revolt" and the army's secret societies. Five plotters were executed and more than a hundred exiled to Siberia. Although the Decembrist Revolt failed, it produced martyrs who, for a century, symbolized the yearnings of Russia's small clique of liberals.

The Autocracy of Nicholas I. Although Nicholas was neither an ignorant nor a bigoted reactionary, he feared that any tinkering with Russia's traditional institutions—like serfdom, which he admitted to be an evil—might cause the nobility to overthrow the monarchy. Consequently, he turned his back on reform and became the most extreme kind of nineteenth-century autocrat. He set up a large secret police, imposed censorship, and did little to ensure the efficiency and honesty of his administration. The only reform he carried out was a codification of Russian law in 1833.

To undercut calls for reform, Nicholas instituted an educational program called Official Nationality. Its slogan, published repeatedly in government documents, newspapers, journals, and schoolbooks, was "Orthodoxy, Autocracy, and Nationalism." The Russian Orthodox faith was to provide the basis for morality, education, and intellectual life. (The church, through control of the schools, was to teach young Russians to accept their places in life and to spurn social mobility.) The autocracy of the tsar was declared to be the only authority strong enough to hold the huge Russian state together and guarantee its prosperity and influence. Nationalism was glorified to convince the Russians that their religion, language, and customs were a source of a unique wisdom that protected them from the moral corruption and political turmoil of the West.

Revolt and Repression in Poland. Poland had remained under Russian domination after the Congress of Vienna, but it had been granted a constitutional government under the Russian tsar. Both Alexander I and Nicholas appointed their brother, the Grand Duke Constantine (1779–1831), to govern Poland. Although both tsars frequently infringed on the constitution and quarreled with the Polish Diet, this arrangement lasted through the 1820s.

In late November 1830, news of recent revolutions in France and Belgium reached Poland and inspired a small insurrection among soldiers and students in Warsaw. The disturbances spread throughout the country, and on December 18, the Polish Diet declared the revolt to be a nationalist movement. When the Diet voted to depose Nicholas as ruler of Poland, the tsar sent in troops and suppressed the uprising. In February 1832, Nicholas issued the Organic Statute, which claimed Poland as an integral part of the Russian Empire. The Polish uprising confirmed all of Nicholas's worst fears and persuaded him to become the gendarme of Europe, ever ready to provide troops to suppress liberal and nationalist movements.

France

Poland's revolt was one of several disturbances inspired by the overthrow of France's Bourbon dynasty in July 1830. Charles X (r. 1824–1830), Louis XVIII's brother and successor, was a firm believer in the divine right of kings. His first action as king was to order France's Chamber of Deputies to indemnify aristocrats who had lost lands in the revolution. He raised the money that was needed by lowering the rate of interest the government paid on its bonds. This alienated members of the middle class who were bondholders. Charles restored primogeniture as a legally mandated system of inheritance, and he enacted a law that punished sacrilege against the Roman Catholic Church with imprisonment or death.

In the elections of 1827, liberals, who had been angered by the king's actions, gained enough seats in the Chamber of Deputies to force him to compromise. He appointed a less conservative ministry. Laws restraining the press and allowing the government to dominate education were eased. Liberals, however, wanted much more—a genuinely constitutional regime. In 1829, the king, deciding that a policy of accommodation had failed, replaced his moderate ministers with a group of ultraroyalists headed by the Prince de Polignac (1780–1847).

The July Revolution. In 1830, Charles X called new elections, and the liberals scored a stunning victory. Instead of accommodating the new Chamber of Deputies, the king tried to destroy it. In June 1830, Polignac had sent a naval expedition against Algeria, and reports of its victory—which founded a French empire in North Africa—reached Paris on July 9. Charles X used the euphoria created by the victory to stage a royal coup d'état. On July 25, 1830, he issued the Four Ordinances, which (1) limited freedom of the press, (2) dissolved the recently elected Chamber of Deputies, (3) restricted the franchise to the wealthiest people in the country, and (4) called new elections under the new royalist franchise.

Reaction was swift and decisive. Liberal newspapers called on the nation to reject the monarch's actions, and the working class of Paris, suffering since 1827 from a downturn in the economy, took to the streets. The king called out troops, and more than 1,800 people died battling in the city. On August 2, Charles X accepted defeat, abdicated, and went into exile. The Chamber of Deputies named a new ministry, composed of constitutional monarchists, and ended the Bourbon dynasty by proclaiming Louis Philippe (r. 1830–1848), the liberal duke of Orléans, king of France.

A fundamental political and social tension underlay the new monarchy. The Revolution of 1830 might have failed if Charles X had provided himself with sufficient troops to maintain order in Paris. Had the aristocratic and middle-class liberals who favored constitutional monarchy not acted quickly, the workers of Paris might have tried to form a republic. Liberals, however, feared popular revolution (such as had swept France in 1792) and had no desire for another *sans-culottes* regime. An alliance between France's hard-pressed laborers and its prosperous middle class won the struggle in 1830, but these groups had different objectives that made it hard for them to stay united.

Louis Philippe. Politically, the so-called July Monarchy was more liberal than the restoration government of the Bourbons. Its new constitution was regarded as the right of its people rather than a concession from their monarch. Catholicism was described as the religion of the majority—but not the official religion. Censorship was abolished. The franchise broadened somewhat, but remained restricted. The king had to cooperate with the Chamber of Deputies and could not dispense with laws on his own authority.

Socially, the new order created by the Revolution of 1830 was quite conservative. The hereditary peerage was abolished in 1831, but the power of the landed oligarchy continued. (Money was the route to influence in a government noted for corruption.) The monarchy took little interest in the plight of the lower classes. The Paris workers in 1830 called for protection of jobs, better wages, and the preservation of the traditional crafts. This kind of economic regulation was inconsistent with the political liberalism of Louis Philippe's government, which viewed the working classes as nothing more than a source of trouble.

Late in 1831, troops suppressed a workers' revolt in the city of Lyons. In July 1832, there was an uprising in Paris occasioned by a funeral for a popu-

Despite laws forbidding disrespect to the government, political cartoonists had a field day with Louis Philippe. Here, an artist emphasizes the king's resemblance to a pear and in the process attacks restraints on freedom of the press. (The Bettmann Archive)

lar Napoleonic general, and again the government called out troops. Over 800 people were killed or wounded. In 1834, a large strike by Lyons silk workers was crushed. Discontent was temporarily smothered, but a lasting peace could only be achieved by an administration that was prepared to address France's serious social and economic problems.

Belgium

The skirmish that established France's July Monarchy ignited revolutionary fires in neighboring Belgium. In 1815, the Congress of Vienna had created a problem by joining Belgium, the former Austrian Netherlands, to the kingdom of Holland. Since the two countries differed in language, religion, and economy, the Belgian upper classes were never reconciled to the arrangement.

Their impetus to organize and to assert their independence came on August 25, 1830. A disturbance erupted in Brussels following the performance of an opera with a revolutionary theme, and the municipal authorities and propertied classes formed a provisional national government to restore order. Attempts at compromise with the Dutch failed, and William of Holland (r. 1815–1840) invaded. The Dutch were defeated by November 10, 1830, and the following year a national congress issued a liberal constitution for Belgium.

The revolution in Belgium upset the boundaries established by the Congress of Vienna, but the major powers were not inclined to intervene. Russia, Austria, Prussia, and other German states were busy suppressing various disturbances elsewhere. France favored an independent Belgium, which it expected to dominate. And Britain was prepared to tolerate a liberal Belgium so long as it was not dominated by another nation.

In December 1830, Lord Palmerston (1784–1865), the British foreign minister, gathered representatives of the powers in London and persuaded them to recognize Belgium as an independent, neutral state. In July 1831, Leopold of Saxe-Coburg (r. 1831–1865) was crowned king of the Belgians. Belgium's neutrality was recognized by the Convention of 1839 and respected until 1914. In that year, a German invasion of Belgium brought Britain into World War I.

Britain

Since George IV (r. 1820–1830) died in 1830, the accession of a new king, William IV (r. 1830–1837), required the calling of a parliamentary election for the summer that France's July revolution took place. The new House of Commons proposed the first major reform of Parliament, but events on the continent seem not to have influenced its members. The passage of the Great Reform Bill (1832) resulted from an accommodation—unique to Britain—between the forces of conservatism and reform.

The inclination to accommodate that was characteristic of British politics had several sources. Since the commercial and industrial classes were larger in Britain than in other countries, every government recognized that the nation's prosperity depended on guarding their economic interests. Britain's aristocratic Whig liberals believed in constitutional liberty and advocated successive moderate reforms instead of revolution. Also, Britain had a long tradition, supported by law and public opinion, of respect for civil liberties.

Catholic Emancipation Act. Repressive conservative government reached a peak under the Tory minister, Lord Liverpool, who had tried to stifle calls for reform by issuing the notorious Six Acts (1819). But in 1820 Liverpool changed his cabinet to create a government more disposed to adjust to changing conditions. It increased economic freedom and repealed earlier restraints imposed on labor organizations.

England's relationship with Ireland brought about another change. In 1800, fearful that Irish nationalists might rebel (as they had in 1798) and offer Ireland to Napoleon as a base for a French invasion of England, William Pitt the Younger persuaded Parliament to pass the Act of Union. Ireland was granted 100 seats in the House of Commons, but only Irish Protestants were permitted to stand for election. During the 1820s, Irish nationalists organized the Catholic Association to agitate for Catholic emancipation, and in 1828, they challenged the law by electing one of their leaders, Daniel O'Connell (1775–1847), to a seat he could not legally occupy. To head off civil war, the British ministry, led by the duke of Wellington and Robert Peel, persuaded Parliament to seat Catholics (the Catholic Emancipation Act of 1829). This, with an earlier repeal of restrictions against Protestant nonconformists (1828), ended the Anglican church's monopoly of British political life.

Catholic emancipation was a liberal measure intended for a conservative purpose: the preservation of order in Ireland. But its passage alienated many of Wellington's Anglican Tory supporters, and the split in the Tory party and an election in 1830 that seated a Parliament disposed to reform led to the fall of Wellington's ministry. King William IV turned to Earl Grey (1764–1845), leader of the Whigs, to form the next government.

Legislating Change. The Whig ministry quickly sent the House of Commons a major reform bill. It proposed replacing "rotten" boroughs with new districts that increased representation for cities and manufacturing areas, and it extended the franchise. When the House of Commons rejected the bill, Grey called for a new election (1831). The new Commons passed the bill, but the House of Lords refused to concur. Mass protest meetings were held throughout the country, and riots broke out. Finally, William IV agreed to create enough new peers to give a third reform bill a majority in the House of Lords, and under this pressure the Lords passed the measure (1832).

The Great Reform Bill expanded the size of the English electorate, but it did not create a democracy. It increased the number of voters by about 50 percent, but it maintained the property qualification for the franchise. It ignored women, and some members of the working class actually lost the right to vote. What the bill achieved was representation in the House of a wider variety of propertied people. This reconciled previously unrepresented economic interests to the political institutions of the country. By admitting people who wanted change to the legislative process, it made revolution in Britain unnecessary.

In the fifteen years that separated the Congress of Vienna from the Revolution of 1830, the Congress system restrained revolutionary and nationalistic activity in Europe. Nonetheless, during the 1820s, political liberalism made inroads into the dominant conservative order, and in 1830, revolutionary and reform movements reappeared. The French replaced the Bourbon monarchy with a more liberal government. Belgium achieved independence under a liberal government. And Great Britain moved slowly toward a more liberal position. The pace of change in Europe was slow, but new political ideas and forces were coming to the fore.

∿ Review Questions

1. What is nationalism? What were the goals of the nineteenth-century nationalists? What were the difficulties they confronted in realizing their goals? Why was nationalism a special threat to the Austrian Empire? What parts of Europe saw significant nationalist movements between 1815 and 1830? Which of these movements were successful? Which failed?

2. What were the tenets of liberalism? What effects did liberalism have on political developements during the early nineteenth century? What relationship does liberalism have to nationalism?

3. What difficulties did the conservatives in Austria, Prussia, and Russia face in the years after the Napoleonic wars? How did they respond on both national and international levels? What were the aims of the Concert of Europe? What did it accomplish and why did Britain withdraw?

4. What political changes took place in Latin America between 1804 and 1824? What were the main reasons for Creole discontent with Spanish rule? To what extent were Creole leaders influenced by Enlightenment political philosophy? Who were the major leaders in the fight for Latin American independence? Why did they succeed?

5. What kind of constitution was decreed for the restored monarchy in France? Was the new government truly constitutional? What did Charles X hope to accomplish? How much support did he have? What were the causes of the Revolution of 1830? What did this revolution achieve? What was its cost?

6. How do you explain the fact that although prior to 1820 Britain was moving down the same reactionary road as the other major European powers, events arrived at a different outcome in Britain? What was the purpose of the Great Reform Bill? What did it achieve? Is it correct to call it a "revolutionary" document?

∿ Suggested Readings

M. BERDAHL, *The Politics of the Prussian Nobility: The Development of a Conservative Ideology, 1770–1848* (1988). A major examination of German conservative outlooks.

R. J. BEZUCHA, *The Lyon Uprising of 1834: Social and Political Conflict in the Early July Monarchy* (1974). An excellent discussion of the tensions in France after the Revolution of 1830.

A. BRIGGS, *The Making of Modern England* (1959). Remains the best survey of English history during the first half of the nineteenth century.

M. BROCK, *The Great Reform Act* (1974). The standard work.

G. A. CRAIG, *The Politics of the Prussian Army, 1640–1945* (1955). A splendid study of the conservative political influence of the army on Prussian development.

J. Droz, *Europe Between Revolutions, 1815–1848* (1967). An examination of Europe as created by the Vienna settlement.

E. Halévy, *England in 1815* (1913). One of the most important and influential books written on nineteenth-century Britain.

E. J. Hobsbawm, *The Age of Revolution, 1789–1848* (1962). A comprehensive survey emphasizing the social ramifications of the liberal democratic and industrial revolutions.

E. J. Hobsbawm, *Nations and Nationalism since 1780: Programme, Myth, Reality*, rev. ed. (1992). The best recent introduction to the subject.

S. Holmes, *Benjamin Constant and the Making of Modern Liberalism* (1984). An outstanding study of a major liberal theorist.

C. and B. Jelavich, *The Establishment of the Balkan National States, 1804–1920* (1977). A standard, clear introduction.

J. Lynch, *The Spanish American Revolutions, 1808–1826* (1973). An excellent one-volume treatment.

C. A. Macartney, *The Habsburg Empire, 1790–1918* (1971). An outstanding survey.

A. Palmer, *Alexander I: Tsar of War and Peace* (1974). An interesting biography that captures much of the mysterious personality of this ruler.

P. Pilbeam, *The 1830 Revolution in France* (1991). An account that emphasizes the restoration accommodation to various interest groups.

N. V. Riasanovsky, *Nicholas I and Official Nationality in Russia, 1825–1855* (1959). A lucid discussion of the conservative idealology that made Russia the major opponent of liberalism.

22

Economic Advance and Social Unrest (1830–1850)

KEY TOPICS IN THIS CHAPTER

~ The development of industrialism and its effects on the organization of labor and the family

~ The changing role of women in industrial society

~ The establishment of police forces and reform of prisons

~ Early developments in European socialism

~ The revolutions of 1848

By 1830, Great Britain had become an industrialized nation, and the rest of Europe was soon to resound with the pounding of machinery and the grinding of railway engines. Between 1825 and 1850, the groups that opposed industrialism made their final protests, and intellectuals articulated major creeds that both supported and criticized the emerging society. These were years of uncertainty, a

∾ Toward an Industrial Society

Industrialism and the urban growth that accompanied it, no less than the political revolutions that derived from the French Revolution, overturned the
Old Regime. The slow but steady conversion of Europe's economy to industrial manufacturing during the first half of the nineteenth century reorganized
society. In unprecedented numbers, people migrated to cities to find work in
the new factories. There they faced radically different conditions of life, and
many found that their skills were of little value in an age of machines.

Britain's Industrial Leadership

The Industrial Revolution, led by textile manufacturing, began in Great Britain
in the eighteenth century. Britain had advantages (natural resources, capital,
technology, food supply, relative social mobility, and strong foreign and domestic markets) that gave it an edge in developing its productive capacities.
It also profited from the fact that for two decades the French Revolution and
the Napoleonic wars disrupted economic activity on the continent and weakened France as a competitor for Atlantic trade. Both the United States and
Canada were rich markets for British goods, and the Latin American Wars of
Independence opened South America to British merchants. From bases in India, Britain dominated the trade of south Asia.

The wealth that Britain acquired through textile production and other
industries (ironmaking, shipbuilding, china production, etc.) was invested in
the development of global networks that enabled Britain to dominate the world
scene in the nineteenth century. British textile mills relied on raw cotton produced by slaves on the plantations of the southern United States. The finished
cloth was shipped to India and elsewhere along sea lanes protected by the
British navy.

By the 1830s, Belgium, France, and Germany were headed down the same
path as Britain. They had a growing number of steam engines in use. Coke
was replacing charcoal in iron and steel production, stimulating exploitation
of the coal fields of the Ruhr and the Saar basins. Large districts of concentrated manufacturing, comparable to the British Midlands, did not yet exist.
There were some pockets of production in cities like Lyons, Rouen, Liège, and
Lille, but most manufacturing took place in the countryside. New machines
were integrated into the existing domestic system; at mid-century, peasants
and urban artisans remained more important politically than industrial factory workers.

The Revolutionary Crisis of 1848–1851

1848

February 22–24	*Abdication of Louis Philippe*
March 3	*Kossuth demands freedom for Hungary*
March 13	*Revolution in Vienna*
March 15	*Habsburg emperor accepts the March Laws*
March 18	*Frederick William IV promises a constitution*
	Revolution in Milan
March 22	*Piedmont declares war on Austria*
April 23	*Election of the French National Assembly*
May 17	*Emperor Ferdinand flees Vienna*
May 18	*The Frankfurt Assembly gathers*
June 2	*Pan-Slavic Congress convenes in Prague*
July 24	*Austria defeats Piedmont*
September 17	*General Jellachich invades Hungary*
October 31	*General Windischgraetz pacifies Vienna*
November 16	*Revolution in Rome*
November 25	*Pope Pius IX flees Rome*
December 2	*Francis Joseph becomes Habsburg emperor*
December 10	*Louis Napoleon and the Second French Republic*

1849

January 5	*General Windischgraetz occupies Budapest*
February 2	*The Roman Republic proclaimed*
March 12	*War resumes between Piedmont and Austria*
March 23	*Piedmont is defeated, Victor Emmanuel II crowned*
March 28	*German crown offered to Frederick William IV*
June 18	*Frankfurt Parliament dispersed*
July 3	*Collapse of the Roman Republic*
August 9–13	*Austria defeats Hungarian forces*

1851

December 2	*Coup d'état of Louis Napoleon*

Population and Migration

As industrialization spread, the population explosion that had begun in the eighteenth century continued. Between 1831 and 1851, France grew from 32 million to 35 million; Germany, from 26 million to 33 million; and Britain, from 16 million to 20 million. Increasingly, these Europeans lived in cities. By mid-century, half the population of England and Wales was urban—as were a quarter of the residents of France and Germany. Eastern Europe, however, remained overwhelmingly rural and little industrialized.

The sheer numbers of human beings exhausted the physical resources of cities. Housing, water, sewers, food supplies, and lighting could not be improved quickly enough to deal with migration from the countryside. Indescribably filthy slums appeared where disease, especially cholera, ravaged the population. Crime became a way of life for those who could make no other living, and human misery and degradation seemed to many contemporary observers to have no bounds.

The situation in the countryside was scarcely better. Liberal reformers had hoped that the changes in land ownership that followed the French Revolution and the emancipation of serfs in Prussia, Austria (1848), and Russia (1861) would transform peasants into progressive, industrious farmers. Instead, most became conservative landholders without enough property to make improvements or, in many cases, to support themselves in an agrarian economy that was becoming increasingly commercialized. By mid-century, the revolution in landholding had improved agricultural production, but at the cost of driving people from the countryside into cities and from Europe into the outside world.

If emancipation movements did little for agrarian economies, they did assist industrialization. In England, France, and the Low Countries, they freed a labor force to move between country and town as needed. In Germany, eastern Europe, and Russia—even after emancipation—such migration was difficult. Consequently, from Germany eastward, the pace of industrialization was much slower.

Europe continued to be haunted by the specter of poor harvests. The century's worst agricultural disaster was the famine Ireland endured from 1845 to 1847. A disease that blighted the nation's potato crop caused about 500,000 Irish peasants to starve to death and hundreds of thousands to emigrate.

Railways

Industrial development in the 1830s and 1840s was driven by the construction of Europe's railway system. The Stockton and Darlington Line opened in England in 1825. The first French company began to operate in 1832, although serious expansion of France's rail system waited until the 1840s. Belgium had begun to run trains by 1835—as had Germany. By mid-century, Britain had 9,797 kilometers of track; France, 2,915; and Germany, 5,856.

Railways epitomized the character of the industrial economy of the second quarter of the nineteenth century: investment in capital goods rather than consumer goods. The construction of railways speeded industrialization in several ways. Trains were the most dramatic application of the steam engine. Railroads sharply increased demand for iron and steel and, therefore, for skilled laborers. Increased manufacturing capacity at forges meant that iron and steel were available to construct ships and machines. And the vast fortunes created by the capital industries were invested to inaugurate other enterprises. Industrialism grew on itself.

∾ The Labor Force

Concentration on capital over consumer production meant that the working class often found little to purchase for the wages earned in the new industries. The early nineteenth-century labor force was extremely diverse: factory workers, urban artisans, domestic system craftsmen, household servants, miners, rural peddlers, farm workers, and railroad navvies. Some workers were reasonably well off, enjoying steady employment and decent wages. Others constituted a "laboring poor" who had jobs, but who earned little more than subsistence wages. Some, such as the women and children who worked naked in the mines of Wales, endured conditions that shocked Europe when they were described by a parliamentary report in the early 1840s.

Only the textile-manufacturing industry became thoroughly mechanized and concentrated in a factory setting during the first half of the century. Industrial factory workers were vastly outnumbered by the skilled artisans who lived in cities or small towns. Industrialization threatened to make the skills of artisans useless and to deprive them of control over their trades. All workers faced possible unemployment with little or no provision for their security. All were aware of the dissolution of traditional social ties maintained by custom and community.

Proletarianization of Factory Workers and Urban Artisans

During the century, both artisans and factory workers underwent a process of *proletarianization.* That means that they lost ownership of the means of production (tools and equipment) and lost control of their trades. They became wage earners. This occurred whenever people with capital constructed factories and purchased what was needed to run them: machinery and raw materials—and labor. The process spread beyond the factory system when inventions, such as mechanical printing presses, took over the work of artisans.

Factory workers, unlike self-employed artisans, had to submit to a kind of discipline that was unpopular and difficult to maintain. The needs of machines—their smooth and profitable operation—determined what was expected of their human operators. Threats and punishments were used to create laborers who could match the regularity of the cables, wheels, and pistons of the machines at which they stood.

Factory conditions were difficult, but workers in textile factories were better off than competitors who resisted the factory mode of production. English handloom weavers, who continued to work in their homes, slipped into ever-deepening poverty as they struggled to match the output of power looms.

Urban artisans were proletarianized more slowly than factory workers, and machinery was only one contributor to the process. Factories did not necessarily harm urban artisans, some of whom prospered from their presence. The construction and maintenance of machines increased demand for metalworkers, and the erection of factories and subsequent expansion of cities benefited the building trades. Lower prices for machine-made textiles reduced the cost of raw materials for tailors and hatters. It was changes in the organization of production inspired by the factory model that threatened the skills and livelihood of urban artisans.

In the eighteenth century and earlier, a guild system had organized production in Europe's urban workplaces. A master (guild member) owned a workshop and the larger equipment. He trained apprentices, who became journeymen owning their own tools. Ultimately, they expected to be admitted to the guild as masters who could set up shops of their own. The guild system gave workers control over labor recruitment, training, pace of production, quality of product, and price.

In the nineteenth century, it became increasingly difficult for guilds to control trades. France had outlawed guilds during the French Revolution; elsewhere in Europe, liberals attempted to ban labor and guild organizations on the theory that they limited economic freedom.

Guild masters also faced increasing competition as machine production invaded craft-dominated industries. In response, many workshops tried to increase efficiency by what was known in France as *confection*, production of standard sizes and styles rather than special orders for individual customers. This practice increased the division of labor, for each of a shop's artisans produced only a part of a more-or-less uniform final product. Consequently, less skill was required and the value of the skill diminished.

Masters also tried to increase production and reduce costs by lowering the wages paid for piecework. This often led to work stoppages or strikes. But immigration from the countryside guaranteed a surplus of relatively unskilled workers who were willing to work for lower wages or under less protected conditions than traditional artisans. This made it difficult for urban journeymen to ascend the ladder and become masters with their own workshops. Increasingly they became lifetime wage laborers whose skills were simply bought and sold according to their fluctuating value in the marketplace.

Working-Class Political Action: The Example of British Chartism

In the 1830s, artisans—proud of their skills and frustrated by their diminishing opportunities for advancement—began to organize movements to protect their social and economic interests. By the middle of the century, they had become the most radical element in the European working class.

In 1836, William Lovett (1800–1877) joined with other London radical artisans to form the London Working Men's Association. In 1838, the group issued the Charter to call for six specific reforms. The Six Points of the Charter were universal male suffrage, annual election of the House of Commons, the secret ballot, equal electoral districts, abolition of property qualifications for members of Parliament, and payment of salaries to members of the House of Commons. The Chartists agitated for their reforms for over a decade. On three occasions the Charter was presented to Parliament, which refused to pass it. Petitions with millions of signatures were sent to the House of Commons. Strikes were called. A newspaper, *The Northern Star*, was published. The Chartists had some success in local government. But Chartism failed to cohere as a national movement, because it split between members who favored violence and those who wanted to use peaceful tactics. The return of prosperity following a depression in the late 1830s and early 1840s also caused

A parliamentary report in the early 1840s revealed the deplorable conditions of women and children working underground in Welsh mines, shocking British public opinion and inspiring labor reforms. [Bildarchiv Preussischer Kulturbesitz]

many working people to lose interest in the movement. Nevertheless, as the first large-scale political movement organized by the working class, chartism provided a model and inspiration for workers throughout Europe who sought some way to improve their situation.

Family Structures and the Industrial Revolution

The European working-class family of the early industrial age is difficult to describe in general terms, for industrialism developed at different rates across the continent. More is known about the family in Great Britain in this period than elsewhere, and many British developments foreshadowed those in other countries.

The Family in the Early Factory System

Before England's revolution in textile production in the late eighteenth century, the individual family was the chief unit of textile manufacture. In the domestic system of family economy, father and mother worked with children as a family unit. They trained and disciplined their children at home, and their home life and their economic livelihoods were much the same. Early textile inventions, such as the spinning jenny, did not change that situation, for the machines could be used at home.

It was the mechanization of weaving that led to major changes. A father who became a machine weaver was employed in a factory, and his work was separated from his home. Still, the adoption of machinery and factory pro-

As textile production became increasingly automated in the nineteenth century, textile factories required fewer skilled workers and more unskilled attendants. To fill these unskilled positions, factory owners turned increasingly to unmarried women and widows, who worked for lower wages than men and were less likely to form labor organizations. [Bildarchiv Preussischer Kulturbesitz]

duction did not destroy the working-class family, for the organization of early English factories allowed the father to preserve certain of his traditional family roles. Early factory owners allowed men to employ their wives and children as their assistants and to transfer parental training and discipline from the home to the factory. This accommodation did not, however, prevent changes in family life caused by the disciplines required for factory work.

A major shift in Britain's family and factory structures took place between the mid-1820s and mid-1830s. Spinning and weaving came under one roof, and factories and machinery grew larger. New machines required fewer skilled operators, but many relatively unskilled attendants. Machine tending became the work of unmarried women and children, for they accepted lower wages and were less likely than adult men to form labor organizations.

The children who stayed in factories were often the children of economically depressed handloom weavers. Wages for skilled adult male factory workers were high enough to allow them to support their families. They kept their wives at home and sent their children to school. The familial links that had organized the work force in the British textile factory for over a quarter-century faded, and men began to supervise women and children who were not their relatives.

Once parents ceased to be present to watch over their children in factories, public concern developed for the child laborer. In 1833, the English Factory Act forbade the employment of children under age nine, limited to nine hours the workday of children below the age of thirteen, and required that these children be given two hours of education a day at company expense.

The effect was to further divide work and home life. Adult males and older teenagers worked twelve-hour days, and younger children worked in relays of four or six hours. This diminished parent-child contact, and the education requirement turned over to schools some of the nurturing and training that traditionally had been done in the home. After this act was passed, many of the British working class demanded shorter workdays for adults. Since they no longer had a relationship with their children at work, they wanted more time to spend with them at home. In 1847, Parliament mandated a ten-hour day.

In the British textile industry by the middle of the 1840s, men of the working class had evolved distinct roles as breadwinners, fathers, and husbands. What occurred in Britain happened elsewhere as industrial capitalism and public education spread. The European family ceased to be an important unit of both production and consumption and became only a consumer. The family did not stop performing as an economic unit, but its members now lived by sharing wages derived from different sources rather than by sharing work in a home or factory. Families linked only by wages might be less closely bound than those that worked together. Wages could be sent over long distances, so children could live and work away from home. But it was also true that some children might stay home longer to accumulate the savings needed to marry and begin their own households.

∽ Women in the Early Industrial Revolution

The industrial economy had an immense impact on the lives of women. By taking virtually all productive work out of the home and allowing many families to live on the wages of the male spouse, it created a new understanding of gender-determined roles. Women were associated with domestic duties: housekeeping, food preparation, child rearing and nurturing, and household management. Men were linked, almost exclusively, with breadwinning. The domestic division of labor into separate spheres that had existed only for the small middle class and the gentry came, during the nineteenth century, to characterize the working class as well.

Changing Expectations in Working-Class Marriage

Many traditional practices associated with the family economy survived into the industrial era. Most women expected to marry as soon as possible, and they sought employment so that they could earn dowries. A girl born in the country often migrated to a nearby town or city for a job as a domestic, sometimes with a relative. If a girl became a factory worker, she might live in a supervised dormitory. Factory owners established these to recruit young workers from families that feared for their safety.

Female workers in nineteenth-century cities faced challenges known to few women of earlier generations. Movement to cities and entrance into the wage economy increased their freedom in the choice of marriage partners.

Women Industrial Workers Explain Their Economic Situation

In 1832 there was much discussion in the British press about factory legislation. Most of that discussion was concerned with the employment of children, but The Examiner *newspaper made the suggestion that any factory laws should not only address the problem of child labor but also, in time, eliminate women from employment in factories. That article provoked the following remarkable letter to the editor, composed by or on behalf of women factory workers, which eloquently stated the real necessity of such employment for women and the unattractive alternatives.*

∽ What are the reasons these women give to explain why they must have manufacturing jobs? What changes in production methods have led women from the home to the factory? Does employment affect whether or not these women will be able to marry?

Sir,

Living as we do, in the densely populated manufacturing districts of Lancashire, and most of us belonging to that class of females who earn their bread either directly or indirectly by manufactories, we have looked with no little anxiety for your opinion on the Factory Bill. . . . You are for doing away with our services in manufactories altogether. So much the better, if you had pointed out any other more eligible and practical employment for the surplus female labour, that will want other channels for a subsistence. If our competition were withdrawn, and short hours substituted, we have no doubt but the effects would be as you have stated, "not to lower wages,

Since there were fewer family and community ties, parents made fewer arranged marriages. There were also more available young men in cities than in rural villages. But since these men had greater mobility in terms of employment, their relationships with women may have been more fleeting. Cohabitation during courtship seems to have been common, and the number of illegitimate births increased. Since marriage usually meant that a woman left the work force to live on her husband's earnings, it might improve her situation. But if her husband became ill or died or deserted her, she returned to the labor market to compete with younger women.

Reliance on the industrial wage diminished marriage's function as an economic partnership and created a new set of gender relationships. By separating the workplace from the home, industrialization made it difficult for women to combine domestic duties with wage employment. When married women worked, it was usually because of dire family necessity. Children were sent out to work more often than wives. This made children an economic asset and encouraged higher birthrates.

The domestic duties of working-class women were unpaid, but essential to their family's wage-based economy. While members of a family worked abroad, someone had to maintain the home front. The separation of home life

as the male branch of the family would be enabled to earn as much as the whole had done," but for the thousands of females who are employed in manufactories, who have no legitimate claim on any male relative for employment or support, and who have, through a variety of circumstance, been early thrown on their own resources for a livelihood, what is to become of them?

In this neighbourhood, hand-loom has been almost totally superseded by power-loom weaving, and no inconsiderable number of females, who must depend on their own exertions, or their parishes for support, have been forced, of necessity into the manufactories, from their total inability to earn a livelihood at home.

It is a lamentable fact, that, in these parts of the country, there is scarcely any other mode of employment for female industry, if we except servitude and dress-making. Of the former of these, there is no chance of employment for one-twentieth of the candidates that would rush into the field, to say nothing of lowering the wages of our sisters of the same craft; and of the latter, galling as some of the hardships of manufactories are (of which the indelicacy of mixing with the men is not the least), yet there are few women who have been so employed, that would change conditions with the ill-used genteel little slaves, who have to lose sleep and health, in catering to the whims and frivolities of the butter-flies of fashion.

We see no way of escape from starvation, but to accept the very tempting offers of the newspapers, held out as baits to us, fairly to ship ourselves off to Van Dieman's Land [Tasmania] on the very delicate errand of husband hunting, and having safely arrived at the "Land of Goshen," jump ashore, with a "Who wants me?" . . .

The Female Operatives of Todmorden

The Examiner, *February 26, 1832, as quoted in Ivy Pinchbeck*, Women Workers and the Industrial Revolution, 1750–1850 *(New York: Augustus M. Kelley, 1969), pp. 199–200.

---

from the workplace made homemaking a distinct occupation with great economic significance. Since a female homemaker was primarily responsible for the purchases that provided her family's food and maintained its shelter, she often took charge of its finances.

⌒ Problems of Crime and Order

The revolutions Europe had experienced at the turn of the century made its propertied classes anxious about social upheaval at a time when the processes of industrialization and urbanization were dislocating many communities. Thousands of people migrated from the countryside to the towns and cities, where they often encountered poverty, disappointment, and frustration. For the first sixty years of the nineteenth century, crime increased slowly but steadily until it reached a plateau.

New Police Forces

The ruling classes developed two strategies for containing crime: improved policing and prison reform. Police forces did not exist until the early nineteenth century, when Europe invented the concept of a permanent police force distinct from an army. Police are a paid, trained group of civilian professionals charged with enforcing law, keeping order, protecting property and lives, investigating crime, and apprehending offenders. Their function is partly preemptive—preventing crime by their visible presence. Theoretically, at least, they have no involvement with politics. The powers and organization of police forces differed from one country to another, but their creation was fundamental to the establishment of an orderly society in Europe.

Professional police forces appeared in Paris in 1828. The same year, the British Parliament authorized police for London's streets. The Londoners came to be called "bobbies" after Sir Robert Peel (1788–1850), sponsor of the bill that established them. Police on the continent were armed; those in Britain were not. All were distinguished by an easily recognizable uniform.

Prison Reform

Before the nineteenth century, Europe had several kinds of prisons: local jails, state prisons (such as the Bastille), and prison ships (hulks). Some Mediterranean nations forced prisoners to work out their terms of incarceration as rowers on galleys. All prisoners lived under wretched conditions. Men, women, and children were housed together. Those who had committed minor offenses were mixed with those guilty of the most serious crimes.

Late in the eighteenth century, the British government began to transport serious offenders to foreign colonies (notably, New South Wales, Australia). The practice continued until the colonies began to object in the middle of the nineteenth century. Britain then established public works prisons to house long-term prisoners.

Reformers, such as John Howard (1726–1790) and Elizabeth Fry (1780–1845) in England and Charles Lucas (1803–1889) in France, exposed the horrendous conditions in prisons and demanded change. But since there was little sympathy for criminals and less popular support for taxes to construct new prisons, governments were slow to respond. In the 1840s, however, both the French and the English launched some bold initiatives based on the idea that crime was the result of character flaws in criminals. They set about designing an imprisonment that would rehabilitate the prisoner. The result was an exceedingly repressive system.

Europeans relied on prison models developed in the United States. All the popular experiments involved separating prisoners from each other in individual cells. In the Auburn system (named for a prison in New York State), prisoners were separated during the night, but worked together during the day. The Philadelphia system kept prisoners rigorously separated at all times. In the Pentonville Prison near London, no prisoner was ever allowed to speak to or see another prisoner. Each wore a mask when in the prison yard, and each had a separate stall in the chapel. The point of the system was to turn the prisoner's mind in on itself—to force it to confront its criminal tendencies. The intense isolation often led instead to mental collapse.

Prisoners were supposed to be trained in some kind of trade or skill while in prison so that they could reemerge as reformed citizens. Those who failed rehabilitation were dealt with very harshly. In 1885, the French government began to send repeat serious offenders to places like the infamous Devil's Island off the coast of South America. The idea was to excise from society the criminal elements that could not be saved.

⌒ Classical Economics

The *classical economists* shaped nineteenth-century attitudes toward commerce. They advocated economic growth through competitive free enterprise and their ideal society consisted of atomistic individuals competing to meet the demands of consumers in the marketplace. They distrusted government action, believing that government's functions were limited to maintaining a sound currency, enforcing contracts, protecting property, and keeping tariffs and taxes low.

Malthus and Ricardo

Classical economic theory, as developed by Thomas Malthus (1766–1834) and David Ricardo (1772–1823), maintained that the condition of the working class could not be improved. It, therefore, confirmed employers' natural reluctance to raise wages and provided arguments justifying opposition to labor unions. Malthus's *Essay on the Principle of Population* (1798) claimed that population must eventually outstrip the supply of food, for population grows geometrically and food production arithmetically. If wages were raised, workers would simply have more children, who would consume the increase. Malthus held out hope that if the working class could be persuaded to aspire to a higher standard of living, increased wages might be spent on consumer goods rather than on children.

David Ricardo's *Principles of Political Economy* (1817) based an "Iron Law of Wages" on Malthus's theories. If wages were raised, more children would be produced. When they entered the labor market, the increased number of workers would lower wages. As wages fell, working people would have fewer children. When a labor shortage developed, wages would rise—and the process would start all over again. The effect, in the long run, was to keep wages at a minimum level.

Government Policies Based on Classical Economics

The major classical economists were British, as was the utilitarian philosopher Jeremy Bentham (1748–1832). Bentham suggested a "principle of utility"—the greatest happiness for the greatest number—as a scientific basis for governing society. In his *Fragment on Government* (1776) and *The Principles* of *Morals and Legislation* (1789), he argued that the application of the principle of utility would end the special interests of privileged groups and remove the legal clutter that prevented justice from being done. Bentham's disciples combined his ideas with those of classical economics and persuaded the House of Commons to pass a new Poor Law (1834). It was premised on the idea that people did not work because they were lazy, and it set up a Poor Law Commission to make sure that the poor were motivated to embrace self-discipline and hard work. Government poor relief was disbursed only in workhouses, where life was designed to be more unpleasant than life outside.

The second British monument to applied classical economics was the repeal of the Corn Laws in 1846. For years, an Anti–Corn Law League, organized by manufacturers, had tried to persuade the government to abolish tariffs protecting the domestic price of grain. That change, they argued, would lead to lower food prices, which would allow them to cut workers' wages. Costs for British manufactured goods would thus go down and their competitive position in the world market would improve. The need to open Britain's ports to foreign grain to counteract the effects of the Irish potato famine also encouraged Parliament to act, and its repeal of the Corn Laws began an era of free trade that lasted until late in the century.

∿ Early Socialism

The socialist movement (either in the form of communism or social democracy) has been one of the major political forces in twentieth-century Europe, but 150 years ago it had no significant following. Early socialists often applauded the productive capacity of industrialism while denying that the free market could adequately produce and distribute goods. An unregulated industrial system, they believed, resulted in mismanagement, low wages, poor distribution, and widespread suffering. Socialists proposed that human society be organized as a community, not an aggregate of atomistic, selfish individuals.

Utopian Socialism

Early critics of industrialism were dubbed *utopian socialists* by their opponents, for their visionary programs often involved the creation of ideal communities with noncapitalistic values. Almost all such proposals involved radical changes in society's attitudes toward sexuality and the family. People who were sympathetic to their economic goals were often alienated by their advocacy of free love and open family relationships.

Saint-Simonianism. Count Claude Henri de Saint-Simon (1760–1825) was the earliest of the socialist pioneers. A liberal French aristocrat, he fought in the American Revolution and welcomed the French Revolution. By Napoleon's day, he had become a writer and social critic. Saint-Simon was convinced that modern society required thoroughly rational management. His ideal government was a board of directors that achieved harmony by coordinating the activity of individuals and groups. In a sense, he was the ideological father of technocracy. He believed that expert management of wealth, not its redistribution, would alleviate poverty and suffering.

Owenism. The first major British advocate of socialism was Robert Owen (1771–1858), a self-made industrialist. In his early twenties, Owen became a partner in a cotton factory at New Lanark, Scotland, one of Britain's largest mills. Owen believed in the environmentalist principles of Enlightenment psychology: human characters could be improved by improving their surroundings. Owen also believed that a company could create a humane industrial environment and make a profit.

He tested his theories at New Lanark. Workers were provided with good quarters. They had abundant opportunities for recreation, and schools were set up for their children. Although Owen himself was a notorious freethinker on matters of religion and sex, he tolerated churches. Incentives were offered to encourage good work, and the factory made a fine profit.

Visitors flocked from all over Europe to see what Owen had accomplished through enlightened management. In numerous articles and pamphlets, and in letters to influential people, he pleaded for a general organizational reform of industry. Finally, he sold his New Lanark factory and, during the 1820s, toured the United States. At New Harmony, Indiana, he founded another model community. It failed, but he was not discouraged. He returned to Britain to promote the Grand National Union, a unification of all the British trade unions. It collapsed in the early 1830s.

Fourierism. In France, Charles Fourier (1772–1837) developed ideas similar to Owen's, but was less successful financially and in attracting public attention. Fourier believed that the industrial order erred in ignoring the passionate side of human nature, the pleasures that people naturally seek. He advocated the construction of communities called phalanxes, where liberated customs would dispel the dullness of factory life.

Agrarian rather than industrial production was to predominate in phalanxes. Sexual activity was to be relatively free, and marriage was to be reserved for later life. Fourier urged that no person be required to perform the same job for an entire day. He argued that people would be happier and more productive if they moved from one task to another. Fourier's discussion of the problem of boredom highlighted one of the key difficulties of modern economic life.

Saint-Simon, Owen, and Fourier expected governments to implement their ideas, but they failed to confront the political difficulties of radical social transformation. Others paid more attention to practical politics. In *The Organization of Labor* (1839), Louis Blanc (1811–1882) called for an end to competition, but not a wholly new society. He believed that giving the vote to workers would empower them to use the political process to reform the system. A state controlled by its working class would finance workshops to employ the poor. In time, such shops might replace private enterprise and re-organize industry to ensure jobs. The state could become the great employer whose employees kept it true to the mission of improving the conditions of labor.

Anarchism

Some social critics of the 1840s opposed any cooperation with industry or government. Some of these *anarchists* recommended violence and terrorism to force change; others trusted to peaceful means.

Auguste Blanqui (1805–1881), a major advocate for terror, sought the abolition of both capitalism and the state. His ideas for a new society were vague, but his strategy for achieving it—the development of a revolutionary vanguard professionally equipped to attack capitalism—foreshadowed Lenin's Russian Revolution. Pierre Joseph Proudhon (1809–1865), author of *What Is Property?* (1840), was a peaceful anarchist who wanted society to be organized on the basis of *mutualism.* He believed that a system of small businesses peacefully cooperating and exchanging goods would make the state redundant. Proudhon influenced the French labor movement, which was less political than comparable movements in Britain and Germany.

Marxism

Too often European socialism is seen as developing naturally or necessarily into Marxism. Nothing could be further from the truth. At mid-century, the opinions of Karl Marx were simply one ingredient among many in the heady mixture of ideas discussed by critics of emerging industrial capitalist society. Marxism differed from its competitors in its claim to a scientific foundation and its insistence on reform through revolution.

Karl Marx (1818–1883) was the son of a German-Jewish family that converted to Lutheranism. He was trained at the University of Berlin, where Hegelian philosophy and radical politics, not Judaism, shaped his education. When editorship (1842–1843) of a radical newspaper (the *Rheinische Zeitung*) caused him to be exiled from his native land, he moved to Paris, then to Brussels, and finally, after 1849, to London. In 1844, he met Friedrich Engels (1820–1895), another young middle-class German. Engels's father owned a textile factory in Manchester, England. The next year, Engels published *The Conditions of the Working Class in England,* a devastating picture of industrial life. Late in 1847, Engels and Marx were asked to write a pamphlet explaining the philosophy of a newly organized (and short-lived) secret society, the Communist League. The league embraced the name *communist* because it was more radical than *socialist.* Communism implied the outright abolition of private property rather than socialism's less extensive rearrangement of society. The *Communist Manifesto,* though only about fifty pages long, was to become the most influential political document in modern European history.

Sources of Marx's Ideas. Marx drew his theories from German Hegelianism, French socialism, and British classical economics. Hegel had explained intellectual progress as a historical process by which a thesis and an antithesis clash until they form a synthesis. What Hegel saw in the history of thought, Marx saw in the history of societies: conflicts between dominant and subordinate social groups that led to the emergence of new dominant groups. The socialists highlighted the significance of property distribution in the formation of classes. And the classical economists produced the analytical tools that enabled Marx to conduct an empirical, scientific examination of industrial capitalist society.

Revolution Through Class Conflict. In *The Communist Manifesto,* Marx and Engels contended that reason provided a simple explanation for the whole of human history: History describes humankind's struggle with the physical world to obtain the goods needed for survival. The structures, values, and ideas of a society are a function of the economy that sustains it. History is driven, Marx claimed, by a conflict between the classes who own and control the means of production and the classes who work for them. Conflict between these groups is not an accidental by-product of mismanagement or bad intentions. It is inherent in the structures of production. Consequently, piecemeal reforms cannot eliminate social and economic evils. A radical social transformation is required, and Marx believed that the natural development of capitalism would inevitably bring about such a revolutionary event.

Marx and Engels believed that class conflict had, early in the nineteenth century, become a simplified struggle between the bourgeoisie and the proletariat—between the middle class and the workers. The nature of capitalism ensured that the struggle would intensify. Capitalist competition and large-scale industrial production would steadily increase the size of the unpropertied proletariat by crushing both traditional and smaller industrial producers into the ranks of the proletariat. As business structures grew ever larger, competitive pressures would squeeze out smaller middle-class units and produce a larger and more miserable proletariat.

Eventually workers, Marx contended, would foment revolution and overthrow the few remaining owners of the means of production. For a time, the workers would organize the means of production through a dictatorship of the proletariat, but this would eventually give way to a propertyless, classless communist society—the end-product of the historical process. Although the final class conflict resembled earlier ones, it differed in a significant respect. The victorious proletariat, by its very nature as a huge majority, could not become a new oppressor class. Having no significant group to oppress, it would function for the good of all.

Marx's prediction of the collapse of capitalism in the later part of the nineteenth century proved to be wrong. Nor did the middle class become proletarianized, as he had expected. Rather, more and more people benefited from the industrial system. Nonetheless, Marxist doctrines appeared to be based on the empirical evidence of hard economic fact. Their scientific aura enhanced their credibility, for during the second half of the century, Europeans were fascinated by all things scientific. Within a generation, Marxism had captured the imagination of many socialists, especially in Germany, and large segments of the working class.

～ 1848: Year of Revolutions

A series of revolutions erupted across the continent in 1848. They had no single cause, but similar conditions encouraged them in many places: severe food shortages, economic depression, widespread unemployment, overburdened poor relief systems, wretched living conditions in cities, and increasing frustration and discontent among the artisan and laboring classes.

The agents of change in 1848, however, were not workers but political liberals from the middle classes who were agitating for more civil liberties, better representative government, and an unregulated economy. Although they preferred to pursue their objectives by peaceful means, they put pressure on governments by appealing for support from the urban working classes. The workers had little interest in liberal political reform. They wanted improved working and economic conditions, and they were prepared to use violence to get them. Everywhere but in France, nationalism also played a part in the uprisings.

The 1848 revolutions were stunning, for never in a single year had Europe known so many major uprisings. Yet, without exception, the revolutions failed. Nationalistic groups turned against each other, and differences in goals soon drove a wedge between the revolutionaries of the middle and working classes.

France: The Second Republic and Louis Napoleon

Now as before, revolutionary tinder first blazed in Paris. During 1846 and 1847, France's economy went into decline, and the regime of Louis Philippe and his minister Guizot seemed adept only at corruption. Liberal opponents of the monarchy organized a series of banquets to rally support for increasing middle-class participation in politics, and angry workers were eager to back any critics of the government. When the king tried to silence his opponents by forbidding the political banquets (February 21, 1848), a crowd of disgruntled Parisian workers took to the streets. The government quickly lost control, and within a few days Louis Philippe had abdicated and fled to England (February 24, 1848).

The National Assembly and Paris Workers. Led by the poet Alphonse de Lamartine (1790–1869), the liberals set up a provisional government to organize an election for an assembly to write a new republican constitution. Various Parisian working-class groups wanted more—a social as well as a political revolution. They demanded posts in the cabinet for their leader, Louis Blanc, and two of his compatriots. These men forced the government to fund public works and relief programs.

On April 23, an election based on universal male suffrage chose a new National Assembly. Moderates and conservatives won most of the seats, for electors in the provinces were not as inclined to radical socialist reform as the workers of Paris. When the new government began to trim back public works projects and relief programs, crowds of unemployed Parisians rioted. Late in June, barricades reappeared on the streets, and the government ordered General Cavaignac (1802–1857) to bring in troops from the conservative countryside to restore order. Over 400 people were killed in two days of combat, and another 3,000 were subsequently hunted down.

Emergence of Louis Napoleon. The so-called June Days ended the drive for social revolution and confirmed dominance of French politics by men who wanted safety for small property. The conservatives were further strengthened when, late in 1848, Louis Napoleon Bonaparte (1808–1873), nephew of the former emperor, won election to the presidency. The voters associated the name of Bonaparte with stability and greatness.

The election of the "Little Napoleon" doomed the Second Republic, for Louis Napoleon was dedicated to his own fame, not to republican ideals. He was the first of the modern dictators, a man who ruled by manipulating unstable politics and exploiting the insecurity of the masses.

Louis Napoleon opposed the National Assembly, claiming that he, rather than it, represented the will of the nation. When the assembly refused to amend the constitution to allow him to run for reelection, he sent troops to disperse it—on December 2, 1851, the anniversary of his uncle's victory at Austerlitz. Over 200 people died resisting his coup, and more than 26,000 were arrested. About 10,000 were transported to Algeria.

In a plebiscite on December 21, 1851, only about 600,000 voters protested Louis Napoleon's actions. And a year later, another plebiscite approved his decision to proclaim himself Emperor Napoleon III. For the second time in just over fifty years, France had turned from republicanism to caesarism.

French Women in 1848. Following the collapse of the July Monarchy (Louis Philippe's abdication), numerous political clubs sprang up. Some, particularly in Paris, mobilized women who wanted to work for women's rights. A radical group—calling themselves *Vesuvians* after Italy's volcano—demanded full equality between men and women in the home, the right of women to serve in the military, and similarity in dress for both sexes. Feminism of this kind remained a politically naive fringe phenomenon, but a more conservative women's movement won some support in the National Assembly. By lauding the importance of the traditional family and motherhood, it defended itself against the charge that feminists wanted to destroy marriage and family life.

The liberal freedoms that suddenly became available in 1848 inspired some women to try, without success, to vote in various elections. Some

Parisian feminists founded a daily newspaper, the *Voix des femmes* (*The Women's Voice*), to demand that special attention be given to women's interests. It pointed out that improvements for men did not necessarily liberate women. A society with the same name as the newspaper was organized to work with male political groups. It cleverly used the conservatives' faith in the importance of the family to make a case for women's rights. Because motherhood and child rearing were so important to society, the *Voix des femmes* argued that women needed educations, employment, economic security, civil and property rights, and the vote.

Feminists met the same fate as the workers who helped launch the revolution of 1848—complete defeat. Women, as well as men, were hurt when the conservative National Assembly cut back relief and public works projects. A subsequent crackdown on political clubs destroyed the arena in which they worked for reform, and soon they were specifically forbidden to participate in any political clubs. The *Voix des femmes* tried to skirt this law by creating labor organizations dedicated to helping working-class women. But two leaders of this movement, Jeanne Deroin (d. 1894) and Pauline Roland (1805-1852), were arrested, tried, imprisoned, and exiled. By the time of Louis Napoleon's triumph in 1852, the feminist movement that had sprung up in 1848 had been eradicated.

The Habsburg Empire: Nationalism Resisted

France's revolution of 1848 shook the Habsburg domains, where the frustrations of liberals and nationalists were building to dangerous levels. The imperial regime was suddenly confronted by revolts in Vienna, Prague, Hungary, and Italy—and affected by disturbances breaking out in Germany.

The Vienna Uprising. The Habsburg troubles began on March 3, 1848, when Louis Kossuth (1802–1894), a Magyar nationalist and member of the Hungarian Diet, called for the independence of Hungary. His speeches inspired students to riot in Vienna. When the army failed to restore order, Metternich resigned and fled the country, and Emperor Ferdinand (r. 1835–1848), who was feeble-minded, promised a moderately liberal constitution. Radicals among the students were not satisfied with this and formed democratic clubs to press the revolution further. On May 17, the emperor and his court fled to Innsbruck and surrendered Vienna to a committee of about 200 people who were primarily concerned with the plight of Viennese workers.

What the Habsburg government feared most was not urban rebellion but an uprising of the serfs. There had already been isolated instances of serfs invading manor houses and burning records. Almost immediately after the Vienna revolt, the imperial government emancipated the serfs in much of Austria, and the Hungarian Diet abolished serfdom in March 1848. These actions headed off the most serious potential threat to order in the empire, and the end of serfdom was among the most important permanent achievements of the revolutions of 1848.

The Magyar Revolt. The Vienna revolt encouraged the Hungarians. The Magyar leaders were primarily liberals backed by nobles who wanted to guard their aristocratic privileges against incursions by the Habsburg government. The Hungarian Diet's reform program, the March Laws, demanded equality of religion, jury trials, the election of a lower chamber, a relatively free press, and payment of taxes by the nobility. Emperor Ferdinand, who had little choice, acquiesced.

The Magyars also wanted a nearly autonomous Hungarian state within the Habsburg domains. The partially independent nation they envisioned required them to annex Transylvania, Croatia, and neighboring parts of the Habsburg Empire. That brought Romanians, Croatians, and Serbs under their control, and these groups resisted Magyarization—particularly the imposition of the Hungarian language. They concluded that their chances for ethnic survival were better under the Habsburg government.

In late March, the Vienna government sent Count Joseph Jellachich (1801–1859) to assist the peoples who were rebelling against the rebellious Hungarians. By early September 1848, he was invading Hungary with the strong support of the opponents of Magyarization.

Czech Nationalism. In the middle of March 1848, with Vienna and Budapest in revolt, Czech nationalists demanded that Bohemia and Moravia be recognized as an autonomous Slavic state within the empire. Conflict immediately developed between the Czechs and the Germans who inhabited these regions.

The Czechs called for a meeting of Slavic peoples—the Poles, Ruthenians, Czechs, Slovaks, Croats, Slovenes, and Serbs—in Prague early in June. Francis Palacky (1798–1876), leader of this first Pan-Slavic Congress, issued a manifesto calling for the national equality of Slavs within the Habsburg Empire and protesting the repression of the Slavic peoples who were under Habsburg, Hungarian, German, and Ottoman domination. The document envisioned a vast Slavic nation or federation extending from Poland south and eastward through Ukraine. Such a state never came into being, but the dream of a unified, independent Slavic people was a useful political tool. Russia invoked Pan-Slavism to win the support of nationalist minorities in eastern Europe and the Balkans and to bring pressure against Austria and Germany.

On June 12, the day the Pan-Slavic Congress closed, an insurrection erupted in Prague. By June 17, General Prince Alfred Windischgraetz (1787–1862) had put it down. The middle class was happy to see the radicals suppressed, and resident Germans approved the smothering of Czech nationalism. A policy of "dividing and conquering" had worked.

Rebellion in Northern Italy. In addition to the Hungarian and Czech revolts, the Habsburg government faced war in northern Italy. On March 18, 1848, a revolution began in Milan, and five days later General Count Joseph Wenzel Radetzky (1766–1858), the Austrian commander, withdrew from the city. King Charles Albert of Piedmont (r. 1831–1849), whose kingdom was in Lombardy (the province of which Milan is the capital), aided the rebels. In July,

Radetzky, reinforced by new troops, defeated Piedmont and suppressed the revolution.

In midsummer the emperor returned to Vienna, where a newly elected assembly was struggling to write a constitution while dealing with radicals who pressed for ever more concessions. When a new insurrection occurred in October, the imperial government reasserted control. Its army bombarded Vienna and crushed the revolt. On December 2, Emperor Ferdinand, now clearly too feeble to govern, abdicated in favor of a young nephew, Francis Joseph (r. 1848–1916).

By January 5, 1849, Austrian troops had occupied Budapest, and by March they had imposed military rule over Hungary. The Magyar nobles attempted one last revolt. But in August, the Austrian army—reinforced by 200,000 soldiers happily furnished by Tsar Nicholas I of Russia (r. 1825–1855)—crushed the Hungarians. Divisions among its enemies and a determination to use military force had enabled the empire to survive the gravest internal challenges.

Italy: Republicanism Defeated

The brief Piedmont-Austrian war of 1848 was only the first stage in Italy's revolution. When King Charles Albert of Piedmont was defeated by the Austrians, Italy's nationalists began to pin their hopes for the unification of their country on their liberal pope, Pius IX (r. 1846–1878). In Rome, however, political radicalism got out of control. On November 15, 1848, a democratic extremist assassinated Count Pelligrino Rossi (1787–1848), the liberal minister of the Papal States. The next day, popular demonstrations forced the pope to appoint a radical ministry, and shortly thereafter he fled to Naples. In February 1849, the radicals proclaimed Rome a republic, and nationalists from all over Italy, most prominently Giuseppe Mazzini (1805–1872) and Giuseppe Garibaldi (1807–1882), flocked to the city. They hoped to use Rome as a base of operations to unite Italy under a republican government.

In March 1849, radicals in Piedmont forced Charles Albert to renew the war against Austria. Prompt defeat led to his abdication in favor of his son, Victor Emmanuel II (r. 1849–1878). Piedmont's surrender meant that the Roman Republic was left to defend itself alone. Since France wanted to prevent the rise of a strong nation on its southern border, it decided to enter the fray. In early June 1849, 10,000 French soldiers laid siege to Rome. The Roman Republic dissolved, and on July 3, Rome fell to the French. (They stayed in Italy to protect the pope until 1870.) Disillusioned by liberalism, Pius IX became an archconservative, and Italy's nationalists were forced to look elsewhere for a leader to unify their homeland.

Germany: Liberalism Frustrated

Revolutionary contagion spread rapidly through the German states of Württemberg, Saxony, Hanover, and Bavaria, where rebels demanded liberal governments and greater national unity. But the most serious disturbances took place in Prussia.

Revolution in Prussia. Since Frederick William IV (r. 1840–1861) preferred to believe that foreign agitators were to blame, he refused to turn his troops on the Berliners who rioted on March 15, 1848. When the royal government failed to overcome its own internal confusion and restore order, the king agreed to convene a constituent assembly to write a Prussian constitution. He also implied that he would work for German unification. For all practical purposes, the Prussian monarchy capitulated.

Frederick William IV appointed a cabinet headed by David Hansemann (1790–1864), a respected moderate liberal. It, however, could not work with the radical democrats seated in the constituent assembly. The king, in frustration, replaced his liberal ministry with a conservative one and, in April 1849, dissolved the assembly and proclaimed a constitution of his own. All adult males were given the vote, but they were divided into three classes, according to the taxes they paid, and limited to voting for representatives from their class. This meant that the major taxpayers—about 5 percent of the population—elected one-third of the Parliament. The ministry reported to the king alone, and the Prussian army swore direct loyalty to him.

The Frankfurt Parliament. On May 18, 1848, representatives from all the German states gathered in Saint Paul's Church in Frankfurt to reorganize the German Confederation. The Frankfurt Parliament intended to write a moderately liberal constitution for a united Germany, but the assembly's liberalism alienated conservatives and members of the working class. Conservatives resented any challenge to the existing political order, and workers and artisans disliked

German revolutionaries behind a street barricade in Berlin prepare for an assault from forces loyal to King Frederick William IV, March 18–19, 1848. [The Bettmann Archive]

liberalism's commitment to free trade—its hostility to the protections the guild system offered labor. At Frankfurt a split developed between liberals and workers, which German conservatives exploited for the rest of the century.

The Frankfurt Parliament also floundered in its discussions of unification. Members could not agree on whether to include Austria in a united Germany. The *kleindeutsch* (small German) faction prevailed over the large German *(grossdeutsch)* party when Austria rejected the whole notion of unification. The numerous nationalities resident within the Habsburg domains feared German domination.

Austria's opposition to unification strengthened support for Prussian leadership of Germany. On March 27, 1849, the parliament produced a constitution and offered the crown of a united Germany to Frederick William IV of Prussia. He rejected the offer, asserting that kings ruled by the grace of God, not with permission from man-made constitutions. His refusal led to the collapse of the Frankfurt Parliament and a defeat from which German liberals never fully recovered. In the end, all the various revolutions accomplished was an extension of the franchise in some of the German states and the establishment of conservative constitutions.

During the first half of the nineteenth century, Europeans confronted unprecedented social challenges. The emerging industrial economy was transforming virtually all their institutions, and social change was encouraging political strife. The liberal revolution that began in 1789 culminated as the uprisings of 1848 were suppressed and Conservatives seized the political initiative.

After 1848, the European middle class ceased to be revolutionary and became increasingly concerned with protecting its property. In particular, it feared radical movements associated with socialism and, eventually, with Marxism.

✑ Review Questions

1. What inventions were particularly important in the development of industrialism? What changes did industrialism make in society? Why were the years covered in this chapter so difficult for artisans? What is meant by "the proletarianization of workers"?

2. In what ways did the industrial economy change the working-class family? What roles and duties did various family members assume? How did the role of women change in the new industrial era?

3. What were the goals of the working class in the new industrial society? How did they differ from middle-class goals? How do you explain the separation of working-class and middle-class goals?

4. How did police change in the nineteenth century? Why were new systems of enforcement instituted? In what ways were prisons improved? How do you account for the reform movement that led to the improvements?

5. How would you define *socialism?* Were Karl Marx's ideas different from those of the socialists?

6. Why did revolutions break out in so many places in 1848? Were circumstances essentially the same or were they different in the various countries? Why did the revolutions fail? What roles did liberals and nationalists play in them? Did they always agree?

∽ Suggested Readings

I. BERLIN, *Karl Marx: His Life and Environment* (1948). An excellent introduction.

P. BROCK, *The Slovak National Awakening* (1976). A standard work.

W. COLEMAN, *Death Is a Social Disease: Public Health and Political Economy in Early Industrial France* (1982). One of the first works in English to study this problem.

I. DEAK, *The Lawful Revolution: Louis Kossuth and the Hungarians, 1848–1849* (1979). The most significant study of the topic in English.

J. ELSTER, *An Introduction to Karl Marx* (1985). The best volume to provide a discussion of Marx's fundamental concepts.

T. HAMEROW, *Restoration, Revolution, and Reaction: Economics and Politics in Germany, 1815–1871* (1958). Traces the forces that worked toward the failure of revolution in Germany.

J.F.C. HARRISON, *Quest for the New Moral World: Robert Owen and the Owenites in Britain and America* (1969). Now the standard work.

G. HIMMELFARB, *The Idea of Poverty: England in the Early Industrial Age* (1984). A Major work covering the subject from the time of Adam Smith through 1850.

M. IGNATIEFF, *A Just Measure of Pain: The Penitentiary in the Industrial Revolution, 1750–1850* (1978). An important treatment of early English penal thought and practice.

D. LANDES, *The Unbound Prometheus: Technological Change and Industrial Development in Western Europe from 1750 to the Present* (1969). The best one-volume treatment of technological development in a broad social and economic context.

W. L. LANGER, *Political and Social Upheaval, 1832–1852* (1969). A remarkably thorough survey, strong in both social and intellectual history as well as political narrative.

J. M. MERRIMAN, *The Agony of the Republic: The Repression of the Left in Revolutionary France, 1848–1851* (1978). A major study of the manner in which the Second French Republic and popular support for it were suppressed.

H. PERKIN, *The Origins of Modern English Society, 1780–1880* (1969). A provocative attempt to look at the society as a whole.

I. PINCHBECK, *Women Workers and the Industrial Revolution, 1750–1850* (1930, reprinted 1969). A pioneering study that remains of great value.

P. ROBERTSON, *An Experience of Women: Pattern and Change in Nineteenth-Century Europe* (1982). A useful survey.

D. SORKIN, *The Transformation of German Jewry, 1780–1840* (1987). An examination of the decades of Jewish emancipation in Germany.

P. STEARNS, *Eighteen Forty-Eight: The Tide of Revolution in Europe* (1974). A good discussion of the social background.

E. P. THOMPSON, *The Making of the English Working Class* (1964). An influential and controversial work.

L. A. TILLY and J. W. SCOTT, *Women, Work, and Family* (1978). A useful and sensitive survey.

H. ZEHR, *Crime and the Development of Modern Society: Patterns of Criminality in Nineteenth-Century Germany and France* (1976). An examination of crimes against property in urban society.

23

The Age of Nation-States

KEY TOPICS IN THIS CHAPTER

~ The unification of Italy and Germany

~ The shift from empire to republic in France

~ The emergence of dual monarchy in Austria-Hungary

~ Reforms in Russia, including the emancipation of the serfs

~ The emergence of Great Britain as the exemplary liberal state and its confrontation with Irish nationalists

Although the revolutions of 1848 collapsed and authoritarian regimes spread across Europe in the early 1850s, within a quarter of a century many of the objectives of early-nineteenth-century liberals and nationalists had been realized. Italy and Germany were each united under constitutional monarchies. The Habsburg emperor accepted a constitution and granted liberties to the Magyars of Hungary. Russia's tsar emancipated the serfs. France again became a republic. Liberalism and even democracy flourished in Great Britain. Paradoxically, most of this happened while conservatives were in power.

Consolidation of States (1854–1900)

1854–1856	*The Crimean War*
1855	*Alexander II becomes tsar*
1859	*Piedmont and France fight Austria*
1860	*Garibaldi invades southern Italy*
1861	*Austria issues the February Patent*
	Proclamation of the Kingdom of Italy (March 17)
	Russia abolishes serfdom
1862	*Bismarck becomes prime minister of Prussia*
1863	*Russia suppresses the Polish Rebellion*
1864	*Danish-Prussian War*
1866	*Austro-Prussian War*
	Venetia ceded to Italy
1867	*North German Confederation formed*
	Formation of the Dual Monarchy: Hungary and Austria
	Britain's Second Reform Act
1868	*Gladstone becomes prime minister of Britain*
1870	*Franco-Prussian war begins (July 19)*
	Third Republic proclaimed in France (September 4)
	Italian state annexes Rome (October 2)
1871	*The German Empire proclaimed (January 18)*
	Paris Commune (March 28–May 28)
	Treaty of Frankfurt between France and Germany (May 1)
1872	*Introduction of the secret ballot in Britain*
1874	*Disraeli becomes prime minister of Britain*
1880	*Gladstone's second ministry*
1881	*Alexander II assassinated; Alexander III succeeds*
1884	*Britain's Third Reform Act*
1886	*Lord Salisbury becomes prime minister of Britain*
1892	*Gladstone's third ministry*
1894	*Nicholas II becomes tsar*

∽ The Crimean War (1854–1856)

The impetus for political change in Europe at mid-century was the Crimean War (1854–1856), a product of a long-standing rivalry between Russia and the Ottoman Empire. Russia had both material and spiritual motives for beginning the conflict. It wanted to annex the Ottoman provinces of Moldavia and Walachia (modern Romania), and the tsar claimed a duty to protect Orthodox Christians resident within the Ottoman Empire.

The other great powers soon became involved. Both France and Great Britain, which had extensive naval and commercial interests in the eastern Mediterranean, opposed Russian expansion. Austria and Prussia disappointed Tsar Nicholas I by remaining neutral. The Austrians had ambitions of their own in the Balkans, and Prussia decided, for the moment, to follow Austria's lead.

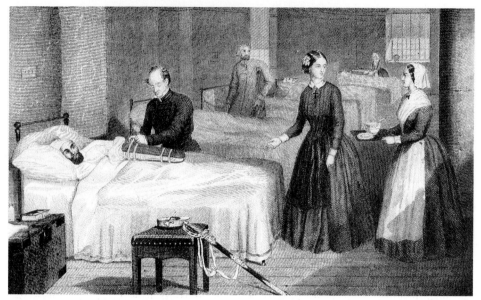

During the Crimean War, Florence Nightingale of Great Britain organized nursing care for the wounded. [The Bettmann Archive]

Both sides conducted the conflict ineptly. Their ill-equipped and poorly commanded armies bogged down along the Crimean coast of the Black Sea. In September 1855, the Russian fortress of Sevastopol finally fell to the French and British, and in March 1856, Russia came to terms. The Treaty of Paris required Russia to surrender territory near the mouth of the Danube River, to recognize the neutrality of the Black Sea, and to renounce claims of protection over Christians in the Ottoman Empire. Austria had already forced Russia out of Moldavia and Walachia. The aura of invincibility that Russia had radiated since the Napoleonic wars was dispersed.

Also shattered was the Concert of Europe, the tradition of nations consulting on foreign policy issues in order to maintain the agreements ratified at the Congress of Vienna. Napoleon III favored redrawing, along lines of nationality, the map of Europe produced by the Congress of Vienna. The Austrians wanted more influence within the German Confederation, but Prussia did not want its role in German affairs subordinated to Austria's. Russia, a chief defender of the Vienna settlement, was determined to counter the humiliation of the Treaty of Paris. And Britain, having stumbled through the Crimean War, was hesitant about any military involvement on the continent.

Confident (after the suppression of the 1848 revolutions) of their control of domestic affairs, nations embarked on aggressive foreign policies. Ambition was limited only by the extent of military and diplomatic resources. The most significant achievements of the era were the unifications of Italy and Germany—events that transformed Europe's international politics.

～ Italian Unification

Romantic Republicans

Nationalists had long wanted to fuse the small principalities of the Italian peninsula into a single state, but opinion differed about what should be done. Following the Congress of Vienna, the "romantic republicans" took the lead in rallying nationalistic sentiment. They organized secret societies throughout Italy and declared the unification of Italy to be a divine mission—a duty to God and to humanity.

In 1831, Giuseppe Mazzini (1805–1872), the most important nationalist leader in all Europe, founded the Young Italy Society. It was dedicated to driving Austria from the peninsula and establishing a republic in Italy. During the 1830s and 1840s, Mazzini and his fellow republican, Giuseppe Garibaldi (1807–1882), led insurrections. Both were involved in the ill-fated Roman Republic of 1849, and throughout the 1850s they conducted what amounted to guerilla warfare. Both men spent much time in exile and became well known in the United States.

More moderate Italians wanted to end Austrian domination, but not establish a republic. For a time, they promoted the papacy as a vehicle for unification. That plan foundered after Pius IX's disastrous experience with the Roman Republic in 1849. But another moderate liberal strategy succeeded. By a Machiavellian process of unification by force of arms and secret diplomacy, the prime minister of Piedmont, Camillo Cavour (1810–1861), created a constitutional monarchy for Italy.

Cavour's Policy

Piedmont (the Kingdom of Sardinia) in northwestern Italy was the most independent of the Italian states. The Congress of Vienna had restored it to create a buffer between the French and the Austrians. During 1848 and 1849, King Charles Albert of Piedmont twice fought Austria. Following his second defeat, he abdicated in favor of his son, Victor Emmanuel II (r. 1849–1878). In 1852, the new king appointed Count Camillo Cavour prime minister.

Cavour began political life as a conservative but gradually moved toward a moderately liberal position. A practical man deeply imbued with the ideas of the Enlightenment, classical economics, and utilitarianism, Cavour made a fortune investing in railroads, reforming agriculture on his estates, and editing a newspaper. He had no respect for Mazzini's romantic ideals or for republicanism. He believed that the unification of Italy was necessary for its economic and material progress.

Cavour worked for free trade, railway construction, credit expansion, and agricultural improvement. Although he felt that material and economic bonds, not fuzzy romantic yearnings, must unite the Italians, he tried to win the support of nationalists of all kinds. To this end, he founded the Nationalist Society which established chapters in other Italian states to press for unification under the leadership of Piedmont. Cavour also solicited help from France.

French Sympathies. Cavour used the Crimean War to establish a role for Italy in European politics. In 1855, Piedmont sent 10,000 troops to assist France and Britain. Participation in the war gave Cavour a seat at the Paris peace conference and an opportunity to raise the Italian question. He left Paris with no firm commitments, but he had impressed the other diplomats and won the sympathy of Napoleon III. For the rest of the decade, he courted international respectability by opposing Mazzini's various nationalist uprisings. Cavour's strategy was to depict Piedmont as a moderate liberal alternative to both republicanism and reactionary absolutism.

In January 1858, an Italian named Orsini tried to assassinate Napoleon III. The incident motivated the French emperor to take a stronger interest in the Italian issue. He liked the idea of continuing his famous uncle's efforts to liberate the peninsula, and he wanted Piedmont as an ally against Austria. In July 1858, Cavour and Napoleon III met at Plombières in southern France and agreed to provoke a war in Italy that would give them a chance to defeat Austria. For its help, France was to receive French-speaking Nice and Savoy from Piedmont.

War with Austria. When Austria objected to Piedmont mobilizing its army early in 1859, Piedmont claimed that Austria had provoked war. France joined in, and Austria was defeated at Magenta on June 4 and at Solferino on June 24.

The war encouraged revolutionaries, who wanted union with Piedmont, to seize control in Tuscany, Modena, Parma, and the Romagna provinces of the Papal States. This alarmed Napoleon III and prompted him to make a separate peace with Austria. Although Cavour felt betrayed, Austria had been driven from most of northern Italy, and Piedmont was able to annex Lombardy. Soon Parma, Modena, Tuscany, and the Romagna voted to become part of the Piedmontese kingdom (see Map 23–1).

Garibaldi's Campaign. At this point, the romantic republicans pressured Cavour into completing the unification of northern and southern Italy. In May 1860, Garibaldi landed in Sicily with more than a thousand soldiers who had been outfitted in the north. He captured Palermo and prepared to invade the mainland. By September, he controlled the kingdom of Naples.

Garibaldi wanted a republican Italy, but Cavour forestalled him by sending Piedmontese troops into the south. They conquered the remaining Papal States—except for the area around Rome, which the French protected for the pope. Faced with the choice of sacrificing either republicanism or hope for national unity, Garibaldi unhappily accepted Piedmontese domination. In late 1860, Naples and Sicily voted to join Piedmont's northern union.

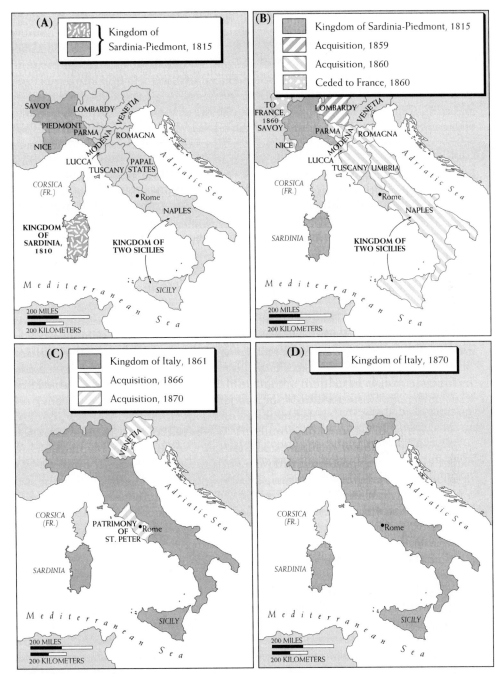

MAP 23–1 The Unification of Italy *Beginning with the association of Sardinia and Piedmont by the Congress of Vienna in 1815, unification was achieved through the expansion of Piedmont between 1859 and 1870. Both Cavour's statesmanship and the campaigns of ardent nationalists played large roles.*

The New Italian State

In March 1861, Victor Emmanuel II was proclaimed king of Italy, and three months later Cavour died. This was unfortunate, for the new state needed the skills of a consummate diplomat. Italy had been more nearly conquered than united. The republicans resented Piedmont's treatment of Garibaldi. The clericals resented its conquest of the Papal States. The economies of north and south were incompatible. The south was rural, poor, and backward. The north was industrializing and developing links to the rest of Europe. Large landholders and peasants peopled the south, while an urban working class emerged as the dominant group in the north. The south employed arms to resist the imposition of Piedmontese-style administration until 1866.

The political machinery the monarchy set up to govern Italy was inadequate. Piedmont's constitution of 1848 provided for a conservative constitutional monarchy with a Parliament of two houses: a Senate appointed by the king, and a Chamber of Deputies elected on a narrow franchise. Since ministers reported to the king, not to Parliament, Parliament had little power. Its leaders often simply avoided problems and kept themselves in power by *transformismo,* the use of bribes to "transform" enemies into friends. Italian politics became a byword for corruption.

Many Italians also believed that their nation would be incomplete until it acquired Venetia and Rome. Italy won the former in 1866, by supporting Prussia in the Austro-Prussian War. In 1870, the Franco-Prussian War forced the French to withdraw the troops that had been guarding Rome since 1849. The Italian state promptly annexed the city and declared it the nation's capital. The Vatican retained its independence, but the papacy remained hostile to the Italian state until 1929, when the two sides concluded a treaty (the Lateran Accord).

By 1870, of the lands Italians thought of as theirs, only the province of Trent and the city of Trieste remained under foreign domination (ruled by Austria). A patriotic desire to liberate *Italia Irredenta* ("Unredeemed Italy") helped persuade the Italians to support the Allies against Austria and Germany during World War I.

∾ German Unification

The most important political development in Europe between 1848 and 1914 was the unification of Germany (see Map 23–2). German unity had been sought by two generations of liberals, but it was the product of conservative moves to outflank liberals.

Although the major German states were linked by trade agreements and railways, their unification seemed remote throughout the 1850s. Liberal nationalists were in retreat after the suppression of the revolts of 1848 and 1849. Frederick William IV of Prussia had quickly given up thoughts of leading the unification movement, and Austria opposed any union that might lessen its influence.

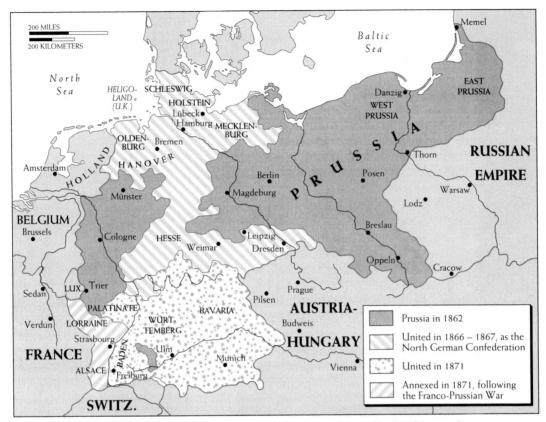

MAP 23–2 The Unification of Germany *Under Bismarck's leadership, and with the strong support of its royal house, Prussia used most diplomatic and military means, on both the German and international stages, to forcibly unify the German states into a strong national entity.*

Prospects for unification suddenly improved, however, when Prussia's internal situation altered. In 1858, Frederick William IV was adjudged insane, and his brother William became his regent and then his successor. William I (r. 1861–1888) was less idealistic than his brother and more of a Prussian patriot. Consistent with Hohenzollern tradition, his first concern was for his troops. In 1860, he proposed enlarging the army, increasing the number of its officers, and extending the period of conscription from two to three years. The Prussian Parliament, whose liberal leaders wanted to avoid increasing the power of the monarchy, refused to approve the necessary taxes. For two years, monarch and Parliament were deadlocked.

Bismarck

In September 1862, William I turned for help to the person who, more than any other single individual, determined the course of Europe's history for the next thirty years: Otto von Bismarck (1815–1898). Bismarck came from Junker stock. He attended university, joined a *Burschenschaft* (one of the politically active student societies), and took an interest in German unification. During the 1840s, he was elected to the provincial diet. Although he was so reactionary as to disturb even the king, he made his mark as a politician, and from 1851 to 1859, he served as the Prussian delegate to the Frankfurt Diet of the German Confederation. Later he became Prussian ambassador to Russia, and he had just been named ambassador to France when William I decided to make him prime minister of Prussia.

Over the years, Bismarck mellowed into a conservative. He opposed parliamentary government, but favored a strong monarchy under a constitution. He understood the importance to a nation of a strong industrial base. And he was, above all, a pragmatic politician—a believer that change was wrought more by power and action than by the discussion of ideas.

As soon as Bismarck became prime minister in 1862, he moved against the liberal Parliament. He contended that the Prussian constitution granted the government the power to impose the taxes it needed to carry out its regular functions. Therefore, the taxes required to expand the army could be collected despite the current Parliament's refusal to vote them. The army and most of the bureaucracy supported Bismarck's interpretation of the constitution, but in 1863, new elections sustained the liberal majority in the Parliament. Bismarck had to find a way to undercut the liberals and solicit popular support for the monarchy and the army. His strategy was to propose using Prussia's conservative institutions to unify Germany.

The Danish War (1864). Bismarck took a *kleindeutsch* (small German) position on unification; that is, he believed that it would be easier for Prussia to dominate a Germany that did not include Austria. The difficulty was to force Austria to accept such an arrangement. Bismarck's strategy was to provoke and win a war with Austria.

A quarrel between Denmark and the German Confederation gave him an opportunity to begin maneuvering. The two northern duchies of Schleswig-Holstein had long been ruled by Denmark, but they were not part of Denmark. Holstein's population was more German than Danish, and it belonged to the German Confederation. When, in 1863, the Danish parliament annexed both duchies, the smaller states of the German Confederation clamored for war. Bismarck proposed that Prussia and Austria handle the situation, and Denmark was easily defeated. In August 1865, the Convention of Gastein declared that Austria would administer Holstein and Prussia, Schleswig.

Meanwhile, Bismarck gained Russia's friendship by supporting its suppression of a revolt in Poland in 1863, and he persuaded Napoleon III to promise neutrality in the event of a future Austro-Prussian conflict. In April 1866, Bismarck concluded a treaty with Italy, promising that it would get Venetia if it joined Prussia in an attack on Austria.

The Austro-Prussian War (1866). Austrian and Prussian forces clashed frequently in Schleswig and Holstein, where Bismarck directed his men to provoke the Austrians by being as obnoxious as possible. On June 1, 1866, Austria appealed to the German Confederation against Prussia. Bismarck, claiming that this action violated Prussia's treaties with Austria, promptly launched the Seven Weeks' War.

Austria was decisively defeated at Königgrätz in Bohemia. Except for Venetia, Austria lost no territory by the Treaty of Prague, which ended the war. But defeat deprived the Habsburgs of the role they had previously played in German affairs. Prussia emerged as the only major power among the German states.

The North German Confederation. In 1867, Prussia annexed Austria's allies in the war (Hanover, Hesse, Nassau, and Frankfurt) and created a confederation that united all of Germany north of the Main River. Each state had its own local government, but all military forces were under federal control. Prussia's king, represented by Bismarck, was president of the federation, which was governed by a bicameral legislature: the *Bundesrat,* appointed by the governments of the states, and the *Reichstag,* elected by universal male suffrage.

The constitution of the North German Confederation (which after 1871 became the constitution of the German Empire) looked more liberal than it was. Its *Reichstag* was chosen by all male citizens, but it had little power. Government ministers were responsible only to the monarch, and only the king's chancellor could initiate legislation. Bismarck, in effect, established a military monarchy over Germany. His liberal opponents acquiesced because, in the end, their desire for national unity proved greater than their commitment to liberal principles.

The Franco-Prussian War and the German Empire (1870–1871)

Events in Spain gave Bismarck an excuse to bring the south German states into Prussia's confederation. In 1868, the corrupt Bourbon queen of Spain, Isabella II (r. 1833–1868), was deposed. Two years later the Spaniards offered their crown to Prince Leopold of Hohenzollern-Sigmaringen, a Catholic cousin of Prussia's William I. Leopold's father, fearing that France would attack Prussia to prevent the Hohenzollerns from establishing themselves in Spain, renounced his son's candidacy (July 12, 1870). William I was relieved that he had not been required, as the French were urging him, to order Leopold to renounce the Spanish throne.

The matter might have rested there had it not been for the impetuosity of the French and the guile of Bismarck. On July 13, the French government instructed its ambassador to Prussia, Count Vincent Benedetti (1817–1900), to ask William I for assurances that he would tolerate no future Spanish candidacy for Leopold. The king refused, and sent Bismarck, who was in Berlin, a telegram describing the meeting. Bismarck, who wanted war with France in order to bring the remaining German states into the Prussian federation, used the king's telegram to incite the war the king hoped to avoid. He released an edited version of the dispatch that made it appear that William I had insulted the French ambassador.

Everything developed as Bismarck expected. France declared war (July 19), and once the conflict erupted, the south German states rallied to Prussia's side. On September 1, at the Battle of Sedan, the Germans beat the French army and captured Napoleon III. Paris was besieged in late September. On January 18, in the Hall of Mirrors at the Palace of Versailles, the German Empire was proclaimed. On January 28, 1871, Paris capitulated, and at the peace conference France ceded control over Alsace and part of Lorraine to Germany.

German unification changed the face of Europe by creating a powerful new state that was far stronger than Prussia had been alone. A humiliated France returned to republican government, and the beleaguered Habsburgs hastened to come to terms with their Magyar subjects. Liberals everywhere were alarmed, for conservative politics now had the backing of the strongest state on the continent.

∾ France: From Liberal Empire to the Third Republic

Historians divide the reign of Emperor Napoleon III (r. 1851–1870) into halves to mark a shift in the year 1860 from authoritarian to more liberal government. Initially, Napoleon III controlled the legislature, censored the press, and harassed political dissidents. He relied on the army, the Catholic clergy, property owners, and businessmen, who were interested primarily in security for property, the papacy, and commerce.

Late in the 1850s, Napoleon III began to suffer reverses abroad that forced him to change his domestic policy. His influence faded in Italy as Piedmont pursued unification. He had little choice but to stand by passively while Prussia reorganized Germany. He was humiliated when France's intervention in Mexico against the Spanish led to the overthrow and execution of the man the French army helped to the Mexican throne, the Archduke Maximilian of Austria (r. 1864–1867).

To shore up support at home for a government weakened by these foreign policy failures, Napoleon III began to make liberal concessions. In 1860, he granted the legislature greater freedom of debate. He concluded a free trade treaty with Britain. He relaxed the laws limiting the press and forbidding labor unions. In 1870, he accepted a ministry formed by moderates in the legislature, and he approved a liberal constitution that made ministers of state responsible to the legislature.

Napoleon III began the Franco-Prussian War hoping that the struggle would consolidate support for the Second Empire. The result was quite the opposite. When news of the emperor's capture at the Battle of Sedan (September 1870) reached Paris, a republic was proclaimed and a Government of National Defense organized. Most of France was ready to sue for peace long before Paris surrendered in January 1871.

The Paris Commune

The new National Assembly, which was elected in February, accepted Prussia's terms for peace and signed the Treaty of Frankfurt. It promised to pay a large indemnity, to permit occupation by Prussian troops until the indemnity was paid, and to surrender Alsace and part of Lorraine. Napoleon III was exiled to England, where he died in 1873.

Many Parisians, who had suffered from the Prussian siege of their city, felt betrayed by the National Assembly's capitulation. On March 28, 1871, they installed the Paris Commune, a municipal government that pledged to administer Paris separately from the rest of France. The National Assembly quickly surrounded Paris with an army and, on May 8, ordered bombardment. On May 21, the day on which the treaty with Prussia was signed, the assembly's forces broke through the city's defenses. About 20,000 Parisians were killed before order was restored.

The short-lived Paris Commune quickly became a legend throughout Europe. Marxists claimed that it was a genuine proletarian government suppressed by the bourgeoisie, but they were wrong. The goal of the commune was not a worker's republic but a nation of relatively independent democratic enclaves. Its suppression was the triumph, not of the middle over the lower class, but of a centralized national government over an alternative form of political organization. In Italy and Germany, armies pulled nations together; in France, an army prevented a nation from coming apart.

The Third Republic

The National Assembly was dominated by monarchists, but it backed into a republican form of government. The monarchists were divided between support for the House of Bourbon and for the House of Orléans. This problem could have been resolved by appointing the Bourbon claimant, the count of Chambord. He had no children and was willing to make the Orléanist heir his successor. But Chambord refused to be king if France retained the tricolor flag of the revolution. Since restoration of the white flag of the Bourbons was too politically reactionary even for the most conservative of the monarchists, negotiations stalemated.

In 1873, the indemnity was paid, and the Prussian occupation ended. The new president of the assembly, Marshal MacMahon (1808–1893), favored restoration of the monarchy—if an acceptable king could be found. But in 1875, the National Assembly, frustrated by the inability of the monarchists to unite, confirmed a political organization: a Chamber of Deputies elected by universal male suffrage, a Senate chosen indirectly, and a president elected by the two legislative houses.

This Third Republic proved much more durable than many expected. It defended itself against General George Boulanger (1837–1891), who wanted to impose a stronger executive authority, and it survived a number of scandals (such as sales of awards of the Legion of Honor and bribes paid politicians by a company constructing a canal in Panama).

The Dreyfus Affair

The Third Republic's greatest trauma was the Dreyfus affair. On December 22, 1894, a French military court found Captain Alfred Dreyfus (1859–1935) guilty of passing information to the German army. But after he was sent to the notorious prison on Devil's Island, secrets continued to flow to the Germans. In 1896, a new head of French counterintelligence reopened the case and found that evidence against Dreyfus had been forged. Suspicion centered on a different officer, but a military court quickly acquitted him of all charges.

Dreyfus was Jewish, and the near-hysterical public debate over his case revealed the extent of French anti-Semitism. The army, the French Catholic church, conservative politicians, and certain newspapers vehemently contended that Dreyfus was guilty. In 1898, the novelist Émile Zola countered with a newspaper article: *"J'accuse"* ("I Accuse"). He contended that the army had consciously denied due process to Dreyfus and had plotted to suppress or forge evidence. The government's response was to convict Zola of libel and sentence him to a year in prison.

The prosecution of Captain Alfred Dreyfus, shown here standing on the right at his military trial, provoked the most serious crisis of France's Third Republic. [The Bettmann Archive]

Zola fled to England, but the political left—liberals, radicals, and socialists—took up Dreyfus's cause. They were eager to embarrass the conservative government by proving that it had denied Dreyfus the rights belonging to all citizens of the republic. They also wanted to humble the military by showing that it had offered up Dreyfus to protect guilty parties in the army. In August 1898, further evidence of forged material came to light, and the officer responsible committed suicide in jail. When a second military trial refused to acquit Dreyfus, the president of France stepped in to pardon him. In 1906, a civilian court set aside the verdicts of both military tribunals.

The Dreyfus case had long-lasting political repercussions. It put conservatives on the defensive, for they had persecuted an innocent man, falsified evidence to protect themselves, and embraced violent anti-Semitism. Support for Dreyfus helped bring the radicals, republicans, and socialists of the left closer together. But divisions and suspicions growing out of the Dreyfus affair continued to divide the Third Republic until France's defeat by Germany in 1940.

∽ The Habsburg Empire

After 1848, the Habsburg Empire became a problem to itself and Europe. The Habsburg response to the revolts of 1848–1849 had been the reassertion of absolutism. Consequently, in an age characterized by national states, liberal institutions, and industrialism, the Habsburg domains remained dynastic, absolutist, and agrarian. Francis Joseph, emperor from 1848 to 1916, was honest and hard-working, but unimaginative. He reacted to events, but rarely commanded them.

During the 1850s, his ministers tried to impose a centralized administration on the empire. It featured an army and bureaucracy staffed by German-speaking Austrians. Internal tariffs in the empire were abolished. Hungary was divided into military districts. The Roman Catholic Church took control of education. National groups, such as the Croats and Slovaks, who had helped the empire defeat the Hungarian rebels of 1848, got nothing in recognition of their loyalty. The government's "neoabsolutism" provoked resentment and opposition. Setbacks in foreign affairs provoked its fall.

Austria's refusal to support Russia in the Crimean War cost the Habsburgs Russia's help in Hungary. An external prop for their power, on which they had relied for half a century, was thus removed. This, together with Austria 's loss of territory to Piedmont in 1859, necessitated radical changes in domestic policy. For seven years, Austria's leaders struggled to construct a viable system of government.

Formation of the Dual Monarchy

In 1860, Francis Joseph issued the October Diploma. It proposed a federated government for the states and provinces of the empire, utilizing a single imperial parliament and local diets dominated by the landed classes. The Magyar nobility of Hungary rejected the plan, so the emperor returned, in 1861, with the February Patent. It established a bicameral imperial parliament (the *Reichsrat*), with an upper chamber appointed by the emperor and an indirectly elected lower chamber. Government ministers reported to the emperor, not the *Reichsrat*. Civil liberties were not guaranteed. Armies could be levied and taxes raised without parliamentary consent. And when the *Reichsrat* was not in session, the emperor could rule by decree. Although the Magyars again refused to cooperate with this plan, the February Patent governed the empire for six years and Austria proper until World War I.

Secret negotiations between the emperor and the Magyars produced no concrete result until 1866, when the Prussians defeated Austria and excluded it from German affairs. This compelled Francis Joseph to come to terms with the Magyars. The result was the *Ausgleich* (Compromise) of 1867, which reorganized the empire as a dual monarchy, Austria-Hungary. Except for a common ruler, Austria and Hungary functioned as separate states. They shared a few ministers—foreign affairs, defense, and finance. But their other departments of government and their parliaments were separate. Each year, sixty parliamentary delegates from each state met to discuss mutual interests. Every ten years, Austria and Hungary renegotiated their trade relationship. This cumbersome machinery, unique in European history, reconciled the Magyars to Habsburg rule by giving them the free hand they had long wanted in Hungary.

Unrest of Nationalities

By acceding to the nationalistic desires of the Hungarians, the Compromise of 1867 increased tensions within the empire. It prompted other ethnic groups to demand comparable recognition of their rights to separate government, self-government, or union with fellow nationals outside the empire. Many peoples—including the Czechs, the Ruthenians, the Romanians, and the Croatians—opposed the Compromise of 1867 because it permitted German-speaking Austrians and Hungarian Magyars to dominate other nationalities.

The Czechs of Bohemia were most insistent in demanding recognition, as had Hungary, as a separate kingdom within the empire (see Map 23–3). Francis Joseph was willing, but the Magyars objected. (They feared having to make similar concessions to their subject nationalities.) Germans resident in Bohemia also worried that the Czech language would be imposed on them. For over twenty years, the emperor placated the Czechs with generous patronage, but in the 1890s, Czech nationalists again became strident. In 1897, Francis Joseph made Czech and German equal official languages in various localities. Angry Germans in the Austrian *Reichsrat* responded by disrupting Parliament; the Czechs replied in kind. As a result, the *Reichsrat* was paralyzed, and the emperor was forced to rule by decree. By 1914, Austrian constitutionalism was dead. It survived in Hungary, but only because the Magyars maintained their political supremacy over other nationalities.

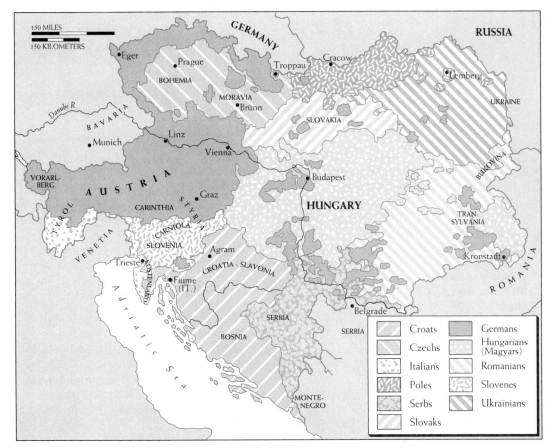

MAP 23–3 Nationalities Within the Habsburg Empire *The patchwork appearance reflects the unusual problem of the numerous ethnic groups that the Habsburgs could not, of course, meld into a modern national state. Only the Magyars were recognized in 1867, leaving nationalist Czechs, Slovaks, and the others chronically dissatisfied.*

Nationalism seems to have become stronger during the last quarter of the nineteenth century and lines between groups more clearly drawn. Language was believed to be the most important defining attribute of a nation. But racial ideologies, which taught that there was a genetic basis for ethnic identities, were also popular. Austria's dominant population was German-speaking and loyal to the emperor, but a significant faction yearned to be part of Bismarck's united Germany. These nationalistic Austro-Germans often hated the non-German subjects of the empire. Many of them were anti-Semites. Their prejudices shaped an Austrian who in the twentieth century became a leader of Germany: Adolph Hitler.

Strife among the nationalities subject to the Habsburg Empire created political instability in central and eastern Europe. Both foreign and domestic policy issues were involved, for nationalists wanted self-determination within

Lord Acton Condemns Nationalism

Lord Acton was a major nineteenth-century English historian and commentator on contemporary religious and political events. In all of his writings, he was deeply concerned with the character and preservation of liberty. His was one of the earliest voices to point to the political dangers of nationalism.

~ Why does Acton see the principle of nationality as dangerous to liberty? Why does he see nationalism as a threat to minority groups? Why does he see nationalism as a threat to democracy?

The greatest adversary of the rights of nationality is the modern theory of nationality. By making the State and the nation commensurate with each other in theory, it reduces practically to a subject condition all other nationalities that may be within the boundary. It cannot admit them to an equality with the ruling nation which constitutes the State, because the State would then cease to be national, which would be a contradiction of the principle of its existence. According, therefore, to the degree of humanity and civilization in that dominant body which claims all the rights of the community, the inferior races are exterminated, or reduced to servitude, or outlawed, or put in a condition of dependence.

If we take the establishment of liberty for the realization of moral duties to be the end of civil society, we must conclude that those states are substantially the most perfect which, like the British and Austrian Empires, include various distinct nationalities without oppressing them. Those in which no mixture of races has occurred are imperfect; and those in which its effects have disap-peared are decrepit. A State which is incompetent to satisfy different races condemns itself; a State which labors to neutralize, to absorb, or to expel them, destroys its own vitality; a State which does not include them is destitute of the chief basis of self-government. The theory of nationality, therefore, is a retrograde step in history. . . .

. . . . [N]ationality does not aim either at liberty or prosperity, both of which it sacrifices to the imperative necessity of making the nation the mold and measure of the State. Its course will be marked with material as well as moral ruin, in order that a new invention may prevail over the works of God and the interests of mankind. There is no principle of change, no phrase of political speculation conceivable, more comprehensive, more subversive, or more arbitrary than this. It is a confutation of democracy, because it sets limits to the exercise of the popular will, and substitutes for it a higher principle.

John Emerich Edward Dalberg-Acton, First Baron Acton, Essays in the History of Liberty, *J. Rufus Fears, ed., (Indianapolis: Liberty Classics, 1985), pp. 431–433.*

the empire and unification with fellow nationals outside the empire. Groups such as Ukrainians, Romanians, Italians, and Bosnians saw themselves as potentially linked to Russia, Romania, Italy, Serbia, or to a yet-to-be established south Slavic or Yugoslav state. The significance of nationalist unrest within the late-nineteenth-century Austrian Empire and its neighbors can hardly be overestimated. It helped spark the First World War, the Second World War, and the current bloodshed in the former Yugoslavia.

～ Russia: Emancipation and Revolutionary Stirrings

Reforms of Alexander II

Russia changed remarkably during the second half of the nineteenth century, for foreign policy reversals (defeat in the Crimean War and humiliation by the Treaty of Paris) compelled the Russian government to reconsider its domestic policies. Nicholas I's son and heir, Alexander II (r. 1855–1881), was well trained for his duties as tsar. Travel within his nation and experience in its government gave him a sense of the difficulties that Russia faced. The debacle of the war made reform both necessary and possible, and Alexander II made the most of this opportunity. He began the most extensive restructuring of Russian institutions since the days of Peter the Great.

Abolition of Serfdom. A profound cultural gap separated Russia from the rest of Europe. Nowhere was this more apparent than in the survival of serfdom in Russia at a time when it had been abandoned by all other European states. Among Western nations, forms of involuntary servitude were maintained only in Russia, Brazil, and certain portions of the United States.

Serfdom was economically inefficient and a constant source of social unrest. In March 1856, at the conclusion of the Crimean War, Alexander II announced his intention to abolish it. He claimed that its abolition was necessary to permit Russia efficient exploitation of its human and natural resources. For over five years, government commissions wrestled over how to implement the tsar's desire. Finally, in February 1861, over opposition from the nobility and the landlords, Alexander II promulgated the emancipation statute.

Former serfs were disappointed, for freedom was not accompanied by land. They were required to pay, over a period of forty-nine years, for the plots they worked—many of which were too small to support them. Payments were made to the government which had already reimbursed the landlords for their losses. The public debt and its interest charges were passed on to the peasants. The procedures were so complicated and the results so limited that many serfs believed that real emancipation was still to come.

Poor harvests made it impossible for many peasants to keep up with the government's payment schedule, and they fell increasingly behind. The situation was not remedied until a widespread revolutionary upheaval—following a Japanese defeat of Russia in 1905—convinced the government, grudgingly, to cancel the remaining debts.

Reform of Local Government and Judicial System. The abolition of serfdom required the reorganization of local government and the judicial system. Vil-

Tsar Alexander II (r. 1855–1881) was assassinated on March 1, 1881. The assassins first threw a bomb that wounded several imperial guards. When the tsar stopped his carriage to see to the wounded, the assassins threw a second bomb, killing him. [Bildarchiv Preussischer Kulturbesitz]

lage communes replaced landlords as the authorities keeping peace among the peasants. The nobility were given a larger role in other aspects of local administration. They sat on provincial and county *zemstvos* (councils) that oversaw things like bridge and road repair, education, and agricultural improvement. Since, however, the councils received inadequate funds, they never developed much vigor.

In 1864, Alexander II promulgated a statute that addressed abuses and inequities in the judiciary. Western European legal principles (equality before the law, impartial hearings, uniform procedures, judicial independence, and trial by jury) became, for the first time, part of Russian practice. Judges still were not genuinely independent, the tsar could change the sentences they handed out, and certain offenses—such as those involving the press—were not tried before a jury. Nonetheless, the new courts improved the efficiency and honesty of law enforcement.

Military Reform. Russia maintained the largest army on the continent. Villages had to meet quotas for recruits, and serfs were often seized from their homes and impressed into service. Once in the army, men rarely saw their families again, for soldiers remained on active duty for twenty-five years and Russian military life was harsh.

Poor performance in the Crimean War prompted the government to enact some reforms. In the 1860s, the period of service was reduced to fifteen years, and discipline was slightly relaxed. In 1874, the enlistment period was lowered to six years of active duty, followed by nine years in the reserves.

Repression in Poland. In 1863, Polish nationalists tried to end Russian dominance of their homeland, and Alexander II responded by trying to "russify" Poland. In 1864, he punished the politically restive nobility by emancipating their serfs. Russian law, language, and administration were imposed throughout Poland, and, until the close of World War I, Poland was treated as a Russian province.

Alexander II entertained no reforms limiting his autocracy, and his programs earned him little gratitude from his subjects. The serfs felt that their emancipation was inadequate. The nobles and the wealthier, educated segments of society resented his refusal to allow them a meaningful role in government.

Although Alexander II became known as the Tsar Liberator, he was never popular. After an attempt was made on his life in 1866, he became increasingly close minded and reactionary. Russia evolved into a police state, and repression fueled the activities of its radicals.

Revolutionaries

One of the most prominent critics of the tsarist regime was an exile, Alexander Herzen (1812–1870), who published a newspaper called *The Bell.* Drawing on the ideas of Herzen and other radicals, students who were disenchanted with the pace of reform in Russia organized a movement known as *Populism.* It wanted to model society after the communal life of the Russian peasants.

In the early 1870s, hundreds of young Russians—both male and female— took their revolutionary message into the countryside. They intended to live with the peasants, to gain their trust, and to teach them about the peasant role in the coming revolution. The bewildered and distrustful peasants turned most of them over to the police. In the winter of 1877–1878, almost 200 were tried. Most were acquitted or given light sentences, because the court believed that a display of mercy would lessen public sympathy for the revolutionaries. The tsar, however, made it known that he favored heavy penalties for anyone involved in revolutionary activity.

This convinced the revolutionaries that they had to attack the tsarist regime directly. Their strategy was terrorism. In January 1878, Vera Zasulich tried to assassinate the military governor of Saint Petersburg. When the jury acquitted her because of her intended victim's reputation for brutality, the verdict encouraged other terrorists.

In 1879, Land and Freedom, the most radical of the revolutionary organizations, split. The faction that advocated educating the peasants soon dissolved. The other, known as People's Will, focused on the overthrow of the autocracy and the assassination of the tsar. After several attempts failed, they succeeded, on March 1, 1881, in hurling a bomb that killed Alexander II. Four men and two women were sentenced to death for the deed.

Alexander III (r. 1881–1894) confirmed all the evils that the revolutionaries saw as inherent in autocratic government. He dedicated his reign to rolling back his father's reforms. He favored government by centralized bureaucracy, not local councils (the *zemstvos*). He built up the secret police and increased press censorship. The reactionary legacy he prepared for his son, Nicholas II (r. 1894–1917), hastened the destruction of Russia's monarchy.

ᰁ Great Britain: Toward Democracy

Great Britain was the model of the confident liberal state with stable political institutions equipped to handle all difficulties and domestic conflicts. Parliament admitted new groups and interests to the political process. The general prosperity of the third quarter of the century mitigated social tensions, and all classes shared a belief in competition and individualism.

The Second Reform Act (1867)

During the early 1860s, pressure began to build to expand the franchise once again. In 1866, a Liberal ministry introduced a reform bill that was defeated. A Conservative ministry then assumed office and surprised everyone by introducing its own reform bill (1867).

Benjamin Disraeli (1804–1881), the Conservative leader in the House of Commons accepted a series of amendments that expanded the electorate beyond the limits earlier proposed by the Liberals and nearly made Britain a democracy. Disraeli believed that reform was inevitable and that the Conservatives' best strategy was to take credit for it. He expected grateful voters of the working class to support Conservative candidates who were responsive to social issues, and he thought that the growing suburban middle class would become increasingly conservative. He was correct. The Conservative Party has dominated British politics in the twentieth century.

Gladstone's Great Ministry (1868–1874)

The voters in the election of 1868 disappointed Disraeli by choosing a prime minister whose term in office (1868–1874) marked the culmination of British liberalism: William Gladstone (1809–1898). Gladstone opened to people from all classes and faiths the institutions that had been the preserve of the aristocracy and the Anglican church. In 1870, competitive examinations for the civil service replaced patronage. In the same year, the Education Act assigned the government responsibility for establishing and running elementary schools. In 1871, the purchase of officers' commissions in the army was abol-

William Ewart Gladstone served in the British Parliament from the 1830s through the 1890s. Four times the Liberal Party Prime Minister, he was responsible for guiding major reforms through Parliament. (Bildarchiv Preussischer Kulturbesitz)

ished, and Anglican religious requirements for the faculties of Oxford and Cambridge universities were removed. The Ballot Act of 1872 introduced voting by secret ballot.

All of these reforms were typically liberal. They ended abuses without destroying existing institutions. They enabled all able citizens to compete on the grounds of ability and merit. They confronted the danger an illiterate citizenry poses to a democratic state. They created new bonds of loyalty to the nation by abolishing sources of discontent.

Disraeli in Office (1874–1880)

Disraeli succeeded Gladstone as prime minister in 1874. The two men had stood on different sides of most issues for over a quarter-century. Whereas Gladstone looked to individualism, free trade, and competition to solve social problems, Disraeli believed in paternalistic legislation and state action to protect the weak.

Disraeli talked much, but had few specific programs or ideas. The significant social legislation of his ministry was the work of his Home Secretary, Richard Cross (1823–1914). The Public Health Act and the Artisans' Dwelling Act (both 1875) improved conditions for the working classes, and expanded protection for their trade unions empowered them to fight for additional reforms.

The Irish Question

From the late 1860s onward, Irish nationalists sought home rule—by which they meant Irish control of Ireland's local government. Gladstone responded with two major pieces of legislation. In 1869, he disestablished the branch of the Anglican church in Ireland so that Roman Catholics were not taxed to support Protestant clergy. And in 1870, his land act provided compensation for evicted Irish tenants and loans for those who wished to purchase land.

The Irish question festered throughout the 1870s. Land was at the center of the problem. An Irish Land League agitated for change and intimidated landlords, who were often English. In 1881, Gladstone strengthened tenant rights, but also issued the Coercion Act, regulations intended to restore law and order to Ireland.

By 1885, Charles Stewart Parnell (1846–1891) had organized eighty-five Irish members of the House of Commons into a tightly disciplined party that often voted as a bloc. In the election of 1885, their votes decided whether the English Liberals or Conservatives would take office. When Gladstone announced his support of home rule, Parnell helped him form a Liberal ministry. The home rule issue, however, split the Liberal Party, and in 1886, some Liberals joined the Conservatives to defeat Gladstone's Home Rule Bill.

Gladstone's Conservative successor, Lord Salisbury (1830–1903), tried a combination of public works, administrative reform, and coercion to reconcile the Irish to English government. In 1892, Gladstone returned to power and proposed a second Home Rule Bill which passed the House of Commons but was defeated in the House of Lords. In 1903, the Conservatives carried out the final transfer of land to tenant ownership, and Ireland became a country of small farms. In 1914, a Liberal ministry took advantage of limitations imposed on the upper house (the House of Lords Act of 1911) to pass the third Home Rule Bill. But its implementation was suspended for the duration of World War I.

Political divisions created by the Irish question made it difficult to resolve other issues. Frustration with the inability of the two traditional parties to enact reforms created an opportunity, by the turn of the century, for a third group to enter British politics: the Labour Party.

Between 1850 and 1875, the contours of the political systems that would dominate Europe until World War I were drawn. The concept of the nation-state had triumphed. Support for governments no longer stemmed from loyalty to dynasties, but from ethnic, cultural, linguistic, and historical bonds and a sense of participation in the duties of active citizenship. The major sources of discontent were unsatisfied aspirations to political power by subject nationalities and labor. These eventually undermined the political structures created during the third quarter of the nineteenth century.

Review Questions

1. Why was it so difficult to unify Italy? What groups were urging unification? Who was Camillo Cavour? How did he succeed where others had failed? What were Garibaldi's contributions to Italian unification?

2. Who was Otto von Bismarck? Why did he want to unify Germany? What attemps at unification had preceded his? Why did they fail? What was his plan for German unification? Why did it succeed? What effect did the unification of Germany have on the rest of Europe?

3. How did France's Second Empire (under Napoleon III) become its Third republic? Why did the Second Empire fall? What problems faced the new republic? Why did the Paris Commune become a legend throughout Europe? What effect did the Dreyfus affair have on the politics of the Third Republic?

4. What changes in government took place in Austria after 1848? What unique problems did Austria have? Were they solved? Why was nationalism a more pressing problem for Austria than for any other nation?

5. What reforms were instituted by Tsar Alexander II? Did he solve some of Russia's domestic problems? Can he be regarded as a "visionary" reformer? Why or why not?

6. How did the politics of the British Liberal and Conservative parties evolve in the period from 1860 to 1890? Who were their leaders? What problems did they confront? What solutions did they favor? How did British politicians handle the "Irish question"? Are there similarities between England's situation with Ireland and the Austrian Empire's struggles with its nationalities?

Suggested Readings

M. BENTLEY, *Politics Without Democracy, 1815–1914* (1984). A well-informed survey of British development.

R. BLAKE, *Disraeli* (1967). The best biography.

J. BLUM, *Lord and Peasant in Russia from the Ninth to the Nineteenth Century* (1961). A clear discussion of emancipation in the later chapters.

G. CHAPMAN, *The Dreyfus Affair: A Reassessment* (1955). A detached treatment of a subject that still provokes strong feelings.

G. CRAIG, *Germany, 1866–1945* (1978). An excellent survey.

S. ELWITT, *The Making of the Third Republic: Class and Politics in France, 1868–1884* (1975). An excellent introduction.

E. HOBSBAWM, *The Age of Empire, 1875–1914* (1987). A stimulating survey that covers cultural as well as political developments.

R. A. KANN, *The Multinational Empire*, 2 vols. (1950). The basic treatment of the nationality problem of Austria-Hungary.

G. KITSON KLARK, *The Making of Victorian England* (1962). The best introduction.

A. J. MAY, *The Habsburg Monarchy, 1867–1914* (1951). Narrates in considerable detail and with much sympathy the fate of the dual monarchy.

C. C. O'BRIEN, *Parnell and His Party* (1957). An excellent treatment of the Irish question.

O. PFLANZE, *Bismarck and the Development of Germany*, 3 vols. (1990). A major biography and history of Germany for the period.

A. PLESSIS, *The Rise and Fall of the Second Empire, 1852–1871* (1985). A useful survey of France under Napoleon III.

D. M. SMITH, *The Making of Italy, 1796–1870* (1968). A narrative that incorporates the major documents.

F. VENTURI, *The Roots of Revolution* (trans. 1960). A major treatment of late-nineteenth-century revolutionary movements.

J. WERTHEIMER, *Unwelcome Strangers: East European Jews in Imperial Germany* (1987). Examines the difficult position of Jews in Wilhelminian Germany.

T. ZELDIN, *France: 1848–1945*, 2 vols. (1973, 1977). Emphasizes the social developments.

24

The Building of European Supremacy: Society and Politics to World War I

KEY TOPICS IN THIS CHAPTER

~ The transformation of European life by the second Industrial Revolution

~ Urban sanitation, housing reform, and the redesign of cities

~ The condition of women in late-nineteenth-century Europe and the rise of political feminism

~ The development of labor politics and socialism in Europe to the outbreak of World War I

~ Industrialization and political unrest in Russia

The growth of industrialism between 1860 and 1914 increased Europe's productive capacity to unprecedented, unparalleled levels. As goods and capital flowed out from Europe across the globe, Europe's politics, economics, and social institutions assumed many of their current characteristics. Nation-states with centralized bureaucracies, large electorates, and political parties emerged. Business developed huge corporate structures. The labor force organized itself into trade unions. Increasing numbers of white-collar workers appeared. Urban life came to predominate throughout western Europe. Socialism became a major political force. Foundations were laid for welfare states and for vast military establishments. Taxation increased accordingly.

Confident in their prosperity, Europeans failed to realize how dependent they were on the resources and markets of the world. Their assumption that European supremacy was natural and enduring was to be challenged as the twentieth century unfolded.

∼ Population Trends and Migration

In 1900, Europe was home to about 20 percent of the world's people, a greater proportion than ever before or since. Its population rose from about 266 million in 1850, to 401 million in 1900, to 447 million in 1910. Thereafter, growth declined or stabilized in advanced nations while increasing in less developed countries.

In addition to its size, Europe's population was more mobile in the second half of the century than ever before. Emancipation of peasants removed legal blocks to migration. Railways, steamships, and better roads increased access to transportation. Offers of cheap land and better wages, which accompanied economic development in Europe, North America, Latin America, and Australia, provided motivation for people to move.

Europeans left their continent in record numbers—more than 50 million between 1846 and 1932. Most went to the United States, Canada, Australia, South Africa, Brazil, or Argentina. At mid-century Great Britain (especially Ireland), Germany, and Scandinavia produced the most emigrants. After 1885, migration from southern and eastern Europe dominated. The exodus solved some of Europe's domestic problems, and relocation of its peoples contributed, along with trade and industry, to the Europeanization of the world. Not since the sixteenth century had European civilization had such an impact on other cultures.

∼ The Second Industrial Revolution

New Industries

The first Industrial Revolution centered on textiles, on iron, and on applications of steam power. The second, which began after 1850, stimulated economic growth by adding production of steel, chemicals, electricity, and oil.

In the 1850s, an English engineer, Henry Bessemer (1830–1898), discovered a process for manufacturing large quantities of steel cheaply. Production in Great Britain, Belgium, France, and Germany rose from 125,000 tons in

European emigrants from eastern Europe wait to board a ship that will carry them to the United States. Between 1846 and 1932, more than 50 million Europeans emigrated to the United States, Canada, South America, Australia, and South Africa. [Bildarchiv Preussischer Kulturbesitz]

1860 to 32,020,000 tons in 1913. The chemical industry also came of age. The Solway process of alkali production allowed more chemical by-products to be recovered and increased production of sulfuric acid and laundry soap. New dyestuffs and plastics were developed. Formal scientific research played an important role in the growth of the chemical industry, and chemists established the modern world's alliance between science and industrial development. Germany took the lead in this process and in fostering scientific research and education.

The most significant changes for industry and daily life resulted from the application of electrical energy to production. Electricity was the most versatile and most transportable source of power ever discovered. It could be delivered almost anywhere to run almost anything—making factory location more flexible and factory construction more efficient. The first major public power plant was constructed in Great Britain in 1881. Soon electric poles, lines, and generating stations dotted the European landscape and electricity began to be marketed to homes.

The internal combustion engine was invented in 1886. A year later, Gottlieb Daimler (1834–1900), a German engineer, put it on wheels and created the automobile. The car remained a novelty that only the wealthy could afford until, in 1909, Henry Ford (1863–1947), the American entrepreneur, de-

Events in the Formation of the Early Twentieth Century

1848	*Britain's Public Health Act*
1851	*France's Melun Act*
1857	*Bessemer steel manufacturing process invented*
1864	*Meeting of the First International*
1869	*John Stuart Mill publishes* The Subjection of Women
1875	*German Social Democratic Party founded*
1876	*Telephone invented*
1879	*Electric light bulb invented*
1882	*England's Married Woman's Property Act*
1884	*Britain's Fabian Society founded*
1887	*Automobile invented*
1889	*Establishment of the Second International*
1895	*Invention of wireless telegraphy*
1900	*Lenin leaves Russia*
1902	*Formation of the British Labour Party*
1903	*British Women's Social and Political Union founded*
	Lenin creates the Blosheviks
	The Wright brothers begin the age of aviation
1904–1905	*Russo-Japanese War*
1905	*Saint Petersburg's Bloody Sunday*
	Russia's October Manifesto
1907	*Norway, first nation to grant women the vote*
1909	*Henry Ford begins mass production of automobiles*
1910	*British suffragettes adopt radical tactics*
1911	*Stolypin assassinated*
1914	*World War I begins*
1918	*Some British women acquire the vote*
1918	*Constitution of the Weimar Republic gives women the vote*
1928	*British women acquire same voting rights as men*

veloped production techniques that made it cheap enough for ordinary people to purchase.

The automobile and new industrial and chemical uses for petroleum had, by the turn of the century, created the first significant demand for oil—and the first great oil companies: Standard Oil of the United States, British Shell Oil, and Royal Dutch. Then as now, Europe depended largely on imported supplies.

Economic Difficulties

Industry and agriculture boomed from 1850 to 1873, but in the last quarter of the nineteenth century economic advance slowed. Bad weather and foreign competition created problems for European agriculture that put a drag on the economy. Many of the emigrants who left Europe during these years came from rural areas or from countries where industrialization was least advanced.

Several large banks failed in 1873. The rate of capital investment slowed, and some industries stagnated for a twenty-year period that many contemporaries regarded as a depression. Overall, however, the second half of the nineteenth century produced improvements in standards of living in industrialized nations. Real wages generally held firm or, in some countries, rose. Many workers still lived and labored in abysmal conditions, however, and there were pockets of *unemployment*—a word that was coined during this period. Labor unrest promoted the growth of trade unions and socialist political parties.

By the end of the century, expansion of consumer demand had revived the economy. Lower food prices allowed all classes to spend a larger portion of their income on consumer goods. The new industries produced new goods. Urbanization created larger markets. New approaches to sales—department stores, chain stores, packaging techniques, mail-order catalogs, and advertising—stimulated consumer demand. Imperialism also generated new consumers for European products abroad.

∽ The Middle Classes in Ascendancy

The sixty years before World War I were the age of the middle classes. The London Great Exhibition of 1851 (housed in a huge solarium called the Crystal Palace) was a monument to the material comforts that industrialization provided for middle-class life. The middle classes, as the largest group of consumers, were the arbiters of taste. Prosperity also made them defenders of the status quo and diminished the enthusiasm some had shown for revolution in 1848. As issues of social equality and political rights were raised, owners of property, small as well as large, worried that socialists and other working-class groups might deprive them of their possessions.

Social Distinctions Within the Middle Classes

The middle classes had never been perfectly homogeneous, and during the nineteenth century they grew increasingly diverse. In the lead were a few hundred families, the owners and managers of great businesses who could afford to live in a splendor beyond the reach of many aristocrats. Behind them were the comfortable small entrepreneurs and professionals—people who could afford private homes; large quantities of furniture, pianos, pictures, books, journals; education for their children; and vacations. With this group might also be numbered people with smaller holdings or lesser educations, but respected, nonmanual employment: shopkeepers, schoolteachers, and librarians.

Last was a wholly new element: white-collar workers who formed a lower middle class or petty bourgeoisie—secretaries, retail clerks, and lower-level bureaucrats. Many had working class origins. Some belonged to unions. But all had middle-class aspirations and consciously distanced themselves from the lifestyle of the lower classes. They actively pursued educational opportunities and career advancement, especially for their children. They spent a considerable portion of their disposable income on consumer goods that kept up a middle-class appearance.

Significant tensions and anxieties marked relations among the groups composing the middle class. Small shopkeepers resented competition from the department stores and mail-order catalog of the great capitalists. Professions grew overcrowded. Those who struggled into the middle class feared being forced out by economic hard times. Nonetheless, during the decades leading up to World War I, the middle class had sufficient cohesion to set society's values and goals.

∼ Late-Nineteenth-Century Urban Life

Between 1850 and 1911, the portion of France's population living in cities increased from 25 percent to 44 percent; in Germany the shift was from 30 percent to 60 percent. Other western European countries experienced similar, unprecedented growth in urbanization.

Migrants to cities from rural areas were uprooted from traditional social ties and condemned to poor housing, social anonymity, and, often, unemployment. Different ethnic groups found it difficult to get along when thrown together—particularly when competing for jobs. The migration of thousands of Russian Jews to western Europe's cities was met by an outbreak of anti-Semitism, which became a factor in politics in the latter part of the century.

The Redesign of Cities

Migration to cities increased demands on their resources and transformed patterns of urban life. During the second half of the century, governments redesigned many European cities. Central areas, which had been home to large numbers of people from all social classes, were transformed into business districts with government offices, large retail stores, and theaters. Residents moved to the peripheries of cities, and commerce, trade, government, and entertainment came to dominate their centers.

The New Paris. The greatest transformation of a major city occurred in Paris. Like most European cities, Paris had evolved with little or no planning. Lavish public buildings and squalid hovels were jumbled together. Streets were narrow, crooked, and crowded. The river Seine, which ran through the center of town, was little more than an open sewer and an obstacle to traffic. In 1850, the government did not even have a complete, correct map of Paris. This was particularly worrisome, for the city's streets had for sixty years provided battlegrounds for insurrections that, as recently as 1848, had toppled French governments.

Napoleon III decided to redesign Paris, and he appointed Georges Haussmann "prefect of the Seine" (from 1853 to 1870) to oversee a vast urban reconstruction program. Whole districts were destroyed to make room for broad boulevards and streets. The wide vistas were both beautiful and functional.

They allowed for the quick deployment of troops to put down riots and eliminated the narrow passages where barricades could be erected. The project was politically astute for a second reason. It created thousands of government-funded jobs, as well as employment in private construction stimulated by public works.

Rebuilding continued under the Third Republic. Many department stores, office complexes, and apartment buildings for the middle class were constructed. By the late 1870s, mechanical trams were operating, and in 1895 construction of the "Métro" (subway) began. New railway stations were erected toward the close of the century. These improvements in transportation linked the refurbished central city to its expanding suburbs.

Development of Suburbs. Redesign of cities displaced many of their residents and raised land values and rents. As both the middle classes and the working class sought alternative housing, suburbs sprang up around cities. They housed families whose breadwinners commuted by the new transportation systems to the town centers or urban factories. European suburbs, unlike those that developed in the United States, often consisted of apartment buildings or closely huddled private houses with small lawns and gardens. Suburban life meant that for hundreds of thousands of Europeans, home and work were more physically separated than ever before.

Urban Sanitation

The growing conservativism of the middle classes stiffened government's resolve to maintain public order. This led to improvements in health and housing for the poor, for it was believed that the well-being of the middle class and the stability of political systems depended on easing the effects of poverty.

The great cholera epidemics of the 1830s and 1840s drove this lesson home. Many common deadly diseases touched only the poor, but cholera struck all classes. Before the development of the bacterial theory of disease late in the century, physicians and sanitary reformers believed that cholera and other illnesses were spread through infection from miasmas in the air. Miasmas were identified by their foul odors and were believed to arise from filth. The only way to rid cities of dangerous, foul-smelling air was to clean them up.

During the 1840s, physicians and government officials began to publicize the dangers posed by human overcrowding and the wastes from some industries. The solution to the health hazard was said to be cleanliness achieved through new water and sewer systems. These facilities were constructed slowly, and some major urban areas did not have good water systems until after the turn of the century. The sewer system of Paris was one of the most famous parts of Haussmann's rebuilding program.

Government Expansion. Concern for public health led to an expansion of governmental power on various levels. Britain's Public Health Act (1848), France's Melun Act (1851), various laws in the still-disunited German states, and addi-

A French Physician Describes a Working-Class Slum in Lille Before the Public Health Movement

It is difficult to conceive of the world before the sanitation movement. The work of medical doctors frequently carried them into working-class areas of industrial cities rarely visited by other members of the middle class. Louis Villermé was such a French physician. He wrote extensive descriptions of the slums and the general living conditions of industrial workers. The passage quoted below, which was published in 1840, describes a particularly notorious section of Lille, a major cotton-manufacturing town in northern France.

∿ What does this physician find most disturbing about the scene he describes? In what way might his description have been designed to call forth sympathy and concern from a middle-class reader? How might the conditions described have led the poor of France toward socialism or radical politics? How would addressing the problem described have increased government's role?

The poorest live in the cellars and attics. These cellars . . . open onto the streets or courtyards, and one enters them by a stairway which is very often at once the door and the window. . . . Commonly the height of the ceiling is six or six and a half feet at the highest point, and they are only ten to fourteen or fifteen feet wide.

It is in these somber and sad dwellings that a large number of workers eat, sleep, and even work. The light of day comes an hour later for them than for others, and the night an hour earlier.

Their furnishings normally consist, along with the tools of their profession, of a sort of cupboard or a plank on which to deposit food, a stove . . . a few pots, a little table, two or three poor chairs, and a dirty pallet of which the only pieces are a straw mattress and scraps of a blanket. . . .

In their obscure cellars, in their rooms, which one would take for cellars, the air is never renewed, it is infected; the walls are plastered with garbage. . . . If a bed exists, it is a few dirty, greasy planks; it is damp and putrescent straw; it is a coarse cloth whose color and fabric are hidden by a layer of grime; it is a blanket that re-sembles a sieve. . . . The furniture is dislocated, worm-eaten, covered with filth. Utensils are thrown in disorder all over the dwelling. The windows, always closed, are covered by paper and glass, but so black, so smoke-encrusted, that the light is unable to penetrate . . . everywhere are piles of garbage, of ashes, of debris from vegetables picked up from the streets, of rotten straw; of animal nests of all sorts; thus, the air is unbreathable. One is exhausted, in these hovels, by a stale, nauseating, somewhat piquante odor, odor of filth, odor of garbage. . . .

And the poor themselves, what are they like in the middle of such a slum? Their clothing is in shreds, without substance, consumed, covered, no less than their hair, which knows no comb, with dust from the workshops. And their skin? . . . It is painted, it is hidden, if you wish, by indistinguishable deposits of diverse exudations.

Louis René Villermé, Tableau de l'état physique *et* moral des emploies dans les manufactures de coton, de laine et de soie *(Paris, 1840), as quoted and trans. in William H. Sewell, Jr.,* Work and Revolution in France: The Language of Labor from the Old Regime to 1848 *(Cambridge: Cambridge University Press, 1980), p. 224.*

tional later legislation introduced new restraints on private life and enterprise. Medical officers and building inspectors were allowed to enter homes and other structures in the name of public health. Private property could be condemned for posing health hazards. Private land could be excavated for the construction of sewers and water mains, and building codes increasingly restrained the activities of private contractors. Acceptance at the close of the century of the bacterial theory of disease—developed by Louis Pasteur in France, Robert Koch in Germany, and Joseph Lister in Britain—increased concern for sanitation and opened the way for greater government intervention in the lives of citizens.

Housing Reform and Middle-Class Values

The wretched dwellings of the poor, which were monuments to bad sanitation, came to be viewed as health hazards for the general public. Middle-class reformers and bureaucrats were shocked by reports describing the domestic arrangements of the lower classes and worried by suggestions that revolutions, like those of 1848, could be caused by the pressures of overcrowded housing.

Reformers looked to housing reform to solve all kinds of medical, moral, and political problems. Proper, decent housing was to foster a good home life, which would create a healthy, moral, content, and politically stable community. It was also believed that the saving and investment required for owning a home would motivate members of the working class to adopt the thrifty habits of the middle classes.

The goal of housing reform was to make it possible for the working class to enjoy a family life much like that of the middle class. At the minimum, this required a dwelling of several rooms with a private entrance and toilet. Private philanthropy made the first attack on the problem. Companies operating on low profit margins or making low-interest loans encouraged housing for the poor. Firms such as the German Krupp armaments concern tried to ensure a contented, healthy, and stable workforce by constructing model industrial communities.

By the mid-1880s, migration into cities had made housing a political issue. In 1885, England lowered the interest rates for the construction of cheap housing. Soon thereafter, public authorities began public housing projects. Similar action, initiated by local municipalities, followed in Germany; in 1894, France made inexpensive credit available for constructing housing for the poor. By 1914, the housing problem had been fully recognized if not adequately addressed.

∼ Varieties of Late-Nineteenth-Century Women's Experiences

Social Disabilities Confronted by All Women

Women in the late nineteenth century, like men, led lives that reflected their social ranks. Yet within each rank, the experience of women was distinct from that of men. Women were economically dependent and legally inferior, whatever their class. Virtually all European women were handicapped with respect to property rights, family law, and education, but by the end of the century improvements had been made in each of these areas.

Women and Property. In most European countries, until the last quarter of the century, married women of all classes could not own property in their own names. Upon marriage, a woman lost control of any property she owned, inherited, or earned, to her husband. Her legal identity was subsumed in his. She had no independent standing before the law. The theft of her purse was a theft of his property. Because European society was based on private property and wage earning, these disabilities put her at a great disadvantage.

Reform of women's property rights came very slowly. Great Britain passed a Married Woman's Property Act in 1882, which allowed wives to own property as individuals. But in France, a married woman could not even open a savings account in her own name until 1895, and married women were not granted possession of the wages they earned until 1907. In 1900, Germany allowed a woman to take a job without her husband's permission, but except for her wages, her husband retained control of most of her property. Similar laws prevailed elsewhere in Europe.

Family Law. Divorce was difficult to obtain, and most nations did not permit termination of a marriage by mutual consent. Expensive court trials were required, and these were beyond the means of women who had no control over their own property.

French law forbade divorce altogether from 1816 to 1884. Thereafter, the chief legal grounds for divorce were acts of cruelty and injury that could be proven in court. In Germany, only adultery or serious mistreatment were recognized as reasons for divorce. In England prior to 1857, divorce required an act of Parliament. Thereafter, divorce could be gained, with difficulty, through the Court of Matrimonial Causes. Adultery was the usual cause for granting a divorce in Britain, but everywhere on the continent a double standard prevailed. A husband's extramarital sexual relations were tolerated much more than a wife's.

Legal codes required wives to obey their husbands, and the Napoleonic Code and the remnants of Roman law still in effect throughout Europe designated women legal minors. In cases of divorce and separation, husbands were usually given custody of children. The authority of fathers over children was extensive. A father could take children away from their mother and give them to someone else for rearing. Only a father, in most countries, could permit a daughter to marry, and in some countries he could force his daughter to wed the man of his choice.

The sexual and reproductive rights of women were seldom discussed in the nineteenth century. Both contraception and abortion were illegal well into the twentieth century, and laws punishing rape worked to a woman's disadvantage. Wherever victims turned—whether to physicians or to lawyers,—they confronted a world controlled by men.

Educational Barriers. Throughout the nineteenth century, women had less access to education than men. Most were given only enough schooling to permit them to do their duties as wives and mothers. Not surprisingly, there were more illiterate women than men, and the absence of a system of private or public secondary education prevented women from acquiring the qualifications needed to enter university.

Universities and professional educations were closed to women until at least the third quarter of the century. The University of Zurich admitted women in the 1860s. Women's colleges were founded at Oxford and Cambridge during the last quarter of the century, but women who passed examinations at those universities were not awarded degrees until 1920 (Oxford) and 1921 (Cambridge). Women were not admitted to lectures at the Sorbonne in Paris until 1880. Not until the end of the century did universities and medical schools in the Austrian Empire allow women to matriculate. Prussian universities did not admit women until after 1900. Russian women did not attend universities before 1914, but could study at other degree-granting institutions. Italian universities were more open to female students and instructors than comparable institutions elsewhere.

Restriction of a woman's access to secondary and university education was justified as a defense of her traditional gender roles and a way to shield her from political radicalism. There was one exception. Elementary teaching, because it was associated with child nurturing, was thought of as a female job. It became a professional haven for women, but the schools that trained women for this work were regarded as inferior to universities.

A few women did enter professions, particularly medicine. Most nations refused to allow women to practice law until after World War I, and many of the American women who founded or taught in the first women's colleges in the United States had to go to Europe to acquire their educations. Female pioneers in these fields faced grave social obstacles, personal humiliation, and outright bigotry. They and their male allies called into question a recently acquired article of middle-class faith: that males and females had distinctly separate spheres of activity. Women were often so acculturated to their roles that they were reluctant to work for liberating changes. They, as well as men, feared that family responsibilities were incompatible with feminism.

New Employment Patterns for Women

The Second Industrial Revolution featured two developments that had a major impact on the economic lives of women. The first was an expansion in the variety of jobs available apart from the learned professions. The second was the reduction of the number of married women in the workforce.

Although the kinds of industrial occupations that women had filled in the middle of the nineteenth century (especially in textile and garment making) shrank, expansion of governmental bureaucracies, large-scale business organizations, and retail stores created new employment opportunities for women. Government-mandated compulsory education increased the need for elementary school teachers. New inventions, such as typewriters and telephones, fostered employment of females.

Employers paid low wages to women in these jobs. The work required low-level skills, and society assumed, quite often knowing better, that women did not need a living wage. They were supposed to be dependents—relying on fathers or husbands for support. A woman could rarely find an adequately paying job or earn as much as a man for comparable work. Men were paid more, for they were assumed to have dependents.

Withdrawal from the Labor Force. Most of the women filling the new service positions were young and unmarried. After marriage, or certainly after the birth of a child, a woman usually withdrew from the labor force. She either did not work or worked at something that could be done at home. Employers in offices and retail stores often limited openings to unmarried women without family responsibilities that might interfere with work schedules.

Many changes discouraged married women from working outside their homes. As wages paid to males increased, the importance of a wife's second income diminished. Improving health conditions meant that as more men lived longer, fewer widows were forced back to work. Smaller family sizes decreased the need for supplementary wages. Working children stayed home longer and contributed longer to the family's wage pool. The cultural dominance of middle-class values—the ideal of the wife as full-time homemaker—also created social expectations that eased women out of the workforce. The more prosperous a working-class family became, the less its women were supposed to be earning money.

The definition of women's chief work as pertaining to the home degraded the economic situation for a woman who had to work outside the home. Because her wages were expected merely to supplement a husband's, she was treated as a casual worker who could be hired and fired according to the whims of the moment.

Working-Class Poverty and Prostitution

Most nineteenth-century cities had a surplus of working women who were not wives or daughters supplementing a family's income. Economic vulnerability and consequent poverty drove many of them into prostitution. Prostitution had always been a way for very poor women to find some income, but in the late nineteenth century it was closely related to the difficulty they had making their way in an overcrowded female labor force. On the continent, prostitution was generally legalized and regulated by governments (led by men). Great Britain preferred largely to ignore its existence.

Most prostitutes were active on the streets for a very few years, generally from their late teens to about age twenty-five. Thereafter, they moved into the regular workforce or married. Very poor women who had recently migrated from nearby rural areas were most likely to become prostitutes. Their trade flourished in cities with large army garrisons or naval ports or, like London, large transient populations. Fewer prostitutes worked in manufacturing towns, where there were more opportunities for steady employment and where community life was more stable.

Women of the Middle Class

A vast social gap separated working-class women from their middle-class counterparts. As their fathers' and husbands' incomes permitted, middle-class women responded to the increasing preoccupation with domestic comfort and helped feed a rapid growth in consumerism in the late nineteenth and early twentieth centuries. They and their numerous domestic servants moved into fashionable new houses constructed in the rapidly expanding suburbs. They filled these homes with manufactured items—clothing, china, furniture, carpets, drapery, wallpaper, and prints. They profited from the improvements that sanitation made in urban life and they enjoyed the new conveniences provided by electrical power.

The Cult of Domesticity. During the first half of the nineteenth century, a middle-class husband expected his spouse to be involved in his business—handling accounts or correspondence. She frequently had little to do with rearing their children, a task that was left to nurses and governesses. By the end of the century, things had changed. Middle-class women, if at all possible, did not work for wages. They were limited to the roles of wife and mother. They often enjoyed great domestic luxury, but at the cost of circumscribed lives, talents, ambitions, and intellects. Their roles reflected a particular understanding of society. Home life was to be very different from life in business and the marketplace. Scores of women's journals urged wives to make their homes private oases where husbands could find refuge from the stresses of the male world.

Marriages were usually arranged for some kind of family economic benefit. (Romantic marriage was viewed as a danger to social stability.) Middle-class women married young and, since the rearing of children had become their chief task, began to have babies immediately. Women received no training for any role other than that of dutiful daughter, wife, and mother.

Within the home, a middle-class woman had weighty duties. She was in charge of a household that could be very large. She oversaw all domestic management and child care. She handled most purchases for her family (which is why so much advertising began to be directed toward women). But there were strict limits set to her initiative. A woman's conspicuous idleness was an important symbol of her father's and then her husband's worldly success.

Religious and Charitable Activities. The churches promoted the cult of domesticity, for it exalted religion for women. Women were expected to attend public worship frequently, to arrange religious instruction for their children, and to see that their families observed domestic religious disciplines and rituals. Prayer was urged as a daily activity for women, who were encouraged to internalize the aspects of Christian faith that stressed meekness and passivity.

Middle-class women were also expected to engage in charitable work—a nurturing activity to which females were said to be innately disposed. Middle-class women oversaw clubs for poor youth, societies to protect poor young women, schools for infants, and societies for visiting and relieving the poor. Charity of this kind was supposed to inspire the poor to emulate character traits exemplified by middle-class women. Charity work gave women an opportunity to expand their spheres of activity. By the end of the century, some were becoming social workers for private, ecclesiastical, and government organizations.

Sexuality and Family Size. Recent studies have called into question older theories about sexual repression in the nineteenth century. Diaries, letters, and early sex surveys indicate that sexual enjoyment, not inhibition, characterized middle-class marriages. Much of the anxiety about sexuality stemmed from the dangers of childbirth, not from a disapproval of sex.

A major change in married sex took place during the second half of the century. Family sizes declined. During the last decades of the century, new contraceptive devices became available and acceptable to middle-class couples, for many couples were eager to limit family size in order to maintain a relatively high level of material consumption. Their children had become much more expensive to rear at a time when expectations for standards of living were rising.

The Rise of Political Feminism

Obstacles to Achieving Equality. Liberal reforms did not automatically benefit women, particularly with respect to politics. Liberal leaders feared that women were unduly susceptible to religious influences that conservatives would use to manipulate their votes. Conservatives were opposed to the break with tradition that was necessary to put this theory to the test.

Women themselves were often reluctant to support feminist causes or particular feminist organizations. For some, other issues took precedence over those relating to gender—things like patriotic struggles for national independence. Among feminists, there were disagreements about which goals for improvement in women's conditions were most important and about the tactics that were appropriate. Except in England, it was often difficult for working-class and middle-class women to cooperate.

Although liberal society and law confronted women with obstacles, they also provided feminists with intellectual tools. As early as 1792, Mary Wollstonecraft (*The Vindication of the Rights of Woman*) had cited revolutionary declarations of the rights of man to argue for comparable rights for women. In 1869, John Stuart Mill (1806–1873) and Harriet Taylor, his wife, published *The Subjection of Women*. It applied the logic liberals used to undermine tyranny to critique woman's place in European society. Socialists often, but by no means always, indicted capitalist societies for their treatment of women.

The fact that early statements of feminist positions were often linked with unorthodox opinions about sexuality, family life, and property made it difficult for feminists to enlist widespread public support. Everywhere in Europe, including Britain, the feminist cause was badly divided over both goals and tactics.

Votes for Women in Britain. Europe's most advanced women's movements were in Great Britain. Millicent Fawcett (1847–1929) founded a moderate National Union of Women's Suffrage Societies that, by 1908, could organize rallies of half a million women. Fawcett's husband was an economist who had served as a Liberal Party cabinet minister, and her tactics were those of English Liberals. She believed that Parliament would give women votes when women demonstrated that they would be respectable, responsible participants in politics.

Emmeline Pankhurst (1858–1928) advocated a much more radical approach. Her husband, who died near the close of the century, had fought for labor and for Irish home rule. Irish nationalists employed numerous disruptive political tactics to promote their cause, and early labor leaders also had confrontations with police over the right to hold meetings. In 1903, Pankhurst and her daughters, Christabel and Sylvia, founded the Women's Social and Political Union. Derisively dubbed "suffragettes," they spent years lobbying for votes for women. By 1910, having failed to move the government, they turned to violent tactics. They organized marches on Parliament and resorted to arson, window breaking, and sabotage of postal boxes. The Liberal government of Henry Asquith imprisoned demonstrators, force-fed those who staged hunger strikes in jail, and steadfastly refused women the franchise. In 1918, gratitude for their contribution to the war effort finally won the vote for some British women.

Political Feminism on the Continent. Although Norwegian women were voting on national issues by 1907, the rest of the continent lagged far behind them and behind the pace set by Britain's feminists. In France, when Hubertine Auclert (1848–1914) began campaigning for the vote in the 1880s, she stood virtually alone. Almost all French feminists opposed violence in any form, and they were never able to organize mass rallies. Their leaders believed that the vote could be achieved through careful legalism. In 1919, the French Chamber of Deputies passed a bill granting the vote to women, but the French Senate defeated the bill in 1922. It was not until after World War II that French women were granted votes.

Political feminism was even more underdeveloped in Germany, where laws actually barred women from participation in political activities. But since no group in the German Empire enjoyed extensive political rights, women were not particularly sensitive to their situation. Calls for rights were regarded suspiciously, as subversive not only of the state but of society. In 1894, the

Union of German Women's Organizations (BDFK) was founded. It was primarily concerned with improving women's social conditions, access to education, and various protections, but by 1902 it was supporting a call for the right to vote. The German Social Democratic Party endorsed women's suffrage, but the party was so disdained by the German authorities and German Roman Catholics that its support raised further objections to suffrage proposals. Women received the vote in Germany in 1918, when defeat abroad and revolution at home influenced the constitution written for the Weimar Republic.

～ Jewish Emancipation

Differing Degrees of Citizenship

Until the late eighteenth century, Europe's Jews generally lived apart from Christians in ghettos or villages, where they were regarded as resident aliens, not citizens. The ideals of the Enlightenment called this custom into question and motivated some reforms. In 1782, Joseph II gave the Jews of the Habsburg Empire more or less the same standing before the law as Christians. The National Assembly of France recognized Jews as citizens in 1789, and, during the turmoil of the Napoleonic wars, Jews and Christians mixed on a relatively equal footing in Italy and Germany. Steps toward political emancipation were, however, subject to repeal when governments changed.

Russia's tradition of harsh discrimination against Jews continued until World War I. The Russian government undermined Jewish community life, limited publication of Jewish books, restricted areas where Jews might live, required internal passports for Jews, banned Jews from forms of state service, and excluded Jews from many institutions of higher education. The police and others conducted *pogroms*—riots organized to disrupt Jewish communities. Hundreds of thousands of Jews fled Russia and eastern Europe for western Europe and the United States. There they encountered prejudice on a personal level, but their legal position became increasingly secure.

Broadened Opportunities

Following the revolutions of 1848, the situation for Jews in western Europe improved. Germany, Italy, the Low Countries, and Scandinavia granted Jews full citizenship. After 1858, Jews could be elected to Great Britain's Parliament, and Austria-Hungary extended full legal rights to Jews in 1867. Jews entered politics and won the highest offices. Politically, they tended to be liberals or, especially in eastern Europe, socialists.

From 1850 to 1880, there was little overt prejudice toward Jews, and many entered professions and occupations previously closed to them. They participated fully in literary and cultural life and became leaders in science and education. The process of their acculturation was encouraged when prohibitions against intermarriages were repealed during the last quarter of the century.

Prejudice against Jews did not, however, disappear. Anti-Semites openly accused Jewish bankers and financial interests of causing the economic stagnation of the 1870s. In the 1880s, organized anti-Semitism erupted in Germany and France. This caused some Jews (Zionists) to work for the establishment of an independent Jewish nation, but most believed that the revival of old prejudices would be temporary and that the liberal legal protections they had acquired over the course of the century would protect them. They were disastrously betrayed by that faith.

～ Labor, Socialism, and Politics to World War I

The industrial expansion that took place in the late nineteenth century increased the size and changed the nature of the urban proletariat. For the first time, factory wage-earners outnumbered artisans and highly skilled workers. Workers had always had to look to themselves to improve their lot, but after 1848, European laborers changed their strategy. They stopped rioting in the streets and trying to revive paternalistic guild systems. They embraced new institutions and ideologies: trade unions, democratic political parties, and socialism.

Trade Unionism

Trade unionism flourished during the second half of the century as governments recognized the right of workers to organize. Unions were legalized in Great Britain in 1871 and allowed to picket in 1875. Napoleon III, his power waning in 1868, allowed weak labor associations, and France's Third Republic legalized unions in 1884. Drives for unionization in Germany met little resistance after 1890.

At mid-century, unions concentrated on organizing skilled workers and improving wages and working conditions. By the close of the century, industrial unions for unskilled workers were being established. These large unions of thousands of members met intense opposition from employers and frequently had to wage long strikes. A majority of Europe's labor force was still not unionized in the decade leading up to World War I.

Democracy and Political Parties

With the exception of Russia, all the major European states established broad-based, if not perfectly democratic, electoral systems in the late nineteenth century. Great Britain passed its second voting reform act in 1867 and its third in 1884. Bismarck decreed universal male suffrage for the German Empire in 1871. The French Chamber of Deputies was democratically elected. Universal male suffrage was adopted in Switzerland in 1879, in Spain in 1890, in Belgium in 1893, in the Netherlands in 1896, and in Norway in 1898. Italy fell into line in 1912.

The broadened franchise fundamentally changed politics. It meant that politicians could not ignore workers and that workers no longer had to go outside institutions of government to voice their grievances. Instead of staging revolts against political authorities, they could hold them accountable at the ballot box. But when European states had narrow electoral bases, most voters were people of property who knew what they had at stake in politics. They were a fairly cohesive group that did not require much party organization. The expansion of the electorate brought into the political processes many voters whose level of political awareness and interest was quite low. The political party—with its workers, newspapers, offices, social life, and discipline—was created to mobilize this new electoral force, which the working class had the potential to dominate.

The democratization of politics presented the socialists with greater opportunities to challenge the traditional ruling classes. The major question for late-century socialist parties throughout Europe was whether the improvement of the lot of the working class was best achieved by revolution or by democratic reform. This issue sharply divided socialist parties, most especially those whose leadership adhered to the intellectual legacy of Karl Marx.

Marx and the First International

In 1864, a group of British and French trade unionists founded the International Working Men's Association—known simply as the First International. It encompassed a vast array of radical political types. Although Karl Marx condemned the whole capitalist system as beyond reform, in his inaugural address to the International, he approved efforts by labor to work within existing political and economic processes. (His private writings, which criticized such reformist activity, were not made public until after his death.)

The violence associated with the doomed Paris Commune of 1871, which Marx had praised as a genuine proletarian movement, cast a pall over socialism. France suppressed socialist activities, and British trade unionists, who received legal protections in 1871, wanted to avoid being associated with the friends of the Commune. Faced with declining support, the First International held its last European congress in 1873, then moved its offices to the United States, and dissolved in 1876.

Although short-lived, the First International had a great impact on the future of European socialism. Throughout the late 1860s, the organization gathered statistics, kept labor groups informed of mutual problems, provided a forum for the debate of socialist doctrine, and extravagantly proclaimed its own influence over contemporary events. These activities helped Marxism triumph over other brands of socialism. The apparently scientific character of Marxism also made it attractive to an age that was enthralled with the progress being made by science.

Great Britain: Fabianism and Early Welfare Programs

Neither Marxism nor any other form of socialism made significant progress in Great Britain, the most advanced industrial society of the day. British trade unions usually supported Liberal Party candidates. In 1892, Keir Hardie became the first independent working man to be elected to Parliament, but the socialist Independent Labour Party, which was founded a year later, attracted little support.

Until 1901, labor took little part in politics. But that year, when the House of Lords removed the legal protection accorded union funds (the Taff Vale decision), the Trades Union Congress responded by launching the Labour Party. In the election of 1906, the new party sent twenty-nine members to Parliament. Trade unionists were not yet advocates of socialism, but they were becoming more militant. There were scores of strikes in the years leading up to the war, and the government assumed a greater role as mediator.

British socialism was primarily the preserve of non-Marxist intellectuals. Britain's most influential socialist group was the Fabian Society. Founded in 1884, it took its name from Q. Fabius Maximus, a Roman general famous for defending Rome by refusing directly to confront Hannibal, a Carthaginian invader. The name symbolized the society's gradualist approach to social reform. Its leading members, Sidney (1859–1947) and Beatrice (1858–1943) Webb, H. G. Wells (1866–1946), Graham Wallas (1858–1932), and George Bernard Shaw (1856–1950), hoped to convince their country of the rational wisdom of socialism. They believed that collective ownership, often at the municipal level, could solve the problems of industry and that the expansion of ownership and state direction of production could be achieved gradually, peacefully, and democratically.

The British government and the major political parties slowly responded to pressures from labor. In 1903, Joseph Chamberlain (1836–1914) split the Conservative Party by waging an unsuccessful tariff-reform campaign intended to finance social reform through higher import duties. After 1906, the Liberal Party, led by Sir Henry Campbell-Bannerman (1836–1908) and by Herbert Asquith (1852–1928) after 1908, pursued a two-pronged policy. Fearful of losing seats in Parliament to the new Labour Party, they restored the former protection of the unions. Then, after 1909, with Chancellor of the Exchequer David Lloyd George (1863–1945) as its guiding light, a Liberal ministry enacted a broad program of social legislation: the establishment of labor exchanges; the regulation of sweatshop trades (tailoring and lacemaking); and the National Insurance Act (1911), which provided unemployment benefits and health care.

Proposals to finance these programs created conflict between the House of Commons and the Conservative-dominated House of Lords. This led to the enactment in 1911 of the Parliament Act, which allowed the Commons to override the legislative veto of the upper chamber. The new taxes and social programs (which were not yet enough to content labor) meant that in Britain, the home of nineteenth-century liberalism, the state was expanding its role in the lives of its citizens.

France: "Opportunism" Rejected

At the turn of the century, Jean Jaurès (1859–1914) and Jules Guesde (1845–1922) led opposing factions of French socialists. Guesde repudiated Jaurès for attempting to work with France's governing ministries. He insisted that socialists could not cooperate with a bourgeois government that they were dedicated to overthrowing. The Dreyfus affair brought the quarrel to a head when, in 1899, Prime Minister René Waldeck-Rousseau (1846–1904) tried to unite Dreyfus's supporters by finding a socialist willing to serve in the French cabinet. Alexander Millerand (1859–1943) accepted the appointment.

Cabinet participation was part of a political strategy that socialists termed "opportunism." In 1904, the Amsterdam Congress of the Second International—a group founded in 1889 to coordinate various national socialist parties and trade unions—condemned opportunism and ordered France's socialists to form a single party. Jaurès acquiesced; by 1914, Socialist Party members were the second-largest group in the Chamber of Deputies. Socialists would not, however, serve in a French cabinet until the Popular Front Government of 1936.

French workers tended to vote socialist, but their unions, unlike those in Great Britain, avoided direct participation in politics. The Confédération Générale du Travail, founded in 1895, saw itself as an alternative to socialist parties. Its leaders embraced the doctrines of *syndicalism*, expounded by Georges Sorel (1847–1922) in *Reflections on Violence* (1908). They believed that the general strike, not the political process, was the tool workers should use to demand reform. Strikes often conflicted with socialist efforts to use the machinery of the state on behalf of workers. Strikes, some of which the government used troops to suppress, were common between 1905 and 1914.

Germany: Social Democrats and Revisionism

The Marxist-dominated German Social Democratic Party, or SPD, was consistently hostile to all nonsocialist governments. The SPD emerged in 1875 from the efforts of Ferdinand Lasalle (1825–1864), a labor agitator who wanted to win a role for the working class in German politics. Since Marxists who opposed reformist politics—particularly Wilhelm Liebknecht (1826–1900) and August Bebel (1840–1913)—helped organize the party, it was, from the start, divided between those who advocated reform and those who trusted only in revolution.

Bismarck, the so-called "Iron Chancellor," opposed socialism. Although no socialists were involved in an 1878 assassination attempt on William I, Bismarck exploited the event to steer laws through the *Reichstag* that suppressed the organization, meetings, newspapers, and other public activities of the SPD. The legislation proved politically counterproductive. From the early 1880s onward, the SPD steadily polled more and more votes in elections to the *Reichstag*.

When repressive laws failed to wean German workers away from socialism, Bismarck designed social welfare legislation to provide a paternalistic, conservative alternative to socialism. In 1883, the German Empire adopted a health insurance measure. A year later, it created accident insurance. In 1889, Bismarck sponsored a plan for old age and disability pensions. Since these programs were funded by contributions from both workers and employers, they constituted a state-organized system of social security that did not require any change in ownership of property or in politics. Germany became the first major industrial nation to enjoy this kind of welfare program.

The Erfurt Program. After Bismarck's forced resignation, Emperor William II (r. 1888–1918) tried to win support from the working class by allowing the antisocialist legislation to expire. The lifting of the repressive laws, which had never prevented members of the SPD from sitting in the *Reichstag*, forced the party to ponder what attitude it ought to assume toward the German Empire.

The SPD's stand (the Erfurt Program of 1891) was formulated by Bebel and by Karl Kautsky (1854–1938). In good Marxist fashion, the party declared its faith in the imminent doom of capitalism and the necessity of socialist ownership of the means of production, but it pledged to pursue these goals through legal political participation, not revolution. Consequently, although in theory the SPD was hostile to the German Empire, in practice it worked within the system.

The SPD's dilemma prompted the most important rethinking within socialist circles of the orthodox Marxist critique of capitalism. Eduard Bernstein (1850–1932), a socialist thinker who had been exposed to Fabianism in Great Britain, questioned Marx's confident prediction that the inadequacies of capitalism would make revolution inevitable. In *Evolutionary Socialism* (1899), Bernstein pointed to developments that did not meet orthodox Marxist expectations: a rising standard of living in Europe and sales of stocks that broadened ownership of capitalist industry. These things increased the size of the middle class instead of forcing it, as Marx had predicted, into the ranks of the proletariat. Moreover, the extension of the franchise to the working class meant that revolution might not be necessary to achieve social change.

Although a heated debate led German socialists to condemn Bernstein's doctrines (dubbed "revisionism"), the SPD pursued a course of action consistent with Bernstein's views. Its trade union members, who were prospering, did not want revolution, and its leaders did not want to provoke the kind of persecution they had experienced under Bismarck. Subsequently, by working for electoral gains, membership expansion, and short-term reform, the SPD succeeded in becoming one of the most important political organizations in imperial Germany.

Russia: Industrial Development and the Birth of Bolshevism

During the last decade of the nineteenth century, Russia entered the industrial age and encountered many of the problems that more advanced nations had experienced fifty or seventy-five years earlier. Alexander III (r. 1881–1894) and his successor, Nicholas II (r. 1894–1917), believed that Russia had to become an industrial power to maintain its international influence. To Sergei Witte (1849–1915), the finance minister appointed in 1892, fell the task of devising a program. He was the epitome of the nineteenth-century modernizer—trusting to planned economic development, protective tariffs, high taxes, the gold standard, efficient management, and the development of heavy industries.

In Russia, as elsewhere, industrialism created considerable social discontent. Landowners resented the profits foreign investors took out of the country. Peasants objected to being taxed to sustain development that did not improve their lives. And a small but significant industrial proletariat protested abysmal working conditions.

Emancipation of the serfs in 1861 had not improved Russian agriculture. Peasants were handicapped by redemption payments, excessive taxes, and falling grain prices. Many owned land communally (through a *mir*, or village) and farmed inefficiently. Many had too little land to support themselves and had to work for the nobility or the *kulaks*, prosperous peasant farmers. To make things worse, between 1860 and 1914, Russia experienced a population explosion: increasing from 50 million to 103 million.

Social discontent motivated the formation of new political parties. The Social Revolutionary Party, founded in 1901, adopted the Populists' agenda of the 1870s: opposition to industrialism and advocacy of an idealized version of the communal life of the Russian peasantry. In 1903, the liberal Constitutional Democratic Party, or Cadets, was formed to work for a regime of ministries, civil liberties, and progressive economic policies maintained by a parliament. The socialist Social Democratic Party appeared in 1898, but its leaders were soon driven into exile.

Lenin's Early Thought and Career. Since Russia had a small working class and no representative institutions, its socialists, unlike socialists elsewhere, despaired of working with the established government. Their commitment to revolution inclined them to a brand of Marxism developed by two exiled leaders: Gregory Plekhanov (1857–1918) and his disciple Vladimir Illich Ulyanov (1870–1924), known as Lenin.

Lenin's father was a high-ranking bureaucrat whose elder son was executed in 1887 for plotting against Alexander III. In 1893, Lenin, while studying in Saint Petersburg, became involved with revolutionary factory workers. He was arrested in 1895 and sent to Siberia. In 1900, he left Russia and spent most of the next seventeen years in Switzerland in the company of the exiled Russian Social Democrats.

Unlike the backward-looking Social Revolutionaries, the Social Democrats were Marxists and modernizers. They favored industrial development, and most believed that Russia had to create a large proletariat before the revolution could begin. Like other socialist groups, they split over the issue of working to reform the system or to overthrow it. Lenin, in *What Is to Be Done?* (1902), condemned any accommodations, such as those practiced by the German SPD. He maintained that revolutionary consciousness would not arise spontaneously from the working class. Only a small, tightly organized, elite party could sustain adequate revolutionary fervor and resist penetration by police spies. He rejected Kautsky's claim that revolution was inevitable and Bernstein's faith that it would arrive democratically. For Lenin, the social transformation Marx predicted would be the work of a small party of professional revolutionaries, not the proletariat.

In 1903, at its London Congress, the Russian Social Democratic Party split. Lenin emerged the leader of a very slim majority of its members, a faction calling itself the *Bolsheviks* ("majority"). Their more moderate opponents were the *Mensheviks* ("minority"). In 1912, the Bolsheviks organized separately.

In 1905, Lenin published a program for revolution in Russia: *Two Tactics of Social Democracy in the Bourgeois-Democratic Revolution*. He grasped better than any other revolutionary the profound discontent in the Russian countryside and argued for an alliance between workers and peasants to overthrow the tsarist regime. In November 1917, his Bolsheviks seized power, but only after other political forces had toppled the government.

The Premature Revolution of 1905. Industrialization, not Lenin, was the source of Tsar Nicholas II's problems. In 1903, he dismissed Witte from office. In 1904, he declared war on Japan, hoping to generate a wave of patriotism. Instead, Russia was defeated, and a political crisis ensued. On "Bloody Sunday" (January 22, 1905), the tsar's troops fired into a crowd of workers in Saint Petersburg who were trying to present a petition asking the tsar to improve industrial conditions.

The incident sparked revolutionary disturbances throughout Russia: sailors mutinied, peasants revolted, the tsar's uncle was assassinated, the liberal Constitutional Democratic Party demanded political reform, students staged strikes, and Social Revolutionaries and Social Democrats stirred up urban workers. Early in October 1905, strikes broke out in Saint Petersburg, and worker groups, called *soviets*, took control of the city. Nicholas II responded with the October Manifesto, a pledge to institute constitutional government in Russia.

Early in 1906, Nicholas II announced elections for a bicameral representative body, the Duma, but he reserved to himself ministerial appointments, financial policy, military matters, and foreign affairs. When the April elections returned a very radical assembly, the tsar again discharged Witte, whom he had recalled, and chose a new adviser, P. A. Stolypin (1862–1911). After only four months, Stolypin persuaded him to dissolve the Duma. A new assembly, which was elected in February 1907, lasted only into June. By limiting the

In this photograph taken in 1895, Lenin sits at the table among a group of other young Russian radicals from Saint Petersburg. [The Bettmann Archive]

franchise, the government finally won election of a more pliable third Duma in late 1907.

Since Nicholas II appeared to have recaptured much of the ground he had conceded, Stolypin set about repressing rebellion and rallying support from property owners. In November 1906, the government canceled payments for land that peasants still owed under the terms of the Emancipation Act of 1861. Peasants were encouraged to assume individual management of their holdings and to abandon the communal system associated with the *mirs*. This, combined with a program offering instruction in farming methods, helped stimulate agricultural production. Moderates approved of the land measures, and many people were eager to compromise with the government to avoid further revolutionary disturbances.

When the unpopular Stolypin was assassinated in 1911, Nicholas II failed to find a competent adviser to replace him. The situation at court was complicated by the increasing influence of Grigory Efimovich Rasputin (1871?–1916), a strange, uncouth monk who claimed to be able to heal the tsar's hemophilic heir. As social discontents demanded, and conservatives rejected, further liberal reforms, the domestic situation became increasingly unmanageable. The tsar again began to hope that a bold move on the diplomatic front might rally the popular support he so desperately needed.

Between 1860 and 1914, two apparently contradictory developments occurred in European social life: the lifestyle of the property-owning urban middle classes became the model to which much of society aspired, while socialists and labor unions demanded a broader redistribution of property.

The working class was not alone in seeking change. Women began to de-

mand a political role and to protest the gender inequalities embedded in law and family life. Their demands, as much as the theories of socialists, would in time raise questions about the adequacy of the much admired late-nineteenth-century middle-class lifestyle.

～ Review Questions

1. How was European society transformed by the second Industrial Revolution? What new industries developed? Which do you think had the greatest impact in the twentieth century? How do you account for European economic difficulties in the second half of the nineteenth century?

2. What were living conditions like in European cities during the late nineteenth century? Why were European cities redesigned during this period? How were they redesigned? Why were housing and health key issues for urban reform?

3. What was the status of European women in the second half of the nineteenth century? Why did they grow discontented with their lot? What factors led to change? To what extent had they improved their position by 1914? What tactics did they use in effecting change? Was the emancipation of women inevitable? How did women approach their situation differently from country to country?

4. What reforms did the emancipation of Jews take in the nineteenth century?

5. What was the status of the proletariat in 1860? Had it improved by 1914? What caused the growth in trade unions and organized mass political parties? Why did socialist parties debate "opportunism" and "revisionism"?

6. How important was industrialism for Russia? Were the tsars wise to attempt to modernize their country? Would they have been better off leaving it as it was? How did Lenin's view of socialism differ from that of the socialists in western Europe?

～ Suggested Readings

I. M. Aronson, *Troubled Waters: The Origins of the 1881 Anti-Jewish Pogroms in Russia* (1990). The best discussion of this subject.

L. R. Berlanstein, *The Working People of Paris, 1871–1914* (1985). Interesting and comprehensive.

D. Blackbourn and G. Eley, *The Peculiarities of German History: Bourgeois Society and Politics in Nineteenth-Century Germany* (1985). An important and probing study.

C. M. Cipolla, *The Economic History of World Population* (1962). A basic introduction.

D. F. Good, *The Economic Rise of the Hapsburg Empire, 1750–1914* (1985). The best available study.

S. C. Hause, *Women's Suffrage and Social Politics in the French Third Republic* (1984). A wide-ranging examination of the question.

G. Himmelfarb, *Poverty and Compassion: The Moral Imagination of the Late Victorians* (1991). The best examination of late Victorian social thought.

E. J. Hobsbawm, *The Age of Capital* (1975). Explores the consolidation of middle-class life after 1850.

S. S. Holton, *Feminism and Democracy: Women's Suffrage and Reform Politics in Britian, 1900–1918* (1986). An excellent treatment of the subject.

K. H. Jarausch, *Students, Society, and Politics in Imperial Germany: The Rise of Academic Illiberalism* (1982). The reaction of the academic community to the threat of socialism.

S. Kern, *The Culture of Time and Space, 1880–1918* (1983). A lively discussion of the impact of the new technology.

S. Kern, *The Culture of Love: Victorians to Moderns* (1992). A major discussion of the manner in which Europeans have thought and behaved in regard to love, family, and sexuality.

D. Landes, *The Unbound Prometheus: Technological Change and Industrial Development in Western Europe from 1750 to the Present* (1969). Includes excellent discussions of late-nineteenth-century development.

G. L. Moose, *German Jews Beyond Judaism* (1985). Sensitive essays exploring the relationship of Jews to German culture in the nineteenth and early twentieth centuries.

P. G. Nord, *Paris Shopkeepers and the Politics of Resentment* (1986). An examination of the political attitudes of Paris shopkeepers in the wake of the redesign of the city.

D. Olsen, *The City as a Work of Art: London, Paris, Vienna* (1986). A splendidly illustrated survey of nineteenth-century urban growth and design.

D. H. Pinkney, *Napoleon III and the Rebuilding of Paris* (1958). A classic study.

H. Rogger, *Russia in the Age of Modernization and Revolution, 1881–1917* (1983). The best synthesis of the period.

C. E. Schorske, *German Social Democracy, 1905–1917* (1955). A brilliant study of the difficulties of the Social Democrats under the empire.

B. G. Smith, *Ladies of the Leisure Class: The Bourgeoises of Northern France in the Nineteenth Century* (1981). Emphasizes the importance of the reproductive role of women.

N. Stone, *Europe Transformed* (1984). A sweeping survey that emphasizes the difficulties of late-nineteenth-century liberalism.

F. M. L. Thompson, *The Rise of Respectable Society: A Social History of Victorian Britain, 1830–1900* (1988). A major survey.

A. B. Ulam, *The Bolsheviks: The Intellectual and Political History of the Triumph of Communism in Russia* (1965). Early chapters discuss prewar developments and the formation of Lenin's doctrines.

A. M. Verner, *The Crisis of Russian Autocracy: Nicholas II and the 1905 Revolution* (1990). A major study of this crucial event.

E. Weber, *Peasants into Frenchmen: The Modernization of Rural France, 1870–1914* (1976). An important and fascinating work on the transformation of French peasants into self-conscious citizens of the nation-state.

25

The Birth of Modern European Thought

KEY TOPICS IN THIS CHAPTER

~ The dominance of science in the thought of the second half of the nineteenth century

~ The conflict of church and state over education

~ The effect of modernism, psychoanalysis, and the revolution in physics on intellectual life

~ Racism and the resurgence of anti-Semitism

~ Late-nineteenth- and early-twentieth-century developments in feminism

---

The political systems, industrialized economies, and middle-class lifestyles that emerged in the late nineteenth century were accompanied by intellectual developments shaping a "modern" mind. These were rooted in the Enlightenment (which contributed confidence in reason and science and a tolerant, cosmopolitan outlook) and the Romantic movement (which fostered respect for feeling, imagination, artistic insight, and the value of individuals). Most of the West's traditional assumptions about nature, religion, and social life were subjected to radical re-examination. As a result, at the turn of the century, European intellectuals were more daring than ever before, but less certain about where their work *might lead. Fading confidence in the reliability of traditional points of view helped some disadvantaged groups, like women, win liberating social reforms.*

∽ The New Reading Public

Advances in Primary Education

In 1850, 50 percent of Europeans were illiterate, and many of those who technically could read and write did so poorly. Thanks to state-financed education, that changed. And during the next half-century, Europe for the first time developed a mass reading public. Hungary led the way, providing elementary education in 1868; Britain, in 1870; Switzerland, in 1874; Italy, in 1877; and France, between 1878 and 1881. Prussia's superior educational system was extended in various ways throughout the German Empire after 1871. By 1900, the literacy rate in Britain, France, Belgium, the Netherlands, Germany, and Scandinavia was 85 percent. Italy, Spain, Russia, Austria-Hungary, and the Balkans achieved rates of only 30 to 60 percent.

The educational crusade embodied the Enlightenment rationalist faith that right knowledge would lead to right action. Both liberals and conservatives believed that literacy would enable newly enfranchised voters to use political power responsibly and that it would help the poor help themselves by making them a more productive labor force. Once the masses were given a taste for education—and realized its benefits—demands for schooling increased. Having created systems of primary education, the major nations, during the World War I era, began to provide secondary education. A generation later, democratic university instruction was under development.

Reading Material for the Mass Audience

Advances in technology lowered publication costs just as the expanding literate population developed an appetite for new kinds of reading materials. The number of monthly and quarterly journals designed for particular groups of subscribers increased. Cheap mass-circulation newspapers, such as *Le Petit Journal* of Paris and the *Daily Mail* and *Daily Express* of London, enjoyed their first heyday.

Because many of the new readers were marginally literate and relatively unsophisticated, the materials produced for them were often mediocre. Newspapers, in particular, exploited stories of sensational crimes and political scandals and carried pages of advertising that made extravagant, unsubstantiated claims. Despite the low level of public taste, the new literacy was the intellectual equivalent of the railroad and the steamship. It enabled people to explore new intellectual territory and, on their own initiative, to enhance their skills and deepen their understandings. Governments and political leaders quickly discovered the power of newspaper editorials to influence voters.

⌒ Science at Midcentury

Comte, Positivism, and the Prestige of Science

During the first half of the nineteenth century, science gained ground as the model for all human knowledge. The link between science and technology in the Second Industrial Revolution made the public more aware of science than ever before. The dominant worldview remained that of Newton: a rational universe that operated according to observable mechanical principles.

Auguste Comte (1798–1857), building on the Enlightenment, claimed that science was the culmination of human intellectual development. In *The Positive Philosophy* (1830–1842), Comte argued that human understanding evolved in three stages: the theological (where natural events are credited to the action of spiritual beings), the metaphysical (where abstract principles, not personified entities, are thought to control nature), and the positive (where natural phenomena are explained by referring them to each other, not to unobservable principles). Comte believed that physical science had entered the positive stage first and that other fields would eventually follow. His argument helped establish the idea that knowledge of all subjects must resemble the kind of knowledge common to the natural sciences. Comte is remembered, in particular, as the father of sociology, for he predicted that things like the laws of physics would be found to explain social behavior.

During the third quarter of the century, talk emerged of a religion of science that would explain all nature without resort to supernaturalism. Men such as Thomas Henry Huxley (1825–1895) in Britain and Ernst Haeckel (1834–1919) in Germany interpreted scientific advances for the general public, while proclaiming the faith that science held the answer to the questions of life. They advocated government support of scientific research and inclusion of science in the curricula of schools and universities.

Darwin's Theory of Natural Selection

In 1859, Charles Darwin (1809–1882) published *The Origin of Species*. The book is one of the seminal works of Western thought, the equivalent in biology of Newton's contribution to physics. Darwin's work has been much misunderstood. He did not originate the concept of evolution, which had been discussed widely before his time. His contribution was a theory proposing a mechanical process to explain how evolution took place: the principle of natural selection. Working independently, his contemporary, Alfred Russel Wallace (1823–1913), came up with the same idea.

Building on one of Malthus's insights, Darwin and Wallace contended that more organisms are created than can survive in their environment. Those

In two works of seminal importance, The Origin of Species *(1859) and* The Descent of Man *(1871), Charles Darwin enunciated the theory of evolution by natural selection and applied that theory to human beings. The result was a storm of controversy that affected not only biology but also religion, philosophy, sociology, and even politics.* [Bildarchiv Preussischer Kulturbesitz]

that have a unique trait that gives them a marginal advantage in the struggle for existence change the nature of their species by reproducing more successfully than their competitors. Since the fittest survive to pass on their unique characteristics, a mechanistic process of "natural selection," not divine choice, shapes the design of living things. Neither Darwin nor anyone else at the time could explain the origin of the chance variations that gave certain individuals advantages over others of their species. Only after 1900—when work on heredity by an Austrian monk, Gregor Mendel (1822–1884), began to circulate—did the mystery of those variations begin to be unraveled.

The theory of evolution by natural selection removed a need for a guiding purpose in nature. It explained a species' traits as the result of its past struggles with the environment, not a deity's plan for its destiny. It called into question a literal interpretation of the biblical narrative of Creation and undermined the deistic argument for God as the author of the universe's design. No God was needed if the universe had no design. And if there was no design, no fixity in nature—nothing but flux and change—might the same thing not also be true of society, values, customs, and beliefs? What was truth in such a world?

In 1871, Darwin published *The Descent of Man* and spelled out the implications of natural selection for the human species. He contended that not only the human frame, but human conscience and religious intuition evolved naturalistically as part of a survival strategy. No God was needed to provide

Darwin Defends a Mechanistic View of Nature

In the closing paragraphs of The Origin of Species *(1859), Charles Darwin contrasted the view of nature he championed with that of his opponents. He argued that an interpretation of organic nature based on mechanistic laws was actually nobler than an interpretation based on divine creation. In the second edition, however, Darwin added the term "Creator" to these paragraphs.*

~ Why does Darwin believe that a mechanistic explanation for creation suggests no less dignity for human beings than an act of special creation by God? How does the insertion of the term "Creator" change this passage? What is the grandeur that Darwin finds in his view of life?

Authors of the highest eminence seem to be fully satisfied with the view that each species has been independently created. To my mind it accords better with what we know of the laws impressed on matter by the Creator, that the production and extinction of the past and present inhabitants of the world should have been due to secondary causes, like those determining the birth and death of the individual. When I view all beings not as special creations, but as the lineal descendants of some few beings which lived long before the first bed of the Cambrian [geological] system was deposited, they seem to me to become ennobled. . . .

It is interesting to contemplate a tangled bank, clothed with many plants of many kinds, with birds singing on the bushes, with various insects flitting about, and with worms crawling through the damp earth, and to reflect that these elaborately constructed forms, so different from each other, and dependent upon each other in so complex a manner, have all been produced by laws acting around us. These laws, taken in the largest sense, being Growth with Reproduction; Inheritance which is almost implied by reproduction; Variability from the indirect and direct action of the conditions of life, and from use and disuse: a Ratio of Increase so high as to lead to a Struggle for Life, and as a consequence to Natural Selection, entailing Divergence of Character and the Extinction of less-improved forms. Thus, from the war of nature, from famine and death, the most exalted object which we are capable of conceiving, namely the production of the higher animals, directly follows. There is grandeur in this view of life, with its several powers, having been originally breathed by the Creator into a few forms or into one; and that, whilst this planet has gone cycling on according to the fixed law of gravity, from so simple a beginning endless forms most beautiful and most wonderful have been, and are being evolved.

Charles Darwin, The Origin of Species and the Descent of Man *(New York: Modern Library, n.d.), pp. 373–374.*

an image for humanity. Not since Copernicus had removed the earth from the center of the universe had human pride received so sharp a blow. With so much at stake, Darwin's theories were slow to win support. The scientific community did not tilt in their favor until the 1920s and 1930s, when developments in modern genetics began to solve some of their puzzles.

Science and Ethics

Debates about *Darwinism* inevitably raised questions about the implications for society of the kind of science it represented. The phrase "survival of the fittest," which Darwin used, was coined earlier by classical economists to affirm the healthiness of competition. Some philosophers hastened to suggest that it might also explain ethics and human relationships.

A British philosopher, Herbert Spencer (1820–1903), was the most famous thinker to apply evolutionary analogies to ethics. He advocated individualism and asserted that competition was essential if society was to progress. The strong had a kind of ethical imperative to subdue the weak, for attempts to spare the weak only served, by perpetuating their inferior traits, to undermine the species. Spencer's arguments were used to justify neglect of the poor and the working class, exploitation of colonial peoples, and aggressive competition among nations.

Social Darwinism of this kind came close to claiming that might makes right, but Thomas Henry Huxley (1825–1895), a vigorous defender of Darwin's, rejected it. He argued that the process of evolution in the physical world was at odds with the development of ethical awareness in human beings. The struggle in physical nature was not the same as the struggle within human nature. Many admirers and practitioners of science disagreed with him. During the second half of the century, they confidently spoke as if they had discovered nearly all that might be discovered and as if the future would do nothing but refine and extend their insights. They expected every human thought, sooner or later, to conform to their current understanding of science.

∾ Christianity and the Church Under Siege

As might be expected from the intellectual attitudes that were in the ascendancy, the nineteenth century was one of the most difficult for organized Christianity. Many intellectuals left the faith. Nation-states, under liberal leadership, curtailed the influence of the church. The expansion and migration of population and the growth of cities challenged traditional forms of ecclesiastical organization. Yet the churches, Protestant and Catholic, made considerable headway among the masses.

Intellectual Skepticism

History. The *philosophes* of the Enlightenment had delighted in pointing out contradictions in the Bible. The historical scholarship of the nineteenth century brought intellectual rigor to the analysis of these texts. In 1835, David Friedrich Strauss (1808–1874) published a *Life of Jesus* that questioned whether the Bible contained any genuinely historical information about Jesus. Strauss explained the story of Jesus as a myth reflecting the aspirations of the people of first-century Palestine.

During the second half of the century, Julius Wellhausen (1844–1918) in Germany, Ernst Renan (1823–1892) in France, and William Robertson Smith (1847–1894) in Great Britain showed how human authors had written and revised various books of the Bible with the problems of the societies in which they lived in mind. Like the Homeric epics, the Bible reflected the concerns of primitive human communities. The doubt these scholars cast on the literal truth of the Bible as a text dictated by God caused a crisis of faith for many literate individuals.

Science. Enlightenment theologians had tried to ground the Christian religion in science, but the scientific discoveries of the nineteenth century tended to undermine faith. Darwin's theory cast doubt on the doctrine of the Creation. The geology of Charles Lyell (1797–1875) suggested that the earth was much older than the biblical records contended. By finding natural causes for floods, mountains, and valleys, Lyell also removed the miraculous hand of God from the physical processes shaping the earth. Anthropologists, psychologists, and sociologists suggested that religious sentiments were nothing but natural phenomena.

Morality. Setting questions of historical validity and science aside, even the worth of Christianity as a moral force came in question. The colorful behavior of certain biblical figures, particularly from the Old Testament, had long embarrassed Christians. But now God Himself was directly criticized. Liberals considered the Old Testament depiction of God as whimsical and vindictive to be unworthy of the progressive, tolerant, rational values that they associated with divinity. The morality of the New Testament view of God—as a being who would sacrifice for His own satisfaction the only perfect man ever to walk the earth—was similarly suspect.

During the last quarter of the century, a different kind of attack was made on Christian ethics. Friedrich Nietzsche (1844–1900), a German philosopher, described Christianity as a religion for sheep—a glorification of weakness rather than the vigor of a full-blooded human life. Christianity was said to demand useless, debilitating sacrifices of the flesh and spirit and not to encourage heroic living.

Theological skepticism was confined largely to the upper levels of educated society, but it cost Christianity much of its intellectual respectability. Fewer educated people joined the clergy, and many were content to lead their lives with little or no reference to organized Christianity.

Increasing secularism—particularly of urban life—was as harmful to faith as direct attacks on it. Cities expanded faster than ecclesiastical institutions and services. Whole generations of the urban poor grew up with little or no experience of the church or training in Christian doctrine.

Conflict of Church and State

For centuries, religious orders or denominations had provided most of Europe's schools. But the governments of the major nations of the late nineteenth century were secular organizations that were often suspicious or resentful of the church. Consequently, a heated debate over religious education erupted in the last quarter of the century.

Great Britain. Great Britain's Education Act of 1870 provided for the construction of state-supported schools run by elected school boards in areas where religious organizations had failed to provide satisfactory educational opportunities. Problems had been created by intense local hostility among competing religious groups. They cooperated only to oppose improvements in education that increased the costs of their schools. In 1902, another Education Act attempted to ensure the quality of all schools by providing state support for and by imposing the same educational standards on both religious and nonreligious institutions.

France. The church-state conflict in Britain was far less intense than in France. France had a dual system of Catholic and public schools, but the Falloux Law of 1850 mandated Catholic religious instruction (under the tutelage of a local priest) in public schools. Increasing hostility between the Third Republic and the conservative clergy of the French Catholic church led to the enactment, between 1878 and 1886, of educational reforms sponsored by Jules Ferry (1832–1893). The Ferry Laws increased the number of public schools, replaced their religious instruction with civic training, and barred members of religious orders from their faculties. After the Dreyfus affair, the radical government of Pierre Waldeck-Rousseau (1846–1904) punished the French clergy for their reactionary politics by suppressing the religious orders; in 1905, the termination of the Napoleonic Concordat separated church and state.

Germany. The most extreme example of church-state conflict was the *Kulturkampf* ("cultural struggle") that Bismarck waged in Germany during the 1870s. When Germany was unified, its Catholic hierarchy wanted freedom for the churches guaranteed in the constitution. Bismarck originally left the matter to the discretion of each federal state, but he soon concluded that the Roman Catholic Church and the Catholic Center Party were a threat to the unity of the German Empire. In 1870 and 1871, he brought Prussia's educational system under state management and forbade clergy (Catholic and Protestant) oversight of schools.

Secularization of education began a concerted attack on the independence of Germany's Catholic church. The May Laws of 1873, which applied to Prussia but not to the German Empire at large, transferred to the state the disciplinary power over the clergy traditionally exercised by the pope and the church. Priests were required to be educated in Germany, to pass state examinations, and to seek state ratification for their appointments to church offices. When many of the clergy refused to obey these laws, Bismarck used police force. In 1876, he either arrested or drove from Prussia all the Catholic bishops. This was the greatest blunder of his career. Persecution created martyrs and increased resistance. By the end of the 1870s, the chancellor had abandoned his attack. He had gained state control of education and civil laws governing marriage, but at the price of provoking long-lasting resentment of the German state among Catholics.

Areas of Religious Revival

The intense hostility of religion's enemies resulted in part from its persistent vitality. The second half of the nineteenth century witnessed the final great effort to Christianize Europe. In Great Britain, both the Anglican church and the nonconformist denominations grew considerably. In Ireland, the 1870s saw a widespread Catholic devotional revival. France's defeat by Prussia resulted in mass pilgrimages by penitents who believed that their sins had caused their nation's defeat. The famous cult of the miracle of Lourdes grew during these years.

Churches of all denominations gave increased attention to the urban poor. Their evangelism was well organized, well led, and well financed. It fell short, not from want of effort, but because the population of Europe outstripped the resources of the churches.

The Roman Catholic Church and the Modern World

The papacy struggled to find a course through the turmoil of a period marked by skepticism and religious revival. The liberal sympathies of Pope Pius IX (r. 1846–1878) vanished on the night in November 1848 when he fled the revolution that tried to restore the Roman Republic. Further embittered by the process of Italian unification, he waged a counteroffensive against liberalism. In 1864, he issued the *Syllabus of Errors*, a condemnation of political liberalism and modern thought that declared that the Roman Catholic faith was incompatible with contemporary science, philosophy, and politics. In 1869, he summoned the First Vatican Council, and a year later, despite opposition from numerous bishops, he promulgated the doctrine of papal infallibility. His assertion that in matters of faith and morals the pope's pronouncements could not be questioned was the most sweeping claim ever made for monarchical papal authority.

Leo XIII (r. 1878–1903), Pius IX's successor, tried to reach an accommodation with the modern age and to address its great social questions. In the philosophical tradition of Thomas Aquinas (1225–1274), he believed that the claims of faith and reason could be reconciled. His encyclicals of 1885 and 1890 permitted Catholics to participate in the politics of liberal states. His most important encyclical, *Rerum Novarum* (1891), defended private property, religious education, and religious control of marriage law. It condemned socialism and Marxism, while affirming the right of workers to organize unions and to demand just treatment from employers. He supported laws and regulations to protect labor and urged that modern society pursue corporate goals benefiting all citizens. He hoped that a corporate model derived from medieval social organization would provide an alternative to both socialism and unrestrained capitalism. Leo XIII's endorsement of Catholic participation in politics led to the establishment of democratic Catholic parties and Catholic trade unions throughout Europe.

Pius X (r. 1903–1914), who has been proclaimed a saint, was not enthusiastic about Leo XIII's social policies, and he set the church squarely against the intellectual currents of his day. He urged the rejection of modern thought and the revival of traditional devotional life. In 1910, he required all priests to take an oath to oppose Catholic Modernism, a movement that accepted the results of modern textual criticism of the Bible.

∾ Toward a Twentieth-Century Frame of Mind

During the last quarter of the nineteenth century and the first decade of the twentieth century, the kind of fundamental reassessment that Darwin's work made necessary in biology began to occur in other disciplines. New concepts challenged the presuppositions of mid-nineteenth-century science, rationalism, liberalism, and bourgeois morality.

Science: The Revolution in Physics

By the late 1870s, some members of the scientific community were voicing concern about the excessive realism of traditional science. They warned that the mechanistic models of Newtonian physics—solid atoms moving in absolute time and space—were only models, not definitive descriptions of reality.

Ernst Mach (1838–1916), in *The Science of Mechanics* (1883), urged scientists to think of their concepts as reports not about the physical world, but about their sensations as observers. All that investigators can know, he warned, are their sensations, not the physical realities that produce these sensations. Henri Poincaré (1854–1912), a French scientist, agreed. He claimed that scientific concepts were hypothetical constructs made by the human mind, not descriptions equivalent to the true state of nature. By World War I, few scientists believed any longer that they could portray the "truth" about physical reality. Their task was to record observations and devise useful hypothetical or symbolic models of nature.

X-rays and Radiation. Laboratory work soon confirmed the provisional nature of scientific knowledge. In December 1895, Wilhelm Roentgen (1845–1923) announced the discovery of X-rays, a form of energy that penetrated various opaque materials. When major steps in the exploration of radioactivity followed within months of the publication of his paper, the comfortably "complete" explanation nineteenth-century physicists thought they had for the world vanished.

In 1896, Henri Becquerel (1852–1908), building on Roentgen's work, discovered that uranium emitted a form of energy resembling the X-ray. A year later, J. J. Thomson (1856–1940), of Cambridge University's Cavendish Laboratory, formulated the theory of the electron. The interior of the supposedly indivisible atom suddenly became a new frontier for human exploration. In 1902, Ernest Rutherford (1871–1937), who had been Thomson's assistant, suggested that radiation was caused by the disintegration of atoms of certain materials and speculated that immense stores of energy were present within atoms.

Theories of Quantum Energy, Relativity, and Uncertainty. The discovery of radioactivity was followed by revolutionary theories that made the certainties trusted by the previous generation of physicists problematical. In 1900, Max Planck (1858–1947) articulated a quantum theory of energy, which describes energy as a series of discrete quantities or packets rather than a continuous stream. In 1905, Albert Einstein (1879–1955) published his first epoch-making papers on relativity. He contended that time and space exist as a combined continuum whose measurement depends as much on the observer as on the entities being measured. In 1927, Werner Heisenberg (1901–1976) stated the uncertainty principle. It postulated that the behavior of subatomic particles is a matter of statistical probability—that it cannot be described with the certainty of a cause-and-effect encounter between solid objects.

The mathematical complexity that substantiates the theories of modern physics makes it impossible for most people to comprehend much science. But the highly visible transformation that science—applied as technology—has worked in daily life has made scientists the best supported and most respected group among Western intellectuals.

Literature: Realism and Naturalism

Between 1850 and 1914, the moral certainties of learned and middle-class Europeans underwent modifications no less radical than their concepts of the physical universe. The *realist* movement in literature tried to observe and describe human beings with scientific objectivity. It rejected the Romantic idealization of nature, poverty, love, and polite society, and portrayed the hypocrisy, the physical and psychic brutality, and the dullness that underlay bourgeois life.

In the preceding generation, writers like Charles Dickens (1812–1870) and Honoré de Balzac (1799–1850) had vividly depicted the cruelty of industrialized societies focused simply on the pursuit of money. Authors such as George Eliot (born Mary Ann Evans) (1819–1880) had paid close attention to the details of their scenes and characters. There had always been room, however, in the works of this period for imagination, fancy, and artistry—and a hope that the world could be improved by human efforts and the application of Christian values. The major figures of late-century realism were less certain that a better life was possible. They saw human beings as animals, subject to passions, to Marx's materialistic determinism, and to the pressures of Darwin's struggle for survival. Society itself seemed designed to perpetuate evil.

Flaubert and Zola. The novel that signaled the advent of realism was *Madame Bovary* (1856), by Gustave Flaubert (1821–1880). It is a story of colorless provincial life and a woman's hapless search for love within and beyond her marriage. It views human existence as devoid of heroism, purpose, or even simple civility.

Émile Zola (1840–1902) articulated the rationale for literary realism. He asserted that human events were as much the products of determinism as events in the physical world and that, therefore, writers should observe and report the characters and actions in their novels as scientists relate the course of laboratory experiments. Zola suggested that literature model itself on medical texts such as Claude Bernard's (1813–1878) *An Introduction to the Study of Experimental Medicine* (1865).

Ibsen and Shaw. The Norwegian playwright Henrik Ibsen (1828–1906) wrote stark, unsentimental dramas depicting crises in domestic life. His intent was to peek beneath the cloak of respectability that middle-class morality tried to drape over the family. His most famous play, *A Doll's House* (1879), describes the awakening of Nora, the spouse of a narrow-minded middle-class man who will not grant her any independence of character or thought. The play ends as she comprehends her situation and leaves him, slamming the door behind her. In *Ghosts* (1881), a respectable middle-class woman must deal with the shame and guilt of passing syphilis, unknowingly contracted from her husband, to her son.

George Bernard Shaw (1856–1950), an Irish playwright who spent most of his life in England, was one of Ibsen's greatest admirers and imitators. His *Mrs. Warren's Profession* (1893) was long censored in England for its blunt treatment of prostitution. In *Arms and the Man* (1894) and *Man and Superman* (1903), Shaw heaped scorn on the Romantic ideals of love and war. In *Androcles and the Lion* (1913), he pilloried Christianity. Shaw made sure that no one missed the point of his plays by attaching long prefaces to them to spell out the social criticism they intended.

Advocates of realism believed that artists ought to portray reality and the commonplace. By dissecting the "real" world and refusing to let public opinion dictate what they wrote, they attempted to change the moral perception of the good life. By forcing audiences to consider unmentionable things, they sought to strip away the veneer of hypocrisy that prevented discussion of important issues. By destroying social and moral illusions, they hoped to compel the public to confront reality. Few, however, of the realist writers who vividly described problems suggested solutions to them. The public was stripped of old values, but not offered new ones.

Modernism

Beginning in the 1870s, a new movement emerged to shape Western arts: *modernism.* Like realism, modernism criticized middle-class society and traditional morality. But modernism's concern was not social reform as much as aesthetics—the production of an artistic experience for its own sake.

In all the arts, modernists abandoned traditional canons of beauty and tried to create new forms. (Many observers ridiculed the new forms as formless.) Modernists also believed that each of the arts should influence the others. Painters gave pictures musical titles: for example, James Abbott McNeil Whistler's (1834–1903) "Nocturnes." Musicians drew material from many sources. Igor Stravinsky's (1882–1971) notorious ballet, *The Rite of Spring* (1913), combined jazz rhythms, dissonance, and anthropological theory. Pablo Picasso (1881–1973) and other artists were inspired by primitive masks they saw in anthropological museums to create the "cubist" style. Cubist paintings simultaneously viewed objects from a variety of angles. England's practitioners of "New Sculpture" mixed materials. Some rejected traditional forms entirely. For all these artists, the immediate aesthetic experience of a work of art overrode all other concerns.

Among the chief proponents of modernism in England were the members of the Bloomsbury Group: authors Virginia (1882–1941) and Leonard Woolf (1880–1969), artists Vanessa Bell (1879–1961) and Duncan Grant (1885–1978), historian and literary critic Lytton Strachey (1880–1932), and economist John Maynard Keynes (1883–1946). Bloomsbury was determined to

Virginia Woolf charted the changing sentiments of a world with most of the nineteenth-century social and moral certainties removed. In A Room of One's Own, *she also challenged some of the received notions of feminist thought, asking whether women writers should bring to their work any separate qualities they possessed as women, and concluding that men and women writers should strive to share each other's sensibilities. [Hulton/Deutsch Collection Limited]*

expose the inadequacy of what it regarded as "Victorian" values, particularly an allegedly repressive Victorian sexual morality.

Strachey, in *Eminent Victorians,* produced a series of biographical sketches less to write history than to heap contempt on famous Victorians. Grant and Bell followed the lead of modernist continental artists. Keynes challenged nineteenth-century economic theory. But no one charted the changing sensibilities of the time with more care and eloquence than Virginia Woolf. Her novels *Mrs. Dalloway* (1925) and *To the Lighthouse* (1927) portrayed a world that had lost most of the social and moral certainties of the nineteenth century.

Continental literary modernism is well illustrated by Marcel Proust (1871–1922). His seven-volume novel, *In Search of Time Past* (issued from 1913 to 1927), used a stream-of-consciousness format that allowed him to explore memories. He would concentrate on a single experience or object and then allow his mind to wander through all the thoughts it evoked. Germany's Thomas Mann (1875–1955) wrote a series of novels—including *Buddenbrooks* (1924) and *The Magic Mountain* (1927)—to explore the social experience of middle-class Germans as they attempted to come to terms with the intellectual heritage of the nineteenth century. In *Ulysses* (1922), James Joyce (1882–1941), an Irish author who spent much of his life on the continent, wholly transformed both the novel and the structure of the paragraph.

Literary modernism flourished in the atmosphere of turmoil and social dislocation created by World War I. The war destroyed many of the political and social systems modernism opposed, and, after war's appalling violence, readers were much less shocked by anything artists could do or say.

Friedrich Nietzsche and the Revolt Against Reason

The legacy of the Enlightenment had been supreme confidence in the power of reason, but, during the second half of the nineteenth century, philosophers began to argue that rational thought had severe limitations. Friedrich Nietzsche (1844–1900), a German philologist, was the most inflammatory of these thinkers. He wanted to tear away the masks of respectable life, but also to discover how human beings made these masks.

In *The Birth of Tragedy* (1872), Nietzsche claimed that the nonrational aspects of human nature were as important and noble as the rational. He insisted that instinct and ecstasy were vital functions and that to limit the human to the rational was to diminish it. In Nietzsche's view, the strength that produced heroes and great artists sprang from something beyond reason. In later works, such as the prose poem *Thus Spake Zarathustra* (1883), Nietzsche criticized democracy and Christianity for empowering the mediocrity of the sheepish masses. He proclaimed the death of God and the rise of the "Overman" *(übermensch),* the embodiment of a heroic humanity free to seek its own fulfillment without illusions. The term was often misunderstood as a reference to a superman or super race, but Nietzsche was no racist or anti-Semite. He idealized a heroism he associated with the Greeks of the Homeric age, a people not yet exposed to the emasculating influence of Christianity and bourgeois morality.

Two of Nietzsche's most profound works, *Beyond Good and Evil* (1886) and *The Genealogy of Morals* (1887), explore the idea that morality is a human convention that has no grounding in external reality. Good and evil, he claimed, do not exist in the world. They are human projections onto the world. Human beings have to forge from their own inner will the truth and values that are to exist in their world. Nietzsche did not condemn morality, but challenged human beings to inquire into its worth and purpose. He urged them to reject the values of Christianity, utilitarianism, and middle-class respectability because he believed they were life-denying. He insisted that people could, if they wanted, create a new moral order based on life-affirming values: pride, assertiveness, and strength.

The Birth of Psychoanalysis

All the major figures of late-nineteenth-century science, art, and philosophy were driven to probe beneath the surfaces of things—of atoms, of reason, of codes of respectability, and of human relationships. Their work dispelled smugness and complacency, but it also undercut self-confidence; such was the effect of psychoanalysis.

Development of Freud's Theories. Sigmund Freud (1856–1939), the founder of psychoanalysis, was the son of an Austrian Jewish family. In 1886, he opened a medical practice in Vienna, where he remained until driven out by the Nazis in 1938. Freud's earliest interests were psychic disorders. In 1885, he went to Paris to observe Jean-Martin Charcot's (1825–1893) use of hypnosis to treat hysteria. In 1895, he and another Viennese physician, Josef Breuer (1842–1925), published *Studies in Hysteria.*

In the mid-1890s, Freud abandoned hypnosis and allowed his patients to talk freely and spontaneously about themselves. Repeatedly, they associated their neurotic symptoms with experiences that brought to mind earlier experiences, going back to childhood. Freud also observed that his patients' problems were often connected with sex, and for a time he wondered if sexual abuse during childhood accounted for their illnesses.

By 1897, Freud had moved beyond this view to a theory of infantile sexuality that scandalized many contemporaries. He claimed that human beings were sexual creatures from birth, that sexual drives and energy do not simply emerge at puberty but exist in infants. This cast doubt on the innocence of childhood and forced people to face up to issues of sexuality and mental health that, in his day, they preferred not to discuss.

In 1900, Freud published his most important book, *The Interpretation of Dreams.* It combined his theory of infantile sexuality with another idea: the psychic significance of dreams. As a rationalist, Freud believed that apparently irrational phenomena, like dreams, must have reasonable, scientific explanations. He concluded that dreams are expressions of unconscious wishes, desires, and drives that waking consciousness suppresses. While awake, the mind censors certain thoughts fundamental to an individual's psychological makeup, but during sleep it expresses them cloaked in symbols. Freud argued that these unconscious drives and desires were clues explaining certain conscious behaviors.

In later works, Freud defended the importance of the human unconscious and developed a model to explain its role in the mind. He saw the mind as an arena where three entities struggled: the "id," the "ego," and the "superego." The id consists of innate amoral, irrational drives for sexual gratification, aggression, and sensual pleasure. The superego internalizes the moral imperatives that society and culture impose on the personality. The ego mediates between the impulsive id and the self-denying superego. Personality, as expressed in everyday behavior, is the product of the ego's efforts to repress impulses of the id and satisfy the demands of the external world embodied in the superego.

Freud never claimed that humankind ought to liberate the id and free itself of all repression. While he believed that excessive repression could lead to mental disorders, he said that civilization and the survival of humankind were impossible without some repression of sexuality and aggression. Freud saw human beings as attaining rationality, not as being inevitably endowed with it. He wanted civilization to prevail, but he warned that immense sacrifice of instinctual drives was required for civilized behavior, and he revealed previously unsuspected obstacles that lay in the way of rationality. Freud believed that the sacrifices necessary to be humane were worthwhile, but he was pessimistic about the future of civilization in the West.

Divisions in the Psychoanalytic Movement. By 1910, Freud had attracted followers, some of whom eventually broke with him. Chief among these was Carl Jung (1875–1961), a Swiss whom Freud regarded as his most promising student. Freud was firmly rooted in the rationalism of the Enlightenment, but Jung shared the religious mysticism of the Romantics. He questioned the primacy of sexual drives in the formation of human personality and of mental disorders. He believed that the subconscious was a soul formed by personal experiences and "collective" memories inherited from one's ancestors. Illness, he claimed, was caused by alienation from useful collective memories.

Although the psychoanalytic movement had fragmented by the 1920s, it had tremendous influence on modern intellectuals—affecting work in psychology, sociology, anthropology, religious studies, history, and literary theory. Its explanations for human behavior have recently been questioned and its future is in doubt, but there is no question about the contribution it has made to the development of the modern mind.

Retreat from Rationalism in Politics

Nineteenth-century liberals and socialists believed in the rationality of human beings. They thought that if given votes and properly educated, individuals would see to their own rational self-interest. German sociologist Max Weber (1864–1920) regarded the development of reason as humanity's major achievement, for reason laid the foundations for civilization: scientific knowledge and bureaucratic organization. Where Marx saw capitalism as the driving force in modern society, Weber saw *bureaucratization.* Bureaucratization is the process whereby labor is divided and individuals acquire a sense of personal identity by finding roles for themselves in large organizations. Also unlike Marx, Weber believed that noneconomic factors account for history's major developments. Weber's *The Protestant Ethic and the Spirit of Capitalism* (1905), for instance, traced capitalism itself to the ascetic religious doctrines of Puritanism. The Puritans, he argued, sought worldly success less for its own sake than to assure themselves that they were God's elect.

Many of Weber's colleagues were less sanguine about human rationality than he was. Gustave LeBon (1841–1931) was a psychologist of mob behavior who pointed out that reason's power faded when people gathered in crowds. In *Reflections on Violence* (1908), Georges Sorel (1847–1922) argued that people were motivated less by reason than by collectively shared ideals. Émile Durkheim (1858–1917) and Graham Wallas (1858–1932) insisted that instinct, habit, and affections had more power than reason to direct human social behavior. All of these theorists suggested that when people made political decisions, they operated not as rational individuals, but as defenders of the groups that gave them their senses of identity.

Racism

The tendency to ignore reason and sacrifice the individual to the group manifested itself in the theories of race that emerged late in the nineteenth century. Racial thinking had a long history, but Count Arthur de Gobineau (1816–1882), a reactionary French diplomat, enunciated the first important theory of race as the major determinant of human history. His four-volume *Essay on the Inequality of the Human Races* (1853–1854) blamed the failings of Western civilization on the degeneration of an original white European race, the Aryans. (Linguists of the late eighteenth century had postulated the existence of Aryans to account for a vanished language that was the common ancestor of most European tongues and Sanskrit.) Gobineau claimed that intermarriage with inferior yellow and black races had weakened modern Europeans by diluting their superior Aryan blood.

Initially, Gobineau's essay had little influence, but racial thinking was encouraged by trends in nineteenth-century science. Anthropologists and explorers adapted Darwin's theory of the survival of the fittest to explain cultural differences, and in 1899, Houston Stewart Chamberlain's (1855–1927) *Foundations of the Nineteenth Century* advanced a theory of biological determinism to integrate information drawn from many different fields. Gobineau had assumed that the "degeneration" of the human race was irreversible, but Chamberlain suggested that careful attention to genetics might enable scientists to breed a new super race.

Chamberlain's work had alarming political implications, for he accused the Jews of being the major threat to Europe's racial regeneration. His opinion was shared by Paul de Lagarde (1827–1891) and Julius Langbehn (1851–1907), who both declared the Jews to be a racial and cultural threat to Germany. Their arguments demonstrate how racism became intertwined with nationalism in the late nineteenth century.

Nationalism had begun as a movement among scholars and liberals who cherished national languages and wanted the map of Europe to acknowledge ethnic identities. From the 1870s onward, however, nationalism became a well-financed, well-organized mass movement that equated nationality with race. It opposed the internationalism advocated by liberals and socialists and worked to create solid, homogeneous states commanding unquestioned loyalty from all their citizens. Nationalism sometimes became a secular religion evangelized by state-supported schools. A powerful ideology promoting conflicts in the early twentieth century, it has recently reemerged following the collapse of communism.

Anti-Semitism and the Birth of Zionism

The rationalism of the Enlightenment had helped dispel some of Europe's traditional religious prejudice against Jews; in the first half of the nineteenth century, Jews won political rights and social acceptance in Britain, France, and Germany. But during the last third of the century, economic pressures created by finance capitalism revived anti-Semitism, particularly among members of the lower middle class.

Anti-Semitic crusades led by Karl Lueger (1844–1910), head of Austria's Christian Socialist Party; Germany's Adolf Stoecker (1835–1909); and the prosecutors of France's Captain Dreyfus convinced many Jews that assimilation was no guarantee of permanent acceptance. Their racist enemies insisted that the problem with Jews was not objectionable conduct that could be unlearned, but the ineradicable defects of inferior blood.

If Jews were unacceptable as citizens of European nations, their only safety lay in establishing their own nation—or so argued Theodor Herzl (1860–1904), founder of the Zionist movement. In 1896, Herzl published *The Jewish State* and argued for an independent Jewish state where the Jews of the world would be assured of the rights that should have been theirs in the liberal states of Europe. Herzl, an Austro-Hungarian, directed his appeal to the impoverished Jews of eastern Europe's ghettos and western Europe's slums. His Zionism linked opposition to anti-Semitism with both liberalism and socialism.

⌁ Women and Modern Thought

Anti-Feminism in Late-Century Thought

Many of the new ideas advanced in the late nineteenth century seemed to confirm old gender stereotypes, representing women as weaker and less able than men. Whatever changes were to be wrought through science, significant reorganization of the home and of male-female relationships was not among them.

Late Victorian biologists and anthropologists tended to lump women with nonwhite races as inferior members of the human family. T. H. Huxley, the popularizer of science, gave lectures presenting what he claimed was scientific evidence of female inferiority. Karl Vogt (1817–1895), a prominent German anthropologist, advanced similar views. And Darwin drew on their work for his *Descent of Man.*

Darwin and Huxley believed that women's opportunities for education should be improved, but they did not advocate admitting women to the scientific community. Male scientists insisted that codes of decency prohibited women from discussing certain subjects, and many claimed that women's limited intellects would depress the level of debate in learned societies.

Freud and his followers were trained as medical doctors at a time when medical education assumed the inferiority of women. Many of Freud's theories were developed using case histories of female patients, but his view of the female psyche is controversial. Some critics argue that Freud portrayed women as incomplete human beings, flawed males who were destined to mental problems. He claimed that they needed motherhood to fulfill themselves, particularly the nurturing of sons. Distinguished women psychoanalysts, such as Karen Horney (1885–1952) and Melanie Klein (1882–1960), have challenged Freud's ideas and attempted to establish a psychoanalytic basis for feminism, but the psychoanalytic profession and academic psychology remain dominated by men. Psychology's influence on child-rearing practices has given men, ironically, an impact in the one area of social activity that had always been dominated by women.

Virtually all of the early sociologists took a conservative view of marriage, the family, child rearing, and divorce. Auguste Comte, drawing on Rousseau, portrayed women as biologically and intellectually inferior to men. Herbert Spencer advocated improving women's lot while accepting as fact their inability to be men's equals. Émile Durkheim described women as creatures motivated by feeling more than intellect. Max Weber favored improvements in social conditions for women, but not changes in their social roles.

New Directions in Feminism

At the close of the nineteenth century, feminist thought revived in Europe and began to raise issues that would not be more fully and successfully explored until after World War II. Many women's organizations concentrated on achieving the vote for women, but consciousness was growing of a broader need to redefine women's relationships to men and society at large—to challenge the double standard of sexual morality and the traditional male-dominated family.

Demands for women's rights often began with campaigns to abolish prostitution, a fate to which poverty drove many lower-class women. Between 1864 and 1886, the English Parliament passed the Contagious Diseases Acts, which gave police in cities with naval or military bases the power to force women suspected of prostitution to undergo immediate examinations for venereal disease. Without legal recourse, those infected were locked up for months in special hospitals. These laws angered middle-class women, for they literally assigned control over women's bodies to men—customers, physicians, and police. By denying poor women the freedoms that all men enjoyed in English society, they implied that all women were less than fully human. Also, they decreed no penalties for prostitutes' customers. Their purpose was, after all, the protection of such men.

Thanks to a campaign waged by Josephine Butler (1828–1906), head of the Ladies' National Association for the Repeal of the Contagious Diseases Acts, the laws were suspended in 1883 and repealed in 1886. The English movement became a model for other nations struggling with the issue of police regulation of prostitution. During the 1890s, the General Austrian Women's Association, led by Auguste Ficke (1833–1916), fought the introduction of legalized prostitution. In Germany, women's groups divided between those who wanted to penalize prostitutes and those who saw prostitutes as victims of male society.

By opposing laws that punished prostitutes while letting their customers go free, feminist groups were challenging society's sexual double standard and, by extension, the traditional relationship of men and women in marriage. Virtually all turn-of-the-century feminists advocated wider sexual freedom for women. Their arguments for contraception were bolstered by appeals to social Darwinism. They claimed that limiting the number of children would ensure that those raised were healthier and more intelligent.

Women Defining Their Own Lives. The European feminist movement hoped to end male-dominated society and create a world in which women were as free as men to determine their destinies. Many feminists were attracted to socialism, for they believed that a classless society would liberate women. Socialist parties tended to have male leaders who—like Lenin, and, later, Stalin—were intolerant of feminist demands for changes in family life or sexual codes. But they were willing to support feminist efforts to improve women's economic situation.

It was within literary circles that feminists most successfully articulated the problems confronting women. Distinguished female writers functioned on a more or less equal footing with men, leading some to wonder whether simple equality was the real issue. In *A Room of One's Own* (1929), Virginia Woolf produced a fundamental text for twentieth-century literary feminism. It described the difficulties that gifted women encounter in being taken seriously as intellectuals, and it argued that a woman who wished to write required complete independence: an income and a room of her own. Woolf also established a new stance for feminist writers. She challenged the idea that women should write like men, and she argued that male and female writers should be able to think as both men and women. This encouraged people to ponder definitions of gender.

By World War I, feminism in Europe was associated in the popular mind with socialism, political radicalism, and attacks on traditional gender roles and morality. As a result, when extreme conservative political movements arose between the world wars, feminism faced stiffened opposition. Even Lenin and Stalin emphasized traditional roles for women and traditional ideas about sexual morality.

By the opening of the twentieth century, European thought had achieved its current contours. Science had revolutionized the way Westerners thought about the world and themselves. Accepting a role for humanity as part of the natural order, not a separate divine creation, scientists tried to find a rational basis for ethics and morality. This led to conflicts between faith and reason and, ultimately, to a loss of faith in reason. Some thinkers questioned whether human beings were subject to control by reason. Political theorists doubted that politics could be entirely rational, and racial theorists claimed that alleged characteristics carried in the blood were as important as character and intellect.

∼ Review Questions

1. Why did science dominate thought in the second half of the nineteenth century? What were some of the major changes in scientific outlook that occurred between 1850 and 1914? What advances took place in physics? How would you define *positivism?* What was the theory of natural selection proposed by Darwin and Wallace? What effect did it have on theories of ethics, on Christianity, and on European views of human nature?

2. Why did Christianity come under attack in the late nineteenth century? What form did the attack take? What political agendas were pursued by popes Pius IX, Leo XIII, and Pius X? Why was Leo XIII regarded as a liberal pope? How do you account for the resilience of the papacy during this period of attack on the church?

3. How were changes in society reflected in the literature of the late nineteenth century? What was the significance of the explosion of literary material? What was literary realism? How was it influenced by science? How did the realists undermine middle-class morality? How did literary modernism differ from realism?

4. How did Nietzsche and Freud challenge traditional middle-class and religious morality? Was Freud a product more of the Enlightenment or of the Romantic movement?

5. How do you account for the fear and hostility many late-nineteenth-century intellectuals displayed toward women? What was Freud's view of women? What were some of the social and political issues that especially affected women in the late nineteenth and early twentieth centuries? How did reformers confront them? What new directions did feminism take?

6. What forms did racism take in the late nineteenth century? How did it become associated with anti-Semitism? What was Zionism? Why did Herzl develop it?

⌇ Suggested Readings

J. L. ALTHOLZ, *The Churches in the Nineteenth Century* (1967). A useful overview.

H. ANDERSON, *Utopian Feminism: Women's Movements in Fin-de-Siècle Vienna* (1993). One of the best treatments of feminism on the continent.

S. AVINERI, *The Making of Modern Zionism: The Intellectual Origins of the Jewish State* (1981). An excellent introduction to the development of Zionist thought.

F. L. BAUMER, *Modern European Thought: Continuity and Change in Ideas, 1600–1950* (1977). The best work on the subject for this period.

P. BOWLER, *The Eclipse of Darwinism: Anti-Darwinian Evolution Theories in the Decades Around 1900* (1983). A major study of the fate of Darwinian theory in the nineteenth-century scientific community.

P. BOWLER, *Evolution: The History of an Idea* (1989). An outstanding survey of the subject.

O. CHADWICK, *The Secularization of the European Mind in the Nineteenth Century* (1975). The best treatment available.

C. M. CIPOLLA, *Literacy and Development in the West* (1969). Traces the explosion of literacy in the past two centuries.

A. DANTO, *Nietzsche as Philosopher* (1965). A helpful and well-organized introduction.

A. DESMOND AND J. MOORE, *Darwin* (1992). A brilliant biography.

P. GAY, *Freud: A Life for Our Time* (1988). The new standard biography.

J. KATZ, *From Prejudice to Destruction: Anti-Semitism, 1700–1933* (1980). An excellent and far-reaching analysis.

W. LACQUER, *A History of Zionism* (1989). The most extensive one-volume treatment.

P. MEISEL, *The Myth of the Modern: A Study in British Literature and Criticism after 1850* (1987). A broad study.

J. R. MOORE, *History, Humanity, and Evolution* (1989). A collection of major essays on evolution that touch upon science, religion, and the question of evolution and women.

G. L. MOSSE, *Toward the Final Solution: A History of European Racism* (1978). A sound introduction.

L. POLIAKOV, *The Aryan Myth: A History of Racist and Nationalist Ideas in Europe* (1971). The best introduction to the problem.

F. M. TURNER, *Contesting Cultural Authority: Essays in Victorian Intellectual Life* (1993). Essays that deal with the relationship of science and religion and the problem of faith for intellectuals.

A. VIDLER, *The Church in an Age of Revolution* (1961). A sound account of the problems of church and state in the nineteenth century.

C. WELCH, *Protestant Thought in the Nineteenth Century*, 2 vols. (1972, 1985). The most extensive recent study.

26

Imperialism, Alliances, and War

KEY TOPICS IN THIS CHAPTER

～ The economic, cultural, and strategic factors behind Europe's New Imperialism in the late nineteenth and early twentieth centuries

～ The formation of alliances and the search for strategic advantage among Europe's major powers

～ The origins and progress of World War I

～ The Russian Revolution

～ The peace treaties ending World War I

During the second half of the nineteenth century, Europe wielded unprecedented worldwide influence. Massive immigration made North and South America, Australia, and New Zealand outposts of European nations that were dividing up Africa into colonies and dictating terms to the countries of Asia.

Europe's dominance created a single world economy that might have increased general prosperity. Instead, competition among the great powers led to a terrible war that undermined Europe's strength and global influence. The peace settlement, which humiliated Germany and provoked its desire for revenge, was followed by the United States' fateful decision to withdraw into disdainful isolation from world affairs.

~ Expansion of European Power and the "New Imperialism"

Europe's power was based on the progress it made during the nineteenth century in science, technology, industry, agriculture, transportation, communications, and military weaponry. These things enabled a few Europeans (or Americans) to impose their wills on peoples many times their number. Westerners also had another advantage. The growth of nation-states, a Western phenomenon, permitted Europeans to utilize their resources to maximum effect. Confidence in the superiority of their civilization made Europeans energetic, if self-righteous, expansionists.

The New Imperialism

Imperialism can be defined as a policy of expanding a nation's power by seeking some form of hegemony over an alien people. Imperialism in earlier ages involved seizing land and settling it with the conqueror's people or establishing trading centers to exploit the resources of a dominated area. The New Imperialism employed these devices and introduced others.

A European nation often began by investing capital in a "backward" country to develop its mines and agriculture, to build railroads, bridges, harbors, and telegraph systems. These ventures employed great numbers of its people, and European states safeguarded their investments by lending local rulers money or by intimidating them into making favorable concessions. As a result, native economies and cultures were transformed.

If these arrangements proved inadequate, the dominant power would take direct control. Sometimes this meant annexation, or it could result in protectorate status whereby a local ruler became a figurehead for European military occupation. A European state might also establish a "sphere of influence" in which it enjoyed commercial and legal privileges without overt political control.

Motives for the New Imperialism: The Economic Interpretation

A need for markets and raw materials is not an adequate explanation for the New Imperialism. Although some European businessmen and politicians

Significant Dates from the Era Culminating in World War I

1871	*Creation of the German Empire*
1873	*The Three Emperors' League*
1875	*The Russo-Turkish War*
1879	*The Dual Alliance (Germany and Austria)*
1882	*The Triple Alliance (Germany, Austria, and Italy)*
1888	*William II becomes the German emperor (kaiser)*
1889–1902	*Boer War*
1890	*Bismarck is dismissed*
1894	*The Franco-Russian alliance*
1898	*Germany begins to build a battleship navy*
1902	*The British alliance with Japan*
1904	*The Entente Cordiale (Britain and France)*
1904–1905	*The Russo-Japanese War*
1905	*The first Moroccan crisis*
1908–1909	*The Bosnian crisis*
1911	*The second Moroccan crisis*
1912–1913	*The First and Second Balkan Wars*
1914 (August)	*Germans attack in the West*
(August–September)	*First Battle of the Marne*
(September)	*Battles of Tannenberg and the Masurian Lakes*
1915 (April)	*Dardanelles Campaign*
(May)	*Germans sink British ship* Lusitania
1916 (February)	*Germans attack Verdun*
(May–June)	*Battle of Jutland*
1917 (February)	*Germans declare unrestricted submarine warfare*
(March)	*Russian Revolution*
(April)	*United States enters war*
(November)	*Bolsheviks seize power*
1918 (March)	*Treaty of Brest-Litovsk; German offensive in the West*
(November)	*Armistice*

hoped that colonial expansion might cure the great depression of 1873–1896, colonies were usually not important markets for imperial nations. It is not even certain that colonialism was profitable. Some individuals and companies made great profits from particular ventures, but the people involved had minimal influence on national policy. Economic interests were involved, but a full understanding of the New Imperialism requires appreciation of other motives.

Cultural, Religious, and Social Interpretations

Advocates of imperialism justified it in various ways. Some argued that European nations had a duty to extend the benefits of their superior civilization to "backward" peoples. Churches demanded that governments furnish political and military support for Christian missions. Some politicians, particularly in Germany, hoped that imperialism might deflect public interest from domestic problems. Joseph Chamberlain (1836–1914), Britain's colonial secretary from 1895 to 1903, argued that Britain might finance a program of domestic reform and welfare from the profits of empire, but most imperial expansion was over by the time he advanced this idea. Some social reformers hoped to use colonies to relieve population pressures in Europe, but most emigrants went to places not controlled by their homelands (e.g., North and South America and Australia).

Strategic and Political Interpretations: The Scramble for Africa

The New Imperialism may have owed more to strategic considerations and national pride than to economics. On the eve of the scramble for Africa, Britain was the world leader. Other nations coveted the strategic advantages and status it derived from its extensive overseas holdings (see Map 26-1).

Great Britain. The completion of the Suez Canal in 1869 stimulated British interest in Africa, for Britain's shortest route to its Indian empire was now through Egypt. In 1875, Disraeli's ministry purchased a major, but not controlling, interest in the canal. In the 1880s, when Egypt's internal stability was threatened, the British intervened. They then moved into the Sudan to protect their position in Egypt. In the 1890s, Britain imposed its will on Zimbabwe and Zambia to prevent expansion by other nations from imperiling its route to India around the Cape of Good Hope.

France. A raid on pirates based in the city of Algiers brought the French to North Africa in 1830. By the 1880s, France was in full control of Algeria, which was attracting thousands of European immigrants. In 1882, France took over Tunisia to prevent it from falling into Italy's hands, and it annexed much of West Africa, the Congo, and the island of Madagascar.

Germany. Small states like Belgium, Portugal, Spain, and Italy were soon seeking to enhance their prestige by acquiring new African colonies or expanding old ones. In 1884 and 1885, Germany declared protectorates over Southwest Africa (Namibia), Togoland, the Cameroons, and East Africa (Tanzania). None of these places was of much value or strategic importance, and Bismarck had no interest in them for themselves. His concern was for Germany's exposed position in Europe between Russia and France. He hoped that African colonies could be used to put pressure on Britain and provide an outlet for France's hostility.

Germany's annexations started a wild scramble for African territory among European nations, and by 1890, almost all of the continent had been parceled out. There were few sound economic or political justifications for this. It was driven by the desire to appear powerful.

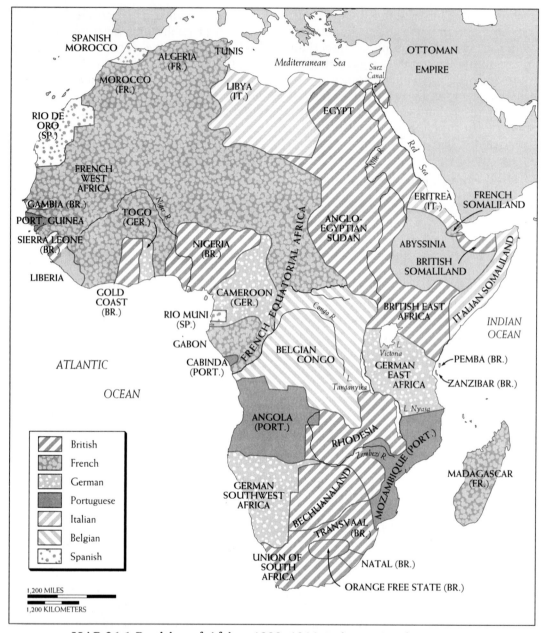

MAP 26-1 Partition of Africa, 1880–1914 *Before 1880, the European presence in Africa was largely the remains of early exploration by old imperialists and did not penetrate the heart of the continent. By 1914, the occupying powers included most large European states; only Liberia and Abyssinia remained independent.*

Reorganizing the Globe

The East. In Asia the emergence of Japan as a great power frightened the Europeans who were interested in China (see Map 26-2). The Russians, who were building a railroad across Siberia to Vladivostok and who feared that Manchuria would be threatened, joined the French and Germans in forcing Japan out of north China's Liaotung Peninsula.

In 1899, fearing that concessions granted to European nations would close China to American trade, the United States proposed the Open Door Policy. British support won agreement from all the powers except Russia that there would be no attempts at annexation of Chinese territory or acquisition of special trade advantages.

American Empire. The United States was only beginning to emerge as a force in international affairs, for until the end of the nineteenth century, its people were focused on westward expansion across the North American continent. Cuba's bid for independence from Spain sparked the United States' interest in international affairs. The Monroe Doctrine of 1823 had proclaimed the Western Hemisphere an American protectorate, and sympathy for the Cuban cause—as well as concern for American investments on the island and its strategic importance in the Caribbean—persuaded the Americans to declare war on Spain.

The Spanish-American War of 1898 won the United States an empire in the Caribbean and the Pacific. The United States assumed an informal protectorate over Cuba and annexed Puerto Rico. Spain was also forced to sell the Philippine Islands and Guam to the United States. The Americans and the Germans divided Samoa between them, and Germany bought Spain's other Pacific islands. The remaining islands in the Pacific were snapped up by France and Britain. Hawaii, which had been under American influence for some time, was annexed in 1898.

∼ The German Empire and the Alliance Systems (1873–1890)

By defeating Austria and France and, in 1871, uniting Germany, Prussia revolutionized European diplomacy. The appearance of a vast new nation of great and growing population, wealth, industrial capacity, and military might threatened to upset the balance of power that had existed since the Congress of Vienna (1815).

Britain and Russia, though the latter had been weakened by the Crimean War, remained formidable. But Austria, threatened with disintegration by the forces of nationalism, was in decline. And France, its prestige damaged by the Franco-Prussian War and the subsequent surrender of Alsace-Lorraine to Germany, had lost its traditional position as the dominant nation in western Europe.

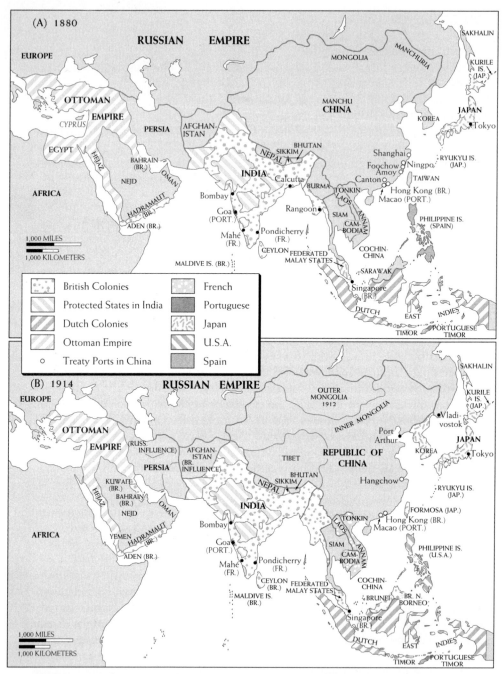

MAP 26-2 Asia, 1880–1914 *As in Africa, the decades before World War I saw imperialism spread widely and rapidly in Asia. Two new powers, Japan and the United States, joined the British, French, and Dutch in extending control both to islands and to the mainland and in exploiting an enfeebled China.*

Bismarck's Leadership (1873–1890)

Bismarck, who hoped to avoid provoking a conflict that might undo his achievements, insisted after 1871 that Germany wanted no more territory. He tried to placate the French, while developing a strategy to isolate them in case he failed. To this end, he sought treaties with Austria and Russia. The "Three Emperors' League" he formed in 1873 collapsed in 1875, when the Russo-Turkish War pitted Russia against Austria in the Balkans.

The tottering Ottoman Empire was an invitation to disorder in the Balkans, but it survived because the European powers could not agree on how to divide it up. When Slavs in Bosnia and Herzegovina revolted against Turkish rule, Slavs in Serbia and Montenegro came to their aid. The rebellion spread to Bulgaria, and Russia entered the fray.

The Ottoman Empire quickly sued for peace, and the resulting Treaty of San Stefano (March 1878) was a triumph for Russia. Slavs in the Balkans were liberated from Ottoman control. Russia annexed territory and won a large monetary indemnity. These developments, however, alarmed other nations. Austria feared growth of Russian influence in the Balkans. The British worried that Russia might alter the European balance of power, possibly seize the Dardanelles, and imperil Britain's control of the Suez Canal.

The Congress of Berlin. Britain and Austria forced Russia to agree to an international conference to review the Treaty of San Stefano. Bismarck's insistence that Germany had no territorial aspirations made him an acceptable international arbiter, and in June–July 1878, a congress met in Berlin under his presidency. Bismarck dubbed himself an "honest broker." The title was justified. His chief aim was to prevent Germany from being drawn into a war between Russia and Austria.

The congress dealt a blow to Russia. Bulgaria, Russia's client, was deprived of two-thirds of its territory and of access to the Aegean Sea. The great powers also compensated themselves for the lands they allowed Russia to keep. Austria-Hungary was authorized to "occupy and administer" Bosnia and Herzegovina, which remained formally under Ottoman rule. Britain took Cyprus, and France was urged to occupy Tunisia.

Although Germany asked for nothing, participation in the congress earned it Russia's resentment. The Balkan states were also annoyed. Romania wanted Bessarabia, which Russia kept; Bulgaria wanted the borders originally granted it by the Treaty of San Stefano; and Greece wanted a share in the Ottoman spoils. Serbia and Montenegro deeply resented Austria's occupation of Bosnia and Herzegovina, as did many of the natives of those provinces. The south Slavic question and the estrangement between Russia and Germany became threats to peace in Europe.

German Alliances with Russia and Austria. Russia's hostility drove Germany closer to Austria. In 1879, a secret treaty created the Dual Alliance, whereby

Bismarck and the young Kaiser William II meet in 1888. The two disagreed over many issues, and in 1890 William dismissed the aged chancellor. [German Information Center]

Germany and Austria agreed to come to each other's aid if either were attacked by Russia. Each was also to stay out of the other's conflicts with other nations. The treaty remained in force until 1918 and was the anchor of German policy. In retrospect, it may have been an error, for it linked Germany's fortunes with those of the troubled Austro-Hungarian Empire. And by isolating the Russians, it pushed them to seek new alliances in the West.

Bismarck never allowed the alliance to drag Germany into Austria's Balkan quarrels. He also made it clear to the Austrians that the alliance was purely defensive and that Germany would never be a party to an attack on Russia. Bismarck believed that monarchical, reactionary Russia would not seek ties with republican France or democratic Britain. In fact, he expected news of Austro-German negotiations to frighten Russia into reconciling with Germany.

In this he was correct. By 1881, he had renewed the Three Emperors' League on a firmer basis. Germany, Austria, and Russia pledged neutrality if any of them was attacked by a fourth power. Austria was granted the right to annex Bosnia-Herzegovina and promised help in closing the Dardanelles to all nations in case of war. The league allayed German fears of a Russian-French alliance and Russian fears of a German-Austrian alliance. It also safeguarded Russia from British plots to win Austria's support for allowing the British fleet into the Black Sea. Most important, the agreement hoped to keep peace in the Balkans between Austria and Russia.

The Triple Alliance. In 1882, Italy crowned Bismarck's policy with triumph. Seeking to strengthen its defenses against France, it asked to join the Dual

Alliance. As a result, Germany had treaties with three of the great powers and friendly relations with the one that held aloof from all alliances, Great Britain. France was thus isolated and neutralized. Bismarck's challenge now was to maintain the complicated system of secret treaties in the face of rivalries among his allies. He succeeded until a change in the German monarchy upset things.

In 1888, Kaiser William II (r. 1888–1918) came to the German throne. At age twenty-nine, he was ambitious, impetuous, imperious, and a believer in the divine right of kings. An injury at birth left him with a physical defect—a withered left arm—for which he overcompensated by vigorous athletic activity, military bearing, and embarrassingly bombastic rhetoric.

Like many Germans of his generation, William II believed that Germany was destined to lead Europe. At the least, he wanted Britain, under the rule of his grandmother Queen Victoria, to accept Germany as its equal. To win a "place in the sun" for Germany, he wanted a navy and colonies like Britain's. This, of course, ran counter to Bismarck's limited continental policy. When Bismarck opposed William's attempts to build up the German navy, William used a disagreement over domestic policy to dismiss him (1890).

With Bismarck in power, Germany had been secure and had earned respect as the guardian of peace in Europe. Germany could not have exercised its leadership role without its great military power. But control of this power required consummate statesmanship, a willingness to exercise restraint, and a clear understanding of the nation's true self-interest.

Forging of the Triple Entente (1890–1907)

Franco-Russian Alliance. Bismarck's retirement led to the immediate collapse of his system of alliances. General Leo von Caprivi (1831–1899), his successor, felt incompetent to manage Bismarck's complicated policy and hoped to secure Germany more simply by drawing closer to Britain. The results were unfortunate. Britain remained aloof, and Russia was alienated.

In 1894, despite their inconsistent political philosophies, France and Russia formed a defensive alliance against Germany. Diplomatic isolation and the need for foreign capital had driven the Russians into the arms of the French, and the French, who were even more isolated than the Russians, were delighted to find any friend who promised to help them against Germany.

Britain and Germany. Britain held the key to the international situation and, initially, it was disposed to favor Germany. Colonial rivalries pitted the British against the Russians in Central Asia and against the French in Africa. Britain had also long opposed Russian control of Constantinople and the Dardanelles and French dominance of the Low Countries.

Despite all this and despite Britain's long history of friendly relations with Germany, within a decade of William II's accession, most Britons had come to think of Germany as the greatest threat to their national security.

What had alarmed them was the foreign and naval policies of the German emperor William II, who coveted Britain's colonial empire and fleet. At first, he tried to win the British over to the Triple Alliance, but when Britain clung to its "splendid isolation," his policy changed. He decided to demonstrate Germany's importance as an ally by making trouble for Britain.

Germany blocked British attempts to build a railroad from Capetown to Cairo. It openly sympathized with the Boers of South Africa, who were fighting British expansion. And in 1898, William began to implement plans for a great German navy by ordering construction of nineteen battleships. In 1900, his government doubled their number.

The architect of the new navy was Admiral Alfred von Tirpitz (1849–1930). He explained that Germany's naval policy was to build a fleet strong enough, not to defeat Britain, but to do sufficient damage to make the British navy inferior to that of other nations. The plan was absurd, for the British, who had greater financial resources than the Germans, could add enough new ships to maintain their advantage over Germany. The main achievement of the policy was to waste German resources by beginning an arms race with Britain.

At first, Britain was not unduly concerned, but the steady growth of the German navy gradually persuaded the British to abandon their traditional policy of "splendid isolation." Widespread international disapproval of Britain's Boer War (1899–1902)—an unequal struggle in which the great empire crushed a rebellion by South African farmers—also convinced the government to seek some treaties of friendship. Between 1898 and 1901, Joseph Chamberlain, the colonial secretary, made several approaches to Germany. But the Germans, confident that a British alliance with France or Russia was impossible, spurned him in the expectation of forcing greater concessions in the future.

The Entente Cordiale. The first breach of Britain's isolation came in 1902, when it concluded an alliance with Japan to defend British interests in the Far East from Russia. Next, Britain overcame its traditional antagonism to France and, in 1904, concluded the Entente Cordiale. This was not a formal treaty with military provisions, but a coordination of the colonial ambitions of the two nations. Britain gave France a free hand in Morocco in return for French recognition of British control over Egypt. The Entente Cordiale was a long step toward the alignment of Britain with one of Germany's great potential enemies.

Britain's new relationship with France was surprising, but even more so was Britain's emerging sympathy for Russia. Russia's government, chastened by a humiliating defeat in the Russo-Japanese War (1904–1905) and shaken by a failed revolution (1905), was sufficiently weakened to dispel Britain's fear of Russian expansion. Britain worried instead that Russia would drift into the German orbit.

The First Moroccan Crisis. At this point, Germany tested the new relationship between Britain and France. In March 1905, William II landed at Tangier, made a speech in favor of Moroccan independence, and implied that Germany had a role in determining Morocco's destiny. This was a challenge to France that Germany hoped would reveal the weakness of France and of Britain's commitment to France.

The Germans demanded an international conference, a forum for a more dramatic demonstration of their power. At the conference, which met at Algeciras in Spain in 1906, the Germans overplayed their hand. Austria sided with Germany, but Spain, Italy, and the United States voted with Britain and France. The Germans received trivial concessions, and France's position in Morocco was confirmed. German bullying had succeeded only in driving Britain and France closer together. Sir Edward Grey, the British foreign secretary, authorized the British and French general staffs to discuss what they might do if Germany attacked France. By 1914, French and British military and naval plans had become so mutually dependent that the two countries were effectively, if not formally, allied.

British Agreement with Russia. As Britain grew closer to France, it grew closer to France's ally, Russia. Germany's growing navy and its ambitions in the Middle East (reflected in a plan to build a railroad from Berlin to Baghdad) prompted Britain to conclude an agreement with Russia (1907) much like the Entente Cordiale. Russo-British disputes in Central Asia were resolved and wider cooperation was promised. A "Triple Entente," an informal, but powerful, association of Britain, France, and Russia, emerged to oppose the "Triple Alliance" of Germany, Austria-Hungary, and Italy. Italy, however, was an unreliable ally, and Germany and Austria-Hungary felt increasingly threatened by encirclement.

William II and his ministers had turned Bismarck's nightmare of the prospect of a two-front war with France and Russia into a reality—and made it more horrible by involving Britain. The equilibrium that Bismarck had worked so hard to achieve in Europe was destroyed. Britain ceased to help Austria block Russia's ambitions in the Balkans, and Germany was unwilling to restrain Austria for fear of alienating its most important ally. The new alliances increased the risk of war and made the Balkans its flashpoint.

～ World War I

The Road to War (1908–1914)

Although the Ottoman Empire was weak, it still held a vital corridor of land running across the Balkan peninsula from Constantinople to the Adriatic. The independent states of Romania, Serbia, and Bulgaria (autonomous, but technically Ottoman) lay to the north; Greece to the south. The territory on the Adriatic coast north of Serbia was part of the Austro-Hungarian Empire. It included Croatia and Slovenia and, since 1878, an "occupied and administered" Bosnia and Herzegovina.

Except for the Greeks and the Romanians, most of the inhabitants of the Balkans spoke variants of the same Slavic language. They felt a kinship with one another strengthened by centuries of foreign domination—Austrian, Hungarian, and Turkish. The nationalistic movements that swept across Europe in the late nineteenth century fanned their desire for independence, and the more radical among them longed to unify the south Slavic (Yugoslav) peoples. Serbia was to be the center of a new nation that would liberate all the Austrian Empire's Slavic provinces, especially Bosnia. Serbia hoped to unite the Slavs as Piedmont had united the Italians and Prussia the Germans.

The Bosnian Crisis. In 1908, a group of modernizing reformers—the "Young Turks"—launched a revolution in the Ottoman Empire. Austria and Russia, which planned to partition the empire, were suddenly alarmed that the revolutionaries might succeed in breathing new life into it. They acted quickly. Russia consented to Austria's annexation of Bosnia and Herzegovina in return for Austria's support in opening the Dardanelles to Russian warships. Austria declared the annexation, but did nothing for Russia when the British and French helped the Turks maintain their hold on the Dardanelles. The Russians were humiliated, for they, a Slavic nation, had let down their "little brothers," the Slavic Serbs who believed that Bosnia belonged to them, not to Austria.

The Austrians had given the Germans no warning before they seized Bosnia. Germany was upset, for as Austria's chief ally, its relations with Russia were strained by the coup. But Germany was so dependent on the Dual Alliance that it had to allow its foreign policy to be made in Vienna. The Triple Entente was, however, similarly strained. The refusal of Britain and France to allow Russia to move into the Dardanelles meant that they had to acquiesce to some future Russian demand if they wanted to retain Russia's friendship.

The Second Moroccan Crisis. In 1911, a second crisis involving Morocco drove France and Britain closer together. When France sent an army to Morocco to put down a rebellion, Germany sent a gunboat named "the Panther" to the Moroccan port of Agadir, allegedly to protect German residents. The British, anticipating the worst, wrongly believed that the Germans meant to seize Agadir and develop it into a naval base on the Atlantic. In 1907, Germany had built its first "dreadnought," a version of a new type of battleship that Britain had launched in 1906. In 1908, Germany had passed still another naval law to accelerate development of its fleet. When negotiations failed to persuade the Germans to slow naval construction, Britain concluded that the security of its island kingdom was at stake.

The crisis passed when France yielded some insignificant bits of the Congo in exchange for German recognition of France's protectorate over Morocco. Its chief effect was to increase Britain's fear of Germany and to forge stronger links between Britain and France. Although there was no formal treaty, German naval construction and the Agadir crisis turned the Entente Cordiale into an alliance, de facto.

War in the Balkans. The second Moroccan crisis provoked another crisis in the Balkans. Italy, desiring the status of a colonial power, planned to take Libya from the Turks. Fearing that the recognition of the French protectorate in Morocco would encourage France to move into Libya before it could, Italy hastened to attack the Ottoman Empire. Italy easily defeated the Turks, and this encouraged the Balkan states to try their luck. In 1912, Bulgaria, Greece, Montenegro, and Serbia jointly defeated the Ottoman Empire. This "First Balkan War" led to a quarrel among the victors over the division of Macedonia, and in 1913, a "Second Balkan War" enabled Turkey and Romania and the other states to strip Bulgaria of much of what it had gained in 1878 and 1912.

The First Balkan War alarmed the Austrians, who were determined to prevent the Serbs from entering Albania and gaining a port on the Adriatic. When the Russians backed the Serbs, Britain sponsored an international conference to resolve the matter (1913). It called for an independent kingdom of Albania. Austria, however, felt humiliated by the airing of Serbian demands, and the Serbs defied the agreement by continuing to occupy parts of Albania until Austria forced them to withdraw. When the Serbs returned in September 1913, after the Second Balkan War, Austria issued an ultimatum, and again Serbia withdrew.

Many Austrians favored an all-out attack on Serbia that would decisively end its threat to the empire, and Russia was pressured by Pan-Slavic sentiments to help the Serbs. Britain, France, Italy, and Germany cooperated in restraining both parties, but each side worried about seeming too reluctant to help its friends.

The crisis of 1913 helped determine the response of the European nations to the events of 1914 that finally precipitated world war. The Russians' allies, having urged them to back down in 1913 as in 1908, were reluctant to restrain them again. The Austrians, having discovered that they got better results from a threat of force than from humiliating debates at international conferences, lost their will to negotiate.

Sarajevo and the Outbreak of War (June–August 1914)

The Assassination. On June 28, 1914, a young Bosnian nationalist shot and killed the heirs to the Austrian throne, Archduke Francis Ferdinand and his wife, as they drove through the Bosnian capital of Sarajevo. The assassin was a member of a terrorist organization called Union or Death (popularly known as the Black Hand). The chief of intelligence on the general staff of Serbia's army had helped plan the crime. His role was not known at the time, but the glee with which the Serbian press reported the event led many Europeans to assume that Serbian officials had been involved.

Germany and Austria's Response. Since the assassination was condemned everywhere in Europe except Serbia, Austrians who favored military action against Serbia as a solution to the empire's Slavic problem believed that the time had come to declare war. Conrad von Hötzendorf, chief of the Austrian general staff, urged an attack, but Count Stefan Tisza, representing the Hungarian portion of the Dual Monarchy, resisted. Count Leopold von Berchtold, the foreign minister, knew that German help was needed to sway the Hungarians to war and that German support would be required in the likely event that Russia intervened to protect Serbia. The ultimate decision, therefore, was Berlin's.

William II and Chancellor Theobald von Bethmann-Hollweg (1856–1921) readily promised German support for an attack on Serbia and urged the Austrians to move swiftly, while the other powers were still angry. The Austrians hoped that Germany's protection would discourage intervention by other powers and allow them to fight Serbia alone, but they were prepared to risk a general European conflict. The Germans, too, recognized the risk of a broader war, but believed they could contain the fight.

Although the decision to support Austria made war difficult if not impossible to avoid, there is no evidence that Germany had long been plotting a war. The subsequent conduct of its leaders suggests that they were reacting to events, not implementing some master plan.

The emperor and his chancellor alone, without consulting their advisers, made the fateful commitment to Austria. William II was motivated by violent passions. He had been the archduke's friend, and he was outraged by an attack on royalty. Bethmann-Hollweg, the chancellor, was less emotionally involved, but he was reluctant flatly to oppose the emperor and to appear "soft" to the military establishment. Moreover, he, like many other Germans, feared for the future. The time had come to take a "calculated risk." Russia was recovering its strength. The Triple Entente was growing more powerful. And Austria was Germany's only reliable ally. While it was dangerous to support Austria, it might have been even more dangerous to withhold support. If Austria failed to crush Serbia, Slavic nationalism could disrupt the empire and invite Russian intervention.

Bethmann-Hollweg hoped that the Austrians would strike swiftly and present the powers with a fait accompli. He believed that fear of Germany would keep Russia from becoming involved. But if not, he was prepared for war with France and Russia. In that case, he convinced himself that he could persuade Britain to remain neutral—despite Germany's continuing provocation of the British with a naval arms race.

The Austrians did not act quickly, and the Serbians returned so soft and conciliatory an answer to the ultimatum that was meant to provoke war that even the mercurial German emperor concluded that there were no longer grounds for hostilities. But the Austrians were determined not to turn back. On July 28, they declared war on Serbia, even though their army could not be ready until mid-August.

The Triple Entente's Response. The Russians responded angrily to Austria's treatment of Serbia. Conservative elements within the Russian government opposed war, fearing that it would lead to revolution. But nationalists, Pan-

Slavs, and the majority of the politically conscious classes demanded action. The government responded by ordering a partial military mobilization that was intended to dissuade Austria from attacking Serbia.

Mobilization of any kind was dangerous, for it was generally seen as an act of war. But Russia's mobilization particularly alarmed the German general staff. Germany's strategy, the Schlieffen Plan, called for an attack on France before Russia could get itself organized to enter the war. Germany now believed that it had no choice but to scramble to mobilize its forces. Perceptions of military necessity began to escalate pressures on nations.

France and Britain were not eager for war. France's president and prime minister were on their way home from a visit to Russia when the crisis flared on July 24. Had they been in Paris, they might have tried to restrain the Russians. But France's ambassador to Russia gave the Russians the same assurances that Germany had given the Austrians. The Austrians, smarting from the humiliation of the London Conference of 1913, rejected a British proposal for another conference. Germany privately supported Austria, while making conciliatory public statements to court British neutrality. Soon, however, Bethmann-Hollweg realized what he should have known from the first. If Germany attacked France, Britain would fight. After July 30, when Austria ordered mobilization against Russia, Germany's sham appeals for Austrian restraint became sincere. But it was too late for Austria to back down without a massive loss of face.

Bethmann-Hollweg resisted enormous pressure to mobilize, not because he hoped to avoid war but because he wanted Russia to act first and appear to be the aggressor. Only then would the German people support the war. Minutes before Germany was set to initiate mobilization, news arrived that Russia had begun. The Schlieffen Plan was put into effect. On August 1, the Germans occupied Luxembourg. An invasion of Belgium two days later violated Belgian neutrality, which Britain had promised to protect in a treaty of 1839. This united the British people against Germany, and when Germany invaded France, Britain entered the war (August 4). As Sir Edward Grey, the British foreign secretary, put it, the lights were going out all over Europe. When they came on again, Europe would be a different place.

Strategies and Stalemate: 1914–1917

Across Europe there was jubilation as the decision to fight released the tensions created by the repeated crises of recent years. No general war had been fought since Napoleon's day, and few anticipated the horrors of modern combat. The dominant memory was of Bismarck's swift, decisive campaigns, whose costs were light and rewards great.

Both sides expected to take the offensive, force a battle on favorable ground, and win a quick victory. The "Allies" (the Triple Entente nations) had superior numbers and financial resources and command of the sea. The "Central Powers" (Germany and Austria) had the advantages of internal lines of communication and of launching the first attack.

Germany's war plan had been developed a decade earlier by Count Alfred von Schlieffen (1833–1913), chief of the German general staff from 1891 to 1906. The German army was to outflank the French defenses by sweeping through Belgium to the English Channel, then wheeling to the south and east to envelop the French and to crush them against German fortresses in Lorraine. The key to the plan lay in making the right wing of the advancing German army immensely strong while deliberately weakening the left, opposite the French frontier. The weakness of the left was meant to draw the French into attacking there while the war was decided by the German right. In the East, the Germans planned simply to defend against Russia until France was crushed. That was expected to take only six weeks.

Helmuth von Moltke (1848–1916), the nephew of Bismarck's most effective general, was given command of the campaign. He, however, lacked the courage to heed Schlieffen's warning that it was necessary to risk Germany's frontier and depend entirely on the strength of the right wing. Moltke added divisions to the left wing—even weakening the Russian front to get them. As a result of his hesitant strategy and of mistakes by commanders in the field, the Schlieffen Plan failed—narrowly.

The War in the West. The French, too, put their faith in an offensive, but with less reason than the Germans. They badly underestimated the numbers and effectiveness of the German reserves and overestimated the importance of the courage and spirit of their own troops. Courage and spirit could not prevail against machine guns and heavy artillery. The French attack on Germany's western frontier failed totally, but defeat was better than partial success. The troops that were freed for use against the main German army helped the French and British stop the German advance on Paris at the Battle of the Marne (September 1914; see Map 26-3).

Thereafter, the war in the West bogged down. Both sides dug in behind a wall of trenches and barbed wire that stretched from the North Sea to Switzerland. Strategically placed machine-gun nests made assaults difficult and dangerous. Both sides, nonetheless, attempted massive attacks preceded by artillery bombardments of unprecedented force. Sometimes assaults that cost hundreds of thousands of lives produced advances measured in mere hundreds of yards. The development of poison gas increased casualties, but not victories. In 1916, the British invented the tank as an effective counter to the machine gun, but the Allied command was slow to grasp its significance for new offensive strategies. For three years, the Western Front moved only a few miles in either direction.

The War in the East. In the East, the war began auspiciously for the Allies. The Russians advanced into Austrian territory and inflicted heavy casualties, but Russian incompetence and German energy soon reversed the situation. A junior German officer, Erich Ludendorff (1865–1937), under the command of the elderly General Paul von Hindenburg (1847–1934), destroyed or captured an entire Russian army at the Battle of Tannenberg and defeated another one

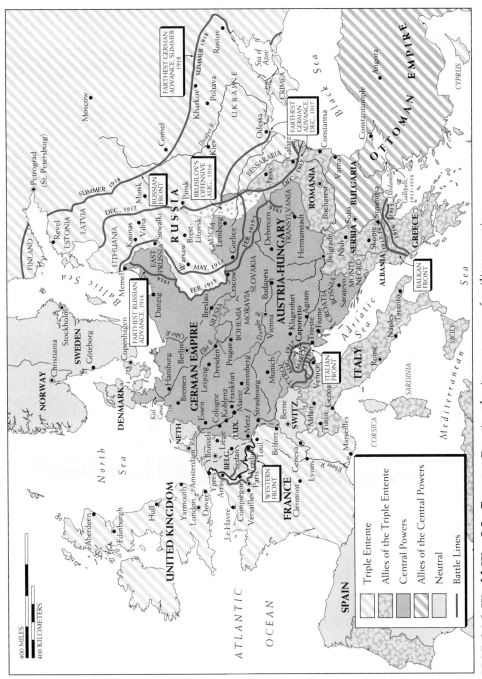

MAP 26-3 World War I In Europe *Despite the importance of military action in the Far East, in the Arab world, and at sea, the main theaters of activity in World War I were in the European areas.*

German infantrymen eating in a trench on the Western Front. Trenches, defended by barbed wire and machine guns, gave the defense the advantage in World War I and prevented breakthroughs. [Bildarchiv Preussischer Kulturbesitz]

at the Masurian Lakes. In 1915, the Central Powers drove into the Baltic states and Russian Poland. They inflicted over 2 million casualties in a single year.

As the battle lines hardened, both sides sought new allies. In 1916, Romania joined the Allies, but was quickly defeated and driven from the war. Turkey, which was hostile to Russia, and Bulgaria, Serbia's enemy, joined the Central Powers. In the Far East, Japan honored its alliance with Britain by overrunning the German colonies in China and the Pacific—and using the opportunity to improve its position against China.

Both sides bid for Italian support. The Allies won by promising the Italians more of what they wanted—spoils from Austria's empire. In a secret treaty of 1915, they agreed to give Italy most of *Italia Irredenta* (i.e., the South Tyrol, Trieste, and some of the Dalmatian Islands), colonies in Africa, and a share of the Turkish Empire. By the spring of 1915, Italy was engaging Austrian armies. The campaign weakened Austria and forced the Germans to divide some of their troops, but Italy's help failed to achieve anything significant for the Allies.

Each side tried to stir up trouble for the other by appealing to nationalistic movements in its opponent's territory. The Germans supported the Irish against Britain, the Flemings in Belgium, and the Poles and the Ukrainians opposing Russia. They tried to persuade the Turks to lead a Muslim uprising against the British in Egypt and India and against the French in North Africa. The Allies had greater success appealing to nationalists who wanted to break free from the Austrian Empire: Czechs, Slovaks, south Slavs, and Poles. A movement seeking Arab independence from Turkey, guided by Colonel T. E. Lawrence (1888–1935) "of Arabia," was especially successful later in the war.

In 1915, Winston Churchill (1874–1965), first lord of the British admiralty, suggested a plan to break the deadlock on the Western Front. He proposed an attack on the Dardanelles and Constantinople. This was to knock Turkey out of the war, relieve the Balkan front, and ease communications with Russia—all at minimal risk. Thanks to British naval superiority and the element of surprise, a naval action alone was deemed sufficient to force the straits and capture the city. If it failed, the fleet could escape with little loss. Success, however, depended on timing, speed, and daring leadership, and the attackers had none of these. Troops were landed, and as Turkish resistance continued, more were added. Before the project was abandoned, the Allies had lost almost 150,000 men and diverted three times that number from more useful occupations.

Return to the West. Both sides turned their attentions back to the West in 1916. General Erich von Falkenhayn (1861–1922), who had succeeded Moltke in September 1914, attacked the French stronghold of Verdun. His goal was not to take the fortress, but to inflict enormous casualties on the French who would have to defend it against superior firepower coming from several directions. The French, however, held Verdun with comparatively few men and inflicted almost as many casualties as they suffered. Verdun's commander, Henri Pétain (1856–1951), became a national hero.

The Allied initiative was a major offensive along the River Somme. Aided by a Russian attack in the East that drew off some German strength and by an enormous artillery bombardment, the Allies hoped at last to break through the German line. But once again, enormous casualties on both sides brought no one a decisive advantage.

The War at Sea. As the war dragged on, control of the sea became increasingly important. The British ignored international laws that protected ships carrying peaceful cargo and imposed a strict blockade to starve out their enemies. The Germans responded with submarine warfare. By threatening all shipping, they hoped to starve Britain. The policies of both nations offended neutrals—especially the United States, which conducted extensive trade in the Atlantic.

In 1915, the British liner *Lusitania* was torpedoed by a German submarine, and 118 Americans were among the 1,200 of its passengers who drowned. When President Woodrow Wilson (1856–1924) warned Germany that a repetition would have grave consequences, the Germans tried to avoid incidents that might bring America into the war. The German fleet that had cost so much money and caused so much trouble ultimately played no significant part in the war. Its only battle, fought at Jutland in the spring of 1916, resulted in a standoff that confirmed British domination of the surface of the sea.

America Enters the War. In December 1916, Woodrow Wilson tried to mediate peace negotiations, but neither side was willing to renounce aims that the

The Outbreak of the Russian Revolution

The great Russian Revolution of 1917 started with a series of ill-organized demonstrations in Petrograd early in March. The nature of these actions and the incompetence of the government's response are described in the memoirs of Maurice Paléologue, the French ambassador.

~ What explanations for the success of the March Revolution can be inferred from this selection? Why might the army have been unreliable? Why did the two ambassadors think a new ministry should be appointed? What were the grievances of the revolutionaries? Why is there no discussion of the leaders of the revolution? What role did the emperor (tsar) play in these events?

Monday, March 12, 1917

At half-past eight this morning, just as I finished dressing, I heard a strange and prolonged din which seemed to come from the Alexander Bridge. I looked out: there was no one on the bridge, which usually presents such a busy scene. But, almost immediately, a disorderly mob carrying red flags appeared at the end which is on the right bank of the Neva, and a regiment came towards it from the opposite side. It looked as if there would be a violent collision, but on the contrary the two bodies coalesced. The army was fraternizing with revolt.

Shortly afterwards, someone came to tell me that the Volhynian regiment of the Guard had mutinied during the night, killed its officers and was parading the city, calling on the people to take part in the revolution and trying to win over the troops who still remain loyal.

At ten o'clock there was a sharp burst of firing and flames could be seen rising somewhere on the Liteïny Prospekt which is quite close to the embassy. Then silence.

Accompanied by my military attaché, Lieutenant-Colonel Lavergne, I went out to see what was happening. Frightened inhabitants were scattering through the streets. There was indescribable confusion at the corner of the Liteïny. Soldiers were helping civilians to erect a barricade. Flames mounted from the Law Courts. The gates of the arsenal burst open with a crash. Suddenly the crack of machine-gun fire split the air: it was the regulars who had just taken up position near the Nevsky Prospekt. The revolu-

other found unacceptable. The war seemed likely to continue until exhaustion felled one or both.

Two events early in 1917 altered the situation. On February 1, the Germans resumed unrestricted submarine warfare. This led the United States to break off diplomatic relations and, on April 6, to declare war on the Central Powers. The decision to enter the war was made easier by an unexpected event that took place in March. Wilson, who could justify war only as an idealistic crusade "to make the world safe for democracy," had been reluctant to join the Allies in defending autocratic tsarist Russia. But in March 1917 the Russian Revolution overthrew the tsarist regime.

tionaries replied. I had seen enough to have no doubt as to what was coming. Under a hail of bullets I returned to the embassy with Lavergne who had walked calmly and slowly to the hottest corner out of sheer bravado.

About half-past eleven I went to the Ministry for Foreign Affairs, picking up Buchanan [the British ambassador to Russia] on the way.

I told Pokrovski [the Russian foreign minister] everything I had just witnessed.

"So it's even more serious than I thought," he said.

But he preserved unruffled composure, flavoured with a touch of scepticism, when he told me of the steps on which the ministers had decided during the night:

"The sitting of the Duma has been prorogued to April and we have sent a telegram to the Emperor, begging him to return at once. With the exception of M. Protopopov [the Minister of the Interior, in charge of the police], my colleagues and I all thought that a dictatorship should be established without delay; it would be conferred upon some general whose prestige with the army is pretty high, General Russky for example."

I argued that, judging by what I saw this morning, the loyalty of the army was already too heavily shaken for our hopes of salvation to be based on the use of the "strong hand," and that the immediate appointment of a ministry inspiring confidence in the Duma seemed to me more essential than ever, as there is not a moment to lose. I reminded Pokrovski that in 1789, 1830, and 1848, three French dynasties were overthrown because they were too late in realizing the significance and strength of the movement against them. I added that in such a grave crisis the representative of allied France had a right to give the Imperial Government advice on a matter of internal politics.

Buchanan endorsed my opinion.

Pokrovski replied that he personally shared our views, but that the presence of Protopopov in the Council of Ministers paralyzed action of any kind.

I asked him:

"Is there no one who can open the Emperor's eyes to the real situation?"

He heaved a despairing sigh.

"The Emperor is blind!"

Deep grief was writ large on the face of the honest man and good citizen whose uprightness, patriotism and disinterestedness I can never sufficiently extol.

Maurice Paléologue, An Ambassador's Memoirs (London: Doubleday & Company, Inc., Hutchinson Publishing Group Ltd., 1924), pp. 221–225. Reprinted by permission.

∿ The Russian Revolution

Russia's March Revolution was neither planned nor led by any political faction. It resulted from the collapse of the monarchy's ability to govern. Tsar Nicholas II was weak and incompetent, and the demands the war put on the resources of his country and government were too great. Military and domestic mismanagement produced massive casualties, widespread hunger, strikes by workers, confusion in the army, and peasant uprising. In 1916, the tsar alienated all political factions by adjourning the Duma, Russia's parliament, and proceeding to rule alone.

The Provisional Government of the Mensheviks

Strikes and worker demonstrations erupted in Petrograd (Saint Petersburg) early in March 1917. When the ill-disciplined troops stationed in the city refused to fire on the demonstrators and restore order, the tsar abdicated (March 15). The Duma reconvened to form a provisional government that was composed chiefly of Constitutional Democrats (Cadets) sympathetic to the West.

Outside the provisional government, various socialists, including both Social Revolutionaries and Social Democrats of the Menshevik wing, organized *soviets* (councils of workers and soldiers). As relatively orthodox Marxists, the Mensheviks believed that Russia had to pass through a bourgeois stage of development before the revolution of the proletariat could be launched. Consequently, they were willing to work, temporarily, with the Constitutional Democrats in a liberal regime.

The provisional government was doomed by its decision to continue the war against Germany, for the war perpetuated the suffering and discontent that had brought down the tsar. When Russia's last offensive collapsed in the summer of 1917, military discipline disintegrated and mass disillusionment undermined loyalty to the government.

Lenin and the Bolsheviks

Opposition to the provisional government by the Bolshevik wing of the Social Democratic Party suggested a scheme to the Germans for subverting order in Russia. They smuggled V. I. Lenin, a brilliant Bolshevik leader, in a sealed train from Switzerland across Germany to Petrograd.

Lenin believed that an opportunity was at hand to realize a key piece of Marxist theory: a political alliance between workers and peasants using the soviets that the Bolsheviks controlled. Lenin attempted a coup following 1917's failed military offensive. When it collapsed, he fled to Finland, and his chief collaborator, Leon Trotsky (1877–1940), was imprisoned. The failure of a right-wing countercoup then gave the Bolsheviks a second chance. Trotsky was released from prison, and Lenin returned. On November 6, Trotsky, leader of the powerful Petrograd soviet, staged an uprising that concluded with an armed assault on the provisional government. Almost as much to their own astonishment as to that of the rest of the world, the Bolsheviks became Russia's rulers.

The Communist Dictatorship

In an election the provisional government had called for late November to select a Constituent Assembly, the Social Revolutionaries won a large majority over the Bolsheviks. The assembly convened in January, but it met for only a day before the Bolsheviks' Red Army dispersed it. In November and January, the Bolshevik government nationalized land ownership and turned it over to peasant proprietors. Factory workers were put in charge of their plants. The debt of the tsarist government was repudiated. Banks were seized by the state, as was the church's property.

The Bolshevik government signed an armistice with Germany in December 1917. On March 3, 1918, by the Treaty of Brest-Litovsk, Russia surrendered claims to Poland, the Baltic states, and the Ukraine. Some territory in the Transcaucasus region went to Turkey, and the Bolsheviks agreed to pay a heavy war indemnity. The price for peace was terribly high, but Lenin had no choice. Russia was incapable of renewing the war effort, and the Bolsheviks needed time to establish control over a devastated, chaotic Russia. Besides, Lenin believed that the war and Russia's example would soon spark communist revolutions across Europe.

Resistance to the Bolshevik takeover continued within Russia until 1921—a civil war between "Red" Russians supporting the revolution and "White" Russians opposing it. In the summer of 1918, the Bolsheviks murdered the tsar and his family, but loyal army officers, with help from the Allies, continued to fight. Trotsky's Red Army, however, established Lenin in firm control.

The End of World War I

The collapse of Russia and the Treaty of Brest-Litovsk were the zenith of German success. Control over eastern Europe and its resources freed Germany to concentrate its forces on the Western Front. This might have tipped things decisively in favor of Germany had not America intervened.

It took about a year for American troops to arrive in significant numbers, and in the interim the bloody deadlock continued. When an Allied offensive in the West failed disastrously, the French army mutinied. The Austrians defeated the Italians at Caporetto and threatened to overrun Italy, but they were checked with the aid of Allied troops.

Germany's Last Offensive

In 1918, Germany decided to gamble everything on one last offensive. Its army again advanced as far as the Marne, where lack of reserves and exhaustion caused it to bog down. The Allies, bolstered by the arrival of American troops, launched an irresistible counteroffensive. The Austrian fronts in the Balkans and Italy collapsed, and the German high command realized that the end was imminent.

Ludendorff was determined that peace should be made before the German army was thoroughly defeated and that civilians should take responsibility for ending the war. President Wilson refused to deal with any German government but a democracy that claimed to speak for the German people. Consequently, Ludendorff had Prince Max of Baden establish such a government and sue for peace on the basis of the Fourteen Points that President Wilson had articulated as America's goals in the war. These idealistic principles included self-determination for nationalities, open diplomacy, freedom of the seas, disarmament, and establishment of a league of nations to keep the peace.

German Republican Government Accepts Defeat

The disintegration of the German army forced William II to abdicate on November 9, 1918. The Social Democratic Party proclaimed a republic to block formation of a soviet government by a Leninist faction. Two days later Germany signed the armistice. The German people were not aware of the dimensions of their defeat, for no foreign soldiers occupied their land. Most expected a mild settlement. Many refused to believe that Germany had been beaten. They claimed it had been tricked by the enemy and betrayed by republicans and socialists at home.

There was little cause for either side to rejoice. Total casualties came to about 10 million dead and twice as many wounded. The economic and financial resources of the European states were badly strained. The victorious Allies, formerly creditors to the world, became debtors to a new American colossus. The old international order was gone. Russia was ruled by a Bolshevik dictatorship fomenting world revolution. Germany was in chaos. Austria-Hungary disintegrated into a half-dozen small states. Overseas colonial empires were shaken. Europe was no longer the center of the world, and memory of the war unnerved Europeans as they confronted an uncertain future.

∿ The Settlement at Paris

Representatives of the victorious states gathered at Versailles early in 1919. The "Big Four" were Wilson of the United States, David Lloyd George (1863–1945) of Britain, Georges Clemençeau (1841–1929) of France, and Vittorio Emanuele Orlando (1860–1952) of Italy. Japan also took an important part in the discussions.

Now, as in Vienna in 1815, diplomats faced the challenge of restoring world order after long, costly wars. But delegates to the Congress of Vienna could confine their thoughts to Europe and, unswayed by public opinion, draw a new map along practical lines determined by realities of power softened by compromise. The negotiators at Versailles in 1919 were less fortunate. They represented generally democratic governments accountable to public opinion. The new nationalism meant that Europe's many ethnic groups would not remain quiet while the great powers distributed them about the map. And propaganda, much of it American, had turned World War I into a moral crusade in which compromise was difficult.

Wilson's idealistic Fourteen Points declared the right of nationalities to self-determination, but the map of Europe could not be drawn to match ethnic groups perfectly with their homelands. Wilson also had to contend with many secret treaties made before and during the war. The British and French electorates had been promised that Germany would be made to pay for the war. Russia had been promised Constantinople in return for recognizing France's claim to Alsace-Lorraine and Britain's control of Egypt. Romania had been promised Transylvania at the expense of Hungary. Italy and Serbia had competing claims to the islands and shores of the Adriatic. The British had encouraged Arab hopes of an independent Arab state carved out of the Ottoman Empire, although that contradicted the Balfour Declaration (1917), which supported Zionist claims to a Jewish homeland in Palestine. Both of these plans conflicted with an Anglo-French agreement to divide up the Middle East.

The national goals of the victors defeated Wilson's idealistic plans for a "peace without victors." France was eager to weaken Germany permanently. Italy still wanted *Italia Irredenta.* Britain pursued its imperial interests. Japan had aspirations in Asia. And the United States insisted on freedom of the seas and on the Monroe Doctrine.

The peacemakers of 1919 also faced a world still in turmoil. Fear of Germany was intense. Bolshevism added new anxieties. The Allies landed small armies at several places in Russia to help overthrow the Bolshevik regime, but the revolution spread. Communist governments were established in Bavaria and Hungary, and there was a communist uprising, led by the "Spartacus group," in Berlin (see Map 26-4).

The Peace

Liberals and idealists who expected a new kind of international order to be achieved in a new and better way were disillusioned. The notion of a peace without victors was jettisoned when the Soviet Union (as Russia was now called) and Germany were excluded from the peace conference. Terms were dictated to the Germans, and the principle of national self-determination was frequently and unavoidably violated. Wilson, who received undeserved adulation on his arrival at the conference, gradually became the object of equally undeserved scorn.

The League of Nations. Wilson made unpalatable compromises in the hope that injustices could be corrected by a new international organization he insisted on establishing, the League of Nations. The league was not an international government, but a group of sovereign states which agreed to consult and submit differences to arbitration. The league had no armed forces of its own, but it planned to enforce its edicts by economic sanctions and military interventions by its members. Any action, however, required the unanimous consent of a council with permanent seats for Britain, France, Italy, the United States, and Japan, and temporary seats for four other states. The exclusion of Germany and the Soviet Union from the league undermined its claim to evenhandedness.

Colonial areas were placed under the "tutelage" of one of the great powers, under league supervision, and encouraged to advance toward independence. This provision had no teeth, and little progress was made. Provisions for disarmament were equally ineffective. Members of the league remained fully sovereign and fully committed to their own national interests.

400 MILES
400 KILOMETERS

North Sea

NORWAY
Oslo

SWEDEN
Stockholm

UNITED KINGDOM

DENMARK

NETH.
BEL.
LUX.

GERMANY
Hamburg
Berlin
Weimar

RHINELAND

LORRAINE
FRANCE
ALSACE

SWITZ.
Munich

TYROL

ITALY
Milan
Rome

TUNISIA
(FR.)

Mediterranean

MALTA (U.K.)

SICILY

Baltic Sea

FINLAND
Helsinki

L. Onega

L. Ladoga

Revel
ESTONIA
Riga
LATVIA

Danzig
EAST PRUSSIA
Kaunas
LITHUANIA

Warsaw
POLAND
Brest-Litovsk

Prague
CZECHOSLOVAKIA
GALICIA
Lvov
RUTHENIA

Vienna
AUSTRIA
Budapest
HUNGARY

Fiume
CROATIA
BANAT
YUGOSLAVIA
Belgrade
BOSNIA
MONTE-NEGRO
SERBIA
Tirana
ALBANIA

GREECE

Dniester R.

Kiev

UKRAINE

TRAN-SYLVANIA
ROMANIA
MOLDAVIA
WALLACHIA
Bucharest
DOBRUJA

Sofia
BULGARIA

TURK.
Istanbul

DODECANESE IS. (IT.)

CRETE

Sea

White Sea
Archangel

Dvina R.

Leningrad (Petrograd 1914-1924)

SOVIET

Volga R.

Moscow

Smolensk

WHITE RUSSIA

UNION

Kama R.

Perm

Samara

Ural R.

Saratov

Tsaritsyn

Don R.

Rostov

BESSARABIA

Dnieper R.

CRIMEA

Black Sea

Batum
TRANSCAUCASIA

Astrakhan

Volga R.

Caspian Sea

Baku

ARMENIA
AZERBAIJAN

Angora (Ankara, 1930)

Smyrna (Izmir, 1930)

TURKEY (Republic, 1923)

KURDISTAN

Tabriz

MESOPOTAMIA
Mosul

Euphrates R.
Tigris R.

IRAN (PERSIA)

Baghdad

CYPRUS (U.K.)

SYRIA (FR. MAND.)

IRAQ (BR. MAND.)

PALESTINE (BR. MAND.)

TRANS-JORDAN (BR. MAND.)

EGYPT (BR. INFLUENCE)
Suez Canal
Cairo

SAUDI ARABIA (1932)

Persian Gulf

	Austria-Hungary, 1914
	Germany, 1914
	Areas lost by Germany in 1919
	Areas lost by Bulgaria
	Areas lost by Russia
	Areas lost by The Ottoman Empire

MAP 26-4 World War I Peace Settlement in Europe and the Middle East *The map of central and eastern Europe, as well as that of the Middle East, underwent drastic revision after World War I. The enormous geographical losses suffered by Germany, Austria-Hungary, the Ottoman Empire, Bulgaria, and Russia were the other side of the coin represented by gains for France, Italy, Greece, and Romania and the appearance, or reappearance, of at least eight new independent states, from Finland in the north to Yugoslavia in the south. The mandate system for former Ottoman territories outside Turkey proper laid foundations for several new, mostly Arab, states in the Middle East.*

Germany. Although a united Germany was less than fifty years old, no one seems to have thought of undoing Bismarck's work and dividing it into its component parts. To protect France against a resurgent Germany, France received Alsace-Lorraine and the right to work the coal mines of the Saar for fifteen years. A belt of land extending from the frontier fifty kilometers east of the Rhine was declared a demilitarized zone. Allied troops were to be stationed west of the Rhine for fifteen years. Britain and the United States promised to defend France if it were again attacked by Germany. And Germany was permanently disarmed.

The East. Poland was reestablished and connected to the sea by a corridor that cut East Prussia off from the rest of Germany. The Austro-Hungarian Empire was broken up into five small successor states. Most of its German-speaking people were gathered into the republic of Austria, cut off from the Germans of Bohemia, and forbidden to unite with Germany. The Magyars retained a much-reduced kingdom of Hungary. The Czechs of Bohemia and Moravia joined with Slovaks and Ruthenians to form Czechoslovakia, which was also home to Poles, Magyars, and several million unhappy Germans. The southern Slavs formed the Kingdom of Serbs, Croats, and Slovenes (Yugoslavia). Italy gained the Trentino and Trieste. Romania acquired Transylvania from Hungary and Bessarabia from Russia. Bulgaria lost territory to Greece, Romania, and Yugoslavia. Finland, Estonia, Latvia, and Lithuania established their independence of Russia.

The Ottoman Empire disappeared. Constantinople became the capital of a republic of Turkey approximately equivalent to Asia Minor. The British established a "mandate" over Palestine and Iraq. The French did the same in Syria and Lebanon. Britain, France, Belgium, and South Africa divided Germany's African colonies. Its Pacific possessions went to Australia, New Zealand, and Japan. In theory, the "advanced nations" were to govern their "mandates" in the interests of native peoples until the latter were ready to govern themselves. In practice, "mandates" were treated as colonies. Twenty years after the signing of the Versailles treaty, not one had achieved independence.

Reparations. The most controversial part of the peace settlement dealt with reparations for the damage Germany did during the war. The American estimate was between $15 billion and $25 billion, an amount Germany could pay. France and Britain, however, worrying about their own debts to the United States, wanted Germany to pay everything, including pensions to veterans and their dependents. Realistically, it was acknowledged that Germany could not pay such a huge sum, whatever it might be. So it was agreed that Germany was to pay $5 billion annually until 1921, when a final figure would be set that would have to be paid off in thirty years. To justify these huge reparation payments, the Allies declared that the Germans were solely responsible for the war.

The Germans, of course, bitterly resented the charge and the blight on their future. They had already lost territories containing badly needed natural resources, and now they were presented with an apparently unlimited reparations bill. Germany's prime minister, Philipp Scheidmann (1865–1939), described the treaty as the imprisonment of the German people, but he had no recourse. The Weimar government that ruled Germany until 1933 never overcame the stigma of accepting the Treaty of Versailles.

Evaluation of the Peace

Few peace settlements have been as severely criticized as the one negotiated in Paris in 1919. Both the defeated and the victorious parties found it wanting. Many criticisms of the Treaty of Versailles are, however, unjustified. It did not dismember or ruin Germany, which, until the worldwide depression of the 1930s began, was recovering its prosperity. The terms the Germans imposed on Russia at Brest-Litovsk (and Germany's plans for Europe, had it won) were far harsher than anything enacted at Versailles. The peace Versailles decreed was, however, unsatisfactory. Dismemberment of the Austro-Hungarian Empire was economically disastrous, for it separated raw materials from manufacturing areas and producers from markets. Realignments of national borders also exacerbated ethnic conflicts. The Germans believed that they had been cheated rather than defeated, and they remained unreconciled to the outcome of the war. And the Allied position was not enhanced by rhetoric professing a higher morality than that reflected in the terms of the treaty.

But the great weakness of the peace treaty was its failure to acknowledge reality. Germany and Russia, although destined inevitably to play important roles in Europe, were excluded from the settlement and from the League of Nations. The treaty also created no machinery to enforce its terms. The Treaty of Versailles was, therefore, neither conciliatory enough nor harsh enough to create a stable world order.

The outburst of European imperialism in the last part of the nineteenth century spread Western influence around the globe. But the world order created by the "New Imperialism" did not endure. A conflict in the Balkans spread to become a war involving all of Europe, and that war affected people under Europe's colonial rule. The principles of nationalism and self-determination, which Europeans invoked to justify the war, inspired Europe's colonies to seek independence and nationhood. A glance at the new map of the world could give the impression that the old imperial nations, especially Britain and France, were more powerful than ever, but that impression would be misleading. The European states had paid an enormous price in lives, money, and will during the war. And by denying their colonies the "universal" rights that they claimed to defend in the war, they created a new source of political instability.

Review Questions

1. To what areas of the world did Europe extend its power after 1870? How did European attitudes toward imperialism change after 1870? Why? What features differentiate the New Imperialism from previous imperialistic movements? What features did they have in common?

2. What role in the world did Bismarck envisage for the new Germany after 1871? How successful was he in realizing his vision? What was Bismarck's attitude toward colonies? Was he wise to tie Germany to Austria-Hungary?

3. Why, at the turn of the century, did Britain abandon its policy of "splendid isolation"? By what stages did it engineer the change? Were the policies it pursued wise ones? Should it have followed a different course?

4. How did developments in the Balkans lead to the outbreak of World War I? What was Serbia's role? Austria's? Russia's? What was Germany's objective in July 1914? Did Germany want a general war?

5. Why did Germany lose World War I? Could Germany have won, or was victory never a possibility? What were the benefits to Europe of the Treaty of Versailles? What were its drawbacks? Was the settlement too harsh or too conciliatory? Could it have secured lasting peace in Europe? How might it have been improved?

6. Why was Lenin successful in establishing Bolshevik rule in Russia? What role did Trotsky play? Was it wise policy for Lenin to take Russia out of the war?

Suggested Readings

M. BALFOUR, *The Kaiser and His Times* (1972). A fine biography of William II.

V. R. BERGHAHN, *Germany and the Approach of War in 1914* (1973). A work similar in spirit to Fischer's (see below) but stressing the importance of Germany's naval program.

R. BOSWORTH, *Italy and the Approach of the First World War* (1983). A fine analysis of Italian policy.

M. FERRO, *The Great War, 1914–1918* (1973). A solid account of the course of World War I.

D. K. FIELDHOUSE, *The Colonial Experience: A Comparative Study from the Eighteenth Century* (1966). An excellent study.

F. FISCHER, *Germany's Aims in the First World War* (1967). An influential interpretation that stirred an enormous controversy by emphasizing Germany's role in bringing on the war.

O. J. HALE, *The Great Illusion 1900–1914* (1971). A fine survey of the period, especially good on public opinion.

M. B. HAYNE, *The French Foreign Office and the Origins of the First World War* (1993). An examination of the influence on French policy of the professionals in the foreign service.

J. M. KEYNES, *The Economic Consequences of the Peace* (1920). The famous and influential attack on the Versailles Treaty.

V. G. KIERNAN, *European Empires from Conquest to Collapse 1815–1960* (1981). A study of the course of modern European imperialism.

L. LAFORE, *The Long Fuse* (1965). A readable account of the origins of World War I that focuses on the problem of Austria-Hungary.

W. L. LANGER, *European Alliances and Alignments*, 2nd ed. (1966). A splendid diplomatic history of the years 1871–1890.

D. C. B. LIEVEN, *Russia and the Origins of the First World War* (1983). A good account of the forces that shaped Russian policy.

Z. STEINER, *Britain and the Origins of the First World War* (1977). A perceptive and informed account of the way British foreign policy was made before the war.

S. R. WILLIAMSON JR., *Austria-Hungary and the Origins of the First World War* (1991). A valuable new study of a complex subject.

27

Political Experiments of the 1920s

KEY TOPICS IN THIS CHAPTER

⌁ Economic and political disorder in the aftermath of World War I

⌁ The Soviet Union's far-reaching political and social experiment

⌁ Mussolini and the Fascist seizure of power in Italy

⌁ French determination to enforce the Versailles treaty

⌁ First Labour government and general strike in Britain

⌁ The development of authoritarian governments in all the successor states to the Austrian Empire except Czechoslovakia

⌁ Reparations, inflation, political turmoil, and the rise of Nazism in the German Weimar Republic

---

The economic and military provisions of the Paris (or Versailles) peace treaties created problems across Europe. By the close of the 1920s, support was building for the brutally authoritarian, territorially aggressive governments that dominated Eu- *rope in the 1930s and 1940s. They were not inevitable. They were responses to failures to secure democratic systems, stable international relations, and economic prosperity.*

638

Major Political Events of the 1920s

1919 (August)	*Weimar Republic's constitution*
1920	*Kapp Putsch*
1921 (March)	*Lenin's New Economic Policy*
(December)	*The Irish Free State recognized*
1922 (April)	*Treaty of Rapallo*
(October)	*Mussolini assumes power*
1923 (January)	*France invades the Ruhr*
(November)	*Hitler's Beer Hall Putsch*
(December)	*First Labour Party government in Britain*
1924	*Death of Lenin*
1925	*Locarno Agreements*
1926	*General strike in Britain*
1928	*Kellogg-Briand Pact*
1929 (January)	*Trotsky expelled from the Soviet Union*
(February)	*Lateran Accord*

~ Political and Economic Factors After the Paris Settlement

New Governments

In 1919, experimental regimes studded the map of Europe. Many countries, though not all, embraced liberal democracy, and for the first time in Europe's history, politicians handling diplomatic and economic matters were responsible to mass electorates. But too often, nations lacked the will and the political skill to make their new systems of government work.

Demands for Revision of the Paris Settlement

Throughout the 1920s, politicians discovered that they could win votes by appealing to various nationalistic concerns and resentments created by the Paris peace treaties. Germany had been humiliated. Various national groups in the successor states of eastern Europe felt that they had been treated unjustly. And France promoted the belief among the victorious powers that the provisions of the treaty were not being adequately enforced.

Postwar Economic Problems

Europeans shared the dream of returning to the economic prosperity of the prewar years. But after 1918, it was impossible to restore to economic life what American President Warren Harding would shortly term "normalcy." During the Great War, Europeans had turned the vast physical power that they had created in the previous century against themselves and devastated the economic foundations of their civilization.

More than 750,000 British soldiers had perished. The combat deaths for France and Germany were 1,385,000 and 1,808,000, respectively. Russia had lost no fewer than 1,700,000 troops. Hundreds of thousands more from other nations had also been killed. Still more millions had been wounded. These casualties represented not only the waste of human life and talent but also the loss of producers and consumers.

At the start of the war, Europe was the financial and credit center of the world. At its end, European states were deeply in debt to each other and to the United States. The Paris settlement imposed heavy financial obligations on the defeated parties. The United States refused to ask reparations from Germany, but it demanded repayment of loans it had made to its allies. The Bolsheviks simply repudiated the debt of the tsarist government, much of which was owed to France. Reparations and debt structures meant that no nation was fully in control of its own economic life. But the absence of international economic cooperation also meant that individual nations felt they had to pursue selfish, nationalistic economic aims.

Market and trade conditions were no longer those that had prevailed before 1914. In addition to the unprecedented loss of life, Europe's transportation systems, mines, and industries had been damaged or destroyed. Russia all but withdrew from the European economic order. The division of eastern and central Europe into a multitude of small states broke up a trade region that had been unified by Germany and Austria-Hungary. Political boundaries separated raw materials from the factories that used them. Railway systems were controlled by two or more nations. Customs barriers appeared where none had been before.

Patterns of international trade changed. The United States, now less dependent on European production, became Europe's major competitor. Combatant nations had financed the war by selling many of their investments abroad. Consequently, European dominance of the world economy diminished. Decline or slowed postwar growth within colonies and former colonies lessened their demand for European goods. The United States and Japan began to penetrate markets in Latin America and Asia that European producers and traders had previously dominated.

New Roles for Government and Labor

In every country, labor unions had supported wartime production by ensuring that workers cooperated with government. Union members had been rewarded with higher wages and union leaders with admission to government councils. The links established between labor leaders and national governments dispelled the internationalism that had characterized the prewar labor movement. They also meant that henceforth government could not ignore labor's demands. This was one of the most significant political changes wrought by World War I.

Since conditions for workers seemed to improve while those of the middle class appeared to stagnate or decline, the middle class grew suspicious of labor's new role and of socialist political parties. Once the vanguard of the liberal revolution, the middle classes became conservative and worked throughout the 1920s to defend the status quo and fend off advances by the working classes. The conservatism of the middle class deepened as fear of Bolshevism spread across the continent.

∼ The Beginning of the Soviet Experiment

Russia's Bolshevik Revolution established the most extensive and durable of the twentieth-century authoritarian governments that came to power in the wake of World War I. The Soviet Union's Communist Party, the greatest single factor shaping the history of Europe in this century, retained power from 1917 until the end of 1991. It was neither a mass party nor a nationalistic one. In its early days, its membership rarely exceeded 1 percent of the Russian population, and for years following 1917 it faced widespread domestic opposition. Communists regarded their revolution not as an event confined to their national history, but as the beginning of a new epoch in the history of humanity. The leaders of the Soviet Union believed they had a duty to export the ideology and doctrines of communism. Opposition to their efforts shaped the foreign policies of Western nations for most of the century.

War Communism

The Red Army, under the organizational direction of Leon Trotsky (1879–1940), eventually overcame internal and foreign military opposition to Russia's new government. The White Russian armies, which opposed the Red Army, failed to organize themselves adequately, and the help the Allies gave them was insufficient. The military threat they posed, however, helped the Bolsheviks justify authoritarian policies. Lenin declared that the Bolshevik Party was empowered as a "dictatorship of the proletariat." A new secret police, the *Cheka*, was established. Political and economic administration became highly centralized. All major decisions were made at the top. An economic policy called "War Communism" was developed. The revolutionary government took over banks, the transportation system, and heavy industries. The state seized grain from peasants to feed soldiers and urban workers. Resistance to these moves was vigorously suppressed.

War Communism helped the Red Army triumph and the revolution survive. But the policy generated domestic opposition to the Bolsheviks. In 1920, the party numbered only about 600,000 members. When many Russians balked at making the sacrifices demanded by central party bureaucrats, the alliance of workers and peasants the Bolsheviks claimed to represent began to come apart at the seams. In 1920 and 1921, there were large strikes at many factories, and peasants resisted the requisition of their grain. In March 1921, the Baltic fleet mutinied at Kronstadt, and the Red Army crushed the revolt with grave loss of life.

The Russian proletariat resisted the Communist Party's idea of a proletariat dictatorship. By late 1920, it was also apparent that working classes in the European nations were not responding to Bolshevik invitations to revolution. For the time being, the Soviet Union was to be a vast island of revolutionary socialism in a global capitalist sea.

The New Economic Policy

Acknowledging reality, Lenin made a crucial strategic retreat. In March 1921, following the Kronstadt mutiny and faced with continuing peasant resistance to grain requisitions, Lenin issued the New Economic Policy (NEP). The government authorized private economic enterprise except in fields involving banking, heavy industry, transportation, and international commerce. The NEP was designed to court the peasants whom Lenin believed held the key to the success of the revolution. It permitted them to sell surplus grain on the open market.

After 1921, the countryside quieted down, and a more secure food supply seemed assured for the cities. Free enterprise flourished in light industry and domestic retail trade. There were, however, virtually no consumer goods for entrepreneurs to buy with the money they made. By 1927, the NEP had returned industrial production to its 1913 level, but it had transformed Russia into a land of discontented small family farmers, private shopowners, and businesspeople.

Stalin Versus Trotsky

The NEP caused sharp disputes within the Politburo, the Communist Party's highest governing committee. Some members saw it as a betrayal of Marxist principles, a partial return to capitalism. So long as Lenin was in control, unity was maintained. But in 1922 he suffered a stroke that led to his death in 1924. The power vacuum created by his disappearance invited an intense struggle for leadership within the party. Two factions emerged—one led by Trotsky and the other by Joseph Stalin (1879–1953), general secretary of the party since 1922. Lenin had stated reservations about both men but was especially critical of Stalin. Stalin, however, had a strong following within the party and control of its day-to-day management.

The issue between Trotsky and Stalin was leadership of the party, but it was cast as a dispute about Russia's path toward industrialization and the future of the communist revolutionary movement. Trotsky, representing a "left" wing, urged rapid industrialization financed through the expropriation of farm production. He wanted to collectivize agriculture and make the peasants pay for industrialization. He also argued that the revolution in Russia could succeed only if similar revolutions took place elsewhere, for Russia needed the help of sympathetic nations to expand its economy. As Trotsky's influence waned, he also became a late, if self-interested, convert to principles of open discussion. He demanded that party members be allowed to criticize government and party policies.

Stalin led the "right-wing" faction that opposed Trotsky. Nikolai Bukharin (1888–1938), the editor of the official party paper, *Pravda (Truth)*, formulated its ideology. Given the uncertain economic outlook of the mid-1920s, he recommended continuation of Lenin's NEP, relatively slow industrialization, decentralized economic planning, and tolerance of modest free enterprise and small landholdings.

Stalin, the son of a poor family, had not spent time in western Europe as had other early Bolshevik leaders. He was much less intellectual and internationalist in his outlook than they, and he was much more brutal. As commissar of nationalities, his treatment of recalcitrant groups within Russia after the revolution had shocked Lenin—though not enough for Lenin to dismiss him. As the party general secretary, a post many disdained as a clerical position, Stalin built a power base within the party's bureaucracy. He was not a brilliant writer or an effective public speaker, but he was master of the crucial, if dull, details of party structure. His control of admission to the party and promotion within it won him the support of the lower levels of the party apparatus in his fights with other leaders.

In 1924, in opposition to Trotsky, Stalin articulated the doctrine of "socialism in one country." It stated that socialism could be achieved in Russia without support from revolutions elsewhere. Stalin thus nationalized what had been an international Marxist movement while cunningly using his control of the Central Committee to edge out Trotsky and his supporters.

By 1927, Trotsky had been expelled from the party and exiled to Siberia. In 1929, he left Russia for Mexico, where he was murdered (presumably by Stalin's agents) in 1940. Trotsky's defeat left Stalin in unchallenged control of the Soviet state. It remained to be seen where he would take it.

The Third International

In 1919, the Soviet communists founded the Third International (known as the "Comintern") to coordinate the European socialist movement. The Comintern aimed at making Lenin's version of socialism the rule for all socialist parties outside the Soviet Union. In 1920, the Comintern imposed the Twenty-one Conditions on any socialist party that wished to join the organization. The Conditions required acknowledgment of leadership from Moscow, rejection of revisionist socialism, and repudiation of previous socialist leaders. Their intent was to end democratic socialism.

Debate about the Conditions split socialist parties, and led to the rise of separate communist and social democratic parties in many European countries. Communist parties modeled themselves after the Soviet party and took orders from Moscow. The social democratic parties pursued social reform through liberal parliamentary politics. Throughout the 1920s and early 1930s, the communists fought each other more intensely than they fought either capitalists or political conservatives.

The Comintern directly and importantly affected the rise of fascism and Nazism. It is difficult to exaggerate the fear aroused in Europe in the 1920s and 1930s by Soviet rhetoric and Communist Party activity. Popular anxieties, which were often exaggerated, were manipulated by conservative and right-wing political groups. The presence of communist parties in Western nations meant that right-wing politicians had a convenient target that they could justly accuse of seeking to overthrow the governments of their respective homelands. Furthermore, right-wing politicians could also accuse democratic socialist parties of facilitating communist takeovers. The division of Europe's political left meant the diminution of its power to oppose right-wing groups.

∾ The Fascist Experiment in Italy

It was in Italy that fear of Bolshevism produced the first western European experiment in political authoritarianism: *fascism*. The term derives from the *Fasci di Combattimento* ("Bands of Combat"), founded in 1919 in Milan by Benito Mussolini (1883–1945). It is applied to a number of the right-wing dictatorships that appeared in Europe between the wars.

Authorities find it hard to formulate a precise definition for fascism, but most fascist states were antidemocratic, anti-Marxist, antiparliamentary, often anti-Semitic, and usually intensely nationalistic. They opposed the spread of Bolshevism and claimed to want to make the world safe for the small property owners of the middle class. Fascists rejected parliamentary politics, for they believed that political parties sacrificed national interests to their petty disputes. By uniting citizens in pursuit of some great national project, fascists hoped to transcend Marxism's class conflicts and liberalism's party struggles. Fascist governments were usually single-party dictatorships that employed terrorism and police surveillance to guarantee absolute loyalty to the state. Unlike the small Communist Party's role in leading the Soviet Union, mass political movements helped organize fascist states.

The Rise of Mussolini

Mussolini recruited followers among Italy's war veterans, many of whom believed that the Paris peace conference had cheated Italy—particularly by denying it control of the city of Fiume at the northern end of the Adriatic Sea. These people also suffered from the effects of inflation and feared the spread of socialism.

Mussolini, born the son of a blacksmith, had worked as a schoolteacher and a day laborer before entering politics. He was first attracted to socialism, and by 1912, he was editor of the movement's newspaper *Avanti (Forward)*. In 1914, he broke with the socialists to support Italy's entry into the war on the side of the Allies. He established his own paper, *Il Popolo d'Italia (The People of Italy)*, served in the army, and was wounded.

Mussolini poses with supporters the day after the black shirt march on Rome intimidated the king of Italy into making him prime minister. [Bildarchiv Preussischer Kulturbesitz]

In 1919, Mussolini was simply one among many politicians and his *Fasci* organization one among many small groups jockeying for position in Italy. Mussolini was an opportunist par excellence. He changed his ideas and principles to suit every new occasion, for he considered action more important than thought or rational justification. His chief goal was political survival.

Postwar Political Turmoil. Postwar Italian politics was a muddle. The Italian Parliament had virtually ceased to function during the war, and many Italians were disillusioned with their government—believing that it had failed at the Paris peace conference to win for Italy the respect and land it deserved.

In 1919, a band of Italian nationalists, led by author Gabriele D'Annunzio (1863–1938), showed how a private military force could succeed where government failed. They occupied Fiume. The Italian army that finally drove them from the city seemed to many people to be less patriotic than D'Annunzio and his men.

Between 1919 and 1921, Italy experienced considerable internal turmoil. There were industrial strikes. Workers occupied factories. Peasants seized uncultivated land from large estates. The nation's Parliament demonstrated no capacity for dealing with the situation. It was dominated by two parties that claimed to represent the working and agrarian classes: a Socialist Party (the split between socialists and communists had not yet taken place) and a new Catholic Popular Party. Since neither group would cooperate with the other, Parliament deadlocked. Many Italians feared that the combination of social upheaval and political paralysis would result in a communist revolution.

Fascist Organization. At first, Mussolini endorsed the factory occupations and land seizures. But when he realized that Italians of the upper and middle classes, pressured by inflation and fearing the loss of their property, were more concerned about order than vague concepts of social justice, he reversed himself. He and his Fascists stepped in and took charge wherever the government failed to act. They formed local squads of terrorists who disrupted Socialist Party meetings, beat up socialist leaders, and intimidated socialist supporters. They attacked strikers and farm workers and protected strikebreakers.

Conservative land and factory owners were grateful, and officers and institutions of the law simply ignored crimes committed by Fascist squads. By early 1922, intimidation had won Fascists control of local governments in much of northern Italy. In the election of 1921, Italian voters sent Mussolini and thirty-four of his followers to the Chamber of Deputies.

In October 1922, the Fascists, dressed in their characteristic black shirts, led a march on Rome. King Victor Emmanuel III (r. 1900–1946), fearing a confrontation, ensured a Fascist seizure of power by refusing to sign a decree authorizing the army to intervene. The cabinet resigned in protest, and on October 29, the monarch asked Mussolini to become prime minister. The next day Mussolini took the train from Milan to Rome, and by the time his marchers arrived, he was the head of the government.

Although Mussolini technically had acquired office by legal means, his party did not hold a majority of votes in the government. His appointment was the result of months of terrorist intimidation. The politicians of opposing parties, whose ineptitude had given Mussolini his chance, were not alarmed. They assumed that his ministry, like others since 1919, would be brief. They failed to comprehend what he was.

The Fascists in Power

Mussolini owed his success to the impotence of his rivals, his effective use of his office, his power over the masses, and his sheer ruthlessness. He employed propaganda to great effect, building a cult of personality. His intelligence and oratorical skill enabled him to hold his own with large crowds and prominent individuals, and many responsible Italians credited him with saving Italy from Bolshevism.

On November 23, 1922, the king and Parliament commissioned him to restore order and granted him dictatorial authority for one year. In 1924, Mussolini had Parliament change the election law to end the confusion created by weak coalition governments. Previously, a party's representation in the Chamber of Deputies reflected the portion of the popular vote it had won. The new election law gave the party that had the largest popular vote (if at least 25 percent) two-thirds of the seats. In the election of 1924, the Fascists took control of the Chamber of Deputies and used their majority to end parliamentary government. A series of laws, passed in 1925 and 1926, permitted Mussolini to rule by decree. In 1926, all other political parties were dissolved, and Italy became a single-party dictatorial state.

Mussolini strengthened his regime by creating a party organization to correspond with each government institution. By the late 1920s, the Grand

Council of the party, which Mussolini controlled, had become the organ of the state that decided who could stand for election to the Chamber of Deputies and which issues the chamber could vote on. The outlawing of other political parties forced citizens to look to the Fascists in their community for political favors.

Fascists also made sure people knew the risk of opposition. Fascist terrorist squads became a government militia. Late in 1924, they murdered Giacomo Matteotti (1885–1924), a prominent non-communist socialist member of Parliament who had criticized Mussolini and exposed the criminality of the Fascist movement. In protest, most opposition deputies withdrew from the Chamber of Deputies. That tactic only gave Mussolini a freer hand.

Accord with the Vatican. In the 1860s, seizure of papal lands by Italy's armies of unification had opened a rift between church and state. After 1870, the popes had remained secluded in the Vatican. By negotiating the Lateran Accord of February 1929 to address the grievances of the papacy, Mussolini persuaded the church to lend respectability to his authoritarian regime. The pope was recognized as the temporal ruler of Vatican City. The state agreed to compensate the papacy for the territory it had confiscated. Catholicism was recognized as the religion of the nation. Church property was exempted from taxes, and church law was given jurisdiction over marriages.

⌒ Joyless Victors

France and Great Britain (helped by the United States) had won the war. Britain had suffered almost no physical damage, and France emerged the strongest military power on the continent. Both nations, however, had lost vast numbers of young men. Their economies had been weakened and their power overseas diminished. Unlike Russia and Italy, neither experienced a revolution or a shift to authoritarian government, but both faced problems.

France: The Search for Security

In France, the 1920s were marked by frequent changes of ministries and drift in domestic policy. Between the end of the war and January 1933, France was governed by no fewer than twenty-seven different cabinets. For five years following the Paris settlement, France's policy was strictly to enforce clauses in the treaty designed to keep Germany weak while building a system of eastern alliances to replace its prewar tie with Russia. In 1920 and 1921, three eastern states that feared revision of the Versailles treaty—Czechoslovakia, Romania, and Yugoslavia—formed the Little Entente. France allied with these states and with Poland, whose independence also depended on the Paris settlement.

This new system of eastern pacts was far weaker than the old Franco-Russian alliance. The new states were no match for Russia, and they were neither united nor reliable. Poland and Romania were more concerned about Russia than Germany, and fear of Hungary drove the Little Entente. If Germany threatened one of these states, it could not depend on the others for help.

Despite its weakness, the formation of this alliance heightened anxieties in the two excluded powers, Germany and the Soviet Union. In 1922, while the European states were holding an economic conference at Genoa, the Russians and the Germans met at nearby Rapallo to sign a treaty of their own. Although the treaty had no secret political or military clauses, the Germans did help train the Russian army, while German soldiers got valuable experience in the use of tanks and planes in the Soviet Union. The treaty increased suspicions about Germany's intentions and prompted France to take action.

Quest for Reparations. Early in 1923, the Allies declared Germany to be in technical default of its reparations payments. Raymond Poincaré (1860–1934), France's nationalistic prime minister, decided to teach the Germans a lesson. On January 11, 1923, he sent a French army to occupy the Ruhr mining and manufacturing district until the reparations were paid. The German government ordered a general strike. But Poincaré sent French civilians to run the mines and railroads, and France prevailed. Germany paid, but so did France. The English, alienated by France's heavy-handed policy, developed increased sympathy for Germany. And the cost of the Ruhr occupation vastly increased inflation, hurting the economies of France and Germany.

In 1924, Poincaré's conservative ministry yielded to a coalition of leftist parties, the *Cartel des Gauches* led by Edouard Herriot (1872–1957). The new cabinet recognized the Soviet Union and adopted a more conciliatory policy toward Germany. Aristide Briand (1862–1932), foreign minister for the remainder of the decade, championed the League of Nations and urged the French not to think that their military power gave them the ability to manage foreign affairs throughout Europe.

When the value of the franc fell sharply in 1926, Poincaré and the conservatives returned to office. For the rest of the 1920s, conservatives remained in power, and France's economy flourished until 1931, longer than that of any other nation.

Great Britain: Economic Confusion

World War I changed Britain's politics, but not its political system. In 1918, Parliament increased the electorate by extending the vote to men at age twenty-one and to women at age thirty. (It was ten more years before women won equal treatment.) The war helped dispel the radical image of the Labour Party, for the war effort was directed by a coalition cabinet that included Labour alongside Liberal and Conservative ministers. Liberal Prime Minister Herbert Asquith (1852–1928) had presided over the cabinet until 1916, when disagreements over management of the war caused him to be ousted by fellow Liberal David Lloyd George (1863–1945). He decided to maintain coalition government until the tasks of peacemaking and domestic reconstruction were finished.

The British economy was depressed throughout the 1920s. Unemployment never dipped below 10 percent and often hovered near 11 percent. There were never fewer than 1 million people unemployed. Government assistance to the unemployed and to widows and orphans increased, but there was no expansion of the number of jobs available. From 1922 onward, life on the "dole" with little hope of employment became the fate of thousands of poor British families.

The First Labour Government. In December 1923, King George V (r. 1910–1936) asked Ramsay MacDonald (1866–1937) to form the first Labour ministry in British history. The Labour Party was socialistic in its platform, but democratic and distinctly nonrevolutionary. MacDonald's version of socialism owed little, if anything, to Marx. He advocated social reform, not nationalization of industry. He also understood that the most important task facing his government was proving to the nation that the Labour Party was responsible. His nine months in office achieved that and, as a consequence, the destruction of the Liberals. The Liberal Party has continued to exist, but the bulk of its voters have drifted into either the Conservative or the Labour ranks.

The General Strike of 1926. The Labour government fell in the autumn of 1924, and the Conservatives governed until 1929. The stagnant economy remained the nation's chief concern. Business and political leaders believed that all would be well if they could restore prewar conditions of trade—particularly the gold standard. In 1925, the government returned to the gold standard, but by setting the conversion rate for the pound too high against other currencies, they raised the price of British goods to foreign customers.

To restore the competitiveness of their products on the world market, British management cut wages to lower costs. Trouble erupted first in the coal industry. It was inefficient and poorly managed and had a long history of unruly labor relations. Negotiations soon broke down, and the coal miners went on strike. Sympathetic workers in other industries supported them with a general strike lasting nine days (May 1926). But in the end the workers capitulated, for high levels of unemployment weakened unions' bargaining positions. After the strike, the government courted labor by erecting new housing and reforming the poor laws. Despite the economic difficulties of these years, the standard of living of most British workers, including those receiving government insurance payments, improved.

Empire. World War I modified Britain's role as an imperial power. The right of self-determination, which Britain claimed to be defending in the war, made it difficult to oppose liberation movements in its colonies.

The growing popularity of Mohandas Gandhi's (1869–1948) Congress Party forced the British to consider eventual self-government for India. During the 1920s, India acquired the right to impose tariffs to favor its industries rather than to protect British manufacturers. British textile producers' access to the Indian market was also limited.

In 1914, the Irish Home Rule Bill had passed Parliament, but its implementation was postponed until after the war. When the war dragged on, Irish nationalists decided they could not wait. On Easter Monday, 1916, they rose up in Dublin. Theirs was the only revolt staged by a national group against any government in wartime. The British suppressed it within a week, but made a grave tactical blunder by executing its leaders. Overnight the rebels became national martyrs, and leadership of the nationalist cause shifted from the Irish Party in Parliament to an extremist group, Sinn Fein ("Ourselves Alone").

In the election of 1918, the Sinn Fein Party won all but four of the Irish parliamentary seats outside Ulster (Northern Ireland). They refused to join the Parliament at Westminster and constituted themselves as the Dail Eireann (Irish Parliament). On January 21, 1919, they declared Irish independence. The military wing of Sinn Fein established the Irish Republican Army (IRA), and a vicious guerilla war soon broke out between the IRA and the British army.

In December 1921, secret negotiations between the two governments resulted in a treaty establishing the Irish Free State as one of the dominions of the British Commonwealth. The six counties of Ulster were granted home rule and allowed to remain part of what was now called the United Kingdom of Great Britain and Northern Ireland. But no sooner had the treaty been signed than a new civil war broke out. Moderates supported the treaty; diehards wanted a totally independent republic. The second civil war continued until 1923. In 1933, the Dail Eireann abolished the oath of allegiance to the British monarch, and the Irish Free State professed neutrality during World War II. In 1949, it declared itself the wholly independent republic of Eire.

∽ Trials of the New Democracies

France and Great Britain had much experience with democratic government. But in Germany, Poland, Austria, Czechoslovakia, and the other successor states that replaced the German, Austro-Hungarian, and Russian empires, parliaments had never exercised genuine political power. It remained to be seen whether they could handle responsibility and whether conservative groups, such as the military, would cooperate with them.

Successor States in Eastern Europe

It had been an article of faith among nineteenth-century liberals sympathetic to nationalism that only good could come from the demise of Austria-Hungary, the restoration of an independent Poland, and the establishment of nation-states throughout eastern Europe. The right to self-determination was to secure popularity for the new states and make them buffers against the westward spread of Bolshevism. From the beginning, however, they were in trouble, for none of the new states had strong economies such as France and Germany had developed in the course of the nineteenth century. They were poor, rural nations trying to compete in an industrialized world economy.

The collapse of the empires that had once imposed restraint on the conduct of ethnic groups freed these groups to demand political self-determination. Majorities in the populations of the new countries refused to make compromises with minorities lest they undermine the identities of their nations. Many minorities wanted independence or union with a nation other than the one that claimed them. The recent breakup of Yugoslavia and Czechoslovakia and the present turmoil in the former Soviet Union are a continuation of this struggle—a struggle that in the period between the world wars led to the rise of authoritarian governments in all the states but Czechoslovakia.

Poland. Poland, divided up by its neighbors, had disappeared from the map late in the eighteenth century. Its restoration, which was something Woodrow Wilson had urged in the Fourteen Points, proved a disappointment to liberals. The Poles' sense of national identity was too weak a bond to overcome disagreements stemming from differences in class, region, and economic self-interest. Sections of the new Poland had been governed for over a century by Germany, Russia, and Austria. Each had its own laws, administration, economy, and history of experience with electoral institutions. A vast number of tiny political parties made it difficult to form a stable parliament, and the constitution gave the executive too little power. In 1926, a military takeover led by Marshal Josef Pilsudski (1857–1935) ended the confusion. At his death, the government passed into the hands of a group of his officers.

Czechoslovakia. Czechoslovakia was the only central European nation to avoid self-imposed authoritarian government. It had unique advantages: a strong industrial base, a substantial middle class, and a tradition of liberal values. During the war Czechs and Slovaks had learned to work together, and in the person of Thomas Masaryk (1850–1937) they had a gifted leader of immense integrity and fairness. His government broke up large estates in favor of small peasant holdings and gave the country the chance to become a viable modern nation.

Some of Czechoslovakia's smaller ethnic groups were unhappy—particularly the Germans of the Sudetenland who found themselves, thanks to the Paris peace settlement, inside the Czech borders. Rather than work with the Czech Parliament, they invited German intervention.

Hungary. Hungary's defeat in the First World War cost it land, but Hungary achieved something it had long sought: separation from Austria. In 1919, Bela Kun (1885–1937), a communist, established a short-lived Hungarian Soviet Republic. The Allies responded by authorizing an invasion by Romania to remove the communists. Kun's government collapsed, and thousands of Hungarians were executed or imprisoned. Hungary's landowners established a regency headed until 1944 by Admiral Miklós Horthy (1858–1957).

Austria. Austria's economy barely functioned, but union with Germany, which would have created a more viable economic unit, was prohibited by the Paris settlement. Throughout the 1920s, the leftist Social Democrats and the conservative Christian Socialists contended for power. Both groups created small armies with which to terrorize their opponents and impress their followers.

In 1933, a Christian Socialist, Engelbert Dollfuss (1892–1934), became chancellor. He tried to steer a course between the Social Democrats and a newly emerging Nazi Party. In 1934, he outlawed all political parties except the Christian Socialists, the agrarians, and the paramilitary groups that composed his "Fatherland Front." He was shot later that year during an unsuccessful Nazi coup. Kurt von Schuschnigg (1897–1977), his successor, presided over Austria until Hitler annexed it in 1938.

Southeastern Europe. Yugoslavia—which, until 1929, was known as the Kingdom of the Serbs, Croats, and Slovenes—had been founded by the Corfu Agreement of 1917. Throughout the interwar period, Serbs dominated its government and clashed violently with the Croats. The Croats tended to be Roman Catholic, better educated, and accustomed to reasonably incorrupt government. The Serbs were Orthodox, somewhat less well educated, and considered (by the Croats) to be corrupt administrators. Though each group predominated in certain areas of the country, each had isolated enclaves in other parts of the nation. Bosnia-Herzegovina also had a significant Muslim population, and Slovenes, Muslims, and other minorities often played the Serbs and the Croats off against each other. Each of the political parties, except for a small Communist Party, represented an ethnic group, not the nation as a whole. In 1929, King Alexander I (r. 1921–1934), a Serb, tried to impose order by outlawing political parties, jailing popular politicians, and declaring a royal dictatorship. He was assassinated in 1934, but authoritarian government continued under a regency for his son.

Elsewhere in the Balkans, other royal dictatorships were imposed. King Carol II (r. 1930–1940) of Romania and King Boris III (r. 1918–1943) of Bulgaria endeavored to control rival ethnic groups and prevent seizure of power by extremist movements. Greece's parliamentary monarchy was plagued by military coups and calls for a republic until 1936, when General John Metaxas (1871–1941) instituted a dictatorship and dispersed Parliament.

The Weimar Republic

The Weimar Republic, named for the city in which its constitution was proclaimed in August 1919, embodied the hopes of German liberals. It was headed by Social Democrats who assumed power following the abdication of Kaiser William II (November 1918). The republic's acceptance of the terms of the Versailles Treaty spared Germany Allied invasion, but many Germans felt little gratitude. They associated the republic with the disgrace and the economic hardship imposed by the treaty.

Throughout the 1920s the republic, which was responsible for implementing the Paris settlement, became an easy target for the very nationalists and military leaders whose policies had caused the war. They blamed the republic and the socialists for Germany's defeat and the grievous consequences. All political groups shared a desire to revise the treaty, but they differed about the means. The degree of loyalty they felt to the Weimar constitution depended upon the extent to which they wanted to revise the Paris settlement with which Weimar was associated.

The Weimar constitution was in many respects a highly enlightened document. It guaranteed civil liberties and provided for universal suffrage and direct election of the *Reichstag* and the president. However, it had crucial structural flaws that allowed its liberal institutions to be overthrown. A system of proportional representation made it easy for small parties to win seats in the *Reichstag*. Ministers were responsible to the *Reichstag*, but the republic's president could appoint or remove its chancellor. In an emergency, he could declare a temporary presidential dictatorship.

The Weimar Republic had not been established by a popular revolution, and it failed to inspire loyalty in many Germans. Some would have preferred a constitutional monarchy. Civil servants, schoolteachers, and judges, who had previously been the Kaiser's devoted agents, distrusted the Social Democrats who dominated republican politics. The officer corps, which profoundly resented the military provisions of the Paris treaty, perpetuated the myth that the German army had surrendered on foreign soil only because it had been stabbed in the back by civilians—particularly by those who founded the republic.

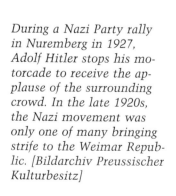

During a Nazi Party rally in Nuremberg in 1927, Adolf Hitler stops his motorcade to receive the applause of the surrounding crowd. In the late 1920s, the Nazi movement was only one of many bringing strife to the Weimar Republic. [Bildarchiv Preussischer Kulturbesitz]

Hitler Denounces the Versailles Treaty

One of the chief complaints of the National Socialist movement was about the unfairness of the Versailles Treaty of 1919. Virtually all German public figures, including leaders of the Weimar Republic, hoped to see that settlement revised. Hitler and his followers made denunciation of the treaty their single most uncompromising demand. In this speech of April 17, 1923, Hitler explained how the treaty had undermined the German nation.

∼ How might the French invasion of the Ruhr and the inflation it produced have contributed to the effectiveness of this speech? To what extent was Hitler's condemnation of the restraints the Versailles Treaty imposed on Germany fair? How does Hitler compare his young Nazi movement with the new Weimar Republic? What makes the one appear strong and the other weak as a supporter of German national goals?

With the armistice begins the humiliation of Germany. If the Republic on the day of its foundation had appealed to the country: "Germans, stand together! Up and resist the foe! The Fatherland, the Republic expects of you that you fight to your last breath," then millions who are now the enemies of the Republic would be fanatical Republicans. To-day they are the foes of the Republic not because it is a Republic but because this Republic was founded at the moment when Germany was humiliated, because it so discredited the new flag that men's eyes must turn regretfully towards the old flag.

It was no Treaty of Peace which was

In March 1920, the right-wing Kapp Putsch (an armed insurrection) erupted in Berlin. Led by a civil servant and supported by army officers, the coup failed, but only after the government had fled the city and German workers had staged a general strike. When later in the month workers in the Ruhr struck, the government sent in troops. Throughout the early 1920s, there were numerous assassinations or attempted assassinations of important republican leaders. And in May 1921, the Allies humiliated the republic by threatening Germany with occupation if it did not accept a preposterous reparations bill of 132 billion gold marks.

Inflation. Borrowing to finance the war and deficit spending after the war created disastrous inflation. As government bonds came due, printing presses poured forth paper money to redeem them. The general strike that German workers staged to counter France's invasion of the Ruhr in January 1923 accelerated economic decline. By November 1923, an American dollar was worth more than 800 million German marks. Money was literally not worth the paper it was printed on. Stores refused to sell goods, and farmers withheld produce from market.

The great inflation of 1923 devastated the lives of many Germans. Middle-class savings, pensions, and insurance policies were wiped out, as were in-signed, but a betrayal of Peace.

The Treaty was signed which demanded from Germany that she should perform what was for ever impossible of performance. But that was not the worst; after all that was only a question of material values. This was not the end: Commissions of Control were formed! For the first time in the history of the modern world there were planted on a State agents of foreign Powers to act as Hangmen, and German soldiers were set to serve the foreigner. And if one of these Commissions was "insulted," a company of the German army had to defile before the French flag. We no longer feel the humiliation of such an act; but the outside world says, "What a people of curs!"

So long as this Treaty stands there can be no resurrection of the German people: no social reform of any kind is possible! The Treaty was made in order to bring 20 million Germans to their deaths and to ruin the German nation. But those who made the Treaty cannot set it aside. At its foundation our Movement formulated three demands:

1. Setting aside of the Peace Treaty.
2. Unification of all Germans.
3. Land and soil to feed our nation.

Our Movement could formulate these demands, since it was not our Movement which caused the War, it has not made the Republic, it did not sign the Peace Treaty.

There is thus one thing which is the first task of this Movement: it desires to make the German once more National, that his Fatherland shall stand for him above everything else. It desires to teach our people to understand afresh the truth of the old saying: He who will not be a hammer must be an anvil. An anvil are we today, and that anvil will be beaten until out of the anvil we fashion once more a hammer, a German sword!

Norman H. Baynes (ed.), The Speeches of Adolph Hitler, *April 1922–1939 (Oxford: Oxford University Press, 1942).*

vestments in government bonds. The ease with which debts and mortgages could be paid off led to speculation in land, real estate, and industry that made great fortunes for some. Union contracts allowed workers to keep up with rising prices, and farmers and food store proprietors could resort to barter. But many members of the middle and lower middle classes were caught in the squeeze. Their desire for order and security at almost any cost contributed to Hitler's rise.

Hitler's Early Career. Adolf Hitler (1889–1945), the son of a minor Austrian customs official, originally hoped to become an artist. As a young man, he sought his fortune in Vienna. There he was supported by his widowed mother, an Austrian orphan's allowance, postcards he painted, and work as a day laborer. There he also became acquainted with Mayor Karl Lueger's (1844–1910) Christian Social Party, a fount of anti-Semitic ideology.

During World War I, Hitler fought in the German army, was wounded, was promoted to corporal, and was awarded the Iron Cross for bravery. The war gave him his first sense of purpose. He became a rabid German nationalist and an extreme anti-Semite. Hatred for Jews led him to oppose everything associated with Karl Marx.

After the war, Hitler settled in Munich and joined a small, nationalistic, anti-Semitic political party. In 1920, it adopted the name National Socialist German Workers' Party—phonetically shortened to "Nazi." The group paraded under a red and white banner with a black swastika, an ancient symbol supposedly representing Germany's "original" Aryan race. The party's platform (the Twenty-five Points) called for repudiation of the Versailles Treaty, unification of Austria and Germany, exclusion of Jews from German citizenship, agrarian reform, prohibition of land speculation, confiscation of war profits, state administration of giant economic cartels, and replacement of department stores with small retail shops.

Originally, the Nazis tried to compete with Marxist political parties for workers' votes by calling for nationalization of industries. When this tactic failed, the Nazis began to redefine *socialism*. In their minds it meant not state ownership of the means of production, but subordination of all economic enterprise to the welfare of the state. The Nazis grew by appealing to every economic group that was under pressure and tailoring their message to their audience. Economically beleaguered war veterans were particularly responsive to their appeals.

Soon after the promulgation of the Twenty-five Points, Captain Ernst Roehm (1887–1934) created a paramilitary organization to serve the party, the *Sturmabteilung* ("storm troopers") or SA. In the mid-1920s, the SA adopted the uniform that caused it to be known as the "brown shirts." Until the Nazis won control of the government, the SA was their chief instrument for intimidating socialists, communists, and other opponents. A private army was a way to skirt the rearmament limitations imposed by the Paris peace settlement and to bring down the Weimar Republic. The republic had no way to control it and the similar paramilitary organizations set up by competing political groups.

On November 9, 1923, Hitler and a band of followers attempted an unsuccessful Putsch at a beer hall in Munich. When local authorities crushed the coup, sixteen Nazis were killed and Hitler was arrested and tried for treason. The trial gave him a national forum for airing his opinions about the republic, the Versailles Treaty, the Jews, and the weakened condition of his adopted country. Sentenced to five years in prison, he served only a few months before being paroled. He passed the time dictating a book—*Mein Kampf (My Struggle)*—and devising a plan to seize political power by legal methods.

The Stresemann Years. Gustav Stresemann (1878–1929), who became chancellor in August 1923, gave new life to the Weimar Republic. He abandoned the expensive policy of passive resistance in the Ruhr and, with the aid of banker Hjalmar Schacht (1877–1970), introduced a new German currency. He helped crush both Hitler's abortive Putsch and smaller communist disturbances.

In 1924, the Allies agreed to a new system of reparation payments. The Dawes Plan, named for American banker Charles Dawes, lowered annual payments and pegged them to fluctuations of the German economy. When the

MAP 27-1 Germany's Western Frontier *The French-Belgian-German border area between the two world wars was sensitive. Despite efforts to restrain tensions, there were persistent difficulties related to the Ruhr, Rhineland, Saar, and Eupen-Malmedy regions that necessitated strong defenses.*

Occupied by the Allies and the United States to 1923

Eupen and Malmédy, to Belgium by Plebiscite, 1920

Saar Basin under the League of Nations, to Germany by Plebiscite, 1935

Demilitarized Areas, a 30 mile-wide strip along the east bank of the Rhine

last French troops left the Ruhr in 1925 (see Map 27-1) and foreign capital began to flow into Germany, employment rose. That year, the election to the presidency of a conservative monarchist and war hero, Field Marshal Paul von Hindenburg (1847–1934), suggested that increasing political and economic stability were reconciling conservatives to the republic.

In late November 1923, Stresemann resigned as chancellor to become foreign minister. In this role, he sought to fulfill the provisions of the Paris settlement, while revising them. His goal was to recover German-speaking territories lost to Poland and Czechoslovakia and to join Austria to Germany. He hoped that a policy of accommodation would restore the respectability and economic stability Germany needed to win international approval.

Locarno. In a spirit of conciliation, foreign secretaries Austen Chamberlain (1863–1937) for Britain and Aristide Briand for France accepted Stresemann's proposal for a fresh start. The result was the Locarno Agreements of October 1925. France and Germany accepted the western frontier established by the Versailles Treaty. No agreement was reached about Germany's eastern frontier, but the Germans signed treaties of arbitration with Poland and Czechoslovakia. France supported German admission to the League of Nations and agreed to withdraw from the Rhineland five years ahead of schedule (1930).

The Locarno Agreements raised hopes across Europe. Chamberlain and Dawes received the Nobel Peace Prize in 1925 and Briand and Stresemann in 1926. In 1928, the leading European nations, Japan, and the United States signed the Kellogg-Briand Pact, renouncing "war as an instrument of national policy."

This much optimism was not justified. France had merely acknowledged that it could not coerce Germany without help. Britain had revealed an unwillingness to uphold the Paris settlement in the east, where Germany disputed its frontiers. Many in France and Germany opposed conciliation. When the Dawes Plan ran out in 1929, it was replaced by the Young Plan (named for its author, American businessman Owen D. Young). Although the Young Plan lowered reparation payments, limited the term for such payments, and removed outside supervision of Germany, there was an intense outcry in Germany against the continuation of any reparations.

The Germans were far from accepting their situation, but another war was not inevitable. Europe, aided by American loans, was recovering its prosperity. A growing economy and further diplomatic adjustments might have rallied the German people behind the Weimar Republic and moderate revisionism. But the Great Depression of the 1930s set Europe on a different path.

At the close of the 1920s, Europe seemed to be emerging from the difficulties created by World War I. Resentments over the peace settlement seemed to abate, and the major powers were cooperating. But the economic and political stability that seemed to be emerging proved illusory, for the world was about to enter the deepest economic depression in modern history. As governments responded to economic collapse, the search for liberty gave way to the search for security. The decade of the 1920s was a time for political experimentation—and the 1930s, for political tragedy.

Review Questions

1. How did the Bolshevik Revolution pose a challenge to the rest of Europe? Why did Lenin institute the New Economic Policy? Was it successful? Could the Russian Revolution have succeeded without Lenin? How did Lenin's policies lead to divisions among Western socialist parties?

2. How did Joseph Stalin come to power? How did he overcome Trotsky's opposition?

3. What is *fascism?* How did the Fascists succeed in obtaining power in Italy? To whom did they appeal? To what extent does Mussolini deserve the credit for his success? How did Mussolini's right-wing Fascist dictatorship compare with Stalin's left-wing Communist dictatorship?

4. Why were Britain and France "joyless victors" after World War I? What weakness did each have? How did World War I change British politics? What caused the decline and fall of the Liberal Party? How successful was the general strike of 1926? By what stages did Ireland win its independence?

5. What foreign policy problems did France face after the signing of the Versailles Treaty? What was the best way to guarantee security for France? Was the invasion of the Ruhr wise? Should France have signed the Locarno pact?

6. Could the Weimar Republic have taken root in Germany, or was its failure inevitable? Between 1919 and 1929, what were the republic's greatest strengths and weaknesses? To what extent did its fate depend more on personalities than on trends in politics and society? Why did the Versailles Treaty loom so large as an issue in Germany's domestic politics?

Suggested Readings

I. BANAC, *The National Question in Yugoslavia: Origins, History, Politics* (1984). An outstanding treatment of the reorganization of eastern European political life.

R. BESSEL, *Political Violence and the Rise of Nazism: The Storm Troopers in Eastern Germany, 1925–1934* (1984). A study of the uses of violence by the Nazis.

K. D. BRACHER, *The German Dictatorship* (1970). A comprehensive treatment of both the origins and the functioning of the Nazi movement and government.

A. BULLOCK, *Hitler: A Study in Tyranny*, rev. ed. (1964). The best biography.

L. FISCHER, *The Life of Lenin* (1964). A sound biography by an American journalist.

P. GAY, *Weimar Culture: The Outsider as Insider* (1968). A sensitive analysis of the intellectual life of Weimar.

N. GREENE, *From Versailles to Vichy: The Third Republic, 1919–1940* (1970). A useful introduction to a difficult subject.

J. HELD, ed., *The Columbia History of Eastern Europe in the Twentieth Century* (1992). Individual essays on each of the nations.

B. JELAVICH, *History of the Balkans*, vol. 2 (1983). The standard work.

P. KENEZ, *The Birth of the Propaganda State: Soviet Methods of Mass Mobilization, 1917–1929* (1985). An examination of the manner in which the Communist government inculcated popular support.

B. KENT, *The Spoils of War: The Politics, Economics, and Diplomacy of Reparations, 1918–1932* (1993). A comprehensive account of the intricacies of the reparations problem of the 1920s.

B. LINCOLN, *Red Victory: A History of the Russian Civil War* (1989). An excellent narrative account.

A. LYTTLETON, *Seizure of Power* (1973). A good narrative of the Italian Fascist rise to power.

A. MARWICK, *The Deluge: British Society and the First World War* (1965). Full of insights into both major and more subtle minor social changes.

J. F. POLLARD, *The Vatican and Italian Fascism 1929–32: A Study in Conflict* (1985). Provides the background to the Lateran Pacts.

S. A. SCHUKER, *The End of French Predominance in Europe: The Financial Crisis of 1924 and the Adoption of the Dawes Plan* (1976). An excellent study of a complicated issue.

D. P. SILVERMAN, *Reconstructing Europe After the Great War* (1982). Examines the difficulties confronted by the major powers.

A. J. P. TAYLOR, *English History, 1914–1945* (1965). Lively and opinionated.

R. TUCKER, *Stalin as Revolutionary, 1879–1929: A Study in History and Personality* (1973). A useful and readable account of Stalin's rise to power.

E. G. WALTERS, *The Other Europe: Eastern Europe to 1945* (1988). An excellent introduction to the problems in the region.

T. WILSON, *The Downfall of the Liberal Party, 1914–1935* (1966). A close examination of the surprising demise of a political party in Britain.

R. WOHL, *The Generation of 1914* (1979). An important work that explores the effect of the war on political and social thought.

28

Europe and the Great Depression of the 1930s

KEY TOPICS IN THIS CHAPTER

∼ Financial collapse and depression in Europe

∼ The emergence of the National Government in Great Britain and the Popular Front in France in response to the political pressures caused by the depression

∼ The Nazi seizure of power in Germany, the establishment there of a police state, and the imposition of racial laws

∼ Planned industrialism, agricultural collectivization, and purges in the Soviet Communist Party and army under Stalin

---

Europe did not share the economic boom that made the 1920s a "roaring" decade for the United States, for its economies did not fully recover from World War I. The Great Depression that began in 1929 was the most severe slump ever experienced by capitalist nations. Business and political leaders despaired at the failure of market mechanisms to restore prosperity, and Marxists rejoiced that the downfall of capitalism was at hand.

Significant Dates from the Era of the Great Depression

1928	*Russia's first Five-Year Plan*
	Nazis win first seats in the Reichstag
1929 (October)	*Wall Street crash*
	Britain's second Labour government
	Collectivization of Russian agriculture
1931 (May)	*Collapse of* Kreditanstalt *in Vienna*
	Britain goes off the gold standard
1932	*Lausanne Conference ends reparations*
(April 10)	*Hindenburg defeats Hitler for presidency*
1933–1934	*Stavisky Affair in France*
1933 (January 30)	*Hitler appointed chancellor*
(February 27)	Reichstag *fire*
(March 23)	*Enabling Act passed*
(July 14)	*Nazis declared Germany's only legal party*
1934 (June 30)	*Murder of SA leadership*
(August 2)	*Death of von Hindenburg*
(December 1)	*Assassination of Kirov*
1935	*Passage of Nuremberg Laws*
1936	*Stalin begins the Great Purge*
(June 5)	*Popular Front government in France under Blum*
1937	*Neville Chamberlain becomes British prime minister*
1938	*Radical ministry in France*
(November 9)	Kristallnacht

⌁ Toward the Great Depression

Three factors heightened the severity and duration of the Great Depression: (1) the financial difficulties created by World War I and the peace settlement, (2) a crisis in production and distribution of goods on the world market, and (3) a failure of the United States and its European trading partners to cooperate.

The Financial Tailspin

The debts European nations incurred during World War I inflated their currencies, and the demand for consumer and industrial goods that the armistice unleashed drove prices still higher. Price and wage increases subsided after 1921, but nations found it difficult to maintain the value of their currencies. The German financial disaster of 1923 and its specter of uncontrolled inflation explain why most governments refused to run budget deficits when the Depression struck.

Reparations and War Debts. French and American politics regarding reparation payments and international war-debt settlements further complicated the picture. France had paid reparations as a defeated nation in 1815 and after

1871. Now that it was a victor, it wanted reparations adequate to finance its postwar recovery. The United States was no less determined to be repaid for the loans it had made to its allies (who were also indebted to each other). Most of the Allies hoped to discharge these obligations by demanding that Germany pay them as reparations.

Reparations and war debts impeded business expansion, capital investment, and international trade. Currency speculation tied up capital that might have funded productive enterprises. Governments imposed controls on credit, trade, and currency. They often imposed high tariffs to curtail importation of foreign goods, for an unfavorable balance of trade meant that a nation lost money it needed to pay its war debts. The financial muddle that resulted hurt trade, production, and employment.

American Investments. In 1924, the Dawes Plan renegotiated reparations and smoothed debt repayments to the United States. Private American capital began to flow to Europe, especially into Germany. This created a short burst of prosperity in Europe after 1925, but in 1928, the booming New York stock market drew money away from European investments. Virtually unregulated financial speculation led to Wall Street's crash in October 1929. U.S. banks had lent customers large amounts of money to invest in the stock market. When the crash made it impossible for banks to recover these loans, banks failed and all kinds of credit diminished or disappeared. Little American capital remained for investment in Europe, and a shortage of capital prevented renewal of loans already made to Europeans.

The End of Reparations. The shortage of American loans contributed to a financial crisis in Europe. In May 1931, a major bank, the Viennese *Kreditanstalt,* collapsed. Government intervention saved Germany's banking system, but Germany could not make its next scheduled reparation payment.

In June 1931, American President Herbert Hoover announced a one-year moratorium on payments of all international debts. This was a sharp blow to France's economy, which relied on German reparations. France had little choice but to go along, for Germany's economy had all but collapsed. In the summer of 1932, the Lausanne Conference ended the era of reparations. Debts owed the United States were settled either through small token payments or default. This did not, however, restore stability.

Problems in Agricultural Commodities

Turmoil in the financial markets was accompanied by a downturn in production and trade. In the 1920s, Europe's capacity to produce goods began to exceed the market for them. This led to factory closings and unemployment. As improved methods of farming, new crop species, expanded tillage, and better transportation increased the world supply of grain, wheat prices fell to record lows. Initially consumers benefited, but the collapse in grain prices meant lower incomes for European farmers at a time when higher wages were raising the cost of the industrial goods they used. Farmers curtailed purchases and began to have difficulty paying off their mortgages and annual business loans.

Countries tried to protect their domestic grain markets by imposing tariffs on imports, but by disrupting trade this may have made things worse. As production outstripped demand and prices plummeted, governments tried to sustain farming by buying agricultural commodities. Government-held reserves soon rose to record levels, and farmers in underdeveloped nations in Asia, Africa, and Latin America could not compete and make enough money to buy finished goods from industrial Europe.

Turmoil in the international agricultural and money markets caused Europe's industries, which depended on foreign customers, to stagnate. Unemployment spread from heavy industries to those producing finished goods. Persistent unemployment in Great Britain and Germany during the 1920s meant that domestic markets in those countries were already "soft." Attempts to restrain spending by governments whose tax bases were shrinking further weakened domestic demand. All these factors interacted to deepen and extend the Great Depression.

Depression and Government Policy

During the Great Depression people with work always well outnumbered the unemployed, and there was economic expansion—particularly in new industries, such as automobiles, radios, synthetics, and service fields. But the general downturn made everyone feel insecure. People in nearly all walks of life feared that it was only a matter of time before they faced poverty or reduced circumstances.

The governments of the late 1920s and the early 1930s were not well suited to deal with these problems. Orthodox economic theory called for them to cut spending to prevent inflation and to wait for market mechanisms to bring the economy back to prosperity. In 1936, John Maynard Keynes's (1883–1946) *General Theory of Employment, Interest, and Money* challenged tradition by arguing that governments could spend their way out of the Depression. But even before that idea took hold, governments across Europe were responding to demands from their electorates to interfere with the economy as never before.

∽ Confronting the Great Depression in the Democracies

Great Britain: The National Government

The Great Depression ended the business-as-usual attitude that had characterized politics in Great Britain and France during the late 1920s. In 1929, a second minority Labour government, headed by Ramsay MacDonald, took office.

George Orwell Observes a Woman in the Slums

Although Great Britain was beginning to emerge from the Great Depression by the late 1930s, much poverty and human degradation remained. This scene, described in 1937 by the social critic and novelist George Orwell (1903–1950), captures a glimpse of the sadness and hopelessness that many British citizens experienced every day of their lives.

~ How does Orwell's descriptive language evoke sympathy for the woman he portrays? What economic conditions led to such poverty? What class attitudes does Orwell begin to explore in this passage?

The train bore me away, through the monstrous scenery of slag-heaps, chimneys, piled scrap-iron, foul canals, paths of cindery mud crisscrossed by the prints of clogs. . . . As we moved slowly through the outskirts of the town we passed row after row of little grey slum houses running at right angles to the embankment. At the back of one of the houses a young woman was kneeling on the stones, poking a stick up the leaden waste-pipe which ran from the sink inside, and which I suppose was blocked. I had time to see everything about her—her sacking apron, her clumsy clogs, her arms reddened by the cold. . . . She had a round pale face, the usual exhausted face of the slum girl who is twenty-five and looks forty, thanks to miscarriages and drudgery; and it wore, for the second in which I saw it, the most desolate, hopeless expression I have ever seen. It struck me then that we are mistaken when we say that "It isn't the same for them as it would be for us," and that people bred in the slums can imagine nothing but the slums. For what I saw in her face was not the ignorant suffering of an animal. She knew well enough what was happening to her—understood as well as I did how dreadful a destiny it was to be kneeling there in the bitter cold, on the slimy stones of a slum backyard, poking a stick up a foul drain-pipe.

George Orwell, The Road to Wigan Pier *(New York: Berkley Medallion Books, 1967; originally printed in 1937), p. 29.*

As the number of Britain's unemployed exceeded 2.5 million in 1931, the ministry split over what to do. MacDonald believed that the budget should be slashed, government salaries reduced, and unemployment benefits cut. This was a bleak program for a Labour government, and many government ministers resisted. The prime minister responded by requesting the resignation of the entire cabinet.

MacDonald arranged for a meeting with King George V, at which he was expected to announce the fall of his government. But instead of resigning, MacDonald agreed to form a coalition cabinet (the "National Government") containing Labour, Conservative, and Liberal members. The facade of a coalition helped the government impose unpleasant measures.

The National Government devised three programs to fight the Depression. It tried to balance its budget by raising taxes, cutting benefits to the unemployed and the elderly, and lowering government salaries. In September 1931, it took Britain off the gold standard and let the value of the pound fall about 30 percent. (This was expected to stimulate exports by lowering the price of British goods abroad.) In 1932, Parliament passed the Import Duties Bill. All goods coming from outside the empire were required to pay a 10 percent *ad valorem* tariff (i.e., not a fixed import fee, but a charge of 10 percent of the cost of each item brought into the country). The gold standard and free trade—hallmarks of a century of British commercial policy—were abandoned.

The National Government's program had some success. Great Britain avoided the banking crisis that hit other countries. Government efforts to keep interest rates down fostered the largest private housing boom in British history, and this helped related industries. In 1934, Britain became the first nation to restore and exceed the 1929 level of production. By 1937, the number of jobless had fallen to just below 1.5 million.

Although Britain's economy was stagnant at the start of the Depression and remained so after the crisis had passed, Britain's political system was never seriously challenged. There were demonstrations by the unemployed, but social insurance kept them from becoming too desperate. The National Government placated employed citizens by seeming to steer a middle course between the extremes of both the Labour and the Conservative parties.

France: The Popular Front

France's Great Depression began later, but lasted longer, than Britain's. The economic slide did not affect the French economy until 1931. Although wages went down, unemployment was not a major problem. Rarely were more than 500,000 French workers without jobs, but relations between labor and management were tense. The government raised tariffs to protect French goods and French agriculture. These measures sustained a home market but did little to combat industrial stagnation.

The first political fallout from the Depression was the election of another Radical coalition government in 1932. The earlier Radical government's policies had allowed rampant inflation to erupt in 1924. This administration pursued a deflationary program. But in the same year that the new ministry took office, the reparation payments upon which the French economy depended stopped. As the economic crisis mounted, political life became difficult and confused.

Right-Wing Violence. Outside the Chamber of Deputies, right-wing groups with authoritarian tendencies forced themselves onto the political scene. These included the *Action Française,* founded in the wake of the Dreyfus affair, and a veterans' organization, the *Croix de Feu* ("Cross of Fire"). More than 2 million people joined these and similar groups. Some advocated monarchy; others wanted military rule. All opposed parliamentary government, socialism, and communism. Their eagerness to end party politics by uniting all citizens in a pursuit of glory for their nation showed a kinship with Fascists and Nazis.

On February 6, 1934, a large demonstration by right-wing groups took place in Paris. When the crowd attempted to march on the Chamber of Deputies, violence erupted. Fourteen demonstrators were killed; scores were injured. It was the largest disturbance in Paris since the Commune of 1871, and it brought down the Radical ministry of Edouard Daladier (1884–1970). A national coalition government composed of all living former premiers was formed. But the demonstration served chiefly to warn the parties of the left that a right-wing coup might succeed in France.

Emergence of Socialist-Communist Cooperation. Between 1934 and 1936, the French left worked at making peace within its own ranks. In 1920, Comintern had split French Socialists, led by Léon Blum (1872–1950), from French Communists. Stalin's fear of Hitler, however, now made cooperation between the two groups possible. Despite mutual suspicions, left-wing parties came together to form the Popular Front in July 1935. Its purpose was to preserve the republic and press for social reform.

The election of 1936 gave the Popular Front a majority in the Chamber of Deputies and, for the first time in France's history, enabled the Socialists, as the largest single party, to form a cabinet. Léon Blum, who assumed the premiership on June 5, was a Jewish intellectual and humanitarian who opposed the communist version of socialism. He saw socialism as compatible with democratic, parliamentary government.

Before the Popular Front came to power, strikes had begun to spread throughout French industry, and the Blum government was immediately challenged by further spontaneous work stoppages. Over 500,000 workers staged sit-ins at their factories. These were the most extensive labor disturbances in the history of the Third Republic, and they alarmed a conservative business community already frightened by the Popular Front's election.

Blum swiftly brought labor and management together. On June 8, he announced an accord that restructured relations between labor and management. Wages were raised—7 percent to 15 percent, depending on the job involved. Employers were required to recognize unions and collective bargaining. The forty-hour week was established, and workers got annual two-week paid vacations. Blum hoped that better labor-management relations would reduce worker hostility to France's social and political institutions and help the economy by increasing domestic consumer demand.

Blum raised the salaries of civil servants and instituted a program of public works. Government loans were extended to small industry. Spending on armaments was increased, and some armament industries were nationalized. A National Wheat Board was set up to manage the production and sale of grain. In the autumn of 1936, international monetary pressure forced Blum to devalue the franc; he did so again in the spring of 1937. The conservative banking and business community was enraged, and, in March 1937, they pressured the ministry to end Blum's reform program. In June 1937, Blum resigned. The

Popular Front ministry held on until April 1938, when it was replaced by a Radical ministry under Daladier.

French industrial production did not return to 1929 levels until 1939. Citizens from all walks of life had reason to wonder if the republic was worth preserving. Business leaders accused it of being inefficient and too subject to socialist pressures. The left remained divided. The right wing hated republics in principle. When the time came in 1940 to defend the republic, too many French citizens doubted whether it was worth the trouble.

∼ Germany: The Nazi Seizure of Power

Germany's Nazi (National Socialist) Party was the most important of the political movements to emerge from the turmoil of the Great Depression. In the late 1920s, the Nazis were a small group that could not seriously contend for power in the Weimar Republic. The change in their political fortunes was wrought by their successful exploitation of fears created by the Depression.

Depression and Political Deadlock

The prosperity of Weimar Germany was undermined when supplies of foreign, especially American, capital dried up in 1928. The coalition of center parties and Social Democrats that headed the republic that year was broken up by disputes over economic policy. Social Democrats defended spending on unemployment insurance and social programs, while conservative parties, frightened by memories of 1923's rampant inflation, insisted on cuts to balance the budget.

President von Hindenburg appointed Heinrich Brüning (1885–1970) chancellor to break the deadlock in the *Reichstag*. Brüning governed through emergency presidential decrees, as authorized by Article 48 of the Weimar constitution. Since divisions among parties prevented Parliament from overriding his decrees, the Weimar Republic became an authoritarian regime.

Unemployment rose from 2,258,000 in March 1930 to over 6,000,000 in March 1932. In the election of 1928, the Nazis won only twelve *Reichstag* seats and the Communists fifty-four. By 1930, the Nazis held 107 seats and the Communists seventy-seven.

The Nazis pursued power by legally campaigning for office while resorting to terror and intimidation. The unemployed hastened to join the storm troopers (SA), who grew from 100,000 in 1930 to almost 1 million in 1933. The SA destroyed decency and civility in political life by viciously attacking opposition parties. At mass rallies resembling religious revivals, Nazis appealed to the pride and frustration of the German nation. They quickly found a following, not just among the unemployed, but among intellectuals and business, military, and media leaders.

Hitler Comes to Power

Brüning survived in the chancellor's office for two years. But when the economy did not improve, Hitler challenged Hindenburg for the presidency. In the election of 1932, Hitler got 30.1 percent of the vote and forced a runoff. In the second election, he polled 36.8 percent. Hindenburg remained in office, but replaced Brüning. The new chancellor, Franz von Papen (1878–1969), was one of a small group of extremely conservative advisers on whom the 83-year-old president had become dependent. Given the continuing paralysis in the *Reichstag*, they virtually controlled the government.

Since the Nazis were the only party with mass support, Papen wanted to win Hitler's cooperation. But he did not want to give him real power. He hoped to convince Hitler that the Nazis could not succeed without the help of the Hindenburg circle. He removed the ban on Nazi meetings that Brüning had imposed and called a *Reichstag* election for July 1932. When the Nazis won 230 seats (37.2 percent of the vote), Hitler demanded appointment as chancellor. Hindenburg refused and called another election in a bid to wear down the Nazis' financial resources. The Nazis lost 34 seats, and their popular vote dipped to 33.1 percent.

In November 1932, Papen resigned. General Kurt von Schleicher (1882–1934), the next chancellor, tried to head off civil war between the left and the right by building a broad-based coalition of conservatives and trade unionists. This alarmed the Hindenburg circle, which did not trust Schleicher's motives, and they persuaded Hindenburg that Hitler was the lesser evil. On January 30, 1933, Hitler was appointed chancellor and Papen vice-chancellor. It was assumed that Papen and a cabinet filled with conservatives could keep Hitler under control.

Hitler had obtained office legally. Therefore, the civil service, the courts, and the other agencies of government could support him in good conscience. He headed a rigidly disciplined party structure, and he was a master of techniques of mass propaganda. He knew how to touch the raw nerves of the electorate, and he won support across the social spectrum, not just, as was once argued, from the lower middle class. In some rural areas and small towns, Roman Catholic voters opposed him. But his following was strong among farmers, war veterans, and the young, whose hopes for the future were imperiled by the Depression. Hitler promised them a defense against communism and socialism, effective government in place of petty party squabbles, and an inspiring nationalist vision of a strong, restored Germany.

Big business once received much of the credit for the rise of Hitler, but there is little evidence that contributions from business leaders made a crucial difference to the Nazi campaign. Hitler's supporters were often suspicious of business and giant capitalism. They wanted a simpler world in which small property would be safe from socialism and capitalist consolidation. The Nazis won out over other conservative nationalistic parties because they better addressed the fears of the German people.

Hitler's Consolidation of Power

Once in office, Hitler quickly consolidated control by winning full legal authority, crushing alternative political groups, and purging rivals within his own party. His opportunity came on February 27, 1933, when a mentally ill Dutch communist set fire to Berlin's *Reichstag* building. The Nazis claimed that the fire was a prelude to a communist assault on the government. Under Article 48 of the Weimar constitution, Hitler issued an emergency decree suspending civil liberties and proceeded to arrest known or alleged communists. The decree remained in effect for as long as Hitler ruled Germany.

In early March 1933, there was another *Reichstag* election. The Nazis received only 43.9 percent of the vote (288 seats), but the removal of all Communist deputies and the political fear aroused by the fire enabled Hitler to get the legislation he wanted. On March 23, 1933, the *Reichstag* passed an Enabling Act authorizing Hitler to rule by decree. Since all legal limits on his power had been removed, he never found it necessary formally to repeal or amend the Weimar constitution.

Hitler knew that he and his party had not been swept into power by destiny. He had worked to get where he was, and he knew how to protect his position. He outlawed or undermined any German institution that might have become a rallying point for his opponents. In early May 1933, the Nazi Party, acting like a branch of government, seized the offices, banks, and newspapers of the free trade unions and arrested their leaders. By July 14, 1933, the National Socialists had been declared the only legal party in Germany. The Nazis then moved against the governments of the individual federal states in Germany, and by the end of 1933, all opposition to them had been silenced.

Hitler's final step was to consolidate his hold on the Nazi Party. His chief concern was his strongest potential rival, Ernst Roehm (1887–1934), commander of the SA, the party's private army of 1 million active storm troopers. On June 30, 1934, Hitler ordered the murders of Roehm and key SA officers. By July 2, more than 100 persons had been killed, including the former chancellor General Kurt von Schleicher and his wife. The regular German army, the only institution that might have prevented the murders, was delighted by the destruction of a group that it saw as trespassing on its territory. On August 2, Hindenburg died, and Hitler claimed the offices of both chancellor and president—making himself sole ruler of Germany and its Nazi Party.

The Police State and Anti-Semitism

Hitler set up a police state under the surveillance of the SS (*Schutzstaffel*, "protective force"), commanded by Heinrich Himmler (1900–1945). This group originated in the mid-1920s as Hitler's bodyguard, and it had evolved into a more elite paramilitary organization than the huge SA. (By 1933, it had about 52,000 members.) It carried out the bloody purges of the party in 1934, and by 1936, Himmler was second only to Hitler in Germany.

Hitler's police state bore down most heavily on Germany's Jews, for anti-Semitism was a key plank in the Nazi program. It was motivated not by religious feeling, but by biological theories of race rooted in late-nineteenth-century science. There were three stages in the Nazi attack on the Jews. In 1933, shortly after assuming power, the Nazis excluded Jews from the civil service and tried, ineffectively, to persuade the public to boycott Jewish businesses. In 1935, a series of measures known as the Nuremberg Laws robbed Jews of rights of citizenship. Professions and key occupations were closed to them. Marriage and sexual intercourse between them and non-Jews were prohibited. In November 1938, under orders from the Nazi Party, thousands of Jewish stores and synagogues were sacked on what became known as *Kristallnacht* ("glass night," from the sound of breaking windows). Henceforth Jews were forbidden to own businesses in Germany. By these means and other acts of public humiliation, the Nazis indoctrinated the population with faith in the concept of a master race of pure German "Aryans" and prepared Germany to accept the "final solution," the extermination of Europe's Jews.

Nazi Economic Policy

Hitler was more effective than any other European leader at dealing with economic problems, and his success ensured loyalty to his tyrannical regime. What he did was to create jobs by mobilizing his nation for a war of aggression. In the process he sacrificed all political and civil liberties, destroyed trade unions, prevented the private exercise of capital, and ignored consumer demand.

Hitler endorsed private property and capitalism, but subordinated all economic enterprise to the needs of the state. He instituted a massive program of public works and spending, much of which was related to rearmament. Workers were often assigned jobs rather than being allowed freely to choose them. The government handled labor disputes through compulsory arbitration, and it enrolled workers and employers in the "Labor Front," a propaganda campaign promoting worker loyalty to the state.

In 1935, Germany renounced the military provisions of the Versailles Treaty and began openly to rearm. In 1936, Hitler commissioned Hermann Göring (1893–1946), head of the air force, to develop a Four-Year Plan to prepare Germany economically and militarily for war. This essentially restored full employment while pandering to the desire of the German people for national vindication.

Women in Nazi Germany

Hitler and other Nazis believed that men and women had separate spheres of activity. Men belonged in the public arena, women in the home. Nazis dismissed the feminist movement as a symptom of cultural decline and urged women to earn respect by fulfilling duties as wives and mothers, not by competing with men.

Young women among an enthusiastic crowd extend the Nazi salute at a party rally in 1938. Nazi ideology encouraged women to favor traditional domestic roles over employment in the workplace and to bear many children. The onset of the war, however, forced the government to recruit women workers. [Bildarchiv Preussischer Kulturbesitz]

These attitudes directly opposed many of the changes that had taken place in German society during the first three decades of the twentieth century. German women had become much more active and assertive. More of them worked in factories or were independently employed. Some had entered the professions. The Weimar constitution, by giving them the vote, had also stimulated a lively discussion of issues surrounding their emancipation.

The Nazis dismissed all this as a sign of cultural weakness and urged women to return to traditional roles. Conservative women welcomed what they saw as official validation of their decision to be homemakers. Men were pleased, for in an era of high unemployment, they were eager to reduce competition from women in the workforce.

Racism colored the Nazi view of women. Nazis argued that the superiority of the German race depended on maintaining the purity of its blood and that women, as mothers, were especially responsible for this. Women were to breed strong sons and daughters for the state, and their role in childbirth was compared to that of men in battle. In both cases, the needs of the nation took precedence over those of individuals. The needs of a nation contemplating war were obvious: a large pool of manpower. It was, therefore, the duty of women to bear many children. The Nazis awarded medals to mothers of large families and sponsored schools to teach women how to rear children—nurturing in them a passionate love for German culture and the motherland.

The Nazis did not reduce the number of women in the workforce. From 1928 to 1939, the proportion of employed German women remained constant at 37 percent. As the war went on, the government recruited more female workers. But Nazi ideology maintained that the kinds of employment women sought outside the home ought to use their gifts as women and never force them to slacken in their duties as wives and mothers.

❦ Italy: Fascist Economics

In Italy, the Fascists substituted discipline for economic policy and creativity. During the 1920s, Mussolini undertook vast public works, such as draining the Pontine Marshes near Rome. The government subsidized the shipping industry and introduced protective tariffs. Mussolini desperately tried to make Italy self-sufficient, but he was unable to stave off the effects of the Great Depression. Production, exports, and wages fell.

The Fascists sought to steer an economic course between socialism and a liberal laissez-faire system. Their policy, known as *corporatism*, organized major industries as syndicates of labor and management. These syndicates were to cooperate in designing a planned economy. The government stepped in when necessary to settle labor disputes, but labor and management were urged to look beyond their private interests to the greater goal of productivity for the nation.

Corporations

After 1930, industrial syndicates were further organized into entities called *corporations*. A corporation united all the people who contributed, from raw materials through finished products and distribution, to a particular kind of productive work (e.g., agriculture or metallurgy). Twenty-two corporations encompassed Italy's whole economy. In 1938, Mussolini replaced the Chamber of Deputies with a Chamber of Corporations. Instead of increasing production, this vast organizational framework spawned bureaucracy and corruption.

Italy's experiment with corporatism did not last long; in 1935, Italy, like Germany, began to structure its economy for military mobilization. When Italy declared war on Ethiopia, the League of Nations imposed ineffective economic sanctions. Taxes rose, and the government imposed a forced loan on the citizenry. (Property owners were required to buy government bonds.) Wages continued to fall, and as international tensions mounted, the state's management of the economy increased. Fascism brought order to Italy, but it was not the order of prosperity.

❦ The Soviet Union: Central Economic Planning and Party Purges

The Decision for Rapid Industrialization

While Western capitalist systems suffered through the Great Depression, the Soviet Union made tremendous economic progress. But Russia achieved its stunning growth during the 1930s only at the cost or degradation of millions of lives.

Through 1927, Lenin's New Economic Policy (NEP), which Stalin supported, guided Soviet economic development. The program relied on private enterprise in rural districts to ensure food supplies for urban workers. Although 1913's industrial production level had been restored by 1927, the Party Congress of 1927 decided to abandon NEP and push for more rapid industrialization. The result was one of the most striking accomplishments of the twentieth century. Russia's economy grew more rapidly than that of any other Western nation during any comparable time period.

By conservative Western estimates, Soviet industrial production—which emphasized heavy machinery and not consumer goods—rose about 400 percent between 1928 and 1940. Russia had plenty of domestic labor, but capital had to be obtained from abroad by selling grain, even if that meant food shortages at home. As in the tsarist past, technology was borrowed from other industrialized nations.

Stalin's strategy was to create a series of Five-Year Plans overseen by the State Planning Commission (Gosplan). The plans set goals for production and organized the economy to meet them. The result was increasing regimentation of the industrial labor force and the peasantry. The task of coordinating all facets of production was immensely complicated, and there was many a slip between the cup and the lip. To elicit cooperation from the Russian people, the government and the Communist Party undertook a vast program of propaganda lauding the Five-Year Plans.

By the close of the 1930s, the results of the three Five-Year Plans were truly impressive. Industries that had not previously existed in Russia now challenged, and in some cases surpassed, counterparts elsewhere. These developments probably enabled the Soviet Union to survive invasion by Germany, but the social and human costs were astounding.

An enormous propaganda effort accompanied the Soviet Five Year Plans. This poster proclaims, "For the betterment of the Soviet people we are building an electricity plant." [Bildarchiv Preussischer Kulturbesitz]

ДЛЯ БЛАГА СОВЕТСКОГО НАРОДА
ПОСТРОИМ НОВЫЕ ЭЛЕКТРОСТАНЦИИ!

The Collectivization of Agriculture

The pursuit of rapid industrialization had enormous consequences for Soviet agriculture. The *kulaks,* cultivators of relatively large properties (less than 5 percent of farmers), prospered under the NEP. They, however, were discontented, for there were few consumer goods for them to buy with the cash they earned. Frequently during the 1920s, they organized movements to withhold grain from the market. The government worried about potential unrest caused by food shortages in the cities.

Following months of difficulty lasting from 1928 into 1929, Stalin came to the decision that agriculture had to be collectivized. His objectives were to end upheavals in the farm sector of the economy, to produce sufficient grain for domestic consumption and export, and to free some peasants to work in the factories of the expanding industrial sector. Stalin basically embraced Trotsky's earlier economic position and unleashed a second Russian revolution of unprecedented violence.

Collective farmers bringing grain to a shipment center. Note that horse-drawn wagons are the only form of transport in this picture; there are no trucks or tractors. [Bildarchiv Preussischer Kulturbesitz]

In 1929, Stalin blamed the *kulaks* for grain shortages and set about eliminating them as a class. (A *kulak* was soon defined as anyone who opposed Stalin.) Peasants and farmers of all kinds united to sabotage collectivization. Between 1929 and 1933, they slaughtered more than 100 million horses and cattle, and the countryside erupted in open warfare. In March 1930, Stalin—claiming "dizziness from success"—called a brief halt to the process.

The drive to collectivize the farms was soon renewed with vehemence. As many as 10 million peasants were killed, and millions of others were dragged off to collective farms or labor camps. Stalin persevered, although turmoil on the land caused agricultural production to fall and famine to spread in 1932 and 1933. Uprooted peasants were moved to thousand-acre collective farms that were worked with state-supplied machinery.

Collectivization dramatically changed Russian farming. In 1928, small peasant holdings accounted for approximately 98 percent of Russia's farms. Ten years later, over 90 percent of the land had been collectivized, and the amount of farm produce handled by the government had risen 40 percent. The government had won control of the food supply and deprived farmers of the power to cause unrest in the cities. But Stalin and the Communist Party failed to achieve their second crucial objective: expanded grain production. That difficulty continues to plague the Soviet Union.

Foreign Reactions and Repercussions

Many foreigners were naively enthusiastic about the Soviet economic experiment, for while the capitalist world languished, the Soviet economy grew at a pace never realized in the West. These observers ignored the shortages in consumer goods, the poor housing, and the social cost of the Soviet achievement. The full extent of human suffering and loss during those years will probably never be known, but it far exceeded the price of Europe's nineteenth-century industrialization, which had so appalled Marx and Engels.

In 1934, Stalin, fearing that Russia might be left alone to face aggression by Nazi Germany, reversed the Comintern policy established by Lenin in 1919 as part of the Twenty-one Conditions. He ordered Communist parties in other countries to cooperate with non-Communist groups against Nazism and Fascism.

The Purges

Stalin's programs aroused internal opposition. In 1929, he forced Nikolai Bukharin, a fervent supporter of the NEP, off the Politburo. Not much is known about continuing resistance at lower levels in the party, but, by 1933, Stalin was afraid that he was losing control. Whether the threat to him was real or imagined, it resulted in the Great Purges, one of the most mysterious and horrendous political events of the twentieth century.

On December 1, 1934, Sergei Kirov (1888–1934), a member of the Politburo, was assassinated. In the wake of the shooting, thousands of people were arrested. Many others were expelled from the party and sent to labor camps. It is almost certain that Stalin authorized Kirov's murder because he feared Kirov as a rival, but Stalin used the charge of direct or indirect complicity in the crime against his opponents.

Between 1936 and 1938, a series of spectacular show trials were held in Moscow. High Soviet leaders confessed to political crimes they had not committed and were convicted and executed. Other party members were tried in private and shot. Hundreds of thousands of people received no trials at all, and no one can explain why some were executed, others sent to labor camps, and still others left unmolested. After the civilian party members had been purged, the prosecutors turned against the army. Officers, including heroes of the civil war, were shot. Hundreds of thousands of members of the party were expelled, and applicants for membership were removed from the rolls. The exact numbers of executions, imprisonments, and expulsions are unknown, but certainly they ran into the millions.

Since no national emergency existed in Russia, the purges astonished Western observers. The scale of the political turmoil was unprecedented, and even the Russians could not comprehend what was happening. If there is a rational explanation, it lies in Stalin's fear for his own power. The purges created a party structure absolutely subservient to him. The "old Bolsheviks" of the October Revolution were destroyed and replaced by newcomers who had little knowledge of old Russia or of the ideals of the original Bolsheviks. They knew no leader but Stalin.

By the middle of the 1930s, dictators of the right and the left had established themselves across Europe. Political tyranny was not new, but these rulers were unique. They were supported by well-organized political parties rooted in nationalism, fear of the Great Depression, and schemes for transforming the social and political order. They monopolized mass communications and used armies, police forces, and party machines to terrorize opponents. Thanks to the technologies of the Second Industrial Revolution, they had unprecedented destructive power at their disposal.

∾ Review Questions

1. What caused the Depression of the 1930s? Why was it more severe and longer-lasting than previous depressions? Could it have been avoided?

2. How successful, respectively, were Britain's National Government and France's Popular Front in dealing with their nations' economic problems? How would you account for the differences? Why did France's

Third Republic have so few supporters?

3. How did the Depression affect Germany? How did Hitler rise to power between 1929 and 1934? Was his dictatorship inevitable? Which played the larger role in his successful seizure of power, his personality or his politics?

4. What were Hitler's economic policies? Why did they work? How does his economic program compare with the economic policies put in place in Britain, Italy, and France? Why were some nations more successful than others in addressing the Depression?

5. What are the characteristics of a "police state"? What is the role of terror and intimidation in the consolidation of an authoritarian regime? Are they necessary to its survival? How did Hitler, Mussolini, and Stalin use terror to achieve their goals?

6. Why did Stalin decide that Russia had to industrialize rapidly? Why did this require the collectivization of agriculture? What obstacles stood in the way of collectivization? How did Stalin overcome them? What caused the purges in the Soviet Union? What groups were the special targets of the purges? Why?

~ Suggested Readings

W. S. ALLEN, *The Nazi Seizure of Power: The Experience of a Single German Town, 1930–1935*, rev. ed. (1984). A classic treatment of Nazism in a microcosmic setting.

N. BRANSON and M. HEINEMANN, *Britain in the Nineteen Thirties* (1971). Primarily considers the social and economic problems of the day.

R. CONQUEST, *The Great Terror: Stalin's Purges of the Thirties* (1968). The best treatment of the subject to date.

R. CONQUEST, *The Harvest of Sorrow: Soviet Collectivization and the Terror-Famine* (1986). A study of how Stalin used starvation against his own people.

B. EICHENGREEN, *Golden Fetters: The Gold Standard and the Great Depression, 1919–1939* (1992). A remarkable study of the role of the gold standard in the economic policies of the interwar years.

R. GELLATELY, *The Gestapo and German Society: Enforcing Racial Policy, 1933–1945* (1990). A discussion of how the police state supported Nazi racial policies.

J. JACKSON, *The Politics of Depression in France, 1932–1936* (1985). A detailed examination of the political struggles prior to the Popular Front.

J. JACKSON, *The Popular Front in France: Defending Democracy, 1934–1938* (1988). The best recent treatment.

H. JAMES, *The German Slump: Politics and Economics, 1914–1936* (1986). A difficult but informative examination of the German experience of the Great Depression.

C. KINDLEBERGER, *The World in Depression, 1929–1939* (1973). An account by a leading economist whose analysis is comprehensible to the layperson.

D.J.K. PEUKERT, *Inside Nazi Germany: Conformity, Opposition, and Racism in Everyday Life* (1987). An excellent discussion of life under Nazi rule.

D. SCHOENBAUM, *Hitler's Social Revolution: Class and Status in Nazi Germany* (1966). A fascinating analysis of Hitler's appeal to various social classes.

D. M. SMITH, *Mussolini's Roman Empire* (1976). A general description of the Fascist regime in Italy.

A. SOLZHENITSYN, *The Gulag Archipelago*, 3 vols. (1974–1979). A major examination of the labor camps under Stalin by one of the most important contemporary writers.

J. STEPHENSON, *The Nazi Organization of Women* (1981). Examines the attitude and policies of the Nazis toward women.

L. YAHIL, *The Holocaust: The Fate of the European Jewry, 1932–1945* (1990). A major recent study of this fundamental subject in twentieth-century history.

Reference should also be made to the works cited in chapters 27 and 29.

29

World War II

KEY TOPICS IN THIS CHAPTER

～ The origins of World War II

～ The course of the war

～ Racism and the Holocaust

～ The impact of the war on the people of Europe

～ Relationships among the victorious Allies and the preparations for peace

---

Idealistic survivors of the First World War hoped that it would be "the war to end all wars," but only twenty years after it ended a second and even more terrible global conflict erupted. In Europe and Asia, democracies fought for their lives against militaristic, nationalistic, author- *itarian, and totalitarian states. Victory did not bring peace, but a Cold War in which the European states were subordinated to two partially or fully non-European superpowers: the Soviet Union and the United States.*

Significant Dates from the Era Culminating in World War II

1919 (June)	*The Versailles Treaty*
1931 (Spring)	*Onset of the Great Depression in Europe*
1933 (January)	*Hitler comes to power*
1935 (March)	*Hitler renounces disarmament*
(October)	*Mussolini attacks Ethiopia*
1936 (March)	*Germany remilitarizes the Rhineland*
(July)	*Outbreak of the Spanish Civil War*
(October)	*Formation of the Rome-Berlin Axis*
1938 (March)	Anschluss *with Austria*
(September)	*Munich Conference; partition of Czechoslovakia*
1939 (August)	*The Nazi-Soviet pact*
(September)	*Germany and the Soviet Union invade Poland; Britain and France declare war on Germany*
(November)	*The Soviet Union invades Finland*
1940 (April)	*Germany invades Denmark and Norway*
(May)	*Germany invades Belgium, the Netherlands, Luxembourg, and France*
(June)	*Fall of France*
(August)	*Battle of Britain begins*
1941 (June)	*Germany invades the Soviet Union*
(July)	*Japan takes Indochina*
(December)	*Japan attacks Pearl Harbor; United States enters war*
1942 (June)	*Battle of Midway*
(November)	*Battle of Stalingrad begins; Allies land in North Africa*
1943 (February– August)	*Allies take Sicily, land in Italy*
1944 (June)	*Allies land in Normandy*
1945 (May)	*Germany surrenders*
(August)	*Atomic bombs dropped on Hiroshima and Nagasaki*
(September)	*Japan surrenders*

∼ Again the Road to War (1933–1939)

World War I and the Versailles Treaty contributed only marginally to the world depression of the 1930s. But in Germany, where payment of war reparations had fueled vast inflation in 1923, Adolf Hitler denounced the peace settlement as the root of all ills. The Nazi Party succeeded, in part, because it appealed to German nationalism and attended to Germany's social problems. Once Hitler became chancellor in January 1933, the nation's foreign policy also centered on these issues.

Hitler's Goals

From his first published manifesto, *Mein Kampf (My Struggle)*, a book he wrote in jail in 1924, to his suicide in his underground bunker in Berlin in 1945,

Hitler's thoughts were centered on race. He considered the German people (the *Volk*) to be a race, and he was determined to push out Germany's 1914 boundaries (the limits to which his predecessors had aspired) to encompass all Germans in a single nation. The new Germany was to include all the Germanic parts of the old Habsburg Empire, including Austria.

A virile, growing Germany would need, however, even more "space to live" *(Lebensraum)*. This was to be acquired by conquering Poland and Ukraine, land occupied by Slavs—a race Hitler considered fit only for servitude. The Jews, another race the Nazis regarded as inferior, were to be removed completely from German territory. Hitler articulated no plan of action. He was a brilliant improviser who kept his goals clearly in sight and exploited opportunities as they arose.

Germany Rearms. When Hitler came to office, Germany was far too weak simply to take the land he wanted. It had first to break the fetters imposed by the Versailles Treaty and restore its formidable military power. In October 1933, Germany—claiming that other powers had not honored promises to disarm—withdrew from an international disarmament conference and from the League of Nations. The following January, Germany signed a nonaggression pact with Poland, an eastern enemy that France had hoped would prevent Germany from risking another war on its western front. In March 1935, Hitler formally renounced the disarmament provisions of the Versailles Treaty. He then established a German air force and reinstated conscription to build an army of 500,000 men.

The League of Nations Fails. In September 1931, two years before Hitler became chancellor, a Japanese invasion of Manchuria had sent China fleeing to the League of Nations for help. A report written by a British diplomat, the Earl of Lytton (1876–1951), condemned the Japanese, but the league failed to act. Japan simply withdrew from the league and remained in Manchuria.

The league's manifest weakness convinced Hitler that it was safe to rearm Germany. As he expected, his action was condemned, but unopposed. France and Britain, having reneged on promises to disarm, were not in a strong position to object. Instead, they tried intimidation. They formed the Stresa Front (June 1935), a pact with Mussolini to cooperate in using force to maintain the status quo in Europe. This arrangement failed as each nation pursued its own interests. Britain, desperate to maintain its superiority at sea, sacrificed France's security by making a separate naval agreement with Hitler. It authorized a German fleet 35 percent as large as the British navy. Italy's ambitions in Africa caused further friction among the Allies, and the result was to grant Hitler a free hand.

Italy Attacks Ethiopia

Mussolini's attack on Ethiopia in October 1935 was intended to avenge a humiliating defeat that Italy had suffered in 1896, to recall Rome's imperial glory, and to distract the Italians from domestic problems. The League of Nations' response advertised its impotence and the timidity of the Allies.

France and Britain hoped to offset the growing power of Germany by appeasing Mussolini. But Italy's aggression so outraged public opinion that their governments were forced at least to appear to resist. The League of Nations, for the first time, voted sanctions—imposing an arms embargo and limiting loans, credits, and trade involving Italy. But Britain and France, fearful of alienating Mussolini, refused to embargo oil, the one thing that could have prevented Italy's victory. The British fleet also allowed Italian troops and munitions passage through the Suez Canal. This totally discredited the League of Nations and its commitment to collective security and drove an offended Mussolini into Hitler's arms. By November 1, 1936, there was open talk of a Rome-Berlin "Axis."

Remilitarization of the Rhineland

The Ethiopian affair diminished Hitler's respect for the Western powers. On March 7, 1936, he probed their resolve by sending a small armed force into the demilitarized Rhineland. This breached the Versailles Treaty and the Locarno Agreements, canceling a key guarantee of French security. France and Britain had every right to resist. Yet neither power did anything but register a feeble protest with the League of Nations. British opinion was opposed to backing France, and the French would not act alone. Both countries were weakened by a growing pacifism.

In retrospect, it is clear that on this occasion the Allies lost a great opportunity to stop Hitler before he became a serious menace. His move into the Rhineland was taken against the advice of his generals, and its failure might have led to his overthrow. At the least, it would have made German expansion to the east dangerous or impossible. The Germans themselves later admitted that the French army could easily have routed the tiny force they sent into the Rhineland.

A rearmed Germany with a defensible western frontier changed the diplomatic game in Europe and prompted the Allies to devise a policy of *appeasement*. It was based on beliefs that Germany's grievances were real and Hitler's goals limited. Horror at the memory of the last war increased public pressure on governments to make concessions to preserve peace, and a firmer policy would have required a rapid rearmament that British leaders, in particular, hoped to avoid. They feared its expense and believed that an arms race had led to World War I. Consequently, Britain hoped for the best; Germany armed; and France huddled behind a newly constructed defensive wall, the Maginot Line.

The Spanish Civil War

The polarization of Europe between democracies and fascist states was made clear when a civil war erupted in Spain in 1936. In 1931, the Spanish monarchy had collapsed, and Spain had become a democratic republic. The republic's program of moderate reform antagonized landowners, the Roman Catholic Church, nationalists, and conservatives—without satisfying peasants, workers, Catalan separatists, or radicals. In February 1936, the Spanish Popular Front (a coalition of republicans, Communists, and anarchists) triumphed at the polls, but losers in the election, especially the Falangists, Spain's fascists, refused to accept defeat. In July, an army led by General Francisco Franco (1892–1975) attacked the republic from Spanish Morocco. This began a civil war, lasting almost three years, that became a training ground for World War II. Germany and Italy sent troops, airplanes, and supplies to support Franco. The Soviet Union aided the republicans, as did many American and European volunteers.

The civil war brought Germany and Italy closer together and led to the Rome-Berlin Axis Pact of 1936. The Axis powers were joined that year by Japan in the Anti-Comintern Pact, an alliance, designed ostensibly, to oppose international communism. Western Europe, especially France, was eager to prevent Spain from falling into the hands of a fascist regime allied with Germany and Italy. But appeasement continued. Although international law permitted the sale of munitions to Spain's legitimate republican government, France and Britain forbade the export of war materials to either side. The United States affirmed neutrality, and Barcelona fell to Franco early in 1939.

Austria and Czechoslovakia

In 1934, Nazis had assassinated Austria's prime minister and tried to seize power. Mussolini, who was not yet allied with Hitler, quickly moved an army to the Austrian border to prevent Germany from intervening to complete the coup.

In 1938, Hitler, now Mussolini's friend, tried again to take over Austria. The Austrian chancellor, Kurt Schuschnigg (1897–1977), refused to be intimidated by threats and declared that the Austrian people would decide the question of union with Germany for themselves. A plebiscite was announced for March 13. To forestall this, Hitler sent his army into Austria on March 12. Mussolini stood quietly by as Hitler entered Vienna amid the cheers of Austrian sympathizers.

The *Anschluss,* the union of Germany and Austria, was a clear violation of the Versailles Treaty. But no nation stepped forward to oppose it. This was doubly alarming, for the process of German expansion was not likely to stop with Austria. Germany now surrounded Czechoslovakia, one of the bulwarks protecting France, on three sides.

The existence of a democratic Czechoslovakia, an ally of France and Russia, was an affront to Hitler, for it had been created partly as a check on Germany. About 3.5 million Germans, residing as a resentful minority in the nation's Sudetenland district, gave him an excuse for intervention. Led by a Nazi, Konrad Henlein (1898–1945), they agitated for autonomy within the Czech state. The Czechs made concessions, but Hitler increased his demands in order to force a confrontation that would destroy Czechoslovakia.

In May 1938, the Czechs reacted to rumors of invasion and mobilized their army. France, Britain, and Russia warned that they would defend the Czechs, and Hitler, who was not yet prepared to attack, was forced to deny that he had designs on Czechoslovakia. Infuriated by this public humiliation, he mobilized his forces. This frightened France and Britain. Neville Chamberlain (1869–1940), Britain's prime minister, was thoroughly committed to the policy of appeasement and determined to keep Britain out of war. He pressed the Czechs to make further concessions, but nothing was enough.

On September 12, 1938, Hitler made a speech at a Nazi Party rally in Nuremberg that prompted rioting in the Sudetenland. The Czechs declared martial law, and German intervention seemed imminent. Between September 15 and 29, Chamberlain made three flights to Germany to negotiate with Hitler. On September 15, Chamberlain forced the Czechs, who were defenseless without the support of their Western allies, to separate the Sudetenland from Czechoslovakia. But a week later, Hitler insisted on German military occupation of the Sudetenland within three days.

Munich

At the last moment, at Chamberlain's request, Mussolini proposed a conference of Germany, Italy, France, and Britain. Meeting in Munich on September 29, it granted Hitler almost everything he wanted. The Sudetenland became part of Germany. This deprived the Czechs of the ability to defend themselves, but Hitler renounced any further territorial ambitions. Chamberlain returned to England to claim that he had made a "peace with honour."

Munich taught Europe that fear of war may bring on war. By giving Germany a hunk of Czechoslovakia, the Munich agreement encouraged Poland and Hungary to lay claims to other parts of the nation. The Slovaks also demanded recognition as a separate state. On March 15, 1939, Hitler swept them all aside by breaking his promises and occupying Prague. If the French and the British had attacked Germany from the west while the Czechs fought in the east, Hitler might have been stopped. A war begun in October 1938 would at least have forced him to fight before he had promises of neutrality and material assistance from the Soviet Union and before he gained control over the resources of eastern Europe.

Poland was Germany's next target. In the spring of 1939, Hitler demanded that Poland restore the formerly German city of Danzig and allow a railroad and a highway through the Polish Corridor to connect East Prussia with the rest of Germany. The Poles refused, and tension mounted. On March 31, Chamberlain announced a Franco-British guarantee of Polish independence. Hitler did not take him seriously, for he knew that Britain and France were not prepared materially or emotionally for war. They also had no means of getting effective help to the Poles.

To defend Poland, England and France needed help from Russia, but there were obstacles to such an alliance. The French and the British opposed communism. Stalin's purge of the Red Army cast doubt on its military effectiveness. And the Russians could not help Poland without being given the right to enter Poland and Romania. Both nations had good reasons to reject this idea.

The Nazi-Soviet Pact

The Russians feared, quite rightly, that the Western powers meant them to bear the burden of a war with Germany. Consequently, they opened negotiations with Hitler, and on August 23, 1939, a Nazi-Soviet nonaggression pact was announced. Its secret provisions, which were soon carried out, divided Poland between the two powers and allowed Russia to occupy the Baltic states and Bessarabia.

The West had offered the Russians danger without prospect of gain. Hitler had countered with an offer of gain without prospect of danger. Stalin was not about to allow ideological disputes to interfere with rational self-interest. Communist parties in the West immediately reversed themselves, ceasing to advocate resistance to Hitler and calling for peace. On September 1, 1939, the Germans invaded Poland. Two days later, Britain and France declared war on Germany.

⌒ World War II (1939–1945)

The German Conquest of Europe

Using a new military strategy, the *Blitzkrieg* ("lightning warfare")—airplanes supporting fast-moving armored columns—Germany quickly defeated Poland. The speed of the German victory astonished the Russians, who hastened to grab parts of Poland before Hitler claimed it all.

Having thus encircled the Baltic countries, Stalin sent in the Red Army. By 1940, Estonia, Latvia, and Lithuania had become puppet states within the "Soviet Union," or the Union of Soviet Socialist Republics (USSR). In June 1940, the Russians forced Romania to cede Bessarabia. In November 1940, they invaded Finland. The Finns resisted fiercely for six months, finally yielding territory to Russia in exchange for guarantees of independence. Russia's expansionism and the poor performance of its army in Finland may have persuaded Hitler to turn against Stalin. In June 1941, just twenty-two months after conclusion of the Nazi-Soviet pact, Germany invaded Russia.

The Western Front was quiet until the spring of 1940. While Hitler and Stalin swallowed Poland and the Baltic states, France remained entrenched behind the Maginot Line. Britain hastily rearmed, and the British navy blockaded Germany. In April 1940, without warning, the Germans invaded and quickly subdued Denmark and Norway. This secured Hitler's northern front and gave him air and naval bases closer to Britain. A month later he struck at Belgium, the Netherlands, and Luxembourg. The Dutch surrendered in a few days and the Belgians, despite French and British aid, less than two weeks later. The British and French armies in Belgium fled to the English Channel at the beaches at Dunkirk. Hundreds of heroic Britons manning small boats rescued over 200,000 British and 100,000 French soldiers, but losses of men and equipment were high.

The Maginot Line ran from Switzerland to Belgium, and the French had expected the Belgians to continue it along their part of the German border. But when France failed to oppose Hitler's remilitarization of the Rhineland in 1936, the Belgians lost faith in France as an ally and declared neutrality. By overrunning Belgium, Hitler was able, therefore, to sweep around the left flank of France's main line of defense. The French army, which was poorly led by aged generals who did not understand tanks and planes, soon collapsed. Mussolini saw a chance for a safe, easy conquest and invaded southern France on June 10. Less than a week later, a new French government headed by the elderly hero of Verdun, Marshal Henri Philippe Pétain (1856–1951), asked for an armistice. Hitler had accomplished in two months what his predecessors had failed to achieve in four years of hard fighting in the previous war.

The Battle of Britain

The fall of France left Britain isolated, and Hitler expected the British to come to terms. In exchange for allowing Britain to retain its empire, he wanted a free hand for Germany on the continent. If there was any chance that the British would consider such terms, it disappeared when Winston Churchill (1874–1965) replaced Chamberlain as prime minister in May 1940.

Churchill had been an early critic of Hitler, the Nazis, and the policy of appeasement. His sense of history, confidence in Britain, hatred of tyranny, and love of freedom made him reject any thought of compromise with Hitler. His great skill as an orator and an author enabled him to inspire his people with the courage and determination to continue what seemed a hopeless fight. Hitler and his allies, including the Soviet Union, controlled all of Europe. Japan was advancing in Asia. The United States, awash in isolationist sentiment, was determined to remain neutral.

One of Churchill's most important achievements was the close relationship he established with the American president, Franklin D. Roosevelt (1882–1945). Roosevelt found ways to help Britain despite strong opposition in Congress. In 1940 and 1941, "neutral" America traded military supplies and badly needed warships for leases on British naval bases. It even convoyed ships across the Atlantic to help Britain survive.

As weeks passed and Britain remained defiant, Hitler was forced to contemplate invasion. That required control of the air. The first strikes by the German *Luftwaffe* (air force) were on airfields in southeastern England in August 1940. If Germany had stuck with this strategy, it might have won control of the air and a chance for a successful invasion. But in early September, the *Luftwaffe*, eager to avenge British bombing raids on German cities, switched its attention to London. For two months, London was bombed nightly. Much of the city was destroyed, and about 15,000 people were killed.

Strategists who had argued that victory could be achieved through air power alone were proved wrong. Casualties were much less than expected, and Britain's morale was not shattered. In fact, the bombings united the British people and made them more resolute. The Royal Air Force (RAF) inflicted heavy losses on the *Luftwaffe*. Aided by a new invention, radar, and an excellent system of communications, the British Spitfire and Hurricane fighter planes destroyed more than twice as many German aircraft as the RAF lost. The Battle of Britain was won in the air, and it forced Hitler to abandon his plans for invasion.

The German Attack on Russia

Hitler had always believed that the conquest of Ukraine was necessary to provide *Lebensraum* ("living space") for the German people. In December 1940, while the bombing of England continued, he ordered his generals to prepare to invade Russia by May 15, 1941 (see Map 29-1). He may have thought that a *Blitzkrieg* victory in the East would undermine Britain's will to fight.

"Operation Barbarossa," the code name for the invasion of Russia, was designed to destroy Russia before winter set in. Success required an early start, but Hitler's Italian alliance held him up. Mussolini had been humiliated when his invasion of France turned into a fiasco. Eager to vindicate himself, he attacked the British in Egypt. Encouraged by initial success, he also invaded Greece from a base that he had seized in Albania in 1939. The British counterattacked in North Africa and drove the Italians back into Libya. And when the Greeks, aided by Britain, pushed into Albania, Hitler was forced to intervene. General Erwin Rommel (1891–1944), "the Desert Fox," was sent to Africa to force the British out of Libya, and an army was dispatched to crush Greek resistance and occupy Yugoslavia. This delayed the start of the Russian campaign by six weeks.

Operation Barbarossa, launched on June 22, 1941, almost succeeded. Despite a later claim by the Russians that the Nazi-Soviet pact was a diversion intended to give them time to prepare for war with Germany, Hitler took them by surprise. Stalin had not fortified his frontier, and he was so panicked that he failed to orchestrate an orderly retreat. In the first two days, 2,000 Russian planes were destroyed on the ground. By November, Hitler had advanced farther into Russia than Napoleon. The German army reached the gates of Leningrad, the outskirts of Moscow, and the Don River. Of the 4.5 million troops with which the Russians had begun the fighting, they had lost 2.5 million; of their 15,000 tanks, only 700 were left. German victory seemed imminent.

The Germans failed, however, to deliver a decisive blow. The Nazi general staff wanted to concentrate on taking Moscow before winter. Although this had not worked for Napoleon, it might have worked now, for Moscow had become the hub of Russia's transportation system. Hitler chose, instead, to divert a large part of his army to the south. By the time he was ready for an offensive near Moscow, it was too late. German soldiers, who lacked ap-

MAP 29-1 Axis Europe, 1941 *On the eve of the German invasion of the Soviet Union, the Germany-Italy Axis bestrode most of western Europe by annexation, occupation, or alliance—from Norway and Finland in the north to Greece in the south and from Poland to France. Britain, the Soviets, a number of insurgent groups, and, finally, America had before them the long struggle of conquering this Axis "fortress Europe."*

propriate dress and equipment, were devastated by the onslaught of winter. Stalin, given a respite, constructed defenses for the city and called in troops from Siberia. The Russians counterattacked, and the Germans began to have Napoleon's nightmares.

Hitler's Plans for Europe

Hitler often spoke of the "new order" that the Nazi's "Third Reich" would establish in Europe. The earlier German Reichs (empires) were those of Charlemagne (the ninth century) and Bismarck (the nineteenth). Hitler claimed that his, unlike those, would last for a thousand years. Hitler seems to have had no single plan for governing either Germany or Europe. He relied on intuition and pragmatism to create patchwork organizations in the lands he conquered. Some districts were annexed by Germany; some were administered directly by German officials; some remained nominally autonomous under puppet governments.

Hitler's regime was probably unmatched in history for its studied use of terror and cultivation of inhumanity. The *Lebensraum* he sought for Germans was to be won by dispossessing people he deemed inferior. In Poland, German colonists evicted natives from their land and used them as cheap labor. A similar fate on a grander scale was planned for Russia. The Russians were to be driven into central Asia and Siberia and kept in check by frontier colonies settled by German war veterans. European Russia was then to be settled by Germans.

Germanization, as well as colonization, was to build the Reich. People who were racially akin to the Germans (the Scandinavians, the Dutch, and the Swiss) were to be reeducated, purged of dissenting elements, and absorbed into the German nation. Selected individuals from lesser races might also be assimilated. A half-million Ukrainian girls were to be dispatched to Germany as servants and potential wives for German men. (About 15,000 were actually sent.)

In practice, Hitler plundered wherever he conquered. Eastern Europe was stripped of everything useful, including entire industries. Russia and Poland offered only land for confiscation, but conquered Western nations were forced to support their armies of occupation at a rate several times above real costs. Germans used the excess to buy up everything they desired, stripping defeated populations of most necessities. The Nazis frankly admitted their eagerness to exploit, to enslave, and to destroy to advance their dream of German glory.

Racism and the Holocaust

The worst abuses of Nazi power were the result not of military or economic policies, but of Hitler's racial doctrines. The Slavs were among the many nationalities labeled *Untermenschen* ("subhumans" who need not be treated as people). The upper and professional classes were entirely exterminated—jailed, deported, or killed—in parts of Poland. Polish schools and churches were closed; the birth rate was kept down by limiting the right to marry; and harsh living conditions were imposed.

Things were even worse in Russia. Hitler characterized the Russian campaign as a war of extermination. Heinrich Himmler, head of the elite SS, had plans to eliminate 30 million Slavs to make room for Germans. Six million

Mass Extermination at Belsen

Hitler's calculated plan to wipe out Europe's Jews, along with millions of other people he considered undesirable for racial and other reasons, was not widely known during the war. Care was taken to keep the mass murders secret. Even when news of them leaked out, many were reluctant to believe what they heard, and participants in the crimes were naturally not eager to talk about them. Kurt Gerstein, a colonel in the SS, was part of the apparatus of extermination. However, unlike most people involved and at great risk to himself, he tried to tell the world what was taking place. The following is an account of what he saw at the death camp at Belsen in 1942.

~ Who participated in the murders of the victims described here? Why did the guards lie to the victims about their fate? Why were all their personal belongings, even their hair, collected? How did the Nazis' treatment of their victims differ from the way in which the strong have brutalized the weak throughout history? What was the basis for the Nazis' choice of victims? How did the rest of the world react to Nazi atrocities? Was a different reaction possible? Was it warranted?

A train arrived from Lemberg [Lvov]. There were forty-five cars containing 6,700 people, 1,450 of whom were already dead. Through the gratings on the windows, children could be seen peering out, terribly pale and frightened, their eyes filled with mortal dread. . . . The train entered the station, and two hundred Ukrainians wrenched open the doors and drove the people out of the carriages with their leather whips. Instructions came through a large loudspeaker telling them to remove all their clothing, artificial limbs, glasses, etc. They were to hand over all objects of value at the counter. . . . Shoes were to be carefully tied together, for otherwise no one would ever again have been able to find shoes belonging to each other in a pile that was a good eighty feet high. Then the women and girls were sent to the barber who, with two or three strokes of his scissors, cut off all their hair and dropped it into potato sacks. "That's for some special purpose or other on U-Boats, for packing or something like that," I was told by an SS-Unterscharfuhrer. . . .

Then the column moved off. Headed by an extremely pretty young girl, they walked along the avenue, all naked, men, women, and children, with artificial limbs removed. I myself was stationed up on the ramp between the [gas] chambers with Captain Wirth.

Russian prisoners of war and deported civilian workers may have died under Nazi rule.

Hitler had a special fate in mind for Jews. He intended to make Europe *Judenrein* ("purified of Jews"). At first, he thought he might send them to the African island of Madagascar, but he ultimately decided on extermination—his "final solution." The Nazis built camps in Germany and Poland where sophisticated technology was developed to kill millions of men, women, and

Mothers with babies at their breasts came up, hesitated, and entered the chambers of death. At the corner stood a burly SS man with a priest-like voice. "Nothing at all is going to happen to you!" he told the poor wretches. "All you have to do when you get into the chambers is to breathe in deeply. That stretches the lungs. Inhaling is necessary to prevent disease and epidemics." When asked what would be done with them, he replied: "Well, of course, the men will have to work building houses and roads, but the women won't need to work. They can do housework or help in the kitchen, but only if they want to." For some of these poor creatures, this was a small ray of hope that was enough to make them walk the few steps to the chambers without resistance. Most of them knew what was going on. The smell told them what their fate was to be. They went up the small flight of steps and saw everything. Mothers with their babies clasped to their breasts, small children, adults, men, women, all naked; they hesitated, but they entered the chambers of death, thrust forward by the others behind them or by the leather whips of the SS [Storm Troopers]. Most went in without a word. . . . Many were saying prayers. I prayed with them. I pressed myself into a corner and cried aloud to my God and theirs. How gladly I should have gone into the chambers with them; how gladly I should have died with them. Then they would have found an SS officer in uniform in their gas chambers; they would have believed it was an accident and the story would have been buried and forgotten. But I could not do that yet. First, I had to make known what I had seen here. The chambers were filling up. Fill them up well—that was Captain Wirth's order. The people were treading on each other's feet. There were 700–800 of them in an area of 270 square feet, in 1,590 cubic feet of space. The SS crushed them together as tightly as they possibly could. The doors closed. Meanwhile, the rest waited out in the open, all naked. "It's done exactly the same way in winter," I was told. "But they may catch their death!" I said. "That's what they're here for," an SS man said. . . . The Diesel exhaust gases were intended to kill those unfortunates. But the engine was not working. . . . The people in the gas chambers waited, in vain. I heard them weeping, sobbing. . . . After 2 hours and 49 minutes, measured by my stop watch, the Diesel started. Up to that moment, men and women had been shut up alive in those four chambers, four times 750 people in four times 1,590 cubic feet of space. Another twenty-five minutes dragged by. Many of those inside were already dead. They could be seen through the small window when the electric light went on for a moment and lit up the inside of the chamber. After twenty-eight minutes, few were left alive. At the end of thirty-two minutes, all were dead.

From *Pius XII and the Third Reich: A Documentation.* Copyright ©1964 by Éditions du Seuil. Reprinted by permission of Georges Borchardt, Inc.

children with maximum efficiency. Before the war was over, 6 million Jews may have died in the *Holocaust.* About 1 million survived, mostly in pitiable condition.

World War II was fought with unprecedented cruelty. When Stalin's armies conquered Poland and entered Germany, they avenged themselves by raping, pillaging, and deporting millions. The British and American bombing of Germany killed thousands of civilians, and the dropping of atomic bombs on Japan inflicted terrible casualties on noncombatants. The Western allies were convinced, however, that Nazi atrocities justified virtually any act that would bring the war to a successful conclusion.

Japan and America's Entry into the War

The assistance that Roosevelt gave Britain would have justified a German declaration of war, but Hitler held back. Isolationist sentiment might have kept the United States out of the war in the Atlantic if war had not been forced on it in the Pacific.

Japan's conquest of Manchuria in 1931 caused the United States to regard it with suspicion. When war broke out in Europe and the Japanese accelerated their drive to dominate Asia, relations further deteriorated. The Japanese allied themselves with Germany and Italy, made a treaty of neutrality with the Soviet Union, exploited France's weakness to move into Indochina, continued their war in China, and planned to take Malaya and the East Indies from Britain and the Netherlands. Only the United States stood in the way.

The Americans had delayed cutting off vital supplies of oil and other materials to Japan for fear of provoking an attack on Southeast Asia and Indonesia. But when Japan occupied Indochina in July 1941, the United States froze Japanese assets and cut off oil supplies. The British and Dutch did the same. The Japanese then decided that to continue their expansion, they had to acquire Indonesia for its oil and Malaya for its rubber and tin.

In October 1941, a pro-war faction led by General Hideki Tojo (1885–1948) came to power in Japan. On Sunday morning, December 7, 1941, while Japanese representatives were discussing a settlement in Washington, Japan launched an air attack on America's chief naval base in the Pacific, Hawaii's Pearl Harbor. The Americans, taken by surprise, lost much of their fleet and many airplanes. For the time being, their capacity to wage war in the Pacific was negated. A day later, the United States and Britain declared war on Japan. Three days later, Germany and Italy declared war on the United States.

The Japanese swiftly captured Guam, Wake Island, and the Philippines. By the spring of 1942, they had won control of Hong Kong, Malaya, Burma, Indonesia, and the Southwest Pacific as far as New Guinea—positioning themselves to attack Australia. The Germans, the same year, almost reached the Caspian Sea in a drive toward Russia's oil fields. In Africa, Rommel closed in on the Suez Canal, pushing the British back to El Alamein, seventy miles from Alexandria. German submarines roamed the Atlantic, making it difficult for allies to keep Britain supplied.

The Tide Turns

The future looked bleak, but more than twenty nations around the world joined to oppose the Axis powers. Great Britain, the Soviet Union, and the United States took the lead. The Russians accepted all the aid they could get, but they did not trust their allies. Complaining of inadequate help, they demanded that the democracies open a "second front" on the mainland of Europe.

Although the United States' potential power was enormous, America was not yet prepared to contribute to an invasion of Europe. Conscription had been introduced in 1940, but the American army was tiny, inexperienced, and ill supplied. American industry was not geared for war, and German submarines made the Atlantic unsafe for shipping troops to Europe. Not until 1944 would conditions be right for an invasion. In the meantime, other developments forecast doom for the Axis.

The Allies' first victory in the Pacific, a battle in the Coral Sea, came in the spring of 1942. The ships Japan lost diminished the likelihood that Australia would be invaded. A month later, the United States defeated the Japanese in a fierce air and naval battle off Midway Island. This minimized the risk of another assault on Hawaii and did enough damage to halt Japan's advance. American Marines then landed on Guadalcanal in the Solomon Islands and began to reverse the momentum of the war. The fight in the Pacific was far from over, but Japan was sufficiently contained to allow the Allies to concentrate their efforts in Europe.

Allied Landings in Africa, Sicily, and Italy. British Field Marshal Bernard Montgomery (1887–1976), after stopping Rommel at El Alamein, began a drive to the west. In November 1942, an Allied force landed in French North Africa, and the American general, Dwight D. Eisenhower (1890–1969), pushed eastward through Morocco and Algeria. By crushing the Germans between them in Tunisia, the two armies won control of the Mediterranean and opened the way for an invasion of Europe from the south.

In July and August 1943, the Allies took Sicily, and Mussolini fell (July 25). Italy did not prove as easy to occupy as the Allies had hoped, for Hitler defended it with the German army. Marshal Pietro Badoglio (1871–1956), leader of the new Italian government, joined the Allies in a fierce fight that strained Germany's thinning resources.

Battle of Stalingrad. The Russian campaign heated up in the summer of 1942, when the Germans resumed the offensive on all fronts. Stalingrad was a key point on the flank of the German army in the south, and Hitler was as determined to take it as Stalin was to defend it (see Map 29-2). The battle of Stalingrad raged for months. More Russians died in this one campaign than did Americans in the entire war. In the end, Russia prevailed. When Hitler overruled his generals and refused to retreat, an entire German army was lost.

Stalingrad was the turning point in the war for Russia. America provided some material help, but increased production from Russian industries that had been moved to or built up in the safe central and eastern regions of the USSR allowed the Soviets to gain and keep the offensive. As Germany's resources dwindled, Russia advanced inexorably westward.

Strategic Bombing. In 1943, the industrial might of the United States began to tell. New technology and tactics greatly reduced the submarine men-

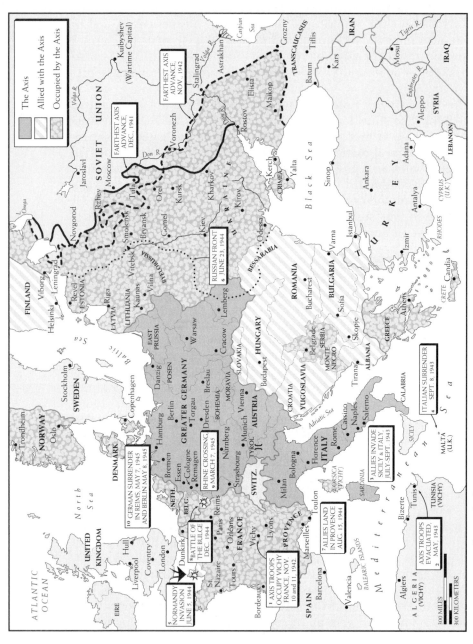

MAP 29-2 Defeat of the Axis in Europe, 1942–1945 *Here we see some major steps in the progress toward Allied victory against Axis Europe. From the south through Italy, the west through France, and the east through Russia, the Allies gradually conquered the continent to bring the war in Europe to a close.*

ace, and American and British air forces began a massive bombardment of Germany that continued night and day. The Americans, who favored a strategy of "precision bombing" limited to military and industrial targets, favored day missions. The British, who believed that precision bombing was impossible, preferred to fly at night and to conduct indiscriminate "area bombing" to undercut the morale of the German people. Neither approach was very effective until 1944, when the Americans introduced long-range fighters that could protect bombers and increase the accuracy of daylight missions.

By 1945, the skies were virtually cleared of German planes, and the Allies could bomb at will. Attacks on industrial targets helped to shorten the war, but terror bombing also continued—even though it seems to have had little effect. An air raid on Dresden in February 1945 was especially savage. It was much debated within the British government at the time and continues to raise moral questions. Whatever else the aerial war over Germany accomplished, it took a heavy toll of the German air force and diverted resources from other military purposes.

The Defeat of Nazi Germany

On June 6, 1944 ("D-Day"), American, British, and Canadian troops under the Allied commander, Dwight D. Eisenhower, landed on the heavily fortified coast of Normandy. Amphibious assaults are especially vulnerable to wind and weather, and the German defenses were strong. But the Allies established a beachhead and began to advance. In mid-August, they landed in southern France; by the beginning of September, France had been liberated.

In December, the Germans launched a counterattack through Belgium's Ardennes Forest and dented the Allied line—making a "bulge" that gave the

The close cooperation between Prime Minister Winston Churchill of Britain and President Franklin Roosevelt of the United States greatly helped to ensure the effective cooperation of their two countries in World War II.

battle its name. The Allies suffered heavy losses, but the Battle of the Bulge was Germany's last Western offensive. The Allies recovered their momentum and crossed the Rhine in March 1945. As German resistance crumbled, there was no doubt that in this war Germany was being defeated on the battlefield.

In the East, the Russians overcame fierce German resistance to advance swiftly on Berlin. Since the Allies refused any terms but unconditional surrender, the Germans fought on as long as possible. Finally, on May 1, 1945, Hitler committed suicide in an underground bunker in Berlin, and the Russians, with the consent of their allies, occupied the city. Instead of the thousand years Hitler had predicted, the Third Reich had survived for twelve.

Fall of the Japanese Empire

The war in Europe ended on May 8, 1945. By then, victory over Japan was also in sight. The longer the war lasted, the more American superiority in industrial production and population began to tell.

In 1943, the American forces, which were still relatively small, began a campaign of "island hopping." Its goal was not to recapture every island Japan held, but to gain strategic sites along the enemy's supply line (see Map 29-3). Starting from the Solomon Islands, the Americans moved northeast toward Japan. In June 1944, they won the Mariana Islands from which bombing raids could be launched on the Philippines, China, and Japan itself. The Philippines were recaptured in October, forcing the Japanese fleet to retreat to its home waters. In 1945, Iwo Jima and Okinawa fell, giving the Americans more bases for bombers, whose missions devastated Japan's industry and disabled its navy.

When the Japanese government, dominated by a military clique, refused to surrender, the Americans made plans for a frontal assault on the Japanese mainland. A million American casualties and greater Japanese losses were anticipated, but at this point science provided the Americans with another option. A secret program had been in progress since the start of the war. Staffed in part by refugees fleeing Hitler, it had been exploring military uses for atomic energy.

On August 6, 1945, an American plane dropped an atomic bomb on the Japanese city of Hiroshima. More than 70,000 of the city's 200,000 residents were killed. Two days later, the Soviet Union declared war on Japan and invaded Manchuria, and the next day a second atomic bomb destroyed Nagasaki. The Japanese cabinet wanted to fight on, but unprecedented intervention by Japan's Emperor Hirohito (r. 1926–1989), who by tradition was aloof from politics, forced the generals to offer terms on August 14. Although the Allies had insisted on unconditional surrender, Harry S Truman (1884–1972)—who became president on April 12, 1945, after Franklin D. Roosevelt died in office—agreed to Japan's request to keep its emperor. The war ended with the signing of a treaty aboard the U.S.S. *Missouri* in Tokyo Bay on September 2, 1945.

Some analysts claim that the bombings were unnecessary to defeat Japan and that their main purpose was to frighten the Russians into respecting America after the war. Others have suggested that the decision to use the bomb

MAP 29-3 World War II in the Pacific *As in Europe, the Pacific war involved Allied recapture of areas that had been quickly taken earlier by the enemy. The enormous area represented by the map shows the initial expansion of Japanese holdings to cover half the Pacific and its islands, as well as huge sections of eastern Asia, and the long struggle to push the Japanese back to their homeland and defeat them by the summer of 1945.*

was almost automatic once the nation had committed to its development. At the time, however, the choice was simple. The bomb ended the war swiftly and saved American lives. Its employment was conscious, not automatic, and required no ulterior motive.

The Cost of War

World War II was the most terrible war in history. About 15 million military personnel died and so did at least as many civilians. Deaths from disease, hunger, and other causes indirectly linked to war raise the number of victims to 40 million. Most of Europe and significant parts of Asia were devastated.

At so terrible a cost, the war bought little peace of mind. The Atomic Age had begun, and people feared that another conflict could extinguish humanity. Everything depended on achieving a stable peace, but even as the fighting ended, conflicts among the victors made prospects for a lasting peace doubtful.

~ The Domestic Fronts

Germany: From Apparent Victory to Defeat

Hitler had expected the techniques of the *Blitzkrieg* to win him a quick victory that would not alter Germany's social or economic life. For the first two years of the war, few sacrifices were demanded from the German people. Spending on domestic projects continued, and food was plentiful. Things changed, however, when the assault on the Soviet Union bogged down. Food imports from the East declined, and Germany had to mobilize for total war.

In 1942, Germany began a push to increase its army and military production. Albert Speer (1905–1981), minister for armaments and munitions, diverted the economy from production of consumer goods to production of military supplies. The output of military products tripled between 1942 and 1944, but began to decline when the army found it necessary to draft workers. Shortages of everyday products became serious, and the standard of living of German workers fell. Prices and wages were controlled, and food rationing began in April 1942. Shortages were severe until food was confiscated from occupied countries. The Nazis preserved their home front by passing its suffering on to their defeated neighbors.

By 1943, labor was also in short supply. Teenagers, retired men, and increasing numbers of women were recruited into the workforce. The Germans closed retail businesses, raised the age for women eligible for compulsory service, shifted non-German domestic workers to wartime industries, closed theaters, moved artists and entertainers into military service, and reduced basic public services such as mail and railways. The Nazis also compelled thousands of people from conquered lands to do forced labor in Germany.

Women had a special place in Hitler's war effort. Propaganda depicted them as mothers and wives who loyally sent sons and husbands off to war. Their other wartime activities were said to be natural extensions of their maternal roles. As air raid wardens, they protected their families. As factory workers, they aided their men on the front lines. As farm laborers, they provided food for soldier sons and husbands. As housewives, their frugal management conserved supplies needed to win the war. And, most important, as chaste wives and daughters, they guarded the purity of the German race.

Hitler and other Germans genuinely believed that a lack of support from the home front had led to Germany's defeat in World War I. They devised a propaganda campaign of unique intensity to make sure this did not happen again. Propaganda Minister Josef Goebbels (1897–1945) exploited radio and films to boost the Nazi cause at home, and the same mass media were used to control occupied lands. The ministry broadcast exaggerated claims of Nazi victories. And when Germany's armies were finally checked on the battlefield, propaganda stiffened resistance by spreading alarm about the consequences of defeat. Allied bombing raids that, beginning in May 1943, devastated one German city after another may have played into the hands of the Nazis. They seemed to confirm propaganda that branded Germany's enemies as ruthless.

The war effort increased the power of the Nazi Party by bringing everything in Germany under its control. During the war, there was virtually no serious opposition to Hitler. In 1944, a few army officers did try to assassinate him, but their failed attempt elicited few signs of popular approval. A radically different state was to emerge from the utter defeat of the Nazis and the consequent devastation of Germany.

France: Defeat, Collaboration, and Resistance

The truce Hitler had made with the French on June 22, 1940, gave the Germans the right to occupy more than half the country, including the Atlantic and English Channel coasts. To prevent the French from turning their fleet over to Britain and continuing to fight in North Africa, Hitler left southern France unoccupied until November 1942. Marshal Pétain set up a dictatorial regime in the city of Vichy and collaborated closely with the Germans in hopes of preserving as much autonomy as possible.

Many conservatives and extreme rightists hoped the Vichy government would end what they considered to be the corrupting influences of liberalism. The Roman Catholic Church supported Pétain, who restored religious instruction in state schools and increased financial support for Catholic institutions. Vichy also endorsed the church's views on family and spiritual values, making divorce difficult and subsidizing large families. The Vichy regime encouraged intense, chauvinistic nationalism and exploited long-standing prejudice against foreigners working in France. Its chief victims were France's Jews. Even before 1942, when Hitler undertook his "final solution," the French were driving Jews from influential posts in government, education, and publishing. In 1941, the Germans began to intern the Jews who lived in occupied France. In the spring of 1942, they started to deport them. Over 60,000 were sent to extermination camps in eastern Europe. The Vichy government had no part in this, but it made no protest.

A few French fled to Britain after their homeland surrendered to the Nazis. There, under the leadership of General Charles de Gaulle (1890–1969), they organized the French National Committee of Liberation, the "Free French." The

Vichy government retained control of French North Africa and France's navy until the end of 1942, but the Free French established a base in central Africa and waged propaganda offensives from London. A serious internal resistance movement did not begin to develop until late in 1942, and the number of its members was small—less than 5 percent of the adult French population.

In early 1944, when it became clear that the Allies were winning, active resistance began on a large scale. General de Gaulle, from his base in London, urged the French to fight their conquerors and the Vichy administration. From Algiers on August 9, 1944, the Committee of National Liberation repudiated the legitimacy of the Vichy government, and French soldiers joined in the liberation of Paris. On October 21, 1945, France voted to end the Third Republic and adopt a new constitution forming the Fourth Republic. Bitter quarrels over who had done what during the occupation were to divide the French for decades.

Great Britain: Organization for Victory

On May 22, 1940, the British Parliament gave the government emergency powers to enable it to institute compulsory military service, food rationing, and economic controls. All British political parties cooperated in a government led by Winston Churchill.

The nation's most pressing military need was for airplanes to fight the Battle of Britain. Lord Beaverbrook, one of Britain's most important newspaper publishers, oversaw their production. A massive campaign to reclaim scrap metal was launched, the first of many appeals to which the civilian population enthusiastically responded in support of the war effort. Factory hours were extended. Women were brought into the workforce in great numbers, and unemployment disappeared. By the end of 1941, Britain's production had already surpassed Germany's.

Germany's "blitz" air attacks during 1940 and 1941 provided the British people with their most dramatic war experiences. Thousands were killed and many left homeless. Families sent children to the countryside for safety. Gas masks were issued to city-dwellers, who sheltered from the bombs in London's subways. Hitler needed most of his air force on the Russian front after the spring of 1941, but he continued to bomb Britain. Bombs killed more than 30,000 Britons before the war ended, although Allied bombers took a much greater toll on the Germans. But in Germany, as in England, bombing, far from breaking people's spirits, seems to have increased their determination to resist.

The British people made many sacrifices. Transportation facilities strained to carry enough coal for domestic heating and fueling factories. Food and clothing were in short supply, so the government imposed strict rationing. Every scrap of land was farmed, increasing tillage by almost 4 million acres. Since gasoline was scarce, private vehicles almost vanished.

Like the Germans, the British used propaganda to further the war effort. The British Broadcasting Company (BBC) urged resistance to the Nazis in programs transmitted abroad in all the European languages. At home, radio serials and Churchill's famous speeches helped bring the nation together.

The Soviet Union: Patriotic Mobilization

No nation suffered greater losses of life and property during the war than the Soviet Union. About 16 million of its people were killed, and vast numbers of its soldiers suffered imprisonment. Hundreds of cities and towns and well over half the nation's industrial and transportation facilities were devastated. Thousands of Soviets became forced laborers in German factories, and Germans confiscated the Soviet Union's grain, mineral resources, and oil.

In the decade leading up to the war, Stalin had made the Soviet Union a highly centralized state that was permanently on something resembling a wartime footing. Stalin worried that the army might siphon power away from the Communist Party, and his purges in the late 1930s had eliminated many officers whose loyalty he doubted. As the war continued, the army did acquire a degree of independence. Generals ceased to be subservient to party commissars. But the military was constrained by the power of Stalin and by the nature of Soviet government and society.

Soviet propaganda differed from that of other nations. Distrustful of the loyalty of its citizens, the government confiscated radios to shield them from German and British propagandists. In cities, the government used loudspeakers, not radios, to communicate. It appealed to patriotism, not Marxist class theory, to marshal support for the war. Stalin even made peace with the Russian Orthodox Church in an effort to win support at home and improve the image of the Soviet Union in regions of eastern Europe where the church was strong.

An active resistance movement quickly developed in the western Soviet Union. The German army advanced so quickly that thousands of Soviet soldiers were stranded behind German lines. Many were shipped to Germany as prisoners of war, but others escaped to become guerilla fighters. In addition to causing trouble for the Germans, these partisans helped keep peasants, who resented the Soviet government's policy of collectivization, from collaborating with the enemy. When the Soviet army moved westward at the end of the war, the partisans rejoined the regular units.

Stalin had entered the war reluctantly, but he emerged a major winner. The Soviet Union established itself as a world power second only to the United States, and the feelings of patriotism and self-sacrifice the war inspired in Russia's people consolidated support for Stalin and the Communist Party more effectively than any strategy they could have devised.

∾ Preparations for Peace

The split that quickly developed between the Soviet Union and its allies came as no surprise. The Soviet Union was openly dedicated to the overthrow of capitalist nations, and those nations were no less open about their hostility to communism. Only the emergency of the war had forced them to put their ideological differences temporarily aside.

Cooperation against a common enemy and effective propaganda did improve attitudes toward the Soviets in the West. But Churchill was determined to halt a Soviet advance into Europe. Roosevelt's hope that the Allies could work together after the war was already fading by 1945. Expectations of a mutually satisfactory peace settlement upheld by continued cooperation were quickly to be disappointed.

The Atlantic Charter

In August 1941, before the Americans went to war, Roosevelt and Churchill met on a ship off Newfoundland to negotiate the Atlantic Charter. It was intended, in the spirit of Wilson's Fourteen Points, to provide a theoretical basis for the peace they sought. The alliance that Russia, the United States, and Britain established in January 1942 was purely military. It left all political questions aside.

Tehran and Negotiations Among the Allies

The leaders of the USSR, Britain, and the United States (the Big Three) first met in Tehran, the capital of Iran, in 1943. Britain and the United States agreed to open a second front in France, and Stalin promised to join the war against Japan once Germany had been defeated.

The most important decision reached at Tehran was the choice of Europe's west coast rather than the Mediterranean as the place to begin the Allied offensive. Britain and the United States failed to realize that this might lead to Soviet forces occupying eastern Europe. In 1943, the Russians were still fighting far behind their own frontiers, and military objectives overrode all other considerations.

By 1944, the situation had changed. In August, Soviet armies reached Warsaw. Expecting imminent liberation, its people rose up against the Germans. But the Russians turned south into the Balkans and allowed the Poles to be annihilated. They occupied Romania and Hungary, realizing the dreams of centuries of expansionist tsars. Churchill was alarmed and went to Moscow to meet with Stalin in October. They agreed to split up the Balkans. The Soviets were to dominate Romania and Bulgaria, the West was to control Greece, and the two sides were to share influence equally in Yugoslavia and Hungary.

The Americans were reluctant to agree to enforce such "spheres of influence." But the three powers easily agreed on plans for Germany—its disarmament, denazification, and division into four zones of occupation: one for each of the Big Three and France. Churchill balked at Stalin's demand for $20 billion in reparations and the requisition of forced labor from all the zones—half of everything going to Russia.

The settlement of eastern Europe was a thorny problem. Everyone agreed that the Soviet Union deserved friendly neighbors, but the Western allies insisted that they be independent, autonomous, and democratic. Western leaders were not eager to see eastern Europe fall under Russian domination, and they were committed to democracy and self-determination. Stalin knew, however, that independent, freely elected governments in Poland and Romania could not be counted on to be friendly to Russia.

Stalin had already established a puppet government in Poland, although there was a Polish government-in-exile in London. Fearful that the Allies would betray him and make a separate peace with Germany, he made all kinds of conciliatory promises. He added some people friendly to the West to Poland's government and signed a Declaration on Liberated Europe that promised self-determination and free democratic elections. Once the war was over, he ignored these agreements.

Yalta

The Big Three held their next meeting at Yalta in the Crimea in February 1945. Western armies had yet to cross the Rhine, but the Soviets were within a hundred miles of Berlin. Roosevelt, faced with the prospect of invading Japan with heavy losses, was eager to bring the Russians into the Pacific war. To encourage their participation, he and Churchill made extensive concessions

The Allied campaign of aerial bombardment did terrible damage to German cities. This photograph shows the devastation it delivered to the city of Cologne on the Rhine. [UP/Bettmann]

to Russia in Sakhalin, the Kurile islands, Korea, and Manchuria. Roosevelt suspected Churchill of maneuvering to maintain the British Empire and disapproved of efforts to set up British spheres of influence in Europe. He saw these as invitations to the Russians to do the same and as sources of future conflicts. Roosevelt, like Wilson, pinned hopes for peace on a united-nations organization. Soviet support for this seemed well worth concessions.

Potsdam

The Big Three met for the last time in the Berlin suburb of Potsdam in July 1945. President Truman replaced the deceased Roosevelt, and Clement Attlee (1883–1967), leader of the Labour Party, had defeated Churchill at the polls. Previous agreements were reaffirmed, but progress on new issues was slow. Russia's western frontier was moved far into what had been Poland and German East Prussia. Poland was compensated by a grant of authority over the rest of East Prussia and Germany east of the Oder-Neisse river line. This, in effect, accommodated the Soviet Union by moving Poland about a hundred miles into Germany. A Council of Foreign Ministers was established to negotiate peace terms with Germany's allies, and Germany was divided into occupation zones. It was not completely reunited until 1990.

The war was slow to come to an official end. Italy, Romania, Hungary, Bulgaria, and Finland did not sign peace treaties until February 1947. The Russians rejected the United States's 1951 treaty with Japan and signed their own agreement with the Japanese in 1956. Potsdam had left much unresolved.

World War II was a response to the resolution of World War I. The two wars might be considered one continuous conflict interrupted by a brief, uneasy truce. But the second war was not inevitable. It was caused by failures of judgment and will on the part of the Western democracies. The United States, potentially the strongest nation in the world, withdrew into short-sighted isolation and failed to respond when ambitious dictators appeared in Europe. Britain and France refused to face up to the threat posed by the Axis powers until war was unavoidable.

In Europe, where World War II began, it ended not—as had World War I—with unsatisfactory peace treaties, but with no treaties at all. Two hostile "worlds" emerged—headed, respectively, by the United States and the Soviet Union. The two lived in what has been characterized as a state of "Cold War." Some analysts spoke of the emergence of a "Third World" of developing nations for whose support the former Soviet Union and the United States competed. Differences among members of this group are so great, however, as to make the term all but meaningless.

~ Review Questions

1. What were Hitler's foreign policy aims? Was he bent on conquest in the East and dominance in the West, or did he simply want to return Germany to its 1914 boundaries?

2. Why did Britain and France adopt a policy of appeasement in the late 1930s? What were its main features? Did the appeasers buy the West valuable time to prepare for war by their actions at Munich in 1938?

3. How was Hitler able to defeat France so easily in 1940? Why was air war against Britain a failure? Why did Hitler invade Russia? Why did the invasion ultimately fail? Could it have succeeded?

4. Why did Japan attack the United States at Pearl Harbor? What was the significance of American intervention in the war? Why did the United States drop atomic bombs on Japan? Did President Truman make the right decision when he ordered the bombs used?

5. What impact did World War II have on the civilian population of Europe? How did experiences on the domestic fronts differ in Great Britain, Germany, and France? What impact did the "Great Patriotic War" have on people of the Soviet Union? Did participation in World War II solidify Stalin's hold on power?

6. What was Hitler's "final solution" for Europe's Jewish population? Why did Hitler want to eliminate Slavs as well as Jews? Has the twentieth century been the "century of Holocaust" or an age of great progress?

~ Suggested Readings

A. ADAMTHWAITE, *France and the Coming of the Second World War, 1936–1939* (1977). A careful account making good use of the newly opened French archives.

E. R. BECK, *Under the Bombs: The German Home Front, 1942–1945* (1986). An interesting examination of a generally unstudied subject.

A. BULLOCK, *Hitler: A Study in Tyranny*, rev. ed. (1964). A brilliant biography.

H. FEIS, *From Trust to Terror: The Onset of the Cold War, 1945–1950* (1970). The best general account.

M. GILBERT, *The Holocaust: A History of the Jews of Europe During the Second World War* (1985). The best and most comprehensive treatment.

J. KEEGAN, *The Second World War* (1990). A lively and penetrating account by a master military historian.

M. KNOX, *Mussolini Unleashed*, (1982). An outstanding study of Fascist Italy's policy and strategy in World War II.

D. C. LARGE (ed.), *Contending with Hitler: Varieties of German Resistance in the Third Reich* (1992). Essays that examine the efforts of resistance to Hitler and their limits.

S. MARKS, *The Illusion of Peace* (1976). A good discussion of European international relations in the 1920s and early 1930s.

M. SHERWIN, *A World Destroyed: The Atomic Bomb and the Grand Alliance* (1975). An analysis of the role of the atomic bomb in the years surrounding the end of World War II.

H. THOMAS, *The Spanish Civil War*, 3rd ed. (1986). The best account in English.

P. WANDYCZ, *The Twilight of French Eastern Alliances, 1926–1936* (1988). A well-documented account of the diplomacy of central and eastern Europe in a crucial period.

G. WRIGHT, *The Ordeal of Total War 1939–1945* (1968). An excellent survey.

30

Europe and the Soviet-American Rivalry Through 1982

KEY TOPICS IN THIS CHAPTER

⌁ The origins of the Cold War and the division of Europe into eastern and western blocs following World War II

⌁ The American domestic scene

⌁ The Soviet Union and the Cold War through the Khrushchev and Brezhnev eras

⌁ Political and economic developments in western Europe during the Cold War

⌁ Decolonization and the conflicts in Korea and Vietnam

⌁ The Arab-Israeli conflict

From 1945 (the end of World War II) until the late 1980s (the end of the Soviet Union), Soviet and American nuclear-armed superpowers waged the "Cold War." Europe's nations lined up on both sides, forming NATO (the North Atlantic Treaty Organization, with the United States) and the Warsaw Pact (with the USSR).

The active role that the United States assumed in world affairs was a major departure from its tradition of isolationism. It reflected a lesson learned from the world wars: the risks involved in assuming that American security was unrelated to developments abroad. America's leaders worried most about the expansion of Soviet power and Communist influence. To counteract these, they assisted Europe with the Marshall Plan and NATO, and intervened in wars in Korea and Vietnam.

⌁ The Emergence of the Cold War

The Lines Drawn and the Iron Curtain

Basic differences of ideology and self-interest lay behind the split that developed between the United States and the USSR. At the end of World War II, the Soviet Union's attempt to expand westward into central Europe and the Balkans and southward into the Middle East was a continuation of policies established by tsarist governments. Britain's role traditionally had been to block these Russian moves, but in the wake of the war only the United States was strong enough to contain the Soviets.

Although American military forces were at their historical peak, American industrial power was unmatched, and the United States had exclusive possession of atomic weapons, it made no attempt to roll back the Soviets. Within a year of the war's end, the United States had reduced its forces in Europe from 3.5 million to 500,000. This was consistent with its plans for peace: support for self-determination, autonomy, and democracy in the political arena and for free trade, freedom of the seas, and unrestrained investment opportunities in the economic sphere. These ideals reflected American principles and served American interests. As the strongest industrialized power in the world, the United States had much to gain from the kind of international order it envisioned.

From the Soviet perspective, the USSR had to extend its borders and dominate formerly independent states of eastern Europe to secure the nation and obtain the compensation due its people for their fearful losses in the war. The Soviets saw American opposition to their expansion as a threat to their security and a denial of their legitimate claims. The Americans saw the growth in France and Italy of large Communist parties directed from Moscow as proof that Stalin was carrying out a worldwide plot to subvert capitalism and democracy. Evidence of hostility among the former allies was not long in coming. In February 1946, Stalin and his foreign minister, Vyacheslav Molotov (1890–1986), openly branded the Western democracies enemies of the Soviets. A month later, Churchill, in a speech in Fulton, Missouri, announced that an "Iron Curtain" had descended on Europe, dividing a free and democratic West from a totalitarian East.

Significant Dates from the the Era of the Cold War

1945	*Yalta Conference; founding of the United Nations*
1946	*Churchill's Iron Curtain speech*
1947 (March)	*Truman Doctrine*
(June)	*Announcement of Marshall Plan*
1948	*Communist takeovers in Czechosovakia and Hungary; State of Israel proclaimed*
1948–1949	*Berlin blockade*
1949	*NATO founded; East and West Germany emerge as separate states*
1950–1953	*Korean conflict*
1953	*Death of Stalin*
1955	*Warsaw Pact founded; Austria established as a neutral state*
1956 (February)	*Khrushchev's Secret Speech denouncing Stalin*
(October)	*Suez crisis and the Hungarian uprising*
1957	*Sputnik launched*
1961	*Berlin Wall erected*
1962	*Cuban missile crisis*
1963	*Test Ban Treaty (Soviet Union and the United States)*
1964	*Gulf of Tonkin Resolution, America in Vietnam*
1967	*Six Days' War, Arab-Israeli conflict*
1968	*Soviet invasion of Czechoslovakia*
1972	*Strategic Arms Limitation Treaty*
1973	*Yom Kippur War*
1975	*Saigon falls to North Vietnam; Helsinki Accords*
1978	*Camp David Accords*
1979	*Soviet invasion of Afghanistan*
1981	*Solidarity founded in Poland*

Early Frustrations of the United Nations

Roosevelt hoped that, following the war, an international body—the United Nations—would emerge to provide a forum where nations could negotiate differences and plan joint military operations to tame aggressors. The United States, in contrast to its rejection of the League of Nations following World War I, signaled its readiness to become a responsible world power by pledging it to support the new organization and provide it a home.

The United Nations, formally founded in February 1945, has two governing bodies: a large General Assembly, representing all member states, and a smaller Security Council. The latter has five permanent seats (Great Britain, France, China, the Soviet Union, and the United States) and two chairs occupied for fixed terms by representatives chosen from other countries. The five permanent members are the major allied powers of World War II. Each has the right to veto any measure brought to the Council.

By the late 1940s, the hope that the United Nations would be able to resolve major conflicts had begun to fade. The United Nations is dependent on

Churchill Invents the "Iron Curtain"

In 1946, Winston Churchill chose an American audience (at Westminster College in Fulton, Missouri) for the speech that contributed the expression "iron curtain" to the language. More important, it defined the existence of what came to be known as the Cold War between the Communist and democratic camps.

~ Why do you think Churchill chose to deliver this address to an American audience? What events and concerns arising at the end of World War II and in the months immediately following had led Churchill to these conclusions? Would Churchill's description have been more accurate had he delivered this speech five years later?

A shadow has fallen upon the scenes so lately lighted by the Allied victory. Nobody knows what Soviet Russia and its Communist international organization intends to do in the immediate future, or what are the limits, if any, to their expansive and proselytizing tendencies. . . .

From Stettin in the Baltic to Trieste in the Adriatic, an iron curtain has descended across the Continent. Behind that line lie all the capitals of the ancient states of central and eastern Europe. Warsaw, Berlin, Prague, Vienna, Budapest, Belgrade, Bucharest and Sofia; all these famous cities and the populations around them lie in the Soviet sphere and all are subject in one form or another, not only to Soviet influence but to a very high and increasing measure of control from Moscow. Athens alone, with its immortal glories, is free to decide its future at an election under British, American, and French observation. The Russian-dominated Polish government has been encouraged to make enormous and wrongful inroads upon Germany, and mass expulsions of millions of Germans on a scale grievous and undreamed of are now taking place. The Communist parties, which were very small in all these eastern states of Europe, have been raised to preeminence and power far beyond their numbers and are seeking everywhere to obtain totalitarian control. Police governments are prevailing in nearly every case, and so far except in Czechoslovakia, there is no true democracy. . . .

. . . I do not believe that Soviet Russia desires war. What they desire is the fruits of war and the indefinite expansion of their power and doctrines. . . .

. . . If the western democracies stand together in strict adherence to the principles of the United Nations Charter, their influence for furthering these principles will be immense and no one is likely to molest them. If, however, they become divided or falter in their duty, and if these all-important years are allowed to slip away, then indeed catastrophe may overwhelm us all.

"Winston Churchill's Speech at Fulton," in Vital Speeches of the Day, *Vol. 12 (New York: City News Publishing), March 15, 1946, pp. 331–332.*

voluntary contributions of money and troops, and its charter forbids it to interfere in the internal affairs of nations. Many of the crises of the late 1940s were classed as internal affairs, and, during that period and throughout the 1950s, the Soviet Union repeatedly vetoed U.N. initiatives.

An American plan to place the manufacture and control of atomic weapons under international control was an early victim of U.N. weakness and the Cold War. It fell through when the Soviers refused to accept on-site inspections of nuclear facilities and limits on their veto power in the United Nations. As a result, the United States continued to develop atomic weapons in secrecy, while the USSR did the same. In 1949, with the help of information obtained by espionage, the Soviet Union exploded its own atomic bomb.

Containment in American Foreign Policy

The Truman Doctrine. In a speech to Congress on March 12, 1947, President Truman set forth what came to be called the Truman Doctrine. It affirmed America's willingness to support "free people who are resisting attempted subjugation by armed minorities or by outside pressures." Truman had in mind immediate aid for Greece and Turkey as they struggled to fend off Communist aggressors, but his statement implied America's willingness to help others who were similarly besieged anywhere in the world.

The Marshall Plan. Western Europe, like Greece and Turkey, was threatened by growing Communist movements. There, however, the cause was postwar poverty and hunger, not direct military pressure. The Americans, in response, devised the European Recovery Program or "Marshall Plan"—named for the secretary of state who introduced it, George C. Marshall (1880–1959). It provided broad economic aid to European states, conditional only on their working together for their mutual benefit. The Soviet Union and its clients were also invited to participate. Czechoslovakia and Finland were willing, and Poland and Hungary were interested. The Soviets however, feared that American aid would draw satellites out of the Soviet orbit and forbade them to take part. The Marshall Plan was a great success. It set the stage for Europe's unprecedented postwar economic growth, thus sapping the strength of Communist parties in the West.

Soviet Assertion of Domination of Eastern Europe

The West believed that communism was inherently aggressive and that a policy of "containment" was needed to halt its spread. The Soviets saw things differently. European powers had invaded Russia once in the nineteenth century (under Napoleon) and twice in the twentieth. Tsarist Russia had governed Poland for over a century and had intervened at the request of the Austrian Empire to put down Hungary's revolution in 1848, and Russia also had a longstanding interest in the area around the Black Sea. Given this history and the extraordinary losses their nation suffered in World War II, it is not surprising that Soviet leaders sought eastern European satellites to serve as buffers against future attacks.

Stalin put an end to multiparty governments behind the Iron Curtain and replaced them with thoroughly Communist regimes completely under his control. In the autumn of 1947, he called a meeting in Warsaw of all Communist parties around the world. There, the old Comintern was reborn as

Cominform (the Communist Information Bureau), an organization dedicated to spreading revolutionary communism throughout the world. Communist leaders in the West who favored working within the political system were replaced by hard-liners who wanted to sabotage it.

In February 1948, Stalin brutally displayed his new policy. Communists expelled the democratic members of what had been a coalition government in Prague and murdered Jan Masaryk (1886–1948), foreign minister and son of Czechoslovakia's founder, Thomas Masaryk (1850–1937). President Eduard Beneš (1884–1948) was forced to resign, and Czechoslovakia was brought under Soviet rule. The Soviet Union forced subject governments in eastern Europe to impose Stalinist policies: one-party political systems, close military cooperation with the Soviet Union, collectivization of agriculture, Communist Party domination of universities and schools, and discouragement of religion.

The Postwar Division of Germany

The Allies had no clear plan for dealing with Germany after its defeat. Although Churchill worried that dismemberment of the nation would encourage Soviet expansion, the invading armies had established occupation zones. The Soviets quickly dismantled the factories in the Eastern Zone, claiming German industrial equipment as war reparations. The Americans feared that such a policy would force the United States to assume financial responsibility for Germany and cause resentment of the West that Communists could exploit. The United States chose, therefore, to make Germany self-sufficient by restoring its industrial capacity. This alarmed the Soviets, who had reason to fear the resurgence of Germany.

Berlin Blockade. In 1948, the Western powers decided to issue a separate constitution and currency for the western sectors of Germany. The Soviets, in protest, withdrew from the joint Allied Control Commission. Berlin, which was under the jurisdiction of all four powers despite being well within the Soviet zone, immediately became a point of contention. The Soviets, fearing that foreign currencies circulating in Berlin would undercut their own, chose to seal the city off by closing the railroads and highways that connected it with West Germany. Their hope was to drive the other Allies out of Berlin.

The West met the Berlin blockade with an airlift of supplies that lasted almost a year. In May 1949, the Soviets yielded and restored access to Berlin. The incident, however, hastened the separation of Germany into two states. In September 1949, West Germany became the German Federal Republic. A month later, the eastern region became the German Democratic Republic. No one had planned or expected this as the outcome of the war.

NATO and the Warsaw Pact

As the USSR became more isolated, the Marshall Plan increased cooperation among Western nations. In March 1948, Belgium, the Netherlands, Luxembourg, France, and Britain signed the Treaty of Brussels, providing for economic and military cooperation. In April 1949, they joined Italy, Denmark, Norway, Portugal, Iceland, Canada, and the United States in a mutual defense pact, the North Atlantic Treaty Organization (NATO). West Germany, Greece, and Turkey soon joined the western bloc created by NATO. For the first time in history, the United States had committed itself to defend allies outside the Western Hemisphere.

In 1949, the states of eastern Europe formed the Council of Mutual Assistance (COMECON) to integrate their economies. Unlike NATO, the eastern alliance was dominated by its superpower, the Soviets. The Warsaw Pact of May 1955, which brought together Albania, Bulgaria, Czechoslovakia, East Germany, Hungary, Poland, Romania, and the Soviet Union, merely recognized a system that already existed. Europe was formally divided between two blocs, antagonists in the Cold War (see Map 30–1).

The Korean Conflict

Following World War II, the United States helped to reconstruct Japan as a democracy and made arrangements for the disposition of its former empire. The Japanese had occupied Korea from 1910 until they were driven out in 1945. Temporarily, the United States and the Soviet Union agreed to divide Korea along the thirty-eighth parallel, anticipating the nation's eventual reunion. By 1948, however, two separate states had coalesced: the north's Democratic People's Republic of Korea, under Kim Il Sung (1912–1994), and the south's Republic of Korea, under Syngman Rhee (1875–1965). The Soviet Union backed the former, the United States the latter.

In late June 1950, North Korea invaded the south, and the United States intervened—supported by a U.N. mandate. Great Britain, Turkey, and Australia volunteered token forces under the command of the American general, Douglas MacArthur (1880–1964). The West regarded the Korean conflict as an extension of its struggle against Communist expansion in eastern Europe, for American policymakers viewed the Communist world as a single unit directed from Moscow.

General MacArthur initially forced the North Koreans to retreat almost to Manchuria. Late in 1950, however, the Chinese, sensing a threat to their border, intervened and pushed the Americans back. U. S. leaders assumed that the Chinese, who since 1949 had been under a Communist government led by Mao Tse-tung (1893–1976), were Moscow's puppets. No one at the time knew of the tensions that existed between the USSR and China. The war bogged down for two years, and on June 16, 1953, an armistice was signed restoring the thirty-eighth parallel as the border between the north and south. The American government claimed success for its Cold War policy of containment.

The formation of NATO and the "police action" in Korea capped the first round of the Cold War. In 1953, Stalin's death and a Korean armistice raised hopes for an easing of tensions. Early in 1955, the Soviets withdrew their army of occupation from Austria, and it became a neutral country. Later that year,

MAP 30–1 Major European Alliance Systems *The North Atlantic Treaty Organization, which includes both Canada and the United States, stretches as far east as Turkey. By contrast, the Warsaw Pact nations were the contiguous Communist states of eastern Europe, with the Soviet Union, of course, as the dominant member.*

France, Great Britain, the Soviet Union, and the United States met in Geneva to discuss nuclear weapons and the future of Germany. Despite public displays of friendliness—"the spirit of Geneva"—the meeting produced few substantial agreements, and the polemics of the Cold War soon resumed.

∼ The American Domestic Scene Since World War II

America's international policy during the Cold War era was influenced by three domestic issues: anti-Communism, the civil rights movement, and economic development.

The Truman and Eisenhower Administrations

President Truman's foreign policy concentrated on opposing Communist expansion in Europe and East Asia. Domestically, his administration alienated conservative Republicans by expanding Roosevelt's New Deal. His opponents' major achievement was passage of the Taft-Hartley Act (1947), which limited various forms of labor union activity.

Against great odds, Truman won the 1948 election. His efforts to institute what he called the "Fair Deal," an expanded role for the federal government in providing economic security, were frustrated as the nation became preoccupied with rumors of Communist infiltration. Senator Joseph McCarthy of Wisconsin led the fight against this perceived danger by ferreting out suspected Communists in all walks of life. Scores of prominent Americans had their patriotism and loyalty questioned, and fear of Communist encroachment helped win election to the presidency in 1952 for the World War II hero, Dwight Eisenhower (1890–1969).

In retrospect, the Eisenhower years seem a period of calm before the storms of the 1960s. The president, who was personally popular, ended the Korean conflict and presided over a nation enjoying general prosperity. (Although he was deliberately less activist than either Roosevelt or Truman, he did begin construction of the vast interstate highway system.) Beneath the apparent quiet, however, disruptive forces stirred. Chief among these were the injustices of racial prejudice and foreign policy commitments that led to American involvement in Vietnam.

Civil Rights

In 1954, the U.S. Supreme Court, resolving the case of *Brown v. Board of Education of Topeka*, declared segregation of blacks and whites in America unconstitutional. Shortly thereafter, the court ordered the desegregation of schools. Some southern states resisted, and in 1957, Eisenhower sent troops into Little Rock, Arkansas, to integrate its schools.

The battle over the schools helped energize a civil rights movement in which American blacks protested segregation in other arenas. In Montgomery, Alabama, in 1955, Reverend Martin Luther King, Jr. (1929–1968), organized a bus boycott that popularized civil disobedience as a strategy for fighting discrimination. Civil rights activists went to jail rather than obey laws they believed to be unjust, and, in 1963, tens of thousands of their supporters staged a famous march on Washington.

The greatest achievements of the movement were the Civil Rights Act of 1964 and the Voting Rights Act of 1965. The former desegregated public accommodations, and the latter enabled large numbers of African-Americans to vote. Although this legislation and continuing pressure for action on housing and job discrimination brought black citizens nearer to the mainstream of American life, much remained undone.

In 1967, lethal race riots broke out in several American cities, and support for the civil rights movement waned. In 1968, the assassination of King cost the movement its most effective national leader, and it was twenty years before another figure of comparable ability, Jesse Jackson (b. 1941), emerged. In the 1980s, Jackson contested the Democratic Party nomination for the presidency (in 1984 and 1988). Although African-Americans have made much progress on civil rights, they still lag behind. And as other groups, particularly Hispanic-Americans, inject their concerns into politics, racial issues become more complicated. The presidential campaign of 1992 and the congressional campaign of 1994 were notable for the absence of discussion of minority issues.

New Social Programs

The civil rights movement was a sign that political liberalism was in the ascendancy by the late 1950s. In 1960, John F. Kennedy (1917–1963) narrowly won the presidential election and launched a bold domestic agenda: the "New Frontier." It was designed to restore activist government after the calm of the Eisenhower years. A space program succeeded in putting a man on the moon. But efforts to expand government-sponsored health care under the Social Security program failed. On civil rights, Kennedy reacted more than he led.

Kennedy's assassination in 1963 mobilized support for bold programs proposed by his successor, Lyndon Johnson (1908–1973). The Civil Rights Act passed Congress in 1964, and Johnson followed with legislation billed as a "War on Poverty." It aimed at increasing employment and providing job training, and added new entitlements to the Social Security program (notably Medicare, medical services for the elderly). Johnson's pursuit of what he called the "Great Society" brought to a close an era of major government initiatives that had begun with Franklin Roosevelt. By the late 1960s, an increasingly conservative electorate was showing a loss of confidence in this liberal approach to government.

The Vietnam War and Domestic Turmoil

Johnson's domestic agenda was overshadowed by his decision, in 1965, to send tens of thousands of American military personnel to Vietnam. This began the longest war in America's history. At home, the war (and the draft) provoked the worst divisions within the nation since the Civil War. Large-scale protests employing the civil disobedience strategies used in the civil rights movement erupted on many campuses. At Kent State University in Ohio in 1970, a National Guard unit that was sent in to restore order killed four protesters.

The unrest in the nation convinced President Johnson that it was futile to seek reelection in 1968, and Richard Nixon (1913–1994) won the White House for the Republicans. Nixon, although an ardent anti-Communist at the vanguard of a new conservative era in American politics, surprised many people by establishing diplomatic relations between the United States and the

People's Republic of China. At the same time, he continued the war against Communism in Vietnam. Half the casualties of that war occurred during his years in office. In 1972, he finally withdrew America from the war and was reelected. Soon thereafter, a scandal began to erode his administration.

The Watergate Scandal

The Watergate scandal, springing from a 1972 burglary of the Democratic Party national headquarters by White House operatives, raised issues of legitimate presidential authority and government's right to intrude into the lives of citizens. In 1973, a congressional committee learned that President Nixon had recorded conversations in the White House. A special prosecutor was appointed to investigate, and in the summer of 1974 the Supreme Court granted him access to the White House tapes. When they revealed that Nixon had ordered federal agencies to cover up his involvement in the burglary, Nixon resigned rather than face impeachment. He was the only president in American history to have done so.

Economic Growth and Changing Fiscal Policy

The Watergate scandal shook the public's confidence in government and delayed government action on other serious issues. Chief among these problems was a rate of inflation fueled by the costs of the war in Vietnam and expanding domestic programs. Gerald Ford (b. 1913), Nixon's successor from 1974 to 1977, and Jimmy Carter (b. 1924), who followed him from 1977 to 1981, struggled with the economy to no avail. In November 1979, Iranians took more than forty Americans hostage. As they languished in Tehran for over a year, support for the Carter administration faded.

In 1980, Ronald Reagan (b. 1911) was elected president by a large majority—and was reelected four years later. He was the first ideological conservative to occupy the White House in the postwar era. In foreign policy, he took a tough line toward the Soviet Union, vastly increasing defense spending. By the end of his second term, he had concluded a major missile reduction treaty with the Soviets. For eight years, he also fought Sandinista Communists in Nicaragua. On the domestic front, Reagan tried to reduce the role of the federal government in American life by enacting a major tax cut and a reform of the tax system. Reduced tax income and enhanced defense spending combined to produce the largest federal deficit in American history. Inflation, however, was controlled, and the economy experienced its longest peacetime expansion.

The conservatism of the Reagan administration offended those Americans who had traditionally supported a liberal political and social agenda. Reagan's policies were seen as hostile to blacks and women. There were several scandals during his presidency that implicated high officials. The most important of these involved a sale of arms to Iran in exchange for the promised release of American hostages held in Lebanon.

In 1988, Reagan's vicepresident, George Bush (b. 1924), was elected to succeed him. Bush hastened to work out a new policy for dealing with the Soviet Union, which had been transformed by its leader, Mikhail Gorbachev (b. 1931). Bush kept the NATO alliance strong at a time when observers were questioning its utility. In 1989, he sent troops into Panama to oust its dictator, Manuel Noriega (b. 1938). In the summer of 1990, he responded to Iraq's invasion of Kuwait by initiating the largest mobilization of American troops since the Vietnam War. Through the United Nations, he forged a worldwide coalition to oppose Iraq's aggression. Operation Desert Storm forced Iraq out of Kuwait early in 1991.

The Persian Gulf War was the high point of the Bush presidency. Thereafter, Bush was faulted for not confronting the economic problems that plagued the nation. In the campaign of 1992, Ross Perot (b. 1930), a Texas businessman, organized a third-party bid for office. The winner, however, was the Democratic nominee, Bill Clinton (b. 1946), governor of Arkansas. Clinton promised to give priority to domestic concerns and launched a bold, but unsuccessful, program of health care reform. In November 1994, Congressional elections established Republican majorities in both the House of Representatives and the Senate.

∾ The Khrushchev Era in the Soviet Union

The Last Years of Stalin

No nation suffered greater losses during World War II than the Soviet Union, whose people hoped that their sacrifices would win them freer, more comfortable lives. They were to be disappointed. The Cold War stance of the United States simply confirmed Stalin in his ways. His police state continued unaltered, its central bureaucracy grew, heavy industry was favored over production of consumer goods, and agriculture remained troubled.

At the start of 1953, there were signs that Stalin might unloose a new series of purges. A group of Jewish physicians was charged with plotting the deaths of important leaders, and claims of an extensive conspiracy appeared in the press. Quite suddenly, however, in the midst of this furor, Stalin died on March 6, 1953. The circumstances surrounding his death are unclear.

For a time, the Presidium (the renamed Politburo) governed the nation as a group, but leadership gradually devolved on the party secretary, Nikita Khrushchev (1894–1971). Although he became premier in 1956, he never enjoyed Stalin's extraordinary power.

Khrushchev's Domestic Policies

The Khrushchev era (1956–1964) retreated from Stalinism, but not from authoritarianism. Politically, this meant that shifts in leadership and party structure could occur by means other than purges. But even reformers were unwilling to eschew repressive measures.

Khrushchev permitted intellectuals somewhat greater freedom to express their opinions, and he often went outside bureaucratic channels to seek information and new ideas. The intellectual liberalization of Soviet life during this period, however, looked good only in comparison with what preceded and followed it. In 1958, Boris Pasternak (1890–1960), author of *Dr. Zhivago,* was not allowed to accept the Nobel Prize for Literature. But, in 1963, Aleksandr Solzhenitsyn (b. 1918) was permitted to publish a novel *(One Day in the Life of Ivan Denisovich)* critical of the Soviet system.

By 1953, the economy had recovered from the war, but food, consumer goods, and housing remained in short supply. Khrushchev tried to improve production of consumer goods by taking steps to decentralize the economy. Steel, oil, and electric-power generation grew, but the consumer sector improved only slightly.

Khrushchev, who recognized that the collectivization of the 1930s had not resulted in an agricultural system capable of feeding his people, removed many restrictive regulations on private farming and made hundreds of thousands of additional acres available for wheat cultivation. Initially, grain production set records, but poor farming techniques caused soil erosion. Yields quickly declined, and the agricultural problem worsened. The Soviet Union continues to import vast quantities of grain, and its need for American grain lay behind the policy of détente that existed between it and the United States for much of the 1970s.

The Secret Speech of 1956. In February 1956, at the Twentieth Congress of the Communist Party, Khrushchev broke with Soviet tradition and made a secret speech (later published outside the Soviet Union) denouncing Stalin. There was shock and consternation in party circles, but the way was opened for limited internal criticism of the Soviet government and the gradual removal of the strongest supporters of Stalinist policies from the Presidium. Communist leaders in eastern Europe took Khrushchev's speech as a signal that they could retreat, not from Communism, but from the Stalinist policies that had been required of them since the late 1940s. The result was a series of crises that made 1956 one of the key years in the Cold War.

The Crises of 1956

Suez. In July 1956, Gamal Abdel Nasser (1918–1970), president of Egypt, nationalized the Suez Canal, which had been under Anglo-French control. In October, war broke out between Egypt, which was supported by the Soviet Union, and the eight-year-old state of Israel, which was closely tied to the West. Britain and France, eager to protect the canal (their access to Persian Gulf oil supplies), intervened. Claiming to separate the combatants, they seized the canal. Israel occupied the Sinai and Britain and France landed troops in the canal zone, but the operation foundered when the United States refused its support and the Soviet Union vigorously protested. The Anglo-French forces withdrew, and Egypt regained control of the canal. Israel left the Sinai and the Gaza Strip the following year.

The Suez incident proved that without U.S. support, the nations of western Europe could no longer use military force to impose their will on the rest of the world. It also demonstrated that the United States and the Soviet Union could restrain their allies from ventures that might lead to wider conflicts.

Poland. In the autumn of 1956, developments in eastern Europe revealed the limited extent to which the governments of Soviet-bloc nations were permitted independent action. The Polish Communist Party and Moscow disagreed over the appointment of a prime minister for Poland. Ultimately, Wladyslaw Gomulka (1905–1982), a candidate acceptable to both the Polish Communists and the Soviets, was chosen. He promised the latter continued Polish membership in the Warsaw Pact. For the former, he proposed an end to collectivization of Polish agriculture and improvement in relations between the government and the Roman Catholic Church. Since the compromise appointment more or less allowed the Polish Communist Party to settle its own affairs, another eastern European country was inspired to seek similar autonomy.

Hungary. In late October, demonstrations in Budapest in support of Poland escalated into street fighting, and the Hungarian Communist Party created a new ministry headed by former premier Imre Nagy (1896–1958). Although a Communist, Nagy wanted Soviet troops withdrawn from Hungary. Ultimately, he favored neutrality for Hungary and withdrawal from the Warsaw Pact. These demands were wholly unacceptable to the Soviets. In early November, they invaded, deposed Nagy (who was later executed), and made Janos Kadar (1912–1989) premier.

Collapse of the 1960 Paris Summit Conference

The events of 1956 demonstrated that European nations could no longer take fully autonomous action. The two superpowers had made this clear to their allies in different ways. The Soviets, feeling more secure, began to talk about "peaceful coexistence" with the United States. The successful launch, in 1957, of the earth's first satellite (Sputnik) confirmed their belief that they had achieved technological superiority over the West. In 1958, they began to negotiate limits on the testing of nuclear weapons with the United States. Tempers flared that year when the Soviets demanded that Allied occupation forces evacuate West Berlin, but, by 1959, tensions had eased enough for several Western leaders to visit Moscow and for Khrushchev to tour the United States. A summit meeting was scheduled for May 1960. Just before the Paris Summit Conference was to convene in 1960, however, the Soviets shot down an American U-2 aircraft that was flying reconnaissance over their territory. Eisenhower accepted responsibility for ordering the surveillance, but refused to apologize to the Soviets. Khrushchev retaliated by scuttling the summit.

Khrushchev's Clashes with John Kennedy

The abortive Paris conference inaugurated the most difficult period in the Cold War. In 1961, newly elected President John F. Kennedy and Premier Khrushchev met in Vienna, and Kennedy left wondering if the two nations could avoid war.

The Berlin Wall. Throughout 1961, thousands of refugees from East Germany crossed into West Berlin. This was a political embarrassment to East Germany and a detriment to its economy. In August 1961, the East Germans, with Soviet approval, created the Cold War's starkest symbol: a concrete wall dividing East and West Berlin. Crossing from one part of the city to the other became possible only at designated checkpoints for people with proper papers. The United States protested and sent Vice President Lyndon Johnson to Berlin to reassure its citizens. But when nothing was done to force the wall's removal, doubt spread about U.S. commitments to West Germany.

The Cuban Missile Crisis. The most dangerous days of the Cold War occurred during the Cuban missile crisis of 1962. In 1957, a revolution led by Fidel Castro had made Cuba, less than 100 miles from the United States, a Communist state and a Soviet ally. Khrushchev's decision to install nuclear missiles on the island prompted an American blockade and a demand for their removal. After a tense week of exchanging threats with the United States, the Soviets backed down.

   In 1963, the United States and the Soviet Union concluded a Nuclear Test Ban Treaty that eased international tensions. The German problem also subsided in the late 1960s, when West Germany, under Premier Willy Brandt (1913–1992), began to improve its relations with the Soviet Union and eastern Europe. Many Russians, however, feared that Khrushchev had tried to do too much too soon—and had done it too poorly. On October 16, 1964, a defeat in the Central Committee of the Communist Party prompted his resignation.

∼ The Brezhnev Era in the Soviet Union

In 1964, Khrushchev was replaced as premier by Alexei Kosygin (1904–1980) and as party secretary by Leonid Brezhnev (1906–1982). In 1977, the Soviets amended their constitution to combine the offices of president and party secretary, and Brezhnev took over—wielding more personal power than any Soviet leader since Stalin.

Invasion of Czechoslovakia

Although the Soviet Union had demonstrated in 1956, in Poland and Hungary, that it would not tolerate independent action by its eastern European neighbors, Alexander Dubcek (1921–1992) experimented, during the "Prague Spring"

The Berlin Wall, erected in August 1961, came to symbolize the tensions of the Cold War era. [Bildarchiv Preussischer Kulturbesitz]

of 1968, with liberalizing Communism in Czechoslovakia. He expanded freedom of discussion and intellectual rights at a time when they were being curtailed in the USSR. The Soviets responded by invading Czechoslovakia and installing leaders more to their liking. Brezhnev also articulated what came to be termed the "Brezhnev Doctrine," a claim that the Soviet Union had the right to interfere in the domestic politics of Communist countries.

Dissidents

Under Brezhnev, the Soviet government also became markedly more repressive at home. Novelist Aleksandr Solzhenitsyn was expelled in 1974, and the government began to harass Jewish citizens, placing obstacles in the path of their emigration to Israel. A small group of prominent dissidents protested. Demonstrations were organized, and some Soviets accused their government of violating human rights. Brezhnev responded by cracking down even more.

Foreign Policy and Relations with the United States

While tightening control over the Communist world, Brezhnev tried to reach an accommodation with the United States. Although he sided with North

Vietnam in its war with the United States his support was limited. He and President Nixon pursued a policy of détente (easing of tensions). And during Gerald Ford's presidency, the United States and the Soviet Union signed the Helsinki Accords (1975), which recognized the Soviet sphere of influence in eastern Europe and the obligation of both nations to safeguard human rights. When President Carter, a strong advocate of human rights, sought to induce the Soviet Union to live up to its commitments, relations between the two countries cooled, and the situation deteriorated further when the Soviet Union invaded Afghanistan in 1979.

Invasion of Afghanistan. It is not clear why the Brezhnev government felt it had to invade Afghanistan. The decision had serious repercussions. The U.S. Senate protested by refusing to ratify a second Strategic Arms Limitation Agreement. American grain shipments to the Soviet Union were cut off, and the United States boycotted the 1980 Olympic Games in Moscow. The war in Afghanistan, which had no clear purpose, grew increasingly unpopular among the Soviet people.

The Reagan Administration. Brezhnev died in 1982, early in the first term of American President Ronald Reagan. Reagan relaxed America's grain embargo and placed less emphasis on human rights. But at the same time, he intensified Cold War rhetoric, increased U.S. military spending, slowed arms limitation talks, deployed a major new missile system in Europe, and proposed the Strategic Arms Defense Initiative. Dubbed "Star Wars" by the press, it foresaw deployment in space of some high-technology defense against nuclear attack. The Star Wars proposal, combined with the Reagan defense spending, forced the Soviet Union to increase military expenditures when it could ill afford to do so. The economic problems that resulted contributed to its collapse.

Communism and Solidarity in Poland

The Polish Communist Party, headed by Wladyslaw Gomulka (1905–1982), began, in 1956, to make peace with the Roman Catholic Church, to halt land collectivization, to establish trade with the West, and to participate in cultural exchanges with non-Communist nations. However, chronic economic mismanagement and persistent shortages of food and consumer goods continued. In 1970, food shortages led workers to strike, most notably in the shipyards of Gdansk. In December 1970, when the government broke the strike at the cost of a number of workers' lives, Gomulka was replaced by Edward Gierek (b. 1913).

For a decade, the Polish economy made very little progress. In early July 1980, a government decision to raise meat prices prompted hundreds of protest strikes across the country. On August 14, workers occupied the Lenin shipyard at Gdansk, and the strike spread rapidly to other facilities connected with the shipbuilding industry. The strikers found a leader in Lech Walesa (b. 1944) and refused to negotiate through the old government-controlled unions. The strike ended on August 31, after the government promised the workers the right to organize Solidarity, an independent union. The new union and Poland's Catholic clergy were also guaranteed access to the news media.

On September 6, Stanislaw Kania (b. 1927) replaced Gierek as head of the Polish Communist Party, and, during the summer of 1981, remarkable changes took place within the party. For the first time ever in a European Communist state, secret elections for a party congress were held. Poland remained governed by a single party, but that party permitted real debate. This extraordinary experiment ended late in 1981, when General Wojciech Jaruzelski (b. 1923) became party head and declared martial law. A number of Solidarity's leaders were arrested, and martial law continued until late in the 1980s. Political repression failed, however, to solve Poland's economic problems.

ᘓ Western European Political Developments During the Cold War

Following World War II, the nations of western Europe endorsed principles of liberal democracy—with the exceptions of Portugal and Spain, where dictatorships survived into the mid-1970s. But the outbreak of that war had made it clear that traditional democracies had inadequacies and that a stable democracy required a social and economic base as well as a political structure. Most Europeans concluded that it was the duty of government to ensure economic prosperity and social security in order to stave off the kind of turmoil that fostered tyranny and Communism.

Christian Democratic Parties

Except for the British Labour Party, democratic socialist parties did not prosper during the Cold War. The policies Europeans embraced were the work, usually, of coalition governments headed by various Christian Democratic parties. These groups were a major new development within postwar politics. Although they were largely Roman Catholic, they differed from the Catholic parties of the late nineteenth century through the 1930s. Those had been very conservative—opposing Communism, but proposing few positive programs. The postwar Christian Democratic parties of Germany, France, and Italy welcomed non-Catholic members and fought for democracy, social reform, and economic growth.

Economic Concerns

Europe's most immediate postwar domestic problems were the physical damage created by the conflict and unresolved issues left over from the 1930s. The most remarkable story was the "economic miracle" that brought unprecedented prosperity to West Germany. In Great Britain, the Labour ministry of Clement Attlee (1945–1950) introduced the welfare state and nationalized a number of major industries, but the British economy failed to prosper. From the 1960s through the 1970s, there were frequent clashes between labor and business interests. When Margaret Thatcher (b. 1925), Britain's first female prime minister, took office in 1979, she campaigned for a freer market economy.

Search for Stability in France

For almost a quarter-century following the end of World War II, France's political stability was threatened by postcolonial struggles in Indochina and Algeria. Charles de Gaulle, wartime leader of the forces of Free France, eventually lost confidence in France's post-war government, the Fourth Republic. He resigned but, in 1958, unrest accompanying France's Algerian war prompted his recall. He imposed a new constitution, the Fifth French Republic, and withdrew from Algeria. (Algerian independence was recognized in 1962.)

For ten years, de Gaulle pursued a course that he considered essential to the maintenance of France's greatness. He was hostile to the United States and Great Britain, insistent on an independent French nuclear capacity, and reluctant to cooperate with NATO. In May 1968, a domestic upheaval revealed the fragility of the Fifth Republic. Hundreds of thousands of workers went on strike. After assuring himself the support of the army, de Gaulle made a televised speech that called his followers into the streets. The strikes ended, but de Gaulle improved the wages and benefits of workers in a bid to secure government stability.

In 1969, the defeat of some relatively minor constitutional changes de Gaulle had proposed prompted his resignation, and political life in France quieted down. De Gaulle's various successors—most important among them Valéry Giscard d'Estaing (b. 1926), a Gaullist, and François Mitterand (b. 1916), a Socialist—have strongly supported European unification.

⁓ Toward Western European Unification

The most important political development in postwar Europe may be the unprecedented steps European nations have taken toward unification. Talks have focused primarily on economic integration, but they have been motivated by the European states' sense that their political power is ineffective.

Postwar Cooperation

European unification could be approached by three paths: political, military, or economic. The economic route was chosen because the other options failed. In 1949, ten European states had organized the Council of Europe, headquartered in Strasbourg, France. Some had hoped that the council might become a parliament of Europe, but none of the major states was willing to surrender any sovereignty to it. The failure of the council to foster political cooperation doomed, therefore, a political or parliamentary unification plan.

Between 1950 and 1954, there was interest in a more thorough integration of military forces. During the Korean War, the United States urged the rearmament of West Germany. This was intended to provide Europe with added protection against Soviet aggression while the United States concentrated on Korea. France, however, still fearful of Germany, proposed the creation of a European Defense Community—a supranational military organization that committed Britain to defend France from future German threats. In 1954, the French Parliament abandoned this idea, and, in 1955, West Germany was permitted to rearm and to enter NATO.

Economic cooperation was easier to arrange than military and political union, for it involved little loss of sovereignty and promised material benefits that would increase support for individual governments. An Organization for European Economic Cooperation (OEEC) had been created by the Marshall Plan, and Europe's leaders concluded that further economic cooperation would avoid the kind of economic turmoil that had, in the past, enabled dictators to win popular support. In 1950, Robert Schuman (1886–1963), France's foreign minister, proposed that coal and steel production in western Europe be integrated. The next year, France, West Germany, Italy, and the "Benelux" countries (Belgium, the Netherlands, and Luxembourg) created the European Coal and Steel Community. It focused on a single sector of the economy, but that sector affected almost all other industrial production. By 1955, coal production had grown by 23 percent, and iron and steel production was up almost 150 percent. The Community's success reduced distrust in government and business circles of the concept of economic integration.

The European Economic Community

The diplomatic isolation of France and Britain that followed the unsuccessful Suez intervention persuaded many Europeans that unified action was necessary to maintain their independence of the superpowers. In 1957, the Treaty of Rome stated the intention of the six members of the Coal and Steel Community to form a new organization: the European Economic Community (EEC). The members of the "Common Market," as the EEC soon came to be called, wanted to eliminate tariffs, guarantee unimpeded flow of capital and labor, and establish similar wages and social benefits in all member states.

The Common Market was stunningly successful during its early years. By 1968, well ahead of schedule, all tariffs among the six members had been abolished. Trade and labor migration grew steadily, and other countries had begun to copy the community and to consider joining it. In 1959, Britain, Denmark, Norway, Sweden, Switzerland, Austria, and Portugal formed the European Free Trade Area, but, by 1961, Great Britain had decided to seek Common Market membership. Twice, in 1963 and 1967, France, under de Gaulle, vetoed British membership, claiming that Britain was too closely tied to the United States to support the EEC wholeheartedly.

The French vetoes demonstrated the major difficulty confronting the Common Market during the 1960s. The EEC's Council of Foreign Ministers was composed of people representing the separate interests of member states. It had more power than the EEC's High Commission, the board of technocrats who proposed policy. Political factors increasingly entered into decisions that should have been made on the basis of economics. France was particularly unwilling to compromise on any issue that it regarded as affecting its sovereignty. Agricultural policy was a major bone of contention.

Despite its problems, the Common Market has prospered and has continued to make proposals for further economic integration (particularly via a common currency). In 1973, Great Britain, Ireland, and Denmark joined. There was some loss of momentum from the late 1970s into the 1980s, when Norway and Sweden, whose economies were relatively strong, declined membership. In 1982, Spain, Portugal, and Greece applied for membership and were eventually admitted.

Early in 1988, the leaders of the EEC ended a decade of drift by announcing an important decision. They targeted the year 1992 for achieving a virtual free-trade zone throughout the Community. In 1991, the Treaty of Maastricht proposed creation of a unified currency and a central bank. A number of states submitted the treaty to referendums. It was rejected by Denmark, only narrowly passed in France, and was confronted with substantial organized opposition elsewhere. Nationalistic concerns and economic pressures arising from the current European recession created resistance to further economic union, and the expectations for 1992 were not fully realized.

∼ European Retreat from Empire

One of the most significant postwar developments has been the development of a so-called Third World political bloc. It is composed of decolonized lands previously administered as part of great European empires (see Map 30-2).

The Effects of World War II

The war itself encouraged decolonization. It drew soldiers stationed in the colonies back to Europe. Japanese conquests ended European domination of some parts of Asia. The dislocations of the war and the postwar economic collapse deprived European nations of the resources needed to maintain empires. They also found it difficult to justify colonial dominance abroad while opposing tyranny at home. The United States, on principle, did not sanction empires. And nationalist movements, which sprang up in many colonial areas, pressed for independence.

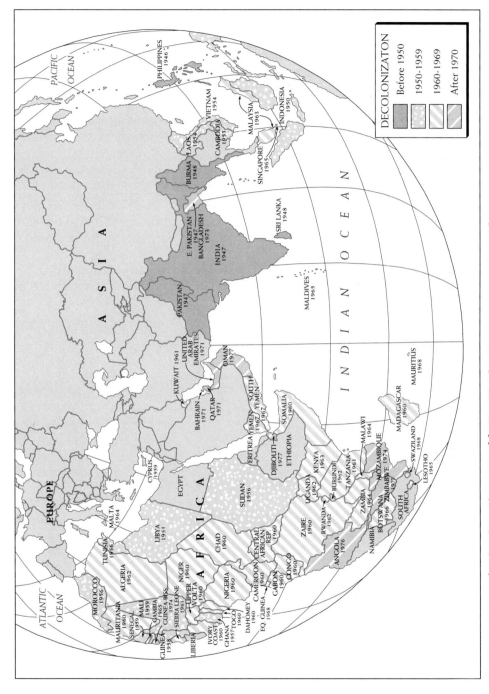

MAP 30–2 Decolonization Since World War II *The Western powers' rapid retreat from imperialism after World War II is graphically shown on this outline map covering half the globe—from West Africa to the Southwest Pacific.*

Major Areas of Colonial Withdrawal

The decolonization process that reshaped the global map proceeded in different ways—sometimes with systematic preparation, sometimes with a hasty retreat. India and Pakistan separated when Britain withdrew in 1947. In 1948, Burma and Sri Lanka (formerly Ceylon) became independent. During the 1950s, Britain tried to prepare some colonies for self-government. Ghana (formerly the Gold Coast) and Nigeria—which became self-governing in 1957 and 1960, respectively—enjoyed planned decolonization. But in areas such as Malta and Cyprus, the British retreat was hastened by militant nationalist movements.

The smaller colonial powers often had no options. The Dutch were forced from Indonesia in 1950. In 1960, great turmoil led to independence for the Belgian Congo (now Zaire). For a long time, France maintained its position in Southeast Asia (where it met defeat in 1954) and in North Africa. President de Gaulle then conducted referendums on independence for the rest of France's colonial possessions. By the late 1960s, only Portugal was still a traditional colonial power, and, in 1975, it relinquished its African colony, Angola. Decolonization is currently occurring in the various republics of the former Soviet Union, where non-European peoples are seeking independence from Moscow.

∿ France, the United States, and Vietnam

Problems relating to decolonization helped transfer Cold War rivalries from Europe to other continents. France's retreat from Southeast Asia, in particular, led directly to American military involvement in Vietnam (See Map 30–3).

Resistance to French Colonial Rule

France had occupied Laos, Cambodia, and Vietnam between 1857 and 1883. Many natives of these areas had been educated by France, and tens of thousands of them had aided France in World War I. Despite this, they suffered discrimination at the hands of their colonial rulers.

Ho Chi Minh. By 1930, nationalistic resistance to French colonial rule was winning a following in Vietnam for Ho Chi Minh (1892–1969) and the Indochinese Communist Party he organized. Ho had traveled widely before World War I and was thoroughly familiar with European affairs. In 1919, he was at the Versailles Conference to urge that the principle of self-determination be applied to his homeland. A year later, the wing of the French Socialist Party to which he belonged formed the French Communist Party, and, in 1923, Ho went to Moscow.

Throughout the 1930s, the French were able to suppress most Communist activity in their colony, but World War II created an opportunity for Ho Chi Minh. France's pro-Vichy colonial governors aroused hostility by collab-

MAP 30–3 Vietnam and Its Neighbors *The map identifies important locations in the long and complex struggle centered in Vietnam.*

orating with Japanese invaders. Ho Chi Minh's participation in the resistance movement won him fame as a nationalist leader. Nationalism was more important than communism in establishing his position.

In September 1945, Ho Chi Minh declared the independence of Vietnam under the Viet Minh, a coalition of nationalists that was soon taken over by Communists. Since there was considerable internal resistance to the Viet Minh from religious groups and non-Communist nationalists, France was able to maintain control. In 1946, France and the Viet Minh declared an armistice, but full-fledged war broke out a year later.

The United States, being opposed to colonialism, had urged France to accommodate Ho Chi Minh. But in 1949, the defeat of Chiang Kai-shek (1887–1975) and the establishment of the Communist People's Republic of China dramatically changed American policy. The French colonial war against Ho Chi Minh now appeared to be a campaign within the Cold War. In May 1950, the United States offered financial support for the French war effort. But despite $4 billion in aid, France's position deteriorated, and in the spring of 1954, the Viet Minh defeated the French at the battle of Dien Bien Phu. Pierre Mendés-France (1907–1982) was elected premier in Paris on a promise to end the conflict.

The Geneva Settlement

In 1954, a conference was held at Geneva to settle the Indochina war. Temporarily, it divided Vietnam at the seventeenth parallel. By 1956, elections were to be held to reunify the country. Meanwhile, the north was to be administered by the Viet Minh from the city of Hanoi; the south, by the French from the city of Saigon. In order to campaign for the elections, each was to have access to the territory of the other. Geneva hoped, in this way, to turn a military conflict into a political one.

The United States, whose thinking about Indochina was colored by the Korean conflict, was not happy with the Geneva solution. Assuming that a North Vietnamese government would, like the government of North Korea, be a Communist puppet state, it negotiated another security agreement similar to NATO, the Southeast Asia Treaty Organization (SEATO). It consisted of the United States, Great Britain, France, Australia, New Zealand, Thailand, Pakistan, and the Philippines.

The U.S. Involvement

As French troops withdrew from South Vietnam, various groups began to fight for power, and the United States stepped in with offers of military and economic aid. The United States backed Ngo Dinh Diem (1901–1963), a strong non-Communist nationalist who had not collaborated with the French. Unfortunately, because America had been committed to France, its support caused Vietnamese nationalists to view Diem with suspicion. In October 1955, Diem established a Republic of Vietnam in the south. By 1956, the United States was training its troops and government officials, paying its salaries, and providing its military equipment.

Diem declared that his government was not bound by the Geneva agreements and would not permit reunification elections. The United States, which had not signed the Geneva documents, supported him. Diem then began an anti-Communist campaign that attacked many people who had participated in the fight against France. His government granted itself extraordinary powers and alienated the peasants by favoring large landowners and replacing elected village councils with appointed officials, many of whom came from the north. (Diem's major support derived from the more than 1 million Vietnamese who migrated to the south after 1954.)

In 1960, the considerable internal resistance that was developing against Diem spawned the National Liberation Front. It pledged to overthrow him, unify the country, reform the economy, and oust the Americans. It was anticolonial, nationalist, and Communist. Late in the 1950s, the government of North Vietnam began to aid its military arm, the Viet Cong, in carrying out a program of terrorism and political disruption in the south. Diem's response to mounting attacks from many quarters was further repression .

On November 1, 1963, Diem was murdered in an army coup. The United States, which was deeply involved in the plot, hoped that the elimination of the Diem regime would clear the way for a new government capable of winning popular support. The United States settled on Nguyen Van Thieu (b. 1923) as the best candidate.

In August 1964, the U.S. Congress responded to an attack on an American ship in the Gulf of Tonkin by authorizing the bombing of North Vietnam. Bombardment continued, with only brief pauses, from February 1965 until early in 1973, and a land war developed involving more than 500,000 American military.

In 1969, President Nixon initiated "Vietnamization," a policy of gradual withdrawal from Vietnam. In January 1973, a cease-fire was arranged. In early 1975, an evacuation of South Vietnamese troops from the northern part of their country turned into a rout when they were attacked by the North Vietnamese. On April 30, 1975, the city of Saigon fell to the Viet Cong, and the Second Indochina War came to an end.

President John Kennedy of the United States and Premier Nikita Khrushchev of the Soviet Union meet in Vienna in 1961. The discussions were very difficult, leaving both leaders with feelings of mutual distrust. [Sovfoto/Eastfoto]

This war in the East had a major impact on the West. For a decade it diverted the attention of the United States from Europe. American prestige suffered, and American commitments to Europe were questioned. Many young Europeans—and not a few Americans—came to see the United States not as a protector of liberty, but as a cruel champion of defunct colonialism.

~ The Arab-Israeli Conflict

British Balfour Declaration

In the Middle East, as in Southeast Asia, postcolonial struggles invited intervention by combatants in the Cold War. Crises in this part of the world centered on relations between Jews and Arabs. In 1897, Theodore Herzl had founded the Zionist movement to push for the creation of a homeland for the world's Jews. Between the world wars, thousands of Jews, mainly from Europe, immigrated to Palestine, which was at the time a British mandate. There they created an organized Jewish community (the *Yishuv*) with political parties, a press, labor unions, and schools. In 1917, the Balfour Declaration promised British support for a Jewish state in Palestine, and Britain tried, rather unsuccessfully, to mediate the frequent clashes that took place between the native Arabs and the Jewish settlers.

Nazi persecution rallied Jews everywhere in support of the Zionist ideal of a Jewish state in Palestine, and the Allies also felt that it was morally right that something be done for Jewish refugees from Nazi concentration camps. In 1947, therefore, the British referred the problem of working out a relationship between Palestinian Arabs and Jews to the United Nations. Over opposition from some Arab groups, the United Nations suggested dividing Palestine between Jews and Arabs.

The Birth of the State of Israel

In May 1948, the Yishuv declared the existence of an independent Jewish state called Israel and chose David Ben-Gurion (1886–1973) as prime minister. The United States quickly recognized the new nation. During 1948 and 1949, Israel fought a war of independence against the Arabs and pushed its borders beyond the limits set by the United Nations (see Map 30–4). By 1949, it had secured its existence, but not its diplomatic recognition by Arab states. Its peace was, therefore, little more than an armed truce.

In 1952, a group of army officers, led by Gamal Abdel Nasser (1918–1970), seized power in Egypt. Four years later, Nasser, an advocate of militant Arab nationalism, precipitated the Suez crisis by claiming jurisdiction over the canal. Israel joined France and Britain in opposing Egypt until a U.N. peacekeeping force separated the warring factions.

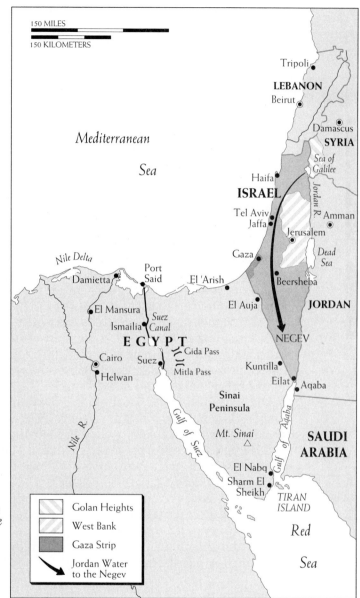

150 MILES

150 KILOMETERS

Mediterranean

Sea

Tripoli

LEBANON

Beirut

Damascus

SYRIA

Sea of Galilee

Haifa

ISRAEL

Tel Aviv
Jaffa

Jordan R.

Amman

Jerusalem

Dead
Sea

Gaza

Beersheba

JORDAN

Nile Delta

Port
Said

El 'Arish

El Auja

Damietta

El Mansura

*Suez
Canal*

Ismailia

E G Y P T

Gida Pass

NEGEV

Cairo

Suez

Mitla Pass

Kuntilla

Helwan

Eilat

Aqaba

Nile R.

Gulf of Suez

Sinai
Peninsula

Mt. Sinai
△

Gulf of Aqaba

**SAUDI
ARABIA**

El Nabq

Sharm El
Sheikh

TIRAN
ISLAND

*Red

Sea*

▨	Golan Heights
▨	West Bank
▓	Gaza Strip
→	Jordan Water to the Negev

MAP 30–4 Israel and Its Neighbors *Israel's occupied territories include lands that were previously part of Syria, Jordan, and Egypt. The future of those lands, their inhabitants, and the refugees who left Israel and its territories lies at the heart of the region's unresolved problems.*

The 1967 Six Days' War

During the uneasy peace that ensued, the Soviet Union's influence with Egypt increased and the United States developed closer ties with Israel. In 1967, President Nasser concluded, erroneously, that the Arab nations had acquired enough arms from the USSR to defeat Israel. He massed troops in the Sinai

Peninsula, tried to close the Gulf of Aqaba to Israeli shipping, and demanded the withdrawal of the U.N. peacekeepers.

On June 5, 1967, the Israeli army, under Defense Minister Moshe Dayan (1915–1981), attacked Egyptian airfields. Although Syria and Jordan immediately came to Egypt's aid, by June 11, Israel had won a stunning victory and ended the Six Days' War. Egypt's army was reduced to a shambles, and Israel occupied the Sinai Peninsula and part of the state of Jordan (an area along the Jordan River known as the West Bank).

Anwar el-Sadat and the Camp David Accords

In 1970, President Nasser died and was succeeded by Anwar el-Sadat (1918–1981). Although Egypt received arms from the Soviet Union, Sadat distrusted the Soviets and ordered them out of his country in 1972.

Sadat believed that another war with Israel was necessary to regain what Egypt had lost in 1967. In October 1973, on the Jewish holy day of Yom Kippur, Egypt and Syria crossed the Suez Canal into Israeli-held territory. The Israelis, who were taken by surprise, initially lost ground. Ultimately, however, they rallied and thrust back the invaders.

The Yom Kippur War introduced a new Arab strategy that was to be deeply troubling to the West. At the start of the war, the major Arab oil-producing states shut off supplies to the United States and Europe to induce the Western powers to restrain Israel. Europeans were especially alarmed, for they had few other major sources of oil to fuel their industries.

In November 1977, Sadat made a dramatic personal gesture. He flew to Israel, with which he was still technically at war, to address the Israeli Parliament and hold discussions with Prime Minister Menachem Begin (1913–1992). For the first time, the head of a major Arab state effectively recognized Israel's existence. Sadat's initiative was roundly condemned by many Arabs, but it made direct negotiations possible. The most important took place in the United States, at Camp David, with President Carter as moderator. The Camp David Accords (September 1978) provided a framework for continuing efforts to bring peace to the Middle East.

A Palestinian refugee problem has been the major stumbling block to an agreement between Israel and the Arabs. The Palestine Liberation Organization (PLO), the major spokesman for the Arabs who were driven from Israeli-occupied lands, has sought a Palestinian state. Israel fears the threat such a state might pose to its survival.

Lebanon and the Intifada

The assassination of President Sadat by Muslim extremists in October 1981 cast doubt on the future of the Camp David process. Further strains developed in late December 1981, when the Israeli Parliament suddenly annexed the Golan Heights. In 1982, Israel invaded Lebanon to destroy PLO bases, and the fragile Lebanese state, already racked by civil war, collapsed.

In 1987, the West Bank area that Israel occupied in the 1967 war became the scene of the *intifada,* an Arab uprising protesting the Israeli presence. The Israelis responded with increasing, often deadly, force, and their actions generated intense controversy at home and abroad. Late in 1988, PLO leader Yasir Arafat (b. 1929) recognized Israel's right to exist and pledged the PLO to refrain from terrorist activity. Earlier that year, the PLO had laid claim to the West Bank and Gaza for a Palestinian state.

The PLO's stance toward Israel softened as a result of the Persian Gulf War. In 1990, only Jordan and the PLO supported Iraq when it invaded Kuwait. The other Arab powers joined the United States in a worldwide coalition opposing the Iraqis. Iraq's defeat was costly for the radical Arab cause, for Saudi Arabia and other wealthy Arab states decreased or ended their financial support of the PLO. By the end of 1991, the PLO found itself increasingly isolated within the Arab world.

During the early 1990s, the United States sponsored peace talks in the Middle East, and in 1993, the Israeli government began to permit meetings between its citizens and the PLO. In September 1993, Israel and the PLO surprised the world community by agreeing to recognize each other and establish Palestinian self-government in Gaza and the city of Jericho. Although radicals on both sides have opposed the agreement signed in Washington, D.C., on September 14, 1993, Israel and various Arab states have since moved toward formal diplomatic recognition. Much instability remains in the region.

During the quarter-century that followed the end of World War II, there was a relative decline in the power of European nations. The United States and the Soviet Union emerged as the globe's new superpowers and launched a struggle called the Cold War.

In Europe, the divided city of Berlin was the scene for confrontations between the superpowers. Elsewhere in the world, there were other points of contact. In Asia, the United States twice intervened against Communist forces: first, with U.N. support in Korea, and second, on its own in Vietnam. The establishment of a Communist government in Cuba created another trouble spot, and the Arab-Israeli conflict in the Middle East invited both Soviet Union and American involvement.

The collapse of the Soviet Union in the mid-1980s concluded the Cold War. The conflict placed heavy burdens on both superpowers but had little impact on Europe, which has achieved unprecedented economic prosperity, political stability, and unity.

Review Questions

1. How did Europe come to be dominated by the United States and the Soviet Union after 1945? Through what stages did the Cold War pass? What was crucial about the years 1956 and 1962?

2. How would you define the policy of *containment?* What were some of the global events in the period from 1945 to 1982 that were influenced by this American policy?

3. How did Khrushchev change the Soviet state that had been created by Stalin's repression? Why did many people inside and outside the Soviet Union regard Khrushchev as reckless?

4. How did western Europe move toward political unity following World War II? How

important was the Marshall Plan to western Europe's development? Were the domestic policies of Charles de Gaulle important for maintaining political stability in France?

5. Why did the nations of Europe give up their empires? How was the process of decolonization carried out? How did the United States become involved in Vietnam? What was the effect of the Vietnam War on Europe?

6. What has promoted conflict between Arabs and Israelis in the Middle East since 1948? Why are the Camp David Accords historically important? What strategies have been used in subsequent peace initiatives?

Suggested Readings

E. BOTTOME, *The Balance of Terror: Nuclear Weapons and the Illusions of Security, 1945–1985* (1986). An examination of the role of nuclear weapons in the Cold War climate.

A. W. DePORTE, *Europe Between the Superpowers: The Enduring Balance* (1979). This remains a significant study.

R. EMERSON, *From Empire to Nation: The Rise to Self-assertion of Asian and African Peoples* (1960). An important discussion of the origins of decolonization.

B. B. FALL, *The Two Vietnams: A Political and Military Analysis*, rev. ed. (1967). A discussion by a journalist who spent many years on the scene.

H. FEIS, *From Trust to Terror: The Onset of the Cold War, 1945–1950* (1970). The best general account.

D. HOLLOWAY, *The Soviet Union and the Arms Race,* (1985). Excellent treatment of internal Soviet decision making.

F. LEWIS, *Europe: Road to Unity* (1992). A discussion of contemporary Europe by a thoughtful journalist.

L. P. MORRIS, *Eastern Europe Since 1945* (1984). Concentrates on the political and economic organization of the Soviet-dominated states.

L. SCHAPIRO, *The Communist Party of the Soviet Union* (1960). A classic analysis of the most important institution of Soviet Russia.

Z. SCHIFF and E. YA'ARI, *Intifada: The Palestinian Uprising—Israel's Third Front* (1990). An analysis of recent developments.

A. ULAM, *The Communists: The Story of Power and Lost Illusions: 1948–1991* (1992). The best account to date of the days of Communist strength and collapse.

M. WALKER, *The Cold War and the Making of the Modern World* (1994). A major new survey.

This eighteenth-century church, designed by Johann Michael Fischer in Ottobeuren, Bavaria, is in the baroque style favored by Catholic countries in the years following the Reformation. The interior explodes with energy and is filled with sculptures and paintings and magnificent woodwork that catch the eye. The intent was to inspire and move the worshipper to self-transcendence.
[Bildarchiv Preussischer Kulturbesitz]

This portrait of Louix XIV of France (r. 1643–1715) proclaims the spirit of the form of monarchy (absolutism) and of the aristocratic social order that flourished in Europe during the eighteenth century.
[Giraudon/Art Resource, NY]

This glimpse into an aristocratic household, Marriage à la Mode: Morning *by William Hogarth (1697–1764), both illustrates and ironically comments on the lifestyle of the wealthy aristocrats who supported the Enlightenment's artists and scholars.* [National Gallery, London. (Superstock)]

Jacques Louis David's portrait of Socrates at his execution combined Enlightenment classicism with the Romantic movement's dramatic emotionalism. [David, Jacques Louis (1748–1825), The Death of Socrates. *Oil on canvas. The Metropolitan Museum of Art, Wolfe Fund, 1931. Catharine Lorillard Wolfe Collection. (31.45)]*

Phillip James de Loutherbourg's A Philosopher in a Moonlit Churchyard *illustrates the Romantics' fascination with history, religion, and mystery in the early nineteenth century.*
[Yale Center for British Art]

The painter of this late-nineteenth-century scene has used a naturalistic style to make a social commentary sympathetic with the spirit of the revolutionary movements of his age. It shows Russian peasants waiting patiently outside a government office while insensitive officials take their time over lunch.
[Bildarchiv PreussischerKulturbesitz]

The nineteenth century's interest in close scientific analysis of nature was consistent with a new artistic movement of the period. The French Impressionists, led by Claude Monet (1840–1926), believed in working rapidly with primary colors to capture the actual impression that natural light makes on the eye of a viewer.

[Monet, Claude. The Picnic. 1840–1926. Hermitage Museum, St. Petersburg, Russia. (Superstock)]

The iconoclastic spirit of the modern age is well represented by artists such as Pablo Picasso (1881–1973), the founder of Cubism. The art of the twentieth century, like much of the era's science, has been driven by a desire to experiment and explore.

[Picasso, Pablo. Les Demoiselles d'Avignon, 1907. Oil on canvas, 8' x 7'8". The Museum of Modern Art, New York, acquired through the Lillie P. Bliss Bequest.]

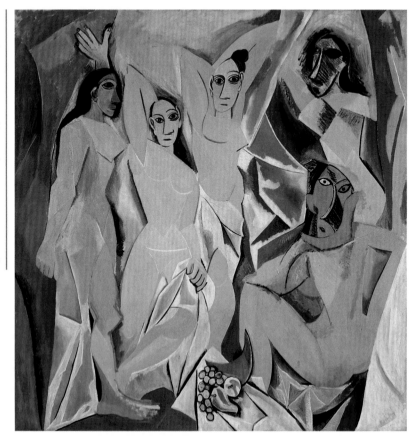

31

Toward a New Europe and the Twenty-First Century

KEY TOPICS IN THIS CHAPTER

~ Unprecedented prosperity and the expansion of the consumer society in western Europe

~ Demographic trends, migrations, and growing ethnic tensions

~ Intellectual and social movements since World War II

~ Perestroika and glasnost in the Soviet Union

~ The collapse of Communism in eastern Europe and the Soviet Union

~ The civil war in Yugoslavia

Life in Western nations has undergone a dramatic transformation during the second half of the twentieth century. Europe has experienced unprecedented economic growth, allowing its consumers more goods and services than ever before. Fewer people are needed to work the land, and more now live in cities. Women have greater visibility in the workplace and in society at large than at any time in history. And the collapse of the Communist governments of the Soviet Union and its eastern European subject states augurs more change for the Western world.

～ European Society in the Second Half of the Twentieth Century

The "Americanization" of Western Europe

During the past half-century, western Europe has been enormously influenced by the United States. Following World War II, Europe's economy was rebuilt by the Marshall Plan and its defense provided by NATO—both American initiatives. Over the years, hundreds of thousands of American military personnel have served in Europe. Thousands of American students have studied there. And literally millions of American tourists have visited.

The result has been an "Americanization," an influence on European cultures that Europeans have much discussed and frequently lamented. American fast food restaurants, such as McDonald's, line the streets of European cities from Dublin to Moscow. American clothing styles—particularly blue jeans—are wildly popular throughout Europe. The shopping centers and supermarkets that Americans pioneered are displacing Europe's traditional sales districts. American television programs and movies are readily available everywhere, and American rock music dominates European popular culture. As a result, the same movie stars and entertainers are idolized on both sides of the Atlantic. Thanks to the media and the power of American corporations, American English seems to be emerging as a common language for Europe's business and academic communities.

A Consumer Society

During the past half-century, the economy of western Europe has been differentiated from that of the East by its extraordinary redirection toward consumer goods. Throughout the Soviet bloc, economic planners put capital investment and military budgets before everything else. As a result, the quality and availability of food and consumer goods decreased. On the other hand, by the early 1950s, western Europeans had an excellent food supply that has only continued to improve, and they have enhanced access to an expanding array of consumer goods and services: automobiles, household appliances, entertainments, clothing, "disposable" conveniences, and vacations—all the appurtenances of the leisured lifestyle.

The Revolutions of 1989

January 11	*Independent parties permitted in Hungary*
April 5	*Solidarity legalized in Poland*
May 2	*Hungary dismantles barriers along its borders*
June 4	*Solidarity victory in Polish elections*
August 19	*Solidarity member appointed premier in Poland*
October 18	*Erich Honecker removed from office in East Germany*
October 23	*Hungary proclaims itself a republic*
October 25	*Gorbachev renounces Brezhnev Doctrine*
November 9	*Berlin Wall opened*
November 19	*Civic Forum organized in Czechoslovakia*
November 24	*Czechoslovak Communist leadership resigns*
December 3	*Czechoslovak ministry with non-Communist members*
December 16–17	*Massacre of civilians in Timisoara, Romania*
December 22	*Ceauşescu government overthrown in Romania*
December 25	*Announcement of Ceauşescu's execution*
December 29	*Václav Havel elected president of Czechoslovakia*

This development has had dramatic political repercussions. Through the limited number of radios, televisions, movies, and videos available to eastern Europeans, they became aware of the discrepancy between their lives and those of Westerners. They intuited the link between Western consumerism and democracy, between free societies and economic policies that minimize government planning. Paradoxically, the consumerism of the West, which has been deplored by Western commentators and Christian moralists, helped generate the discontent in the East that brought down its Communist governments.

Population Changes

Despite horrendous losses in war, Europe's population has grown during the course of the twentieth century. Between 1913 and 1985, the number of its inhabitants has increased over 44 percent.[1] Large as this is, population growth elsewhere in the world has outpaced Europe's. Whereas in the first decade of the century Europeans accounted for approximately 20 percent of the world's people, today they represent about 11 percent. This shift has changed Europe's place in the world and accounts in part for growing pressure on resources from non-European regions. Growth in their numbers has forced Europeans to live more closely together than ever before. Population density rose from 66 people per square kilometer in 1920 to 101 in 1985. The most densely populated regions are the Netherlands, Belgium, England, western Germany, and Italy.

The chief factors behind Europe's remarkable population growth are increased life expectancy and reduced infant mortality rates. Both are the results

---

[1]Information on population and most of the other statistical information in this chapter is taken from Gerold Ambrosius and William H. Hubbard, *A Social and Economic History of Twentieth-Century Europe* (Cambridge, Mass.: Harvard University Press, 1989).

of medical advances and improved living standards. Despite regional variations, life expectancy has now increased almost uniformly across the continent.

While mortality rates have declined, so has Europe's birthrate. Beginning in the 1920s, birth control information and contraceptives became widely available. A "baby boom" occurred in the decade and a half following World War II, but after peaking in 1964, Europe's birth rate has declined to extremely low levels. The advent of the birth control pill during the 1960s, the legalization of abortion in many countries, and changing social attitudes may explain this trend. Over the century, the average European family has decreased from five or more children to two.

Modern European Household Structures

Although the media gives attention to unconventional lifestyles, the half-century following World War II has seen an increase in the number of married people in Europe. Previously, many women remained unmarried all their lives, but few do now. Women are also marrying at a younger age than before, particularly in eastern and southern Europe.

At the same time, traditional expectations for marriage have changed. Family size is smaller, and marriages tend to be of shorter duration. Divorce laws have eased across the continent, although not until after 1980 in the nations of southern Europe where the Roman Catholic Church is strong. In the Scandinavian countries, more children are being born out of wedlock. Quite often, parents live together without being married. Single motherhood has been made economically easier by government-sponsored programs that provide care for children. Despite the attention these developments have received, they have not become the norm anywhere in Europe. But the growing tendency toward small families has resulted in an increase in single-person households. Because women tend to live longer than men, these consist overwhelmingly of widows.

The Movement of Peoples

External Migration. In the decade and a half after 1945, about 500,000 Europeans emigrated annually. This was the largest outward migration since the 1920s, when the rate reached 700,000 persons per year. Unlike the emigration of the second half of the nineteenth century, which was largely of rural populations, the later migrants included educated city dwellers.

On the other hand, the decolonization of the postwar period prompted many Europeans to return from overseas. More than 1 million French colonials relocated to France at the end of the Algerian War. British citizens returned from various parts of their empire. The Dutch came home from Indonesia, and the Portuguese from Mozambique and Angola.

Decolonization also provoked migration to Europe by non-European inhabitants of former colonies. Thousands came to Great Britain from India,

Pakistan, and Africa. France received many from Indochina and the Arab world. This influx has created conflict. In Great Britain during the 1980s, racial incidents led to angry clashes between police and non-European immigrants. In France, where a tight job market has led some working-class voters to resent job competition from North African immigrants, an extreme right-wing group led by Jean-Marie LePen (b. 1928), known as the National Front, has gained strength.

Internal Migration. World War II and its aftermath dislocated countless people. Many cities had been bombed or overrun by invading armies. Germany had imported hundreds of thousands of foreign workers to support its war effort. There were thousands of prisoners of war for whom to find places. Changes in the borders of nations forced people to move.

Before the construction of the Berlin Wall, about 3 million East Germans migrated to West Germany. But once Soviet domination was established, it was impossible for eastern Europeans to move to other parts of Europe. Most of Europe's internal migration was then confined to the West, where it was motivated, after the late 1950s, by a search for economic opportunity. By 1960, several hundred thousand workers were entering France and Germany annually. They were welcome during years of prosperity, but in the mid-1980s, when European economies began to slow, these "guest workers" were increasingly resented. Some in Germany began to suffer violent attacks early in the 1990s.

In the late 1980s, political changes began again to prompt migration in Europe. In 1988 and 1989, thousands of refugees, trying to escape from eastern Europe, hastened the collapse of its Communist governments. Their fall cleared the way for more Easterners to migrate west, and the civil war in the former Yugoslavia created yet more refugees. Unfortunately, all this happened at a time when Europe struggled with an economic recession. Mass resentment of the newcomers has persuaded several European nations to take steps to restrict migration.

Urban Expansion. The long-established tendency for Europeans to leave the country for the city has increased during the last half-century. With the exception of Albania, at least one-third of the population of each European nation now lives in urban areas. City dwellers constitute about 75 percent of the residents of western Europe. In Mediterranean Europe, little has been done to control urban development and there is enormous pressure on services (water, electricity, sanitation, and police), housing, and medical facilities. In many cases, urban growth has caused serious pollution.

A Second Agricultural Revolution

Never before have so few Europeans (about 10 percent) been involved in agriculture, but never has so much food in such variety been available to them. During the Great Depression and World War II, there was a steep drop in agricultural production in Europe. The two decades after the war, however, saw a remarkable recovery. European farming became more mechanized. New kinds of fertilizers were introduced, and better methods were developed to control crop diseases. Although not without problems related to environmental concerns, these changes have doubled Europe's agricultural output and launched a second agricultural revolution.

The Welfare State

The Great Depression, the rise of authoritarian states, and the mobilization of large groups of people to fight World War II changed the way Europeans thought about the powers of government. This change encouraged development of the modern welfare state. Prior to World War II, there were two basic models for social legislation: the German and the British. The program Bismarck enacted in Germany affected all workers and was designed to diminish their support for the German Social Democratic Party's campaign for enfranchising the masses. In Great Britain, where all classes had access to the political system, social insurance was targeted at the very poor.

After World War II, the belief developed that social insurance against predictable risks should be available to all citizens. In 1942, in Great Britain, a report by William B. Beveridge (1879–1963) made the case for universal coverage, and the Labour Party ministry of Clement Attlee (1883–1967) began Europe's first welfare state. Its centerpiece, the National Health Service, provided universal access to medical care. Debates over universal coverage delayed similar legislation in France and Germany until the 1970s, but the spread of welfare legislation within western Europe was encouraged by the Cold War. Since Communist states promised (even if they could not often deliver) their people enormous social security and full employment, capitalist nations had to safeguard their stability by making similar pledges.

The systems of government-furnished services now established in Europe are beginning to encounter criticism, for their financial support was premised on the assumption of a growing population. As the portion of the population consuming services (the sick, the injured, and the elderly) increases relative to the able-bodied workers who pay taxes, the cost of government services has become burdensome.

New Patterns in the Work and Expectations of Women

More Married Women in the Workforce

At all levels in society women have, since World War II, become much more prominent in public life. The number of married women with jobs outside their homes, from both the middle and the working classes, has risen sharply since the turn of the century. Low birthrates during the 1930s meant that there were relatively few young, single women seeking employment in the years just after the war. Society made adjustments that enabled married women to replace them in the job market.

Children in the twentieth century have not been expected to contribute significantly to family incomes. Instead, the state requires them to spend their time in school. When families require more income than one member can provide, both parents usually seek employment. Financial need has brought many married women who have children into the workforce, but there is considerable evidence that many of these women also seek jobs to contribute to a sense of personal fulfillment.

New Work Patterns

Stages in female work patterns in the late twentieth century display much more continuity than they did in the nineteenth century. Single women enter the workforce after completing their educations and keep their jobs after marriage. Lengthening life spans have left modern Western women with years to fill in which no children of their own are dependent on them. Women also now have options not available to earlier generations. They often, particularly in urban settings, decide to begin bearing children at a later age and to have fewer of them. Some forego childbearing altogether. Both men and women continue to expect to marry, but marriage does not always imply an intention to have children. New careers open to women and the desire of some couples to maintain high standards of living have contributed to the West's declining birthrates.

Women in the New Eastern Europe

Under Communism, women in eastern Europe generally enjoyed social equality and many government-financed benefits. Well over 50 percent of women in these societies usually worked—both because they could and because it was expected of them. There were, however, no significant women's movements agitating for women's rights. Feminist groups, like all independent associations, were regarded with suspicion by totalitarian governments.

The new governments recently established in the former Communist states of eastern Europe are free, but have so far ignored women's issues. The economic difficulties they face may endanger funding for various health and welfare programs that benefit women and children. It is uncertain whether a free-market economy will allow eastern European women the extensive maternity benefits to which they have been entitled. And during economically difficult times of adjustment to a free market, women may find themselves being laid off before men and offered new jobs later than men.

∼ Transformations in Knowledge and Culture

Intellectual life has been transformed in the twentieth century. Larger numbers of people from diverse backgrounds are recruited into higher levels of education than ever before. Many traditional intellectual assumptions have been challenged, and the West's dominant religion, Christianity, has struggled to remain relevant in the midst of this intellectual ferment.

Communism and Western Europe

The Intellectuals. Throughout the century, western Europe has had organized Communist parties and intellectuals sympathetic to communism. During the 1930s, when the Great Depression caused liberal democracies to flounder and right-wing regimes to spread across Europe, some people saw in communism a means to protect humane values. Many European university students affiliated with the Communist Party, and they, together with older intellectuals, visited the Soviet Union and praised Stalin. Some were ignorant of Stalin's reign of terror; others closed their eyes to it, believing that humane ends might be served by inhumane means; a few defended the terror as warranted. During the late 1920s and the 1930s, communism became for some Europeans little less than a substitute religion. Following World War II, a group of former Communists described their attraction to and disillusionment from the movement in a book entitled *The God That Failed* (1949).

Four events helped disillusion the West's pro-Communist intellectuals: the purge trials of 1936, the Spanish Civil War (1936–1939), the Nazi-Soviet pact of 1939, and the Soviet invasion of Hungary in 1956. Yet disillusionment with the Soviet Union or with Stalin did not always lead to disillusionment with Marxism or radical socialist criticism of European society. Some commentators urged the establishment of alternative Communist governments based on non-Soviet models. During the decade after World War II, Yugoslavia provided an example of one such alternative. Some radical students and a few intellectuals in the late 1950s drew inspiration from China. Other groups hoped for the development of a European Marxist system. The collapse of Communist governments in eastern Europe and the Soviet Union has, however, raised questions about Marxism's future as an influence on European intellectual life, and in the wake of these developments, some Communist parties have dropped the "Communist" label and embraced a socialist designation.

Existentialism

The intellectual movement most characteristic of mid-twentieth-century European culture was existentialism. As a movement, it was badly divided, for existentialist philosophers disagreed on major issues. But in general, it continued the revolt against reason that began in the nineteenth century.

Friedrich Nietzsche (see Chapter 25) and Søren Kierkegaard (1813–1855), a Danish author who received little attention until after World War I, were the forerunners of existentialism. Both rejected the dominant Hegelian philosophy of their day and its attempt to explain life in abstract categories.

Kierkegaard criticized the same tendencies in the established churches. In *Fear and Trembling* (1843), *Either/Or* (1843), and *Concluding Unscientific Postscript* (1846), he argued that Christian truth could not be captured in creeds, doctrines, and ecclesiastical organizations. It was grasped only by people who endured extreme situations. Passion, he claimed, was the only human faculty adequate to comprehend truth.

The intellectual and ethical crises created by World War I brought Kierkegaard's thought to the fore and revived interest in Nietzsche's critique of reason. That war caused many people to doubt that human beings could control their destiny or make historical progress. Its destructiveness undercut faith in the redemptive power of reason, for the war's most terrible weapons were the products of rational technology. The nineteenth century's sunny faith in orderly human development was one of the casualties of war at the start of the twentieth century.

The major existential writers were two Germans—Martin Heidegger (1889–1976) and Karl Jaspers (1883–1969)—and two Frenchmen—Jean-Paul Sartre (1905–1980) and Albert Camus (1913–1960). Although they often disagreed, they all, in one way or another, questioned the primacy of reason and scientific understanding as approaches to comprehending the human situation. The Enlightenment tradition taught that analysis, the division of human experience into component parts, was the path to understanding. But existentialists argued that the human condition was greater than the sum of its parts. It could only be grasped as a whole.

The Romantics of the early nineteenth century had also questioned reason, but much less radically. They believed that truth could be grounded in imagination and intuition. The existentialists dwelt primarily on the obliterating extremes of human experience: death, dread, fear, and anxiety. They believed that confrontations with ultimates, such as death, compel human beings to formulate ethical values for themselves. Traditional religion, rational philosophy, intuition, or social customs cannot help them. Each person is endowed with a dreadful freedom, a need to create value.

The attraction of existentialism, like communism, was very much a response to a mood that existed in Europe before and just after World War II. During the 1960s, turmoil over Vietnam and the youth rebellion created a different social environment that redirected European intellectual concerns.

Expansion of the University Population and Student Rebellion

At the turn of the century, no more than a few thousand people were enrolled in universities in any major European country. But by the 1980s, even though university education was less common in Europe than in the United States, that figure had risen to hundreds of thousands. Higher education is now available to people from a variety of social and economic backgrounds and, for the first time, to women.

The expanding population of university-educated people is related to a surge of intense self-criticism among Europeans. Millions of citizens have been trained in skills of critical thinking that once were the preserve of small, literate elites, and television has given critics wide audiences. More scientists, historians, economists, literary critics, and other professional scholars have been produced during the last seventy-five years than have existed in total in all of human history. The great intellectual developments of the last three centuries thrived primarily outside the university, but in the twentieth century, most intellectuals seek a university home.

One unexpected result of the rising population of students and intellectuals was a rebellious student movement that began in the United States in the early 1960s, thrived as opposition grew to the war in Vietnam, and then spread to Europe and other parts of the world. It was usually associated with antimilitarism and a radical critique of American politics, although in eastern Europe the Soviet Union was the target of some of its resentment. The movement also rejected middle-class values, traditional sexual mores, and traditional family life.

The student movement reached its peak in 1968. In that year, American students demonstrated against U.S. involvement in Vietnam, French students at the Sorbonne in Paris instigated a serious challenge to the government of Charles de Gaulle, and students helped promote a move in Czechoslovakia toward liberal socialism. These protests failed to alter the policies of the governments at which they were directed, and by the early 1970s, the era of the student rebellion seemed to have passed. European students continued to oppose nuclear weapons—particularly the placement of American nuclear missiles in Europe. But from the middle of the 1970s, students maintained a generally radical political stance without engaging in the kinds of disruptive protests that marked the 1960s.

Students and Popular Music

Rock music, which first appeared in the 1950s, is the best-known and most characteristic product of the waning twentieth century's student (or youth) culture. It has become part of the fabric of contemporary life—so much so that lyrics by the Beatles, a British rock group that became wildly popular in the 1960s, may be the most widely dispersed poetry in world history. Rock's appeal has transcended nationality and has done at least as much to homogenize European culture as advertising or the European Economic Community. Rock music has also been an effective vehicle for youth's critique of contemporary society. Rock stars, symbols of daring and heroic self-assertion, have championed subjectivity and individualism and have helped to energize important political movements in both democratic and Communist nations.

Environmentalism

Consumer goods were in short supply after World War II, which created a demand that fueled economic expansion through the 1960s. During this period, the public paid scant attention to the ethical implications of growth and its effect on the environment. Concern for the environment emerged in the 1970s. By the 1980s, it had acquired real political clout. Among the most important of the politically active environmental groups were the Club of Rome (founded in 1972) and the German Greens. In 1979, the Greens formed a political party that immediately became an electoral force.

Several developments lay behind the increasing sensitivity to the environment. The Arab oil embargo of 1973–1974 alerted Europeans to the degree to which their lifestyle was dependent on imports of natural resources that were in limited supply. At the same time, the dire environmental consequences of three decades of economic expansion were becoming impossible to ignore—fish were disappearing from major river systems because of industrial pollution, and acid rain was killing forests. Also, the anxiety created by the nuclear threat of the Cold War and descriptions of the nightmares that would follow accidents at nuclear reactors began to have an effect on voters.

The German Green movement shared the views of the radical student groups of the late 1960s from which it recruited members. It was anticapitalistic—holding business responsible for pollution. It was peace-oriented—opposing nuclear arms. But unlike the earlier student groups, the Greens chose to compete in the electoral process rather than use mass demonstrations to intimidate governments. They had modest success, winning seats in the West German Parliament and some local councils.

The 1986 meltdown of nuclear reactors at Chernobyl in the Soviet Union raised environmental issues that no government in Europe could ignore. There were many deaths and injuries, and the Soviet government had to relocate tens of thousands of people. Clouds of radioactive fallout spread across Europe, posing a threat to the health of its people and their food supplies.

Chernobyl demonstrated that environmental issues transcend national borders, and it prompted governments, in both the East and the West, to begin to take action. Environmental groups now command a significant share of votes. And as the European Economic Community solidifies, it will likely impose environmental regulations on business and industry. The nations of eastern Europe face a particularly daunting challenge—cleaning up vast polluted areas while trying to catch up economically with their Western neighbors.

Developments in Feminism

Feminist and environmental groups now provide the ongoing critique of society that formerly was the mission of Europe's socialist parties. European feminism has developed a new focus since World War II that reflects the influence of the most widely read feminist book of the postwar era: Simone De Beauvoir's *The Second Sex* (1949). Early feminism was a political movement that pressed for equal rights for women. Recent feminism has a broader agenda, a critique of all aspects of European culture. Radical feminists have asserted that European society inherently represses women, and they have insisted on the necessity of guaranteeing women control over their own lives. Whereas feminists once sought the same legal and civil rights as men, they have now turned to the pursuit of personal independence and issues that are unique to women.

∽ The Christian Heritage

Christianity has been hard-pressed during the twentieth century. Material prosperity, political ideologies, environmentalism, gender politics, and simple indifference have replaced religious faith for many people. But Europe's Christian churches still exercise considerable influence. In Germany during World War II, churches were among the few major institutions not wholly subdued by the Nazis. After the war, in Poland and elsewhere in eastern Europe, the Roman Catholic Church kept opposition to Communism alive. In western Europe, religious affiliation provides a basis for Christian Democratic parties. And churches everywhere have heightened concern about colonial exploitation, nuclear weapons, human rights, and other moral issues.

Neo-Orthodoxy

The rational optimism that characterized scholarship in the nineteenth century encouraged its liberal theologians to soften the concept of sin—to portray human nature as not far removed from divinity. The horror of World War I destroyed that illusion, and the *neo-orthodox* movement responded by emphasizing the importance of Christian insights neglected by liberals—the power of evil and the human potential for self-destructive conduct.

Karl Barth (1886–1968), a Swiss pastor and theologian, produced the most influential neo-orthodox Christian reflection on the lessons of war. In *A Commentary on the Epistle to the Romans* (1919), Barth claimed that Christian faith sprang from a sense of God's transcendence and humankind's dependence. Under Kierkegaard's influence, Barth returned to the Reformation theology of Martin Luther. He envisioned God as the "wholly other" who is encountered in the extreme moments of life when people are forced to confront their insufficiencies.

Liberal Theology

Neo-orthodoxy did not end the liberal tradition in Christian theology. Its strongest defender was a German-American, Paul Tillich (1886–1965). Where Barth saw God as dwelling outside humankind, Tillich believed that evidence for the divine was to be found in human nature and culture. Rudolf Bultmann (1884–1976), likewise, produced a brilliant analysis of the development of the Christian Scriptures that rejected supernaturalism as a basis for Christian faith. His work was popularized by an Anglican bishop, John Robinson (b. 1919), author of *Honest to God* (1963). Another British liberal Christian and literary scholar, C. S. Lewis (1878–1963), attracted millions of readers with amusing and accessible explications of doctrine. His best-remembered work is *The Screwtape Letters* (1942). In recent years, Protestant voices such as these have faded from the European religious scene.

Roman Catholic Reform

The most significant postwar changes in Christian institutions have occurred in the Roman Catholic Church. In 1959, Pope John XXIII (r. 1958–1963) called the twenty-first ecumenical council, popularly known as Vatican II. By 1965, under the guidance of John's successor, Paul VI (r. 1963–1978), the council had carried out the most extensive reform of Catholicism that has taken place, some would say, since the sixteenth century. Catholic liturgy was rewritten, and the Latin mass gave way to celebrations in the vernacular. The pope permitted freer relations with other Christian denominations, gave more power to bishops, and made the church more representative of the world at large by appointing cardinals from former European colonies.

While granting these liberal reforms, Pope Paul VI and his successors have rejected others. They have firmly upheld celibacy for priests, maintained prohibition of contraception, and opposed ordination for women. These policies have increased resentment among the laity and made it difficult for the church to recruit people for the priesthood and the religious orders.

Paul VI's successor, John Paul I, reigned for only thirty-four days. He was followed by the youngest pope to be elected in more than a century, Karol Wojtyla, archbishop of Cracow. Wojtyla, who took the name John Paul II, has defended traditional positions, stressing the authority of the papacy and limiting doctrinal and liturgical experimentation. He has also pursued expansion of the church in the non-Western world, stressing the need for social justice while limiting the political activity of priests.

John Paul II's opposition to communism strengthened the spirit of freedom in eastern Europe that brought down its Communist regimes. As a cardinal in Poland, he had clashed with Poland's Communist government. After his election to the papacy, he visited Poland and supported the Solidarity movement. His encouragement of popular resistance to eastern Europe's Communist governments during the 1980s opened a new chapter in the relationship of church and state in modern Europe.

∾ The Collapse of European Communism

Gorbachev Redirects the Soviet Union

Brezhnev died in 1982, and his immediate successors, Yuri Andropov (1914–1984) and Constantin Chernenko (1911–1985), died after short periods in office. In 1985, Gorbachev came to power and launched what proved to be the last attempt to reform the Soviet system. The policies he initiated unloosed forces that within seven years unseated him and ended Communist rule and the Soviet Union as it had existed since the Bolshevik Revolution of 1917. Behind these events were a stagnating Soviet economy, a lost war in Afghanistan, and growing resentment of the lack of openness in political life.

In the early 1980s, the Soviet Union faced a paradoxical situation. Militarily it was at its peak, for the Cuban missile crisis had determined the Soviets to embark on an extensive military buildup. Diversion of resources to the military, however, caused other aspects of the Soviet economy to stagnate. Its overall rate of economic growth declined, and progress in all but military technology slowed. Shortages in all kinds of consumer goods were extensive, and discipline was fading from the workforce. Efforts to match the military buildup that Ronald Reagan ordered in the United States in the 1980s imposed strains on this overextended system that led to its collapse.

Gorbachev had earned a reputation early in his career for impatience with the inefficiencies of the Soviet system. He believed that drastic change was needed to restore the Soviet Union's political and economic health. Consistent with the tradition of his nation, he tried to impose reform from above. He was not opposed to socialism or to the intellectual framework of Soviet Communism. His hope was to restore what he believed was the original Bolshevik vision, a dream that had been clouded by corruption and political terror.

***Economic* Perestroika.** Initially, Gorbachev attacked the way the party and the state bureaucracy managed the Soviet government and economy. A new policy called *perestroika* ("restructuring") was proposed. Various centralized economic ministries were considerably reduced in size, and a larger role was allowed at the local level for private enterprise. Early in 1990, Gorbachev began to abandon traditional Marxist ideology. He advocated private ownership of property and a freer market.

In addition to moving away from centralized planning, Gorbachev and his supporters were critical of corruption and inefficiency in the economy and the party bureaucracy. They implemented numerous organizational changes, but to little avail. The Soviet economy stagnated—even declined—and shortages of food, consumer goods, and housing became chronic. Old-fashioned Communists blamed this on the abandonment of centralized planning. Their democratic opponents cited the slow pace of reform and urged a more rapid move to a free-market economy.

Glasnost. Failure on the economic front drove Gorbachev to attempt bold political initiatives. He allowed what was for the Soviets an extraordinarily wide-ranging public discussion and criticism of Soviet history and Communist ideology. Thanks to his policy of "openness" *(glasnost)*, some of the leaders who had suffered in Stalin's purges of the 1920s were again recognized for their contributions to Soviet history. Workers were allowed to criticize party officials and the government's economic plans. Censorship was relaxed. Free expression was encouraged. Dissidents were released from prison, and in the summer of 1988, Gorbachev allowed a party congress to conduct full debates.

The government's tolerance for open discussion allowed many suppressed issues to surface. Throughout its history, the Soviet Union had been an empire composed of diverse peoples. Some had been conquered by the tsars; others, such as the Baltic states, had been occupied under Stalin. Glasnost allowed these people to voice their discontents, and Gorbachev proved particularly inept at dealing with ethnic demands for political autonomy.

Gorbachev soon moved from glasnost to perestroika in the political arena. In 1988, a new constitution permitting openly contested elections was adopted, and real political campaigning, a new experience for the Soviet people, preceded the election of a new Congress of People's Deputies in 1989. The Supreme Soviet, which chose Gorbachev as president in 1989, was the scene of lively debates.

1989: Year of Revolution in Eastern Europe

The Soviet Union maintained tight control over eastern Europe throughout the Cold War era, intervening militarily to end political experiments in Hungary in 1956 and in Czechoslovakia in 1968. In 1968, the Soviets articulated the Brezhnev Doctrine, a declaration of their right to interfere in the domestic affairs of any Communist country. They did not again carry out this threat in an eastern European country, but in 1981, Poland's Communist government headed off Soviet intervention by imposing martial law on itself and suppressing Solidarity. Before Gorbachev, reform seemed unlikely anywhere in eastern Europe.

Solidarity Reemerges in Poland. During the mid-1980s, Poland's government relaxed martial law. By 1984, several leaders of Solidarity had been released from prison and had begun, in defiance of the terms of their release, to work for free trade unions and democratic government. An active underground press appeared, and several dissenting political organizations emerged. These groups pointed to Poland's deteriorating economy as proof that here, as elsewhere, Communist governments could not deliver growth and prosperity.

During 1987, the government freed the last of its Solidarity prisoners. In 1988, when strikes occurred that even the leaders of Solidarity had not anticipated, the Communist government failed to reimpose control. The government legalized Solidarity, and the union's founder, Lech Walesa, was again thrust into the public spotlight—to mediate between the government and the more independent elements within the union movement.

General Jaruzelski, Poland's Communist ruler—with the tacit consent of the Soviet Union—repealed martial law and promised free elections to a parliament with increased powers. In the elections of 1989, the Communists lost overwhelmingly to Solidarity candidates. Jaruzelski, unable to find a Communist who could form a majority coalition, turned to Solidarity. On August 24, 1989, negotiations with Lech Walesa led to the naming of Poland's first non-Communist prime minister since 1945, Tadeusz Mazowiecki (b. 1927). Gorbachev approved his appointment.

Why Historical Truth Became Important to Dissidents in Eastern Europe

G. M. Tamás is a leader of an opposition party in present-day Hungary. In this passage, he explores the manner in which eastern European and Soviet dissidents used the rights guaranteed in the Helsinki Accords of 1975 to document the repression of the Communist regimes. He contends that telling these truths and bearing witness helped both to spread information and to embarrass the Communist governments by showing how they violated the agreement they had signed.

~ How did the right to free expression become so closely related to the telling of historical truth? What does Tamás mean by the right to historical truth? What was the importance of the Helsinki Accords in establishing it? Why did the dissidents believe more strongly in the value of the rights guaranteed in the Helsinki Accords than did some people in the West?

The first, most important human right for dissident intellectuals was the right to freedom of expression. But freedom of expression meant a licence to tell the truth, especially the truth about the Communist system, the truth about the martyrdom of East European peoples under the Gulag regime. The moral attitude which emerged from this simple idea of uncensored truth-telling was that of *bearing witness:* so the chief genre of dissident writing is neither philosophical treatise nor poetry, but *testimony.* Martyrs are . . . witnesses. The eloquence of their martyrdom, where the whole community was martyred, created a new symbolic community: the community of those who suffered and lived to tell and

The Soviets and Revolutionary Developments. It had taken a decade of struggle to establish Poland's Solidarity government, but within a few months of that event, Communist governments had fallen throughout eastern Europe. Except in Romania, the transition was relatively peaceful.

None of these revolutions could have succeeded if the Soviet Union had revived its policy of military intervention. But in October 1989, Gorbachev formally renounced the Brezhnev Doctrine. For the first time since the end of World War II, the people of eastern Europe were free to shape their own political destinies, and thousands of them took to the streets to denounce Communist Party domination and to express a desire for democracy.

The peaceful character of these revolutions may have owed something to the shock that much of the world felt, in the spring of 1989, at China's violent repression of pro-democracy protesters in Beijing's Tiananmen Square. The Communist Party officials of eastern Europe and the Soviet Union clearly decided at some point in 1989 that they could not risk offending world opinion by behaving in a similar manner.

were ready to suffer again for the right to tell.

The irresistible force of this surge of testimony was lethal, because in spite of denial, a sometimes almost psychotic refusal to know, everyone half-consciously knew that it was true. . . .

In the struggle for the right to historical truth, for the right to bear witness (where history and morals, strangely, become one), dissidents were harassed, persecuted and punished. They continued to document these new abuses—one of the chief tasks of the dissident movement was to write its own chronicle, a testimony this time on the fate of the witnesses themselves. They did not at first demand the usual fundamental human rights: their emphasis was on the Word. They did not set up political parties or organize conspiracies. They wanted to expose unspeakable, even unimaginable crimes and show the continuity of the Great Terror through the servility and mendacity of their present. The rulers were told that the communiqués they had signed guaranteed the right to free speech, peaceful assembly and the like. "Why, therefore, cannot people say what they believe to be the truth?". . . .

In the West, little of this passion for historico-moral truth was understood. But the West's shaky faith in the universality of its basic principles (human and civil rights) was challenged by the East European dissidence: people putting themselves at risk for the pious and dull commonplaces of the Helsinki accords. The unasked-for support for Western constitutional principles by trustworthy people, made so by their willingness to suffer for those principles, gave a new distinction to a certain idea of natural right; the dissidents' behaviour forced the ideas of the American Revolution on to the political agenda after two hundred years. This was a universalist discourse common to both systems, and the debate conducted within it was won by the West and its allies, the dissidents. No *Realpolitik* could ever have won that controversy.

G. M. Tamás, "The Legacy of Dissent: How Civil Society Has Been Seduced by the Cult of Privacy," The Times Literary Supplement, May 14, 1993, p. 15.

Hungary Moves Toward Independence. Among eastern European nations, Hungary demonstrated the most economic independence of the Soviet Union. Its government had stressed production of food and consumer goods and permitted a small stock exchange. During the early months of 1989, while events unfolded in Poland, Hungary's Communist government took other independent actions. In January, it authorized independent political parties. Then it opened the border between Hungary and Austria to permit free travel—the first breach of the Iron Curtain. Thousands of East Germans seized the opportunity to escape to West Germany via Hungary and Austria.

In May, the Hungarian premier who had been installed after the Soviet intervention in 1956 (Janos Kadar, b. 1912) was voted from office by Parliament. Hungarians demonstrated their approval by rallying in the thousands at a funeral honoring Premier Imre Nagy, who had been executed in 1956. The Hungarian Communist Party changed its name to the Socialist Party and permitted opposition political parties to organize. In October, Hungary was promised free elections. And by 1990, a coalition of democratic parties had won control of Parliament and the country.

The Breach of the Berlin Wall and German Reunification. Nothing in Europe so symbolized the tension of the Cold War as a divided Germany and the Berlin Wall, which had been erected in 1961 to halt the flight of East Germans to the West. In the autumn of 1989, the movement of tens of thousands of East Germans into West Germany through Hungary and Austria incited demonstrations in many German cities. The streets filled with people demanding democracy and an end to Communist Party rule.

Gorbachev informed the heads of the East German Communist Party that the Soviet Union would no longer support them, and, with startling swiftness, they abdicated in favor of a younger generation of Communist leaders. In November 1989, the government of East Germany ordered the opening of the Berlin Wall. That week, one of the most emotional events of the past fifty years took place: tens of thousands of East Berliners crossed into West Berlin to celebrate, to visit families, and to shop with money provided by the West German government. Shortly thereafter, free travel began between East and West Germany. East Germany's Communist Party was thoroughly discredited, and in 1990, free elections brought conservatives to power who proposed rapid unification with West Germany.

The developments in East Germany had broader ramifications for international relations than the changes in Poland and Hungary, for they raised the issue of the restoration of a united Germany. Helmut Kohl (b. 1930), chancellor of West Germany, drafted a tentative plan for reunification, and, late in 1989, the ministers of the European Economic Community accepted the principle of one Germany. The United States, the Soviet Union, Great Britain, and France all concurred, and by early 1990, the citizens of the two Germanies had expressed their desire to come together.

The Velvet Revolution in Czechoslovakia. Hard-liners in the Czechoslovak Communist Party, who had been restored to power by the Soviet invasion that ended the "Prague Spring" of 1968, enjoyed undisputed authority for twenty years. But late in 1989, a series of events dubbed the "Velvet Revolution" caused their rule in Czechoslovakia to unravel. In November 1989, street demonstrations and well-organized political opposition drove them from office. The pattern was similar to developments elsewhere: older Communists resigned in favor of younger ones, who tried to hang on to power by proposing inadequate reforms.

The Czech leader of the popular resistance to the Communist Party was Václav Havel (b. 1936), a playwright of international standing who had endured frequent political imprisonment. Havel's group, which called itself Civic Forum, negotiated a series of reforms with the government: an end to the political dominance of the Communist Party, inclusion of non-Communists in the government, elimination of Marxist education, removal of travel restrictions, and relaxation of censorship.

Early in December, the tottering Communist regime admitted that the invasion of 1968 had been a mistake, and the Soviet Union and other Warsaw Pact states did likewise. Shortly thereafter, Civic Forum forced the resignation of Gustav Husak (b. 1913), president of Czechoslovakia since 1968. A free election for his successor was guaranteed, and on December 29, 1989, Havel was chosen president. Alexander Dubcek, leader of the "Prague Spring," returned as chairman of the Parliament.

Violent Revolution in Romania. The most violent upheaval of 1989 occurred in Romania, where Nicolae Ceauşescu (1918–1989) had ruled unopposed for almost a quarter-century. Romania was a one-party state with total centralized economic planning. Ceauşescu, who had long been at odds with the Soviet government, maintained a Stalinist regime in the face of Gorbachev's reforms. On December 15, trouble erupted in Timisoara in western Romania, when government security forces tried to arrest a clergyman campaigning for rights for Romania's ethnic Hungarians. Demonstrators shouted defiance at Ceauşescu at a major rally in Bucharest a few days later, and by December 22, the city was in full revolt. Fighting broke out between the army, which supported the revolution, and the security forces, which remained loyal to Ceauşescu. Ceauşescu and his wife tried to flee, but they were caught, secretly tried, and executed by firing squad on December 25. The shooting between the army and the security forces then stopped, and a provisional government in Bucharest announced that the first free elections since the end of World War II would take place in the spring of 1990.

The Collapse of the Soviet Union

Gorbachev ended support for the Communist governments of eastern Europe because he believed that the Soviet Union could no longer afford the expense of upholding their authority. Similar difficulties also plagued efforts to sustain the Soviet Communist Party at home. Gorbachev hoped to create a new political structure—a strong presidency filled by election in the Supreme Soviet—with a base of support extending beyond the Communist Party. In early 1990, he proposed to the party's Central Committee that it relinquish the party's monopoly of power, and, after intense debate, it concurred. Gorbachev did not want to abandon communism (at least not socialism), but he did want to open the political process to competition. At the same time, he expected the Soviet Union to remain a single strong state under a powerful central government. Gorbachev soon found himself reacting to events rather than controlling them (in the face of steadily declining popularity). Three major political forces challenged him. One consisted of groups considered conservative in the Soviet context. They wanted to rely on traditional Soviet instruments of control to deal with the country's economic stagnation and social turmoil. In 1991, Gorbachev added some of these people to his government to help him deal with opposition from a second group. Its leader, Boris Yeltsin, pushed for rapid progress toward a market economy and a more democratic government. In 1990, Yeltsin became president of the Russian Republic, the largest and most important of the Soviet Union's constituent units.

A third force came into play in 1989: regional unrest in some of the Soviet Union's republics. This discontent was not new, but in the past it had been repressed by military or Communist Party action. Initially, the strongest outcries came from the three Baltic republics: Estonia, Latvia, and Lithuania. They had been independent until the eve of World War II, when the Soviet-German Nonaggression Pact assured Stalin that Hitler would not stand in the way of their annexation by the USSR. During 1989 and 1990, the parliaments of the Baltic republics sought to increase their independence from the Soviet Union. Lithuania actually declared independence.

Unrest also developed in the Soviet Islamic republics in central Asia. Riots broke out in Azerbaijan and Tadzhikistan. Throughout 1990 and 1991, Gorbachev tried to negotiate new constitutional arrangements between the republics and the central government. His failure may in time be seen as the most important reason for the Soviet Union's rapid collapse.

The August 1991 Coup. In August 1991, the conservative forces that Gorbachev had brought into the government attempted a coup. Armed forces occupied Moscow, and Gorbachev was placed under house arrest while on vacation in the Crimea. On the day of the coup, Boris Yeltsin, from the top of a tank stationed in front of the Russian Parliament building, denounced the reactionaries and called on the world to help maintain movement toward democracy in the Soviet Union.

Within two days, the coup collapsed, and one of the largest demonstrations in all Russian history erupted in Moscow to celebrate its failure. Gorbachev returned to Moscow, humiliated and victimized by men he had brought into the government. The Communist Party, compromised by its role in the coup, lost its effectiveness as a political force, and Yeltsin's power increased. Constitutional arrangements between the central government and the individual republics were revised to create the Commonwealth of Independent States, and on December 25, 1991, Gorbachev stepped down and the Soviet Union ceased to exist.

Crushing the Russian Parliament. As president of Russia, Boris Yeltsin headed the largest, most powerful state in the new Commonwealth. Initially, he enjoyed great popularity in Russia and throughout the Commonwealth, but by 1993, he was facing serious economic and political problems. Opposition to Yeltsin, personally as well as to his reforms, developed in the Russian Parliament. Parliament was populated mostly by former Communists who were leery of reform, and relations between them and the president soon reached an impasse. In September 1993, Yeltsin suspended Parliament, and it responded by deposing him. Parliamentary leaders tried to provoke popular uprisings against Yeltsin, but the military backed Yeltsin and surrounded the Parliament building with troops and tanks. On October 4, 1993, after pro-Parliament rioters had rampaged through Moscow, Yeltsin ordered the tanks to attack and crush the revolt.

This action consolidated Yeltsin's position and authority, and all the major Western powers, deeply concerned by the turmoil in Russia, supported

After the failed coup in August 1991, Boris Yeltsin soon displaced Mikhail Gorbachev as leader of the new Commonwealth of Independent States. Here they appeared jointly before the Parliament of the collapsing Soviet Union.

him. In December 1993, Russians elected a new Parliament and approved a new constitution. Parliamentary authority has been limited and the president has been granted extensive powers.

Russia's future remains uncertain. Yeltsin's victory increased his dependence on the military, and his nation's continuing economic problems breed unrest. In the December 1993 elections, radical nationalists who are openly intolerant of non-Russian ethnic groups and who advocate rebuilding Russia's empire made an alarmingly strong showing. Power struggles in Russia may stay within constitutional limits, but events have evolved so rapidly and so unexpectedly that no reliable predictions can be made.

The Future of the Commonwealth of Independent States

The Commonwealth of Independent States is a loosely organized federation of fifteen republics that were formerly part of the USSR (see Map 31-1). Since serious differences exist among these states, the status of their federation is quite shaky. Many of the republics have ethnic minorities that are dominant groups in neighboring republics. Persecution of these minorities is a source of tension within and between republics that may lead to military confrontations. In the past Russia, the largest of the republics, has exploited these tensions to play groups off against each other to its advantage.

The economy of the Commonwealth as a whole, as well as those of each of the individual republics, remains weak. The consumer shortages that existed before 1991 continue, and it is uncertain how much economic aid the West will be willing to supply to help guarantee the Commonwealth's political stability. Some conservative institutions also survive to hinder the Commonwealth's moves toward democracy. Secret police still exist and operate independently. The former Soviet army has not been dismantled, although

MAP 31-1 Republics of the Former Soviet Union *In December 1991, the Soviet Union broke up into its fifteen constituent republics, which are now loosely joined in the Commonwealth of Independent States.*

various republics are competing for control of its weapons and the allegiance of its troops stationed on their soil. In the current volatile situation, leaders can quickly lose popular support. The crucial question is whether they and their successors will continue to advocate democracy or will decree a return to authoritarian government.

The Collapse of Yugoslavia and Civil War

The Communist government of Yugoslavia had long been distinct from those of the other eastern bloc nations dominated by the Soviet Union. The country's leader, Marshal Tito, had acted independently of Stalin in the late 1940s. Thereafter, Yugoslavia pursued a foreign policy that was independent of the

Soviet Union. After Tito's death in 1980, Yugoslavia became increasingly unstable and has now erupted in civil war.

Yugoslavia, which was created after World War I, is home to six national groups: Serbs, Croats, Slovenes, Montenegrins, Macedonians, and Bosnians. They have been quarreling for centuries, and each has staked historical claims to a particular region: Serbia, Croatia, Slovenia, Montenegro, Macedonia, and Bosnia-Herzegovina (see Map 31-2). These regions, which were separate republics within Yugoslavia, have mixed populations. Many Serbs, for instance, live outside Serbia.

Tito, the Communist leader of Yugoslavia, muted ethnic differences by complex power-sharing arrangements and by a cult of personality that made

MAP 31-2 The Nations in the Center of Europe *The rapid changes in eastern Europe during the close of the 1980s brought to the fore various long-standing ethnic tensions in the region. This map shows national and ethnic borders and major ethnic enclaves within areas generally dominated by a single ethnic group.*

loyalty to him the linchpin for the nation. After Tito's death in 1980, Yugoslavia had serious economic problems that undermined its central government, and in the late 1980s, the old ethnic differences flared up. Nationalist leaders came to power—most notably Slobodan Milošević (b. 1941) in Serbia and Franjo Tudjman (b. 1922) in Croatia. The Serbs contended that Serbia was not powerful enough within the Yugoslav federation and that Serbs living in other parts of Yugoslavia suffered discrimination (especially from Croats). The Croats and Slovenes, on their part, created tension by pushing hard for rapid movement toward a market economy. During the summer of 1990, in the wake of the upheaval in the former Soviet bloc, Slovenia and Croatia seceded from Yugoslavia, and won recognition from the European Community.

From this point on, violence escalated steadily. Serbia was determined to maintain a united Yugoslavian state under Serbian control. Croatia was equally determined to secure independence. Croatian Serbs, who demanded protection, provided the Serbian army with a pretext to attack Croatia. By June 1991, war had erupted between the two republics.

The struggle took a new turn in 1992, when Croatian and Serbian forces decided to divide Bosnia-Herzegovina. The Muslims in Bosnia were caught between the opposing forces, and the Serbs, in particular, began a process of "ethnic cleansing," a euphemism for the murder or dispossession of large numbers of Bosnian Muslims. Unremitting Serbian bombardment of Sarajevo, the capital of Bosnia-Herzegovina, brought the Yugoslavian civil war to the attention of the world, and the United Nations tried, unsuccessfully, to mediate an end to the conflict.

∾ Problems in the Wake of the Collapse of Communism

The collapse of communism in eastern Europe and the former Soviet Union means that nations in those areas have a chance to restore civil liberties and develop standards of living comparable to those in western Europe. But the problems facing the Communist successor states are enormous. Unemployment is widespread. Existing plants and factories are obsolete, and some are causing the worst environmental pollution in the world. Hundreds of thousands of people are migrating from eastern to western Europe, looking for work. There, they encounter resentment, opposition, and violence.

The nations of western Europe, struggling with economic problems of their own, are hesitant to send economic aid to the East. Western Europeans are also grappling with the issue of how the former Communist economies can be related to the European Economic Community. Eastern Europeans are pushing for rapid integration, but western Europeans fear that close ties with the East could undermine their prosperity.

The freedom made possible by the fall of Communist governments has, thus far, been used to pursue ethnic goals that lead almost inevitably to domestic political turmoil. In 1993, disagreements between Czechs and Slovaks led them to split Czechoslovakia into separate states. With exceptions (Aus-

An elderly parishioner walks through the ruins of St. Mary's Roman Catholic Church in Sarajevo. The church was destroyed by Serb shelling in May 1992. [Reuters/Bettmann]

tria, Romania, Bulgaria, and Greece), all of the nations between Germany and the Commonwealth of Independent States have existed as distinct political units with their present borders only since World War I. Between World War I and 1989, all of them spent time under either fascist or Communist governments. After World War II, only Germany and Austria developed strong democracies. No one knows if democratic governments can cope with the disorder, economic stagnation, and competing ethnic claims that now exist within the former Communist states or whether these nations will resort to some illiberal alternative.

The collapse of European communism has also profoundly altered international relations. The demise of the Warsaw Pact has raised questions about the future of NATO, whose primary function had been to deter a Soviet attack on western Europe. Many have argued that NATO should become an instrument to preserve international order, but its failure to play an effective role in ending the Yugoslav civil war raises doubts about its effectiveness in such a role.

Serious challenges loom ahead for the West as it struggles to create a just and stable world order. Ethnic tensions and militant nationalism, sources of the great wars of the twentieth century, are again on the rise. Faltering economies are heightening tensions. And crises springing from the environment, population growth, and resource shortages loom.

Although solutions to these and other problems will not be easy, the traits persistent in Western cultures—concern for constitutional government, tension between sacred and secular, pursuit of science and rationalism, and a penchant for self-criticism—offer hope. Although they have not ensured the moral excellence of Western civilization, they have given that civilization the ability to correct and redirect itself and to raise questions about the nature of the good life and the good society. Such questions must be asked before improvement and reform *can be attained. Those who most sustain Western culture today are probably those who, in its midst, most criticize it and demand that it justify itself.*

～ Review Questions

1. In what specific ways has Europe been "Americanized" in the second half of the twentieth century? How do you account for the trend toward a consumer society in the West? What population changes and migration patterns have marked the period since World War II? How have they affected Europe's economy and society?

2. How have women's social and economic roles changed in the second half of the twentieth century? What tensions and difficulties have new work patterns created for women? What changes and problems have women faced amidst the political instability in eastern Europe?

3. What changes have taken place in the pursuit and diffusion of knowledge in the twentieth century? What has been the effect of the communications revolution? What has been the effect of the expansion of universities? Has Western intellectual life become more unified or less so? Why?

4. What contributions did Nietzsche and Kierkegaard make to existentialism? What did Sartre mean when he said that existentialism was a philosophy of anguish and despair? To which crises of the twentieth century was existentialism a response?

5. By what stages did communism collapse in eastern Europe and the former Soviet Union? How important was Gorbachev in transforming the political and economic atmosphere of the Soviet Union? Why did he fail? How do the revolutions of 1989 compare with those of 1848?

6. How did Marshal Tito maintain political stability in Yugoslavia after 1945? Why have violence and civil war steadily escalated there in the 1990s? What are the problems and opportunities that the collapse of communism has presented to Europe?

～ Suggested Readings

G. Ambrosius and W.H. Hubbard, *A Social and Economic History of Twentieth-Century Europe* (1989). The best one-volume treatment of the subject.

P. Baldwin, *The Politics of Social Solidarity: Class Bases of the European Welfare State 1875–1975* (1990). An excellent analysis of the political forces that allowed the welfare state to come into being.

I. Banac (ed.), *Eastern Europe in Revolution* (1992). Excellent articles on the events of 1989 and afterwards.

E. Bramwell, *Ecology in the 20th Century: A History* (1989). Traces the environmental movement to its late-nineteenth-century origins.

R. Crossman (ed.), *The God That Failed* (1949). Essays by former Communist intellectuals.

P. Desai, *Perestroika in Perspective: The Design and Dilemmas of Soviet Reform* (1989). A thoughtful essay on Gorbachev's reforms.

A. N. Dragnich, *Serbs, and Croats: The Struggle in Yugoslavia* (1992). An introduction to the historical roots of the current struggle.

M. Ellman and V. Kontorovich, *The Disintegration of the Soviet Economic System* (1992). An overview of the economic strains that the Soviet union experienced during the 1980s.

W. F. Hanrieder, *Germany, America, and Europe: Forty Years of German Foreign Policy* (1989). A major survey.

H. S. Hughes, *Sophisticated Rebels: The Political Culture of European Dissent, 1968–1987* (1988). A series of thoughtful essays on recent cultural critics.

T. Judt, *Past Imperfect: French Intellectuals, 1944–1956* (1992). An important study on French intellectuals and communism.

C. Lemke and G. Marks (ed.), *The Crisis of Socialism in Europe* (1992). Essay on the difficulties now confronted by socialism.

R. Maltby (ed.), *Passing Parade: A History of Popular Culture in the Twentieth Century* (1989). A collection of essays on a topic just beginning to receive scholarly attention.

P. H. Merkl, *German Unification in the European Context* (1993). The first major essay on the impact of German unity.

G. Montefiore, *Philosophy in France Today* (1983). A good introduction to one of the major centers of contemporary thought.

B. Nahaylo and V. Swoboda, *Soviet Disunion: A History of the Nationalities Problem in the USSR* (1990). A discussion of one of the major areas of political difficulty today.

S. P. Ramet, *Social Currents in Eastern Europe: The Sources and Meaning of the Great Transformation* (1991). A broad survey of eastern European social life and popular culture on the eve of the revolutions of 1989.

G. Ross, *Workers and Communists in France: From Popular Front to Eurocommunism* (1982). A useful survey.

J. Ruscoe, *The Italian Communist Party, 1976–1981: On the Threshold of Government* (1982). Examines the party at the height of its influence.

H. A. Turner, *Germany from Partition to Reunification* (1992). The best brief introduction.

Index

Sozzini, Faustus, 264
Sozzini, Lelio, 264
Space program:
  Soviet Union, 719
  United States, 715
Spa Fields, 494
Spain, 108
  and ancient Greece, 32
  and ancient Rome, 89, 91
  Bourbons, 398, 472, 497
  Cortes, 237, 497
  in eighteenth century, 350–51
  empire, 238–40
    African colonies, 611, 612
    Bourbon reforms, 398
    colonial government, 397–98
    discovery and explorations,
      238–40, 245–47
    North America, 395
    and Spanish-American War, 613
    trade regulation, 397–98
    (see also Latin America, colo-
      nialism)
  fascism in, 683
  Ferdinand and Isabella, 237,
    238–39, 245
  foreign relations:
    France, 289, 316
    Great Britain, 294–97
    Netherlands, 291–94
    Portugal, 291
  Hohenzollerns in, 545
  Humanism in, 244–45
  inflation, sixteenth century, 291
  literacy, late nineteenth century,
    587
  literature, sixteenth and seven-
    teenth centuries, 338–39
  as maritime power, 350–51
  monarchy:
    eighteenth century, 350–51
    fifteenth century, 238–40
  nation-building, 238–40
  New World riches, 290–91
  Philip II, 284, 288, 289–94
  political parties:
    Falangists, 683
    Spanish Popular Front, 683
  Punic empire, 89
  religion:
    Inquisition, 239, 245
    Islam (Moors), 239, 291
    Jews, 239
    Roman Catholicism, 239, 247,
      284, 290, 293, 316
    toleration, 239
  Renaissance, 237, 238–40, 244–45
  wars and warfare:
    England, 294–97, 308
    Habsburg-Valois wars, 285
    Napoleonic Wars, 470, 472
    Netherlands, 291–94
    religious wars (1556-1603),
      289–97
    Spanish-American War, 613
    Spanish Civil War, 682–83, 744
    Spanish Revolution of 1820, 497
    Thirty Years, War, 297–303, 308
    Turks, 291
    War of Devolution, 322
    War of Jenkins's Ear, 402–3
    War of the Spanish Succession,
      322, 325–27, 350
Spanish American War, 613

Spanish Armada, 289, 294, 297, 350
Spanish Civil War, 682–83, 744
"Spanish Fury," 293
Spanish Infanta, 308, 316
Spanish Popular Front, 683
Spanish Succession, War of the, 322,
  325–27, 363, 398
Sparta (see Ancient Greece)
Spartacus, 96, 101
Spartacus group, 633
Spectator, The, 418
Speeches on Religion to Its Cultured
  Despisers (Schleiermacher), 483
Speer, Albert, 698
Spencer, Herbert, 591, 604
Speyer, Diet of, 261
Spheres of influence, 702, 704, 722
Spice trade, 245
Spinning jenny, 385, 517
Spinoza, Baruch, 344–45
Spirit of the Laws, The (Mon-
  tesquieu), 424, 426–27
Spiritual Exercises (Ignatius of Loy-
  ola), 272
Spiritual Franciscans, 174, 217
Spiritualists, 264
Spitfire plane, 687
Sputnik, 719
Spy flights, United States over Soviet
  Union, 720
Sri Lanka, 728
SS (Schutzstaffel), 670, 690–91
Stadtholder, 292
Stäel, Madame de, 480
Stagirus, 65
Stalin, Joseph, 605, 606, 642–43, 667,
  674, 675–77, 684, 685, 687,
  688, 701, 702, 703, 711, 713,
  717–18, 756
Stalingrad, battle of, 693
Stamp Act, 407, 408
Stamp Act Congress, 407
Standard Oil, 563
Star Wars (see Strategic Defense Ini-
  tiative [Star Wars])
State, Council of, 493
State Planning Commission (see
  Gosplan)
Statutes of Provisors, 267
Steam engine, 386, 512
Steel, manufacturing of, 561–62
Steele, Richard, 418
Stein, Baron von, 471
Stendhal, 480
Stephen II, Pope, 150–51, 152
Stephen IX, Pope, 167
Steward, in late Middle Ages, 189
Stoa, 74
Stoa Poikile, 74
Stock market crash of 1929, 663
Stockton and Darlington Line, 514
Stoecker, Adolf, 603
Stoics, 74, 111
Stolypin, P. A., 582, 583
Storm troopers (see Sturmabteilung
  [SA])
Strachey, Lytton, 598, 599
Strasbourg, 263, 265, 266, 299, 725
Strategic Arms Limitation agree-
  ment, 722
Strategic bombing, World War II,
  693–94
Strategic Defense Initiative (Star
  Wars), 722

Strauss, David Freidrich, 591
Stravinsky, Igor, 598
Stream-of-consciousness, 599
Streltsy, 364, 365, 366
Stresa Front, 681
Stresemann, Gustav, 656–58
Strikes, labor, 576, 579, 649, 654,
  667, 722–23
Struggle of the orders, ancient Rome,
  84–85
Stuarts, 285, 295, 296, 306–15
Student protests:
  of 1960s, 745–46
  Vietnam War, 715–16, 745
Studia humanitatis, 228
Studies in Hysteria (Freud and
  Breuer), 600
Sturmabteilung (SA), 656, 668, 670
Sturm und drang, 479
Subjection of Women (Mill), 573
Submarine warfare, in World War I,
  627
Submission of the Clergy, 268
Suburbs, late nineteenth century,
  566
Subways, 566
Succession, Act of, 268
Successor states, 650–52
Sudan, 611
Sudetenland, 651, 683, 684
Suez Canal, 611, 615, 682, 692, 733
  Suez Crisis, 718–19, 733
Sugar, 398, 400, 406
Suger, Abbot, 180
Sulla, L. Cornelius, 100–101
Sully, Duke of, 315, 316
Sumer and Sumerians, 5, 6, 16
  religion, 6–7
Sumerians, 1
Summa, 202
Summa Theologica (Thomas
  Aquinas), 202
Sumptuary laws, 195
Sun King (see Louis XIV of France)
Sunna, 144
Sunnis Muslims, 144
Superego, 601
Superstitions, 336–37
Supremacy, Act of (1534), 268
Supreme Soviet, 751, 755
Survival of the fittest, 588–90, 591,
  602–3
Swabia, 164
Sweden, 301
  Charles XII, 357, 367
  in eighteenth century, 357
  foreign relations:
    France, 301
    Netherlands, 301
  Protestant Reformation in, 270
  wars and warfare:
    Great Northern War, 357, 367
    Hohenzollerns and, 361
    Thirty Years' War, 301, 316, 357
Swiss Brethren, 264
Swiss Confederacy, 303
Switzerland, 158, 300, 576
  civil wars, 263
  Middle Ages, 180
  primary education in, 587
  Protestant Reformation in, 253,
    262–63
  Roman Catholicism in, 262
Syllabus of Errors, 594